Russian Politics Today
Stability and Fragility

Russian Politics Today: Stability and Fragility provides an accessible and nuanced introduction to contemporary Russian politics at a time of increasing uncertainty. Using the theme of stability versus fragility as its overarching framework, this innovative textbook explores the forces that shape Russia's politics, economy, and society. The volume provides up-to-date coverage of core themes – Russia's strong presidency, its weak party system, the role of civil society, and its dependence on oil and gas revenues – alongside path-breaking chapters on the politics of race, class, gender, sexuality, and the environment. An international and diverse team of experts presents the most comprehensive available account of the evolution of Russian politics in the post-Soviet era, providing the tools for interpreting the past and the present while also offering a template for understanding future developments.

Susanne A. Wengle is Associate Professor of Political Science at the University of Notre Dame, and concurrent faculty at the Keough School for Global Affairs. Her research examines post-Soviet political economy and engages with the study of markets in that context and beyond. Her publications include *Post-Soviet Power: State-Led Development and Russia's Marketization* (2015) and *Black Earth, White Bread: A Technopolitical History of Russian Agriculture and Food* (2022).

T0320843

Russian Politics Today

Stability and Fragility

Edited by

Susanne A. Wengle

University of Notre Dame, Indiana

Shaftesbury Road, Cambridge CB2 8EA, United Kingdom

One Liberty Plaza, 20th Floor, New York, NY 10006, USA

477 Williamstown Road, Port Melbourne, VIC 3207, Australia

314–321, 3rd Floor, Plot 3, Splendor Forum, Jasola District Centre, New Delhi – 110025, India

103 Penang Road, #05–06/07, Visioncrest Commercial, Singapore 238467

Cambridge University Press is part of Cambridge University Press & Assessment, a department of the University of Cambridge.

We share the University's mission to contribute to society through the pursuit of education, learning and research at the highest international levels of excellence.

www.cambridge.org
Information on this title: www.cambridge.org/highereducation/isbn/9781009165914

DOI: 10.1017/9781009165921

First published 2023

Printed in the United Kingdom by TJ Books Limited, Padstow Cornwall 2023

A catalogue record for this publication is available from the British Library

ISBN 978-1-009-16591-4 Hardback
ISBN 978-1-009-16590-7 Paperback

Additional resources for this publication at www.cambridge.org/wengle

Cambridge University Press & Assessment has no responsibility for the persistence or accuracy of URLs for external or third-party internet websites referred to in this publication and does not guarantee that any content on such websites is, or will remain, accurate or appropriate.

Contents

Figures, Maps, and Tables

FIGURES

MAPS

TABLES

Contributors

ŞENER AKTÜRK is Professor in the Department of International Relations at Koç University, Istanbul. His research focus is the comparative politics of ethnicity, religion, and nationalism. His book, *Regimes of Ethnicity and Nationhood in Germany, Russia, and Turkey* (2012) received the 2013 Joseph Rothschild book prize from the Association for the Study of Nationalities. He has published in *World Politics, Perspectives on Politics, Comparative Politics, Journal of Ethnic and Migration Studies, Post-Soviet Affairs, Mediterranean Politics, Social Science Quarterly, European Journal of Sociology, Nationalities Papers, Problems of Post-Communism, Turkish Studies, Middle Eastern Studies, Osteuropa, Ab Imperio*, in several other journals, and in various edited books.

STEPHEN CROWLEY is professor at the Department of Politics, Oberlin College. He has written widely on the politics of Russia and Eastern Europe, with a focus on labor and the political economy of postcommunist transformations. His most recent book is *Putin's Labor Dilemma: Russian Politics between Stability and Stagnation* (2021).

NATALIA FORRAT is a postdoctoral researcher at the Weiser Center for Emerging Democracies, University of Michigan, and the author of a forthcoming book on the social roots of authoritarian power in Russia. She was a predoctoral fellow at the Center for Democracy, Development, and the Rule of Law, Stanford University, and a postdoctoral fellow at the Kellogg Institute for International Studies, University of Notre Dame. Her research focuses on authoritarian power, state–society relations in authoritarian regimes, state and civil society organizations, and civic resistance and mobilization. Her work has been published in *Post-Soviet Affairs* and *Comparative Politics*.

JORDAN GANS-MORSE is Associate Professor of Political Science at Northwestern University. His research focuses on corruption, the rule of law, property rights, and political and economic transitions, primarily with an emphasis on the former Soviet Union. He is the author of the book *Property Rights in Post-Soviet Russia: Violence, Corruption, and Demand for Law* (2017), as well as a number of other publications that have appeared in leading journals including *American Journal of Political Science, American Political Science Review, Comparative Political Studies, Journal of Law, Economics, and Organization*, and *Post-Soviet Affairs*.

SCOTT GEHLBACH is Professor, Department of Political Science and Harris School of Public Policy, University of Chicago. He is a political economist and comparativist whose work is motivated by the contemporary and historical experience of Russia, Ukraine, and other postcommunist states. He has made numerous contributions to the study of autocracy, economic reform, political connections, and other important topics in political economy.

LEO GRANBERG is Professor Emeritus of Rural Studies at Aleksanteri Institute, University of Helsinki, and an affiliate at the Institute for Russian and Eurasian Studies, Uppsala University. His research focuses on social and economic changes in European countryside, local development in Russia, and the global food system. His studies are based on field research in different regions of Russia and in other previously socialist countries. He is the author of *The Other Russia: Local Experience and Social Change* (2017, with Ann-Mari Sätre) and *Evaluating the European Approach to Rural Development* (2015, edited with Kjell Andersson and Imre Kovách), among other works.

SAMUEL A. GREENE is Professor of Russian Politics and Director of the King's Russia Institute at King's College London. He is the author of *Moscow in Movement: Power and Opposition in Putin's Russia* (2014) and coauthor, with Graeme B. Robertson, of *Putin v. the People: The Perilous Politics of a Divided Russia* (2019).

LAURA A. HENRY is Professor in the Department of Government and Legal Studies at Bowdoin College, Maine. Her research investigates Russia's post-Soviet transformation with a particular focus on civil society, citizen activism, and environmental politics. Henry is the coauthor (with Lisa McIntosh Sundstrom) of *Bringing Global Governance Home: NGO Mediation in BRICS States* (2021) and the author of *Red to Green: Environmental Activism in Post-Soviet Russia* (2010). She is also the coeditor of *Russian Civil Society: A Critical Assessment* (2006). Her work has appeared in *Environmental Politics*, *Global Environmental Politics*, *Post-Soviet Affairs*, and *Europe–Asia Studies*, among other journals.

ALEXANDER SASHA KONDAKOV is an assistant professor at the School of Sociology, University College Dublin. He is also an editor for the *Journal of Social Policy Studies* published by the Higher School of Economics in Moscow. He has held positions in the Aleksanteri Institute, in Helsinki, Finland, the Woodrow Wilson Center in Washington, DC, and the University of Wisconsin-Madison. Kondakov's work is primarily focused on law and sexuality studies, more specifically on queer sexualities, and his research has been published in journals such as *Sexualities*, *Social and Legal Studies*, *Feminist Legal Studies*, and *European Journal of Criminology*.

JODY LAPORTE is the Gonticas Fellow in Politics and International Relations at Lincoln College, University of Oxford. Her teaching and research centers on the politics of nondemocratic regimes in post-Soviet Eurasia. She holds a Ph.D. from the University of California, Berkeley. Her work has been published in *Comparative Politics*, *Post-Soviet Affairs*, *Sociological Methods and Research*, *Political Research Quarterly*, *Slavic Review*, and *PS: Political Science and Politics*.

MARLENE LARUELLE is Research Professor at the Elliott School of International Affairs, George Washington University, where she is Director of the Institute for European, Russian and Eurasian Studies (IERES), Director of the Illiberalism Studies Program, and a Co-Director of PONARS (Program on New Approaches to Research and Security in Eurasia). Her research explores how nationalism and conservative values are becoming mainstream in different cultural contexts. She focuses on Russia's ideological landscape and its outreach abroad. She has recently published *Memory Politics and the Russian Civil War: Reds versus Whites* (2020, with Margarita Karnysheva) and *Is Russia Fascist? Unraveling Propaganda East and West* (2021).

TETYANA LOKOT is Associate Professor in Digital Media and Society, School of Communications, Dublin City University. Her research focuses on protest and digital media use in networked authoritarian states, as well as internet freedom, censorship, and internet governance in Ukraine, Russia, and Eastern Europe. She is the author of *Beyond the Protest Square: Digital Media and Augmented Dissent* (2021).

LAUREN A. MCCARTHY is Associate Professor of Legal Studies and Political Science at the University of Massachusetts Amherst. She is also a Research Fellow at the Center for the Study of Institutions and Development, Higher School of Economics in Moscow. Her research focuses on the relationship between law and society in Russia, police and law enforcement institutions, civilian oversight, and the issue of human trafficking. Her book *Trafficking Justice: How Russian Police Enforce New Laws, from Crime to Courtroom* (2015) explores how Russian law enforcement agencies implemented laws on human trafficking. Her research has been supported by the Fulbright Institute for International Education, the Kennan Institute, and the Aleksanteri Institute in Helsinki, Finland.

STANISLAV MARKUS is an associate professor of international business at the University of South Carolina. He received his Ph.D. from Harvard University and his undergraduate degree from the University of Pennsylvania. He works on corporate political strategy and economic development, especially in Russia and other emerging markets. His book *Property, Predation, and Protection: Piranha Capitalism in Russia and Ukraine* (2015) was awarded the Stein Rokkan Prize for Comparative Social Science Research. His research has also been published in the leading peer-reviewed journals in political science, including in *Comparative Political Studies, World Politics*, and *Academy of Management Review*.

ILYA MATVEEV is a researcher with the Public Sociology Laboratory, St. Petersburg, Russia. His research interests include post-Soviet politics and political economy, and he has published in *Europe–Asia Studies, East European Politics*, and other journals.

ALEXANDRA NOVITSKAYA is a postdoctoral fellow at the Russian Studies Workshop, Indiana University Bloomington. She holds a Ph.D. in Women's, Gender, and Sexuality Studies from Stony Brook University. Her research interests include queer migration and asylum, and post-Soviet politics and geopolitics of gender and sexuality. She has held visiting research appointments at New York University and the University of Illinois at Urbana-Champaign. She has published articles and book chapters in *NORMA: International Journal of Masculinity Studies, Russian Review, Post-Soviet Affairs*, and the *Routledge Handbook of Gender in Central-Eastern Europe and Eurasia*.

EVGENIA OLIMPIEVA is a doctoral candidate at the University of Chicago. Her research revolves around authoritarian politics with a focus on the personnel politics in the bureaucracies. In her dissertation she shows how strategic appointment of prosecutors in Russia's regions contributed to the consolidation of Putin's regime.

ORA JOHN REUTER is Associate Professor of political science at the University of Wisconsin-Milwaukee and Senior Researcher at the International Center for the Study of Institutions and Development at the Higher School of Economics in Moscow. His research focuses on authoritarianism, political parties, and elections, with a particular emphasis on Russia. He is the author of *The Origins of Dominant Parties: Building Authoritarian Institutions in Post-Soviet Russia* (2017) as well as many articles on Russian politics in outlets such as *American Political Science Review, Journal of Politics, World Politics*, and *Comparative Political Studies*.

ANN-MARI SÄTRE is Professor in Eurasian Studies and Research Director at the Institute for Russian and Eurasian Studies at Uppsala University. Her research focuses on the performance of the Soviet/Russian economy, in particular on women's work, poverty, local development, social policy, and processes of social marginalization in Russia. She is the author or coauthor of several books including *Environmental Problems in the Shortage Economy: The Legacy of Soviet Environmental Policy* (1994); *The Other Russia: Local Experience and Societal Change* (2017), together with Leo Granberg; and *The Politics of Poverty in Contemporary Russia* (2019).

ANTON SHIRIKOV is a Postdoctoral Scholar at the Harriman Institute, Columbia University. He studies propaganda, misinformation, and trust in authoritarian and democratic regimes, as well as elites and institutions in postcommunist countries. Before academia, he was a journalist and editor in Russian independent media.

RUDRA SIL is Professor of Political Science at the University of Pennsylvania where he is also the Director of the Huntsman Program in International Studies and Business. His areas of expertise include Russian/post-Soviet studies, comparative postcommunism, international development, the politics of labor, and qualitative methodology. He is the author, coauthor, or coeditor of seven books and has published articles in a wide range of outlets, including *Comparative Political Studies*, *International Studies Quarterly*, *Perspectives on Politics*, *Journal of Theoretical Politics*, *Europe–Asia Studies*, and *Post-Soviet Affairs*.

LAURA SOLANKO is Senior Adviser at the Bank of Finland Institute for Emerging Economies (BOFIT), responsible for the analysis of Russian economic policies, banking sector developments, and energy markets. Her current research is on empirical banking and on political economy, with research projects on political lending cycles in Russia and on the effects of sanctions on listed European firms. Her research has been published in *Journal of Banking and Finance*, *Public Choice*, *Review of International Economics*, and *Russian Journal of Money and Finance*.

MIKHAIL STROKAN is a Ph.D. candidate in political science at the University of Pennsylvania, where he is completing a dissertation comparing the evolution of policymaking and governance structures in the oil and gas industries in post-Soviet Russia, Azerbaijan, and Central Asia. He holds master's degrees from Syracuse University and St. Petersburg State University and specializes in the politics of natural resources with a focus on the former Soviet Union.

DAVID SZAKONYI is Assistant Professor of political science at George Washington University and co-founder of the Anti-Corruption Data Collective. His research focuses on corruption, clientelism, and political economy in Russia, Western Europe, and the United States. He is also a Research Fellow at the International Center for the Study of Institutions and Development at the Higher School of Economics in Moscow. His book *Politics for Profit: Business, Elections, and Policymaking in Russia* (2020) examines why businesspeople run for elected political office worldwide and whether individuals with private-sector experience make better policy decisions.

ANDREI P. TSYGANKOV is Professor in the Departments of Political Science and International Relations, San Francisco State University. He teaches Russian/post-Soviet comparative politics, and international politics. He is a contributor to both Western and Russian academia. He has co-edited collective projects and published books including *Anti-Russian Lobby and American Foreign Policy* (2009), *Russia and the West from Alexander to Putin* (2012), *The Strong State in Russia* (2014), *The Routledge Handbook of Russian Foreign Policy* (2018, editor), *Russia and America* (2019), and *Russian Realism* (2022), as well as many journal articles. Tsygankov has also published a well-received textbook, *Russia's Foreign Policy* (2006, six editions).

SUSANNE A. WENGLE is N. R. Dreux Associate Professor of Political Science at the University of Notre Dame. Her main research focus is Russia's post-Soviet political and economic transformation. She is the author of numerous articles and two books: *Black Earth, White Bread: A Technopolitical History of Russian Agriculture and Food* (2022) and *Post-Soviet Power: State-Led Development and Russia's Marketization* (2015). Her research has been supported through research funding from a variety of international sources, including the Swiss National Science Foundation, the European Commission, the Swedish Collegium for Advanced Studies, the Neubauer Collegium for Culture and Society, and the Östersjöstiftelsen.

SARAH WILSON SOKHEY is Associate Professor in the Department of Political Science at the University of Colorado Boulder and a Faculty Associate at the University's Institute of Behavioral Science. Her book *The Political Economy of Pension Policy Reversal in Post-Communist Countries* (2017) examines backtracking on social security reforms in the wake of the 2009 financial crisis, and won the Ed A. Hewett Book Prize from the Association for Slavic, East European, and Eurasian Studies.

NIKOLAY ZAKHAROV is Senior Lecturer of Sociology in the School of Social Sciences at Södertörn University, Sweden. The main focus of his research is global racism and antiracism, religion, and nationalism in Eastern Europe. He is the author of *Attaining Whiteness* (2013), *Race and Racism in Russia* (2015), and *Post-Soviet Racisms* (2017, with Ian Law). His most recent articles appeared in *Nationalities Papers* and *Journal of Religion in Europe.*

Preface

When the Soviet Union ceased to exist in 1991, the future of Russian politics was uncertain. The first decade of the country's post-Soviet transformation was marked by economic collapse and political disorder. Centrifugal forces and power struggles that had their roots in the late Soviet era accelerated and led to a historic unraveling of institutions and an acute questioning of established ideals. Upon ascending to the presidency of the Russian Federation, Vladimir Putin declared war on chaos and promised to restore a strong state. Over the course of two decades, the Putin administration strengthened some political institutions, while weakening others. Similarly, some elements of ideational politics were readopted and shored up with elements from Soviet-era politics and imperial Russian traditions.

Importantly, though, the real political history of the young Russian Federation defied virtually all predictions that had been advanced by scholars and policy-makers about how institutions would take shape in the early 1990s. Although democratic forces seem to have strengthened in the late 1980s and 1990s, Russian politics now combines formally democratic institutions with highly centralized and authoritarian power structures. Similarly, while the country privatized the large majority of state-owned factories and farms and created market institutions, Russia's economy contains statist features, and economic nationalism exists side by side with market forces and private entrepreneurship. Many new actors and concerns have shaped the political agenda in the post-Soviet era for sure, but the state remains a central force in many aspects of Russian life. Societal influence on politics forms a complex and dynamic picture in which some groups have gained prominence, while others are repressed and excluded.

In the years between 1991 and 2022, evolving institutions, newly emerging political actors, and shifting ideational politics together forged a political order that has come to be known as high Putinism – an order in which power rests almost exclusively in the presidency. The dynamics shaping Russian politics today and the trajectory of change that have contributed to the creation of the current order are high-stakes topics that require continued in-depth analysis for three simple reasons: They shape everyday realities for millions of Russian citizens, Russia remains an influential regional hegemon in Eurasia and an important actor in global politics. While this book focuses squarely on domestic political, economic, and social trends, the underlying assumption of the chapter selection is that an understanding of these trends is indispensable for anyone interested in Russia's domestic politics as well as its role as a global power.

As this book goes to print, in June 2022, Russia's war in Ukraine, which Russia started on February 24, 2022, is still referred to as a special operation by the state-controlled media, and an unprecedented crackdown has muted societal criticism. The Prologue details the main aspects of the war that are known to date; the full extent of the war's implications for Russian politics is not yet apparent. Indeed, the future of Russian politics is perhaps as uncertain as it was during the turbulent days of 1991. What we do know is that the war is exceedingly risky, and that the Putin regime will have to contend with and justify the mounting human and economic costs of the war. Time will tell whether the political institutions will prove robust enough to insulate the Russian population, or fragile and unable to deflect discontent.

A paired central concept – stability and fragility – informs the analysis in all the chapters of *Russian Politics Today*. The book familiarizes students with political, economic, and social trends in contemporary Russia, mostly focusing on the past thirty years, but also bringing Soviet and imperial history to the discussion, if the issue at stake requires it. The book relies on contributions by a distinguished group of international scholars who explain empirical trends and cutting-edge research by political scientists in accessible terms. The chapters cover well-established themes in Russian politics, such as the strong presidency, the weak party system, foreign policy, and civil society, combining them with chapters on environmental politics, on the politics of race, class, gender, and sexuality, and on protests. Dedicated chapters address and explain the role of uniquely important and new actors in Russian politics, such as Russia's oligarchy and the Orthodox Church. The book also conveys diverse political, social, and economic trends across the country's large territory, with one chapter addressing the political tensions of center–region relations, another that examines everyday life on Russia's margins, and yet another that details some of the political dynamics unfolding in the Russian Arctic.

Together the chapters seek to teach the lesson that we should not think of Russian institutional change, ideational trends, and interest formation as in some way failed "outcomes" of a historical trajectory that was meant to lead to convergence with an imaginary West. Neither does it treat February 2022 as a preordained outcome of an inherently authoritarian and aggressive state. Instead, students are encouraged to learn about the political, economic, and social processes that have taken shape in Russia over the past thirty years through close study of historical trends. The aim is to help them develop a keen eye and open mind to grasp the newly emerging institutions, ideas, and interests. The concepts of stability and fragility give the volume coherence. All contributing authors have identified stabilizing forces that have helped elites maintain power and authority in one form or other, contrasting them with sources of disruption that may undermine the established order. Stability and fragility are concepts that serve as a kind of template to understand contemporary and future developments in Russian politics. They allow students to address questions related to the nature of the political regime under Putin. They are tools to analyze changing political dynamics without the underlying narrative that Russia should have progressed toward democracy, or was meant to backslide toward an authoritarian order. *Russian Politics Today* thereby allows students to gain a dynamic and multifaceted understanding of the evolving political struggles of post-Soviet Russian politics.

Russian Politics Today consists of three parts: "Political Institutions," "Political Economy," and "Politics and Society." The themes in each section speak to the "three Is" that are the focus of academic and public policy debates on contemporary Russia: *institutions*, *ideas*, and *interest*. A series of chapters introduces students to some of the most important *institutional changes*: on the presidency, center–region relations, the electoral institutions and the party system, legal institutions, the institutional underpinnings of Russia's economy, and the institutional power of the Orthodox Church. Virtually all chapters address in some way or the dynamics of authoritarian control and the opposition it generates; the chapter on center–region relations addresses the centralization of power, the chapter on protests discusses the shrinking space for public expressions of popular grievances, as do the chapters on new and old media and the social roots of societal compliance. Several chapters explore shifting *ideational and identity aspects* of Russian politics, such as the chapters on race and exclusion, on gender, on conservatism, and on ethnicity and religion. Other chapters – on oligarchs, on labor, and on the rise of economic inequality – address how *interest and interest groups* have emerged and evolved. Finally, a chapter on the role of oil and gas addresses whether we can think of Russia as a typical "petrostate," and a chapter on environmental politics explains how Russia's extraordinary natural resources create environmental vulnerabilities and shape environmental politics. There are many points of connection between the chapters; these are explicitly flagged in the book and will allow students to gain a nuanced and multifaceted understanding of the complex political landscape in contemporary Russia. Note that a number of themes and events, such as corruption and the annexation of Crimea for example, do not receive attention in a dedicated chapter, not because they are not important, but because they are relevant for multiple aspects of Russian politics and are discussed in several chapters.

Each chapter contains a number of elements that are designed to make the volume a useful teaching tool. Each chapter opens with an image that adds a visual component to the narrative of central themes, and an epigraph that allows students to hear the voice of the chapter's protagonists. The bulk of the chapter narratives focus on conveying the main trends in Russian politics since 2000, when Vladimir Putin became president of the Russian Federation, yet each of the contributors also provides information on historical precedents. The chapters are pitched to students with little prior knowledge of Russian politics or history, but they are nevertheless written to convey at times complex political dynamics and intricate histories.

Theoretical debates in comparative politics and other academic disciplines do not take center stage, but inform authors' take on the topics they cover. The textbook also provides Discussion and Exam Questions for each of the chapters. Discussion Questions are open-ended and provoke students to reflect on key aspects of the themes discussed in the chapter, and at times to take a stance on controversial issues; they appear at the end of each chapter. Exam Questions are shorter and are meant to be a test of students retention of core elements of the chapter; they are available as an online resource for instructors at www.cambridge.org/wengle. This website also includes external links to vetted video and audio content, such as documentaries and news coverage. Finally, the companion website provides links to vetted video and audio content, such as documentaries or news coverage. The book is authored by a distinguished group of senior and mid-career scholars with international reputations as well as by younger scholars who are pursuing new and ambitious projects. Contributors all have an established track record of publishing in their subfields; they have institutional homes in the United States and Europe and have taught Russian politics in one form or other.

KEY FEATURES, IN BRIEF

Russian Politics Today provides in-depth treatment of a broad range of themes in Russian politics across and within the three broad topics – political institutions, political economy, and society. It also presents a compelling overall framework by highlighting forces of stability vs. fragilities. The chapters are pitched to readers with very limited prior knowledge and include basic information on each topic, while also relying on cutting-edge research. The book thereby offers an accessible but nuanced treatment of a high-stakes topic.

The textbook is made up of twenty-one chapters, most of them relatively short. A few core chapters are somewhat longer, either because they lay the foundation for other chapters in the section (for example, on the presidency) or because they cover very large themes (for example, on foreign policy). Instructors can select themes that fit their syllabi and can pair chapters with one or more readings, either with an academic journal article or with a news media report, depending on the level of the class.

The book offers a teaching tool for instructors teaching Russian Politics, Russian Society, or Russian History; sections of classes such as World Politics or Foreign Governments; and many other courses.

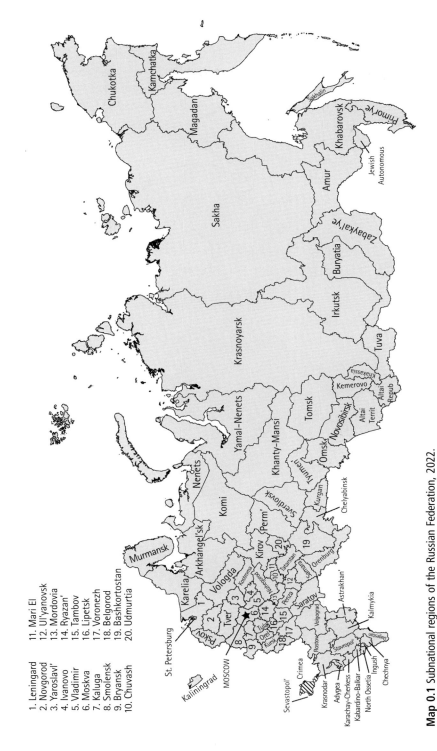

1. Leningard
2. Novgorod
3. Yaroslavl'
4. Ivanovo
5. Vladimir
6. Moskva
7. Kaluga
8. Smolensk
9. Bryansk
10. Chuvash

11. Mari El
12. Ul'yanovsk
13. Mordovia
14. Ryazan'
15. Tambov
16. Lipetsk
17. Voronezh
18. Belgorod
19. Bashkortostan
20. Udmurtia

Map 0.1 Subnational regions of the Russian Federation, 2022.

Note: Crimea has been occupied by Russia since 2014, but is not recognized as a territory of the Russian Federation by the international community.

Credit: Matthew Sisk, Lucy Family Institute for Data & Society, University of Notre Dame.

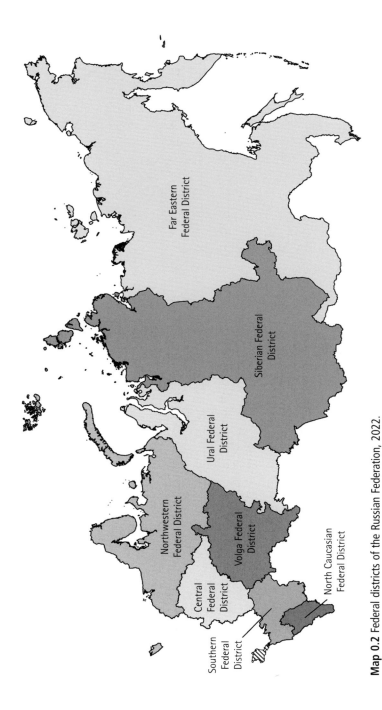

Map 0.2 Federal districts of the Russian Federation, 2022.

Note: Crimea has been occupied by Russia since 2014, but is not recognized as a territory of the Russian Federation by the international community.

Credit: Matthew Sisk, Lucy Family Institute for Data & Society, University of Notre Dame.

Prologue: Russia's War in Ukraine

When Russia invaded Ukraine in February 2022, an era seemed to come to an end. Driven by a desire to bring Ukraine back into Russia's sphere of influence, Vladimir Putin's Russia launched an extremely destructive military campaign. Russia's aggression, while not surprising, and expected by many Ukrainians, was also not preordained. It was perhaps the worst possible of many outcomes of the past thirty years of Russian history. The chapters that follow will help to explain the complex political dynamics that precipitated these events.

As this book goes into print, the war is ongoing. The editor and contributing authors have done their utmost to update the chapters to reflect rapidly changing dynamics. That said, the textbook was conceived in the spring of 2021 and the chapters were written in the fall of that year. This prologue, finalized in May 2022, serves as a short primer on the war; updates will be available on the textbook's dedicated website.

On February 24, 2022, Vladimir Putin announced the invasion of Ukraine, calling it a "special military operation" to liberate the country from an illegitimate, Western-supported government. In the initial attack, the Russian military simultaneously targeted Kyiv, Chernihiv, Sumy, and Kharkiv in the north of the country, Kherson and Melitopol' in the south, as well as Donetsk and Luhansk regions in eastern Ukraine. Within only a week of the invasion, it seemed clear that Russia's attack had not gone as planned. Not only did the Russian military face far more resistance than they had expected from Ukrainian forces and volunteer soldiers, but President Volodymyr Zelensky and his government also remained steadfast in their willingness to defend Kyiv and the country as a whole.

In an iconic YouTube video filmed in an outdoor location in Kyiv, Zelensky affirmed his and his chief advisors' commitment to remain "here" (*tut*). The significance of this statement emerged within days, as it became clear that Vladimir Putin and his advisors had expected that Zelensky would either flee the country or be captured. This was but one of the many ways in which the conflict did not unfold as the Kremlin had expected. Russia was unable to establish air superiority, which in turn hampered the advance of ground troops that appeared poorly coordinated and suffered from disruptions in supply lines. By early April, the Russian military was forced to retreat from the suburbs of Kyiv. Although the Russian government framed this as a tactical redeployment, it clearly exemplified its failure to take Ukraine's capital, topple the Zelensky government, and install a pro-Russian regime.

After the retreat of Russian forces, it emerged that Russian occupying forces had not only indiscriminately destroyed administrative and residential buildings, but directed extreme violence against ordinary civilians. In the towns of Bucha and Irpin, more than 1,200 civilians were found dead, some with their hands bound, many unburied or in mass graves. Surviving residents told investigators that they had been kept captive and tortured. Retreating Russian forces had also left booby traps and mines. Ukrainian authorities are filing criminal charges with the International Criminal Court against individual Russian soldiers for war crimes. Russian authorities, meanwhile, denied being involved in civilian deaths, which were claimed to have been staged by Ukrainian forces and were presented as "fake news" in the Russian media.

This lie was only one piece of a much bigger propaganda war that the Russian government is waging through state-controlled media channels. The war is portrayed as the liberation of Ukrainians who have been captured by fascist, aggressive pro-Western forces and committed genocide against Russian speakers in Ukraine. The West and NATO are shown as encircling Russia and threatening its security. Since many Russians receive their news from state-controlled media, much of the population is scarcely aware of the brutal realities of the war. Russia has blocked Western news and social media sites that report on the war. Although it is difficult to ascertain exactly how Russians view the war, it is likely that a majority of Russians support it. Respondents in a Levada Center poll published on April 22, 2022, shows that 45 percent "definitely support," and a further 29 percent "probably support," the war. The group that "definitely supports" the war had declined by 8 percentage points, down from 53 percent a month earlier. These results need to be interpreted with caution – opinion polls are a flawed tool in this context, because an unknown share of respondents fears repercussions for giving the wrong answer. Even in Moscow, populated with more educated, younger, and more liberal citizens than other parts of the country, a majority of respondents said the conflict was initiated by either the United States or NATO, and they see the "special military operation" as either successful or quite successful. Older generations of Russians are far more supportive of the war, while younger Russians are about equally split in either supporting or opposing the war (www.levada.ru/2022/04/28/konflikt-s-ukrai noj-i-otvetstvennost-za-gibel-mirnyh-zhitelej/).

Russian citizens who speak out against the war face extreme difficulties expressing their views. The government has effectively silenced anyone who voices criticism of the war, of the government's lies, and of the militant nationalism that justify it. By early May 2022, more than 5,500 people had been detained in protests across 77 cities, according to OVD-Info, a civil society organization monitoring protests and arrests (https://ovd.news/news/2022/03/06/spiski-zaderzhannyh-v-svyazi-s-akciyami-protiv-voyny-s-ukrainoy-6-marta-2022-goda). In March, a number of laws were passed that criminalized criticism of the war and the spreading of "fake news" about the military and other state organizations, punishable by fines and up to fifteen years in prison. Vladimir Putin dismissed domestic opponents of the war as gnats and traitors who were deliberately trying to weaken the country and who should be forced to leave Russia. The last remaining independent Russian news outlets, such as Ekho Moskvy, Dozhd, and *Novaya Gazeta*, had to close, and many journalists were forced into exile. Regular civilians, teachers for example, were denounced as traitors by colleagues if they made remarks critical of the war.

This is not to say that dissenting voices cannot be heard inside Russia. An employee of Channel One, Russia's most prominent state-run TV channel, interrupted a regular news program with a sign warning Russians about the lies of state media. There are many activists – students, feminist groups, artists, and others – who are staging public art, organizing flash mobs, and sharing information about the war on Telegram channels. One group put antiwar messages (for example, "Next stop – North Korea") on banknotes, and others help Ukrainians who have been shipped to Russia from the war zone. Activists, though, face an extremely difficult situation in Russia's current political context. Rather than fighting the government from within, many pro-Western, young, liberal urbanites have left the country, precipitating an unprecedented exodus of highly skilled professionals.

The world's response to the war has varied. In many East European countries, and in Poland in particular, a grassroots humanitarian movement has mobilized to assist the millions of Ukrainians who have been forced to leave their homes and seek refuge abroad. The Russian government defied international norms by invading a sovereign country, which prompted the United States and Western Europe to provide billions of dollars in weapons and aid to Ukraine. These countries have also imposed exceedingly harsh sanctions on Russia, which amount to what is now called "economic warfare" by both sides of the conflict. Sanctions have escalated since the onset of the conflict, starting with sanctions on key financial institutions, the freezing of assets belonging to Russian elites and the government, and the removal of many of Russia's banks from the SWIFT system. After atrocities committed by Russian troops were revealed, Western governments have also started boycotting Russian energy. Russia's energy exports to Europe may be the most critical element of sanctions against Russia. Unlike the United States, many European countries are dependent on Russian energy. The EU has been slow to propose a boycott, though on April 8 the EU imposed its first ban on Russian coal, and in May 2022 the EU made a commitment to phase out oil, gas, and coal purchases over time. While the West has been united in its response to Russia, China and India have been hesitant to condemn the Russian invasion and have cooperated with Russia to help the country soften the blow of Western sanctions. China has been buying large quantities of rubles, and India is still importing Russian oil and other commodities.

It is already clear that the war it will inflict tremendous costs. According to the UN Office of the High Commissioner, 2,345 Ukrainian civilians had died as of late April 2022, although this is presumed to be an undercount. The violence has caused more than 5 million Ukrainians to flee the country, and many others have been forced to leave their homes. While the Russian Ministry of Defense has reported the deaths of only 1,351 soldiers as of late April, the UK Defence Ministry estimates that likely around 15,000 Russian troops have been killed. The economic sanctions have led to inflation and threaten to isolate the Russian economy, with effects that are felt by regular Russian citizens. The aggregate impact of the war and of sanctions on Russia's economy is expected to add up to an 8–15 percent decline in the country's GDP in 2022. The long-term impact of the isolation of Russia's economy is not yet known. The effects of the war are also being felt across the world. Energy and fertilizer prices have skyrocketed. As the fighting has disrupted Eurasian grain production, many countries in Africa and the Middle East are experiencing food shortages.

While the long-term consequences of the war for Ukraine, Russia, Europe, and the world are yet unfathomable, it is certain to mark a watershed in Russian politics as well as Russia's relations with its neighbors and with the West.

Susanne Wengle, with Katherine Mansourova
Chicago, May 2022

1 | Stability and Fragility in Contemporary Russian Politics

SUSANNE A. WENGLE

Fig. 1.1 Navalny mural being painted over by St. Petersburg municipal worker, April 28, 2021. Credit: Anton Vagonov / Reuters / Alamy Stock Photo.

> It's all in your hands!
>
> Lyubov Sobol, "Pora deistvovat'"

Abstract

Contemporary Russian political dynamics are shaped by exceptionally strong conservative forces that stabilize a prevailing order, but also contain many sources of potential destabilization and change. By the beginning of 2022, Russia's political order was dominated by President Vladimir Putin and his loyalists within formal institutions, such as United Russia, and informal networks of power led by political and economic elites. There are no political actors who are both powerful and critical of this order, which has been called "high Putinism." A majority of citizens supported the concentration of power over the previous two decades and contributed to its consolidation through their beliefs and actions. All major channels of communication are firmly controlled by actors committed to disseminating the value, even necessity, of the current order. This highly centralized political order made it possible for Putin to launch a brutal and wholesale war on Ukraine in February 2022. Over the course of the past decade, three key pillars of support for the political current order and the war have been strengthened: (i) the state's ability to instrumentalize formal institutions to prolong Putin's and United Russia's hold on power, (ii) the fact that the state controls virtually all media outlets, and (iii), finally, the government's ability to generate relative economic prosperity. The war and sanctions are acutely threatening Russia's economy, and have led to a crackdown on the last remaining independent media outlets.

Whether or not this political constellation will turn out to be stable or fragile depends in large part on whether citizens continue to support Putin. An increasingly assertive foreign policy toward the West had bought high approval ratings for some years. Despite its virtual monopoly over the levers of power, the Putin government has been increasingly afraid of street protest and has gone to great lengths to silence a small but vocal opposition, led by Alexei Navalny. Discontent stemming from failing institutions, pervasive corruption, mounting inequality, and economic hardship has the potential to undermine the balance between stability and fragility in contemporary Russian politics. The outcome of the war in Ukraine will certainly be a watershed moment, although we do not yet know how the war will end. The future of Russian politics will hinge on answers to the question whether Russian citizens will continue to support the Putin government, even with mounting economic and human costs of the war.

1.1   "It's All in Your Hands!" . . . Or Is It?

On September 17, 2021, on the eve of Russia's tense 2021 parliamentary elections, **Lyubov Sobol**, one of Russia's leading opposition leaders, had a message for Russian citizens. "The future of our country depends on you," she pleaded via a video message disseminated on YouTube. Not on the president, whose name she did not actually mention, not on **United Russia**, the dominant party, not on bureaucrats, or on the **FSB**, the country's security service. Sobol is a close ally of **Alexei Navalny**, who nearly died in 2020 after a politically motivated poisoning and was imprisoned at the time of the elections. A few things were remarkable about Sobol's plea: First, she charted the path to change as a simple one – citizens could use a right they had, that is, the right to vote. Go vote, she said, for the candidate who has the strongest chance of winning against United Russia, also known as the "party of power," which has loyally approved all laws favored by the Kremlin. Navalny and Sobol's organization had in fact developed an app that citizens could download, **smart.vote** (*umnoe golosovanie*) that identified these candidates in all voting precincts; many were members of the Communist Party, with no affiliation to Navalny's network. Secondly, she justified the urgency of citizens taking action by bringing up a range of issues that Russians care about – inflation, pensions and salaries, the ailing healthcare system, schools, roads with potholes, and, finally, the dishes that families could afford to serve for New Year, Russia's most important holiday. Change, and the future of all of these issues, she urged citizens, is "all in your hands" (*vse v vashe rukakh*).

To perhaps no one's surprise, the 2021 parliamentary elections turned out to be skewed in favor of United Russia. The smart.vote app was removed from Apple's and Google's app stores, and from the Russian messaging platform Telegram, just days before the elections, as these companies yielded to pressure from the Russian government. Evidence of irregularities and fraud surfaced in the aftermath. In Moscow and St. Petersburg, candidates supported by the smart.vote initiative seemed to have won the majority of districts, but early leads were erased as the results from the country's controversial electronic voting system were tallied. Protests on the day after the elections were small; they had been prohibited by authorities due to COVID-related prohibitions on large gatherings. The official result was that United Russia won 324 out of 450 seats (72 percent) in the Russian **Duma**. **Vladimir Putin** and the party of power had consolidated their hold on the country's political institutions. Russia's war on Ukraine, which started on February 24, 2022, made clear that power and authority had indeed been extremely concentrated in preceding years.

Sobol's plea and the outcome of the 2021 elections may appear to be proof that citizen action is futile and that the channels of democratic accountability are incapable of shaking the solid foundation of power. These events stand for more than that, however, because they raise the question: Who can effect change, and how? In 2022, with Ukraine under siege, these questions are more urgent than ever before.

If we look closely at the events surrounding the 2021 elections, we learn a few important lessons about Russian politics over the past thirty years. The notion that citizens are stewards of their own future, of course, runs counter to the conviction of foreign and Russian observers that the Russian state, with Vladimir Putin at its helm, is principally in charge of charting the country's path. Yet, Putin's leadership is not unopposed even today, when presidential power is arguably as strong as it has ever been over the past thirty years. Though the Russian political system concentrates power in the executive, and mechanisms of popular accountability are nearly absent, parliamentary politics still matter and citizens' votes confer legitimacy on those in public office. And, while Putin's insistence on Russia's great power status and the stoking of patriotism and traditional values have resonated, everyday problems of citizens remain salient political concerns. The far-reaching sanctions that were imposed in February and March 2022 had an immediate and crippling effect on the Russian economy. We also learned that the opposition's use of social media, and in particular a new technology and the information it disseminated, actually helped sway citizens. In 2021, the government deemed the smart.vote app threatening enough to lean on Apple, Google, and Telegram. In 2022, new laws were passed to criminalize anyone opposing the war on any media platform.

Up until February 2022, it seemed that a broader range of political, social, and economic actors played a role in contemporary Russian politics than we might glean from a typical news report on Russia, which tends to take for granted that Putin presides over every move on the chessboard of Russian politics as a grand master. The war in Ukraine will be a watershed in Russian politics. On the one hand, the attack on Ukraine seems to have been initiated by an increasingly isolated president. State-controlled media are uniform in disseminating a narrative that emanates from the Kremlin – calling the war a "special operation" to liberate Ukraine from Western occupation. On the other hand, even in this extreme situation, it is still the case that Vladimir Putin relies on support from political and economic elites and the broader public.

To understand contemporary Russian politics, this book suggests that we need to depart from a Kremlin- or Moscow-centered view of Russian politics and take a closer look at how politics appears from multiple perspectives and geographical locations, and what motivates a variety of political, social, and economic actors. Only if we gain a better understanding of the urgency of citizens' changing needs and the tools and strategies of both the Putin government and a savvy and resilient opposition will we get a better idea of the stability and fragility of **Putinism**. The next sections of this chapter (1.2–1.5) introduce key sources of stability and fragility and locate them in the context of the past thirty years of Russian history. Section 1.6 addresses how Russia's search for a position in global politics and global markets has influenced domestic trends. It bears noting that, while the focus in this book is primarily on domestic politics and socioeconomic trends and actors, Russia's foreign politics and the country's integration into global markets played an important role throughout this period. The former receives a dedicated chapter in Part I of the book, and the latter is the background for chapters in Part II of the book. The final sections of this chapter, 1.7 and 1.8, provide an overview of the book and conclude by addressing the changing nature of Russia's political regime.

1.2   Thumbnail Sketch of Thirty Tumultuous Years

The year 2021 marked the thirtieth anniversary of the official dissolution of the **Soviet Union** on New Year's Eve 1991. Since the **Bolshevik Revolution** in 1917, the Soviet Union's social, economic, and political order represented the twentieth century's most important alternative to liberal democracy and capitalism. Social progress and industrial modernity were the goals, while establishing a **planned economy** and a **Leninist party** was the path pursued by Soviet leaders for more than seven decades. By the 1980s, it had become increasingly clear that central planning could not keep up with rapidly evolving consumer expectations. In 1985, **Mikhail Gorbachev** initiated *perestroika*, a series of reforms that were meant to decentralize the economy and democratize political decisionmaking. The planned economy, however, was exceedingly difficult to transform because it was both extremely hierarchical and made up of a myriad of informal practices and networks. Instead of improving economic efficiency, the reforms exacerbated shortages and worsened the economic situation for many Russians. Meanwhile, another set of reforms, *glasnost*, was meant to bring more transparency to contemporary and historical events, especially the terror and human toll of the Stalin years. *Glasnost* contributed to the blossoming of civil society and reexamination of Soviet-era atrocities, but this in turn led to an acceleration of independence movements by ethnic and national minorities, who were increasingly unwilling to see their future determined in Moscow. Gorbachev had attempted to reform the Soviet-era system of governance to make it more responsive to citizens' needs, but rapidly unfolding events overtook his ability to transform the socialist system. The Soviet Union collapsed and ceased to exist in 1991, when its constituent republics (the former **soviet socialist republics, SSRs**) declared their independence, led by Lithuania and Georgia in the spring of that year, followed a few months later by Estonia, Latvia, Belarus, and Ukraine.

The **Russian Federation**, along with each of its new neighbors, was then faced with the exceedingly challenging task of building institutions that could govern the newly independent countries. The **Cold War** had contributed to the widespread perception that socialism and capitalist democracy were competing opposites. The collapse of communism in the Soviet Union, and with it the principal competing social order of the twentieth century, buoyed the "end-of-history thesis," shaping expectations in Russia and abroad that formerly socialist countries would now proceed to converge toward more democratic governance and capitalist markets. Although there were disagreements and a great deal of uncertainty about how precisely the reconstruction of an entire social, political, and economic order would proceed, it was quite clear that what was ahead was a historic transformation of the fundamental institutions of the state, the economy, and society. The country's constitution, voting and party system, markets for goods and services, and property rights, along with a myriad of other institutions, rules, and laws, had to be redrafted more or less from scratch. It soon became clear that, rather than the somewhat mysterious forces of convergence, the process of institution-building in post-Soviet Russia was profoundly shaped by Soviet and prerevolutionary history, along with the domestic and international political dynamics that unfolded in the early 1990s.

The historical background of the Soviet-era precedents and **Boris Yeltsin**'s presidency in the 1990s were crucially important, and each of the chapters that follow details how they shaped contemporary Putinism. The main purpose of this introductory chapter is to lay out a conceptual framework centered on **stability** and **fragility**. Unlike in other textbooks on Russian politics, the democracy–autocracy continuum is not the master narrative of this book, although regime dynamics are addressed in the conclusion of this chapter. The approach chosen here is that each chapter details how particular elements of democratic governance initially emerged and then faltered. With the emphasis on the concepts of stability and fragility, *Russian Politics Today* offers a template with which to assess an inherent and often-neglected dynamism in Russian politics. It teaches students to identify sources of stability and fragility, thereby equipping them not only with a grounded and informed understanding of Russian politics today, but also with a tool to reassess political dynamics as the country's future unfolds.

1.3   Stability and Fragility

Russian politics has always contained both exceptionally strong **conservative forces** that stabilize a prevailing order and many sources of potential destabilization. This was no less true in 1917, on the eve of Russia's **October Revolution** that defined the country's history to this day, than it was in 2021, when multiple grievances and the increasingly stifling authoritarianism of the Putin era brought thousands of protesters to the streets. In the years leading up to the Bolshevik Revolution, Russia had been embroiled in a costly war abroad and its citizens at home were divided between those who were hungry and those who were not. The promise of peace and bread made by the Bolshevik revolutionaries, and by **Vladimir Lenin** as their leader, proved to be enough to destabilize the imperial order and usher in its collapse in 1917. In retrospect, the late imperial and late Soviet regimes were more brittle than they appeared in the years before these two episodes of cataclysmic change. A similar kind of fragility also characterized the Soviet social and political order, which unraveled as outlined above, when Mikhail Gorbachev initiated reforms that loosened central control and opened the airwaves for genuine public discourse. Twice, then, in relatively recent memory, Russia found that an apparently solid and strong social order was more fragile than it appeared; or, to rely on Alexei Yurchak's cogent words, "everything was forever, until it was no more" (Yurchak 2005).

Today, Russia's political order is sustained through formal institutions that centralize power in the executive, powerful informal networks among politicians, economic, and media elites, rents from the hydrocarbon sectors, and the cultural clout of the **Russian Orthodox Church**. At the same time, poverty and rising inequality, discrimination against those who do not fit the mold of nationalist and religiously conservative Russia, and various (often local) grievances have the potential to destabilize Putin's Russia, making the current order more fragile than it appears. Each of these dynamics – that is, the sources of regime resilience and vulnerability – has a history and current manifestations. This chapter introduces some of the main pillars of stability and potential fragilities in contemporary Russian politics that are detailed in later chapters.

1.4   Forces of Stability

Vladimir Vladimirovich Putin has occupied the apex of Russian political power and shaped Russian politics for more than two decades. After a career in the KGB (the Soviet secret service), Putin, then aged forty-seven, was handed the reins of power and government by an ailing President Boris Yeltsin on New Year's Eve 1999. The 1990s had been a perilous decade for most Russian citizens; a decade that had started with exuberant hope for a better future and more comfortable lives quickly became marked by economic hardship, the rise of physical violence, and a profound sense of disorientation that stemmed from the disappearance of the Soviet Union (Woodruff 1999; Volkov 2016, Oushakine 2009). By 1999, it had become increasingly obvious that the state's authority was exceedingly weak and that Boris Yeltsin was unable to solve the many big and small problems that Russians faced. Vladimir Putin promised to restore order and strengthen the state to bring prosperity to Russians in the new millennium. In the years that followed, the president moved swiftly to centralize political authority, to regain control over valuable economic assets, and to implement reforms that had been proposed in the 1990s but never carried out. Control and centralization of formal institutions went hand in hand with the development of informal and personalistic networks of power; in aggregate these have been called **patronalism** (Hale 2014) or *sistema*, "the system" (Ledeneva 2013). Patronal networks comprise a complex and dynamic set of informal institutions that channel resources and appoint cadres. High-ranking members of the military, the secret service, and the police, collectively known as the *siloviki* (literally "people of force" or "strongmen"), are especially influential in many of these informal and hierarchical networks, but others are led by Russia's new **oligarchs**, only some of whom are connected to *siloviki* circles.

While the Yeltsin years were marked by centrifugal forces that undermined the central government's ability to initiate reforms that state-building and market construction called for, the early Putin years saw reassertion and strengthening of the institutions of the state. Meanwhile, the first decade of the new millennium saw buoyant oil prices and an economic recovery, which led to higher household incomes and allowed the state to improve social spending and to raise pensions and state-sector salaries. Though Putin officially gave up the formal office of the president to **Dmitry Medvedev** between 2008 and 2012, he was reelected after these four years. The political order he has established since then has been exceptionally durable. In contemporary Russia, there are virtually no political actors who are both powerful and critical of the president and his inner circle, forming a political order that has been called "**high Putinism**" (Sharafutdinova 2020). A number of parties, including the **Liberal Democratic Party of Russia (LDPR)**, **Rodina**, and the **Communist Party of the Russian Federation**, hold seats in the Duma and in regional parliaments, but they have not opposed United Russia's agenda in any meaningful way. The most vocal and committed group of Putin critics is led by Alexei Navalny and his team, whom the Putin administration calls the "**nonsystemic**" opposition. Navalny has tried to unify a large, but loosely organized set of local groups and independent political actors capable of channeling discontent.

Despite mounting concerns about elite corruption and nearly a decade of slower economic growth, many Russians support the order that Putin created, either because they approve of the president himself or because they do not think any other leader would be capable of leading the country into the future. The most important pillars of the current order are:

- the **superpresidency** – institutions that centralize power in the executive branch;
- the state-controlled media that have conveyed the perspective of the Kremlin; and
- a mixed economy that has brought relative prosperity and economic security for many Russian citizens.

1.4.1   The Superpresidency

A central pillar of the durability of Putinism lies in the extraordinary formal and informal power residing in the executive branch, known as Russia's superpresidency (see Chapter 2). The Russian Federation is formally a semi-presidential political system, and the constitution divides power among the three branches of government and horizontally distributes authority between the federal center and regional administrations. Yet, since the Yeltsin presidency, Russian leaders have decisively altered these arrangements, centralizing power and striving to establish what is called the "**power vertical**" (*vertikal' vlasti*). The chapters that follow detail many instances and examples of how Vladimir Putin instrumentalized the formal powers of his office to strengthen his hold on power. An early turning point was a 2004 law that abolished direct elections of regional governors, instead giving the Russian president the right to appoint them. The law was passed swiftly by both chambers of the Russian legislature, before being signed by the president; it was not challenged by the Constitutional Court, even though it ostensibly violated the rights of Russia's regions granted by the constitution. A few years earlier, in 2000, seven new administrative regions had been created, each headed by a newly appointed leader, the *polpred*, directly chosen by and accountable only to the president's office. Perhaps the most blatant example of the president's reliance on instrumentalizing institutions to extend his hold on power was the constitutional amendment passed by the Duma in 2020 that lengthened the presidential term, allowing Putin to stay in office until 2036.

Over the past twenty years, many steps have contributed to the strengthening of Putin's hold on the executive branch. What is more, formal institutions have served in various ways to eliminate critics and possible opponents. They have been used against oligarchs, most notoriously against **Mikhail Khodorkovsky** (former owner of **Yukos**, Russia's largest oil company in the 1990s, which produces approximately 20 percent of Russia's oil output), as well as against **Vladimir Gusinsky** and **Boris Berezovsky**, both of whom emerged as media tycoons in the same decade. These and many other oligarchs were convicted of tax fraud and corporate wrongdoing, and either jailed or forced to flee Russia. Laws have also been used to arrest protesters and therefore suppress the expression of societal discontent. The members of the punk rock band **Pussy Riot**, an outspoken and courageous group of artists, were convicted under a law against hooliganism for the unsanctioned performance of a critical punk rock song in Moscow's Cathedral of Christ the Savior. In 2013, in the aftermath of their trial, a new law against **blasphemy** made slights of religious believers a criminal offense. The same year, legislation known as the "**gay propaganda**" **law** was passed to prohibit the distribution of information related to "non-traditional sexual orientation," ostensibly to protect children from being exposed to information that undermines traditional family values. This law, too, has been widely used as a tool to discourage and crack down on societal critiques of Putin's nationalist and traditionalist agenda. Finally, since 2020 the Russian state has frequently referred to **COVID-19**-related restrictions on large gatherings to arrest participants of street protests critical of Putin.

1.4.2   State-Controlled Media

A second powerful tool that strengthens the Putin government is control of the country's media, especially TV channels, which are the main source of news and information for most Russian citizens. The collapse of the Soviet Union and, with it, the state's monopoly on the ownership of the news media created a whole new media landscape in Russia, with many new print publications and TV channels founded by enthusiastic media entrepreneurs and backed by oligarchic capital.

Journalists and owners of these news outlets provided critical coverage of some of the postcommunist period's most catastrophic events, such as the war in **Chechnya**, the sinking of the *Kursk* **submarine**, and the **Beslan hostage crisis**. It gradually became clear, however, that these media outlets often reflected the interests of their oligarchic owners, especially when it came to whitewashing their role in the property struggles through which they had accumulated vast fortunes (see Chapter 17). When Putin became president, the government sought to reclaim the state's control of media outlets. One of Russia's main TV channels, **NTV**, had not backed Putin in the 2000 presidential election. In the spring of 2001, the channel's owner, Vladimir Gusinsky, was arrested and subsequently forced to flee Russia, and his media empire was taken over by Gazprom, the state-owned energy company. Along with NTV, Putin seized control of **Channel One** (formerly ORT), which in the 1990s was formally state-owned but de facto had been controlled by the oligarch Boris Berezovsky. Together with a third national television network, **Rossiia-1**, these channels provided increasingly bland and noncritical media coverage during the first decade of the 2000s.

A few islands of independent media, such as the radio station **Ekho Moskvy**, the newspaper *Novaya Gazeta*, and the TV station **Dozhd**, survived for some time, though they reached only a small segment of liberal urbanites. Meanwhile, however, the number of internet and social media users exploded. By 2011, the opposition had realized that social media could be an indispensable tool in coordinating protests against election fraud and corruption.

After Putin reclaimed the presidency in 2012, the state's control of Russia's media expanded further. The owner of **VKontakte**, Russia's main social media platform, was forced to sell the network to Alisher Usmanov, an oligarch close to and loyal to the Kremlin. The editors-in-chief of several high-profile media outlets that had maintained some independence were fired or resigned under pressure; these included the editor of the respected business daily *Vedomosti* and the editor of **Lenta.ru**, until then Russia's top news website. (Galina Timchenko, Lenta.ru's editor, and many of her staff members subsequently founded **Meduza**, an online media venture based in Latvia that is one of the few remaining independent media outlets covering Russian news.)

Although many Russian journalists are highly skilled professionals, most TV and print media do not see their role as an independent fourth estate, counterbalancing the powers of government. Throughout the mass protests in Ukraine in 2013, the annexation of Crimea in 2014, the Russian-controlled separatist movement in eastern Ukraine, and most recently the all-out war on Ukraine, Russia's media have provided a uniform message for citizens that reflects the Kremlin's nationalist and aggressive rhetoric. Not only did Russian state-controlled media avoid any criticism of Russian policy, but they also came to serve as tools to promote loyalty, galvanize support for the war in Ukraine, and vilify critics as enemies of Russia.

By 2021, the remaining independent print media, including most prominently *Novaya Gazeta*, were operating under heavy constraints. Moreover, as the 2021 elections approached, the government was increasingly willing to restrict online media. Few could have anticipated, however, the dramatic increase in censorship that accompanied Russia's invasion of Ukraine the following year – events that unfolded as this volume went to press. After February 2022, most of Russia's remaining independent media, including Ekho Moskvy and Dozhd, were forced to close. Putin's control of the media is now nearly complete.

1.4.3 Russia's Mixed Economy

A third enormously important stabilizing force in Russian politics is the mixed economy, that is, a statist economy that also tolerates markets and private ownership (Wengle 2015). Thanks to this economic model, and supported by profits from the oil and gas sectors, Russian citizens have experienced two decades of relative prosperity and macroeconomic stability. Although economic growth has slowed since 2010 and creeping inflation has been a worry for citizens, over the past thirty years the Russian economy has evolved to change citizens' everyday life in ways that make Russians feel more comfortable. A new car, nice furniture and durable consumer goods, vacations abroad, and restaurant meals have all come within reach of Russia's emerging middle class and define how they think of the Putin period.

This is in stark contrast to the economic realities of the Yeltsin years and the late Soviet period. The Soviet planned economy had directed and allocated vast resources to politically important sectors, which allowed the Soviet Union to score victories in the Cold War that prioritized military, space, and satellite technologies. At the same time, the socialist planned economy was not very responsive to consumer demand and was plagued by chronic, and increasingly frequent, shortages of many goods. Soviet citizens had to navigate shortages using informal networks, often dedicating significant time and resources to locating and securing popular consumer goods. The 1990s were marked by enormously disruptive economic crises: Nearly every Russian citizen's quality of life was adversely affected by hyperinflation, unemployment, nonpayment of wages, and other calamities. Oligarchs seemed to be the only beneficiaries, and they squirreled away vast fortunes into foreign assets and offshore accounts.

Many citizens, meanwhile, were faced with poverty, a shock for Russians who had grown up with full employment, stable prices, and the universal access to healthcare and education of the Soviet era. The economic crises gave rise to a profound disappointment with market reforms that had brought so few of the tangible rewards they had promised. The state, meanwhile, could not afford to protect citizens with social programs; it was unable to collect taxes, and the government incurred debts and budget deficits. In the run-up to the 1995 parliamentary elections, Boris Yeltsin's popularity had plummeted. With reelection in jeopardy, Russia's first democratically elected president turned to American advisors to run his political campaigns and to Russia's most powerful oligarchs to shore up both the campaign and the state budgets. In return, Yeltsin handed over highly valuable shares of state-owned enterprises to these oligarchs in a program known as "loans for shares," essentially giving away many of the crown jewels of the Soviet industry to a new and tiny group of well-connected elites (see Chapter 12).

After 2000, Vladimir Putin pursued a far more statist economic policy than Yeltsin had, although many of the liberal economic advisors remained influential for some years. Most importantly, the Russian government under Putin moved rapidly to reassert the state's control over the lucrative hydrocarbon sectors that had been partially privatized in the 1990s. This, together with high energy prices in the early twenty-first century, allowed the government to bolster public revenues and allowed for more generous spending, in turn a central prerequisite for the relative prosperity of these years. At the same time, Putin realized that the new class of powerful oligarchs was among the most likely political challengers – they owned TV networks, allowing them to sway the Russian electorate, and they could finance political opponents. Oligarchs derived their political power largely from controlling large enterprises in the natural resource sector or media empires. Putin thus reclaimed the state's ownership of energy assets, and led a broader campaign to "tame" the energy and media oligarchs though a variety of carrots and sticks. Oligarchs essentially were left with a choice either to be loyal and benefit from a new order, or to be prosecuted, exiled, or even killed.

After about the mid-2000s, the Russian state was able to appropriate the proceeds from the hydrocarbon sectors and force oligarchs to invest in Russian assets. While it renationalized the country's largest oil company, Rosneft, a move that reasserted state control of the economy, the government also often pursued liberal economic policies, for example by liberalizing capital markets. With growing state revenues, the state subsidized and supported other sectors it deemed strategically important – aviation and agriculture, for example – helping Russian companies compete with foreign and global corporations. Today, Russia's economy still relies on the state-dominated hydrocarbon sector, but many other sectors are privatized, and some of them deliver innovative products and services to Russian consumers. Russia's bureaucracy and public-sector employment have also grown, in turn creating a new middle class. State-sector employees lead relatively secure and comfortable lives: Not only can they rest assured that their wages will be paid by the state, but they also still enjoy the tangible comforts of a consumer-oriented market economy that were so conspicuously absent in the late Soviet period. Not surprisingly, Russia's state-employed middle class has proved to be supportive of Putin's order (Rosenfeld 2020).

This prosperity is now acutely under threat, as economic sanctions imposed after February 2022 have had immediate and serious consequences for the Russian economy. Sanctions initially targeted the financial ties of Russian companies and elites, as foreign-denominated assets were frozen and some banks were banned from the SWIFT system, which facilitates international bank transfers. Many multinational corporations, though, reacted to events by pulling out of the Russian market, especially companies with consumer-facing brands, such as Ikea, H&M, Starbucks, and McDonald's. The Russian stock market was closed for a month after February 25, 2022. The short-term effects of these sanctions included the precipitous devaluation of the ruble, while the price of goods increased, hurting Russian consumers who had already been concerned with years of creeping inflation. Some foreign companies continue to pay employees, but these jobs will likely disappear, unless the war ends. The medium- and long-term consequences of the war will depend on how well the Putin government can insulate the Russian economy from these shocks and possible future boycotts of Russian energy. Whether high-quality food staples and consumer goods will be available and affordable is one of the key variables that may sway Russian citizens.

1.4.4   Popular Support for Putinism?

Although all three pillars of strength and stability in Putin's increasingly authoritarian order rest on the state's control of formal institutions, informal networks of power, and material assets, citizens also play a critical role in strengthening Putin's power from below. Through their actions and beliefs, citizens and social actors enforce and co-construct power together with agents of the state. A large majority of Russians are supportive of Putin's leadership and consolidation of power, and the president consistently receives high and very high popularity ratings in public opinion surveys (see, for example, Greene and Robertson 2020; Chapter 18). Importantly, Gulnaz Sharafutdinova (2020) shows that this kind of support is both manufactured and genuine, that is, it is both generated by propaganda that molds popular attitudes and an expression of widely held sentiments that value the apparent achievements of the Putin period.

What precisely drives popular support for Putin, and whether or not it will prove robust through coming months, has become an extremely urgent question as the war in Ukraine rages on. Will Russians continue to support Putin and believe his version of the nature of the "special operation" as the costs of war and sanctions mount? On the one hand, extremely centralized political institutions, control of the media, and the severity of the crackdown on protests suggest that it will indeed be very hard for citizens to oppose the war. On the other hand, most Russian citizens are vulnerable to price increases of basic consumer goods, and images of the real brutality of the war are available online and via social media. Many young Russians, including many supporters of Alexei Navalny, oppose the war. Mothers and families of fallen

Russian soldiers will not be misled that this is a bloodless and welcome liberation. The sorrow and concerns of this group may change the minds of fellow citizens, especially if inflation accelerates and jobs disappear, though only time can tell.

1.5   Fragility

Citizens do have the potential to disrupt the existing order through protests and collective action. During the Soviet era, expressions of popular dissent were either violently repressed during the Stalin years, or more subtly discouraged with punitive measures that could marginalize a citizen who voiced discontent. Yet, in the twentieth century, Russian society asserted its will against an apparently strong established order that sought to control citizens, not once, but twice: in the years leading up to the October Revolution and in 1991. For many Russians today, for better or worse, Putin's order gives the impression that it is durable and, were it not for Putin's own mortality, that it may last forever. Given Russia's history of harboring the potential for sudden ruptures and upheaval, though, we need to look more closely to find the fissures and fragilities in the current order. We find them in the

- weakness of formal institutions;
- prospects of a fraught transfer of power;
- pervasive corruption; and
- economic stagnation.

1.5.1   Weakness of Formal Institutions

A first fragility of the political institutions in Putin's Russia lies in the weakness of many formal institutions. This is not to say that Russia does not have any sophisticated and complex institutions that function well and achieve stated objectives. Russia's ministries and bureaucracies are staffed by many committed and competent specialists who make sound policy recommendations and apply the rule of law. Some formal institutions, though, are weakened by the primacy (and more recently increasing isolation) of the presidential system and the workings of informal networks. The media and elections are both formal institutions that illustrate this dynamic: Their ability to act as mechanisms of accountability and to disseminate information is undermined if and when they are instrumentalized to spread propaganda and cement the power of one elite group. Another example is environmental regulations that are skirted when they negatively affect powerful allies of the president. In this case, the weakness of formal institutions is evident in the detrimental effects of these practices on shared environments and commons, for example in the disruption of reindeer herds in the Arctic or the pollution of salmon spawning grounds in Kamchatka. Indeed, to Russian citizens these kinds of institutional failures have often been most noticeable when they involve local concerns and compromise regional or municipal authorities. The expropriation of parkland and the failure to provide municipal waste disposal services are two grievances that have repeatedly generated public protests in recent years.

Emphasizing personalistic and centralized authority structures as sources of fragility may seem paradoxal, as section 1.4 identified them as pillars of strength of Putin's order. The point here is that these kinds of institutions create incentives for political actors and bureaucrats to "look up" to power elites as the relevant and decisive constituencies, rather than having to serve society. In the long run, this impedes institutions' ability to carry out the functions that they are tasked with, which in turn creates societal problems, grievances, and sources of instability.

1.5.2 Fraught Transfer of Power

A second fragility of the current political order is related to the first: In a highly personalistic political system the transfer of power is inherently fraught (Frye 2020). If power and authority coalesce and rest in one person, the end of that person's tenure in office creates a high level of uncertainty about formal and informal rules and expectations. The political stability of many post-Soviet successor countries was disrupted when the first post-Soviet presidents were forced to hand over the reins of power as old age impeded their ability to preside over the institutional apparatus that they had fostered during the preceding decades. Most recently this has been the case in Kazakhstan, where protests and elite infighting led to violence and political turmoil in January 2022.

In Russia, two transfers of power have taken place between 1991 and today. When Yeltsin's health deteriorated in the late 1990s, he moved quickly to appoint a loyal successor, rather than run the risk of a powerful opponent turning against him, his family, and his network. Putin, by contrast, has chosen to tweak formal institutions to allow him to stay in power legally. In 2008, at the end of Putin's first two terms in office, the president formally stepped aside and assumed the office of prime minister for four years, while simultaneously transferring some powers from the presidency to the prime ministerial office and lengthening the presidential terms from four to six years. The 2020 constitutional amendment was a bolder change of a formal institution. It annulled the term limits of Russia's 1993 constitution (though only for the sitting president), thereby allowing Putin to hold the reins of power through 2036. Both of these changes were made in the name of stability. Note that this is part of Russian political discourse that portrays Western-style democracy, and Ukrainian-style longing for it, as specters of undesirable disorder and chaos that must be avoided in Russia. In the winter of 2011, Putin's reclaiming of the presidency sparked mass protests; by 2020, by contrast, citizens' response to the far-reaching constitutional amendments was muted, in part also because the referendum to approve them coincided with the disorienting early months of the COVID-19 pandemic. At the same time, many Russians have not opposed these steps to consolidate and lengthen Putin's time in office and have gone along with increasingly blatant corruption.

1.5.3   Corruption

A third fragility of Russia's political order relates to corruption. During the past twenty years, Putin-era elites have amassed vast fortunes through schemes that typically either divert resources from lucrative hydrocarbon extraction or siphon resources from the state sector. Corruption takes many forms; government contracts for public works that overpay a favored contractor, who in turn underdelivers on the promised good, are a fairly typical example. (This kind of corruption happens despite a sweeping law, passed in 2012, that all Russian companies must publicly report state procurement contracts. Here, too, we see the existence of a formal institution – the procurement system, meant to increase transparency of how public funds are spent – that has not achieved its stated objective of increasing account-ability and curbing corruption.) Many Russian citizens largely accept even pervasive corruption as an unavoidable fact of politics, but that does not mean that they are indifferent to how the country's resources are distributed. It is a common sentiment

Fig. 1.2 "We did not elect crooks and thieves!" Russian citizens protesting in Novosibirsk, December 10, 2011. Credit: AFP / Stringer / AFP / Getty Images.

that elite stealing is not particularly objectionable, as long as these elites also guarantee that regular citizens have "normal," or acceptable, standards of living.

During the 2011 wave of protests, Navalny dubbed United Russia the "Party of Crooks and Thieves" ("*Partiia Zhulikov i Vorov*"), a nickname that has stuck and tainted the party since then. Detailed revelations, researched and disseminated by the Foundation against Corruption via YouTube, about precisely how much wealth prominent political figures have amassed were viewed by millions of Russians. They resonated in a context of growing wealth and income inequality, which meant that many Russians gained the impression that elites had assumed all of Russia's wealth, leaving only crumbs for regular citizens. The anticorruption revelations also helped Alexei Navalny and his team gain prominence as credible critics of the Putin establishment. Disgust with corruption helped Navalny unify a multivocal and diverse group of citizens who had become disillusioned with the current order for a whole host of different of reasons, often connected with the malfunctioning of formal institutions and the blanket dominance of pro-Putin politicians.

1.5.4 Economic Stagnation

A fourth fragility emanates from a stagnating economy. Although the Russian economy has delivered relative stability and prosperity compared to the late Soviet period and the 1990s, it remains dependent on energy revenues, and low global oil prices lead to dwindling tax revenues and export earnings. Periods of global economic crisis, such as the one triggered by the 2008/09 subprime mortgage crisis and the 2020 COVID-19 crisis, have threatened the stability of the Russian economy via the low energy prices that characterized recessions. Global economic or financial crises are thus recurring sources of instability for the Russian economy. The Russian government has set up a stability fund to cushion the effects of these crises on the domestic economy but, while helpful, these funds need to be maintained and are not unlimited. There are also domestic sources of economic hardship for Russian citizens. During Putin's second stint in office, that is, since 2012, the Russian economy has grown much more slowly and has created unequal opportunities. Some sectors are thriving and offer employment for qualified, well-trained professionals, but others are stagnating and in some regions of the country poverty has increased. What is more, legislative reforms that had a sharply negative effect on household incomes were enacted despite being deeply unpopular. The 2005 reforms of in-kind entitlements, called the *l'goty* reforms, were in fact the first time the Putin government encountered widespread disapproval and street protests (Wengle and Rasell 2008; Chapter 13). Citizens' reactions to pension reforms implemented in 2018 mirrored those of 2005, even if the government had become far less tolerant of public protest in the intervening years. Up to 2022, the credibility of the government's claim that a strong leader and paternalistic government is the only appropriate form of governance for Russia largely hinged on its ability to deliver relative prosperity. After the onset of sanctions, the government's credibility will at least in part depend on how they affect regular citizens.

All these sources of fragility within the current political order relate to its shortcomings in addressing societal grievances of various kinds. Personalistic institutions fail to address societal problems, because institutions and local politicians serve power elites, rather than society. The informal networks of economic and political power are so tightly and intricately tied up with the maintenance of a small circle around Putin that a transfer of power brings about the threat of major destabilization and shock to the political system. Finally, Russians increasingly believe that informal power networks serve kleptocratic elites who do not share the country's wealth with regular Russians. The Putin government clearly fears citizens' discontent and societal demands to share power and wealth. This fear has accelerated the repression of any kind of popular protest. The ferocity of the crackdown on antiwar protests by the Russian National Guard (Rosgvardiia) in 2022 makes it increasingly apparent that Russia has turned into an authoritarian police state.

1.6   Russia's Place in the World

Russian politics, then, revolves around the strong presidency, coopted institutions, a powerful but loyal group of oligarchs, citizens at large, and a vocal, but largely powerless and decapitated opposition. Like all other countries, Russian domestic political dynamics are also shaped by powerful global economic, political, and ideational forces. There are many sources of stability and fragility emanating from the global arena that have either helped or challenged Russian political actors as they sought to build institutions domestically. Global capital and energy markets greatly affect Russian economic policies as well as regular Russian citizens. Putin's domestic political rhetoric both echoes and contributes to shaping a global backlash against liberalism, globalization, and identity politics; the latter has emerged as a powerful ideational current in many political struggles across the world in the first decades of the twenty-first century.

Russia's role in global politics and its integration into markets is unique because of its history and status as the heir of the Soviet Union and, for much of the twentieth century, a global superpower and the main adversary of the capitalist West. After 1991, the young Russian Federation had to reestablish foreign relations with large and powerful countries such as the United States and China, as well as with its new neighbors, the former soviet socialist republics. Russia also entered a renewed relationship with the EU and its member countries, which had variegated relations to Russia. The Soviet Union, of course, had a history of struggles and ties with all these countries, but most of them were a function of the Soviet Union's ideological and power position as the leader of the communist world. Russia's stepping into the shoes of the Soviet empire, as it were, raised protracted conundrums about how precisely the country should engage with the world and its neighbors. Russia retained the Soviet Union's nuclear arsenal, for example, but would it retain the power and international status that these weapons had previously conferred? Yeltsin's team of liberal reformers embarked on a program of radical economic liberalization, but should some Russian producers be protected from global competition? Russia's quest to find a place in the world raised many such fraught questions that Russian elites and society have grappled with over the past three decades (see Chapter 8).

Not surprisingly, Russia continued to have a close relationship with most of the fifteen newly independent countries on its borders. The majority of Soviet successor states formed the **Commonwealth of Independent States** (the CIS), although Ukraine never joined, and other countries, including Georgia, have since withdrawn their membership. Strong ties were in part the result of the fact that many ethnic Russians were resident in neighboring countries after 1991. The Russian Federation took a keen interest in their citizenship and cultural rights in those countries, where nationalist sentiments often dominated domestic politics. Russia and its neighbors also generally maintained strong economic relations, and consistent demand for Russian products by neighbors has certainly been one of the sources of Russia's economic stability. Economic ties are in part a result of Soviet-era planning: Railways, electricity, and pipeline networks are material links that act as hardwired connections between Russia and other former Soviet republics. There are other legacies that have facilitated intraregional ties, such as a common *lingua franca* and a shared system of regulating food safety, for example. The **Eurasian Economic Union** (EEU) is the region's international organization that seeks to provide a framework for trade and cooperation among its members, Armenia, Belarus, Kazakhstan, Kyrgyzstan, and Russia.

This does not mean, though, that neighborly economic relationships did not also raise many thorny issues. Among these are the price of energy that Russia sets for neighboring countries, as well as what these countries charge for the transit of Russian oil and gas. Despite a shared history and infrastructural ties, the relationship between Russia and some of its neighbors has often been fraught, as those neighbors sought to gain genuine independence and keep Russian influence at bay. This was especially the case for the Baltic countries, Ukraine, and Georgia, countries with strong independence movements in the late Soviet period. Nowhere is the struggle between new nationhood and inherited ties to Russia more salient and explosive than in Ukraine, a country caught between close ties to Russia and a strongly held desire among many citizens to join the West. Ukraine has long played a pivotal role in Russian foreign and domestic politics, and Russia justifies the current war in Ukraine as a legitimate security concern and a reaction against a purported aggression by the West.

The past thirty years have brought enormous change in Russia's relationship with the West, that is, with both the United States and Europe. For much of the early

1990s, this relationship was characterized by a shared hope for an equal partnership and cooperation to bring about a more peaceful world order. Progress on dismantling the most lethal weapons in both countries' nuclear arsenals and cooperation in global nonproliferation efforts were common goals. The economic hardship and chaos of the 1990s, which democratization and liberalization had brought to Russia, however, contributed to a growing disappointment with these "Western" models. NATO expansion in Eastern Europe and the bombing of Belgrade during the Yugoslav wars were widely seen as a betrayal by Western powers. (The Russian Federation has always maintained that Secretary of State James Baker had ruled out the expansion of NATO in Eastern Europe in 1990; the United States disputes that this was a formal promise.) Russia's economy, meanwhile, was increasingly import-dependent, foreign debt ballooned, and Russia received **International Monetary Fund** (IMF) loans and Western aid. The Russian government seemed to lose autonomy over its economic policy. The ruble crisis in 1998, triggered by the **Asian financial crisis**, led Russia to default on its foreign debt, dealing another blow to an already troubled economy. All of this contributed to a profound sense of disillusionment and vulnerability for Russian citizens.

During Putin's first two terms in office, the Russian government still sought to engage with Western powers in an equal partnership. Tensions between Russia and the United States mounted during the first administration of President Barack Obama, however, marked by growing distrust and misunderstanding due to NATO expansion and ongoing conflicts in Libya and Syria. The 2014 **Sochi Winter Olympics** were still meant to be a kind of showcase event that would demonstrate to global audiences that Russia was a modern and "normal" country. A few months before the Olympics, Mikhail Khodorkovsky was released from prison and allowed to emigrate. Yet Russia and Western countries disagreed sharply about how to respond to the rapidly unfolding events in Ukraine that year, defined by an ongoing struggle between pro-Western civil society groups and pro-Russian elites. Russia's **annexation of the Crimean peninsula** in March 2014 and Russia's support of separatists in eastern Ukraine in the years that followed marked a sharp turning point in Russia's relationship with the West and epitomized Russia's far more assertive stance in global politics. Russia's foreign policy turn was accompanied by increasingly fierce anti-Western rhetoric at home – state-dominated media variously describe Russia as under siege by the West and as the lone defender of "traditional" values in a world swayed by decadent, liberal values. Russia's antagonistic relationship with the West, then, also helped boost its credentials as a leader in a global anti-"Western," antiliberal alliance. Russia has rhetorically and materially given support to nationalist, conservative, and far-right causes in Eastern and Western Europe.

While the Russian government needed to find ways to get along with former enemies and friends, and new neighbors, Russian companies had to learn how to compete with foreign and transnational corporations. The Soviet planned economy had exported gas to global markets since the 1970s and had trade relations with friendly socialist countries in Eastern Europe, Asia, Africa, and Latin America. Yet, with the collapse of the planned economy and the privatizations of the 1990s, Russian companies faced an entirely new set of opportunities and challenges. The opening of Russia's markets in the early 1990s overwhelmed many Russian producers: Collective farms and food-processing companies, for example, could not compete with imported commodities. They did not have access to capital to update machinery and had too little income to pay salaries to workers, who migrated from rural areas to cities. Unable to keep up with the hyperefficient farms in the United States, Argentina, and Brazil, many Russian farms went bankrupt, and cheap American chicken legs reached Russian stores.

The Putin government responded to the shock of the 1990s with a dual policy that embraced global market forces when they seemed to offer Russian producers something that they could not obtain domestically, but also at times actively and strategically limited market access for foreign competitors. During President Putin's first term in office, Russia pursued policies that promised full membership of the most powerful multilateral institutions that govern the global economy. In some institutions, Russia inherited the seat and representation of the Soviet Union, as in the IMF, but in others, such as the **World Trade Organization** (WTO), it had to fulfill a number of conditions to attain membership. Membership of the WTO was an ambitious goal that led Russia to pursue trade and financial market liberalization for much of the early 2000s, although it often found ways to use loopholes to protect particular industries. As a result of these policies, Russia became more globally integrated than it had ever been, although integration is dominated by the country's export of hydrocarbons, metallurgical products, and other raw materials. Because Russia exports more energy and metals than any other product, the price volatility of these commodities on global markets has the potential to be highly destabilizing for the Russian economy (see Chapter 10). Over time, though, other sectors have become more globally competitive: Russia has become the world's largest wheat exporter, selling wheat to more than a hundred countries across the world. While Russia is an important global economic actor, it also remains the most influential economy in Eurasia, maintaining strong ties with most of its neighbors and among emerging economies, such as the **BRICs** (Brazil, Russia, India, and China). What is interesting, though, is that, as Russia has become more integrated than ever, it has also shifted to take on leadership of antiglobalization movements across the world.

The sanctions and countersanctions that followed the annexation of Crimea constrained Russia's engagement with Western economies in important ways, though they have also served to reorient external economic relations with other countries, including China. Russia's war on Ukraine will forever change Russia's role in the world, regardless of its outcome. Although events are unfolding as this book goes into print, global reactions to the war have resulted in the virtual isolation of Russia from Western countries, with yet-uncertain consequences for relations with other post-Soviet neighbors and with China.

1.7   Outline of the Book

This book is organized into three parts:

 I Part I focuses on the core institutional landscape of Russian politics.
 II Part II explores how Russia's economy shapes politics, and vice versa.
 III Part III details how the state and society interact.

   The boundaries between these three parts are permeable – some chapters in the third part (social forces) would not be out of place in the first (political institutions). Economic actors are also social and political actors, of course. Race, gender, and sexuality are intentionally positioned in Part I, because Russian racism and patriarchy constitute political institutions, even if they are sometimes viewed as social forces, placed at the end of edited volumes on Russian politics or not covered at all. Finally, there are many points of connection across chapters and between parts – they will be flagged as such in the chapters and together facilitate a multifaceted understanding of central themes in Russian politics. Corruption, for example, is a pervasive feature of Russia's political and economic scene, and hence features in several chapters.

1.7.1   Foundational Political Institutions

Russian politics is about the constitution, laws, the structure of government, such as federalism, and electoral and party systems. The first part of the book introduces these foundational institutions that underpin Russian political dynamics. The starting point here is that the collapse of the Soviet Union was also the end of the world's most powerful one-party state, and that therefore the Russian Federation had to rebuild many of its most basic political institutions. Rather than following some teleological trajectory toward Western liberal democracy, Russian governance institutions changed in ways that few observers predicted. On the one hand, these institutions have all served to strengthen Putin's political order and reduced the points of access. On the other hand, we will also see institutional dysfunction and grievances that have emerged, which in turn expose important fragilities.

   Chapter 2 focuses on the Russian presidency; Jody LaPorte shows how Putin has taken advantage of both the formal prerogatives of the presidency and his informal command over the "power vertical" in order to consolidate power. Ora John Reuter and David Szakonyi show in Chapter 3 that Russia is an electoral authoritarian regime. They explore party competition and voting in this regime, as well as the nature and extent of electoral manipulation, which has emerged as one of the main grievances motivating the opposition. Yet the drama of politics is not just about the government's workings and laws as "parchment institutions" – we also need to understand the ways in which institutions allow, or hinder, citizen influence on politics. In Chapter 4, Lauren McCarthy shows that Russia has a dualistic legal system: Many laws are applied impartially by judges concerned with maintaining a just and legal order, while others are used as political tools by elites. In Chapter 5, Evgenia Olimpieva shows that the dynamics of center–region relations in Russia established during the Putin presidency are at the heart of both the strength and the fragility of Russia's authoritarian regime. Politics also involves struggles in the symbolic realm that can legitimize elites' hold on power and marginalize groups. In Chapter 6, Nikolay Zakharov details how racial categories and antiracism feature in Russian politics. In Chapter 7, Alexander Kondakov and Alexandra Novitskaya show that Vladimir Putin's political rhetoric is saturated with masculinist tropes that intend to legitimize the centralization of power, but have also contributed to increasing violence against women and the LGBTQ+ community. Finally, Andrei Tsygankov details how Russia's great power ambitions have shaped the country's foreign policy toward its neighbors, the West and Asia, in Chapter 8. Tsygankov also explains Russia's war on Ukraine and addresses the role of the military in Russian politics.

1.7.2 Political Economy

The second part of the book explains how economic actors and material resources have shaped Russian politics. The Russian economy has changed no less dramatically than the country's political system, from a planned economy, via a "Wild East" market economy, to a new type of state–oligarch pact that skims profits, but also seeks to provide a basic income and essential services for all citizens. Eight decades of a Soviet ideology that emphasized economic rights, full employment, and middle-class luxuries (such as chocolates and ice cream) for all citizens molded expectations of what the government should provide. We will see that these expectations continue to shape Russian political dynamics. The turmoil and hardship of the 1990s that accompanied the economic liberalization and privatization of the Yeltsin years remained in recent memory and have further strengthened the political imperative that the state needs to provide at least a basic income. Against this background, the Putin government tried to win approval by focusing on raising standards of living. Putin's first eight years in office happened to coincide with a remarkable global boom, which raised energy prices and therefore hydrocarbon revenues. At the same time, Russia's economy is crisis-prone and has had difficulty generating growth and innovation, which in turn has cast doubt on the claim that Putin's economic order is indeed viable in the long run. The ability to provide for basic needs, and now to withstand the effects of sanctions, is a key source of stability and fragility in Russian politics.

Chapters in the political economy section detail these complex dynamics; many of the chapters also address the effects of sanctions imposed after 2014 and in 2022. In Chapter 9, Jordan Gans-Morse introduces some of the institutional underpinnings of Russia's economy and details the struggles by firms to secure property rights and enforce contracts. The chapter by Laura Solanko, Chapter 10, shows how Russia is vulnerable to economic and financial crises that emanate from the global economy. The chapter discusses how this, together with the hardship caused by the economic policies of the 1990s, has led the Putin government to chart a path that seeks to secure economic stability, but compromises on structural and institutional reforms. Chapter 11, by Mikhail Strokan and Rudra Sil, describes the role of oil and gas in Russia's economy and politics, detailing the evolution of the Russian petrostate amid shifting global challenges and opportunities. Chapter 12, by Stanislav Markus, traces the emergence of a social class known as the oligarchs, the transformation of their relationship with the Kremlin, and the reasons for their current political silence. Ilya Matveev and Sarah Wilson Sokhey address inequality and social policy in Chapter 13, and Stephen Crowley details the role of labor unions and workers in Putin's Russia in Chapter 14. Finally, the chapter by Ann-Mari Sätre and Leo Granberg, Chapter 15, gives an impression of the economic lives of Russians outside the major metropolitan areas.

1.7.3   State–Society Relations

Laws and institutions order society in powerful ways, but they are effective only if large parts of society willingly submit and conform. Even the most powerful state cannot rule without consent, and authoritarian governments face a challenging task of maintaining consent and compliance, while suppressing dissent and opposition forces. Russia has a large, multiethnic, and highly educated population, with diverse values and concerns. Soviet-era ideology held that social forces work in unison with the state toward a better future; artists, writers, and youth and community groups were organized in unions that were funded by the state and motivated by goals congruent with the state's vision of socialism. Censorship of the media and literature was the norm until Mikhail Gorbachev launched *glasnost* in 1986. Soviet-era multiethnic policies explicitly tried to manage diversity with a particular approach that designated certain **"titular" nationalities** with rights and privileges such as native-language instruction and affirmative action.

With the collapse of the Soviet Union, many of these forms of state involvement in social life disappeared. The post-Soviet period has also seen a revival of ethnic identity and religious practices. In the 1990s, writers and artists were free to write, but were also no longer supported by a state pension. Russian artists, in fact, emerged as the most vocal and critical opposition of the Putin government

(Wengle, Monet, and Olimpieva 2018). The chapters in Part III detail politics as the interaction between the Russian state that seeks to manage and control, and society that either complies or resists these efforts. Society is neither always loyally subservient, nor always a priori oppositional. Russian politics is about compliance and opposition, the former contributing to stability and the latter opening the possibility for change. Marlene Laruelle's Chapter 16 details the conservative social ideational movements in Russian politics, highlighting the prominent role of the Russian Orthodox Church. In Chapter 17, Scott Gehlbach, Tetyana Lokot, and Anton Shirikov discuss changes in Russia's media landscape over the past three and a half decades, from the liberalizing reforms of the Gorbachev era, through the freewheeling media environment of the 1990s, to the consolidation of state control under Vladimir Putin. In Chapter 18, Natalia Forrat unpacks how Russian citizens view the state and how these views have contributed to the stability of Putinism. Sam Greene's Chapter 19 presents a framework to understand protests in Russian politics as a learning process, in which authorities and citizens test and experience where power lies, then wield that power once they find it. Greene also shows how the main concerns of societal forces that have opposed the state have changed over time. Laura Henry sheds light on the importance of environmental grievances in post-Soviet politics and illustrates this point with a case study of environmental concerns in the Russian Arctic in Chapter 20. Şener Aktürk's contribution in Chapter 21, finally, highlights the changing role of ethnicity and religion in Russian politics from imperial Russia to the Putin era.

1.8 Russia's Regime: From a Fledgling Democracy to an Increasingly Controlling Authoritarian Order

Through the lens of these different themes and chapters, we gain a new and original picture of the transformation of Russia's political regime from a hopeful fledgling democracy, to a hybrid regime, to an increasingly controlling authoritarian order. As recently as 1991, Russian citizens seemed to have won the ability to shape the future of their country. Since the mid-1980s, Mikhail Gorbachev had spearheaded reforms that were meant to democratize and decentralize authority and bring more transparency to Soviet politics. In August 1991, a conservative coup to reverse these gains failed. Demands by independence movements in constituent Soviet republics had unleashed centrifugal forces that led to the collapse of the Soviet Union in December of that year. Boris Yeltsin became president of the Russian Federation based on a promise to lead the country into a new age of democracy. Streets were filled with Russians who celebrated social and political change that would give citizens more control over government and the economy. Two decades later, large groups of protesters again gathered in central squares of major cities to demonstrate against widespread fraud during the 2011 presidential elections that had brought Putin back to power. As competitive elections are the foundation of any democratic order, Russian citizens interpreted these irregularities as a clear signal that the country's political path had diverged from the promise of 1991. The poster in the hands of the protester in Figure 1.2 reads "We did not elect crooks and thieves," capturing precisely this disappointment. Another decade later, in 2021, it became clear that the Russian government had learned to use violence against street protest. Anyone who still had the courage to take to the streets to demand change was threatened with criminal charges and a prison sentence.

We see aspects of regime change reflected in various spheres of Russia's recent political history, not only during elections and street protest, but also in everyday media coverage of political events and civil society activism across the country. What is important, though, is that Russian politics is often characterized by a kind of dualism: Institutions still serve some of their core functions, but are also utilized to strengthen Putinism and make it more resilient against the fragilities outlined above. We see this clearly in the case of elections: They are still important and serve as a mechanism for citizens to choose representatives, but are also, at the same time, a tool of the Putin government to legitimate its hold on power. The vast majority of Russian laws are respected, but some rules are bent and instrumentalized to keep Putin elites in power. Russia's media landscape had initially facilitated the flow of information among social actors and between society and the state, but has increasingly become a propaganda tool that generates support for the government's chosen path. Finally, the constitution of the Russian Federation nominally upholds civic, human, and minority rights, but has not prevented crackdowns on protest. What is more, recent constitutional changes and new laws have created a political reality that can favor ethnic Russians over minorities, husbands over wives, and heterosexual marriages over the relationships of queer Russians. All the chapters that make up this volume either directly or indirectly address the dynamics of authoritarian control and the opposition it generates, tracking stability and fragility and the uneven and complex evolution of each of the different realms of governance.

Prominent Russian political commentators have long argued that "sovereign democracy" or "managed democracy" are more proximate to Russian culture and history than liberal democracy, and are therefore more suitable governance arrangements for the country. The implication of this argument, of course, is that the move away from a freer polity and more citizen involvement in the 1990s, toward a more controlling and hierarchical governance under Putin, was appropriate, even inevitable. The detailed evidence that the authors of this book present, though, points away from the conclusion that an open democracy never had a chance in Russia. Instead, we see that the country's leaders – first Yeltsin and then Putin – consciously used various tools to cement and strengthen their authority at the expense of formal institutions. Neither societal forces nor economic elites were strong enough to oppose them, often not because they did not want to, or because they were somehow culturally not disposed to do so, but because they were still relatively young and weak (Gel'man 2015). In Russia's twenty-first-century history, these have been mutually reinforcing dynamics: The stronger the presidency and the state, the more diminished the capacity of social actors, economic elites, and young institutions to oppose them. At the same time, the Russian state and Russian society are not opposed to each other as the oppressor and the oppressed (Yaffa 2020); rather, they emerge in tandem, each playing an important role in how Russia's post-Soviet history unfolds, as the chapters that follow show.

What does the future hold for Russian politics? What are Russia's chances of moving away from the repressive aspects of the current order, either gradually or through wholesale change, and toward a form of government that is less controlling and centralized, allowing citizens more involvement, and with freer exchange of information? Summer 2022, as this volume goes into print, is indeed a devastating moment for Russian politics. Nevertheless, no authoritarian order is completely stable, and the war, for all its horrors, will be a formidable test of the stability and resilience of Putinism.

This book suggests a way to think of the future of Russian politics by assessing the balance of stabilizing and conservative forces, vis-à-vis the fragility injected by discontent, protests, and other factors that boost support for Russia's "nonsystemic" opposition. Future analysis of Russian politics could proceed as follows: We could look for evidence that points to the strength of stabilizing forces, such as a loyal middle class and the tamed oligarchy as stable bulwarks of support for an autocratic order. We would then weigh and balance these findings with signs that the Russian citizenry ultimately has a mind of its own and is increasingly frustrated by malfunctioning institutions and tightening repression. If the former evidence is stronger, there is no reason to expect that the current institutional order will erode or be challenged in fundamental ways in the near future. If the latter types of signs multiply and strengthen, we may conclude that a redistribution of power is only a matter of time. The increasing prominence of an opposition leader who is able to mobilize discontent and unify a diverse group of Putin critics, or the emergence of irreconcilable intraelite differences, could lead to mounting protests or a coup.

This framework to assess strengths and weaknesses rests on a notion of politics in which a strong political system is one where power is divided, with institutions channeling the interests and concerns of different social groups, each acting to check and balance the power of other institutional realms. A weak political system, by contrast, is one that ignores social concerns and grievances. This is, of course, in essence a notion of politics and institutions that originates in French and British Enlightenment thought and underlies the constitutions of the Western democracies. Russian political thinkers have countered that, in the Eurasian and Russian historical context, a strong political system hinges not on these imported and foreign notions, but on the authority of a paternalistic sovereign state that provides for the people. Is it then a misguided idea to take the notion of the division of powers to Russia, and assess contemporary Russian institutions through this lens?

Though cognizant of this kind of ideational transplant, there are two reasons why this textbook nevertheless relies on "Western" ideas of the strengths and weaknesses of a polity to assess contemporary Russian politics: First, the constitution of the Russian Federation is in fact largely modeled on a federal democracy that formally divides and shares power between institutions and levels of government. It is still the main institutional architecture of the Russian government and of state power, even if the swift centralization of power in Moscow and in the presidency has partially undermined the division of power. Secondly, in the highly globalized world of the twenty-first century, ideas travel at lightning speed, despite governments' attempt to control information and shape worldviews. The Russian state media can try very hard to shape the hearts and minds of citizens to view a paternalistic and hierarchical "strong hand" as a mode of governance appropriate for Russia. Yet this will not keep a sizeable and possibly growing share of (mostly young) citizens from knowing and striving for alternative forms of government, be that the established "Western" ideas or whatever other forms of governance they may hope to establish in Russia.

The war in Ukraine is extremely risky for the Putin regime. As costs are mounting, both in terms of human lives and economic turmoil, it has to continue to convince citizens that the war is justified to maintain stability. Only time will tell if the regime will succeed with these efforts in the long run, which will also shed light on the question posed at the outset of the chapter: Who holds Russia's future in their hands?

DISCUSSION QUESTIONS

1. What are some of the ways in which the fallout from the failed economic reforms of the Yeltsin era influenced political dynamics under Putin?
2. What are some of the sources of stability in contemporary Russian politics? Which do you think is the most important?
3. Do Russia's formal institutions strike you as strong or weak? Justify your answer.

REFERENCES

Frye, Timothy. 2020. *Weak Strongman: The Limits of Power in Putin's Russia*. Princeton: Princeton University Press.

Gel'man, Vladimir. 2015. *Authoritarian Russia: Analyzing Post-Soviet Regime Changes*. Pittsburgh: University of Pittsburgh Press.

Greene, Samuel A., and Graeme B. Robertson. 2019. *Putin v. the People: The Perilous Politics of a Divided Russia.* New Haven: Yale University Press.

Hale, Henry. 2014. *Patronal Politics: Eurasian Regime Dynamics in Comparative Perspective.* Cambridge: Cambridge University Press.

Ledeneva, Alena V. 2013. *Can Russia Modernise?* Sistema, *Power Networks and Informal Governance.* Cambridge: Cambridge University Press.

Oushakine, Serguei A. 2009. *The Patriotism of Despair: Nation, War, and Loss in Russia.* Ithaca: Cornell University Press.

Rosenfeld, Bryn. 2020. *The Autocratic Middle Class: How State Dependency Reduces the Demand for Democracy.* Princeton: Princeton University Press.

Sharafutdinova, Gulnaz. 2020. *The Red Mirror: Putin's Leadership and Russia's Insecure Identity.* Oxford: Oxford University Press.

Sobol, Liubov. 2021. "Pora deistvovat'. Unichtozhaem Putina." On Alexei Navalny's YouTube channel, September 17, www.youtube.com/watch?v=eBbXfhnGAL8.

Volkov, Vadim. 2016. *Violent Entrepreneurs: The Use of Force in the Making of Russian Capitalism.* Ithaca: Cornell University Press.

Wengle, Susanne. 2015. *Post-Soviet Power: State-Led Development and Russia's Marketization.* New York: Cambridge University Press.

Wengle, Susanne, Christy Monet, and Evgenia Olimpieva. 2018. "Russia's Post-Soviet Ideological Terrain: Zvyagintsev's Leviathan and Debates on Authority, Agency and Authenticity." *Slavic Review*, 77(4), 998–1024.

Wengle, Susanne, and Michael Rasell. 2008. "The Monetization of *L'goty*: Changing Patterns of Welfare Politics and Provision in Russia." *Europe–Asia Studies*, 60(5), 739–56.

Woodruff, David. 1999. *Money Unmade: Barter and the Fate of Russian Capitalism.* Ithaca: Cornell University Press.

Yaffa, Joshua. 2020. *Between Two Fires: Truth, Ambition and Compromise in Putin's Russia.* New York: Tim Duggan Books.

Yurchak, Alexei. 2005. *Everything Was Forever, Until It Was No More: The Last Soviet Generation.* Princeton: Princeton University Press.

PART I
Political Institutions

2 Russia's Superpresidency

JODY LAPORTE

Fig. 2.1 President Vladimir Putin chairs a meeting with members of the Security Council in Moscow on February 21, 2022. Credit: Alexey Nikolsky / AFP / Getty Images.

> Russia needs a strong state power and must have it.
>
> > Vladimir Putin, "Russia at the Turn of the Millennium"

> The notorious vertical power is not just a construction but it's a redistribution of authority and power. It's a search for the best possible organization of the state so that each level of the state is most effective.
>
> > Vladimir Putin, "Full Text: Vladimir Putin Interview"

Abstract

This chapter examines the workings of Russia's superpresidency. It explains how Russia's executive branch of government arose out of the politics of the early 1990s, and it shows the ways that it has evolved since then. Russia's constitution grants the president a wide range of responsibilities and prerogatives, many more than we usually associate with a presidential system of checks and balances. This chapter elaborates the formal powers of the president and explains what makes a "superpresidency" different from other types of political executives. The constitutional powers allocated to the president are only one part of how authority functions in Russia, however. The personal characteristics of the individuals who have occupied the office, their leadership style, and the political context in which they operate have also all shaped how the superpresidency works in practice. This chapter introduces the concept of Vladimir Putin's "vertical of power" in order to understand how decisionmaking authority has been consolidated in the office of the president over the past twenty years. Finally, we will see how Putin has managed to circumvent presidential term limits to extend his time in office. It concludes by highlighting the sources of stability and fragility within the superpresidency. With a very powerful executive and a strong vertical of power, Russia's political system has become highly personalized around the figure of the president. Consequently, the stability of this system will depend in large part on the president's ability to maintain the support of political elites and Russian citizens as he fights a costly war and needs to respond to increasingly painful sanctions.

2.1   Introduction

One of the most important aspects of Russian politics today is the presence of a very powerful president. **Vladimir Putin**'s position is so strong that he has not only managed to stay in power for more than twenty years, but has also successfully amended the **constitution** to allow him to remain president through 2036. The institutions that concentrate authority and resources in the office of the president and allow for this kind of dominance over other branches of government are known as Russia's **superpresidency**. In early spring 2022, it also became clear that the concentration of power has paved the way for a war on Ukraine that has cost the lives of thousands of Ukrainians and thrown Russia's economy into a tailspin.

Scholars often look to the organization and powers of a country's **executive branch** in order to understand how politics works. Political scientists commonly distinguish between presidential, parliamentary, and **semi-presidential** systems of government (Stepan and Skach 1993). Presidential systems are those in which the executive is headed by a directly elected president, who serves for a fixed term in office and whose survival in office does not depend on the confidence of the country's legislature. In parliamentary systems, the executive is not popularly elected, but rather originates in the legislature, and the government depends on a legislative majority to continue serving in office. Semi-presidentialism is a hybrid system of government, in which the executive is composed of both a president who is directly elected and a prime minister who arises out of the legislature.

The format of the executive influences not just the day-to-day running of government, but also the relationship between different political actors, the types of policies that are likely to result, and the long-term prospects for regime stability. But these categories are not always helpful to elucidate the functioning of Russia's executive branch. As this chapter shows, the executive in Russia is formally classified as semi-presidential. However, Russia's president is allocated far more power than other branches of government. It is thus best described as a system of super-presidentialism, given the wide range of responsibilities that are afforded to the presidency.

What is more, three individuals have held the office of president since Russia gained independence in 1991, and each of them has brought his own style, resources, and personal background to the position. **Boris Yeltsin** served as Russia's first president. He took office when the post was created in the last months of the Soviet period and led Russia through the transition to independence and the reforms of the 1990s. When he gave up the position on December 31, 1999, Yeltsin appointed his prime minister, Vladimir Putin, as his chosen successor to serve as acting president until new elections could be held. At the time, many considered Putin to be a surprising pick as Yeltsin's chosen successor, given his quiet demeanor and seeming preference to operate behind the scenes. Vladimir Putin was officially elected to the post of president in March 2000, and he quickly set about consolidating power. After serving two four-year terms from 2000 to 2008, Putin stepped aside in acknowledgment of the constitutionally mandated limit on consecutive terms in office. Between 2008 and 2012, Putin's deputy, **Dmitry Medvedev**, served as president, while Putin took the position of prime minister. In 2012, Putin was reelected to the presidency and has held office since then.

This chapter begins by tracing the origins and evolution of Russia's executive, examining how the office of the president was shaped in important ways by the politics of the late Soviet period and Russia's first years of independence. Next, it addresses the formal powers of the president, which constitute the first important pillar of the superpresidency. Russia's constitution grants the president a wide range of responsibilities and prerogatives, many more than we usually associate with a presidential system of checks and balances. The chapter then examines the informal practices that define the presidency and how the individuals who have held the office and the circumstances they faced have shaped political dynamics. Finally, the chapter turns to how Putin has managed to circumvent presidential term limits to extend his time in office. It concludes by examining how the superpresidency – and the personalist political system that it has created – is a source of both stability and fragility in Russian politics today. With such a powerful executive and a strong

vertical of power, President Putin is viewed by many as the central figure in Russian politics and the personal guarantor of political stability. The success of this arrangement depends in large part on the ongoing support of both political elites and average citizens. In this way, the functioning and future of the superpresidency are a question not just of political institutions, but also of the operation of Russian politics, economics, and society.

2.2   Evolution of Russia's Executive

The institution of a directly elected president in Russia dates back to the last months of the Soviet Union. In March 1991, Soviet authorities held a public referendum on the question of creating a new post – that is, president of the Russian Soviet Federative Socialist Republic – within the already-complex Soviet political structure. This proposal, which had been championed by then-chair of the Supreme Soviet, Boris Yeltsin, passed with significant popular support. The presidency that had been created was formally relatively weak, with many constraints on its power, including restrictions on the ability to appoint ministers and other officials, limited veto powers, and constraints on the ability to reorganize or dissolve other state bodies (Easter 1997). Nonetheless, the first presidential elections in Russian history were held three months later, on June 12, 1991. As Timothy Frye (1997, 536) notes, there was very little uncertainty about what the outcome of these elections would be: "Almost all observers expected Yeltsin to win." Indeed, Yeltsin won these elections by a landslide, thereby gaining a critical incumbency advantage to become the president of a newly independent Russia, a country that at that point did not yet exist.

The ensuing months were tumultuous, as the Soviet Union careened toward collapse. In August 1991, Yeltsin became the public image of the anti-Soviet movement, as he led citizens in mobilizing against an attempted coup by conservative and military officials. Yeltsin's popularity soared in the aftermath. This weakened the position of **Mikhail Gorbachev,** who was the general secretary of the **Communist Party of the Soviet Union** and still formally the highest-ranking official in the Soviet Union. However, Yeltsin became the de facto leader of the USSR in its waning months. In November 1991, he was given the power to rule by emergency decree for one year, which he used to launch an ambitious set of economic reforms. He also named himself as his own acting prime minister and defense minister, effectively subordinating those roles into the powers of the president.

When the Soviet Union was dissolved on December 25, 1991, fracturing into fifteen independent states, Gorbachev formally handed the reins of power to Yeltsin, who became president of the newly sovereign country of Russia. Yeltsin and a team of young reformers quickly introduced an extensive range of political and economic reforms. This led to ongoing conflicts with the legislature, whose members grew resentful at being sidelined by the president. The executive and legislative branches found themselves at loggerheads over how to divide responsibilities between them. A protracted struggle ensued; over the next eighteen months, seven different constitutional drafts were proposed, discussed, and ultimately rejected.

The institutional stalemate continued until September 21, 1993, when Yeltsin prompted a constitutional crisis by dissolving the parliament and suspending the existing Soviet-era constitution. He announced new legislative elections, as well as a public referendum on a new constitution. Parliamentary leaders rejected this action as an attempted *coup d'état* and moved to impeach Yeltsin, setting up a parallel government led by Vice President Aleksandr Rutskoi. Thousands of citizens took to the street in protest. Troops from the security services were deployed to keep order, and the parliament building (known as the White House) was sealed off with barricades. On October 3, pro-parliamentary demonstrators stormed the White House and occupied the building. The next morning, under orders from President Yeltsin, the Russian Army began shelling the White House. Parliamentary leaders quickly conceded, and leaders of the insurrection were arrested. According to official statistics, 147 people were killed during the ten-day standoff, making this the country's deadliest use of military force against protesters since the Russian Civil War in 1917 (Suny 2010, 523).

Yeltsin issued a new proposal in November 1993 that greatly expanded the powers of the president. Yeltsin himself had appointed the members of the working group to draft the new constitution, which included his direct subordinates and other employees within the executive branch. As a result, the new constitution laid out a semi-presidential system of government, in which the executive is composed of both a popularly elected president and a prime minister who derives from and is responsible to the legislature. But despite the presence of a dual-headed executive, Yeltsin's constitution concentrated more power in the presidency than any of the previous proposals that had already been rejected. With the parliament disbanded, the draft was not subject to oversight or revision by other bodies before it was put to a public vote. The draft was approved by popular vote in the constitutional referendum and parliamentary election held on December 12, 1993.

The constitution also reorganized the legislature into a bicameral body consisting of the **Duma** (the lower house) and the Federation Council (the upper house). The Duma, which is composed of 450 members who are elected every five years, is generally seen as the stronger of the two bodies, particularly in legislative matters. All proposed legislation must be considered by the Duma before moving to the Federation Council; the Duma also takes the lead on reconciling legislation that is subsequently amended or rejected by the Federation Council. In addition, the Duma is tasked with confirming the president's pick for prime minister. In contrast, the

Federation Council mainly deals with issues of concern to the subnational regions and is generally seen as the weaker of the two bodies. It is structured much like the US Senate, being composed of two representatives from each administrative district in the country. The first Federation Council was directly elected in December 1993. Since then, selection to the Federation Council has been indirect. Senators are currently nominated by the legislature and governor in each federal region with considerable input from the Presidential Administration – a process that has consequences for the makeup and political tendencies of the body.

The 1993 constitution is still largely in force today although, as the rest of this chapter shows, the presidency has evolved in important ways since then. One major change was enacted in 2008, when the length of presidential terms was extended from four years to six. A second major revision concerned the number of terms a president can serve. The 1993 constitution specified that individuals could serve no more than two consecutive terms as president. In 2020, with President Putin anticipating the end of his second term in office in a row, and fourth in total, Russians voted in a controversial referendum to amend the constitution, removing the restriction on "consecutive" terms and resetting Putin's term clock. This change has enabled Putin to continue as president through 2036.

2.3   Formal Powers of the Presidency

Semi-presidentialism entails inherent ambiguities. Across different country cases, the actual division of power and responsibilities between the president and the prime minister varies significantly over time, which can create tensions and uncertainties.

Russia's constitution resolves these tensions by vesting an enormous amount of power in the president. Timothy Colton and Cindy Skach (2005, 119) note that the de jure powers of the Russian president in fact go far beyond those of most other presidents, even in presidential systems. The president serves not just as head of state, but as "guarantor of the constitution itself." The president is tasked with defining "the basic directions of the domestic and foreign policy of the state" and representing the Russian Federation in domestic and foreign affairs. He can both initiate legislation and veto it, issue decrees and directives that hold the same weight as official legislation, call referendums, and enact states of emergency. The president has wide powers of appointment, with responsibility for selecting and dismissing ministers; he also nominates candidates for the Constitutional Court, the Supreme Court, and the Procuracy General. The president even has the power to dissolve the Duma under certain circumstances (Frye 1997).

In contrast, the powers of both the prime minister and the legislature are far more limited. The prime minister is responsible for managing the day-to-day running of government. This generally includes making proposals to the president, aligning policy across different sectors and branches of government, submitting the annual budget to the Duma, and bearing responsibility for public order and the rule of law. At the same time, the parliament is noticeably weaker than the executive. It "does not have the right to reject individual ministers. It has scant oversight powers. Although it can investigate the president and the government, it lacks the resources to do so and almost never does so in fact. Ministers do not answer to the parliament and are not summoned to testify before it. The parliament has no ability to monitor the military, the police, or the organs of state security" (Fish 2005, 205).

In a crucial difference from most semi-presidential systems, in Russia the prime minister does not originate in the legislature, but rather is appointed by the president and then moves to the legislature for confirmation. Technically, the Duma can veto the president's pick. But, for this to happen, the Duma must reject the candidate in three separate votes, at which point the legislature is automatically dissolved and new parliamentary elections are held. Thus, the parliament does play a role in the selection of prime minister, but contradicting the president jeopardizes the survival of the legislature itself. This game of brinkmanship is usually implicit in these negotiations but, as discussed below, occasionally it becomes explicit. Moreover, this appointment process means that the prime minister does not have to represent the majority party in the legislature. The president can appoint a bureaucrat to the post, as he did with the appointment of Mikhail Mishustin in 2020. Mishustin is an economist who had served as director of the Federal Taxation Service for the decade prior.

This imbalanced division of power has led many political scientists to reclassify Russia's institutions as a case of "superpresidentialism." Steven Fish (2003, 200) describes superpresidentialism as occurring in

> an apparatus of executive power that dwarfs all other agencies in terms of size and the resources it consumes; a president who enjoys decree powers; a president who de jure or de facto controls most of the powers of the purse; a relatively toothless legislature that cannot repeal presidential decrees and that enjoys scant authority and/or resources to monitor the chief executive; provisions that render impeachment of the president virtually impossible; and a court system that is controlled wholly or mainly by the chief executive and that cannot in practice check presidential prerogatives or even abuse of power.

The formal powers allocated to the president are only one part of how authority functions in Russia, however. In order to understand how the superpresidency works in practice, we must also consider the personal characteristics of the individuals who occupy the office, their leadership style, and the political context in which they operate. The next sections consider the informal sources of authority that Russia's presidents have brought to the position and how Russia's presidency has functioned in practice over the past three decades.

2.4   The Yeltsin Presidency: Competitive Authoritarianism

As Russia's first president, Boris Yeltsin presided over the creation of the super-presidential system, in which the executive – and the president, in particular – possessed a large number of formal powers. In practice, however, Yeltsin faced significant practical constraints on his authority that prevented him from capitalizing on those formal powers available to him.

Russia was not a democracy during this period; elections were not sufficiently free or fair to satisfy democratic standards. But, during Yeltsin's presidency, power over political decisionmaking was still spread across many different actors and institutions. Steven Levitsky and Lucan Way (2010) have suggested that this model of politics – which does not quite fit the criteria for democracy, but also falls short of fully consolidated dictatorship – can be called "**competitive authoritarianism.**" In competitive authoritarian regimes, political incumbents routinely abuse state resources in order to stay in office, but they lack the capacity to fully eliminate the constraints on their authority. As we will see, this is a good description of Russian politics in the 1990s.

2.4.1   Legislative Politics

One constraint on Yeltsin's power arose from the functioning of the legislature. Throughout his two terms in office, Yeltsin found it difficult to get his policy agenda passed through the parliament. To some extent, this was due to the fractured political nature of the Duma itself. Both the 1993 and 1995 parliamentary elections produced a fragmented Duma, with its seats spread across many parties, none of which had a majority. More generally, as Henry Hale (2005b) has shown, political parties were very weak in Russia at this time, with few resources, a lack of party discipline, and low levels of mass support. It was thus perhaps inevitable that Yeltsin would find it difficult to enact a stable pro-governmental majority in the Duma that could be relied upon to carry out his legislative agenda.

At the same time, while the legislature included multiple pro-presidential political groupings, the largest number of seats went to those parties that were antagonistic to Yeltsin's agenda. This was particularly true following the 1995 parliamentary elections, returning a legislature that was led by the Communist Party, which sought to reverse Yeltsin's political and economic reforms. From then onward, Yeltsin found himself at loggerheads with the Duma. Through the second half of the 1990s, Russia became stuck in a suboptimal equilibrium of having undertaken partial reforms. That is to say, some important steps toward political and economic liberalization had been taken. But, due to opposition from the legislature – and increasingly from other actors as well – the country failed to implement further policies that would stabilize this trajectory (Hellman 1998). Even as the Duma managed to pass meaningful legislation on a variety of issues, Yeltsin himself increasingly tried to bypass the legislature altogether to advance his political agenda. In the absence of a Duma majority, Yeltsin made use of his decree powers, rather than attempting to pass bills through the normal channels (Chaisty 2003; Chaisty and Schleiter 2002).

The relative weakness of Yeltsin's position also made it difficult for him to form a government. For example, in March 1998, President Yeltsin dismissed Prime Minister Viktor Chernomyrdin, who had held the post for more than five years, and nominated the young Sergei Kirienko in his place. The Duma twice voted to reject this appointment, but on the third time conceded and upheld the nomination. Months later, in the aftermath of the August 1998 Russian financial crisis, Yeltsin attempted to reinstate Chernomyrdin in the role of prime minister. Again, the Duma voted twice against his confirmation. However, in contrast to the outcome earlier in the year, this time it was Yeltsin who backed down and withdrew the nomination in lieu of the more popular Yevgeny Primakov.

2.4.2 Russia's Regions

The limitations of Yeltsin's position also manifested in the relationship between Russia's regions and the central government in Moscow. The 1993 constitution laid out a federal system of government, comprising eighty-nine "federal subjects" – that is, regional units, including republics, cities, and autonomous regions (see Chapter 5). Yet, in Russia's system of "asymmetrical federalism," there was wide variation in the level of political autonomy accorded to these units. More importantly, the division of powers between the center and the periphery was not clearly laid out. The constitution specified a number of responsibilities that were to be shared by the central government and the regional units, but it gave little guidance as to how this cooperation might be negotiated. It also failed to grant any specific powers directly to the regions.

The constitution allowed the federal government to allocate some of its powers to individual federal subjects (and vice versa), but crucially allowed these deals to be negotiated on a case-by-case basis. Through the mid-1990s, dozens of these individual treaties were signed. Many of these agreements granted the provinces considerable sovereignty over their economic resources and political affairs, including in some cases the ability to design their own administrative institutions, establish their own banks, and conduct independent foreign relations with other countries (Petrov and Slider 2007; Ross 2012; Stoner-Weiss 2006). Even in the absence of such concessions, other regional leaders assumed these responsibilities in practice, routinely ignoring national-level policies and directives issued by the president.

2.4.3   State Capture

Yeltsin's authority was undermined by the weakness of the Russian state. As Levitsky and Way (2010 188) point out, the dissolution of the Soviet Union "triggered bureaucratic chaos." As the administrative structure of the state collapsed, civil servants became more concerned with extracting personal gain than in performing their duties (Solnick 1998). These problems were exacerbated by the severe economic crisis that accompanied the collapse of the Soviet state, which left the government unable to regularly pay pensions and public-sector salaries. Without an organizational structure, a clear sense of purpose, or stable paychecks, government officials could not rely on state agencies to follow orders from the federal center or to implement political decisions.

Additionally, the Kremlin consciously undertook the decision to cut back on public spending as part of Yeltsin's economic reforms. This particularly affected the security services and defense forces. As Brian Taylor (2018, 52) has shown, between 1992 and 1999, the Russian military's budget was cut by 62 percent. Thus, while the Soviet military had been the largest in the world, "throughout the 1990s there were frequent predictions of its imminent collapse" (Taylor 2018, 39). This had significant implications not only for the armed forces' ability to defend against foreign threats, but also for enforcing property rights, maintaining rule of law, and combating domestic extremists. Unemployed or underemployed police and special forces officers, for example, worked freelance as enforcers of private property rights for the newly emerging class of **oligarchs** (Volkov 2002). The defense agencies also failed to reliably carry out their normal functions, such as securing the country's borders, suppressing succession movements, and combating extremism. The effects of this were seen in the disastrous Chechen wars (discussed further in Chapters 5 and 21).

In the absence of a strong, impartial state, institutions became "captured" by an emerging group of extremely wealthy businessmen – known as the oligarchs – who gained significant political influence and used that to bend state policies to their own advantage. As Chapter 12 outlines, Yeltsin's economic reforms created the oligarchs, who had amassed wealth during Russia's privatization programs. They were the winners of reform and came to control many of the country's most valuable resources and companies. Through both formal and informal channels, they also constructed robust lobbying networks that penetrated all levels of the state. This allowed them to block the implementation of policies they opposed and gave them increasing sway over political decisions, especially during Yeltsin's second term in office.

2.4.4   Yeltsin as a Leader

Lastly, factors that were specific to Yeltsin and his leadership style undoubtedly shaped his approach to the presidency. Some scholars have claimed that, having made his reputation as a reformist, Yeltsin maintained a personal commitment to democratic governance. In this view, he was personally disinclined to centralize power any further than was necessary (Levitsky and Way 2010, 191). Others highlight his "indifference to detail and his extended absences" (White 1999, 224), suggesting that this hands-off approach precluded micromanaging and inherently allowed many voices to participate in the policymaking process, even if only through benign neglect.

Yeltsin struggled to maintain the mass political support necessary to consolidate his position or at times even to advance a coherent political agenda. While Yeltsin ascended to the presidency on a wave of mass support, during his two terms in office he had difficulty retaining the confidence of Russian citizens. Sometimes this was due to the problems discussed above, including concerns such as corruption and the weak rule of law. In addition, Russia emerged from the Soviet Union as a very poor country. Yeltsin's government undertook the difficult task of enacting market reforms, which were designed to shift the country from the communist-era central planning and a **command economy** to liberal market capitalism. Many of these policies – for example, the removal of price controls, opening of international trade, and expansion of private enterprise – were seen in the West as positive developments. But in the short term, as the country dealt with rampant inflation and financial crises, these circumstances created very challenging economic conditions for average citizens.

All this made Yeltsin unpopular with many Russian voters, who saw their quality of life decline quite significantly. The weakness of Yeltsin's political position can be seen in the serious electoral challenges that he faced. Russia's elections each involved too much voting fraud and governmental manipulation to be considered free and fair. But rather than cruising to overwhelming victory, as many autocratic rulers do, Yeltsin and his allies had to campaign hard for narrow wins. For example, in the 1993 parliamentary election (held jointly with the constitutional referendum discussed above), Yeltsin "had to bargain extensively with regional officials to guarantee victory" and, "despite massive resource advantages, pro-Yeltsin forces fared poorly" (Levitsky and Way 2010, 293). By the time he stood for reelection in 1996, his approval ratings were below 10 percent. He faced a serious challenge from Communist Party candidate Gennady Zyuganov, and in advance of the vote there was genuine uncertainty about who would win.

A final point to consider is the impact of Yeltsin's health problems. Rumors about his drinking habits abounded throughout his presidency. Observers speculated that he seemed drunk in his public appearances, as he stumbled on his feet, struggled to answer questions from the press, and behaved erratically. He also experienced a series of heart attacks during his first term of office. In the months leading up to the 1996 presidential elections, he required quintuple bypass surgery and spent months recovering. His health deteriorated increasingly during his second term in office, and his absences from office grew more frequent and longlasting. By the end of his presidency he was rumored to be spending little time engaged in the day-to-day running of the country. "By the time he resigned … he was largely an absentee president" (Graham 2000, 362).

2.5   Politics in the Putin Era: Strengthening the Power Vertical

Vladimir Putin has taken a very different approach to the presidency. Putin became president on December 31, 1999, having assumed the post of prime minister only a few months earlier. At the time, many considered Putin to be a surprising pick as Yeltsin's successor. He had spent most of his formative professional years in the Soviet security services, having worked for sixteen years as a foreign intelligence officer in the KGB, including five years undercover in East Germany. It was only after the collapse of the Soviet Union that he pursued a political career, first working in a series of positions in the St. Petersburg city administration. In 1996, Putin moved to Moscow and embarked on a meteoric rise through ever-more-powerful posts within Yeltsin's executive apparatus. In July 1998, he was appointed director of the Federal Security Service (FSB), the successor agency to the Soviet-era KGB. Then in August 1999, he became prime minister, a post that positioned him to inherit the presidency.

From his first years of office, Putin worked to create a very powerful presidency by strengthening the "vertical of power." In the "vertical of power" (*vertikal vlasti*), politics is understood as a system of hierarchical relationships organized under the president, rather than a horizontal system of competing checks and balances. Given the sheer disarray of authority structures under Yeltsin, Putin's successful reassertion of power and the establishment of the "vertical" took many observers by surprise. But Putin has continued to affirm the importance of a tight hierarchy of power relationship throughout his time in office. In March 2020, after twenty years in power, he reflected: "I am completely convinced that a strong presidential vertical is necessary for our country. The current situation in the economy and in the security sphere yet again reminds us … that we need this for stability" (Seddon 2020).

The resources, strategies, and decisions that allowed Putin to function as a much stronger president than his predecessor warrant close attention.

2.5.1   Subordinating the Legislature

As we saw above, Yeltsin struggled to build a cohesive and stable majority in the Duma that could be counted on to support his political program. In contrast, Putin enacted a number of changes that strengthened the executive's control over the legislature. This allowed him to pursue policymaking more efficiently and using formal channels, without needing to negotiate and compromise too much along the way.

One change concerned the composition of the upper house, the Federation Council. From its inception, the Federation Council was designed as a way for the regions to be represented in national-level policymaking. Thus, in the 1990s, membership of this upper house was made up of the heads of the regional executives and legislatures, and they used this role to powerfully shape policy decisions. In 2000, the Kremlin introduced new rules that changed who should hold these seats. Rather than the regional leaders taking up the seats themselves, they now chose representatives to hold those seats for them. While this may sound like a small change, in practice it gave the Kremlin much more influence over the selection of senators. "According to one commentator, presidential staff ... recommended or approved the appointment of up to 80 per cent of the Federation Council's new intake" (Chaisty 2008, 434). A significant portion of senators did not even have ties to the regions that they represented.

Perhaps the most transformative event in legislative politics, however, was the creation of a ruling party, which provided Putin with a stable presidential majority in the legislature. The initial step in this process began early in Putin's first term, when several pro-Kremlin parties that were represented in the Duma formed a presidential coalition. This allowed them to build a procedural majority and take control of several key posts in the Duma (Chaisty 2008). In December 2001, **United Russia** was officially established through the merging of a number of these existing parties. While the party centrally serves as a vehicle to advance Putin's policies, its core principles of pragmatism, competence, and stability appealed to Russian voters, who were disillusioned with the communism-versus-capitalism debate that had structured politics through the 1990s. From its inception, United Russia has been the majority party in the Duma, and its presence has helped to increase legislative speed and efficiency. As a result, Putin has not needed to use his decree powers in the same way that Yeltsin did, but instead has enacted his policy agenda directly through the formal legislative channels.

At the same time, Russia's legislature is not simply a "rubber-stamp" parliament. Taylor (2014, 245) has suggested that under Putin, "although the Duma formally has the power to discuss and amend laws, its real function is simply to pass laws" without having much influence over them. In contrast, however, Ben Noble (2020) shows that Russia's legislature frequently does amend the draft laws, including those that are sponsored by the executive. Rather being than an argument for the strength of the legislature over the executive, however, Noble theorizes that this outcome reflects the legislature's role in resolving disputes between competing interests within the executive branch.

2.5.2   Reining in the Regions

Putin also curbed the power of the regional governors by creating a system of parallel authority in each region that existed under the Kremlin's control. First, seven federal districts were created, with an eighth (the North Caucasus) added in 2011, and a ninth (Crimea and Sevastopol) in 2016. Each district was appointed a new official, called the "authorized representative" of the president. These envoys (*polpredy*) were tasked with monitoring each region's political and economic performance, while also bringing local policies into alignment with federal initiatives. Crucially, their job was to homogenize the districts' relationship with Moscow by eliminating the outsized privileges that certain regions had negotiated under Yeltsin.

A second change concerned the procedures for selecting regional governors. In 2004, direct elections for governor were eliminated and replaced with a new indirect selection procedure through the regional assemblies. In practice, this gave the Kremlin more power to influence these decisions. The Kremlin also gained the power to remove regional executives. While some of the powerful governors from the Yeltsin era retained their positions through Putin's first two terms of office, most were removed by 2012. The Kremlin reinstated direct elections for regional governors in 2012, although this change was more superficial than it seemed. As Darrell Slider (2019, 124) notes: "Governors, elected or not, serve only if they are acceptable to Putin. They will still be evaluated by the Kremlin, and the process of elections is tightly controlled to prevent 'accidental' candidates from winning."

The creation of United Russia further strengthened these dynamics. Scholars have shown that ruling parties serve important functions in helping nondemocratic rulers to govern effectively across their territories (Blaydes 2010; Brownlee 2007; Geddes 1999; Magaloni 2006), and this is certainly true in Russia. Regional governors are expected to join United Russia. By 2010, the party held a majority in eighty-two of eighty-three of the country's regional assemblies (Slider 2019). Thus, in addition to legal measures, the internal workings of the party allow the Kremlin to exercise control over the regions through political means as well.

2.5.3   Taming the Oligarchs

One of the most important steps Putin took to strengthen the power vertical was to reduce the power of the oligarchs. In the spring and summer of 2000, state authorities opened a series of criminal investigations into the previous privatization deals and business affairs of many of the major oligarchs. Vladimir Gusinsky and Boris Berezovsky came under the strongest pressure, likely because their control of major media networks was seen as giving them outsized political influence with voters. Gusinsky owned the independent Media-Most conglomerate, including the popular NTV channel, and was seen as critical of Putin. In June 2000, authorities arrested Gusinsky on charges of misappropriation of funds. The following month, under considerable pressure from the Kremlin, he turned his media assets over to the state-controlled Gazprom in exchange for his freedom and fled into exile. Boris Berezovsky, who had actively supported Putin's rise to power before becoming one of his fiercest critics, came under fire later that year. In response to investigations into alleged fraud in his privatization deals, Berezovsky fled Russia and sought political asylum in the UK. He was convicted in absentia of embezzlement, and the government took control of ORT, his formerly extensive media holdings.

This campaign came to a head in October 2003, when prosecutors arrested Mikhail Khodorkovsky, owner of Yukos Oil Company. Yukos was one of the biggest oil companies in the world, having acquired a number of Siberian oil fields in the privatization frenzy of the 1990s, and Khodorkovsky was the richest man in Russia at the time. But he was also believed to be offering financial support to Putin's political rivals. In October 2003, Khodorkovsky was arrested and charged with fraud and tax evasion on the order of $27 billion. He was eventually found guilty and sentenced to nine years in a Siberian prison; he was pardoned and released in December 2013. Meanwhile, Yukos was dismantled. The company declared bankruptcy and its assets were sold off – largely to the Russian state – at discount prices. The Yukos affair, as it came to be known, had several consequences. It gave the government the upper hand financially against the oligarchs, as it left a larger portion of the economy – and, in particular, major sections of the oil and gas industry – in state hands. It also had the effect of politically intimidating other economic elites, as the Yukos affair set an example of what would happen to those who dared to dabble in opposition politics.

This is not to say that the oligarchs have been eliminated entirely under Putin. Not everyone faced such severe sanctions. Putin's approach to dealing with most of the oligarchs has been described as one of a "grand bargain," in which economic elites were allowed to maintain their companies and fortunes as long as they agreed to support Putin's government (Tompson 2005, 168). As a result, the oligarchs were not eliminated, but rather subordinated to the government's political agenda. As Chapter 12 elaborates, wealthy individuals continue to exist in Russia today, though their status is largely dependent on their connections to the Kremlin.

2.5.4   Rise of the *Siloviki*

A final aspect of Putin's consolidation of power concerned the people who hold government posts. By the end of the Yeltsin era, the most powerful ruling elites—that is, the individuals who had the most influence on policymaking—were the oligarchs and members of Yeltsin's immediate family. In the first years of Putin's presidency, this changed dramatically. A large number of officials from the armed forces and security agencies – known as **siloviki**, as they derive from the country's power structures (*silovye struktory*) – were appointed to high-ranking political and administrative positions.

These appointments extended far and wide. Individuals who had previously served in the Ministry of Defense, the Ministry of Internal Affairs, the FSB, and the Foreign Intelligence Service (SVR) were recruited into civilian branches of government to serve as ministers, deputy ministers, and heads of departments. Olga Kryshtanovskaya and Steven White (2003, 296) calculate that more than one-third of all deputy ministers appointed in the first three years of Putin's presidency came from a military or security background, including appointments to the Ministries of Justice, Economic Development, Communications, Foreign Affairs, and Transport. The *siloviki* also took up many posts within the Russian federal structure, serving as regional governors and presidential representatives across the federal districts.

Scholars have debated how much these appointments have been part of a deliberate plan to "securitize" the Russian regime. Some have argued that the *siloviki* form a coherent political network and a powerful interest group. Taylor (2018) has argued that this statist ideology has come to define "**Putinism**" and that the emphasis on law, order, and political stability has driven many of the policy decisions during Putin's presidency. Petra Schleiter (2013) notes that it has coincided with increasing authoritarianism during this period. Kryshtanovskaya and White (2003) claim that this was part of a larger trend in Russia toward "militocracy" – that is, a regime ruled by military and security officers. They point to the fact that these appointments coincided with broader institutional reforms that have centralized the power ministries and brought them under the president's control. Others have argued that the role of *siloviki* has been overestimated – in terms of both the quantity of *siloviki* recruited into government (Rivera and Rivera 2014) and the quality and coherence of their worldview (Renz 2006).

Despite these debates, it seems clear from the past twenty years of Russian politics that Putin has surrounded himself with advisors that he knows and trusts. Observers have noted that he values personal loyalty, and that he has increasingly relied on his network of former colleagues from his days in the St. Petersburg city government, the *siloviki*, and his personal associates to govern (Petrov and Slider 2007). These new networks replaced the Yeltsin-era oligarchs and the ruling elites of the 1990s, but they have also created a more personalist regime and new patronage networks that rest on the president's personal authority to guarantee political stability (Baturo and Elkink 2016).

2.5.5   Political Resources of the Presidency

Putin has managed to align both the formal and the informal sources of authority to create a very powerful and highly centralized presidency. Yet, to understand the functioning and ongoing stability of this system, we must also appreciate the wide array of political resources under his control.

The executive branch includes a large and complex set of administrative agencies and offices that serve to support and implement the president's decisions. Employing more than 3,000 staff members, the Presidential Administration includes more than twenty-one directorates, and dozens of presidential representatives designated to liaise with the State Duma, Federation Council, and the federal districts. It also includes a series of powerful advisory bodies, such as the Security Council, established in 1994 to manage foreign and security issues; and the State Council, created in 2000 to handle issues relating to the subnational districts and center–periphery questions. This vast bureaucracy is overseen by the president's chief of staff, who serves as head of the Presidential Administration and "operates as a sort of eminence grise of the federal executive" (Willerton 2018, 29).

In addition to these administrative resources, Russia's president also controls a significant coercive apparatus. The "power ministries" (*silovye ministerstva*) refer to the wide variety of military troops and law enforcement agencies that are tasked with defending the country and maintaining domestic order. These include the Ministry of Defense and the Ministry of Emergency Situations, as well as the intelligence bodies that serve as successors to the Soviet-era KGB – such as the Federal Security Service (FSB), the Foreign Intelligence Service (SVR), the Federal Guards, and the Presidential Security Service. These military and intelligence agencies sit separately from the Ministry of Internal Affairs (MVD), which itself oversees the domestic police agencies, Internal Troops, and directorates for specialized crimes such as counterterrorism. Other "quasi-power ministries" – such as the Ministry of Justice and the Federal Procuracy – fall outside the president's direct command, but in practice often serve as an extension of the executive branch (Taylor 2011). These structures have been reconsolidated and substantially rebuilt under Putin. With major increases in military spending from 2000 onward and the appointment of Putin loyalists to head the security agencies, the coercive apparatus has served as an important part of Putin's restoration of the power vertical. It also continues to function as a key source of political stability in Russia today.

2.6 Circumventing Presidential Term Limits

Russia's 1993 constitution limited presidents to no more than two consecutive terms of office. This clause led to significant speculation about Putin's long-term plans for staying in power and his options for doing so. It also has important implications for the country's political stability. Hale (2005a, 2011) has characterized Russia's regime as one of "patronal presidentialism," in which political and economic elites derive their status and resources through their personal relationship with the president. In these systems, when impending term limits create uncertainty about the president's intentions, elites will search for a new patron to serve their interests, and this can lead to the premature collapse of the regime.

This section outlines the ways in which Putin has managed to circumvent presidential term limits and secure his hold on power. The issue arose first in 2008 when Putin shifted power to his prime minister and temporary successor, Dmitry Medvedev, and again in 2020, when he solved this problem once and for all by changing the constitution.

2.6.1   The Putin–Medvedev "Tandem"

By Putin's second term in office (2004–08), many observers began to speculate about his longer-term plans and Russia's political future. Questions arose about who might become the next president, how competitive the selection process might be, and how a turnover in power might be negotiated. On one hand, some worried that Putin would ignore the constitution's provisions and stay on for a third term, thus undermining any chance for rule of law in Russia. On the other hand, there were concerns that Russia's political stability rested on him remaining in office, and that a turnover in power might expose the fragility of the country's regime.

In early December 2007, Putin solved this problem by announcing that he had selected Medvedev, his deputy prime minister, to serve as his successor. Medvedev had been trained as a lawyer and had worked with Putin in the St. Petersburg city government in the 1990s. Medvedev officially accepted the nomination as presidential candidate for United Russia on December 17 and immediately announced that, if elected, he would appoint Vladimir Putin to be his prime minister. Medvedev won the presidency in March 2008. His inauguration was held on May 7, and he followed through on his promise to make Putin his prime minister the next day.

This maneuver created what came to be known as the "Putin–Medvedev tandem," and it allowed Putin to retain political power while formally ceding the presidency to Dmitry Medvedev. Medvedev served in office for one term, from 2008 to 2012, and throughout this period there was significant speculation about the degree to which he wielded actual power or was simply a figurehead for Putin's work behind the scenes. After all, within Russia's dual-headed executive, the prime minister had always taken a back seat to the powers of the president. Medvedev was generally considered to be slightly more liberal in his outlook and brought in advisors who were legal scholars and colleagues from St. Petersburg, rather than relying on the *siloviki* that Putin had appointed. He also pursued some domestic reforms in areas such as economic modernization and diversification, as well as reform of law enforcement structures. At the same time, such measures were limited, and they were not accompanied by radical changes in the balance of power within the Presidential Administration.

2.6.2   Putin's Return to Power and 2020 Constitutional Reforms

As Medvedev neared the end of his first term, many began to question whether he would run for a second, or if Vladimir Putin would seek to return to the presidency. Given that the constitution bars candidates from serving as president for more than two *consecutive* terms, Putin was eligible to run for the presidency again in 2012. This question was answered in September 2011, when Medvedev publicly suggested at the United Russia Party Congress that Putin enter the presidential elections in 2012. Putin accepted the nomination and became the party's candidate in the forthcoming elections, winning his third term of office in March 2012. Opposition groups accused the government of rigging the election and engaging in voting fraud, sparking some of the biggest protests in nearly two decades (Smyth 2020). On the same day as his inauguration, in May 2012, Putin nominated Medvedev to the office of prime minister, effectively switching places. Medvedev served in that role until January 2020.

Putin was reelected in 2018 and was soon again confronted with the problem of term limits. According to the constitution, he would need to step down in 2024. As before, speculation ensued about the future of Putinism, the fate of Russia's regime, and whether Putin would step down or find a new way to navigate these constraints. In January 2020, in his annual State of the Union address, Putin announced the possibility of amending the constitution. He proposed amending fourteen articles of the constitution, concerning not just revisions to the president's powers but also thresholds for the national minimum wage and pensions; enshrining marriage as a relationship between a man and a woman; and codifying Russian as the country's national language. Most important, however, was the clause removing the phrase "in a row" from the clause on presidential term limits, and excluding all previous presidential terms that were served before the amendment came into force. This meant that Putin would be eligible to serve two further six-year terms after 2024, potentially enabling him to stay in office until 2036. These amendments were approved by 78 percent of Russian voters in a national referendum on July 1, 2020, and took effect three days later.

2.7   Conclusion: Stability and Fragility in Russia's Superpresidency

The superpresidency has been a central feature of Russian politics since independence. However, the specific way in which it functions has depended not just on the formal powers outlined in the constitution, but also on who holds the office and the political resources, goals, and leadership style that they bring to the job. Over the past twenty years, politics in Russia have become much more centralized around the figure of the president. Within this personalist system, the president is often seen as the ultimate arbiter of political decisions, with few autonomous institutions or elite coalitions that serve as reliable checks on his power.

These dynamics have important implications for how we think about the sources of stability and fragility in Russian politics. Empirical studies have shown that personalist regimes are shorter-lived than many other forms of nondemocratic rule, which scholars have attributed to the challenges of doling out patronage, the narrowness of an individual ruler's support base, and the difficulties in planning for succession (Geddes 1999; Meng 2020; Svolik 2012). Furthermore, in such systems, regime longevity depends in part on the sheer popularity of the ruler, and the popular tide on this point can turn rather quickly (Kuran 1991).

Yet, while these patterns may be true in the aggregate, they do not necessarily suggest that Russia's regime is particularly unstable. As mentioned briefly above, Hale (2011, 9) has pointed out that politics in Russia is not primarily organized around abstract principles or impersonal institutions, but rather around "the personalized exchange of concrete rewards and punishments through chains of actual acquaintance." In this system of patronalism, "power goes to those who can mete these out, those who can position themselves as *patrons* with a large and dependent base of *clients*." Viewed through this lens, the durability of Russia's personalist regime depends centrally on the patronal president's ability to retain the support of his clients – that is to say, his advisors and other political and economic elites, as well as society at large.

Ultimately, the stability of Russia's superpresidency will be based on a number of factors. Foremost among these will be the president's ability to maintain a strong vertical of power, using both the mechanisms of patronage and cooptation, as well as the negative inducements of repression against those who defy the regime. With the war in Ukraine, the Kremlin will also have to find the resources to fight an increasingly costly war abroad, while cushioning the impact of economic sanctions at home. Both will be exceedingly challenging, even for a regime that has extensive control of domestic institutions. There are many aspects of Russian politics, society, and the economy that are largely beyond the government's control, including the price of oil and other major exports, the performance of the Russian economy under sanctions, and demographic trends. Many of these will be discussed in upcoming chapters that show just how deeply entangled the superpresidency is with nearly every aspect of Russian politics and society.

DISCUSSION QUESTIONS

1. What explains Russia's superpresidency? How and why were Russia's rulers able to create such a powerful presidency? Was it inevitable?
2. What impact do institutional and noninstitutional factors have on the nature and functioning of Russia's executive?

3. How and why has the power of Russia's presidency varied over time?

4. What, if any, constraints exist on the power of the presidency in Russia?

REFERENCES

Baturo, Alexander, and Johan A. Elkink. 2016. "Dynamics of Regime Personalization and Patron–Client Networks in Russia, 1999–2014." *Post-Soviet Affairs*, 32(1), 75–98.

Blaydes, Lisa. 2010. *Elections and Distributive Politics in Mubarak's Egypt.* Cambridge: Cambridge University Press.

Brownlee, Jason. 2007. *Authoritarianism in an Age of Democratization.* Cambridge: Cambridge University Press.

Chaisty, Paul. 2003. "Defending the Institutional Status Quo: Communist Leadership of the Second Russian State Duma, 1996–1999." *Legislative Studies Quarterly*, 28(1), 5–28.

2008. "The Legislative Effects of Presidential Partisan Powers in Post-Communist Russia." *Government and Opposition*, 43(3), 424–53.

Chaisty, Paul, and Petra Schleiter. 2002. "Productive but Not Valued: The Russian State Duma, 1994–2001." *Europe–Asia Studies*, 54(5), 701–24.

Colton, Timothy J., and Cindy Skach. 2005. "A Fresh Look at Semipresidentialism: The Russian Predicament." *Journal of Democracy*, 16(3), 113–26.

Easter, Gerald M. 1997. "Preference for Presidentialism: Postcommunist Regime Change in Russia and the NIS." *World Politics*, 49(2), 184–211.

Fish, Steven M. 2003. "The Impact of the 1999–2000 Parliamentary and Presidential Elections on Political Party Development." In Vicki L. Hesli, William M. Reisinger, and Sally J. Kennedy (eds.), *The 1999–2000 Elections in Russia: Their Impact and Legacy*, pp. 186–212. Cambridge: Cambridge University Press.

2005. *Democracy Derailed in Russia: The Failure of Open Politics.* Cambridge: Cambridge University Press.

Frye, Timothy. 1997. "A Politics of Institutional Choice: Post-Communist Presidencies." *Comparative Political Studies*, 30(5), 523–52.

Geddes, Barbara. 1999. "What Do We Know about Democratization after Twenty Years?" *Annual Review of Political Science*, 2(1), 115–44.

Graham, Thomas E. 2000. "The Fate of the Russian State." *Demokratizatsiya: The Journal of Post-Soviet Democratization*, 8(3), 354–75.

Hale, Henry E. 2005a. "Regime Cycles: Democracy, Autocracy, and Revolution in Post-Soviet Eurasia." *World Politics*, 58(1), 133–65.

2005b. *Why Not Parties in Russia? Democracy, Federalism, and the State.* Cambridge: Cambridge University Pres

2011. "Formal Constitutions in Informal Politics: Institutions and Democratization in Post-Soviet Eurasia." *World Politics*, 63(4), 581–617.

Hellman, Joel S. 1998. "Winners Take All: The Politics of Partial Reform in Postcommunist Transitions." *World Politics*, 50(2), 203–34.

Kryshtanovskaya, Olga, and Steven White. 2003. "Putin's Militocracy." *Post-Soviet Affairs*, 19(4), 289–306.

Kuran, Timur. 1991. "Now out of Never: The Element of Surprise in the East European Revolution of 1989." *World Politics*, 44(1), 7–48.

Levitsky, Steven, and Lucan A. Way. 2010. *Competitive Authoritarianism: Hybrid Regimes after the Cold War.* Cambridge: Cambridge University Press.

Magaloni, Beatriz. 2006. *Voting for Autocracy: Hegemonic Party Survival and Its Demise in Mexico.* Cambridge: Cambridge University Press.

Meng, Anne. 2020. "Winning the Game of Thrones: Leadership Succession in Modern Autocracies." *Journal of Conflict Resolution*, 65(5), 950–81.

Noble, Ben. 2020. "Authoritarian Amendments: Legislative Institutions as Intraexecutive Constraints in Post-Soviet Russia." *Comparative Political Studies*, 53(9), 1417–54.

Petrov, Nikolai, and Darrell Slider. 2007. "Putin and the Regions." In Stephen K. Wegren (ed.), *Putin's Russia: Past Imperfect, Future Uncertain*, 2nd ed., pp. 75–97. Lanham MD: Rowman & Littlefield.

Putin, Vladimir. 1999. "Russia at the Turn of the Millennium [Rossiia na rubezhe tysiache-letii]." *Nezavisimaya Gazeta*, December 30, translation at https://pages.uoregon.edu/kimball/Putin.htm#lessons%20for%20RUS.

2006. "Full Text: Vladimir Putin Interview." *Financial Times*, September 10, www.ft.com/content/76e205b2-40e5-11db-827f-0000779e2340.

Renz, Bettina. 2006. "Putin's Militocracy? An Alternative Interpretation of *Siloviki* in Contemporary Russian Politics." *Europe–Asia Studies*, 58(6), 903–24.

Rivera, David W., and Sharon Werning Rivera. 2014. "Is Russia a Militocracy? Conceptual Issues and Extant Findings Regarding Elite Militarization." *Post-Soviet Affairs*, 30(1), 27–50.

Ross, Cameron. 2012. "Federalism and Defederalisation in Russia." In Graeme Gill and James Young (eds.), *Routledge Handbook of Russian Politics and Society*, pp. 140–52. London: Routledge.

Schleiter, Petra. 2013. "Democracy, Authoritarianism, and Ministerial Selection in Russia: How Presidential Preferences Shape Technocratic Cabinets." *Post-Soviet Affairs*, 29(1), 31–55.

Seddon, Max. 2020. "Vladimir Putin Sets Stage for Retaining His Grip on Power." *Financial Times*, March 10, www.ft.com/content/5abff7d6-62c3-11ea-a6cd-df28cc3c6a68.

Slider, Darrell. 2019. "A Federal State?" In Richard Sakwa, Henry E. Hale, and Steven White (eds.), *Developments in Russian Politics*, pp. 119–32. Durham, NC: Duke University Press.

Smyth, Regina. 2020. *Elections, Protest, and Authoritarian Regime Stability: Russia 2008–2020.* Cambridge: Cambridge University Press.

Solnick, Steven Lee. 1998. *Stealing the State: Control and Collapse in Soviet Institutions.* Cambridge, MA: Harvard University Press.

Stepan, Alfred, and Cindy Skach. 1993. "Constitutional Frameworks and Democratic Consolidation: Parliamentarianism versus Presidentialism." *World Politics*, 46(1), 1–22.

Stoner-Weiss, Kathryn. 2006. *Resisting the State: Reform and Retrenchment in Post-Soviet Russia.* Cambridge: Cambridge University Press.

Suny, Ronald Grigor. 2010. *The Soviet Experiment: Russia, the USSR, and the Successor States*, 2nd ed. Oxford: Oxford University Press.

Svolik, Milan W. 2012. *The Politics of Authoritarian Rule.* Cambridge: Cambridge University Press.

Taylor, Brian D. 2011. *State Building in Putin's Russia: Policing and Coercion after Communism.* Cambridge: Cambridge University Press.

2014. "Police Reform in Russia: The Policy Process in a Hybrid Regime." *Post-Soviet Affairs*, 30(2–3), 226–55.

2018. *The Code of Putinism.* Oxford: Oxford University Press.

Tompson, William. 2005. "Putting Yukos in Perspective." *Post-Soviet Affairs*, 21(2), 159–81.

Volkov, Vadim. 2002. *Violent Entrepreneurs: The Use of Force in the Making of Russian Capitalism.* Ithaca: Cornell University Press.

White, Stephen. 1999. "Russia." In R. Elgie (ed.), *Semi-Presidentialism in Europe*, pp. 216–31. Oxford: Oxford University Press.

Willerton, John P. 2018. "Presidency and the Executive." In Richard Sakwa, Henry E. Hale, and Stephen White (eds.), *Developments in Russian Politics 9*, 9th ed., pp. 18–37. London: Bloomsbury Academic.

3 Party Politics and Voting in Russia

ORA JOHN REUTER AND DAVID SZAKONYI

Fig. 3.1 Vladimir Putin at United Russia convention, 2017. Credit: CC by 4.0, http://creativecommons.org/licenses/by/4.0, via Wikimedia Commons.

I remember well how and under what conditions United Russia was created. We all know that it was my initiative. In reality, I started it, and created this party. The need for it was vital, first of all, for the strengthening of Russian statehood and the consolidation of society. And the country was in such a state, as you all well remember and know: There was a threat of its disintegration, and this threat was real; in legal and political terms, the country was really a patchwork territory.

> Vladimir Putin, "Speech to United Russia Party Congress"

Abstract

Russia is neither a democracy nor a monolithic, one-party state, but rather an electoral autocracy in which multiparty elections are the primary means of acquiring power. Though these elections are not free and fair, they enable political competition among a variety of political actors. This chapter describes the key parties, movements, social cleavages, and issues that drive electoral behavior in this system. The chapter also highlights the undemocratic features of the system that constrain full and fair competition. These include the role of the hegemonic party, United Russia; the constraints placed on opposition forces; and the use of electoral manipulation by the regime. By examining the many tensions inherent to electoral autocracy, the chapter demonstrates how elections can both stabilize the regime and undermine it.

3.1   Introduction

The collapse of the Soviet Union in 1991 ended seventy years of one-party rule in Russia. After the transition, Russia adopted a constitutional framework that featured multiparty elections as the primary means of acquiring power. Campaigns in the 1990s were competitive and hard-fought. A multitude of parties formed, opposition candidates routinely defeated incumbents, and Russia's legislature, the State **Duma**, emerged as a lively and influential representative body.

But this period of pluralism was short-lived. In the 2000s, Russia's incipient democracy degenerated into what political scientists call an **electoral autocracy**, a regime type in which multiple parties are allowed to compete, but elections are *not* free and fair. Russia's leaders – President **Vladimir Putin** primary among them – are chosen in multicandidate elections and claim their right to rule on the basis of those electoral mandates. But the Kremlin manipulates those elections to such an egregious extent that they fail to meet minimal democratic standards.

Russia's electoral autocracy has several key features that this chapter highlights. One is the dominant party, **United Russia**. In the early 2000s, the Kremlin cultivated a single ruling party that helps coordinate pro-regime candidates, dominate elections, and ensure legislative discipline. A second feature of the system is that certain moderate opposition parties are allowed to compete in and even, in rare cases, win elections. These parties – primarily the **Communist Party of the Russian Federation (CPRF)**, Just Russia, and the Liberal Democratic Party of Russia (LDPR) – publicly, and often harshly, criticize the regime on matters of public policy, but they stop short of calling for Putin's removal. Third is the so-called **nonsystemic opposition** – whose most prominent representative is protest leader **Alexei Navalny**. The nonsystemic opposition is excluded from elections and takes an uncompromising stance against the regime, routinely calling for Putin to allow free elections and step down. The nonsystemic opposition, especially in recent years, focuses primarily on issues of corruption, electoral manipulation, and abuse of power.

The final element that we highlight is electoral manipulation itself. The regime uses a panoply of tactics to limit competition and prevent electoral upsets. These include ballot fraud, media censorship and propaganda, exclusion of opposition candidates, and voter intimidation and repression. These measures are effective but costly. Russians find them distasteful, and the regime must limit its use of fraud or risk unrest.

Thus, Russia today is neither a democracy nor a monolithic one-party state. It is an electoral autocracy. In concluding the chapter, we highlight the ways that this electoral arrangement both stabilizes and undermines the stability of the regime. On the one hand, there is the ever-present risk that the opposition could actually win even highly managed elections. Giving opposition parties and voters a chance to engage in public politics allows them to organize and promote their grievances, an inherently risky proposition. And the illicit manipulation that is required to contain competition also risks backlash.

At the same time, Russia's leaders seem keen to retain elections for a variety of reasons. They grant legitimacy and help regime leaders keep track of citizen demands. Indeed, even imperfect elections can function as primitive accountability mechanisms. Elections and legislatures also help the regime coopt and control the opposition. Thus, any serious study of Russian politics must concern itself with electoral processes.

3.2 From One Party to Many: Parties and Elections from the CPSU to Yeltsin

Elections are the central institutions that enable representation and accountability in modern polities. And, because parties allow for the aggregation and articulation of complex societal interests, most political scientists view parties as essential to the proper functioning of electoral democracy. Thus, the development of these institutions is seen as crucial for the development of democracy in Russia. This section charts the recent history of parties and elections in Russia.

3.2.1 Parties and Elections in the Soviet Union

From 1917 to 1991, the Soviet Union was a one-party state ruled by the **Communist Party of the Soviet Union (CPSU)**. The USSR under the CPSU was a classic example of what political scientists call a **"party-state,"** a form of government where a single political party exercises unrivaled, collective control over all levers of state power and policymaking. The CPSU's monopolistic role in Soviet politics was explicitly articulated in the Soviet constitution:

The leading and guiding force of Soviet society and the nucleus of its political system, of all state organizations and public organizations, is the Communist Party of the Soviet Union. The Communist Party, armed with Marxism-Leninism, determines the general perspectives of the development of society and the course of domestic and foreign policy of the USSR. (Article 6, 1977 Soviet Constitution)

In order to exercise this control, the CPSU relied on an organizational structure that paralleled and supervised the formal organs of government. Every policymaking institution in the USSR – whether it was the cabinet of ministers, a regional administration, or a local city council – was directed and overseen by party structures. The Central Committee of the CPSU and the Politburo, a small committee of party officials drawn from the Central Committee, asserted collective party control over this hierarchy.

Aside from policymaking, the CPSU also monopolized access to political office. The party maintained and curated a list of posts in both the party and government that were to be filled only by CPSU appointees. This system was called the *nomenklatura*. By managing the ranking of officials on these lists, the CPSU ensured its political dominance over elite politics in the USSR.

In the Soviet party-state, it should come as no surprise that elections were also a one-party affair. Elections in the USSR were held to local councils called "soviets" and to the parliaments of the USSR and its constituent republics (Supreme Soviets). The policymaking powers of these legislative bodies were limited, and they existed primarily to rubber-stamp laws that were conceived by party organs. Elections to these bodies were single-candidate elections; ballots contained only the name of the party-nominated candidate for a given seat. The only way that a voter could vote against the CPSU candidate was by spoiling the ballot paper, an act of dissent that was rare.

Despite the lack of choice, Soviet elections saw high levels of participation. Although certainly inflated, official turnout figures routinely registered above 99 percent. Such astronomical participation rates were achieved via thoroughgoing mobilization and propaganda. At election time, voters were bombarded with exhortations to vote. Such messages were carried by mass media, employers, educational and cultural organizations, and, most of all, party agitators, who were charged with visiting every voter's home before election day.

3.2.2 A Thousand Flowers Bloom: Pluralist Politics in Transitional Russia

The reforms of *glasnost* (openness) and *perestroika* (restructuring), initiated by **Mikhail Gorbachev** in the late 1980s, began a process that would lead to the rapid disintegration of one-party rule and a complete transformation of Russia's party system. By relaxing restrictions on organization and speech, *glasnost*-era policies led to an explosion of "informal" public associations that sprang up to articulate and defend a diverse array of interests. In 1989, multicandidate legislative elections were held for the first time in Soviet history, and in 1990 the CPSU's "leading role" was removed from the Soviet constitution. Political organization was effectively legalized, and hundreds of movements and proto-parties sprang up over the course of 1990 and 1991.

In August 1991, newly elected Russian president **Boris Yeltsin** banned the CPSU, bringing an end to seventy years of Communist Party hegemony in Russia. A new era of pluralist politics had begun. Yet during these early years of transition (1991–93), Russia's emergent political movements remained highly amorphous and disorganized. Most lacked the classic hallmarks of political parties, such as distinctive platforms, formal organization, or linkages with voters. Russia's legislature, the Supreme Soviet, had been elected when Russia was still part of the Soviet Union, and contained no formal political parties. Nonetheless, discernable blocs took shape. On one side were the "democrats," allies of Yeltsin who advocated a market economy, liberal democratic reforms, and a Western orientation in foreign policy. Opposite Yeltsin were a mélange of nationalist and pro-communist forces. The latter opposed market reform, the destruction of the Soviet centralized state, and rapprochement with the West. Nationalist groups, for their part, focused more on issues of identity and culture. They railed against engagement with the West and argued that Western-style liberalism would lead to a degradation of traditional "Russian" values. Politics in the transition era degenerated into a polarized deadlock between supporters of Yeltsin and his communist/nationalist opponents. In October 1993, this polarization reached fever pitch and was resolved only when Yeltsin used force to dissolve the Supreme Soviet and began drafting a new constitution.

The 1993 constitution created the basic system of representative government that exists in Russia to this day. The main elements of that system are:

- a directly elected presidency with elections;
- a directly elected lower house, called the State Duma, with 450 seats up for election every five years; and
- an upper house called the **Federation Council,** which – similar to the United States Senate – seats representatives from each of Russia's federal subjects. From 1993 to 1995 this body was directly elected, but its members have been indirectly elected since 1995.

From the beginning, the State Duma has been the main arena for party politics in Russia, and the December 1993 State Duma elections can be considered the founding elections for Russia's party system. For the first time in Russian history, political parties freely competed with only limited interference from the state. Indeed, parties aligned with Yeltsin – such as Russia's Choice – failed to gain a majority, despite their close ties to the president. In just four short years, Russia's party system had transitioned from one in which all political activity was monopolized by a single political party to one in which state-backed parties could be defeated, often handily, at the ballot box. The mixed electoral system in place, by which half of Duma seats were allotted to political parties according to proportional representation and half according to single-member districts, provided fertile conditions for a large number of viable parties as well as nonpartisan deputies with concentrated geographical support. Such competition remained a hallmark of elections in the 1990s, with hotly contested parliamentary elections being held in 1995 and 1999 and a closely fought presidential election in 1996.

The main parties that arose in the early 1990s reflected the ideological tendencies that had emerged during the transition period. The communist banner was taken up by the Communist Party of the Russian Federation, which emerged as a successor to the CPSU. The Communists took the most votes in both 1995 and 1999 and were the main opposition to Yeltsin in the 1990s. The most important nationalist party to emerge was the Liberal Democratic Party of Russia, which surprised observers by winning the most votes in the 1993 elections. Though Yeltsin himself never joined or even unequivocally supported a political party, his agenda was supported by various centrist and democratic parties, such as Yabloko, the Party of Russian Unity and Accord, Russia's Choice, and Our Home Is Russia. The latter two were called "**parties of power**" because they were supported by the Kremlin.

These main parties shared the ballot with scores of smaller parties as well. Some of these served important social groups, such as farmers, women, veterans, or environmental organizations, but many others served as fly-by-night virtual parties that existed only to service the electoral ambitions of a single politician. This fractionalization reached its peak in the 1995 elections, when forty-three parties ended up on the ballot and almost half the vote went to parties that received less than 5 percent of the vote.

The party system was also volatile; in both 1995 and 1999 more than 40 percent of the vote went to parties that were brand-new. Most of these parties had vague platforms and weak brands, which made it hard for voters to know what parties stood for. Politicians frequently switched from party to party, which made it hard for voters to hold politicians accountable. Aside from the CPRF, most parties were chronically underfinanced and had no grassroots organization to speak of.

For these reasons, many candidates saw little benefit in party affiliation and chose instead to run as independents. In the 1999 elections, 105 of the 225 district seats were won by independents. Many candidates, and even whole parties, were little more than the puppets of prominent **oligarchs**, financial–industrial groups, or regional political bosses. This tendency reached its zenith in the 1999 Duma elections, which largely revolved around a brutal struggle between a series of "governors' parties" that had been formed to advance the presidential ambitions of regional power-brokers.

The fractious fluidity of Russian party politics made the State Duma a lively political arena. Because the decree powers of the Russian president are limited, Yeltsin had to push major policy initiatives through the Duma as legislation. This made the Duma – and in turn party politics – central to Russian politics. But Yeltsin and his allies lacked a stable majority, so major policy initiatives had to be passed via negotiation, logrolling, and compromise. The Communists emerged as Yeltsin's main opponents in the Duma, and the two sides repeatedly locked horns over market reform. In the 1996 presidential elections, Yeltsin narrowly escaped defeat at the hands of Gennady Zyuganov, the leader of the CPRF. The Communists and their allies never attained their own majority in the Duma, but together they were able to stymie many of Yeltsin's reform initiatives and, in 1998, even forced him to accept a Communist-backed candidate for prime minister. While Yeltsin and his allies often managed to salvage their agenda by building coalitions, relations with a fractionalized Duma were a constant source of headaches for the Kremlin. This was a lesson that Yeltsin's successor, Vladimir Putin, would not forget.

In sum, the 1990s saw Russia transition from the monolith of single-party rule to a fragmented multiparty system. High levels of volatility and weak party labels undermined the ability of the party system serve as a mechanism for representation and accountability. But, despite the chaos, elections were highly competitive. Although Russia's democracy was far from perfect, opposition parties had real chances to access power at the ballot box, and the party system was not dominated by Kremlin influence. In the new millennium, this would all change.

3.3   Electoral Autocracy in Putin's Russia

In the 2000s, Russian electoral politics underwent a complete transformation. Over the course of that decade, the Kremlin came to exert more and more control over the electoral process. Today, Russia is what political scientists call an electoral authoritarian regime. This refers to authoritarian regimes that allow multiparty elections, with some modicum of competition. But elections in such systems are not free and fair. Incumbents use their privileged access to state resources to control and manipulate elections and tip the electoral scales in their favor. Steven Levitsky and Lucan Way (2002, 52) describe such systems as those in which "formal democratic institutions are widely viewed as the principal means of obtaining and exercising political authority. Incumbents violate those rules so often and to such an extent, however, that the regime fails to meet conventional minimum standards for democracy." As we will see in the following sections, multiparty elections are very much alive and well in Russia; there has been no return to a single-party state. Russia's leadership claims its legal and moral right to rule on the basis of electoral mandates. At the same time, the Kremlin uses a variety of means – media control, repression, electoral fraud, and institutional manipulation – to disadvantage the opposition.

Accompanying this change has been the transformation of Russia's party system. Over the course of the 2000s, the Kremlin took a much more assertive role in curating Russia's party system. In particular, it explicitly lent its support to a single "party of power," United Russia, and did everything it could to build a stable one-party majority in the Duma. Russia is now a **dominant party system** – a system where multiple parties compete, but the playing field is dominated by a single party. Such systems can be distinguished from single-party systems, best exemplified by the Soviet Union, because opposition parties are allowed to exist and compete. But such systems are also distinguishable from competitive, multiparty systems because one party is hegemonic. The following section describes the key political parties and movements active in Russia's electoral authoritarian regime

3.3.1 United Russia

The hard-fought 1999 State Duma elections saw the Kremlin-backed party Unity win only 18 percent of Duma seats, far from the majority needed to turn Putin's legislative agenda into reality. In a bold move to consolidate political power, Vladislav Surkov, the deputy chief of the Presidential Administration, encouraged leaders from Unity to begin negotiations to merge with the party Fatherland-All Russia (FAR), a rival party in the Duma. With backing from President Putin, the All-Russian Party "Unity and Fatherland – United Russia" (known as United Russia, Yedinaia Rossiia) was founded in 2001 as a merger between Unity, FAR, and two smaller groups of nonpartisan deputies.

Over the next decade, the Kremlin invested considerable resources into building United Russia into an electoral juggernaut. First, intense bargaining and recruitment efforts led to independent deputies, regional legislators, and perhaps most importantly powerful governors joining its ranks. United Russia promoted its brand as the party preferred by President Putin, who to this day enjoys immense popularity among the Russian electorate. Putin and his advisors carefully communicated to both national and regional elites that membership in United Russia would be crucial for career advancement. Unlike Yeltsin, who had shied away from endorsing a single party of power, Putin signaled that members of United Russia would receive legislative privileges as well as appointments to regional governorships.

By the 2003 national parliamentary elections, this process of cooptation had delivered the Kremlin an absolute majority of seats in the State Duma. United Russia has also been the main beneficiary from the government periodically reforming the electoral system. By 2007, all seats in the State Duma were allocated according to proportional representation. This change, alongside onerous registration requirements for smaller parties and the imposition of a minimum electoral threshold to win seats, helped United Russia achieve and maintain its desired two-thirds majority of seats since 2007. At the subnational level, the party has consistently controlled majorities in all regional legislatures and city councils. In addition, most governors and mayors are members of United Russia.

United Russia performs a number of important functions in Russia's political system. First, the party is best understood as a coalition of pro-regime elites, particularly legislative deputies and other leaders at the subnational level. In the 1990s, regional leaders built impressive political machines that both ensured their longevity in power and created difficulties for the federal center to project influence. By creating a party of power, the Kremlin has been able to coopt, rather than repress, these regional machines into a more coherent, manageable political bloc (Reuter 2017). Recognizing Putin's popularity as well as the Kremlin's newfound resources from rising oil prices, regional elites more readily signed onto the United Russia project. The result has been a more unified political bloc, able to recruit strong candidates and present a nationwide party brand to voters. That has driven impressive electoral gains as well as deterring elite defections, which are often the death knell of dominant parties in other political settings (Reuter and Szakonyi 2019).

From a policymaking standpoint, the emergence of a dominant party has helped the Kremlin ensure elite loyalty and push through its legislative agenda at multiple levels of government. Whereas in the 1990s the multiparty Duma consistently presented a roadblock to the Yeltsin administration, United Russia leaders have brought together pro-regime deputies in consolidated factions marked by strict voting discipline. The Kremlin has had little difficulty getting its bills passed through the State Duma.

Interestingly, the influence of United Russia is much more limited in the federal executive branch. Most appointed officials working for the federal government are nonpartisan. While a handful of high-ranking ministers have joined the party, President Putin has not. Rather than becoming a member, he often strategically chooses to endorse the party in the run-up to elections, and has served a four-year term as party chair coinciding with his time as prime minister. Maintaining a reasonable amount of distance between himself and the party allows him more political flexibility as well as autonomy, especially when the party's popularity declines. Putin's reluctance to officially join also circumscribes the party's policy influence. Whereas the Communist Party dictated most decisions in the Soviet Union, the Kremlin, not United Russia, sets the agenda in Russia. United Russia's role revolves more around organizing and structuring relations with elites, recruiting candidates, and coordinating campaigns.

Beyond helping organize elites, United Russia exists to win elections. To do so, the party has built an impressive grassroots organization that facilitates voter mobilization. Deployed mainly in the run-up to elections, local government officials, company directors, and teachers all staff thousands of primary party

Table 3.1 Percentage of Duma seats held by major parties, 2000–2026

Political Party	Duma Convocation					
	Third (2000–03)	Fourth (2003–07)	Fifth (2007–11)	Sixth (2011–16)	Seventh (2016–21)	Eighth (2021–26)
United Russia	18%*	68%	70%	53%	76%	72%
Fatherland-All Russia	10%					
Communist Party	20%	12%	13%	21%	9%	13%
LDPR	4%	8%	9%	13%	9%	5%
Just Russia			8%	14%	1%	6%
Motherland	9%	8%				
Yabloko	5%					
SPS	7%					
New People						3%
Turnout	61.9%	55.7%	63.7%	60.2%	47.9%	51.7%

Note: This table shows the percentage of seats won by each party according to the initial election results.
* United Russia was known as Unity prior to 2001.
Source: Russian Election Commission, www.vybory.izbirkom.ru/.

organizations with the express goal of getting United Russia candidates into elected office at all levels. They are aided by an expansive youth wing, Young Guard (Molodaia Gvardiia), at one point numbering more than 170,000 members. Young Guard agitates in support of United Russia candidates as well as identifying promising young political leaders for later recruitment into the party. Between elections, party activity is considerably more subdued, mainly consisting of meetings and trainings around important political campaigns.

3.3.2 Cleavages Driving Russian Politics

Russian politics is more than just an ongoing referendum on President Putin. Significant cleavages exist within society, and these cleavages drive voting behavior. The first cleavage maps well on traditional left/right dimensions similar to those observed in political settings in the West. Many voters on the Russian left feel a strong nostalgia for life under the Soviet Union, often as a result of disappointment with how the transition to capitalism has gone in Russia over the past three decades. These left-oriented voters generally support efforts to reassert state control over the economy, to provide a strong welfare state including employment guarantees and other societal benefits, and to limit Russia's engagement with the West. As we will see, the CPRF has worked hard to cultivate this base, in particular by espousing the symbols and rhetoric of its Soviet-era precursor.

Support for policies generally considered to the right is somewhat weaker but still visible within Russian society. Voters on the right throw their lot behind more pro-market reforms that emphasize more individual responsibility and a reduced role for the state in the lives of the average citizen. Importantly, voters in Russia can place political parties on this left/right ideological spectrum, which indicates that voters are able to distinguish among the policy platforms of parties (Hale and Colton 2010). Party affiliation in Russia is rooted, at least in part, in programmatic support, and not just clientelist or personalist appeals.

A second major cleavage is rooted in issues of cultural identity. Conservatives in Russia favor a return to more traditional values in society, such as an expanded role for the **Russian Orthodox Church,** support for clearly defined gender roles, and a much more antagonistic view of the West, both on cultural and on foreign policy grounds (Laruelle 2009, 119–52). Liberals, on the other hand, emphasize the importance of human rights and civil liberties, often embracing progressive causes and cultural diversity. In contrast to conservatives, who may hold a special fondness for the monarchic rule of tsarist times, Russian liberals want to see the government work harder to protect political and economic freedoms rather than restrict them for the sake of economic and/or political stability.

United Russia has strategically positioned itself in the middle of both cleavages. Its right/centrist position on the first cleavage has enabled the party to straddle complex issues and construct its big tent. On economic issues, United Russia is perceived to be an advocate for the maintenance of pro-market reforms, and therefore lies somewhat to the right of center, especially in comparison to the CPRF. Although United Russia has also espoused an array of socially conservative policies (for example, with regard to LGBTQ+ issues), overall its positions are actually more liberal than those of the median Russian voter.

Just as United Russia has pitched its big tent to attract as many voters as possible from both sides of the spectrum, the party itself houses a diverse set of wings trying to pull it in liberal and conservative directions. This emphasis on satisfying all the wings, particularly around election time, also generates a watered-down party platform with few specific policy prescriptions. But centrism prevents opposition parties from coordinating against the ruling party, and this catchall approach has been quite effective electorally.

Beyond these ideological pulls, United Russia's popularity owes much to its close association with President Putin and his strong approval ratings, which regularly exceed 60 percent. As the primary party of the regime, United Russia enjoys unparalleled state support during elections. This backing, though, has not been enough to stem the slide of the party in the eyes of the public. By 2021, stagnant economic growth, along with corruption allegations, had sent United Russia's support on a downward trajectory. While it remained the most popular party in the country – thanks to a strong core of support among regime voters that feel a psychological attachment to it – its support dwindled to its lowest ever point.

Opposition to United Russia comes in many forms, though in general opposition parties enjoy rather weak support among the Russian population. Between Putin's personal popularity and electoral manipulation (see below), the regime gives the opposition little opportunity to build its support base. But, as we discuss below, some of the opposition's weakness also arises from its own miscalculations and internal divisions.

Russian opposition parties generally fall into two camps: the systemic and the nonsystemic opposition. On the one hand, the systemic opposition parties, such as the LDPR and Just Russia at times may oppose certain policies pursued by the Kremlin, but they acknowledge the legitimacy of the government and even praise Putin's leadership at the top. This political loyalty to the regime bakes them into the "system." That political support is often rewarded by the Kremlin with a variety of perks and privileges. Leaders of systemic opposition parties regularly appear on state television promoting their parties and can even secure significant access to policymaking, whether in the form of a governorship or various concessions within regional legislatures.

Nonsystemic opposition parties not only oppose the regime's policies, but also often openly advocate the removal of the current leaders from power. In electoral authoritarian regimes, much of the political struggle often revolves around issues of regime type itself. Many nonsystemic opposition voters are motivated to participate in politics by human rights violations, electoral manipulation, and violations of personal freedom that are perpetrated by the regime. Declaring the Putin government authoritarian and illegitimate, these parties have historically excluded most possibilities of cooperating with the regime and have found themselves excluded from most if not all policymaking. Notably, the terms "systemic" and "nonsystemic" are helpful in simplifying the differing openness to cooperating with the regime, but parties do change strategies over time and sometimes do not neatly conform to a simple designation as either inside or outside the system.

3.3.3   Systemic Opposition in Russia

3.3.3.1   Communist Party of the Russian Federation

Continuing the role it played during the Yeltsin administration in the 1990s, the Communist Party of the Russian Federation remains the largest opposition party in the country. As Table 3.1 indicates, the CPRF has consistently won roughly 10–20 percent of the vote throughout the Putin era. In recent years, CPRF members have won election to governorships in a handful of cities and regions (such as Khakassia in 2018 and Ulianovsk in 2021). Ideologically, the CPRF has strayed from its communist roots on many issues. The party has in part betrayed these roots by becoming more receptive to some pro-market reforms as well as by accepting democracy as the mechanism for selecting political leaders. Although still championing an enlarged role for the state in the economy, the party no longer advocates the dogmatic nationalization of the past, and has in fact accepted financial support from big business. Much foreign policy rhetoric from the CPRF still maligns cooperation with the West, but the overall agenda pushes for Russian national interests, rather than the more imperial ones of its predecessor.

That said, there is still significant continuity with the party's socialist past. The CPRF forcefully advocates a robust welfare state, including enhanced support for pensioners and protections for the working class. Support from these two groups has provided the party with a strong grassroots core ready for mobilization, which the party has often deftly activated when more neoliberal policies have been proposed by the Putin government. The party's protest potential, while often muted during the significant 2011–12 wave, does keep the regime on its toes. In fact, the CPRF helped lead protests and fight proposed reforms to the pension system in both 2005 and 2018 (Robertson 2009; Dollbaum 2021).

In more recent years, the CPRF has started to straddle the line between systemic and nonsystemic opposition. During the Putin period, its leaders, in particular party chair Gennady Zyuganov, have been open to negotiation, compromise, and cooperation with United Russia, and with the Kremlin more broadly. Historically, this moderation has allowed the party to extract significant concessions, such as leadership positions in legislative bodies (Reuter and Robertson 2015).

Yet the party's original base is aging, and Zyuganov will soon be entering his third decade at the top. New wings within the party are pushing for more vocal opposition to the Kremlin. Many leftist radicals and liberals alike see a takeover of the CPRF as their best chance to achieve regime change from within. Indeed, Communist Party candidates have been the main beneficiaries of Alexei Navalny's Smart Voting efforts which seek to coordinate nonsystemic opposition votes behind political forces already working within the system. This internal dissension presents great difficulties for the party. Strengthening its opposition to the regime may threaten the CPRF's core base of pensioners and laborers. But relying too heavily on these two groups creates risks of political obsolescence.

3.3.3.2   Liberal Democratic Party of Russia

The other major systemic opposition party is the Liberal Democratic Party of Russia. Despite its name, the politics of the LDPR are anything but liberal or democratic in the traditional sense. Its founder and longtime leader, Vladimir Zhirinovsky, took pride in being one of the most ultranationalist, outlandish personalities in Russian politics. Launching his career shortly after the fall of the Soviet Union, Zhirinovsky quickly made a national name for himself with constant stream of vicious xenophobic rhetoric, crude drunken jokes, and barbarous policy ideas. The most egregious examples include building a barbed-wire fence around the entire North

Caucasus, providing free vodka for men, and shooting all Russia's birds to prevent the spread of avian flu.

As shocking as his rants were, the LDPR enjoyed stable electoral support, and it is the only party, aside from the CPRF, that has won seats in every Duma convocation since 1993. Disregarding Zhirinovsky's many public stunts (which he admitted should not be taken at face value), the LDPR's platform provides little specificity beyond a blend of staunch anti-Westernism, populism, and nationalism. The party has been one of the more stalwart backers of the regime and has been rewarded handsomely for its loyalty. Zhirinovsky died in April 2022, so the party's future is uncertain.

3.3.3.3   Just Russia

As the third party to consistently secure seats in the Putin era, Just Russia professes the least degree of formal opposition to the regime. Founded in 2006 as a pet project of the Kremlin, Just Russia was designed to support the left flank of United Russia and lure voters away from the CPRF. Three smaller parties – Russian Party of Life, Rodina, and the Russian Pensioners Party – ultimately merged, with Sergei Mironov taking the reins of the new bloc. Mironov's close working relationship with Putin dates back to their early careers in St. Petersburg and renders real opposition inconceivable.

Since its founding, Just Russia has focused mainly on social issues, from fighting corruption to introducing progressive taxation and increasing redistribution. Yet, for all its quasi-socialism, the party has courted big businesspeople in the regions as candidates and its leaders in Moscow are very wealthy in their own right. Overall, the party's populist, anti-Western ideology has not sufficiently differentiated itself from either the Communist Party or United Russia, and each Duma election cycle holds out a real possibility of the party not clearing the electoral threshold. Yet, seemingly against the odds, Just Russia has survived and continued to control seats, a far cry from the promise of a second party of power that its founders envisioned.

3.3.4   Nonsystemic Opposition

Nonsystemic groups in Russia come from across the political spectrum, but in recent years the most prominent nonsystemic groups have come from the liberal wing of the political spectrum. For most of the Putin regime, liberal parties have found themselves outside the formal corridors of power. The situation was different in the 1990s, as their policy proposals calling for freer markets, greater democracy, and closer engagement with the West won over a substantial part of the electorate. But, as many Russians grew frustrated with the travails of the transition from communism, support for such ideas and for the politicians who continued to advocate them declined.

Although a substantial number of highly educated Russians still espouse liberal views, the parties claiming to represent their positions remain weak, fragmented, and often hamstrung by personal divisions. The nonsystemic opposition has failed to coalesce into a coordinated group of opposition-minded elites cooperating to remove the regime from power. Some of the damage has been self-inflicted, as too many strong personalities have prevented the emergence of either a single individual or a corresponding party carrying the mantle of Russian liberalism into electoral battle. At the same time, of course, the playing field is severely tilted against all nonsystemic opposition parties: Parties and candidates are prevented from registering, leaders are openly harassed, state media outlets block coverage of their activities, and election administrators use all sorts of election-day tricks to ensure United Russia wins out.

Even amidst these widespread pressures, several liberal parties continue to operate and contest power. The most prominent and popular party is Yabloko, the Russian word for "apple" but also an acronym for the party's founders last names. Led by Grigory Yavlinsky since its founding, Yabloko has survived a tumultuous political trajectory. Early in the Yeltsin period it ranked among the loudest voices for pro-market reforms, before a falling-out with Yeltsin left it outside formal power structures. But the party continued to win seats in the Duma until 2003, when the full brunt of the Kremlin's efforts to institutionalize the party system around United Russia began to take shape. As the media environment closed, Yabloko struggled to communicate its political messages to voters, while the arrest of Mikhail Khodorkovsky in 2003 deprived the party of a key source of financing. Yabloko-affiliated candidates have continued to be allowed to run for office at all levels of government, but the number of their victories has dwindled over the past two decades. Even amidst this electoral drought, Yabloko's party platform has remained consistent. The pillars include support for democratic reform (and accordingly criticism of the regime's growing authoritarianism), free elections, engagement with the West, and protection of human rights.

To the right of Yabloko on economic issues lie a number of market–liberal parties. In the early 2000s, this banner was carried by the Union of Right Forces (Soyuz Pravykh Sil, SPS). Another merger of likeminded opposition parties, SPS first contested the 1999 elections led by Boris Nemtsov, a first deputy prime minister during the Yeltsin administration who made his name by championing pro-market reforms. Appealing to the business community and young people alike, SPS was able to secure twenty-four seats in that Duma convocation (7 percent) and worked closely with the first Putin administration on reforming the economy. Yet rising administrative pressure, smear campaigns orchestrated by the Kremlin, and the loss of key financial backers began to weigh on the party's electoral prospects. SPS's leadership, and Nemtsov in particular, soon become some of Putin's most outspoken and influential critics and led a new coalition called Solidarnost that brought together other extreme opponents of the regime. All but banned from participating in elections, opposition leaders huddling under this umbrella have relied instead on street protests to call attention to a decline in democratic quality, human rights protections, and other political freedoms. In 2015, Nemtsov was murdered in brazen fashion close to the Kremlin, presumably as punishment for his political activism. The subsequent hurried investigation into the killing is seen by many in the opposition as persuasive evidence of the Kremlin's involvement.

For years the Russian opposition had failed to get behind a single opposition leader to guide the movement to unseat Putin and his party. That began to change with the rise of Alexei Navalny, a relatively young lawyer and anticorruption activist who began his political career investigating graft within large state-owned enterprises in the 1990s. Navalny grasped early on not only the extent of corruption within the Putin government, but also its potential for catalyzing and mobilizing opposition against the regime. Expert use of social media, beginning with blogs and then migrating over to YouTube, Facebook, and VKontakte (among others), quickly increased his audience and transformed him into one of the most prominent political voices on the Russian Internet (Dollbaum, Lallouet, and Noble 2021). Crisp, professionally shot videos accuse high-level politicians such as President Putin, former prime minister **Dmitry Medvedev** and former procurator general Yury Chaika of turning ill-gotten gains into lavish palaces and country houses. On YouTube, these videos attract tens of millions of views and have sparked massive protests against corruption in Russia's elite.

In 2013, Navalny launched his formal political career by running for the position of mayor of Moscow, capitalizing on his fame as Russia's most prominent anti-corruption crusader. His second-place finish with 28 percent of the vote further spooked the Kremlin, which was already wary of his growing support among Russia's so-called creative class: young, highly educated urbanites, often populating the country's intellectual and cultural elite. From that point forward, the Kremlin began deploying its repressive toolkit to stop Navalny's political star from rising any further. Convicted of corruption in 2013 in what many viewed as a politically motivated case, he was legally banned from running for any political office and therefore unable to contest the 2018 presidential elections.

In August 2020, Navalny fell critically ill on a commercial flight over Siberia. The Russian government reluctantly allowed his medical evacuation to Germany, where he lay in a coma for months before miraculously recovering. Later evidence would implicate a team of **FSB** (Federal Security Service) officers in following his movements for years and then attempting to poison him. In January 2021, Navalny defiantly returned to Russia only to face another set of trumped-up criminal charges and ultimately a three-and-a-half year jail sentence. He has since become Russia's most famous political prisoner, though it remains to be seen how long his political movement can survive the intense stranglehold the Russian government has applied to him and his comrades-in-arms.

3.3.5   Presidential Electorates in Russia

While Duma elections are the main arena for party politics in Russia, presidential elections can be viewed as far more consequential, given that they determine who holds Russia's most powerful office. From 1993 to 2012, presidential elections were held every four years, but they are now held every six years. A two-round system is used, so that a runoff between the top two is held if no candidate receives a majority in the first round. Yeltsin was first elected president in 1991, an election that was held under Soviet law when Russia was still part of the Soviet Union. Yeltsin won a second term in 1996, narrowly outpacing his communist challenger Gennady Zyuganov. The 2000 presidential election was held in a competitive environment, but Putin was able to win comfortably.

Since then, presidential elections – in 2004, 2008, 2012, and 2018 – have been lopsided affairs, won handily by Vladimir Putin (or Dmitry Medvedev in 2008). As we outline below, ballot-box fraud is commonly used in presidential elections, but outright fraud accounts for a relatively small share of Putin's vote totals. The vast majority of the votes that Putin receives are cast by Russian voters themselves. Why do these tens of millions of voters support Putin? The short answer is that he is by far the most popular politician in Russia. Since he rose to power in 2000, Putin's popularity rating has averaged more than 70 percent, and it was routinely higher than 80 percent in the years following the annexation of Crimea. Even at its lowest point, Putin's popularity has never sunk below 60 percent.

So what draws Russian voters to Putin? Surveys indicate that a number of factors drive the vote for Putin. First, many voters are drawn to Putin's policy positions (see Hale and Colton 2009, 2017). In the previous section we described United Russia's electorate, which is broadly similar to Putin's electorate. Putin and United Russia occupy almost identical spots on the ideological spectrum, and the demographic profile of Putin voters is broadly similar to that of United Russia voters. Thus, for example, center-right voters – those who support market reforms undertaken in Russia over the past thirty years – are more likely to favor Putin over other major presidential candidates. In recent years, issues of identity and culture have taken a more prominent role in Russian political debates. On these issues, Putin has positioned himself as a moderate cultural conservative – a promoter of traditional "Russian" values, the Orthodox Church, and the traditional family. Voters who prioritize these issues have been increasingly drawn to Putin in recent years.

Another major issue that drives the vote for Putin is foreign policy. Here the story is somewhat complicated. On the one hand, Putin has traditionally positioned himself near the center of the political spectrum on foreign policy issues. And, contrary to some popular depictions, he is viewed by voters as actually being *more* pro-Western than most other prominent politicians in Russia. Voters who thought that Russia should treat the West as an ally or friend have traditionally been more likely to vote for Putin than voters who thought that the West should be treated as an enemy or rival. At the same time, Putin has taken a more confrontational posture toward the West in recent years. This has allowed him to expand his support among nationalist voters. Putin increasingly draws support from voters who think that Russia must defend its interests – especially in Ukraine and the rest of the former Soviet space – against Western hegemony.

Demographically, Putin's support base has traditionally been a pastiche. He typically draws support from both old and young, the educated and uneducated, the wealthy and the poor. In recent years, however, he has increasingly lost support among urban dwellers, especially young white-collar professionals in the private sector. Interestingly, there is also an emergent gender gap in Russian elections. In recent years, Putin has been losing support among men and gaining support among women.

Voters are also drawn to Putin because they like his character (Hale and Colton 2017). Surveys indicate that voters identify a number of positive personality traits in Putin. First and foremost, they view him as strong and competent. In a 2016 survey, 77 percent of respondents said they viewed Putin as "smart and knowledgeable." Seventy-four percent said they thought he was a "strong leader." Many voters also view him as "honest and trustworthy" (54 percent). Interestingly, these views do not extend to all his personality traits, as 56 percent of respondents in the aforementioned survey said that Putin "did not think about the interests of regular people" (Reuter and Szakonyi 2021, 299). This discrepancy is instructive. Putin is not a populist. He is not particularly charismatic, is not a strong public speaker, and does not appear often in public. Rather, many Russians are drawn to Putin because they think he is an effective and capable leader (Wengle and Evans 2018).

Finally, one of the most important factors driving the vote for Putin is performance assessments. Many vote for Putin not because of his ideas, but rather because they believe that Putin has performed well in office. In a 2012 postelection survey, 51 percent of Putin voters said that they chose him because of his work as president; only 15 percent said it was because of his personality, and 11 percent said they voted for him because they liked his program.

After the chaos and disruption of the 1990s, many voters credit Putin with restoring order and stability in Russia. Others believe that Putin has helped restore Russia's influence in the world. But economic performance is the metric that matters most. Economic evaluations are one of the most consistent predictors of voting behavior around the world. Voters tend to reward politicians when the economy is doing well and punish them when the economy declines. Russia is no different in this regard. Studies show that the popularity of Russia's presidents closely tracks perceptions of economic performance (Treisman 2011). In the midst of economic depression during the 1990s, Yeltsin's popularity sank to single digits. By contrast, Putin's first two terms were accompanied by robust economic expansion. To this day, many voters credit Putin with Russia's economic recovery.

It must be stressed that all of the aforementioned attitudes are shaped by the authoritarian nature of Russia's system. For one, media bias portrays Putin's character, policies, and performance in a positive light. Blame for policy failures is deflected from Putin and placed on state bureaucracies (Rozenas and Stukal 2019), while foreign policy victories are attributed almost solely to him. Putin's main rivals – for example, Alexei Navalny – are denied public platforms, such as state television, which they could use to criticize the regime. It is little wonder, then, that consumption of state television has become one of the strongest predictors of voting for Putin in recent years.

3.3.6   Explaining Electoral Participation

The decision of who to vote for comes second to another fundamental choice: whether to vote at all. Participation in Soviet elections was near 100 percent, a figure that was partly manufactured, but also reflected the mass mobilizational nature of the Soviet regime. The novelty of participating in the nation's first multiparty elections kept many voters coming to the polls in the late Soviet years, but in the 1990s turnout levels came down from the stratosphere to a level that was comparable with other electoral democracies. Turnout in presidential elections – which are viewed as more consequential than others – has typically averaged around 70 percent. As Table 3.1 shows, turnout in State Duma elections between 1993 and 2011 averaged around 60 percent. This is somewhat lower than in many European parliamentary elections, but about average for a developing country and significantly higher than many midterm elections in the United States, for example.

However, one of the most noteworthy changes in Russian electoral politics over the past decade has been a drop in participation rates. The trend has been most marked in regional and local elections, where turnout levels routinely drop below 20 percent. In State Duma elections there has also been a large decline in turnout – in 2016 and 2021 the official turnout figures were 48 percent and 52 percent, respectively. These figures are inflated by some fraud, so the true figures are likely somewhat lower.

Why is electoral participation declining in Russia? Several answers suggest themselves. First, as discussed below, elections in Russia have become increasingly tainted by fraud, repression, media bias, and opposition exclusion. This, along with the regime's legitimate popularity, makes outcomes all but certain. Some voters believe it is pointless to participate in elections where the winner is preordained.

A second reason relates to the regime's own electoral strategy. The authorities in Russia are ambivalent about the political value of encouraging very high turnout. On the one hand, high turnout legitimizes the regime's electoral mandate. But a politically active electorate also poses dangers for an autocracy like Russia. Politicized voters are more likely to become informed about politics, possibly learning about government malfeasance and opposition politicians. This can lead to demands for representation and accountability. In this regard, an apathetic citizenry can be less threatening.

Kremlin strategists have taken this lesson to heart. In recent years, the authorities have taken steps to depoliticize election campaigns and ensure that they are devoid of political intrigue or controversy. The regime invests little effort into classical mobilizational strategies – get-out-the-vote efforts, media campaigns, and so forth. It refrains from taking clear policy stances and discourages its candidates from engaging in debates with the opposition. In 2016, the decision was made to move State Duma elections to September, so that the campaign would occur in late summer, a traditionally quiet time in Russia, when many voters are on vacation.

This raises the question of why people still vote at all in Russia. As in democracies, the main driver of turnout is civic duty: a feeling that one has a moral obligation to vote, irrespective of the candidates or issues at hand. In the 2016 State Duma elections, 69 percent of respondents in the Russian Election Study said that a feeling of civic duty compelled them to vote (Reuter 2021). Scholars debate the sources of civic duty, but the concept is often linked to reverence or respect for the state. Since opposition voters in Russia increasingly view the state as penetrated and corrupted by the Putin government, surveys indicate that opposition voters are much less likely to state that they feel a duty to vote (Reuter 2021). This leads opposition supporters to participate in elections at much lower rates than regime supporters. In the 2016 State Duma elections, 67 percent of regime supporters stated that they had voted, compared to just 55 percent of opposition supporters.

Aside from one's attitude toward the regime, some of the most important predictors of turnout in Russia are similar to the factors that predict turnout in democracies. Voters who have more time and resources are more likely to pay the "costs" of voting: Older and wealthier voters are consistently more likely to turn out (for example, White and McAllister 2007; McAllister and White 2017). Until recently, education was also positively associated with turnout, but this relationship has waned in recent years. Gender is also important, as women are much more likely to vote.

There are also important "undemocratic" factors that drive turnout patterns in Russia. Many Russian voters are induced, cajoled, or even coerced to vote. This is especially true for public-sector employees – for example, in schools, universities, hospitals, prisons, the military, and other government offices – who often face pressure from their employers to vote at election time. This practice is also common in large and state-owned factories. Surveys show that up to one in four workers are asked by their employers to vote at election time, and studies show that these tactics help to boost turnout (Frye, Reuter, and Szakonyi 2014).

3.4   The Use of Electoral Manipulation and Fraud

At least since 2003, the Putin government has relied on electoral manipulation and fraud to ensure that regime-affiliated candidates win elections by comfortable margins. The regime rarely wants to take chances around elections: Losing seats to the opposition means sharing power and rents, a slippery slope that could eventually result in the complete ouster of the government. Therefore, authorities go to great lengths not only to shift the playing field to its own advantage, but also to limit any backlash by citizens angered by the use of undemocratic practices to win elections.

Manipulations begin long before election day, as the authorities restrict the opposition's ability both to contest elections and to attract support. State-owned media outlets denigrate opposition politicians, deny airtime to voices critical of the regime, and cast Putin/United Russia in a mostly glowing light. Even if they are able to surmount the extraordinary roadblocks the regime uses to deny ballot access (Szakonyi 2022), regime challengers face an uphill battle to raise money to fund their campaigns and to deploy activists to mobilize support on the ground. Opposition politicians who dare to test these institutional restrictions often face outright harassment and repression, as the case of Navalny demonstrates.

Further actions are taken the day of the vote. Although the government has prided itself on installing video cameras in electoral precincts and taking other measures to prevent fraud, independent election monitors often capture pictures and videos of poll workers stuffing ballot boxes or simply making up numbers on electoral returns. Other schemes are more devious, such as the organizing of "carousels" by which voters are illegally bussed to multiple precincts on election day. Electronic voting was first introduced in 2020 as a way to increase turnout amidst the coronavirus pandemic by allowing Russians to vote from the safety of their home. However, serious concerns were raised during both the constitutional referendum of that year and the next year's Duma elections about electronic votes being illegally added to United Russia tallies. Because directives coming from the top place pressure on poll workers to deliver a certain percentage of the vote for United Russia candidates, those responsible for orchestrating the fraud face little to no punishment for their actions.

How many of the regime's electoral victories are the product of fraud? Sophisticated detection techniques have helped academics and other election analysts place bounds on the extent of electoral fraud in each election, even if coming up with precise number is a near-impossible task. For example, a field experiment randomly deploying election monitors to Moscow precincts in the 2011 Duma elections estimated that roughly one-quarter of United Russia's final vote total in the city was due to fraud (Enikolopov et al. 2013). Each election, Golos, the leading electoral monitoring organization, documents thousands of citizen reports of electoral fraud, from voters being coerced or bribed, to actual witnesses of ballot-box stuffing.

The regime works hard to limit the spread of information about the electoral manipulations it undertakes. In fact, many core regime supporters believe that elections are free and fair and, when presented with information to the contrary, withdraw their support for the government (Reuter and Szakonyi 2021). After corruption, electoral fraud ranks among the most explosive political issues in Russia. Blatant electoral fraud helped trigger the 2011–12 wave of protests, which saw the largest demonstrations since the fall of the Soviet Union.

This presents the regime with a tradeoff. The use of fraud and other electoral manipulations may be critically important for United Russia to maintain power, especially as its popularity has lagged. But the more that word gets out that fraud is being used to prop up the regime during the elections, the greater the potential for the opposition to mobilize its own supporters in protest, and even peel off some support from the regime, thereby threatening the regime's hold on power. In neighboring post-Soviet countries, such as Ukraine, Georgia, and Kyrgyzstan, electoral fraud has touched off revolutions that led to the unseating of authoritarian incumbents. Thus, the Kremlin is highly sensitive to the potential downsides of blatant fraud. In response, the Russian government has opted for a strategy of fraud paired with concealment. It hopes that by restricting the ability of citizens to learn about the problems with elections, either through independent media, election monitors, or the opposition, it can continue to manipulate elections without paying significant public consequences. So far, this strategy has been relatively successful, but it remains to be seen how much the government can undermine free elections without the general public taking serious offense and demanding change.

3.5 Electoral Autocracy in Russia: Stability and Fragility

Multiparty elections have been a central feature of Russian politics since 1991. And, even though the regime has become increasingly autocratic over the past two decades, elections remain a core part of the system. Because competition is constrained and results are partially manipulated, these elections do not serve as reliable mechanisms of democratic accountability. So, one might ask: As an autocratic regime, why would Russia bother retaining elections at all? Political scientists have suggested several answers. For one, Russians demand multiparty elections. Surveys show that Russians believe their leaders should be elected and that party competition is important (Hale 2011). Indeed, the regime stakes its legitimacy on winning these elections. In the Soviet era, the CPSU justified its rule by claiming that it was building a better society, one based on socialism. Contemporary Russian leaders justify their rule on the basis of an electoral mandate. Putin wins elections, so the story goes, and this gives him the right to rule.

Elections also operate as an imperfect accountability mechanism that bolsters popular support for the regime. Studies show that even autocratic elections can induce leaders to provide more and better services to the public (Beazer and Reuter 2022). Elections provide other political benefits as well. Election outcomes, for example, provide information on the source, location, and distribution of grievances against the regime. What bothers voters? Which voters are upset? Where do they live? What types of policy appeals might assuage their concerns? Regular elections allow the regime to gather valuable information that can be used to forestall threats before they become critical.

Elections also allow the regime to gather information on the opposition – its strengths, its vulnerabilities. In turn, by winning elections – and crushing the opposition – the regime is able to signal its strength (Magaloni 2006). Winning elections by huge margins demonstrates to would-be opponents that attempts to challenge the regime are likely to fail. For this reason, the regime prefers to win elections by large margins.

Finally, elections provide the institutional means for coopting the opposition and channeling its demands. By inviting (some) opposition forces to participate in elections, the regime is able to take certain demands off the streets so that they can be dealt with in a controlled, legislative environment. At the elite level, the regime is often able to diffuse opposition by offering its leaders plum legislative positions and other sinecures (Reuter and Robertson 2015).

At the same time, elections are not without risk. That the Kremlin sees risks in elections is self-evident: It carefully manages the playing field so that opposition parties are not able to mount a real challenge. But even carefully controlled elections can pose challenges for an authoritarian regime. The act of manipulation itself presents threats. As the previous section discussed, Russian voters find fraud distasteful, and there is always the risk that heavyhanded manipulation tactics will produce a popular backlash.

More generally, elections give citizens and the opposition a chance to engage in public politics. Electoral campaigns give opposition forces a chance to form organizations and build capacity. Voting allows citizens to register their grievances with the regime. Over time, demands for representation and accountability can grow. If these demands become too pressing, even highly managed elections can produce surprise victories for the opposition.

3.6   Conclusion

Elections are thus a source of both stability and fragility for the current electoral authoritarian regime in Russia. The creation and development of the dominant party

United Russia have enabled the regime to consolidate electoral control and manage elites and political institutions across the country. Voters still gravitate to both Putin's policies and his personality, which, in turn, helps United Russia defeat its opponents. Yet the regime's ability to carefully manage electoral politics is predicated on manipulating institutions, coopting and repressing opposition parties, and, sometimes, orchestrating fraud. By ensuring that United Russia can dominate elections, these machinations improve the regime's short-term hold on political power, but this has also created long-term vulnerabilities that challengers may be able to exploit in the future.

DISCUSSION QUESTIONS

1. Do elections contribute to or undermine regime stability in Russia?
2. Why does Vladimir Putin win elections by such large margins?
3. Why was Putin able to succeed in creating a party of power while Yeltsin failed?
4. What are the dilemmas facing the "systemic" opposition in Russia?
5. Would you vote for Putin if you lived in Russia? Why or why not? Would your grandmother?

REFERENCES

Beazer, Quintin H., and Ora John Reuter. 2022. "Do Authoritarian Elections Help the Poor? Evidence from Russian Cities." *Journal of Politics*, 84(2), 437–54.

Dollbaum, Jan Matti. 2021. "Social Policy on Social Media: How Opposition Actors Used Twitter and VKontakte to Oppose the Russian Pension Reform." *Problems of Post-Communism*, 68(6), 509–20.

Dollbaum, Jan Matti, Morvan Lallouet, and Ben Noble. 2021. *Navalny: Putin's Nemesis, Russia's Future?* London: Hearst.

Enikolopov, Ruben, Vasily Korovkin, Maria Petrova, Konstantin Sonin, and Alexei Zakharov. 2013. "Field Experiment Estimate of Electoral Fraud in Russian Parliamentary Elections." *Proceedings of the National Academy of Sciences*, 110(2), 448–52.

Frye, Timothy, Ora John Reuter, and David Szakonyi. 2014. "Political Machines at Work Voter Mobilization and Electoral Subversion in the Workplace." *World Politics*, 66(2), 195–228.

Hale, Henry E. 2011. "The Myth of Mass Russian Support for Autocracy: The Public Opinion Foundations of a Hybrid Regime." *Europe–Asia Studies*, 63(8), 1357–75.

Hale, Henry E., and Timothy J. Colton. 2009. "The Putin Vote: Presidential Electorates in a Hybrid Regime." *Slavic Review*, 68(3), 473–503.

    2010. "Russians and the Putin–Medvedev 'Tandemocracy.'" *Problems of Post-Communism*, 57(2), 3–20.

    2017. "Source of Ruling Party Dominance in Non-Democratic Regimes: The Surprising Importance of Ideas and the Case of United Russia." Working Paper, George Washington University (Washington, DC).

Laruelle, Marlène. 2009. *In the Name of the Nation: Nationalism and Politics in Contemporary Russia.* Basingstoke: Palgrave Macmillan.

Levitsky, Steven, and Lucan A. Way. 2002. "The Rise of Competitive Authoritarianism." *Journal of Democracy,* 13(20), 51–65.

Magaloni, Beatriz. 2006. *Voting for Autocracy: Hegemonic Party Survival and Its Demise in Mexico.* Cambridge: Cambridge University Press.

McAllister, Ian, and Stephen White. 2017. "Demobilizing Voters: Election Turnout in the 2016 Russian Election." *Russian Politics,* 2(4), 411–33.

Putin, Vladimir. 2016. "Speech to United Russia Party Congress." June 27, http://old.iltumen.ru/content/vladimir-putin-vystupil-na-xv-sezde-partii-%C2%ABedinaya-rossiya%C2%BB.

Reuter, Ora John. 2017. *The Origins of Dominant Parties: Building Authoritarian Institutions in Post-Soviet Russia.* Cambridge: Cambridge University Press.

2021. "Civic Duty and Voting under Autocracy." *Journal of Politics,* 83(4), 1602–18.

Reuter, Ora John, and Graeme B. Robertson. 2015. "Legislatures, Cooptation, and Social Protest in Contemporary Authoritarian Regimes." *Journal of Politics,* 77(1), 235–48.

Reuter, Ora John, and David Szakonyi. 2019. "Elite Defection under Autocracy: Evidence from Russia." *American Political Science Review,* 113(2), 552–68.

2021. "Electoral Manipulation and Regime Support: Survey Evidence from Russia." *World Politics,* 73(2), 275–314.

Robertson, Graeme. 2009. "Managing Society: Protest, Civil Society, and Regime in Putin's Russia." *Slavic Review,* 68(3), 528–47.

Rozenas, Arturas, and Denis Stukal. 2019. "How Autocrats Manipulate Economic News: Evidence from Russia's State-Controlled Television." *Journal of Politics,* 81(3), 982–96.

Szakonyi, David. 2022. "Candidate Filtering: The Strategic Use of Electoral Manipulations in Russia." *British Journal of Political Science,* 52(2), 1–22.

Treisman, Daniel. 2011. "Presidential Popularity in a Hybrid Regime: Russia under Yeltsin and Putin." *American Journal of Political Science,* 55(3), 590–609.

Wengle, Susanne, and Christine Evans. 2018. "Symbolic State-Building in Contemporary Russia." *Post-Soviet Affairs,* 34(6), 384–411.

White, Stephen, and Ian McAllister. 2007. "Turnout and Representation Bias in Post-Communist Europe." *Political Studies,* 55(3), 586–606.

4

Law, Legal Enforcement, and the Courts

LAUREN A. MCCARTHY

Fig. 4.1 Sentencing of eleven defendants accused of being involved in the St. Petersburg metro bombing, St. Petersburg, December 10, 2019. Credit: Olga Maltseva / AFP / Getty Images.

> People need to understand once and for all – you've got to follow the law all the time, not just when they have you by the you-know-where.
>
> Vladimir Putin (quoted in RIA Novosti, "20 vyskazyvanii Putina")

Abstract

Despite the common perception of Russia as a lawless place where an all-powerful president can do what he likes, or one with corrupt law enforcement and courts that are deeply mistrusted by citizens, Russia is indeed a country of laws. It is governed by a constitution and by laws passed through a bicameral legislature and signed by the president. Courts decide cases, criminal defendants are prosecuted, and businesses and individuals can sue one another when relationships go sour or damages have been done. Legal actors are acutely aware of what the laws say and how they are written and are careful to rely on the text of the law when making decisions. Behind the formal institutions of law, however, also lie informal practices. We often refer to this as the difference between the "law on the books" and the "law in action." How law operates and is implemented, in other words, often matters more than how the law is written. This chapter will introduce both the formal and informal aspects of law in today's Russia. These two aspects of the law combine to produce a system that is dualistic. It is both politicized – used to repress opposition and dissent – and ordinary – serving the needs of the average citizen – at the same time. The chapter will also demonstrate the importance of law and the legal system in the consolidation of President Vladimir Putin's power.

4.1   Introduction

The idea of **rule of law** gives us a framework for thinking about how law and legal institutions should work. In brief, the rule of law means that people are treated equally regardless of who they are or who they know, that written-down legal procedures are applied consistently by an independent judiciary, and that legal institutions are accessible to ordinary people and can provide an enforceable, meaningful remedy when something goes wrong. In addition to these criteria, we can also judge a legal system on whether it follows the "spirit of the law," whether, at a basic level, people believe that the law is fair and reasonable, and that it is not used for overt political purposes. Of course, no country has ever truly reached this ideal, and Russia is no exception, as noted so colorfully by **Vladimir Putin** in this chapter's epigraph.

Law, however, is a cornerstone of the Putin regime's stability. If we look closely, most of the political and societal changes that have happened over the past twenty years have been based in law rather than outright repression. And the Putin regime has taken great pains to keep its behavior within the law on the books. To give two prominent examples, Putin did not run for a third term in 2008 even though he was popular enough to do so, instead respecting the constitution and becoming the prime minister for four years, handing the presidency to **Dmitry Medvedev**. Before his term was set to be up in 2024, he used a legal process – amending the constitution – to ensure his ability to stay in office for longer if he so desired. This is not an unusual path. The concept of **autocratic legalism** suggests that democratically elected would-be dictators often use the law as a means to consolidate their power, slowly eating away at the courts' independence, the constitution, and other structures of checks and balances until they face little institutionalized opposition and the public is increasingly unable to remove them from power. This mostly happens through legal and constitutional changes made by a compliant legislature and upheld by a compliant court system. In other words, they use the letter of the law to violate its spirit. Far from shying away from the law or ruling by decree, autocracies like Putin's Russia are masters at creatively using the law to achieve their political goals. This happens, for example, through vaguely written laws that leave significant room for interpretation, courts that move politicized cases that include "state secrets" to closed hearings beyond the reach of the public, and the system's limitations on people's ability to bring complaints to the court about rights violations.

In Russia today, the legal issues we usually hear about are the highly politicized cases such as the prosecutions of Mikhail Khordokovsky or **Alexei Navalny**, or the passage of controversial laws like those limiting free speech and freedom of assembly, prohibiting citizens or the media from taking antiwar positions, or targeting the Russian LGBTQ+ population. These issues demonstrate that law has been an important tool in Vladimir Putin's consolidation of political power. Yet at the same time, and much of the time, the law works as it should. Police find and arrest criminals, people get divorced and sue each other for harms they experience, and businesses and individuals successfully take government agencies to court. Even though during the Putin era the number of Russians who say that courts and law enforcement institutions deserve full trust has rarely topped 30 percent (Levada Center 2021), court caseloads have steadily increased over the past three decades, and many disputes are resolved through the ordinary operation of the law. In these ordinary cases, the system's faults tend to be more the result of perverse incentives for its actors rather than power-hungry, amoral, or corrupt police, investigators, prosecutors, and judges (though these certainly exist too). That both of these aspects of the legal system, the political and the ordinary, can exist at the same time is the nature of legal **dualism**.

4.2 A Brief History of Law and Legal Reform in Russia

4.2.1 Soviet Law

Legal dualism has a long history in Russia. During the Soviet period, law, particularly criminal law, was used by the state to help consolidate its power and to rid itself of enemies, real or perceived. Flexible laws like those on prohibiting "counterrevolutionary activity" and those against "anti-Soviet agitation or propaganda" gave the legal system wide leeway to imprison or execute those who did not conform to the USSR's rigid ideological agenda. In 1938, at the height of Stalinist repression, more than 2.7 million people were imprisoned in the GULAG system, a network of prisons throughout the Soviet Union. Historians estimate that between 16 million and 18 million people spent time in these prison camps between 1930 and 1960. Though the greatest excesses of the law were curbed in the 1960s and 1970s under Nikita S. Khrushchev and Leonid I. Brezhnev, the law remained an important tool in the state's toolbox, while citizens could rarely protect themselves from the state by using the law. During the Soviet period, judges were elected for five-year terms and were required to be members of the **Communist Party of the Soviet Union**, and the party had control over their budgets, housing allocations, and other perks. Consequently, it was not surprising that they were politically reliable and compliant. They were often at the receiving end of telephone calls from party officials who would tell them how to decide cases in their courtrooms. This "telephone law" was a hallmark of the Soviet era, and often its beneficiaries were well-connected or high-ranking party officials.

At the same time, throughout Soviet history, ordinary people often went to court to solve ordinary problems, in particular the sorts of problems where courts were unavoidable – divorce, child support, and so on. Low-level Soviet justice came with a heavy dose of moralism, with judges often berating litigants for not living up to the ideal of a model Soviet citizen. This went hand in hand with harsh punishment even for minor infractions. But many courts operated as intended, and people could receive justice, albeit in this Soviet style. Prior to the Soviet Union's collapse in 1991, **Mikhail Gorbachev** tried to move the USSR toward a rule-of-law–based state (*pravovoe gosudarstvo*) and to depoliticize the legal system by giving judges lifetime tenure, expanding rights, and creating a Constitutional Oversight Committee. But these changes were short-lived and, after the collapse of the country, many new legal institutions needed to be created.

4.2.2   Yeltsin-Era Legal Reforms

The first post-Soviet Russian constitution, passed by a national vote in 1993, emerged from a heated conflict with the legislature, which resulted in **Boris Yeltsin** ordering the military to fire on the White House, the legislature's home. Despite this rocky start, the 1993 constitution represented a significant break with the Soviet past, introducing the separation of powers, popular sovereignty, federalism, and a host of civil and political rights such as freedom of speech, assembly, and religion. It created a new Constitutional Court and jury trials, but also retained several Soviet characteristics, including guarantees to social rights such as education, healthcare, and pensions. In the 1990s, new legal institutions were created or repurposed to meet the demands of a market economy and encourage foreign investment. In addition, Russia enacted significant criminal procedure reforms to give defendants more due process, created a new system of economic courts (*arbitrazh*), and increased judicial independence (Solomon and Foglesong 2000).

Nevertheless, there were still many longlasting legacies of the Soviet system to deal with, in particular, the reliance on informal methods of getting things done, whether in business or in personal relationships. Law had a difficult time displacing networks as the way to solve problems (Hendley 1999). For example, instead of taking a contract dispute to court, a business could hire muscle to pressure the other person to fulfill the contract through threats of, or actual, violence. Likewise, the dualistic nature of the Soviet system also left its mark. Russian citizens tended to mistrust the courts and the legal system. Courts were still seen as a place where power, connections, or money could influence the outcome of a case rather than a decision being fair and impartial. Police also had significant problems with corruption and involvement with organized crime as the state often turned a blind eye to low-level corruption, given the poor salaries paid to officers. These situations were compounded by severe underfunding of the court system and police, sometimes leading to local arrangements whereby businesses sponsored a local court or police station by providing basic necessities such as paper, pens, and photocopiers. Yet, despite these misgivings, just as in the Soviet period, Russians continued to use the court system when necessary, and the system retained its dualism.

4.2.3 Putin- and Medvedev-Era Legal Reforms

The early Putin period saw the development of several key pieces of legislation to update Soviet-era codes and practices. These were most notable in the area of criminal procedure, where police, investigators, and prosecutors were still operating under a code created in the 1960s. Most notably, the new Criminal Procedure Code passed in 2001 gave more rights to defendants. This included limiting the use of pretrial detention, requiring police to get judicially approved warrants for many investigative activities, and allowing defendants to have lawyers during the preliminary investigation period. It also introduced the idea of oral presentation of evidence by the prosecution and defense in the courtroom, whereas previously the judge had relied solely on the file of case documents to make a decision. These reforms resulted in a drastic reduction in the pretrial detention population and an increase in probationary sentences as opposed to prison. Between 1999 and 2012, the prison population dropped from 389,000 to 206,000, though it has returned to an upward trajectory since, with 463,000 in prison at the end of 2019 (Paneyakh and Rosenberg 2018; Glikin 2020).

On the civil side, a new Civil Code was passed in 2003. Businesses and individuals had significant success in suing the government for wrongful actions by government officials or failure to fulfill contractual obligations (Trochev 2012). They also gained confidence that the law could offer them a solution in resolving problems with each other, such as disputes over property rights, failure to fulfill contractual obligations, or state officials' miscalculation of taxes due. Putin has also made it a priority to adequately fund the court system, lessening each court's reliance on locally powerful government and business actors, including making long-overdue repairs to courthouses, introducing computers throughout the system, making court data public and transparent, and increasing judges' salaries.

Other reforms during the first Putin presidency focused on shifting the balance of power between law enforcement agencies, moving investigative powers from the powerful Procuracy (described below) to a newly created Investigative Committee (IC) in 2007. The head of the IC is a direct presidential appointee not subject to control by any other agency. The IC was also given the power to investigate misconduct by other law enforcement agencies, resulting in several large scandals, with agencies undertaking high-profile arrests and prosecutions of each other (Taylor 2011). This change was widely seen as an attempt by Putin to ensure that law enforcement agencies would remain in competition with each other for resources, prestige, and power. This is a common tactic of authoritarian rulers, who need to have strong security services to make sure they can limit any significant opposition from society, but do not want them to be so strong that they could become disloyal and overthrow the leader. In that vein, in 2016, another major change was to centralize all riot police into a single National Guard (Rosgvardiia), whose head serves at the pleasure of the president.

In the four years of Dmitry Medvedev's presidency, he made legal reforms a centerpiece of his legislative agenda, hoping to rid the country of its legal nihilism by providing strong, independent judicial institutions. Under Medvedev, the police saw their first post-Soviet overhaul, in 2011 in the wake of several high-profile acts of police misconduct including torture, extrajudicial killings, and a shooting spree in a grocery store. The law renamed the police from their Soviet-era name (*militsiia*) to police (*politsiia*), gave them new uniforms, put all officers through a recertification process, and reduced the force's personnel by 20 percent, raising salaries for those who remained (Taylor 2014). It also centralized financing for the public order police, the branch that most ordinary people are likely to encounter on a day-to-day basis, and the agents most likely to engage in low-level corruption. Unfortunately, the reform had very little impact in changing police practices, formal or informal. While the police retained most of their preexisting power, there were some small nods to public dissatisfaction with their work, such as requiring police to wear a badge so it was easier to report an officer for misconduct, and adding public opinion to their yearly assessment criteria.

4.2.4   Putin's Repressive Legal Turn

Putin's third term, beginning in 2012, brought with it an increased politicization of the law. Following unexpected mass protests in response to falsification of **Duma** elections in 2011, the Putin administration ratcheted up its use of the law to crack down on dissent and opposition activity and to cement his turn toward traditional moral values. Particularly affected were the rights to freedom of speech, freedom of assembly, and freedom of association. Some of the many restrictions on freedom of speech included laws prohibiting "offending the feelings of religious believers," outlawing cursing in public places, known as the "blasphemy law," and a ban on "gay propaganda" to minors, which essentially outlawed any public expression of LGBTQ+ identities or support for the LGBTQ+ movement. Freedom of assembly was curtailed by the passage of a variety of laws introducing fines and even criminal penalties for participation in unauthorized protests (local authorities must approve the time and place of a planned protest; otherwise it is considered unauthorized). Finally, freedoms of association and of speech were impacted by the laws on "foreign agents" passed early in Putin's third term, which limited the ability of nongovernmental organizations that engage in "political activity," loosely defined, to accept any foreign funding for their activities. Having the status of a foreign agent means submitting quarterly financial reports to the Ministry of Justice, and having to label everything as produced by a foreign agent, a negative connotation in the minds of most Russian citizens. Failure to register and failure to label can both result in fines, and in extreme cases, as with the 2021 case against the well-known human rights group Memorial, have resulted in court decisions liquidating an entire organization.

In 2020, the foreign agent law was expanded to include individuals, nonregistered organizations, journalists, and media outlets, and the Ministry of Justice quickly moved to use the law, listing individuals and organizations on the register at, on average, a pace of two per week. In addition, in 2015, the government passed the Law on Undesirable Organizations, which banned many foreign groups from operating in Russia entirely and penalized Russian citizens who worked with them. Russian law enforcement has also increasingly used anti-extremism laws, passed in 2012 to crack down on opposition, which include the offenses of public calls to separatism, incitement to hatred, public justification of terrorism, and inducing, recruiting, or otherwise involving others in mass unrest. These laws, which carry heavy prison sentences, have been used to ban websites and materials that the courts declare extremist, as well as to prosecute religious minorities (primarily Jehovah's Witnesses and various Muslim groups), people who post critical content on social media (for example, speaking out against the annexation of Crimea), and, most notably, banning all entities associated with Alexei Navalny. They have also been used to prosecute actual extremists, such as neo-Nazi and terrorist groups, and to ban ultranationalist materials and those promoting terrorism.

During the war against Ukraine, this repressive legal turn took an even harsher tack. Reporting "false information" about the Russian military is now criminalized and can result in a range of penalties from large fines to fifteen years in prison. The chilling effect of this law was immediate. Many independent media outlets closed, international media removed their reporters from Russia, and still others decided they would no longer report on the war. In addition, people have been charged with various other criminal offenses for antiwar activity, including hooliganism, vandalism, and extremism (OVD-Info 2022).

All of these laws were written in vague, broad language, enabling easy enforcement and conviction. And each was then applied seemingly indiscriminately in criminal cases to discourage others from engaging in similar behavior. One blatant example of this was the prosecutions of more than thirty people, commonly referred to as the Bolotnaia Case, after protests of Putin's 2012 inauguration turned violent (OVD-Info 2014). Rather than focusing on prosecuting the protest's organizers, most people charged with criminal offenses were ordinary participants and sometimes even bystanders, sending the rather effective message that anyone could be a target, thereby discouraging future participation. The coronavirus pandemic has provided new opportunities for the Russian state to use law in a repressive manner. New laws prohibited any form of gathering, even individual protesters holding signs, as a public health measure to prevent the spread of coronavirus. With this same rationale, the government also decreased public access to the courts for most of the pandemic, allowing only the participants in the case to be present in the courtroom.

Putin's legal reforms culminated in July 2020 with the passage of more than 200 constitutional amendments in a national vote. Most notable for its "reset" of the presidential clock, the amendments also increased presidential power vis-à-vis the legislature and the judiciary, expanded the power of the Procuracy, and limited the powers of the Constitutional Court (Pomeranz 2020).

4.3   Courts and Judges

4.3.1   Courts

At the top of the Russian judicial hierarchy stand two courts, the Supreme Court and the Constitutional Court. Established in 1991, the Constitutional Court is a stand-alone court that can hear any questions about the constitutionality of Russian legislation and executive actions. Until the 2020 constitutional amendments, it could also accept direct appeals from citizens who had had their constitutional rights violated. Now those citizens must go through all possible levels of appeal before making these claims. The Constitutional Court has mostly been supportive of the recentralization of power under Putin and has rarely gone against the government on important political cases, yet it also frequently rules pieces of legislation passed by the Duma unconstitutional. Its record is therefore mixed, and experts such as Alexei Trochev and Peter Solomon (2018) have explained this by referring to its behavior as "pragmatic"– prioritizing its continued existence as an institution over everything else.

The other two court structures, the courts of general jurisdiction and the arbitrazh courts, run in parallel, with a unified Supreme Court taking appeals from both systems (see Figure 4.2). At the very bottom of the courts of general jurisdiction hierarchy are the Justice of the Peace (JP) courts. These courts deal with minor civil (property disputes under 100,000 rubles, land title challenges, and uncontested child custody cases), criminal (punishment less than three years' imprisonment), and minor administrative (misdemeanor) offenses subject to fines. In her study of these courts, Kathryn Hendley (2017) shows that the operation of "everyday" justice in today's Russia is nothing like the politicized cases that tend to grab headlines. In the JP courts, which in 2020 handled 30 percent of criminal cases, and an astonishing 88 percent of civil cases and 75 percent of administrative violations (Sudebnyi Departament 2021b), the main challenges are the crushing workloads for the judges – around 200 cases per month – and uneducated litigants who often appear in court unprepared or without proper documents. These courts are where the average Russian citizen is most likely to encounter the legal system, particularly in the many situations where the court's jurisdiction is impossible to avoid.

The next court in the hierarchy is the district court, which is where most criminal and civil cases not heard by the JP courts have their first hearing, and where any appeals from the JP courts go. Finally, there are regional high courts, one for each Russian region. These mostly function as appeals courts, although they do occasionally hear cases for the first time, usually only the most grave crimes, including things such as murder, rape, and espionage. At the top of the hierarchy is the Supreme Court, which primarily serves as the highest-level appeals court, reviewing potential legal errors committed by lower courts. It also oversees the operation of the law more generally and, if necessary, can issue "explanations" of how particular types of cases and issues should be decided by lower courts.

Russia also has a separate set of courts for business disputes, called the arbitrazh courts, created after the fall of the Soviet Union to deal with the new market economy. Each region has an arbitrazh trial court where cases are heard for the first time and, if either side is dissatisfied, they can appeal the case for either a retrial of the facts or for a legal error. As of 2018, the system of arbitrazh courts was regularly hearing more than 2 million cases a year; this dropped slightly during the pandemic, but caseloads have steadily increased since the courts were established in the early 1990s (Sudebnyi Departament 2021a). This indicates that businesses find them an efficient and predictable place to settle disputes, which is an important and noteworthy change from the immediate post-Soviet period, when many preferred to use other means to solve their problems. Prior to 2014, the arbitrazh system had its own Supreme Arbitrazh Court, standing equal to the Supreme Court and the Constitutional Court. In 2014, however, it was merged into the Supreme Court, with its judges demoted to an Economic Collegium within that body. While the stated rationale for this merger was to standardize decisions between the two sets of courts by having one unified court at the top, many speculate that the efficiency, fairness, and transparency of the arbitrazh courts made for a potential alternative power center for business interests and was not consistent with Putin's broader recentralization of power.

From 1998 until 2022, when it was kicked out because of the war in Ukraine, Russia was also a member of the Council of Europe, which meant that, if it violated a citizen's rights, that citizen could sue Russia in the European Court of Human Rights (ECHR). The list of violations is specific and outlined in the European Convention on Human Rights, including the right to life, the right to a fair trial, the right to liberty and security, freedom of thought, conscience, religion, speech, assembly, and association, and the right to be free from inhumane or degrading treatment. The ECHR requires that the citizen must first try to use the national judicial process to get a remedy, but after that they can appeal to the ECHR. When Russia was a member, if its citizen won, Russia had to pay compensation. The ECHR could also have requested that Russia take steps, by changing their laws or policies, to make sure that the same type of violation did not happen again in the future. Citizens took advantage of this in large numbers. From the time of joining, cases coming out of Russia flooded the ECHR and, as of 2020, Russia was the country with the second-largest number of judgments by the ECHR, behind only Turkey, and still had more than 13,500 cases pending (ECHR 2021a). The Russian government prevailed in only

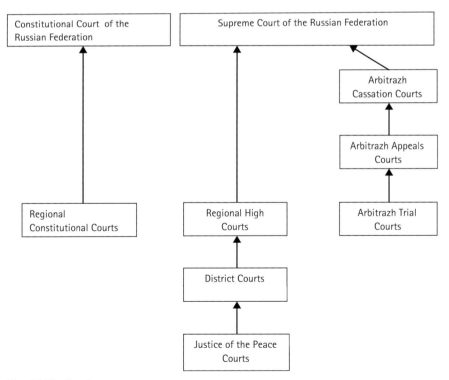

Fig. 4.2 The Russian court system.

6 percent of the cases in which there had been a judgment (ECHR 2021b). In 2015, in anticipation of a 1.9 billion euro judgment against the Russian government in the Yukos case, the Duma passed a law that declared ECHR rulings unenforceable if they contradicted the Russian constitution, leaving the ultimate decision on any individual case up to the Russian Constitutional Court. (The Yukos case refers to a suit taken to the ECHR by the former owners of the company, alleging that the Russian Federation had violated the human rights of Yukos shareholders through what constituted an arbitrary expropriation.) In 2020, the supremacy of domestic law over international law officially became part of the Russian constitution, which covers judgments not only by the ECHR, but also by other international tribunals, including those that arbitrate business disputes.

4.3.2   Judges

One of the most important reforms undertaken by Gorbachev and continued into the post-Soviet era was the selection of judges by merit rather than party loyalty and connections. In the post-Soviet period, judges were even further insulated from political pressure by the creation of a Judicial Qualification Commission (JQC), which put decisions about discipline and dismissal for bad behavior in the hands of their peers. Now anyone with five or more years of experience working in a legal profession and who is over twenty-five years of age can apply for an open spot. Judges receive lifetime tenure after a three-year probationary period, with the exception of justices of the peace, who are selected for five- to ten-year terms depending on local legislation. All must retire at age seventy. If selected by the JQC, a potential judge's nomination is sent through the judicial bureaucracy to the president, who then makes the final decision on appointments. While this gives the president quite a lot of power to prevent "problematic" judges from getting on the bench in the first place, it is a tremendous improvement from the Soviet-era judicial selection process in that it prioritizes merit and competence. In reality, however, many old practices still persist. Networks developed through previous work in the judicial system continue to be a significant advantage for those applying to judgeships, giving them an advantage over equally qualified candidates coming from other legal backgrounds (Dzmitryieva 2021). In addition, changes to the JQC's composition now mean that one-third of each body is made up of members from outside the judiciary, which in practice means regime loyalists or former security service officials.

The 2020 constitution cemented the gradual erosion of judicial independence that has occurred over the Putin period. It gave the Federation Council (upper house of the legislature) the power to remove any Constitutional Court, Supreme Court, cassation, or appellate judge for undermining the "honor and dignity" of the judiciary on the recommendation of the president. It also reduced the size of the Constitutional Court from nineteen judges to eleven, all of whom are appointed by the president. Further legislation prohibited the publication of dissenting opinions by Constitutional Court judges (Pomeranz 2021).

4.4 Legal Actors

In Russia, law is an undergraduate degree. After finishing a five-year legal education, graduates can take a variety of possible career paths. Having a basic legal education qualifies a graduate as a jurist (*iurist*). If they take and pass the bar exam, they become a member of the bar and gain the title of *advokat*. *Advokaty* have a monopoly on criminal defense work in the courts and must pass a qualifying exam, but all other people with a law degree can work in any legal field with the exception of notaries and judges, who must also pass an exam. Lawyers might work for the state as criminal investigators, prosecutors, or judges, in one of many state bureaucracies, or in private practice as *advokaty*, litigators (for all but criminal cases), in-house lawyers, corporate lawyers, or notaries (Hendley 2019).

Many graduates of law schools go into the security services as police, prosecutors, or investigators. The police, otherwise known as the Ministry of Internal Affairs (MVD), form a large and complex organization (Proekt 2020). It employs around 700,000 people, with multiple divisions, including traffic, patrol police, and investigations. Most police activity takes place at the regional and local levels in cities and towns. The police's main jobs are maintaining public order, fighting crime, and protecting health and safety. When a crime occurs, their operative agents gather the initial evidence to open a case. This evidence is then passed on to an investigator whose job it is to compile the evidence into a case file for trial and decide on the charges. If the crime is of minimal severity, the investigator is usually in the MVD, but if it is more serious it goes to an investigator in the Investigative Committee. The Investigative Committee was created in 2007 to deal with more serious crimes, such as corruption, violent crime, extremism, and organized crime. The **FSB** (Federal Security Service) is also active in law enforcement, but focuses primarily on terrorism, border security, and domestic intelligence gathering.

The entire criminal justice process is overseen by the Procuracy. The Procuracy (*prokuratura*) is a uniquely Russian institution which is in charge of overseeing the police, prosecuting court cases for the state, and using their power of "general supervision" (*nadzor*) to revisit any cases to ensure that the law has been properly observed. Though it lost some of its Soviet-era powers in the 1993 constitution and subsequent criminal justice reforms, in the Putin era the Procuracy has been very successful at clawing back some of its previous powers. This culminated in the 2020 constitution, which restores the Procuracy's constitutional duty – previously it was only included in laws – to oversee the observance of the constitution, all laws of the Russian Federation, the rights and freedoms of individual citizens, and all criminal prosecutions. As has happened with other law enforcement agencies, like the Investigative Committee and the National Guard, this expansion of powers also came with greater presidential control, including the power to hire and fire the procurator general and all regional-level heads of the Procuracy.

These law enforcement institutions all retain much of their Soviet character even more than two decades after the collapse of the Soviet Union. Though there have been some attempts to limit and reorganize their powers vis-à-vis each other, most reforms to law enforcement have failed in changing the organizations' culture and mindset. This has allowed informal practices to persist and new ones to blossom, which has led to significant challenges in the administration of justice; these are discussed further in the last section of the chapter.

4.5   Legal Processes

There are three primary types of cases in Russian law: civil, criminal, and administrative. Civil cases between two individuals, criminal cases, and administrative violations receive hearings in the courts of general jurisdiction, while civil cases dealing with businesses are heard in the arbitrazh courts. Looking at each kind of case can tell us something important about how the Russian legal system operates.

4.5.1   Criminal Cases

Like in most countries, a criminal case (theft, drug possession/use, assault, murder) in Russia goes through a fairly standard procedure: investigation, indictment, prosecution, and, if there is a conviction, sentencing (Paneyakh et al. 2012). All convicted parties have ten days to appeal their conviction, which they can do to question the procedure and the law's application, or to request a full rehearing of the evidence. Each step, and the agency responsible for carrying it out, is laid out in the Criminal Procedure Code. Each year the Russian courts handle around 750,000 criminal cases (Sudebnyi Departament 2021c). As you may have noticed from the photograph of the criminal proceeding at the start of the chapter, defendants in Russian courtrooms sit in a cage rather than next to their defense lawyer, a practice that many have suggested undermines the presumption of innocence. Most criminal cases are heard by single judge panels, though there are approximately thirty crimes in Russia where the defendant can opt for a jury trial (Kovalev and Nasonov 2021). Russian juries are composed of six to eight people, depending on whether they take place at the district or regional court level. Jurors do not have to reach a unanimous verdict, though they are encouraged to try, and their time for deliberation is limited to three hours. Should they tie, the defendant is acquitted. Despite the fact that most Russians believe that jury verdicts are more fair and the acquittal rate is significantly higher, the jury procedure is used very rarely in Russia. In 2020, only about 1,000 defendants throughout the country opted for a jury trial. One reason is that, like in many other countries following a civil law tradition, prosecutors are able to appeal an acquittal. If successful, which over 60 percent of them were in 2020, a new trial is ordered (Klimacheva 2021). There is no limit to the number of times this process can take place, and there have been several high-profile political cases in which jury acquittals were overturned multiple times, and then retried until a jury finally reached a guilty verdict. Guilty verdicts can also be appealed by the defendant and are heard by the Supreme Court.

The criminal justice system in Russia is marked by **prosecutorial/accusatorial bias**, which means that once a case is started conviction is highly likely. In fact, the 2020 acquittal rate in Russia is just 0.02 percent, meaning 99.98 percent of defendants in criminal cases are convicted (Klimacheva 2021). While legal systems with a civil law tradition like Russia's are more likely to have high conviction rates than common-law systems like those of the United States and the UK, where acquittals happen in 15–20 percent of cases, Russia is still an outlier when compared with countries like France and Germany, which have acquittal rates of 3–5 percent (Solomon 2018).

Since 2003, defendants in criminal cases also have the option to accept a "special procedure" (*osobyi poriadok*), a form of plea bargain. In this system, the defendant agrees to the charges against them for a punishment that does not exceed two-thirds of the maximum penalty outlined by the Criminal Code, but only if that maximum is under ten years. The courtroom processing of these cases is short and limited to the judge checking to see that there is sufficient evidence to support the charge in the case file, but the defendant gives up the right to appeal on the facts (they can still appeal based on violations of legal procedure). For the defendant, this limits the time they spend in detention waiting for trial and – given the high conviction rates – allows them some control over the process and perhaps a more lenient sentence. In fact, many are given probationary sentences instead of real jail time. For the police and prosecutors, the shortened procedure means that they have to use fewer resources to investigate and prosecute the case and that their work can be of lower quality. Consequently, it is no surprise that this process is now used in half to two-thirds of criminal cases. There is some question about how good a deal this is for defendants, as sentences given out in "special procedure" agreements do not actually differ that much from sentences given out by judges for similar crimes (Titaev and Pozdniakov 2012).

4.5.2   Civil Cases

Civil cases include things like torts (people suing each other for harms caused), contract and property disputes, tax disputes, and family matters such as child support, alimony, and inheritance. As Hendley (2017) has shown, civil cases reveal the main paradox of the Russian legal system in the post-Soviet era – people distrust the courts, but use them anyway. Unlike criminal cases, which the state initiates, the filing of a civil case shows a citizen's willingness to put a dispute in the hands of the court, a neutral third party, for resolution. There are certainly some situations where going to court is a requirement, rather than a choice; for example, a court order is required to collect child support, and for tax assessments, wage disputes, and debt cases. But the massive growth in the use of the civil law system is an indication that, for the most part, ordinary law works in Russia and that people can get what they need from the legal system. From 1997 to 2020, the number of civil cases in Russian courts went from 3.9 million to 20.7 million, with steady growth every year even through the coronavirus pandemic (Paneyakh and Rosenberg 2018; Sudebnyi Departament 2021b). At the same time, some citizens do express hesitancy to use the courts in situations where the opposing party has more economic power than they do, leading to a situation of legal "triplism" – ordinary, economic, and political cases – in the Russian courts rather than legal dualism (Hendley 2017).

4.5.3 Administrative Violations

For much of the post-Soviet period, administrative violations would have hardly merited their own section in a discussion of Russian law. Offenses that fall under the Code of Administrative Violations are usually petty misdemeanor violations that are disposed of with a fine. However, one of the most effective ways that the Putin administration has used the law to silence opponents and to keep protest under control is by making ordinary activities into administrative, and sometimes criminal, violations. The most notable of these is protests. While freedom of assembly is guaranteed by the constitution, gatherings must be authorized by local authorities before taking place. If the gathering is not authorized, which most are not, anyone participating can be arrested and charged with the administrative violation of participating in an unauthorized gathering. If they do this three times within a year, they can be charged with a criminal offense with potential jail time. This legal tool has become one of the primary ways of politicizing the law and repressing opposition. For example, after the 2017 protests against corruption, around 5,000 people were charged with administrative violations, and several more were criminally charged. After the 2019 protests in Moscow, fourteen were convicted and sentenced to up to three and a half years in prison (OVD-Info 2020). In protests in early 2021 in support of Alexei Navalny, more than 11,000 people were arrested across Russia. Many were charged with administrative violations and fined, but more than 150 others were charged with criminal violations and prosecuted (OVD-Info 2021). During the first days of the war in Ukraine, the government continued to use administrative violations to crack down on antiwar protests, arresting and charging more than 13,000 in the first two weeks alone. The Duma approved adding a new administrative violation, "public activities aimed at discrediting the use of Russia's military," which can include any statements opposing the use of the military, even on social media. This law carries a two-strike penalty, turning the administrative violation into a criminal activity if the law is broken twice within one year (McCarthy 2022), and it quickly became a favorite of the Russian police and court system.

4.6   Informal Institutions of the Law

4.6.1   Incentives

In this section, we will turn to look at some of the ways that law operates behind the scenes. To do this, we need to introduce the idea of incentives. Incentives are the forces that drive human behavior. For each person they might be different, but they often involve the basics: making enough money to provide for yourself and your family, living in a pleasant place, and/or increased social or professional status. When thinking about the informal processes that have developed in the Russian legal system, one of the most important things to remember is that actors in the Russian legal system are people too, and their behavior is driven by incentives. It is also important to note that, while there is corruption in the legal system – falsification of evidence by police, paying to close (or open) an investigation, judges taking bribes to decide cases in a particular way – many of these outcomes are responses to perverse incentives.

These incentives are most visible in the criminal justice system whose actors face strict numerical performance assessment criteria. These performance assessment criteria create incentives for particular behaviors. For police, the most important statistic is the number of criminal cases they have cleared, which requires identifying a suspect and gathering enough evidence to hand off the case to a prosecutor. They must do this within time limits set by the Criminal Procedure Code (two months to complete an investigation from the date the case is opened), and each year their performance in clearing cases must compare favorably to the year before. If not, it is a black mark on their record. Prosecutors are assessed based on their success at getting convictions. Judges too must be attentive to their acquittal rates, their "reversal" rate – how many of the cases they decided on are then overturned on appeal – and also to staying within the Criminal Procedure Code's time limits which require that a case be scheduled for trial within fourteen days of it arriving on the judge's desk. For all legal actors, failure to successfully navigate these incentives can lead to reassignment, disciplinary measures, or dismissal and will certainly eliminate the possibility of being promoted to a higher position.

When put together into one criminal justice system, the incentives of each of these actors work together to create a machine that is focused more on hitting numerical targets than the quality and thoroughness of investigations, and where convictions are the only marker of having done a good job (Paneyakh 2014; McCarthy 2014).

Informal pressures to act cooperatively and close relationships between actors in the system (most work in the same building) make the likelihood of judges holding police and investigators accountable even smaller. Once the case has been passed on to the next person in the chain, it is unlikely to be revisited, since the objective of the person – clearing the case, investigating the case, and so forth – has already been met. In addition, solving "serious" cases is rewarded more highly than smaller, more insignificant cases like petty theft of, for example, a wallet, cell phone, or jewelry, which are also nearly impossible to clear. The entire system is also filled with paperwork, with everything requiring documentation. Finally, law enforcement has a fairly strict hierarchy in which superiors are assessed based on their subordinates' performance. As a result, there is significant downward pressure to meet statistical targets and also not to draw any unwanted attention from the higher-ups.

4.6.2   Strategies and Tactics

In order to meet the strict statistical targets and keep their superiors happy, legal actors in the criminal justice system employ a number of clever work-arounds and tricks to help their efficiency and outcomes. To overcome the massive documentation requirements, police often copy and paste their police reports, typos and all, for situations of mass arrests, so that they only have to fill in a few details. To increase their efficiency in the face of high caseloads and strict time limits, judges will often copy wholesale from the prosecutor's indictment, adding only the few required paragraphs with the decision and sentencing information.

In the investigation of criminal cases, we see similar behavior. Police try to avoid opening a case at all. If they cannot avoid opening a case, they try to do most of the investigative work beforehand so they do not run into the time limits until they know they can meet them; or they can pin the blame for unsolved crimes on someone they know did not do it. Sometimes this tips over the line into clear misconduct, with police using excessive force or other manipulation to get people to confess to crimes they did not commit, particularly people of marginalized social status – substance abusers, homeless people, or immigrants. When these behaviors are rewarded by better case clearance rates and possible promotion or salary bonuses, it is no surprise that they tend to become part of the police's standard operating procedures rather than existing as one-off instances committed by bad officers who are later punished. As Ella Paneyakh and Dina Rosenberg (2018) show, we tend to see overrepresentation of particular groups of people in the criminal justice system – unemployed people, those with previous convictions, and those who engage in manual labor (who are often migrants) – all of whom are less likely to be able to mobilize resources to defend themselves. As in many other legal systems, money matters. Those who can mount a vigorous legal defense are likely to cause delays in the smooth processing of cases and are therefore less likely to be targets, unless their targeting is political.

Jury trials are another place where we can see these informal incentives play out. Prosecutors know that there is a roughly 25 percent chance that they will lose in a jury trial, but only thirty crimes are eligible. Consequently, if a defendant opts for a jury trial, the prosecutor can simply change the charge to something that is not jury-eligible. On the other hand, if the proof is strong, a prosecutor has a strong incentive to let the jury decide, as they usually give out harsher sentences than judges do, which also aligns with prosecutorial incentives rewarding convictions on serious crimes.

We can also see incentives at work in the "special procedure." If police can pressure a defendant to admit to the charge and move the case to special procedure, they can cover up shoddy investigative work and guarantee a case closure, as long as the judge is willing to look the other way in their review. For prosecutors, the procedure guarantees a conviction. Likewise with the process of "reconciliation" between the two parties, which is available for low-level crimes, most often property crimes: The offending party pays some sort of restitution to the person whose property was damaged or stolen. This procedure also guarantees a successful case outcome and thus is very attractive to police and prosecutors. Finally, because of their incentives to convict, judges often prefer to deal with the issue of poor evidence by giving probationary sentences, even for very serious crimes, rather than acquitting or sending the case back for further investigation, which would reflect poorly on other actors in the system. Despite seeming at odds with the spirit of the law, all of these tactics persist precisely because they work.

These strategies and tactics are not wholly one-sided. Clever defense lawyers have also adapted their own work to use knowledge of how the system works to their clients' advantage. Sometimes this involves establishing informal ties with police, investigators, and prosecutors to be able to influence their decisionmaking at all stages of the investigation, but particularly before the case is even opened. Another commonly used tactic is the careful monitoring of the entire process for procedural errors committed by the police or investigators; if any errors are committed, they are used either to negotiate with the authorities directly, or to challenge the entire investigation in court.

4.6.3   Reforms?

The challenges of reforming these informal legal practices are immense but not insurmountable. An insightful study by Ekaterina Travova (2019) suggests the sorts of changes in incentives that could be effective. Before more recent reorganizations, there were two law enforcement agencies that dealt with drug crimes in Russia, the MVD and the FSKN (Federal Service for Drug Control). One of these agencies (the MVD) uses year-to-year statistical performance to assess success – the agency is competing against its previous year totals – and the other (the FSKN) uses cross-agency statistical performance to assess success – the local agency is competing against all other local agencies, so the target number is not known in advance. Russian law enforcement agencies have a well-established history of planting drugs, particularly to nudge the case into a more serious category as measured by drug weight. Travova found that the likelihood that drugs would be planted was related to the incentive system. She looked at each agency's likelihood of "finding" an amount of drugs with a weight just above the threshold and found that the MVD was more likely to have drug busts that barely crossed the threshold than the FSKN, signaling that they had planted just enough extra evidence to move the case into the more serious category. Driven by the need to match or exceed their previous year's targets, and by the incentive system that rewards more serious crimes, the MVD had a stronger propensity to engage in evidence falsification because it knew in advance the targets it had to hit. While this offers a suggestion for how incentives could be realigned, an organization's culture is always extremely challenging to change, and if change comes it is usually very slow. Few legal actors have an incentive to believe that new reforms are going to actually stick, and will likely carry on with their preexisting practices until they are absolutely sure that change will be long-term rather than a short-term experiment.

For an authoritarian government, there is also a downside to criminal justice reform. One of the many tools in the authoritarian toolbox is the power to pass vague criminal laws, prosecute people under them, and then ban people with criminal records from participating in particular aspects of public life. In Russia, the statistical assessment criteria can then be put to work to signal the importance of charging people with that particular crime. One example is the extremism law. Anyone who has been convicted of extremism or who is affiliated either currently or in the past with any organization that has been declared extremist is banned from running for political office (this is also true of people affiliated with organizations that are labeled foreign agents). Even displays of material from any of these organizations on private social media can make a person the subject of extremism charges. As of June 2021, this includes all organizations that are affiliated with opposition activist Alexei Navalny and any projects that he has been involved in, including local campaign offices and the "smart vote" campaign, and law enforcement bodies are being encouraged to pursue these cases. Once they begin, they are trapped in a cycle requiring them to find increased numbers of extremism cases from year to year. Thus, these perverse incentives can serve as a powerful tool in the authoritarian consolidation of power.

4.7 Conclusion

In addition to the nuts and bolts of how the Russian legal system works, this chapter has revealed two important things about the law in Putin's Russia. The first is that law retains its long history of dualism, with political cases and ordinary cases coexisting in the same system and sometimes even in the same courtroom with the same judge. Through the lens of civil and arbitrazh lawsuits, we see a system that more or less functions for ordinary people and businesses. And while it is true that Russians, like others, do not love going to court because of the time, resources, and stress that it causes, they have done so with increased frequency since the end of the Soviet Union. In its ordinary operation, the criminal justice system has both formal and informal procedures and practices. Police, prosecutors, and judges are acutely attuned to the formal requirements of the law, yet this does not always produce justice. The perverse incentives in the system mean that, once a case is opened and makes its way into the system, it is nearly impossible to turn the machine off and get an acquittal. The messages from the top also relentlessly stress the importance of conviction, with the longtime head of the Investigative Committee Aleksandr Bastrykin regularly noting that he considers even a 1 percent acquittal rate to be too high. Consequently, many criminal defendants have turned to the off-ramp of special procedures or other cooperation agreements to spare themselves the wait for an inevitable conviction and/or to try to gain a more lenient sentence.

The second important takeaway is to understand the importance of law in Putin's political project of creating stability through the consolidation of power, and as a tool to gain legitimacy and to suppress opposition. We can see this in the variety of reforms to the criminal justice system, with regular shuffling of powers between security agencies to keep them on their toes and maintain their focus of loyalty on the center. Law has also been used in a more instrumental fashion against individual opponents of Putin's regime to pressure people to stay quiet, to threaten them with criminal prosecution so they leave the country, or to actually imprison them and remove them from political life. Using the law to challenge the state on rights issues has also become increasingly difficult in Putin's third presidential term. While many Russians have tried to claim their rights in the European Court of Human Rights, laws and the new constitutional amendments have made this increasingly challenging. In sum, the law has provided much of the bedrock of stability on which Putin's system depends. It remains to be seen whether it may be a source of fragility as well.

DISCUSSION QUESTIONS

1. What are the short- and long-term consequences of a dualistic legal system?
2. Why do powerful authoritarian leaders like Vladimir Putin rely so heavily on the law to accomplish their goals?
3. Do you think the Russian legal system satisfies the criteria of the rule of law? Why or why not?

REFERENCES

Dzmitryieva, Aryna. 2021. "Becoming a Judge in Russia: An Analysis of Judicial Biographies." *Europe–Asia Studies* 73(1), 131–56.

ECHR (European Court of Human Rights). 2021a. "Analysis of Statistics 2020," www.echr.coe.int/Documents/Stats_analysis_2020_ENG.pdf.

2021b. "Violations by Article and State," www.echr.coe.int/Documents/Stats_violation_1959_2020_ENG.pdf.

Glikin, Konstantin. 2020. "Chislo zakliuchennykh v Rossii vpervye stalo men'she 0,5 mln" *Vedomosti*, August 8, www.vedomosti.ru/society/articles/2020/08/13/836640-chislo-zaklyuchennih.

Hendley, Kathryn. 1999. "Rewriting the Rules of the Game in Russia: The Neglected Issue of Demand for Law," *East European Constitutional Review*, 8(4), 89–95.

2017. *Everyday Law in Russia.* Ithaca: Cornell University Press.

2019. "Nature versus Nurture: A Comparison of Russian Law Graduates Destined for State Service and for Private Practice." *Law and Policy*, 41(2), 147–73.

Klimacheva, Kira. 2021. "Sud prisiazhnykh v Rossii. Proshloe, nastoiashchee, i budushchee." Pravo.ru, August 24, https://pravo.ru/story/233124/.

Kovalev, Nikolai, and Sergei Nasonov. 2021. "The Russian Jury Trial: An Ongoing Legal and Political Experiment." In Nancy S. Marder, Sanja Kutnjak Ivković, Shari Seidman Diamond, and Valerie P. Hans (eds.), *Juries, Lay Judges, and Mixed Courts: A Global Perspective*, pp. 237–60. Cambridge: Cambridge University Press.

Levada Center. 2021. "Doverie obshchestvennym institutam," October 6, www.levada.ru/2021/10/06/doverie-obshhestvennym-institutam/.

Maggs, Peter, Olga Schwartz, and William Burnham. 2020. *Law and Legal System of the Russian Federation.* [Huntington, NY]: Juris Publishing.

McCarthy, Lauren A. 2014. "The Day-to-Day Work of the Russian Police," *Russia Analytical Digest*, no. 151, 5–8.

2022. "Why Putin Uses Russian Law to Crack Down on Dissent." *Washington Post*, April 7, www.washingtonpost.com/politics/2022/04/07/autocrats-russia-kremlin-protest-fines-jail/.

OVD-Info. 2014. "Politichskie repressii v Rossii v 2011–2014 godu. Ugolovnye presledovaniia," https://reports.ovdinfo.org/2014/cr-report/.

2020. "Posle leta. Moskovskii eksperiment prodolzhaetsia," https://ovdinfo.org/reports/mgd2-2019.

2021. "Crackdown on Peaceful Protests in January–February 2021 in Russia," https://ovdinfo.org/reports/winter-2021-supression-en#1.

2022. "Antiwar Prosecutions: An OVD-Info Guide," https://ovd.news/news/2022/04/07/antiwar-prosecutions-ovd-info-guide.

Paneyakh, Ella. 2014. "Faking Performance Together: Systems of Performance Evaluation in Russian Enforcement Agencies and Production of Bias and Privilege." *Post-Soviet Affairs*, 30(2–3), 115–36.

Paneyakh [Paneiakh], Ella, Mikhail Pozdniakov, Kirill Titaev, Irina Chetverikova, and Marina Shkliaruk. 2012. *Pravookhranitel'naia deiatel'nost' v Rossii. Struktura, funktsionirovanie, puti reformirovaniia, chast' 1: Diagnostika raboty pravookhranitel'nykh organov*

RF i vypolneniia imi politseiskoi funktsii. St. Petersburg: European University at St. Petersburg Research Institute for the Rule of Law.

Paneyakh, Ella, and Dina Rosenberg. 2018. "The Courts, Law Enforcement, and Politics." In Daniel Treisman (ed.), *The New Autocracy: Information, Politics, and Policy in Putin's Russia*, pp. 217–48. Washington, DC: Brookings Institution Press.

Pomeranz, William. 2020. *Law and the Russian State: Russia's Legal Evolution from Peter the Great to Vladimir Putin.* New York: Bloomsbury Academic.

2021. "Putin's 2020 Constitutional Amendments: What Changed? What Remained the Same?" *Russian Politics*, 6(1), 6–26.

Proekt. 2020. "Triumf boli," February 19, www.proekt.media/research/zarplata-siloviki/.

RIA Novosti. 2008. "20 vyskazyvanii Putina, stavshikh aforizmami." May 7, https://ria.ru/20080507/106744531.html.

Solomon, Peter H. Jr. 2018. "Accusatorial Bias in Russian Criminal Justice." In Marina Kurkchiyan and Agnieszka Kubal (eds.), *A Sociology of Justice in Russia.* pp. 170–204. Cambridge: Cambridge University Press.

Solomon, Peter H. Jr., and Todd Foglesong. 2000. *Courts and Transition In Russia: The Challenge of Judicial Reform.* Boulder, CO: Routledge.

Sudebnyi Departament. 2021a. "Obzor sudebnoi statistiki o deiatelnosti federal'nykh arbitrazh-nykh sudov v 2020 godu," www.cdep.ru/userimages/OBZOR_STAT_arbitrazh_2020.pdf.

2021b. "Obzor sudebnoi statistiki o deiatelnosti federal'nykh sudov obshchei iurisdiktsii i mirovykh sudei v 2020 godu," www.cdep.ru/userimages/OBZOR_stat_SOU_2020.pdf.

2021c. "Otchet o rabote sudov obshchei iurisdiktsii po rassmotreniiu ugolovnykh del po pervoi instantsii," www.cdep.ru/index.php?id=79&item=5671.

Taylor, Brian D. 2011. *State Building in Putin's Russia: Policing and Coercion after Communism.* New York: Cambridge University Press.

2014. "Police Reform in Russia: The Policy Process in a Hybrid Regime." *Post-Soviet Affairs*, 30(2–3), 226–55.

Titaev, Kirill, and Mikhail Pozdniakov. 2012. *Poriadok osobyi – prigovor obychnyi. Praktika primeneniia osobogo poriadka sudebnogo razbiratel'stva (gl. 40 UPK RF) v rossiiskikh sudakh.* St. Petersburg: European University at St. Petersburg Research Institute for the Rule of Law.

Travova, Ekaterina. 2019. "Under Pressure? Performance Evaluation of Police Officers as an Incentive to Cheat: Evidence from Drug Crimes in Russia (May 30, 2019)." CERGE-EI Working Paper Series No. 637, https://ssrn.com/abstract=3396357.

Trochev, Alexei. 2012. "Suing Russia at Home." *Problems of Post-Communism*, 59(5), 18–34.

Trochev, Alexei, and Peter H. Solomon. 2018. "Authoritarian Constitutionalism in Putin's Russia: A Pragmatic Constitutional Court in a Dual State." *Communist and Post-Communist Studies*, 51(3), 201–14.

5 The Pendulum of Center–Region Relations in Russia

EVGENIA OLIMPIEVA

Fig. 5.1 Vladimir Putin speaks in front of a map of the Russian Federation during his annual news conference in Moscow, December 19, 2019. Credit: Bloomberg / Bloomberg / Getty Images.

> Governing Russia is not difficult, but it is completely pointless.
> Attributed to Tsar Alexander II of Russia

Abstract

The dynamics of center–region relations in Russia established by Vladimir Putin over the past two decades are at the heart of both the strength and the fragility of Russia's authoritarian regime today. This chapter provides a history of changing relations between the federal center, the Kremlin, and Russia's diverse subnational territories and highlights a central tradeoff that characterizes this relationship. The federal government has to balance two competing imperatives in its relationship to the regions and decide between a higher level of political control on the one hand, and more responsiveness to local needs on the other. The chapter consists of four sections. The first section considers Soviet legacies and political events that characterized Russia's transition from the Soviet Union. The second looks at Yeltsin's presidency, which was characterized by empowerment of Russian sub-national units and the promises of federalism and democracy, but also extreme weakness of the federal state and threats to Russian statehood. The third section focuses on recentralization dynamics that characterized center–region relations under Putin during his first two terms as a president. The final section considers increasing powers gained by the president in recent years vis-à-vis the regions against the background of persistent issues of regional governance that the regime has been unable to solve. The chapter demonstrates that centralization reforms both strengthened Putin's regime by establishing a system of control over regional actors and failed to build in the flexibility and responsiveness needed to address local needs.

5.1   Introduction: From Hyperfederation to Hypercentralization

Russia's center–region relations can best be characterized with a metaphor of a pendulum swinging between periods of centralization and decentralization. The extreme centralization of the authoritarian Soviet state, which Russia was a part of, was followed by the rapid disintegration of the USSR and the disorganized decentralization that characterized the era of **Boris Yeltsin**. **Vladimir Putin**, in turn, rapidly initiated policies and constitutional changes that marked the beginning of a new era of hypercentralization and a reestablishment of clear hierarchies of levels of government. These trends are important, because the nature of Russia's political system has long been heavily influenced by the relationship between the Kremlin and Russia's diverse territories. While Russia's constitution formally proclaims the country's federal structure, the country today is a highly centralized authoritarian state in which most of the meaningful levers of governance are located in Moscow. At the same time, genuine federalism in Russia has existed at times, but is best understood as having occurred at historical moments when incumbent structures of control collapsed, de facto weakening the center vis-à-vis the regions.

The highly centralized administrative structures of the Soviet state and of Putin's Russia have in part arisen as a response to objective challenges faced by the country for decades, even centuries. The Russian state has to content itself with a large territorial expanse, extreme subnational inequality, a long history of centrally planned development, political opportunism of local elites, and separatist threats. While these structural conditions are undeniably important, the reconstruction of a centralized state under Putin today has directly contributed to the withering away of Russia's democracy and to the strengthening of a personalist and entrenched authoritarian regime. This chapter will outline how the dynamics of center–region relations in Russia established by Vladimir Putin are at the heart of both the strength and the fragility of the country's authoritarian regime today. It will proceed chronologically, first introducing the late Soviet era and its legacies, then describing the tumultuous 1990s heralded by Yeltsin's ascent to power, and finally detailing Putin's policies before and after his return to the presidency in 2012.

The changing federal–regional power balances are important because they bring to light a key dilemma that authoritarian regimes frequently face: the choice of strategies that ensure that the federal government can exercise and maintain a high degree of political control, but that come at the expense of the effective mechanisms of governance. Allocating greater independence to the regions and introducing (or allowing for) bottom-up, democratic levers of control to replace the oversized state and partial decentralization are necessary to create a more efficient system of governance, but unlikely in the context of a regime that fears for its own survival. At the same time, the regime's disregard for local needs and its inability to provide for them may pave the way for discontent and political instability. We see evidence of regime weakness in the declining support for the **United Russia** party and in Putin's waning popularity as well as in recent waves of protest across the country. The war Russia is waging against Ukraine and the ensuing sanctions will further lead to deprioritization of economic development in the regions. Unable to address its weaknesses, the regime will be forced to turn to more violent methods of control. As the regime fears for its survival, the levels of state violence will only grow.

5.2 Soviet Legacies of Ethnic Diversities, Inequalities, and Governance

As the former linchpin of the Soviet Union and the largest of the fifteen republics, the Russian Federation (RF) is the union's most direct descendant. It inherited many of the powers and struggles of its Soviet predecessor. This section will consider two key Soviet legacies consequential for Russia's center–region relations: the country's ethnically defined and multi-tier administrative system and its deep-rooted intraregional inequalities.

5.2.1   Administrative Divisions of the USSR and Russia

Governing Russia has always been a challenge due to the country's sheer size and geographic diversity. The country's struggle to control and govern its farflung territories goes back centuries to Russia's predecessor states: Kyivan Rus', the Russian Empire, and the USSR. These states were formed in part as the result of "internal colonization," a process in which an expansive state is both the subject and the object of colonization, as it pushed its own frontier to explore ever more distant territories and native populations (Etkind 2013). In Russian history, the colonized territories were frequently sparsely populated and less economically developed than the heartland. They were also home to diverse populations.

In fact, Russia's most immediate predecessor, the USSR, was not only the largest country in the world but also one of the most diverse, with more than 100 nationalities residing on its vast territories. Russia inherited its administrative structure directly from the Soviet Union, which was designed in part to accommodate the country's ethnic diversity. Special territorial divisions were created corresponding to the major ethnicities residing in the area, often referred to as "**titular**" **nationalities**. In particular, the USSR incorporated two types of republics. The top-tier administrative level consisted of the fifteen soviet socialist republics (SSRs) or union republics, with Russia being one of the fifteen as the Russian Soviet Federative Socialist Republic (RSFSR). Within the union republics, there were smaller autonomous soviet socialist republics (ASSRs), which accommodated and represented smaller nationalities. These units are particularly important for the story of Russian center–region relations and will be referred to in this chapter as **autonomous republics.**

Even smaller ethnicities were administratively represented by autonomous areas or okrugs and one autonomous region or oblast. Unlike the autonomous republics, these areas were typically very small and thinly populated, which is still true today. Sometimes, the ethnic identity endowed upon a territory was more of a feature of Soviet state-building than a translation of genuine ethnic identity into an administrative structure (Hale 2003). Even in the ethnic administrative units, the proportion of the titular nationality rarely exceeded that of the ethnically Russian population.

In addition to containing smaller ethnically rooted administrative divisions, union republics were also divided into administrative units that were not ethnically defined. These administrative borders were either inherited from the Russian Empire (the former *guberniias*) or created later for the convenience of governance. Hence, administratively, the Soviet Union had a two-tier system, and the RSFSR was essentially a federation within a federation. This *matrioshka* or Russian nested doll–like administrative structure will be consequential for the events that unfolded during the dissolution of the USSR and the conception of Russia as an independent state.

Table 5.1 Subnational units of Russia, 2021

Ethnic "States"	Ethnic Territories	Administrative Territories
- 21 (22) ethnically defined republics (sing.: *respubliki)*	- 4 autonomous areas (sing.: *avtonomnyi okrug* or *AO)* - 1 autonomous region (sing.: *avtonomnaia oblast')*	- 9 territories (sing.: *krai)* - 46 regions (sing.: *krai)* - 2 (3) cities of federal importance (sing.: *gorod federal'nogo znacheniia)*

Note: The numbers in parentheses include the annexed subjects Crimea and Sevastopol.

Contemporary Russia inherited the administrative divisions from its Soviet predecessors. According to the constitution, the Russian Federation is composed of eighty-five units, frequently referred to as "regions," which are officially titled the **federal subjects** (see Table 5.1). Russia's administrative structure can be confusing as there are six different types of subnational administrative units that are all considered federal subjects. The most common way to conceptualize subnational units of Russia is to understand them as falling within three main categories: ethnic "states," ethnic territories, and regular administrative territories.

The exact number of regions has changed over the past twenty years. Some subnational units were merged as part of the recentralization agenda of the Putin era, considered below. Two new regions were added after the annexation of the Crimean peninsula: Crimea and the City of Sevastopol. These territories are recognized as annexed by the international community, yet they were swiftly written into the Russian constitution in 2014 as subjects of the Russian Federation: Crimea received the status of a republic and Sevastopol that of a city of federal importance.

5.2.2   Intraregional Inequalities

Russia's regions are also shaped by significant intraregional inequalities in part as the result of eight decades of Soviet economic planning. Soviet regions varied widely in size of population, territorial expanse, resource endowment, and industrialization. Similar to Soviet Russia, modern Russia can be divided into three larger regions: the developed industrial regions of the European parts of the Urals, the resource-rich Far East and northern Siberia, and the less developed areas of the North Caucasus and southern Siberia (Zubarevich 2005).

Due to the harsh climate characteristic of many regions of Russia, the country's regions also vary in the extent of attractiveness for human settlement. The Soviet practice of state-led development, however, encouraged the development of remote areas that had been challenging spaces for modern urban life. In the Soviet era, inequalities in terms of income, development, and habitatbility were ameliorated through a panoply of equalizing policies and distributive mechanisms. A centralized political system redistributed resources between the regions, and the planned economy equalized wages and social services across the country, as well as prices for food and consumer goods, transport subsidies, and many more features of social and economic life.

The Soviet Union thereby dealt quite effectively with inequalities built into the country's geography and maintained towns across the country's large territory through these various redistributive policies. At the same time, years of Soviet-era state-led development also created a situation in which some Russian towns and villages were heavily supported by the state and subsidies in ways that proved extremely costly and ultimately unsustainable in a market economy. With the dissolution of the USSR and its central planning, the state's ameliorating hand vanished, and inequalities across the Russian regions were exacerbated.

5.3   Nationalist Movements and Regional Empowerment

Every year on June 12, Russians celebrate Independence Day, marking the day Russia acquired its sovereignty. A reasonable question to ask is: sovereignty and independence from whom? For a colonial state, as Russia has always been, celebrating independence, that is, the loss of its colonies, presents a historical paradox (Shevtsova 2014). Yet, for many Russians, the collapse of the Soviet Union in 1991 and the attainment of sovereignty meant the long-desired independence from the old Soviet elites. These processes were welcomed as heralding the dawn of a new era. However, the young Russian Federation faced many old problems. The decentralization processes unleashed during the final years of the USSR's existence, especially the political struggle between **Mikhail Gorbachev** and Russia's new leader Boris Yeltsin, provided conditions for the creation of federalism in the country but also left it struggling to govern its incalcitrant and newly empowered, but highly unequal, subnational units.

5.3.1   From Decentralization to the Dissolution of the USSR

The Soviet Union embodied a federal ideal in its name and in its constitution. In reality, however, the Soviet state was highly centralized and delegated little real authority to the socialist republics. Centralized economic planning and governance of such a vast and unequal country contributed to the economic stagnation that began under Leonid Brezhnev in the 1960s. Debates about whether and how to decentralize planning and governance started in the 1970s, as the *nomenklatura* – key Soviet administrators – considered that some degree of decentralization might facilitate economic recovery. However, it was not until Mikhail Gorbachev launched his sweeping reform agenda of *perestroika* (reconstruction) that major steps to devolve meaningful economic and political authority to lower levels of government were taken (Starodubtsev 2018, 36).

In the process of *perestroika*, the sovereign rights of union republics were formally expanded. Union-level political elites took many of these formal changes as empty slogans because in practice the government of the USSR could invalidate any of the republican laws (Kahn 2002, 92). Gorbachev seemed to want to decentralize, but stopped short of introducing genuine federalism, which would have entailed the simultaneous weakening of the central government structures and the organs of the **Communist Party of the Soviet Union** (CPSU) that were still based in Moscow. The republics were not satisfied with these partial measures and pushed for more sovereignty and independence. Starting with the Baltic states, the republics began to announce their sovereignty and established the primacy of republican over union laws. This is known as the **Parade of Sovereignties** – the avalanche of sovereignty and independence claims of the union republics that unfolded from 1988 to 1990. By 1990, all union republics had declared sovereignty, and some had even proclaimed full-fledged independence from the Soviet Union.

The Soviet government headed by Gorbachev was unwilling to turn to force to stop these processes. A combination of the rejection of Joseph Stalin's methods (thanks to the reforms of Nikita Khrushchev's Thaw) and Gorbachev's personal convictions played a role in this (Shevtsova 2011). Because of this, he is considered a "traitor" by some in Russia. Gorbachev fought to maintain the Soviet Union but in the end was unable to control the centrifugal forces he had unleashed. These processes, fueled by an attempted coup by Soviet hardliners who opposed Gorbachev's reforms, culminated in the *raspad* or dissolution of the Soviet Union. The country seized to exist on December 8, 1991, as the result of signing of the **Belovezha Accords** by the leaders of Russia, Ukraine, and Belarus.

5.3.2   The "War of Laws" between Yeltsin and Gorbachev

The events that led to the dissolution of the USSR had important and direct consequences for the future of Russia and its relationship with its own subnational units. Not only did the country emerge from this period as an independent state, but it also emerged struggling to maintain its unity and statehood. The disintegration processes that unfolded in the USSR unleashed similar processes on the territory of Russia. The development of aspirations for sovereignty and independence in Russia's regions was a direct, but unintended consequence of Gorbachev's desire to save the unity of the USSR in combination with his conflict with Yeltsin, who at the time was growing in popularity as the leader of the RSFSR (Starodubtsev 2018, 40).

Both Gorbachev and Yeltsin exploited the two-tier administrative system of the Soviet state described in previous section; they tried to buy the loyalty of Russia's subnational units and encouraged independence movements in regions that had previously expressed no sovereignty claims. The two leaders competed in the extent of sovereignty they were willing to offer to regions in exchange for their loyalty, which is now remembered as the "**War of Laws.**" In an attempt to weaken Yeltsin, Gorbachev pushed for more sovereignty of republics located within the territory of the RSFSR (Herrera 2005, 144). In particular, he passed a law that provided sovereignty not only to the top-tier members of the union (the SSRs) but also to the second-tier units – most importantly, the ethnic republics on the territory of Russia, such as Tatarstan and Bashkortostan. The law essentially implied that the second-level autonomous republics on the territory of Russia had acquired the same weight in the Soviet Union as Russia itself.

This was a big blow to the status of the RSFSR and to Yeltsin's own personal ambitions, as it reduced Russia's weight in the union and essentially amounted to the loss of de jure control of its territories. In response, on June 12, 1990, the Supreme Council of the RSFSR, chaired by Yeltsin at the time, declared the country's sovereignty. As part of this declaration, Yeltsin not only established the supremacy of Russia's laws over the USSR's, like the republics that participated in the Parade of Sovereignties, but also promised sovereignty to *all* subnational units of Russia, making the status of regular regions, ethnic republics, and autonomous okrugs all equivalent.

By equalizing the status of regular regions and ethnic regions, Yeltsin ensured their support for the Russian government and hoped for their loyalty to himself personally. To regain the support of the ethnic regions, he traveled around Russia, famously encouraging them to "take as much sovereignty as you can swallow" as members of the Russian state. Following the declaration and Yeltsin's tour, an avalanche of sovereignty claims followed. Although hesitant at first, regional elites quickly saw a political opportunity in taking the leadership role in sovereignty claims (Kahn 2002, 107).

Gorbachev's attempts to keep the Soviet Union together and his struggle to undermine Yeltsin had unexpected consequences that paved the way for further and deeper decentralization not only of the union, but also of Russia itself. Since, as he himself later explained, Yeltsin had decided to "fight fire with fire" and offered more sovereignty to Russia's regions to keep them part of the country, they were encouraged and legitimized to demand more sovereignty and independence. On the one hand, this created conditions for the birth of Russia's federalism. On the other hand, the competition between the two power centers that existed in parallel – the old union center headed by Gorbachev and the RSFSR government headed by Yeltsin – delegitimized the lawmaking authority of both. This undermined respect and norms of obedience not just to Soviet legislation, but to any central or federal legislation, setting a dangerous precedent for the future of Russia.

5.4   Yeltsin's Federalism "by Default"

Similar to the Soviet Union, the young Russian Federation pronounced itself a federal state. It could be argued that Russia's own center–region relations never came close to being genuinely federal as none of the formal documents that governed the country allocated sufficiently exclusive powers to the subnational units. Yet Russia in the 1990s poses a striking difference to a unitary centralized Soviet state. The former was a federal state "by default" due to the vast amounts of de facto power possessed by its subnational units vis-à-vis the federal center (Petrov 2010). On the one hand, these processes threatened Russia's statehood and deepened the issue of Russia's intraregional inequalities. On the other hand, they contained a democratic promise because, for a brief moment in Russian history, the federal center was constrained in its decisionmaking and was forced to negotiate with subnational units about their priorities and how they wanted to be governed.

5.4.1   The Rise of Governors

One of the outcomes of decentralization that unfolded on the territory of Russia was the rise of powerful new actors in Russia's regional leaders. These leaders are usually referred to as **governors**, even though the official title varies from one region to another. Importantly for symbolism, governors in the republics were given the title of "president" to highlight their even footing with the president of Russia (even though their powers were never comparable). Originally appointed by the center as heads of local administration, governors became elected leaders under Yeltsin. While regions received the right to elect their own leaders for the first time in 1991, the practice was suspended until 1995 because Yeltsin feared that former communist bosses would be elected.

Regional leaders had a lot of power thanks to their **political machines** – institutional conditions and informal networks that facilitate clientelism or the practice of exchange of material benefits for votes. Since the privatization of the Soviet economy had been delegated to the governors, they found themselves in a position of control over significant economic assets, and their political machines frequently included newly emerging business elites (Orttung 2004; Chebankova 2010). Access to political machines was not a guarantee: Building and maintaining them required political talent and savviness. Many former communist leaders failed to become competitive politicians (Hale 2003).

In addition to networks and institutional legacies, governors frequently had control over the electoral commissions and media outlets and were able to influence local branches of the federal state institutions such as the tax police, security services, judges, and prosecutors. Finally, governors also held a powerful formal channel of influence as members of the **Federation Council** – the upper chamber of

Russia's parliament. This allowed them to impact federal politics directly, and they successfully protected their interests and the interests of their regions by vetoing laws passed in the **Duma** (Remington 2007).

The excessive power of governors was both unpopular among Russians and problematic in many ways. The Russian economy suffered from the governors' collusion with powerful businesses and their promotion of protective policies that were detrimental to economic growth. Economic reforms designed in the center were frequently ignored in the regions, interregional trade barriers were a common practice, and powerful regional governors helped local businesses avoid federal tax bills (Wengle 2015; Berkowitz and DeJong 1999; Ponomareva and Zhuravskaya 2004). Inability to access tax revenues had dramatic consequences, undermining the Russian state's capacity to perform its basic functions, such as fulfilling its obligations to pensioners, paying state employees, maintaining the army, and securing the vast Soviet chemical and nuclear arsenal the country had inherited.

At the same time, the governors' ability to check the federal executive was particularly important in the context of the 1993 constitution adopted under Yeltsin, which maximized presidential powers (Gel'man 2015, 55). The constitution contributed to the creation of a system of **superpresidentialism** in Russia characterized by excessive powers of the president in terms of access to resources and control over expenditures and the ability to govern by decree, to subordinate the judiciary, and to limit parliamentary checks and balances (Fish 2000). In the absence of horizontal constitutional constraints, the vertical constraints imposed by regional leaders became even more important for Russia's future as a democracy.

5.4.2   Recalcitrant Regions and Asymmetric Federalism

The federal center headed by President Yeltsin entered the democratic period of Russia's history weak vis-à-vis the newly empowered and emboldened subnational units. Norms of obedience to the federal agenda were replaced with the new practice of center–region bargaining. Economically rich autonomous republics were positioned especially well for this new setup, as they combined ethnically rooted legitimacy and the capacity to credibly threaten Russia's integrity and the functioning of its economy.

Now that Russia was no longer part of the Soviet Union, new rules for center–region relations needed to be established. The first attempt to establish such rules was the creation and signing of the Federativnii Dogovor or the **Treaty of Federation** (Hiatt 1992). All regions could sign the treaty, but not on the same terms. In fact, the treaty provided huge privileges to the ethnic republics, establishing what is often referred to as **asymmetric federalism**, which implies that uneven rights and privileges are provided for different types of subnational units. Despite the privileges allotted to the ethnic republics, the treaty was not signed by the oil-rich Tatarstan and Chechnya.

To appease Tatarstan, a special appendix to the treaty was added accommodating its demands. Yet, the region proceeded to hold a referendum on its independence from Russia, which was later deemed unconstitutional by Russia's Constitutional Court (Shapiro 1992). More than 60 percent of the residents of Tatarstan voted for independence, but the region remained part of Russia. The referendum was a way for the leaders of Tatarstan to gain leverage against the Kremlin. The events unfolded more bitterly in Chechnya, which fought for complete independence from Russia. In 1994, the Russian Army entered the region, marking the beginning of the first of the two bloody Chechen wars that took thousands of lives.

Yeltsin's constitution, adopted in 1993, replaced the dysfunctional treaty and created a new, formally symmetrical system of center–region relations, which was once again resisted and boycotted by some of Russia's regions. Yet the 1993 constitution established the modern administrative system, in which regular regions have the same status as ethnic republics, territories, and cities of federal significance as federal subjects. While the 1993 constitution made subnational units of Russia equal on paper, asymmetry in privileges and differential treatment continued to exist in an ad hoc, aconstitutional manner, in part as a way to address the internal threats of destabilization.

5.4.3 Bilateral Agreements and Fiscal Decentralization

Despite the adoption of the new constitution, Yeltsin continued to accommodate regions through so-called **bilateral agreements**. In the period between 1994 and 1998, forty-six bilateral treaties were signed (Ross 2005), granting special political and economic conditions for the signatories. At times, agreements endowed regions with extraordinary rights that violated the constitution. For example, the bilateral agreement signed with Tatarstan in 1994 granted it the right to establish a national bank and conduct relations with foreign states independently of Russia. While in the beginning the bilateral agreements were signed only with ethnic republics, eventually this practice spread to regular regions as well. Bilateral agreements deepened the asymmetry and divided the country into regions that lived by the rules written in the constitution and those that had special privileges.

Bilateral agreements were a symptom of rapid and chaotic decentralization. With the central state gone, the regions were left with new responsibilities that frequently exceeded their financial means. Left to fend for themselves and newly accountable to the public, richer regions in particular were protective of their resources. By 1993, as many as thirty of them refused to pay taxes, waging a "tax war." At the same time, most of the regions depended to some extent on federal support. Bilateral agreements were first and foremost a way to find a compromise about who had authority over taxes, federal benefits, grants, and other financial transfers, although they covered many other issues as well.

Governing a country which is as economically unequal as Russia is impossible without some extent of economic redistribution. Yet, in the 1990s, matters of taxation and redistribution were not determined by an objective need for public provision. The central government's willingness to sign bilateral agreements aimed to stabilize the country and prevent further political disintegration. As a consequence of this, richer and more powerful regions – the regions that could both threaten and lobby Moscow – received major tax cuts (Treisman 1996). But the provision of public goods was also politically motivated and aimed to buy political support for Yeltsin personally. Regions that voted in pro-center way and supported Yeltsin in the presidential elections were favored by the fiscal flows (Popov 2004).

The period of the 1990s was a tumultuous time defined by a tug of war between the federal center and Russia's regions or, more specifically, between President Yeltsin and Russia's powerful regional governors. While the regions fought for the sovereignty that had been promised to them by Yeltsin during the transition, they also undermined the capacity of the Russian state and stood in the way of economic reform. The inability of the federal state to fulfill its basic financial obligations threatened the country's statehood and, importantly, disillusioned many Russians with the democratic project. Yet, the 1990s was also a period of democratic hope. Governors posed a real constraint on federal power and in many ways tied the hands of the president of Russia. For a brief moment in the history of Russia, center–region relations resembled federalism. This complicated period in Russia's history ended in 1999, when Boris Yeltsin resigned from his presidential seat and appointed Vladimir Putin in his place. Putin would go on to win the presidential election in 2000 and would take decisive steps to rebuild the hierarchical structure of Russian state, undoing constraints that the regions and their leaders imposed upon the federal center and the president of Russia.

5.5   Putin's Recentralization Efforts

Center–region relations became Putin's central agenda after coming to office in 2000. Emboldened by his victory in presidential elections in 2000 and with Duma support as the result of the victory of the Unity party (the predecessor of United Russia) he had backed in the 1999 parliamentary elections, Putin began to push for "federal reforms." These reforms were in reality antifederal and mark an important turning point toward centralization in center–region relations. They involved decisive steps that reduced the influence of Russian governors, empowered the federal center vis-à-vis the regions, and ultimately recentralized Russia's political and administrative systems. Within a very short timespan, Russian federalism was significantly curtailed, and governors were transformed from representatives of the regions at the federal level to representatives of the federal center in the regions. The effect of Putin's reforms was contradictory. On the one hand, they put an end to the political chaos of the Yeltsin era and brought more predictability and manageability to the Russian political processes. On the other hand, challenges in regional development and inequalities remained, and new threats to Russia's fledgling democracy were created.

5.5.1 Federation Council Reform

During Yeltsin's presidency, governors successfully defended their interests in the Federation Council, Russia's upper chamber, and vetoed presidential decrees and laws adopted by the Duma (the lower chamber). Since 1995, governors have sat on the council *ex officio*, meaning that they were granted a seat by virtue of holding the post of governor. However, this appointment procedure was not written into the constitution, and in August 2000 Putin passed a law that changed how the Federation Council was formed. From then on, the upper chamber comprised permanent fulltime appointees nominated by the regions' local executive and legislative bodies.

The appointees were not directly accountable to the electorate and constantly resided in Moscow, which made them more vulnerable to the influence of the Kremlin elites. Losing the seat in the Federation Council also made governors generally more vulnerable to coercion, as it stripped them of the immunity to criminal investigation (Ross 2003). To appease the governors, Putin established another organ, the **State Council**, as an advisory body to the president. Having a seat on the State Council, in theory, granted governors the ability to influence federal politics directly. However, since the State Council is subordinated to the executive branch and is merely a consultative organ, its members have little actual power.

As a result of Putin's reform of the Federation Council, any real regional influence over federal politics was eliminated, and the council ceased to be a body representative of the interests of regional elites, let alone regional communities. The newly created State Council failed to become an organ representing regional interests in place of the Federation Council. Lack of genuine regional representation diminished the ability of the federal center to make effective regional policy (Turovsky 2007).

5.5.2 Eliminating the Governors' Popular Mandate

Governors presented a threat to Putin not only as members of the Federation Council, but also as ambitious and popular politicians. Reintroduction of popular elections of governors in 1996 led to increased popularity and national recognition of many regional leaders, which worried Putin, who always paid close attention to his own approval ratings as well as those of his potential opponents. In general, a governorship was considered a highly powerful and desirable position that required a lot of political skill and was perceived as a path toward the presidency.

Boris Nemtsov is an example of a politician who gained national recognition as a successful governor. In the 1990s, Nemtsov and his team turned Nizhny Novgorod Oblast into a pioneer region in terms of privatization of state assets and attraction of foreign investment, which contributed to his popularity (Mommen 2016). In 1997, Nemtsov transitioned into federal politics and was appointed by Yeltsin as the first deputy prime minister of Russia. Nemtsov was considered to be a possible presidential candidate and Yeltsin's successor. However, with the election of Vladimir Putin, Nemtsov moved into opposition and became one of Putin's most significant critics, mobilizing popular protests and criticizing Russia's intervention in Crimea. As Nemtsov was working on a report on Russia's involvement in Ukraine in 2014, he was shot near the Kremlin. Nemtsov presents an example of how regions can produce nationally popular politicians who are potentially threatening to a personalist ruler like Putin.

To address the issue of threats stemming from governors, in 2001, Putin introduced a law that allowed the president to fire a governor for legal violations. The law served as a potential deterrent that could be used against noncompliant governors. But this was only the first step. In 2004, capitalizing on the hostage situation in the city of **Beslan** in the region of North Ossetia – one of the worst terrorist attacks in Russian history – Putin blamed Russia's decentralized system for the tragedy and passed a set of sweeping centralization and securitization reforms. Most importantly, a law was passed that canceled the popular elections of governors. From this point on, the governors would be confirmed in their post by regional legislatures after being proposed by the president. This move changed the incentive structure of governors and reoriented their loyalties away from local electorate and toward the president (Sharafutdinova 2010), reducing their political status. Even when a governor was reappointed, the importance of the post had decreased. From being powerful politicians, governors were turned into federal managers and administrators.

Turning the governors from political figures to appointed administrators had consequences for regional economic development. Putin's recentralization agenda sent a signal to local executives that loyalty was more important than economic performance. Since the survival of Putin's regime hinged on the delivery of votes (as electoral authoritarian regimes usually do), the Kremlin prioritized electoral over economic performance in the regions. The first and foremost task of the governors was (and still is) to deliver election results in the presidential and national and regional parliamentary elections. Unlike in China, in Russia economic development did not matter for reappointment of local executives (Rochlitz 2016; Reuter and Robertson 2012). In fact, some of the worst-performing governors were reappointed in 2005, even some known for their criminal activities (Gel'man 2009; Zhuravskaya 2010). In general, economic development mattered for promotions of higher-level bureaucrats only in regions where electoral victory was guaranteed and where there were no local political threats (Reuter and Buckley 2019).

5.5.3   Administrative Recentralization

Even before his direct attack on governors, Putin introduced a full-scale federal reform, the goal of which was to strengthen governmental agencies and their territorial departments in the regions. Unlike in the United States, federal bureaucracies such as the tax police, the judiciary, the Procuracy, and central electoral commissions are built into a single federal hierarchy. Yet, in the 1990s, the governors had ways of influencing these agencies. They often had a say in the appointments and incorporated personnel of these institutions into their informal networks. At times, security agencies informally protected governors' business interests (Volkov 2016) and collaborated with them in corporate takeovers (Rochlitz 2014). The tight relationship that governors had with territorial branches of federal institutions and institutions of law and order in particular made it difficult, almost impossible, for the federal government to implement its policies in the regions. Many of the laws and decrees were ignored, since the center possessed neither monitoring nor coercive capacity in the regions.

To address these issues, Putin created a supraregional level of federal bureaucracy by organizing all of country's regions into seven **federal districts**, each of which was headed by a *polpred* (presidential representative or envoy). These envoys allowed the new president to intercept power from Yeltsin-era local elites and to establish control over the regional governors. Restoring the coercive capacities of the federal state was the primary purpose of this additional bureaucratic level. This can be seen by looking at the backgrounds of people appointed as *polpredy*. Five of the seven appointees had backgrounds in security services and the military (Taylor 2011, 131).

Rather than giving envoys direct power over the governors – which would have made them too powerful – they were made responsible for the vetting and replacement of the heads of local branches of the federal institutions of coercion. Moreover, the introduction of federal districts headed by presidential appointees allowed employees to rotate between the presidential and regional bureaucracies, which affected their professional incentives and made the president an important player in career advancement (Goode 2011, 57). The envoys not only monitored people working in the federal institutions, but they also monitored governors themselves. In particular, they were tasked with collecting compromising information about governors' activities.

5.5.4   Legal and Fiscal Recentralization

One of the main aims and outcomes of Putin's early reforms was the unification of Russia's legal sphere and the removal of special privileges acquired by the regions under Yeltsin. Governors and local legislatures were threatened with removal if legal acts violated the constitution or "the unity of legal and economic space" of the

Russian Federation. Swift and decisive centralization reforms on multiple fronts at once made this threat credible. As a result, the majority of bilateral agreements were rapidly canceled, and local legislation was edited to come into line with the constitution. By 2003, the era of bilateral treaties was largely over, as most of them were either annulled or had lost power.

With bilateral agreements gone, a more unified system of taxation was introduced. In general, the taxation system was reformed in a way that led to centralization of financial resources. The Kremlin's new policies redistributed resources away from the regions. As the result, regional budgets relied less and less on financial flows that stemmed from regional sources and more on federal redistribution. The amount of federal transfers also increased, in part due to the sudden influx of oil money that refilled Russia's federal coffers and in part due to more efficient tax-collection practices. Reliance on federal transfers led to the regions being dependent on the federal center, which justified the need for increased federal monitoring. As the result, most regions, wealthy or poor, but especially poor, found themselves in the state of dependence on the federal center. Yet, from the perspective of political control, it was a convenient strategy. While federal transfers helped ameliorate intraregional inequality that had resulted from the transition to a market economy in the 1990s, the issue of the lack of fiscal autonomy of many regions of Russia remained unresolved (De Silva et al. 2009, 46).

The centralization reforms of Vladimir Putin's first two presidential terms were contradictory. On the one hand, the reforms were systematic steps taken to improve the governability or "manageability" of the Russian state. Indeed, the state's capacity to implement policy across the country's broad territories was revived in important ways. Putin's reforms solved some of the most glaring problems of the Yeltsin era that had been impediments to economic development. The dramatic fiscal asymmetries and inequalities in center–region relations were evened out. Legal order was established, and a formal relationship between the center and Russia's regions was introduced in place of the chaotic bargaining that had defined Yeltsin's era. Yet, the sole focus on reestablishing federal control led to a failure to create a system that prioritized economic development. It is also hard to separate the administrative logic of the reforms from their political effects. Putin's reforms created new threats to Russia's fledgling democracy as the constraints on federal power and on the power of Putin personally were removed, creating the dangers of executive overreach and authoritarian backsliding.

5.6   Putin's Return and Hypercentralization

The years since Putin's return to power in 2012, following the hiatus of **Dmitry Medvedev**'s presidency, have been marked by the continuation and intensification of the same centralization trends described in previous sections. Policies adapted by the federal center after 2012 have been particularly antiregional. While the elections of governors were reinstated as a compromise to political opposition, they did not improve the mechanisms of regional representation. The position of governor was stripped of its political representative functions and further turned into that of a regional manager. In this period, the most antiregional policy of appointment was implemented since the time of Russia's conception as an independent state. Russia's center–region relations can now be characterized as hypercentralized and hyper-presidentialized, as control of regional politics is concentrated in the federal executive. Yet, where the presence of the federal state is needed, such as in Chechnya for the protection of human rights, the Kremlin is absent.

5.6.1   Antiregional Appointees

Popular elections of governors were restored by Dmitry Medvedev in January 2012 in response to the popular uprisings of 2011 against fraudulent parliamentary elections and Putin's return to power. The elections were reintroduced in part to divert dissatisfaction and the popular demand for representation to the local level (Smyth and Turovsky 2018). To maintain control of the political dynamics in Russia's regions, the Kremlin had to ensure that only loyal candidates could be elected. This meant that the return of the gubernatorial elections was accompanied by serious barriers to entry (Ross 2018). By controlling which names appeared on ballots in the regional gubernatorial elections, the Kremlin was able to preclude a return to genuine popular representation in the regions. Although elected on paper, regional governors remain essentially appointed by Putin, with elections serving as a kind of confirmation of the appointment.

An important antiregional practice characteristic of this epoch is the more frequent appointment of so-called outsiders or *variagi*. Outsiders are people without regional ties who have not lived in the region long enough to have made connections there and to know its particularities. The local ties of a federal representative, which is what governors have become under Putin, form one of a few remaining channels of influence and lobbying for local interests. The more foreign to the region appointees are, the more focused they are on the federal center. Local elites representing business and regional interests are less able to influence or lobby such representatives directly.

The practice of appointment of outsiders started as early as 2000 when Putin first came to power. While in the period from 2012 to 2015 about half of appointees were outsiders, by 2018 the appointment of outsiders became a regular practice, marking the peak of antiregional politics (Kynev 2020). The governors have now been relabeled by the Kremlin as "managers" (*menedzhery*) and "technocrats" (*tekhnokraty*), which is meant to highlight the allegedly new business or corporate approach to governance as well as the Kremlin's message that people that sent by the center are more efficient in leading local economies precisely because of their apolitical character.

The typical image of a new governor is a relatively young, unambitious technocrat from Moscow, without any knowledge of or connections with the region. Similar to *polpredy,* the pool of governors in recent years has been increasingly dominated by *siloviki*, literally "wielders of force" or people who serve or have served in the defense, security, and law enforcement institutions. Moreover, almost all new governors owe their career to Vladimir Putin personally (Warsaw Institute 2018). There are a handful of oldtimers who have been in their posts for more than a decade. Yet, they also owe the permission to stay in power to Vladimir Putin, as it was the 2020 amendments to the constitutional "annulling" (*obnulenie)* of governors' terms – originally limited to two – that permitted them to stay in power. Career dependency on the president is one example of "presidentialization" of center–region relations characteristic of this time.

5.6.2   All Power to the President

The administrative reform of the early Putin years contributed to the strengthening and centralization of the Russian state. When Putin returned after the hiatus of Medvedev's presidency, centralization continued but this time through "presidentialization," that is, the rapidly increased importance of presidential decisionmaking. The 2020 amendments to the Russian constitution regarding the Procuracy (Russia's key law-and-order institution) and Constitutional Court are examples of further institutional weakening of the regions vis-à-vis the president (see also Chapter 4).

In the 1990s, Russia's Procuracy had a significant amount of decisionmaking power in terms of the appointment of its regional branch heads. The procurator general – the highest-ranking bureaucrat in the institution of the Procuracy – appointed prosecutors at the top of regional branches following prior consultation with the region about the candidate. Starting in 2014, the law was changed and the candidates were to be merely proposed by the procurator general while the president himself made the appointments. As the result of the constitutional amendments of 2020, the procedure of consultation with the regions as well as the role of procurator general in the appointment process were removed completely. Now the president appoints regional prosecutors in consultation with the Federal Assembly (an institution that does little to represent the regions, as we saw in the previous section).

When it comes to the 2020 constitutional amendments regarding the Constitutional Court, we similarly observe "presidentialization." Article 125.5 now states that, upon presidential request, the Constitutional Court can check the legality of regional laws adopted by the regional legislature before they are published. As a result, this amendment further increased presidential powers vis-à-vis the regions (Grigoriev 2021). Thus, the 2020 constitutional amendments and the federal laws that followed moved Russia further away from the possibility of establishing federal relations with regions and increased the concentration of power to control the regions in the president's hands.

5.6.3   The Problem of Chechnya

For centuries, Chechnya and Russia have had a complicated history. Chechnya was annexed by Russia in the nineteenth century as the result of the expansion of the Russian Empire into the Caucasus, which was followed by a deportation of Chechens to Turkey. Under Stalin, Chechens were accused of collaboration with the Nazis, and once again tens of thousands of Chechens were forcibly deported to nearly uninhabitable areas in Central Asia. When the Soviet Union fell apart, Chechnya along with other regions of Russia proclaimed its sovereignty. However, it went much further than the rest. **Dzhokhar Dudayev** – a native of Chechnya and a radical leader who came from a family that had experienced Stalin's deportations – pushed for complete independence of Chechnya from Russia (Barber 2011). This culminated in two devastating Chechen wars (1994–96 and 1999–2005) that took tens of thousands of lives on both sides.

The two wars decimated the region, and Grozny, its capital, was largely destroyed. Putin's approach to the problem of Chechnya following the war was twofold. First, he funded the rebuilding of the region, especially the capital, and continued to fund the region's budget. Even today, more than 80 percent of Chechnya's budget comes from federal transfers. Secondly, and in contrast to other regions of Russia, despite the levels of financial support from the center, the region gained substantial independence to the point that today Chechnya is essentially an enclave that lives by its own rules. While hypercentralization is a way in which the Kremlin approaches the control of the majority of Russia's regions, for Chechnya, Putin has introduced a distinctly hands-off approach.

Today, even though the region is technically subordinate to Russian legislation, in practice the lives of Chechens are often governed by custom and sharia law, even though many, especially women, seek protection from it from the state law (Lazarev 2019). Chechnya is truly an enclave as it is out of reach even for the all-powerful *siloviki*, including the **FSB** (Federal Security Service) (Slider 2008). In exchange for autonomy, **Ramzan Kadyrov** – Chechnya's leader – expresses unwavering loyalty to President Putin personally. Among other things, he delivers exceptionally high (at times, exceeding 100 percent) turnout and vote results for Putin himself and for the United Russia party (Keating 2012). Kadyrov has also been an ardent and vocal supporter of the war Putin began against Ukraine in 2022, with Chechen paramilitaries participating in the conflict.

Ramzan Kadyrov has governed Chechnya with very few checks on his power, having constructed what amounts to a largely authoritarian religious state within the Russian state. Under Kadyrov's regime, dissent and opposition are not tolerated and are punished in cruel ways (Human Rights Watch 2016). Reports of human rights violations against journalists and activists appear with horrifying frequency. But, even for the average citizen who is not challenging Kadyrov, the situation in Chechnya can be grim, especially for women and LGBTQ+ persons, whose rights are regularly violated. Women frequently become victims of domestic violence in Russia in general but in Chechnya especially. Those escaping the region and seeking refuge have been forcibly returned to their homes. Women also become victims of honor killings. The antigay violence perpetrated by security services has reached a level of a full-scale purge (Lokshina and Knight 2021). The leadership of Chechnya is not simply aware of, but encourages, such violence, because it solidifies Kadyrov's legitimacy among radical and conservative groups.

The Kremlin knows of this situation but turns a blind eye. In fact, in 2021, Vladimir Putin endorsed another term of Kadyrov's regime, praising him for the "safety" that has been established in Chechnya (Lokshina 2021). While it is true that Chechnya has not seen violent conflict since the end of the Second Chechen War, questions arise about the true costs of Kadyrov's regime and the Kadyrov–Putin deal. The center's willful noninterference in Chechnya's business costs thousands of human lives: lost or ruined not as the result of civil war, but as the result of the war that Kadyrov has unleashed on his own people. The Russian federal government is responsible for protecting the rights of all its citizens. In most regions of Russia, the federal government is overly involved in regulating regional matters. Yet, in Chechnya, where this is much needed for the protection of citizens, protection by federal laws and authorities is largely absent.

In sum, center–region relations following Putin's return to power have been characterized by further centralization. While elections of governors were restored, outcomes remain largely controlled by the federal center, and regional gubernatorial elections did not become a channel of genuine regional representation. The increasing number of outsiders in these positions marked the peak of antiregional policy in Russia. In addition to being further centralized, center–region relations in Russia have been "presidentialized," reflecting similar trends in the rest of the political system. Amendments made to the constitution in 2020 solidified these trends by increasing the role of the president in appointments of federal bureaucrats and turning the Constitutional Court into a potential weapon against incalcitrant regions. The hypercentralization trends did not touch the region of Chechnya, however, where at least some federal involvement is most needed to constrain the authoritarian powers of its leader Ramzan

Kadyrov and to impose accountability for the human rights violations committed by his supporters.

5.7 Conclusion

Russia's gradual but persistent move toward authoritarianism has been intertwined with the processes of recentralization that followed the period of significant de facto decentralization of the 1990s, when the major levers of power formerly located in Moscow shifted to the regions. While strong regional governors dictated the politics of the 1990s, their political autonomy and influence had been largely eliminated by the end of Putin's second term in office. From being political representatives of regions at the federal center, governors became bureaucrats appointed by the center to supervise the implementation of federal policies in the regions.

During his first two presidential terms, Putin managed to unify the legal space and even out the legal asymmetries between the regions in Russia, putting an end to the bilateral agreements and curbing local legislation that was inconsistent with the constitution. His policies improved the state's administrative capacity to implement laws. The fiscal capacities of the federal state have been recovered. Yet, these changes have come at the expense of Russia's fledgling federalism and democracy. The ultimate result of these reforms has been a return to a unitary state, which functions today to support Putin's personalistic authoritarian rule. The return of Putin to power in 2012 marked a continuation and an intensification of the same trends, with a focus on increasing the relative weight and tools of regional control available to the president personally.

On the one hand, the system of center–region relations created by Putin contributes to the strength of his regime. The uncertainty associated with regional elections has been largely eliminated. The coercive capacity of the state has been restored and used effectively against regime's opponents. Preemptive measures that could ameliorate future threats to the president from the regions have been put in place. Yet the fact that such measures had to be introduced suggests that threats are expected to arise. Recent massive protests in Khabarovsk against the criminal prosecution and removal of the popularly elected governor **Sergei Frugal** is one example of a regional reaction to federal involvement that has gone too far (Lokhov 2020). Another such example is the recent protests in support of Russia's opposition leader **Alexei Navalny**, which notably unfolded not just in Moscow but swept the entire country and touched more than 100 Russian cities (Troianovski, Kramer, and Higgins 2021).

Intraregional inequalities have changed over time but today they are rooted in failed political institutions rather than in the country's geography and in Soviet legacies. The model of development that satisfies the task of political control is inefficient and prone to corruption. Decentralization and the creation of meaningful systems of control from below offer the main solution to the issues of intraregional inequality and stagnating economic growth. Yet, Russia's regime is unlikely to turn to this solution, because free and fair elections would threaten its hold on power. Especially in the context of the ongoing war that Russia is waging against Ukraine, any decentralization is out of question. Increasing the levels of coercion to prevent public dissent is the strategy that the regime will likely continue to pursue instead – a demonstration of force, yet a sign of deep-rooted weakness.

DISCUSSION QUESTIONS

1. What are some of the issues of Yeltsin's era that Putin's centralization reforms succeeded in resolving? In what ways did the reforms fail?
2. What explains the importance of governors in Russian politics? What are some of the positive and negative consequences of Putin's policies vis-à-vis the governors?
3. What is the relationship between Russia's federal government and Chechnya? Does this policy imply weakness or strength on the part of the federal center?

REFERENCES

Barber, Tony. 2011. "Obituary: Dzhokhar Dudayev." *Independent*, October 23, www.independent.co.uk/news/people/obituary-dzhokhar-dudayev-1306699.html.

Berkowitz, Daniel, and David N. DeJong. 1999. "Russia's Internal Border." *Regional Science and Urban Economics*, 29(5), 633–49.

Chebankova, Elena. 2010. "Business and Politics in the Russian Regions." *Journal of Communist Studies and Transition Politics*, 26(1), 25–53.

De Silva, Migara O., Galina Kurlyandskaya, Elena Andreeva, and Natalia Golovanova. 2009. *Intergovernmental Reforms in the Russian Federation: One Step Forward, Two Steps Back?* Washington, DC: World Bank.

Etkind, Alexander. 2013. *Internal Colonization: Russia's Imperial Experience.* Cambridge: Polity Press.

Fish, M. Steven. 2000. "The Executive Deception: Superpresidentialism and the Degradation of Russian Politics." In Valerie Sperling (ed.), *Building the Russian State: Institutional Crisis and the Quest for Democratic Governance*, 1st ed., pp. 177–92. Boulder, CO: Westview.

Gel'man, Vladimir. 2009. "Leviathan's Return: The Policy of Recentralization in Contemporary Russia." In Cameron Ross and Adrian Campbell (eds.), *Federalism and Local Politics in Russia*, pp. 17–40. New York: Routledge.

2015. *Authoritarian Russia: Analyzing Post-Soviet Regime Changes.* Pittsburgh: University of Pittsburgh Press.

Goode, J. Paul. 2011. *The Decline of Regionalism in Putin's Russia: Boundary Issues.* New York: Routledge.

Grigoriev, Ivan S. 2021. "What Changes for the Constitutional Court with the New Russian Constitution?" *Russian Politics*, 6(1), 27–49.

Hale, Henry E. 2003. "Explaining Machine Politics in Russia's Regions: Economy, Ethnicity, and Legacy." *Post-Soviet Affairs*, 19(3), 228–63.

Herrera, Yoshiko M. 2005. *Imagined Economies: The Sources of Russian Regionalism.* Cambridge: Cambridge University Press.

Hiatt, Fred. 1992. "Russia, Ethnic Regions Sign Treaty Sought by Yeltsin to Preserve Unity." *Washington Post*, April 1, www.washingtonpost.com/archive/politics/1992/04/01/russia-ethnic-regions-sign-treaty-sought-by-yeltsin-to-preserve-unity/421c88ff-3a61-48c9-99b6-36ca366877e0/.

Human Rights Watch. 2016. "'Like Walking a Minefield': Vicious Crackdown on Critics in Russia's Chechen Republic." Human Rights Watch, www.hrw.org/report/2016/08/31/walking-minefield/vicious-crackdown-critics-russias-chechen-republic.

Kahn, Jeffrey. 2002. *Federalism, Democratization, and the Rule of Law in Russia.* Oxford: Oxford University Press.

Keating, Joshua. 2012. "Chechen Precinct Gives 107 Percent." *Foreign Policy*, March 6, https://foreignpolicy.com/2012/03/06/chechen-precinct-gives-107-percent/.

Kynev, Alexander. 2020. "The Membership of Governors' Teams in Russia's Regions, and the Key Features of the Formation of Regional Administrations 1991–2018." *Russian Politics*, 5(2), 154–89.

Lazarev, Egor. 2019. "Laws in Conflict: Legacies of War, Gender, and Legal Pluralism in Chechnya." *World Politics*, 71(4), 667–709.

Lokhov, Pyotr. 2020. "The Region's Biggest Protest Ever, Tens of Thousands Rally in Khabarovsk to Defend Their Arrested Governor." Meduza, July 11, https://meduza.io/en/feature/2020/07/11/the-region-s-biggest-protest-ever.

Lokshina, Tanya. 2021. "Kremlin Endorses Another Term for Kadyrov and His Brutal Chechen Regime." Human Rights Watch, www.hrw.org/news/2021/06/24/kremlin-endorses-another-term-kadyrov-and-his-brutal-chechen-regime.

Lokshina, Tanya, and Kyle Knight. 2021. "No End to Chechnya's Violent Anti-Gay Campaign." Human Rights Watch, www.hrw.org/news/2021/08/31/no-end-chechnyas-violent-anti-gay-campaign.

Mommen, Andre. 2016. "Boris Nemtsov, 1959–2015: The Rise and Fall of a Provincial Democrat." *Demokratizatsiya: The Journal of Post-Soviet Democratization*, 24(1), 5–28.

Orttung, Robert W. 2004. "Business and Politics in the Russian Regions." *Problems of Post-Communism*, 51(2), 48–60.

Petrov, Nikolai. 2010. "Federalism." In Michael McFaul, Nikolai Petrov, and Andrei Ryabov (eds.), *Between Dictatorship and Democracy: Russian Post-Communist Political Reform*, pp. 213–38. Washington, DC: Carnegie Endowment.

Ponomareva, Maria, and Ekaterina Zhuravskaya. 2004. "Federal Tax Arrears in Russia: Liquidity Problems, Federal Redistribution or Regional Resistance?" *Economics of Transition*, 12(3), 373–98.

Popov, Vladimir. 2004. "Fiscal Federalism in Russia: Rules versus Electoral Politics." *Comparative Economic Studies*, 46(4), 515–41.

Remington, Thomas F. 2007. "The Russian Federal Assembly, 1994–2004." *Journal of Legislative Studies*, 13(1), 121–41.

Reuter, Ora John, and Noah Buckley. 2019. "Performance Incentives under Autocracy: Evidence from Russia's Regions." *Comparative Politics*, 51(2), 239–58.

Reuter, Ora John, and Graeme B. Robertson. 2012. "Subnational Appointments in Authoritarian Regimes: Evidence from Russian Gubernatorial Appointments." *Journal of Politics*, 74(4), 1023–37.

Rochlitz, Michael. 2014. "Corporate Raiding and the Role of the State in Russia." *Post-Soviet Affairs*, 30(2–3), 89–114.

2016. "Political Loyalty vs. Economic Performance: Evidence from Machine Politics in Russia's Regions." Higher School of Economics Research Paper No. WP BRP 34.

Ross, Cameron. 2003. "Putin's Federal Reforms and the Consolidation of Federalism in Russia: One Step Forward, Two Steps Back!" *Communist and Post-Communist Studies*, 36(1), 29–47.

2005. "Federalism and Electoral Authoritarianism under Putin." *Demokratizatsiya: The Journal of Post-Soviet Democratization*, 13(3), 347–72.

2018. "Regional Elections in Russia: Instruments of Authoritarian Legitimacy or Instability?" *Palgrave Communications*, 4(1), 1–9.

Shapiro, Margaret. 1992. "Tatarstan Votes for Self-Rule, Repudiating Russia and Yeltsin." *Washington Post*, March 23, www.washingtonpost.com/archive/politics/1992/03/23/tatarstan-votes-for-self-rule-repudiating-russia-and-yeltsin/6f780a8f-bbf6-4092-8f1e-b7aa7badbcd0/.

Sharafutdinova, G. 2010. "Subnational Governance in Russia: How Putin Changed the Contract with His Agents and the Problems It Created for Medvedev." *Publius: The Journal of Federalism*, 40(4), 672–96.

Shevtsova, Lilia. 2011. "Gorbachev and Yeltsin: Reformer and Terminator." February 1, https://carnegiemoscow.org/2011/02/01/gorbachev-and-yeltsin-reformer-and-terminator-pub-42455.

2014. "Russia Day – Independence From Itself?" June 12, https://carnegiemoscow.org/commentary/55904.

Slider, Darrell. 2008. "Putin's 'Southern Strategy': Dmitriy Kozak and the Dilemmas of Recentralization." *Post-Soviet Affairs*, 24(2), 177–97.

Smyth, Regina, and Rostislav Turovsky. 2018. "Legitimising Victories: Electoral Authoritarian Control in Russia's Gubernatorial Elections." *Europe–Asia Studies*, 70(2), 182–201.

Starodubtsev, Andrey. 2018. *Federalism and Regional Policy in Contemporary Russia*. New York: Routledge.

Taylor, Brian. 2011. *State Building in Putin's Russia: Policing and Coercion after Communism*. Cambridge: Cambridge University Press.

Treisman, Daniel. 1996. "The Politics of Intergovernmental Transfers in Post-Soviet Russia." *British Journal of Political Science*, 26(3), 299–335.

Troianovski, Anton, Andrew Kramer, and Andrew Higgins. 2021. "Aleksei Navalny Protests Constitute Biggest Russian Dissent in Years." *New York Times*, January 21, www.nytimes.com/2021/01/23/world/europe/navalny-protests-russia.html.

Turovsky, Rostislav. 2007. "The Mechanism of Representation of Regional Interests at the Federal Level in Russia: Problems and Solutions." *Perspectives on European Politics and Society*, 8(1), 73–97.

Volkov, Vadim. 2016. *Violent Entrepreneurs: The Use of Force in the Making of Russian Capitalism*. Ithaca: Cornell University Press.

Warsaw Institute. 2018. "Technocrat or Silovik – Special Report on Russian Governons [*sic*]." Warsaw Institute, warsawinstitute.org/technocrat-silovik-special-report-russian-governons/.

Wengle, Susanne. 2015. *Post-Soviet Power: State-Led Development and Russia's Marketization.* New York: Cambridge University Press.

Zhuravskaya, Ekaterina. 2010. "Federalism in Russia." In Anders Åslund, Sergei Guriev, and Andrew Kuchins (eds.), *Russia after the Global Economic Crisis*, pp. 59–77. Washington, DC: Peterson Institute for International Economics.

Zubarevich, Natalia. 2005. *Sotsial'noe razvitie regionov Rossii. Problemy i tendentsii perekhodnogo perioda*, 8th ed. Moscow: Editorial URSS.

6

The Politics of Race, Racism, and Antiracism

NIKOLAY ZAKHAROV

Fig. 6.1 Activists from ultranationalist organizations taking part in the "Russian March" on the outskirts of Moscow, National Unity Day, November 4, 2011. Credit: Alexey Sazonov / AFP / Getty Images.

> I saw black people play in Shakespeare's comedies. I don't know when we will have a white Othello … You see, that's absurdity. Political correctness pushed to such absurdity won't end well.
>
> Sergei Lavrov (cited in TASS, "US's Political Correctness")

Abstract

This chapter will discuss how race resonates in Russia, paying special attention to the current developments in racial politics. Contemporary racial politics in Russia is ambivalent and complex. Russian citizenship does not depend on racial or ethnic belonging but on civic loyalty. Nevertheless, despite all the calls for a civil Russian nation, we witness the growing importance of racial discourse, promoting an ethnoracial understanding of Russianness. This chapter examines racialization processes in Russia against the backdrop of a conservative turn in Vladimir Putin's politics. It shows that deeply rooted legacies of racial thinking and practices continue to inform current conceptions of identity in the post-Soviet space. It then argues that racial issues in Russia should be regarded neither as something extreme and abnormal, nor as a disease infecting only certain political figures and subcultures. It is the racialization of mainstream political discourse in Russia – whether it be left, right, or liberal – that encourages the practices of race and the formation of racial identity, leading to new forms of racial governance. Racialization coexists uneasily with the official policy of antifascism. This dualism characterizes post-Soviet racial public discourse and policy leading to uncertainty about Russian identity and to tensions in Russian politics.

6.1   Introduction

The Russian and Soviet governments have long maintained that racism did not exist before the breakup of the Soviet Union and that in its current form it is neither a serious nor a systemic social problem. Contemporary racial politics in Russia is ambivalent and complex precisely because racism has been anathematized for decades by the state and its leaders, who made race a legally unacceptable means for identity construction. The Russian government discourages openly racist political views, and in recent years the punishment for racist violence has been strengthened. Apart from antisemitism, observers and analysts of Russian politics, too, have long largely ignored racism, and the concept of race as an analytical tool to study historical and political processes in Russia has also been traditionally quite limited. In Russia, as in many other societies, people normally do not explicitly categorize each other as belonging to a different race, nor do they reference distinct racial categories as forces that organize their social lives. Yet, this chapter makes the case that the concepts of race and racism reveal important dynamics in Russian identity politics.

In the Russia of **Vladimir Putin**, antifascism has become a new national ideology, and antiracism is the professed official policy of the Russian government (Laruelle 2021). The radical right in Russia has been suppressed by the authorities, with many of its leaders under arrest, and official political discourses have never claimed that belonging to the Russian nation is biologically determined (Arnold and Umland 2018). Nevertheless, deeply rooted legacies of racial thinking and practices continue to inform current conceptions of identity in the post-Soviet space. What is more, a large share of Russia's population holds a primordialist view of racial and ethnic identity and firmly believe that it is possible to deduce a person's origin from their physical appearance (Matusevich 2008). Applying racialized categories is thus not merely a phenomenon typical of extremist groups; the ideology of race is deeply embedded into Russian identity politics, and racism is in many ways normalized, even if many forms of racism are invisible to authorities.

With the waning over the past thirty years of the communist internationalist narrative, which portrayed racial issues as a problem of the capitalist West, the workings of racial thinking and the mechanics of racialized exclusions in Russian politics have received increasing attention. It is now widely accepted in academic debates that racism is a problem in Russian society (ECRI 2019). Sergei Belikov (2011, 38–39) estimates that the membership of skinhead racist gangs in Russia has risen to 50,000, which Richard Arnold (2009) judges to be roughly half of the total skinhead movement in the world today. In general, studies on racism in contemporary Russia focus on the analysis and critique of political and scientific programs as well as quasi-scientific pamphlets containing racist themes, and on monitoring racist violence and legal prosecutions (Shnirelman 2011; Zakharov 2015; Avrutin 2022). This chapter will discuss how race resonates in Russia, paying special attention to current developments in racial politics.

6.2   Key Definitions: What Does Race Mean in Russia?

The relative marginality of the concept of race (*rasa*) is particularly evident if we compare the Russian context with the North American and West European contexts, where the concept was a very important tool for understanding the social and political order after World War II (Rainbow 2019). The most obvious reason for the marginality of race as an analytical category in Russia is the absence of census records and other institutionalized uses of race. This complicated the presentation of race as indicative of a distinct social group who possess a particular identity and interests and hindered any recording of social conflict between racially defined groups. In the North American case, it was possible for groups bounded by racial identity to be analyzed as, for example, important participants in the political process, and census data dominated the study of race relations for decades (Banton 1998).

In the Russian case, researchers' focus was thus on functioning of state classification systems (Miller, Sdvizhkov, and Schierle 2012; Sokolovskiy 2020). The officially recognized categories of nationality (*natsional'nost'*), estate, class, faith, and gender both reflected and contributed to formulating cultural difference and representations of social groups, and "racial others." In Russian identity politics, notions of the "racial other" are deeply intertwined in the contemporary discourse on Russianness. There is also something fundamentally problematic for observers about the clear definition of what "Russian" means. This is a question not only of choosing "Russianness" as a cultural, political, or "ethnoracial" entity in the public discourse (Tolz 2001), but also of how to translate it accurately into English. "Russians" can be used for *russkie*, which means Russians by ethnocultural nationality, and *rossiiane*, which refers to citizenship. Historical research has made it abundantly clear that Russians are not a "pure race," of course, as this group has intermingled with and assimilated members of many other ethnic groups, and it is well established that "race" is an ideological construction. The idea of race as it has been shaped historically constitutes the ethnoracial imaginary through the social process of **racialization**.

Race should be seen in the Russian context as a form of practical knowledge that emerges from racialization processes, rather than as a well-defined and generally understood concept. This notion of racialization processes, or race as practical knowledge, is the most appropriate tool for analysis of racial politics in Russia because it acknowledges that racial discourses emerge from and structure social relations. The relationship between material and spiritual "Russianness" – between blood and culture, in other words – is shaped by multiple ideational strands and practices concerned with the preservation and reproduction of social traits and rules. This discourse includes ideas related to the rise and decline of civilizations, to progress, and to the "quality of people," usually references to population health and resilience. Ideologically these ideas draw from a broad panoply of intellectual traditions – from conservative Christian values to national Bolshevism, from neo-liberal social Darwinism to militant fascist doctrines. Practically, these ideas are applied in official and everyday practices. Practices of race are instrumental in nation-construction, for example, as institutions clearly offer rewards in their welfare policies, and there are incentives associated with being (or becoming) "Russian," even if the word "race" is rarely pronounced in official contexts. Applying the framework of racialization also helps us to explain why, for example, of all migrants, it is those different in appearance who become victims of profiling in Russia during police checks. Examining the role of racial discourse in the building of Russian identity will also help to unpack the logic behind the growing neo-imperialism and the ongoing memory wars in Russia.

6.3   Historical Roots of Racism and Antiracism in Russian Politics

To discern the historical roots of contemporary Russian racism, researchers have looked for traces of racism in repressive Soviet population policies and to the history of imperial Russia (Rainbow 2019; Avrutin 2022). Russia does not have a history of racialized slavery, which has long served as the key institution assisting the development of racist theories and practices elsewhere. We do see, though, that race was clearly present in earlier Russian scientific discourse, even if "at no point were racial concepts allowed to carry the day in politics or science" (Weiner 2002, 50). Instead of an explicit reliance on race as a concept, then, we need to discern how the Russian state has, over centuries, constructed patterns of governance and domination that have been articulated through twin hierarchies of backwardness and civilization, multiple forms of racialization, ethnophilia, and primordialism, separations between Russia's "West" and its "Orient," and undercurrents of "Great Russian chauvinism." Historically, Russian scientific discourse in anthropology (*fizicheskaia antropologiia*) and ethnology provided the intellectual foundations for Russification, Sovietization, ethnic cleansing, and postcommunist racial and ethnic hostility. At the same time, they also informed the **antiracist** agenda both in research and in politics. This ambivalence is central for the understanding of Russian engagements with racial issues. These historical academic debates continue to influence racial politics in contemporary Russia.

6.3.1 Imperial Russia

Imperial Russian governance was shaped by a central imperial–missionary orientation. Following the Tatar–Mongol invasion and its founding as the Moscow Great Princedom, Russia's rule was shaped by what are known as "anti-Horde" sentiments, referring to the Mongol Empire (thirteenth–fourteenth centuries) and the Kazan Khanate (fifteenth–sixteenth centuries). The Russian state sought to inferiorize, Christianize, and "civilize" the diverse groups of people living in its borderlands. The construction, labeling, and manipulation of ethnic and racial hierarchies formed a central part of Russian imperial governance involving differentiations in status, character, and civilization (Brower and Lazzerini 2001). At a time when the state hosted the largest population of Jews in the world, official state antisemitism was also a key dimension of Russian imperial racism, involving segregation, forced assimilation, and persecution. The Pale of Settlement existed from 1791 to 1917, confining Jewish residency to areas including Moldova, Belarus, Lithuania, most of Ukraine, and eastern parts of Latvia and Poland. Longstanding repressive policies and hostility were further institutionalized in the discriminatory and restrictive May Laws, enacted in 1882. Genocidal persecution of Jews, the pogroms, swept across the Russian Empire from the 1880s onward, leading to mass emigration. Official antisemitism and the Pale of Settlement officially ended with the 1917 Revolution, but pogroms were still being carried out during the Russian Civil War of 1918–21 (Budnitskii 2012).

Contrary to these racialized practices, though, Russian public intellectuals in imperial Russia placed more importance on the social milieu in the nature/nurture debates that were popular during the late nineteenth century. Russian socialists also opposed biological determinism, regarding economic forces as defining the "struggle for existence" and ultimately characterizing the level of development in any given society. Marina Mogilner (2013) notes that even the most educated Russian nationalists, who were oriented toward Western standards of nationalism, were extremely careful with the race–nation idea. The development of racial imagination was impeded both by religious fundamentalism and by an apocalyptic vision of modernity characterized by ressentiment toward the industrial West.

The most influential Russian thinkers and public intellectuals rejected interpretations of social development that were borrowed from natural sciences, whether evolutionism or social Darwinism (Vucinich 1988). The categories of "estates" referring to nobility, peasants, urbanites, and the clergy were the key pillars on which the Russian sociopolitical hierarchical order was built. The presence of the virtually impenetrable boundaries between social estates, which existed for many centuries and largely defined the historical specificity of Eastern Europe, are often regarded as having impeded the process of representing the population as consisting of distinct races (Etkind 2011). One of the most famous sayings of Nikolai Danilevskii – "Neither true modesty nor true pride can allow Russia to consider itself European" – sums up the ambivalent logic of prerevolutionary Russia's engagements with race. That is to say, the lower standing of Slavs within the master narrative of European history prevented Russians from subscribing to the notion of racial hierarchies that had evolved in Northern Europe. At the same time, uncertainty on the part of Russians concerning their own identity, as well as their awareness of the existence of a huge gap between upper and lower social groups, facilitated their engagement with racial theories, exactly as was previously the case in Western Europe (Tolz 2012, 192).

6.3.2   Soviet Russia

Official Soviet ideology condemned racism and fascism as absolute evils and considered both to be outgrowths of capitalist development and colonialism. In line with this take on racism and antiracist propaganda, then, racism in the Soviet Union was never presented as a social problem in public discourse, leading to the notion that racism was "absent" in Soviet Russia. W. E. B. Du Bois noted during his extended visits to the Soviet Union in 1926 and 1959 that Russians were seemingly unconscious of race (Baldwin 2002). There are, however, many witnesses of the widespread everyday racism in the Soviet Union:

> Somebody could hit you simply because you were different – different skin colour, different views. But subconsciously he did not know what he was doing. He did not understand it was racism. The word "racism" did not exist in everyday speech, only in the speeches of Soviet propaganda. (Ali Nassor interviewed in Beresnev 2005)

The Soviet understanding of race also reflects the complicated relationship between different social and ethnic groups in different time periods. Eric Weitz (2002, 5) states in this respect that

At the more open and tolerant end of the spectrum, the Soviets allowed people to choose their nationality upon reaching age sixteen. In its most exclusive and racialized articulation of the meaning of nationality, the Soviet Union rounded up and deported every single member of targeted populations, bar none, stamping every purported member of the group with racial stigmas.

Race and ethnicity as concepts were clearly separated in scholarly discourse. Nevertheless, Soviet nationalities policies, with their primordialist understanding of ethnicity, gave rise to exclusionary practices that operated much like race-based exclusion. Viktor Shnirelman (2011) argues that it was the ethnic experience itself that was linked for decades in Russia to forms of discrimination reminiscent of racial discrimination. This was especially obvious in the discrimination experienced by the Roma communities, a traditionally itinerant ethnic group that has historically been marginalized in Russia like elsewhere in Europe. Ian Law (2012, 147–48) states in his examination of the Soviet racialization of Roma that

[the] Soviet logic of anti-Roma racism ... constructed key ideological linkages between the central elements: a genetic inferiority, a foreign asocial group in need of nationalizing, a pre-modern backward culture in need of nationalizing, a pre-modern backward culture in need of Soviet modernization, a parasitic group that fed on "real" workers, a population out of control and in need of sterilization, a criminal group in need of the prison or the labor camp, inveterate drunks who needed sobering up and overall a "brown," "dark" presence that needed managing, regulating and controlling.

Soviet race policies were very much informed by anticolonial rhetoric. Soviet anticolonialism was centralized and subordinated to achieving the aims of the socialist project and geopolitical influence. This constituted an obstacle to any grass-roots anticolonial mobilization and deprived the subalterns of their voice. The civilizing mission conducted by the Soviet state has led to an interpretation of socialist modernization as internal colonization (Gouldner 1977), whereby both colonialism and anticolonialism can be regarded as important logics within the Soviet project. Liah Greenfeld (1990, 588) claims, for example, that "Ressentiment, not social concerns, fueled Russian national consciousness." She adds (Greenfeld 1990, 590) that

Russian nationalism was ethnic, collectivistic, and authoritarian. Constructed in this manner, Russian national identity provided the ground for individual self-esteem; on the face of it, the comparison with the West was moved to a new plane where Russia, by definition, was in no way inferior.

For Russian citizens, national identity during the Soviet period often involved an identification with the state (*derzhava*). Such an identification generated a particularly Soviet Russian nationalism, whereby a truly Soviet Russian blurred "Russianness," which meant that Russians considered themselves the "most Soviet of all Soviets." Russian nationalism, as an ethnic identifier, was discouraged and associated with anti-Bolshevik and anti-Soviet sentiments. The Soviet semi-official xenophobia was a mechanism for bolstering identity under conditions that hindered the formation of a Russian nationalist self-image within the multinational socialist empire.

6.4   Post-Soviet Politics of Race

With the collapse of the Soviet Union, the identification of belonging in respect to Russia found itself hovering in both economic and political terms between the so-called First World and Third World. The Soviet project sought to successfully carry out an ambitious task, namely, to be a great power, or "white," without being European or racist. Contemporary Russia's identity-building project attempts to solve the same complex task with one variable fewer, that is, simply by becoming "white."

The economic and political traumas have been so profound that they affect the social order as a whole and the self-identity of each citizen, transforming daily practices, hopes, and worldviews, and how people regard each other. Among the most striking changes is the wide dissemination of ideas of racial hierarchy by intellectuals, practices of racist exclusion of migrants, and racist violence on the streets.

6.4.1   Academic and Public Intellectual Discourse on Race

While biological conceptions of race are no longer an acceptable scholarly framework in the West, there has been a genuine renaissance in Russia of biological racism among Russian intellectuals. This is manifest, for example, in attempts to revitalize a "science of race" (*rasologiia* in Russian), which is a rough analogue of Nazi Germany's *Rassenkunde*. Numerous books and other texts on the subject, and translations of "classical" scholarly works, such as Hans F. K. Günther's *Racial Science of the German People*, have been published in Russia over the past decade. Even though these publications comprise an ad hoc conflation of alarmist resentment and tendentious pseudoscientific theories, they nevertheless have had a very strong influence on both public and intellectual discourse (Bassin 2017).

The official position of Russian anthropologists in relation to the idea of "race" rejects racist postulates on the hierarchy of races, but at the same time describes the idea that there are no discrete racial features as "deeply mistaken" (Alekseeva and Yablonsky 2002, 5). Criticizing the decline of the school of scientific racial studies in the West, Russian physical anthropologists also harshly criticize the "politically correct" position of Western social science, which regards racial studies as "racist science" and which treats the category of race as constructed (Gerasimova and

Vasiliev 2004, 12). At the Fourth Russian Congress of Ethnographers and Anthropologists, the leading Russian physical anthropologist Aleksandr Zubov (2003, 22) argued that

[A] serious unbiased scientific approach from the anthropological point of view to the question of the different existing human races could defeat racialism. The idea that there are no human races can only do harm to humanity and humanism, and it is for the most part only a political conception.

Antisemitism is a form of racism that has historically been prevalent in Russia. Aleksandr Dugin is an influential public intellectual who played an important role in introducing European extreme-right ideas into intellectual discourse in Russia and in connecting Russian and European far-right politicians (Shekhovtsov 2017). In part because of Dugin's and other neo-Eurasianists' prominence in contemporary Russia, antisemitism remains a strong intellectual current, although levels of anti-semitism are relatively low among the general public. Vadim Rossman (2013) identifies five different types of antisemitism in Russia. First there is a type of antisemitism where Jews are seen as rootless and homeless cosmopolitans, cultural enemies of Russia; the second position sees Jews as religious enemies of Russian Orthodoxy; thirdly, in the discourse of National Bolshevism Jews are archcapitalists and natural enemies of Russian socialists; fourthly, Jews are constructed as a racial foe, for example, in neo-Nazi propaganda. Lastly, antisemitism is apparent in neo-Eurasianism where Dugin constructs Jews as geopolitical enemies of continental civilizations such as Eurasia.

Intellectuals in the national republics of the Russian Federation contribute to racialization through their endeavors to represent their history as colonial (Zakharov and Law 2017). Myths of ethnic descent are focused on genealogical ancestry, and local elites in areas that have been annexed go so far as to define themselves racially in terms of having a different lineage than either the perceived colonizers or the populations they themselves have governed (Shnirelman 2015). This combines ancestral race-thinking with the phenotypical race-thinking that has been predominant in the ethnic core of the empire. While race is usually thought of as a "type" in the Russian intellectual tradition, ethnic minorities more often use race as a "lineage." Thus, the discourses of race in post-Soviet Russia encompass both the horizontal (classifications by "racial type") and the vertical (classifications by descent) dimensions. Vertical dimensions comprise an element in founding myths that emphasize the historical importance and continuity of the group.

6.4.2   Racialization of Migrants

Racialized discourse and racist practices are perhaps most apparent in connection with migration, the treatment of migrants, and migration policies. At a time when many Russians lost status as workers employed in formerly prestigious professions, such as heavy industry and the state sector, some members of ethnic groups traditionally employed in the service sector and in trade became successful capitalists. This led what has been called "ethnotrauma" and self-racialization. During the first decade of the postcommunist transformation, ethnic Russian resentment was directed primarily against representatives of minority diaspora groups who had become successful entrepreneurs (Gudkov 2004), including Armenians and Jews. Antimigrant sentiment was a bottom-up popular sentiment and was shared and fueled by prominent political figures. Surveys indicate that Russian respondents "are typically much more favorably inclined toward migrants of the same race and nationality as the majority in the country" (Drobizheva 2009, 200). Other surveys have revealed that tensions between ethnic groups are perceived to be the second most important conflict in Russian society, with the clash between poor and rich the most concerning one (Chernysh 2011, 37–39).

Racial discourse concerning labor migrants in Russia has been shaped by these economic tensions as well as by the construction of Russian state- and nationhood. The corresponding ideological work, conducted mainly by the state and the elites, operates as securitization and crisis management. One of the most widely shared notions on migration is that population movement by foreign citizens should be controlled and regulated by the state to forestall a purported "invasion of migrants." Prominent Russian political figures have made their position on this public, also expressing the view that migrants themselves must observe the values that give coherence to Russian society. Paradoxically, it is the lack of such cohesion today that gives rise to ambiguities in the interpretations of Russianness and in the use of racial discourse in the nation-building policies. The Russian government asserts the national feelings of Russians in terms of a civic obligation, rather than an ethnic group, a position that derives from a *derzhavnik* (etatist) position. Nevertheless, institutions exist that are designed to implement so-called nationality policies that mostly focus on the prevention of ethnic conflicts.

Elements of ethnonationalistic populism with racial undertones are occasionally added to public statements on migration, including statements concerning the need to limit migration or grant preferential treatment to the Indigenous inhabitants of one city or other in respect to employment opportunities. Policymakers typically think in terms of "established residents" versus "outsiders," rather than in terms of "racial purity," but the tendency to essentialize differences and biologize the particular features of Russians is clearly evident at times. Public sentiments and reactions to them on the part of ruling elites are particularly relevant in connection with the de jure absence of racial politics in Russia. For example, Aleksandr Tkachev, the governor of Krasnodarsky Krai and the head of the Committee of the State **Duma** on Nationalities Issues, declared in 2002 that "surnames ending in 'ian,' 'dze,' 'shvili' and 'ogly' are as illegal as their bearers" (quoted in Shnirelman 2011, II 35). Note that these endings are common in last names originating in the South

Caucasus; Tkachev's claim is thus clearly discriminatory. Widespread "Slavs only" disclaimers in employment and housing advertising are sustained by unspoken social rules rather than by legal practices. However, such unofficial practices maintain racial hierarchies: the distinctions between "black" and "white," with Russianness and whiteness mutually reinforcing one another (Avrutin 2022; Zakharov 2015).

Eugene Avrutin (2022) describes strategies used by racialized minorities to avoid ethnic profiling. They may limit their movement or spend as little time as possible in public spaces where they could easily be identified. Some alter their appearance or refrain from wearing conspicuous clothing or accessories that draw attention to their ethnic origins. To pass for light-skinned Slavs, women color their hair or wear European-style clothing, while men put on baseball caps to partially cover their face. Almost all migrants carried small sums of cash to be offered as a bribe in case they were detained for a document check.

While both the "invasion of migrants" and the West are constructed as threats to Russianness, they also symbolize that Russia is entering and embracing the new global order. Vladimir Putin (2012b) begins "Russia: The National Question," published during his presidential campaign, with a reference to the migration processes unfolding elsewhere. Commenting on the "decline of Europe," he stated that: "There are neighborhoods and entire cities where generations of immigrants are living on welfare and do not speak the language of the host country." "Indigenous populations are shocked by the aggressive pressure on their traditions and way of life and are seriously threatened by the possibility of losing their national identity," continues Putin (2012b). Thus, Putin's administration not only supported the European far right but also contributed, with new conservative discourses and with the models of racial governance for his admirers around the world.

6.4.3   Street Politics and the Russian Far Right: Victims and Perpetrators

Russian racial politics takes shape also at the grassroots level through the public display of racism, street marches by right-wing groups, and race riots. A key event for many right-wing groups is the so-called Russian March, staged for the first time in 2005 (Zuev 2013). Over the years, this has been organized by the Movement against Illegal Immigration (DPNI), which coordinates the march in different Russian cities. December 11, 2010, was marked by the worst racial riots in Moscow history, known as Manezhnaia Square events (Zakharov 2013). A large crowd, estimated at about 5,000 protesters, gathered and used violence against anyone they happened to catch on Manezhnaia Square near the Kremlin who was "non-Slavic" in appearance. This mass protest expressed the widespread public revulsion, affecting the political sphere, caused by the shoddy official investigation into the murder of Yegor Sviridov, a soccer fan rooting for the popular Russian team Spartak. Sviridov was allegedly killed by a group of "individuals of a Caucasian nationality," a term used to refer ethnic minorities native to the North Caucasus. Moscow city police proved incapable of stopping the crowd and violence. Three years later, a second murder of a Russian national, Yegor Shcherbakov, was ascribed to a perpetrator of "non-Slavic appearance." The public reaction to this event was a gathering of angry crowds threatening anyone who appeared to belong to an ethnic minority in the Moscow borough of Biriulevo on October 13, 2013. Again, metropolitan police clashed with protesters, but did not disperse the crowds, and authorities were at a loss to how to react to public anger and racism directed against migrants from the North Caucasus.

These events were remarkable in terms of both their significance and their consequences, and, therefore, they should be considered not only as episodes of racist violence but, more importantly, as a collective action involving ideological, material, and organizational resources to achieve political goals. The Manezhnaia Square events clearly demanded a response from President **Dmitry Medvedev** and Prime Minister Vladimir Putin. Both leaders addressed the events and warned that any further protests would be stopped, but they also made references to the need to end "uncontrolled migration" and deal with the corrupt law enforcement system that allowed illegal migratory flows. President Medvedev assured the public that the situation was under control and that the organizers of the "pogrom" were to be found and punished. Vladimir Putin laid flowers at the grave of the murdered soccer fan Sviridov and made accusations against certain corrupt Moscow investigators who had allegedly released a gang of murderers in exchange for a bribe. He also condemned the riot for being a manifestation of "xenophobia."

These actions made manifest the ambivalence of the government's position vis-à-vis the racism that motivated the antimigrant protests and movement. It was condemned, but at the same time solutions to the problem were located in a better-functioning official migratory system, not directly addressing the racist violence that had taken place. In his annual televised dialogue with Russian citizens, Putin stated that Russian liberals should understand the necessity of "law and order" to respond to problems related to migratory flows. He also said that the government was there to implement the will of the majority, because "otherwise liberal intellectuals would have to shave off their beards, put on helmets, and go out on the streets to fight with radicals" (Putin 2010). The implied meaning, of course was that physically weak liberals and intellectuals (in itself a racialized and derogatory image) would never protect the people, while a strong government would. Such statements are used in Russia in order to normalize the discourse of the movement against immigration. Racism in contemporary Russia is denied, just as it was in the Soviet Union. Yet, the Russian leadership increasingly uses racial rhetoric in a concerted attempt to reclaim it from the movement. Simultaneously the state widely uses the judiciary detain of far-right activists under Article 282 of the Russian

Federation's Criminal Code, which requires the imposition of a criminal penalty for inciting hatred on racist grounds. Prior to the 2006 mass protests in Kondopoga, racist violence in Russia had never taken the form of collective action. However, beginning with the Kondopoga events, when the protests led to pogroms of those who had come from the North Caucasus, not only neo-Nazi gangs but also "ordinary" Russian people were participants in racist attacks. Moreover, those active in the 2010 Manezhnaia Square and the 2013 Biriulevo events considered the Russian political establishment to be their opponents, who combined racist rhetoric with a liberal migrant policy. Unsurprisingly, of the two possible targets of attack – the presumably corrupt establishment and migrants with non-Slavic appearance – the state chose to discharge its anger against the migrants. Putin warned the middle class that their stable status quo and structural advantages could be maintained only by means of strict state control and more powerful state organs.

Richard Arnold and Andreas Umland (2018) argue that racist violence in Russia mirrors the representation of the respective ethnic minority in Russia, with the main ethnic minority groups that are targeted being people from the Central Asian former Soviet republics and from the Caucasus. The decline in racist crimes after the year 2014 indicates the change in engagement with racial discourse and increasing control over grassroots racist movements. By emphasizing the reconstruction of firm vertical structures of government and disseminating imperial propaganda in various forms – from the liberal empire advocated by Anatoly Chubais to the Eurasian empire of Aleksandr Dugin – the political elite controls many of the key elements of the racial discourse formulated by Russian nationalists. The "primordial stability" of Putin's rule is also imposed using concepts, such as *narod* (nation) and *Rodina* (Motherland), both of which derive from the concepts of kinship and lineage.

6.5   Ambiguities of Recent Developments

Mikhail Gorbachev's and Boris Yeltsin's idea of "entering world civilization" implied that the realization of the Soviet project had led both the country and the society away from the path of civilization. But if during the Yeltsin and early Putin era the racial discourse reflected the role of ethnotrauma in the "affective production of the suffering subject" (Oushakine 2009, 83–84) that had lost in the global competition, the more current transition redefines Russianness as a privileged position. As Putin incorporated a conservative populism into the official political position of the Russian government, some elements of racial discourse moved from the far-right margins to the official discourse. At the same time, monopolization of the nationalist agenda by the state led to the increasing repression of oppositional ethnonationalists and the prohibition of openly racist organizations and slogans.

6.5.1 Russia as the True Europe: Geopolitics of Race and Identity Politics

The main intellectual sources of Putin's new authoritarian ideology are the "conservative synthesis" and the "Russian idea," which is an idiosyncratic mix of the social thought of religious philosophers of the late nineteenth and early twentieth centuries (see Chapter 16). There is a significant diversity in the sources of ideas, which has hampered the articulation of a coherent, clear-cut ideological program. The official ideology is in fact often reduced to little more than patriotism and the proclaimed goal and promise that "'our' people should have a better life." The Russian people and the civic nation of *rossiiane* (Russian citizens) are represented as endowed with special features, such as exceptional talent and strength, and deserving of conditions that allow for the fulfillment of the remarkable potential of "our people." Both this potential and the Russian people's alleged readiness for self-sacrifice to bring it to fruition are alleged, but political discourse is rarely clear in what is meant by "our people": It refers variously to the civic nation (*rossiiane*), the peoples of the so-called Russian World (*russkii mir*) (Suslov 2018), or ethnic Russians (*russkie*).

Operationally, the ambiguity in how to understand Russianness reflected the tendency for the "Russian idea" to represent Russianness as a mystically messianic and universalist quality that had nothing at all to do with blood. This ambivalence highlights the instrumental and populist rhetoric of Russian political elites. Scholarship on this topic has identified anti-Western sentiments, antisemitism, and antimigrant stances as the few more or less constant and essential elements of nationalist discourse in Russia (Laruelle 2019). At the same time, however, much of the rhetoric of race can be seen as Russia's reaction to globalization and a hatred of the Westernization of global culture that turned toward decadence and away from traditional values (Zakharov 2012). The Russian notion of a "civilized country," often employed in connection with anti-Western rhetoric, has long been and remains a synonym for racial whiteness.

During the presidency of Vladimir Putin, the theme of the twilight and decadence of the West, coupled with the conception that Russia is the "true Europe," has become dominant in both public and official discourse. These discourses often contain racial undercurrents. There are at least two crucial racial themes in the Russian discussions of (a) Europe being swamped by a flood of "black" migrants, including those arriving from the new, "undercivilized" European Union member states; and (b) physical degradation as a result of the demographic crisis and the legitimization of "political correctness" (Zakharov 2015). The following comments by the mayor of Moscow, Sergei Sobianin (2011), in an interview with the most popular talk radio station in Moscow, reveal his first concern:

> When I first went to Paris I didn't even understand where I was – there are people there whose skin is not Paris-colored, and the number of migrants who have already settled there and are already living there has, I think, reached nearly half the population of Paris.

A statement by Dmitry Rogozin (2004), the former chair of Rodina (the Motherland Party) and deputy prime minister, shows another clear example of the kind of reasoning that claims that Russians are the true Europeans: "Russia is the authentic Europe, without the domination of gays, without pederast marriages, without false punk culture, without flunkeyism toward America. We are true Europeans, we have always survived, we have proven our Europeanness in wars against both the Crusaders and the Mongols – each and every time."

At the same, time, Russia claims that Western Europe does not recognize this feature of Russia's true – that is, "white" and "traditional" – Europeanness. The Russian nationalist Valery Solovei (2007, 15) complains that: "even in the face of invasions by other races, Europeans do not regard Russians as their brothers." Viacheslav Nikonov, another influential pro-Kremlin politician and dean of Moscow State University, recasts the same argument, but also adds that race is the main source of misunderstanding on the international level: "such an attitude toward us [Russians] is connected not least of all with the fact that we are white. Europe and America expect from us the same type of behavior as the Western white man. And they are very upset when our reaction is different. They think that we should constantly demonstrate to them our European image, but Russia is an independent civilization because of its entire historical experience" (Nikonov 2012).

Russian anti-Western rhetoric has turned into an insistence that Russia is the European power that is truly white and truly traditional, contrasting this with the West European path that has allowed LGBTQ+ people and immigrants from non-Western cultures to thrive in public spaces. In this respect, those constructing a new Russian identity today are leading a fierce fight against what they understand as "political correctness."

6.5.2 Antiracism and Antifascism in Russian Politics

Meanwhile, the official policy remains that the Russian Federation combats racism, and in fact the Putin government has recently carried through several successful measures that aim at combating racism. These include measures to address ethnic, racial, and religious hatred as an aggravating circumstance in relation to crimes such as homicide. Other measures prohibit the use of racially and ethnically offensive images and expressions in commercial advertising, and the establishment of an institutional framework for the protection of the rights of ethnic minorities and Indigenous peoples, coordinated by the Council for Interethnic Relations. In an article on the national question from January 23, 2012, Putin explicitly engaged with the debate concerning the ideas of those who advocate the racialist outlook in Russia saying that "it is the shortest path toward the destruction of the Russian nation and Russian statehood" (Putin 2012a). In fact, Putin has consistently favored representing Russia as a civilization or empire in these or similar terms, arguing that "attempts to promote the idea of creating a Russian 'national' mono-ethnic state contradict our thousand-year-old history" (Putin 2012a). Those who oppose Putin's vision, such as Konstantin Poltoranin, the former chief spokesman for the Federal Migration Service (the state body responsible for policies relating to migrants and refugees), have been fired. Poltoranin expressed racist views in an interview with the BBC, saying:

> What is now at stake is the survival of the white race. This is what we feel in Russia. We want to make sure the mixing of blood happens in the right way here – not the way it has happened in Western Europe, where the results have not been good (Sandford 2011).

Both hate crimes and racist rhetoric have declined since 2014, when the increasing confrontation with the West and with Ukraine demanded both a strengthening of the authoritarian regime at home and new "antifascist" arguments in Russia's soft power abroad. Antiracism is an important tool in Russian foreign policy. The Russian Foreign Ministry, for example, publishes an annual report on "The Glorification of Nazism and the Spread of Neo-Nazism and Other Practices that Contribute to Fueling Contemporary Forms of Racism, Racial Discrimination, Xenophobia, and Related Intolerance." Russia successfully promotes the image that it supports religious dialogue and combats Islamophobia. However, the ambivalence of the antiracist message in Russian foreign policy is easily seen in Sergei Lavrov's comment on the Black Lives Matter (BLM) movement and Western "political correctness," both of which are portrayed by high-ranking politicians and pro-Putin media elites as excesses of Western liberal democracies: "Probably, everyone wants to get rid of racism, and we never doubted that. We were the pioneers of the movement for equal rights of people of any skin color. But there is a risk of reaching the other extremity, what we observed during the BLM events and the aggression displayed against white people, white US citizens" (TASS 2021). Like Lavrov, Putin avoids the terms "ethnic conflict," representing all Russian military campaigns either as antiterrorist operations or as humanitarian aid. In the officially sanctioned discourse, the identity of Russians is based on their solidarity with the authorities.

Many of the antiracist statements remain at the level of rhetorical acts, and there are still many problems related to racist policies and public attitudes that are not addressed. No meaningful political action prevents attacks on Roma settlements by the police. There are also no policies to prevent or address the exploitative work conditions of ethnic minority workers and non-Russian citizens from Central Asia, and action against discrimination in access to jobs is also urgently needed. The practice of racial and ethnic discrimination by state officials – preventing former Soviet citizens from acquiring Russian citizenship – against groups such as the Meshketian Turks also continues. The effective combating of racial and ethnic hate speech in the media, on the Internet, and in political discourse, the activities of extremist organizations involved in racial and ethnic violence, and the disproportionate harassment, arrest, and detention of Roma, Africans, and people originating from the Caucasus area by police and law enforcement officials: All remain to be addressed.

In sum, it should be emphasized that, while the negative connotations of the term "racist" are officially retained, the terms "racism" and "fascism" are often used as empty signifiers, representing symbolic evils. They are used to encourage patriotism and loyalty to the Russian government. To be antiracist, then, means to celebrate Russian foreign policy. The alleged tolerance of Russians toward the "other" and their antifascism are celebrated as innate characteristics of Russianness. The state and the state-controlled media now use hatred of racism and its identification with the fascist atrocities of World War II, which was shaped by Soviet indoctrination, to run "antiracist campaigns" against the allegedly racist/pro-fascist policies of states with which Russia happens to be in conflict (Georgia, the Baltic states, Ukraine). It is the toolkit that can be used in the same fashion that antiracist rhetoric was used against the United States during the Cold War. In order to justify the prosecution of the band Pussy Riot, Putin (2012a) even claimed that one of the members "hanged an effigy of a Jew and said that Moscow should be rid of such people" before their show in the church. Through this intentional misinterpretation of what was originally an antiracist message, Putin made use of racial discourse to legitimize internal repressive policies in the eyes of observers.

6.6   Conclusion

In Russian studies, researchers use the term "race" and its derivatives, such as racism and racialization, as analytic tools to reveal and identify processes of exclusion, the assignment of identity, the construction of hierarchies, and the conduct of purges. Such research has revealed a very telling discrepancy between official rhetoric and actual practices both on the institutional level and on the everyday microlevel of interactions between people. Russia is perhaps the clearest example of the primordial understanding of ethnicity and nation pervading popular discourse and everyday interactions. Most Russians rely on the preexisting Soviet understanding of Russianness as a social norm rather than as representing a particular ethnic group.

Although victims, journalists, and human rights advocates alike interpret physical and symbolic violence against individuals who are "visibly different" as racially motivated, invocations of "race" in Russia were never straightforward, with little agreement about whether "race" correlates with skin color, ethnicity, citizenship, or social status. In addition, prospects for understanding and interpretation are made more difficult by the fact that much of what is discussed today in connection with race and racism is in fact related more to the political rhetoric of the Russian government. The paradox is that in Russia antiracist rhetoric continues to remain the norm, and that racism within the context of political polemics is always normatively labeled "fascism." Political competitors, in fact, began accusing each other of racism and fascism during the period of *perestroika*, when the division between pro-Western liberals and nationalists became obvious and significant.

The discourse of race brings together two sets of opposing ideas: While it affirms that Russians participate in the achievements of Europe, it also anchors the authenticity of "Russianness" in juxtaposition to an imagined hostile West. Since the disintegration of the Soviet Union, race imagery has in fact been used as a reliable anchor keeping Russia firmly within the "family of civilized peoples." All Russian presidents have unreservedly defined their nation as a "great power," but the great power image and the ongoing process of nation-building under the conditions of globalization have been accompanied by the exploitation of racial discourses. Russian isolationism is also employing the racial discourses depicting the Russian nation as a unique and superior civilization based on its innate "cultural code" and the moral values that are allegedly inscribed in the Russian "genetic code."

Racial issues in Russia should be regarded neither as something extreme and abnormal, nor as a disease infecting certain political figures and subcultures. It is the racialization of mainstream political discourse – whether it be left, right, or liberal – that encourages the practice of actual racism and the formation of racial identity, leading to new forms of racial governance.

DISCUSSION QUESTIONS

1. What role do racialization processes play in nation-building in contemporary Russia?
2. How did the economic dislocation caused by market reforms affect Russia's racial politics?
3. Explain the racial politics of Soviet internationalism.

REFERENCES

Parts of this chapter first appeared in Nikolay Zakharov, *Race and Racism in Russia* (Basingstoke: Palgrave Macmillan, 2015).

Alekseeva, Tatiana, and Leonid Yablonskii. 2002. *Problema rasy v rossiiskoi fizicheskoi antropologii.* Moscow: Institut Etnologii i Antropologii RAN.

Arnold, Richard. 2009. "'Thugs with Guns': Disaggregating 'Ethnic Violence' in the Russian Federation." *Nationalities Papers*, 37(5), 641–64.

Arnold, Richard, and Andreas Umland. 2018. "The Radical Right in Post-Soviet Russia." In Jens Rydgren (ed.), *The Oxford Handbook of the Radical Right*, pp. 582–607. Oxford: Oxford University Press.

Avrutin, Eugene. 2022. *Racism in Modern Russia: From the Romanovs to Putin.* London: Bloomsbury Publishing.

Baldwin, Kate. 2002. *Beyond the Color Line and the Iron Curtain: Reading Encounters between Black and Red, 1922–1963*. Durham, NC: Duke University Press.

Banton, Michael. 1998. *Racial Theories*. Cambridge: Cambridge University Press.

Bassin, Mark. 2017. "What Is More Important: Blood or Soil?" In Mark Bassin and Gonzalo Pozo (eds.), *The Politics of Eurasianism: Identity, Popular Culture and Russia's Foreign Policy*, pp. 39–58. London: Rowman & Littlefield.

Belikov, Sergei. 2011. *Britogolovye: vse o skinkhedakh. Ekskliuzivnye materialy*. Moscow: Knizhnyi Mir.

Beresnev, Valeriy. 2005. "Budet rasizm v zakone." Fontanka, 27 September, www.fontanka.ru/2005/09/27/149898/.

Brower, Daniel, and Edward Lazzerini (eds.). 2001. *Russia's Orient, Imperial Borderlands and Peoples, 1700–1917*. Bloomington: Indiana University Press.

Budnitskii, Oleg. 2012. *Russian Jews between the Reds and the Whites, 1917–1920*. Philadelphia: University of Pennsylvania Press.

Chernysh, M. 2011. "Standarty zhizni i sotsial'naia struktura russkikh." In Y. Arutiunian (ed.), *Russkie. Etnosotsiologicheskie issledovaniia*, pp. 22–40. Moscow: Nauka.

Drobizheva, Leokadiia. 2009. *Rossiiskaia identichnost' v Moskve i regionakh*. Moscow: MAKS Press.

2011. "Identichnost' i etnicheskieustanovki russkikh v svoei i inoetnichnoi srede." In Y. Arutiunian (ed.), *Russkie. Etnosotsiologicheskie issledovaniia*, pp. 83–99. Moscow: Nauka.

ECRI (European Commission against Racism and Intolerance). 2019. "ECRI Report on the Russian Federation (Fifth Monitoring Cycle)." ECRI Secretariat, Strasbourg.

Etkind, Alexander. 2011. *Internal Colonization: Russia's Imperial Experience*. Cambridge: Polity.

Gerasimova, M., and S. Vasiliev. 2004. "Iz istorii formirovaniia antirasistkoi ideologii v otechestvennoi antropologii." *Rasy i narody*, 30, 5–14.

Gouldner, Alvin. 1977. "Stalinism: A Study of Internal Colonization." *Telos*, 34, 5–48.

Greenfeld, Liah. 1990. "The Formation of the Russian National Identity: The Role of Status Insecurity and Ressentiment." *Comparative Studies in Society and History*, 32(3), 549–91.

Gudkov, Lev. 2004. *Negativnaia identichnost'*. Moscow: Novoe Literaturnoe Obozrenie.

Laruelle, Marlene. 2019. *Russian Nationalism: Imaginaries, Doctrines, and Political Battlefields*. London: Routledge.

2021. *Is Russia Fascist?* Ithaca: Cornell University Press.

Law, Ian. 2012. *Red Racisms: Racism in Communist and Post-Communist Contexts*. Basingstoke: Palgrave Macmillan.

Matusevich, Maxim. 2008. "An Exotic Subversive: Africa, Africans and the Soviet Everyday." *Race and Class*, 49(4), 57–81.

Miller, Aleksei, Denis Sdvizhkov, and Ingrid Schierle (eds.). 2012. *Poniatiia o Rossii*. Moscow: Novoe Literaturnoe Obozrenie.

Mogilner, Marina. 2013. *Homo Imperii: A History of Physical Anthropology in Russia*. Lincoln: University of Nebraska Press.

Nikonov, Viacheslav. 2012. "Rossiia luchshe svoego imidzha na Zapade" (interview with Yurii Solomonov). *Nezavisimaia Gazeta*, 31 January, www.russkiymir.ru/russkiymir/ru/publications/interview/interview0233.html.

Oushakine, Serguei. 2009. *The Patriotism of Despair: Nation, War and Loss in Russia*. Ithaca: Cornell University Press.

Putin, Vladimir. 2010. "Razgovorov s Vladimirom Putinym," December 16, http://premier.gov.ru/events/news/13427/.

2012a. "Putin, Merkel i chuchelo evreia." Interfax, online, November 16, http://interfax.ru/world/txt.asp?id=276315.

2012b. "Russia: The National Question," RT Online, January 23, http://rt.com/politics/official-word/migration-national-question- putin-439/.

Rainbow, David (ed.). 2019. *Ideologies of Race: Imperial Russia and the Soviet Union in Global Context*. Montreal: McGill-Queen's Press-MQUP.

Rogozin, Dmitrii. 2004. "My i est' nastoiashchaia Evropa." *Zavtra*, 1(89), online, 19 January, http://zavtra.ru/denlit/089/131.html.

Rossman, Vadim. 2013. *Russian Intellectual Antisemitism in the Post-Communist Era*. Lincoln: University of Nebraska Press.

Sandford, Daniel. 2011. "Russia: Racism and Abuse in Asylum Centres." BBC News, 20 April, https://www.bbc.co.uk/news/world-europe-13131359.

Shekhovtsov, Anton. 2017. *Russia and the Western Far Right: Tango Noir*. London: Routledge.

Shnirelman, Viktor. 2011. *Porog tolerantnosti*, vol. II. Moscow: Novoe Literaturnoe Obozrenie.

2015. *Ariiskii mif*. Moscow: Novoe Literaturnoe Obozrenie.

Sobianin, Sergei. 2011. Interview on Ekho Moskvy, online, 16 February, http://echo.msk.ru/programs/beseda/750466-echo/.

Sokolovskiy, Sergey. 2020. "Mixed, Merged, and Split Ethnic Identities in the Russian Federation." In Zarine L. Rocha and Peter J. Aspinall (eds.), *The Palgrave International Handbook of Mixed Racial and Ethnic Classification*, pp. 315–33. Basingstoke: Palgrave Macmillan.

Solovei, Valerii. 2007. "Predislovie ko vtoromu izdaniiu." In Vladimir Avdeev, *Rasologiia. Nauka o nasledstvennykh kachestvakh liudei*, 2nd expanded ed., pp. 8–17. Moscow: Belye Al'vy.

Suslov, Mikhail. 2018. "'Russian World' Concept: Post-Soviet Geopolitical Ideology and the Logic of 'Spheres of Influence.'" *Geopolitics*, 23(2), 330–53.

TASS. 2021. "US's Political Correctness Taken to Absurdity Not to End Well, Says Lavrov." TASS, April 1, https://tass.com/politics/1273135.

Tolz, Vera. 2001. *Russia: Inventing the Nation*. London: Arnold.

2012. "Diskurs o rase. Imperskaia Rossiia i Zapad v sravnenii." In Miller, Sdvizhkov, and Schierle (eds.), *Poniatiia o Rossii*, pp. 145–94.

Vucinich, Alexander. 1988. *Darwin in Russian Thought*. Berkeley: University of California Press.

Weiner, Amir. 2002. "Nothing but Certainty." *Slavic Review*, 61(1), 44–53.

Weitz, Eric. 2002. "Racial Politics without the Concept of Race: Reevaluatin Soviet Ethnic and National Purges." *Slavic Review*, 61(1), 1–29.

Zakharov, Nikolay. 2012. "Modernization as Representation: The Russian Case." *Journal of Sociology and Social Anthropology*, 15(65), 194–205.

2013. "The Social Movement against Immigration as the Vehicle and the Agent of Racialization in Russia." In Kersin Jacobsson and Steven Saxonberg (eds.), *Beyond*

NGO-ization: The Development of Social Movements in Central and Eastern Europe, pp. 169–91. Farnham: Ashgate.

2015. *Race and Racism in Russia.* Basingstoke: Palgrave Macmillan.

Zakharov, Nikolay, and Ian Law. 2017. *Post-Soviet Racisms.* Basingstoke: Palgrave Macmillan.

Zubov, Aleksandr. 2003. "Mif o nereal'nosti vnutrividovogo raznoobraziia chelovechestva." In Galina Aksianova (ed.), *Nauka o cheloveke i obshchestvo. Itogi, problemy, perspektivy*, pp. 11–23. Moscow: Institut Etnologii i Antropologii RAN.

Zuev, Dennis. 2013. "The Russian March: Investigating the Symbolic Dimension of Political Performance in Modern Russia." *Europe–Asia Studies*, 65(1), 102–26.

7 The Politics of Gender and Sexuality

ALEXANDER SASHA KONDAKOV AND ALEXANDRA NOVITSKAYA

Fig. 7.1 "#Yes, I will choose [a future with same-sex families]!" A drawing created in response to a homophobic video demonizing same-sex families in Russia, 2020. Credit: https://twitter.com/pendeltur1, used with permission.

> Even though a man has a wife,
> He still prefers to sodomize.
> He takes young lads to bed
> Due to his drinking bent.
>
> Traditional Russian folksong (Kon, *Liki i maski*)

Abstract

Drawing on feminist and LGBTQ+ scholarship, this chapter discusses the role of gender and sexuality in Russian politics, which has risen in significance over the past two decades. It addresses Soviet legacies of gender and sexual norms in contemporary Russia, the use of homophobia by Putin's regime, and feminist and LGBTQ+ grassroots mobilizations. Most notably, the chapter shows how the Russian government has instrumentalized homophobia via the infamous "gay propaganda" legislation and the utilization of the concept of "traditional family values." Domestically, the regime's application of political homophobia has resulted in a discursive othering of LGBTQ+ Russians, as well as a marked increase in anti-LGBTQ+ violence and discrimination. Internationally, the Russian government's efforts advance its anti-"Western" stand and allow it to claim leadership in global conservative alliances. At the same time, this regime of repression has resulted in a proliferation of varied forms of feminist and LGBTQ+ resistance, paradoxically becoming a legitimate part of Russian opposition politics. The chapter concludes by discussing ways in which the diverse front of Russian LGBTQ+ and feminist activists have responded to the sexism, heteronormativity, and silencing efforts of the government and mainstream Russian society.

7.1   Introduction

Over the course of the past two decades, issues related to gender and sexuality have become central to how the Kremlin governs the Russian population and shape many policy areas. Gender and sexuality have long played a crucial role, because they are symbolically represented in the government's core message, addressed to both domestic and international audiences. On the domestic level, the government of **Vladimir Putin** conveys to people that they are supposed to feel injured by the dissolution of the Soviet Union and consequent economic changes. This narrative is geared to resonate especially with men invested in the idea of "traditional" masculinity, which implies the role of "provider" for the family – a role many men are ultimately failing at because of the upheaval in Russia's economic order. As for international audiences, the main addressee is an imagined liberal "West" whose global LGBTQ+ rights agenda is openly opposed by the Kremlin, the guarantor of "traditional values" – a concept deployed strategically to counter the universalizing principle of human rights promoted by Western societies. This constructs Russia as a powerful player on the global stage, regardless of the scale and value of its actual economic, political, and cultural contributions.

In this chapter, we first set the scene with a short historical introduction of the issues as they developed in the last years of the USSR (the "late Soviet epoch") and Russia of the 1990s. Gender and sexuality were silenced topics during Soviet rule. Formal gender equality between men and women, assumed in the Soviet period to have been achieved early on, shut down any discussion of the gender issues faced by Soviet citizens. LGBTQ+ identities were either banned by criminal law since 1934 or silenced as a mental illness, and thus could not be discussed in public, as they were perceived as criminal and shameful. A further development was the sudden and radical change from silencing in the late Soviet epoch to the emergence in the 1990s of a public sphere oversaturated with sex. With the policy of *glasnost* right before and right after the fall of the USSR, the discussion of sexuality rapidly flourished. This, however, invited new calls for stability and regulation, and it also established the link between sexual diversity and the dissolution of the Soviet Union, as well as with the "Westernization" of the Russian public sphere.

After this brief history, the chapter explores how these contextual conditions explain the success of the Kremlin's misogynist and homophobic policies in the 2000s and 2010s. We show that, with the ascendance of Putin, gender and sexuality played an even more important part in Russian politics. Putin's promises of domestic political stability and revanchism against the "West" for its role in destroying the USSR resulted in both greater regulation of sexuality and open confrontation with some liberal democracies on the global scene. Putin's first two presidential terms were marked by an increasing regulation of gender relationships through the reinforcement and stabilization of "traditional" positions of men and women. This was achieved through economic incentives (such as "maternity capital," initially a lump sum given to a family for having a second child, expanded in 2020 to include first-time parents) and symbolic policies (such as the political elites' embrace of the **Russian Orthodox Church**'s vision of gender roles). Meanwhile, LGBTQ+ issues were not explicitly addressed and did not yet play any significant role in domestic politics, because they were not prioritized by domestic or international actors. However, after Putin's return to the presidency in 2012, legislation targeting LGBTQ+ communities became a central legitimizing tool and cornerstone of the Kremlin's policies. This was a reaction to a greater emphasis from liberal democracies worldwide on reframing human rights as inclusive of LGBTQ+ communities. These shifts in global politics created an opportunity for the Kremlin to claim a radical value-centered opposition to the "West" through domestic politics exactly at the time of political crisis of legitimacy faced by Putin's third administration, as shown below.

We conclude the chapter with the argument that with declining economic growth, as the regime's legitimacy becomes fragile, symbolic issues come to play an increasingly important role in Russian politics on various levels. Gender and sexuality politics are an effective way for the Kremlin to amass populist legitimacy at home and promote conservative values abroad. It is important to keep in mind that symbolic issues have very real impacts on contemporary Russian life, ranging from increasing misogynist and homophobic violence to the economic isolationism of Russia in the global context. Whether these policies will endure is an open question. The Kremlin's policies face significant and growing resistance inside Russia as support for LGBTQ+ people grows and LGBTQ+ organizations mobilize to oppose the government's agenda.

7.2   Sexuality and Gender in the USSR

The USSR was established in 1917 in the aftermath of the October Revolution spearheaded by the Bolsheviks, a radical communist movement. The revolutionaries' overarching goals centered on the struggle against the imperial government by the working class and peasants. From the very beginning of the Soviet rule, gender and sexuality were on the Bolsheviks' agenda, though actual policies changed dramatically over the course of the seven decades that followed the October Revolution.

7.2.1   Sexuality and Gender from Early Soviet Progressivism to Stalin's Terror

The franchise for women, the decriminalization of male homosexuality, and even some limited recognition of same-sex marriage between women in the 1920s were among the Soviet state's early achievements (Healey 2001). The Bolsheviks introduced progressive gender legislation, expanded women's rights, encouraged women to fully participate in social and public life, and gave them, among other things, access to easy divorce, birth control (including abortion), and childcare (Gapova 2022). **Women's emancipation** and their ensuing mobilization into the workforce were required for the young Soviet state's pursuit of rapid modernization. The decriminalization of male homosexuality took place not because Bolshevik lawmakers were particularly supportive of queer sexuality; rather, they saw tsarist antisodomy statutes as remnants of the old worldview.

Despite early Soviet progressivism in the 1920s, the fight against gender and sexuality oppression was soon recalibrated. By the mid-1930s, Soviet society was moving away from the spirit of social experimentation and toward social conformity. In this vein, Joseph Stalin announced by authoritarian decree that gender equality had been fully achieved in the USSR and, therefore, the "women's issue" must be considered closed for discussion (Racioppi 1995). Meanwhile, abortion was prohibited and criminalized until after Stalin's death some twenty years later (Johnson 2009). Although the Soviet project of equality between women and men ensured women's equal mobilization into the public sphere, there was no corresponding movement to challenge either traditional gender roles of men or the centrality of motherhood to women's lives. As a result, for most Soviet women, equality actually meant a **"double shift"** where they had to juggle fulltime careers with housework and childcare, with little help from their male partners. Not surprisingly, by the late Soviet period, most women grew resentful of the idea of gender equality, viewing it as yet another ruse of Soviet propaganda. Moreover, despite formal equality and even the presence of quotas for women in low-level politics, Soviet women never had real access to the highest echelons of power in the **Communist Party of the Soviet Union (CPSU)**. There were only four women in the Politburo throughout the entirety of Soviet history, and no woman ever occupied the position of leader of the CPSU. Thus, political power, influence, resources, and decisionmaking in the Soviet Union remained dominated by men.

In the same period in the 1930s, Stalin also signed an instruction to criminalize consensual male homosexuality, later known as **Article 121**, Section 2, in the Russian Soviet Criminal Code (Healey 2001). Under this criminal statute male same-sex relations, defined as "buggery" (*muzhelozhstvo*), were punished by many years in prisons or labor camps. Importantly, the recriminalization of male homosexuality was carried out under the auspice of fighting fascism, thus placing homosexuality in opposition to the ideal Soviet citizen. "Destroy the homosexuals," famously argued Soviet writer Maxim Gorky in 1934, "[and] fascism will disappear" (cited in Essig 1999, 5).

According to different estimates, from 1934 to 1993, between 38,000 and 250,000 men were convicted under Article 121 (Valodzin 2020). Although female same-sex desire was not criminalized outright, same-sex-desiring women faced persecution at the hands of punitive Soviet medicine, which categorized lesbian sexuality as a mental illness, leading to forced institutionalization and social stigma (Essig 1999). The Soviet lesbians who avoided encounters with the Soviet psychiatric system faced oppression on other fronts, such as community surveillance and the symbolic threat of the Article 121 against male homosexuality (Stella 2015). In any case, from the 1930s, the regime of silencing of gender and sexuality via criminal and medical persecution was established in the Soviet Union and lasted until the end of the 1980s, when the country started to collapse (Essig 1999; Naiman 1997).

7.2.2 Sexuality and Gender in Late Socialism and *Perestroika*

One of the effects of a **regime of silence** around gender and sexuality in the Soviet Union was that it curtailed the production of knowledge and limited the circulation of ideas about gender and sexuality. It was prohibited to speak about homosexuality outside the criminal law and to speak about gender outside the recognition of equality between men and women guaranteed by the Communist Party. As such, the regime was maintained by both the censorship apparatus (state officials checking texts and other forms of expression before publication on compliance with party instructions) and self-censorship (authors limiting what they might have wished to say due to the fear of unfortunate consequences). Outside criminal law, medical discourse referred to homosexuality with Soviet doctors understanding same-sex desire as deviant (Alexander 2018). Until the 1980s, there was almost nothing published on LGBTQ+ topics in the Soviet press, no films were made, and very little literature alluded to homosexuality. In fact, some Soviet authors were even imprisoned for their homosexuality under Article 121, which was also used politically, targeting the regime's critics and political nonconformists (Healey 2017).

Grassroots organization was very limited, too, and the first LGBTQ+ organizations would not emerge until the 1980s.

Another effect of official silencing is that it facilitated the production of a parallel underground reality (Kondakov 2019). Under the cover of secrecy, some Soviet citizens could enjoy relative freedom, and LGBTQ+ communities were part of this underground. At the same time, it was also common for dissidents and other underground communities to maintain conservative attitudes toward gender and sexuality, and they were in fact often opposed to official insistence on gender equality (Zakharova 2013). In 1979, when a group of young Leningrad women published a *samizdat* (self-published) anthology *Woman and Russia*, in which they, for the first time in Soviet dissident history, attempted to discuss specifically women's experiences under communism, the authors faced double pressure. They were criticized by fellow dissidents for raising what were seen as trivial or marginal issues. They were also prosecuted, to the point of prison and exile, by the authorities for challenging the USSR's official image of a society free from social problems such as sexism and misogyny (Vasiakina, Kozlov, and Talaver 2020). Regardless of this, the underground was a diverse space inhabited by contradictory and controversial personae. Thus, in 1980s Leningrad, the first relatively visible LGBTQ+ organization Krylia (Wings) was formed. It offered support to people convicted for consensual same-sex practices under Article 121 and advocated the decriminalization of homosexuality. As *perestroika* marched on, a flurry of other, often short-lived but visible, LGBTQ+ grassroots organizations emerged. The scale of this underground life was evidenced at the beginning of the 1990s when the first LGBTQ+ festivals in Moscow and Leningrad (now St. Petersburg) brought together "tens of thousands" of people (Essig 1999, 133–34). Silencing had simply created an underground, one much larger than could have been imagined.

By the beginning of **Mikhail Gorbachev**'s time as the last Soviet ruler, the USSR was very fragile and was already slipping into an economic and political crisis. As a way to address impending problems, Gorbachev initiated a wide policy of liberalization reaching across all areas of Soviet life. Part of his liberalization efforts was the policy of *glasnost* (literally, "voicing") aimed at freeing the public sphere from censorship constraints to allow an open discussion of the state and political problems it faced. This period witnessed the beginning of frank public conversations around sexuality, showing not only Soviet people's eager interest in the issues, but also their lack of sexual culture and their unpreparedness to talk about sex openly (Plakhov 1993). Although Gorbachev went on to become a Nobel Peace Prize laureate for his efforts in transforming the Soviet Union and its relationship with the West, his reforms did not save the country from collapse. By late 1991, the Soviet state ceased to exist. But then, by 1993, the Russian Federation had emerged from its ruins and adopted its own constitution, this time explicitly based on a human rights framework.

The dissolution of the USSR meant many things for the people experiencing it and for the world: Gender and sexuality were about to become central to contemporary Russian politics. The 1990s were the opposite of the late Soviet epoch: Instead of silencing, sex was everywhere in TV programs, film, theater, newspapers, pop music, and so on, and LGBTQ+ topics thus entered official public discussions (Borenstein 2008; Gradskova 2020). A social transformation also took place within gender relations, shaking the habitual division of labor in Russian families: Manual laborers lost much of their symbolic power as well as their jobs; entrepreneurship became a more important virtue and strategy of survival than in a socialist state; and many women had to take care of their families as working men struggled with adapting to the new realities (Utrata 2015). At the same time, as any feminist or gender equality discourse was viewed as a holdover from Soviet times, Russians embraced more traditional ideas of femininity and masculinity (Zdravomyslova and Temkina 2005). For example, women activists who filled a nascent civil society sphere studiously avoided identifying the NGOs they headed, or themselves, as "feminist" even if their work was to advantage women's rights (Johnson 2009). Additionally, conservative forces behind organized religion (Christianity, Islam, and Judaism are considered the three major religions in Russia) started to take over after decades of Soviet oppression (Stoeckl 2020; Shnirelman 2019). In the 1990s, some churches, especially the Russian Orthodox Church, acquired new adherents in great numbers and real estate properties all over Russia as well as, together with all this, political influence.

Following the dissolution of the USSR, and throughout the 1990s, many residents of the newly established Russian Federation felt that the country was approaching the twenty-first century in ruins, shock, and gloomy despair. The public sphere remained unregulated, enabling all kinds of actors to do whatever it took to sell their product. Thus, after decades of discursive abstention, post-Soviet audiences were hungry for sex and keenly consumed sexual content. At the same time, the collapse of the Soviet Union and the period of unregulated economic reforms that followed left the population substantially impoverished and devastated. The newly emerging state structures, based on the market economy, were weak. The rule of force governed everyday life in cities and towns across Russia. Therefore, by the late 1990s, the promise of order and stability was attractive, and the newcomer president Vladimir Putin undoubtedly took advantage of Russians' longing for order. Gender and sexuality politics played a significant role in this process.

7.3 Gender and Sexual Politics in the Twenty-First Century

The Soviet-era criminalization of consensual male homosexuality, enshrined in Article 121, was repealed in 1993 under pressure of both international organizations such as the Council of Europe and local LGBTQ+ communities that had no other goal but the struggle against legal oppression (Kondakov 2021a). In 1999, Russian psychiatrists stopped classifying homosexuality as a mental illness (Essig 1999). These early victories, however, did not pave the way for more equality in the gender and sexuality domain during the following decades under Putin.

At the turn of the new millennium, Putin's ascent to power rested on the promise of bringing order and stability to the country shaken by the lawlessness and permissiveness of the first post-Soviet decade. This promise relied heavily on Putin's personality, as he fit the image of an average Russian man who was suffering the consequences of the Soviet collapse and, finally, standing up for himself because he could not tolerate the humiliation and indignation any longer. This revanchist image played an important role in securing political legitimacy and popular support. Specifically, it referred to a version of masculinity that combined a strongman with a common man – part James Bond and part simple Russian *muzhik* (practical, down-to-earth guy) – which brought Putin admiration from some women and respect from some men (Sperling 2015; Novitskaya 2017). This image became a central element of political rhetoric of the Putin administration and affected Russian political life in different ways.

7.3.1   Machismo, Sexism, and Homophobia in Russian Politics

From the very beginning of Putin's presidency, the administration's political message heavily relied on his gender performance: Vote for me and I will make men men again, I will take revenge for the decade of national emasculation, and I will empower this country's damaged masculinity. This message was communicated through a barrage of images depicting Putin engaging in highly masculinized activities such as hunting, piloting jets, rescuing animals, and performing martial arts, which flooded both Russian and world media. In contrast to his predecessor President **Boris Yeltsin** – who, by the end of his presidential tenure, had acquired the image of a hapless and out-of-control drunk unable to rule the country – the sober, tough, and serious Putin projected confidence and reliability.

Feminist scholars have pointed out close crosscultural associations between both masculinity and national leadership, and masculinity and global power (Alarcon, Kaplan, and Moallem 1999; Yuval-Davis 1997). For this reason, political leaders have been seen as embodying **hegemonic masculinity** (Connell and Messerschmidt 2005), that is, the "ideal" of manliness all men in a given society supposedly aspire to. Political weakness, in turn, has often been associated with femininity (Weber 1994). To the overwhelming majority of commentators both outside and within Russia, the "Putin-based nation-rebuilding scheme" (Johnson 2014, 584) is a clear illustration of these associations. The economic chaos of the 1990s was perceived by Russians as having a "feminizing," that is, weakening, effect on the country. In these gendered terms, Russia was imagined as a feminized nation "brought to its knees" by global powers. Putin's performance of hegemonic masculinity played a significant role, as it symbolized what some scholars define as the "remasculiniza-tion" of the country, that is, the restoration of Russia's strength and international prestige (Riabov and Riabova 2014, 23). As a result, machismo as a strategy of political legitimation has facilitated the strengthening and stabilization of the normative patriarchal gender structure of contemporary Russian society. It was partly inherited from Soviet times, where equality between the sexes meant equal integration of women and men into the workforce, and yet a lack of access to decisionmaking for women (Sperling 2015).

Since the beginning of Putin's rule, women have continued to be underrepresented in Russian politics: The highest number of female **Duma** MPs reached around 16.4 percent after the 2021 elections. The few women who do ascend to roles in the country's highest-level political institutions informally still have less power (Johnson and Novitskaya 2022). According to Janet Elise Johnson (2018), despite the gradual increase in the number of women recruited as formal participants in the government, such as the Duma MPs, governors, heads of various committees, and so on, they are typically delegated to a limited set of roles. They tend to serve as **"showgirls"** – that is, celebrities elected to the Duma to attract voters and increase its popularity, or as **"cleaners"** – that is, women appointed to elite positions to "clean up" the messes made by their male predecessors. Over the years, Duma "showgirls" have included several former Olympian gymnasts and actresses, a ballerina, an opera singer, and even the very first woman in space – cosmonaut Valentina Tereshkova. "Cleaners" include the Chair of the Federation Council **Valentina Matvienko**, who in her previous position as the governor of St. Petersburg served as Putin's loyal "representative" and was expected to bring law, order, and prosperity to the city decayed by her predecessor's corrupt politics (Stolyarova 2008). Extreme loyalty to the regime is crucial for nearly all of these women, as they sponsor and promote laws serving its interests, no matter how misogynist or homophobic they may be. When **Yelena Mizulina**, currently a senator, chaired the Duma's Committee on Family, Women, and Children Affairs, she sponsored the infamous 2013 "gay propaganda" legislation as well as authoring, in 2012, the State Family Concept policy paper that defined a "traditional" heterosexual family with multiple children as the national ideal and condemned homosexuality, abortion, and childbirth out of wedlock (Muravyeva 2014). Another Duma "loyalist," Irina Yarovaia, drafted the **"foreign agent" law** which targets NGOs by stigmatizing them as traitors and spies. LGBTQ+ organizations were the first to be included in the list of "foreign agents," prompting many to shut down. Finally, cosmonaut Tereshkova's most significant and also outstandingly loyal contribution to Russian law was her 2020 proposal for a constitutional amendment that would nullify Putin's presidential terms and ensure his rule until at least 2036.

In the absence of a strong feminist movement in Russia, heteronormative patri-archy had remained virtually unchallenged, making machismo a profitable political enterprise. Furthermore, the presence of women politicians does not translate into women-friendly or pro-gender equality policymaking. As of 2021, there are no high-ranking women politicians with an explicitly pro-women's rights agenda or who would openly self-identify as feminists. Neither "showgirls" nor "cleaners" advocate for gender equality or women's issues; quite the opposite, in fact, is true. Domestic and intimate partner violence continues to be a serious social problem disproportionately impacting Russian women's health, wellbeing, and human rights. Yet it remains unrecognized by the law (Muravyeva 2021). Since the emergence of Russia as an independent state, there have been sixty unsuccessful initiatives to institute antidomestic violence legislation; however, none made it even to the first review by the Duma (Rivina 2021). Recent attempts included the short-lived amendments to Article 116 of the Russian Criminal Code which, in 2016, distinguished "close-person" (that is, domestic) violence as a separate category. The amendment faced backlash from the Russian Orthodox Church and other religious organizations, as well as from conservative politicians and pro-government NGOs. Claiming the law contradicted Russian "traditional values," the critics interpreted it as a direct attack on the family itself, which led to the amendment's repeal in 2017. All subsequent legislative proposals to combat domestic violence have been met with similar criticisms and labeled as threatening to Russian "traditional values" (Muravyeva 2021). Furthermore, many feminist NGOs and grassroots activists involved in antidomestic violence campaigns have faced state persecution, ranging from individual arrests and fines, to being placed on the "foreign agents" list. Oksana Pushkina, one of the legislation's architects who was a Duma MP in 2016–21, was not allowed by her party, **United Russia**, to run for reelection in 2021, likely due to her pro-feminist stance and work on the proposal. Human rights activist Alena Popova, who also lobbied on behalf of the domestic violence legislation and ran on an explicitly feminist platform as a pro-opposition candidate in the same elections, lost the race to a pro-government candidate known for his homophobic, patriarchal, and nationalist views.

The regime of hegemonic masculinity that proliferated in Russian politics under Putin ensures that, in formal politics, women amplify patriarchy as political subjects rather than challenging the existing status quo. Hegemonic masculinity and the machismo of Putin's regime also simultaneously rely on and sustain political homophobia, which the regime then uses strategically as yet another source of legitimacy and symbolic power.

7.3.2   LGBTQ+ Identities and Political Invisibility

The end of Article 121 appeared to be a milestone. The 1990s brought sexual freedom, and with these victories grassroots mobilization significantly declined. Yet, it turned out that the LGBTQ+ politics of the 2000s were instead marked by **political invisibility** combined with a marketization of gay life.

Gay visibility, that is, the ability to make political demands on the basis of being "out and proud," is a foundational concept in Western LGBTQ+ politics. Yet the experiences of nonheterosexual and gender-diverse persons in Russia challenge the belief that "political existence and membership of the body politic is contingent on public visibility" (Wilkinson 2020, 234). At the turn of the twenty-first century, LGBTQ+ Russians remained politically "invisible" as their identities continued to be semi-private, semi-visible, and underarticulated: LGBTQ+ commercial venues welcomed customers, but any political claim would sound excessive and was, ultimately, unspeakable (Barchunova 2010; Sarajeva 2011). In other words, there had been a developed infrastructure of gay clubs, gay press, gay literature and music, gay dating websites, and gay meeting spaces; hence their rights were limited to consumption and participation in gay culture. At the same time, they remained vulnerable to homophobic violence and discrimination without any legal protection mechanism in place, and their right to a family was never recognized by the state (Nartova 2004). Thus, the regime of nonnormative sexuality's silence was reproduced in a new market situation in post-Soviet Russia (Kondakov 2019).

By the mid-2000s, a new generation of LGBTQ+ activists began to organize, however. Their agendas were charted around the concept of LGBTQ+ human rights that presupposes visibility at least in terms of a clear identification of the subject of rights: In order to claim rights and antidiscrimination protections, one has to have a clearly defined identity and a corresponding embodiment of it. These LGBTQ+ activists formed NGOs, which pursued various strategies ranging from supporting cultural initiatives, setting up community centers, monitoring LGBTQ+ discrimination, and lobbying local governments to approve annual pride events and same-sex marriage (Kondakov 2013). Activist efforts to claim human rights were mostly met with resistance from all sides including government officials, the general public, and the very LGBTQ+ individuals these NGOs represented (Soboleva and Bakhmetjev 2015). In 2009, for example, activists complained that there were no Russian LGBTQ+ communities in the Western sense of the word and that ordinary LGBTQ+ individuals did not appreciate or support their efforts (Sozaev 2010). The latter seemed to prefer to live in a state of invisibility which precluded public rights-based activism.

The participation of ordinary LGBTQ+ people in visible activism was determined by fears and avoidance of direct political confrontation – behaviors that have their own Soviet legacies. The LGBTQ+ political subject which emerged in post-Soviet Russia has been influenced by the long-established tradition of "kitchen talk": informal, clandestine underground resistance to totalizing state power practiced in the company of likeminded people and always in semi-private spaces epitomized by the image of one's kitchen (Kondakov 2019). The monopolization of the official discourse and imposition of surveillance over its citizens destroyed the notion of the private sphere in the USSR, which led to the emergence of alternative underground spaces. After the collapse of the Soviet Union, the market offered a commodified version of the same alternative space, this time in the form of gay-themed businesses and, more recently, online venues. Consequently, this reliance on alternative spaces has influenced post-Soviet LGBTQ+ politics toward invisibility. This way, LGBTQ+ activism based on visibility politics is seen as illegitimate nonsense (Brock and Edenborg 2020).

To sum up, in early post-Soviet Russia, the Yeltsin government did not concern itself with LGBTQ+ politics. A strong grassroots movement for decriminalization of male homosexuality and international pressure rapidly resulted in the repeal of the Soviet antihomosexuality law in 1993. This gave the impression that the LGBTQ+ movement had achieved what it had struggled for, given the background of sexual permissiveness confused with freedom as various sexualities were publicly marketed through commercial venues, shows, and the press. As a result, by the time the second generation of LGBTQ+ activists claimed rights publicly in the mid-2000s, their voice was unwanted: People on the ground felt threatened by exposure, while the government felt annoyed by the activists pointing out their failures. Western governments were the only appreciative audience and, consequently, the only participants in early LGBTQ+ pride parades apart from a few local activists. With the rise of Putin and his heavier reliance on the selling of masculinity in return for political legitimacy, this situation changed in the 2010s.

7.3.3   Instrumentalization of Homophobia and LGBTQ+ Hypervisibility

The landscape of sexual politics in post-Soviet Russia shifted again after the **2011–12 protests**, a period that could be characterized by **LGBTQ+ hypervisibility** (Wilkinson 2020). Over the past ten years, gay rights have become a highly volatile political currency in both domestic and foreign affairs. Putin's power seemed at its most fragile during the "Russian Winter," a series of protests started in December 2011, triggered by the perception that elections were rigged (Clément and Zhelnina 2020). After serving as the prime minister during the presidency of **Dmitry Medvedev** (2008–12), Putin returned with a third presidential bid, which was seen as a cynical authoritarian move and met with wide public protest. Large crowds on the streets of big cities and small towns across Russia apparently made the Kremlin tremble in fear. Even though Putin's return to the highest position in the state was not really questioned and he certainly "won" the elections, it was still necessary to calm the crowds and ensure stable rule for the entire term. Various enactments of Putin's hegemonic masculinity had already been played out for years before this crisis, except for the one that promised exceptional political gains: Against the background of international concern over LGBTQ+ rights in the world, why not protect "normal *muzhiks*" from gay people?

From this moment onward, state-sponsored homophobia became a part of public discourse. It forced an unprecedented visibility onto the LGBTQ+ community

(Novitskaya 2017; Edenborg 2017). However, LGBTQ+ Russians had virtually no power to broker the conditions of their newly established highly visible positions: Both internal and external powers forced them to come out. Apart from Putin's personal issues with legitimacy in the aftermath of the Russian Winter, it was also a time of a global polarization of norms governing LGBTQ+ rights (Altman and Symons 2016). This process is characterized by a sharp divide internationally between those who support gay rights and those who do not. However, this is not just rhetorical support: Each "camp" is expected to adopt legislation in accordance with their stance. The gay-supportive part of the world legalizes same-sex marriages; meanwhile, the nonsupportive part reinforces legal and cultural persecution of same-sex desire. In Russia, outright criminalization seemed to be too extreme, but legalizing homophobia in the form of a ban on "gay propaganda" was a viable alternative (Healey 2017). In any case, even though the "supportive" camp obviously makes the lives of some LGBTQ+ people easier, neither camp is directly concerned with people's actual wellbeing. Instead, the international norm polarization in LGBTQ+ rights discourse is a highly abstract political competition which offers domestic and international gains in terms of legitimacy, recognition, and symbolic exceptionalism (Essig and Kondakov 2019). In other words, in the early 2010s, LGBTQ+ rights became *the* issue worldwide, putting individual LGBTQ+ people in a spotlight where some may enjoy recognition and a chance to speak up in the conditions of relative safety, whereas others may feel exposed and vulnerable standing before a massive repressive state apparatus. The latter situation can be referred to as the hypervisibility of LGBTQ+ Russians (Wilkinson 2020).

In Russia, this struggle resulted in an increase in anti-LGBTQ+ legislation. Even before the introduction of the "gay propaganda" bill at the federal level, many attempts at discriminating against LGBTQ+ Russians had been made. In the 2000s, "gay propaganda" existed as an idea in law enforcement practices, but it was not a law, and it was not used politically to make any point or to enact a certain kind of masculinity. Rather, it was a practice typical of post-Soviet conservatism, targeting the proliferation of public discussions about sex, especially gay sex, as the latter was cast in a heteronormative society to be a more provocative topic (Kondakov 2022). Hence, even without any official ban on information about homosexuality, regional law enforcement agencies cited other pieces of legislation and arbitrarily used the notion of "gay propaganda" to enact Soviet-style censorship:

In March 2006, the procurator's office of Rostov Oblast issued a warning to two local TV channels (TRK Pul's and TV-Company EkspoVIM) for broadcasting text messages "that contained propaganda of a nontraditional sexual orientation." In the procurator's warning, it was stated that "propaganda of homosexuality is banned in Russia" (Kochetkov and Kirichenko 2009, 70).

This is an excerpt from a human rights organization's report documenting all instances of banning "gay propaganda" across Russia even in the absence of any "gay propaganda" law. It turned out that this practice of law enforcement agencies was quite widespread and included the censorship of various media (newspapers, TV, radio) and of the activities of local LGBTQ+ groups (banning public events or the official registration of their organizations). Throughout the 2000s, this practice existed without sending any political messages, but rather operating under the guise of legality to reproduce dated Soviet practices such as censorship, so common in the USSR.

At the same time, legislative initiatives were beginning. The **first propaganda law** was enacted in 2006 by Riazan' Oblast, a subnational region in central Russia. The regional law existed largely under the radar until it was discovered by LGBTQ+ activists a few years later. At the time, several federal legislators in the State Duma attempted to recriminalize male homosexuality, introducing a corresponding bill in 2002. The attempt failed because the Duma's legal department found it "illogical in the absence of victims" to pass such a law (Kondakov 2022). Starting in 2003, Duma deputies changed their tactics and proposed several criminal law proposals that would ban the "propaganda of homosexuality" (Healey 2017). These proposals were also rejected by the legal department with the reasoning that it was impossible to criminalize "propaganda" of something (homosexuality) that was not itself criminal. Importantly, the Duma's efforts to criminalize "gay propaganda" failed in the period before Putin's declining legitimacy in 2011–12.

Yet, as the Russian Winter protests erupted, the Kremlin sought populist legitimacy strategies that could stabilize the Putin-era political order. Political homophobia and the "gay propaganda" ban in particular became one such tactic first adopted by regional parliaments. Arkhangel'sk was the first region to adopt another installment of the "gay propaganda" law in fall 2011; Kostroma, St. Petersburg, Vladimir, Krasnodar, Samara, Magadan, Novosibirsk, Bashkortostan, Irkutsk, and Kaliningrad followed the "gay propaganda" strategy in 2012 (Fedorovich, Yoursky, and Djuma 2020). The adoption of "gay propaganda" legislation in all these regions received extensive media publicity. The St. Petersburg champion of the law, Vitaly Milonov, utilized the bill to secure a place in the federal legislature. With this increasing popularity a federal "gay propaganda" bill was debated throughout 2012; it was eventually adopted by the Duma and signed into law by Putin in June 2013. Known as **Article 6.21** of the Russian Code of Administrative Offences, it bans "propaganda of nontraditional sexual relationships," a phrase used to refer to LGBTQ+ sexualities in Russian law.

Article 6.21 does exactly what law enforcement agents had been doing without it: It censors media for publications on LGBTQ+ topics and provides an official excuse to ban LGBTQ+ political events (public rallies, pride parades) by threatening organizers with huge fines and foreign nationals with deportation and placing a hold on activities (for NGOs or media). Legally, it protects children from "harmful" content, but no harm to actual children is required to be proven in court for the law to be enforced – the damage can be merely potential. Hence, this piece of legislation does not address any specific social issue or any existing concern: It regulates a fantasy about someone being potentially harmed by something vaguely referred to as "propaganda of nontraditional sexual relationships." The law has never been meant to address any real issue at all; rather, the law's function is to send a symbolic message to the public: Enemies are within, and they are targeting the most vulnerable areas of our cultural identity, such as gender and sexuality but, once you unite around your leader, the trouble can be overcome. The Russian "gay propaganda" law was a piece of legislation meant to work politically to reinforce Putin's legitimacy.

Has the tactic worked? In 2013, the majority of Russians indeed liked the idea of the law: Popular support for the law ranged between two-thirds, according to the Levada Center (2013), to as high as 86 percent, according to a government-controlled pollster (BBC Russia 2012). Support was also voiced by some members of the Russian LGBTQ+ community, who saw in the law a chance to protect themselves from hypervisibility (Soboleva and Bakhmetjev 2015). A more recent poll indicates that, as this discussion progressed, Russians moderated their opinions toward LGBTQ+ people and did not support discrimination overall, which is a typical fluctuation on highly discussed issues (BBC Russia 2019). Thus, the law evidently had legitimacy at the beginning, but its power deteriorated over time, and more legislation was needed to ensure the stability of the Putin regime. As it was, several more bills that reinforced "**traditional family values**" and opposed same-sex relationships were introduced thereafter and were endorsed with Putin's signature: from the law banning the adoption of Russian children by nationals of countries where same-sex marriages are legal, to the 2020 codification of **marriage as a strictly heterosexual institution** in the Russian constitution. The latter legislation was included in the 2020 referendum where Russian citizens voted "yes" or "no" on a package of 206 constitutional amendments at once. This referendum was held at the height of the COVID-19 pandemic and included issues as diverse as the new definition of marriage as a union between a man and a woman and a reset of Putin's presidential term clock.

Russian domestic political dynamics are intricately linked to, and premised on, global symbolic politics. In fact, the very idea of a "gay propaganda" law was borrowed from a similar policy implemented by Margaret Thatcher's government in the UK in the late 1980s, albeit the latter was on a much more modest scale – it was applied only in schools there. In the UK, the law survived up until the end of the twentieth century unnoticed and hardly ever enforced (Burridge 2004). Still, in the "West" LGBTQ+ rights have become respected domestically and promoted worldwide only recently. At a time when an apparently weakened Russia struggled to find its place in the international arena, the "propaganda law" allowed the Kremlin to send a very clear message to conservative and homophobic governments across the globe to unite behind this prohibitive agenda and to oppose the "West." The message was there even before domestic developments in Russia: Prior to the introduction of regional and nationwide antigay legislation, Russia's representatives had already been promoting a "traditional values" approach to the interpretation of human rights in the UN (Wilkinson 2014). This approach excuses human rights abuse by claiming prevalence of national traditions over the respect of personal dignity and life. These efforts have also been supported by financial investments coming from the transnational conservative **"antigender" movement**, with Russia involved with such major players as the Catholic and Orthodox Churches and the "World Congress of Families" (Essig and Kondakov 2019). As a result, Russia's relationship with Western democracies around this topic has become strained. However, no real power appears to be forming around Putin, either. Hence, the "gay propaganda" law seems to work only partially here: It signals opposition to the "progressive" global players, but without revealing any alternative power.

The most striking geopolitical deployment of political homophobia occurred when **Russia invaded Ukraine in February 2022**. Since the 2014 Revolution of Dignity (also known as Euromaidan), Russian official discourse has regularly interpreted Ukraine's intent to integrate with the European Union as a move away from "traditional values" toward Western "immorality," exemplified by LGBTQ+ rights. By 2022, as Russia started a war in Ukraine, these discourses had become central to the government's justification of the war and violence it unleashed. For instance, in his lengthy diatribe just prior to the invasion, Putin falsely claimed that the war was Russia's last-ditch effort to protect itself from the West, which was going to use Ukraine to harm Russia, specifically, by threatening its "traditional values":

> They [the West] sought to destroy our traditional values and force on us their false values that would erode us, our people from within, the attitudes they have been aggressively imposing on their countries, attitudes that are directly leading to degradation and degeneration, because they are contrary to human nature. This is not going to happen (Fisher 2022).

Putin's claims were fully endorsed by Patriarch Kirill, the leader of the Russian Orthodox Church (a close ally of the Kremlin), who made explicit the link between the "traditional values" discourse, political homophobia, and the war in Ukraine. In a pro-war sermon, he argued that the invasion was necessary to protect Donetsk (a Russia-backed breakaway territory in eastern Ukraine) from "eight years of attempts to destroy its principal nonacceptance of [Western] values," manifested in gay pride parades:

Today, a loyalty test exists for this power [the West and its values], a kind of pass to that "happy" world, a world of excessive consumption, a world of illusory "freedom." Do you know what kind of test it is? It's a very simple and simultaneously terrible test: It is a gay pride parade. The demands of many to have one are the very loyalty test for that most powerful world; and we know that if people or countries reject these demands, they cannot enter that world and become alien to it (Patriarch Kirill 2022).

By equating LGBTQ+ rights with the West, and by positioning Donetsk (and Russia) as its extreme opposites, the patriarch deployed political homophobia to present Russia's war in Ukraine in civilizational terms – notwithstanding the fact that Donetsk was never under any pressure to hold a gay pride parade. Thus, the instrumentalization of LGBTQ+ rights in Russia's war in Ukraine represents the moment at which the lines between symbolic politics and *Realpolitik* became increasingly blurred.

Nevertheless, the resistance to political and state-sponsored homophobia has been increasing as well. Although many LGBTQ+ organizations had to shut down under pressure from the state and the authorities, others continued to grow and secure support from across the spectrum of civil society and political opposition. Prominent opposition leaders such as **Alexei Navalny** openly express their support for LGBTQ+ rights, which would have been unheard of in the past, before the "gay propaganda" era when Russian political opposition did not consider homophobia a human rights issue and distanced itself from gay activists (Sperling 2015). Issues of LGBTQ+ rights also receive wide and sympathetic coverage in the progressive Russian media, such as *Novaya Gazeta* and Dozhd. In 2017, it was *Novaya Gazeta* that first reported on the "gay purges" taking place in Chechnya, bringing global attention to the unprecedented violence against Chechen gay and bisexual men that was happening at the time.

The Internet continues to be an important tool in LGBTQ+ activism, which takes many forms: from creating websites and podcasts dedicated to queer art or Soviet and post-Soviet queer history (a topic still largely underresearched) to using social media hashtags in online flash mobs in support of gay rights. One case is highly illustrative: In 2020, as the constitutional amendment vote was underway, a pro-state media company created a viral video ad which showed a grim and dystopian "future Russia" where gay marriage was the norm, and gay parents could adopt orphans, thus oppressing "traditional" families. The only way to prevent such a future, the ad suggested, was to vote "yes" to the amendments. The ad received backlash on social media, including an artistic flash mob in which anyone could create a drawing celebrating same-sex families and share it online under the "Yes, I will choose [such a Russia]" (#DaVyberu) hashtag (see Figure 7.1). The flash mob generated hundreds of pictures, suggesting that an increased number of Russians are willing and able to express solidarity with their fellow LGBTQ+ citizens. Thus, although the "gay propaganda" law's stated purpose was to censor LGBTQ+ identities, paradoxically not only did it make them hypervisible, but it also helped mobilize LGBTQ+ communities across Russia and, to a degree, helped legitimize them in the eyes of progressive parts of society.

Similarly, with the growing availability and popularity of social media, feminist activists were able to promote women's rights to large audiences, resulting in a sea change regarding Russians' attitudes to feminist values, which even recently were less than favorable (Sperling and Sundstrom 2021). For most Russians, their first exposure to explicit feminist politics was in 2012, when the self-proclaimed feminist punk band **Pussy Riot** was subjected to disproportionately harsh punishment for their anti-Putin performance ("punk prayer") at the Christ the Savior Cathedral in Moscow. The band members were arrested and, in a highly publicized trial, sentenced to two years of prison labor for "hooliganism motivated by religious hatred." Public opinion on the trial was divided: Many agreed with the authorities about Pussy Riot's "despicable" offense, and President Putin himself commented that Pussy Riot had "dishonored women" and that, "in order to stand out and promote themselves in some way, they crossed every line" (Johnson et al. 2021, 10). Others viewed them as victims of the regime and as a symbol of Putin's crackdown on public protest. Along with the spread of social media activism, it is likely that Pussy Riot's position as political prisoners gradually helped popularize and legitimize feminism in the eyes of many Russians. The band's outspoken feminist beliefs paved the way for different forms of online feminist activism, which has since proliferated in Russia. For example, via the use of hashtags and sharing of personal stories, Russian feminists initiated broad discussions about sexism, harassment, women's sexuality, bodily autonomy, and the need for domestic violence legislation. Contemporary feminists also pursue intersectional, coalitional agendas organizing behind a wide variety of social justice causes, including environmentalism, refugee and migrant support, and prisoners' rights. One remarkable example of feminist mobilization is the campaign in support of Yuliia Tsvetkova, a feminist and LGBTQ+ artist-activist who, since 2019, has been persecuted for violation of the "gay propaganda" law and alleged dissemination of pornography for her drawings of women's bodies. To show solidarity with Tsvetkova and raise awareness of her case, feminists and allies have staged public protests and online flash mobs, eventually pressuring the authorities into dropping some of the charges (Lamekhov 2021). Finally, feminist and LGBTQ+ activists were at the forefront of the opposition to Russia's war on Ukraine in 2022. The government's efforts to squash the antiwar protest with censorship and prison terms did not stop activists from mobilizing against the war through public protest, collective antiwar statements, and the anonymous guerrilla-style dissemination of truthful and accurate information about the war.

7.4   Conclusion: From Criminalization to Instrumentalization

From the Soviet suppression of homosexuality to the contemporary "gay propaganda" law, gender and sexuality occupy a significant place in Russian symbolic politics. We reviewed two cases to establish how the Russian government relied heavily on manipulations with gender and sexuality in the 2000s–10s in order to preserve regime stability. In the first case, women in power were allowed a limited number of roles to amplify, not to challenge, the dominant patriarchal power structures. In the second case, we show how homophobic political rhetoric uses LGBTQ+ people as a target to generate hate and convert it to political legitimacy.

Legacies of Soviet and post-Soviet sexuality politics have made this strategy viable, though likely only temporary, for a regime that sees its political power in jeopardy. The Soviet experience of silencing depended on a strong fear of exposure among LGBTQ+ people, which explains the silence on and even support for the "gay propaganda" law from some activists and progressive social groups. What is more, the post-Soviet rhetoric that insists on the necessity of order and stability associates open and unabashed expressions of sexuality with the 1990s and the excessive marketing of sexual content of the time, as well as with foreignness and Westernization. As a result, the majority of Russians initially supported the "gay propaganda" law and by doing this also supported the current power that promises to tackle the associated issues. Given that today LGBTQ+ rights have global currency, this policy also is a strong point against the liberal "West." This, however, does not translate into real empowerment or institutional building of an alternative illiberal "camp" on a global scale. Most of the effects of this symbolical struggle are, therefore, felt on the domestic level as, internationally, homophobia fails to serve as a uniting moral value sufficiently strong to juxtapose itself to "West"-supported universal human rights.

Although the major objective of the "gay propaganda" law had been for it to act as a largely symbolic remedy for the fragility of Putin's deteriorating legitimacy, the law in fact has had very real consequences. It is being implemented as censorship legislation across Russia with hundreds of cases piling up on judges' tables to this day (Utkin 2021). The law has also had unintentional but predictable implications regarding anti-LGBTQ+ violence in the country: Cases of hate crime against LGBTQ+ people started to rise after the adoption of the "gay propaganda" law in 2013, doubling by 2015 (Kondakov 2021b). This trend culminated in a local crackdown when more than a hundred people were simultaneously targeted by law enforcement agents in the Republic of Chechnya in 2017 (Brock and Edenborg 2020). Further, the law incentivized Russian LGBTQ+ people to seek refuge in other countries as both everyday and state violence increased (Novitskaya 2021). Finally, contrary to the law's purpose, publications on LGBTQ+ topics in fact increased (Pronkina 2016) and LGBTQ+ themes in the Russian media became hypervisible. The law thereby raised awareness of LGBTQ+ subjects among some Russian citizens and has generated a certain degree of popular support for LGBTQ+ communities.

Both cases, as well as the broader context discussed in this chapter, demonstrate that gender and sexuality are among the central concerns of the Russian government and are critically involved in contemporary Russian political dynamics. Even though specific circumstances vary, and every new issue appears to require novelty and reframing, symbolic matters such as questions of gender and sexuality underpin the legitimacy of power and are utilized to shore up the stability of the incumbent order.

DISCUSSION QUESTIONS

1. What role have gender and sexuality played in Soviet and post-Soviet politics?
2. What can studying gender and sexuality teach us about symbolic politics?
3. What is the status of women in Russian politics, and what obstacles do they face?
4. What can the case of Russian LGBTQ+ communities tell us about the complexity of gay visibility politics?
5. How can LGBTQ+ rights be instrumentalized in domestic and international politics?

REFERENCES

Alarcon, Norma, Caren Kaplan, and Minoo Moallem (eds.). 1999. *Between Woman and Nation: Nationalisms, Transnational Feminisms, and the State.* Durham, NC: Duke University Press.

Alexander, Rustam. 2018. "Soviet Legal and Criminological Debates on the Decriminalization of Homosexuality (1965–1975)." *Slavic Review*, 77(1), 30–52.

Altman, Dennis, and Jonathan Symons. 2016. *Queer Wars: The New Global Polarization over Gay Rights.* Cambridge: Polity.

Barchunova, Tatiana. 2010. "Shift-F2: Female-to-Female Intimacy Offline and Online (Krasnoiarsk and Novosibirsk Cases)." *Anthropology of East Europe Review*, 28(2), 242–70.

BBC Russia. 2012. "Opros. Bol'shinstvo rossiian – za zapret gei-propagandi," April 19, www.bbc.com/russian/russia/2012/04/120419_vtsiom_gay_law_moscow.
    2019. "Pochti polovina rossiian za ravnye prava dlia LGBT. No bol'shinstvo geev ne liubit," May 23, www.bbc.com/russian/news-48378460.

Borenstein, Eliot. 2008. *Overkill: Sex and Violence in Contemporary Russian Popular Culture.* Ithaca: Cornell University Press.

Brock, Maria, and Emil Edenborg. 2020. "'You Cannot Oppress Those Who Do Not Exist': Gay Persecution in Chechnya and the Politics of In/Visibility." *GLQ: A Journal of Lesbian and Gay Studies*, 26(4), 673–700.

Burridge, Joseph. 2004. "'I Am Not Homophobic But . . . ': Disclaiming in Discourse Resisting Repeal of Section 28." *Sexualities*, 7(3), 327–44.

Clément, Karine, and Anna Zhelnina. 2020. "Introduction to the Special Issue: Imagining a Link between Local Activism and Political Transformation: Inventions from Russia and Eastern Europe." *International Journal of Politics, Culture, and Society*, 33(2), 117–24.

Connell, Raewyn W., and James W. Messerschmidt. 2005. "Hegemonic Masculinity: Rethinking the Concept." *Gender and Society*, 19(6), 829–59.

Edenborg, Emil. 2017. *Politics of Visibility and Belonging: From Russia's "Homosexual Propaganda" Laws to the Ukraine War*. London: Routledge.

Essig, Laurie. 1999. *Queer in Russia: A Story of Sex, Self, and the Other*. Durham, NC: Duke University Press.

Essig, Laurie, and Alexander Kondakov. 2019. "A Cold War for the Twenty-First Century: Homosexualism vs. Heterosexualism." In Richard C. M. Mole (ed.), *Soviet and Post-Soviet Sexualities*, pp. 79–102. London: Routledge.

Fedorovich, Ivan, Yuri Yoursky, and Vitalii Djuma. 2020. *Permit, Do Not Prohibit: How Laws on the Prohibition of "Gay Propaganda" Operate in the Russian Federation*. Tallinn: ECOM, https://ecom.ngo/wp-content/uploads/2020/09/ECOM_LAW_en_a4.pdf.

Fisher, Max. 2022. "Putin's Case for War, Annotated." *New York Times*, February 24, www.nytimes.com/2022/02/24/world/europe/putin-ukraine-speech.html.

Gapova, Elena. 2022. "The Russian Revolution and Women's Liberation: Rethinking the Legacy of the Socialist Emancipation Project." In Katalin Fábián, Janet Elise Johnson, and Mara Lazda (eds.), *The Routledge Handbook of Gender in Central-Eastern Europe and Eurasia*, pp. 115–22. London: Routledge.

Gradskova, Yulia. 2020. "Personal Is Not Political? The Sexual Self in Russian Talk Shows of the 1990s." *Sexuality and Culture*, 24, 389–407.

Healey, Dan. 2001. *Homosexual Desire in Revolutionary Russia: The Regulation of Sexual and Gender Dissent*. Chicago: University of Chicago Press.

2017. *Russian Homophobia from Stalin to Sochi*. London: Bloomsbury Academic.

Johnson, Janet Elise. 2009. *Gender Violence in Russia: The Politics of Feminist Intervention*. Bloomington: Indiana University Press.

2014. "Pussy Riot as a Feminist Project: Russia's Gendered Informal Politics." *Nationalities Papers* 42 (4): 583–90.

2018. *The Gender of Informal Politics*. Cham: Springer.

Johnson, Janet Elise, and Alexandra Novitskaya. 2022. "Gender and Politics." In Darrell Slider (ed.), *Putin's Russia: Past Imperfect, Future Uncertain*, 8th ed. Lanham, MD: Rowman & Littlefield.

Johnson, Janet Elise, Alexandra Novitskaya, Valerie Sperling, and Lisa McIntosh Sundstrom. 2021. "Mixed Signals: What Putin Says about Gender Equality." *Post-Soviet Affairs*, 37(6), 507–25.

Kirill, Patriarch. 2022. "Patriarshaia propoved' v nedeliu syropustnuiu posle liturgii v Khrame Khrista Spasitielia." March 6, www.patriarchia.ru/db/text/5906442.html.

Kochetkov, Igor, and Ksenia Kirichenko. 2009. *Polozhenie lesbiianok, geev, biseksualov, transgenderov v Rossiiskoi Federatsii*. Moscow: Russian LGBT Network.

Kon, Igor. 2006. *Liki i maski odnopoloi liubvi. Lunnyi svet na zare.* Moscow: AST.

Kondakov, Alexander. 2013. "Resisting the Silence: The Use of Tolerance and Equality Arguments by Gay and Lesbian Activist Groups in Russia." *Canadian Journal of Law and Society/La Revue Canadienne Droit et Société*, 28(3), 403–24.

2019. "Rethinking the Sexual Citizenship from Queer and Post-Soviet Perspectives: Queer Urban Spaces and the Right to the Socialist City." *Sexualities*, 22(3), 407–17.

2021a. "Challenging the Logic of Progressive Timeline: Queering LGBT Successes and Failures in Ireland and Russia." *Sexualities* (online).

2021b. "The Influence of the 'Gay-Propaganda' Law on Violence against LGBTIQ People in Russia: Evidence from Criminal Court Rulings." *European Journal of Criminology*, 18(6), 940–59.

2022. "Non-Traditional Sexual Relationships: Law, Forgetting and the Conservative Political Discourse in Russia." In K. Miklóssy and M. Kangaspuro (eds.), *Conservatism and Memory Politics in Russia and Eastern Europe*, pp. 45–61. London: Routledge.

Lamekhov, Denis. 2021. "Khabarovskii sud otmenil reshenie o zaprete pablika khudozhnitsi Iulii Tsvetkovoi 'Monologi Vagini.'" *Daily Afisha*, October 28, https://daily.afisha.ru/news/56131-habarovskiy-sud-otmenil-reshenie-o-zaprete-pablika-hudozhnicy-yulii-cvetkovoy-monologi-vaginy/.

Levada Center. 2013. "Strakh drugogo. Problema gomofobii v Rossii." March 12, www.levada.ru/2013/03/12/strah-drugogo-problema-gomofobii-v-rossii/.

Muravyeva, Marianna. 2014. "Traditional Values and Modern Families: Legal Understanding of Tradition and Modernity in Contemporary Russia." *Journal of Social Policy Studies*, 12(4), 625–38.

2021. "Domestic Violence Legislation in Russia: Campaigning for Change." In Beatriz Garcia Nice, Anya Prusa, and Olivia Soledad (eds.), *Pathways to Justice: Gender-Based Violence and the Rule of Law*, pp. 1–18. Washington, DC: Woodrow Wilson International Center for Scholars.

Naiman, Eric. 1997. *Sex in Public: The Incarnation of Early Soviet Ideology.* Princeton: Princeton University Press.

Nartova, Nadia. 2004. "Lesbiiskiie sem'i. Real'nost' za stenoi molchaniia." In Sergei Ushakov (ed.), *Semeiniye uzy. Model dlia zborki*, pp. 292–315. Moscow: Novoie Literaturnoie Obozreniie.

Novitskaya, Alexandra. 2017. "Patriotism, Sentiment, and Male Hysteria: Putin's Masculinity Politics and the Persecution of Non-Heterosexual Russians." *NORMA: International Journal for Masculinity Studies*, 12(3–4), 302–18.

2021. "Sexual Citizens in Exile: State-Sponsored Homophobia and Post-Soviet LGBTQI+ Migration." *Russian Review*, 80(1), 56–76.

Plakhov, Andrei. 1993. "No Sex in the USSR." In Martha Gever, Pratibha Parmar, and John Greyson (eds.), *Queer Looks: Perspectives on Lesbian and Gay Film and Video*, pp. 177–85. New York: Routledge.

Pronkina, Yelena. 2016. "Osobennosti LGBT-diskursov rossiiskikh media, initsiirovannogo diskussiiami o regulirovanii seksual'nosti." *Journal of Social Policy Studies*, 14(1), 71–86.

Racioppi, Linda. 1995. "Organizing Women before and after the Fall: Women's Politics in the Soviet Union and Post-Soviet Russia." *Signs: Journal of Women in Culture and Society*, 20(4), 818–50.

Riabov, Oleg, and Tatiana Riabova. 2014. "The Remasculinization of Russia? Gender, Nationalism, and the Legitimation of Power under Vladimir Putin." *Problems of Post-Communism*, 61(2), 23–35.

Rivina, Anna. 2021. "Domestic Violence in Russia: Existing and Proposed Legislation." In Beatriz Garcia Nice, Anya Prusa, and Olivia Soledad (eds.), *Pathways to Justice: Gender-Based Violence and the Rule of Law*, pp. 170–73. Washington, DC: Woodrow Wilson International Center for Scholars, www.wilsoncenter.org/publication/pathways-justice-gender-based-violence-and-rule-law.

Sarajeva, Katja. 2011. *Lesbian Lives: Sexuality, Space and Subculture in Moscow*. Stockholm: Acta Universitatis Stockholmiensis.

Shnirelman, Victor. 2019. "Russian Neoconservatism and Apocalyptic Imperialism." In Mikhail Suslov and Dmitry Uzlaner (eds.), *Contemporary Russian Conservatism: Problems, Paradoxes and Dangers*, pp. 347–78. Brill: Leiden.

Soboleva, Irina V., and Yaroslav A. Bakhmetjev. 2015. "Political Awareness and Self-Blame in the Explanatory Narratives of LGBT People amid the Anti-LGBT Campaign in Russia." *Sexuality and Culture*, 19(2), 275–96.

Sozaev, Valerii. 2010. "LGBT-dvizhenie v Rossii. Portret v inter'iere." *Gendernie issledovaniia* (20–21), 90–126.

Sperling, Valerie. 2015. *Sex, Politics, and Putin: Political Legitimacy in Russia*. Oxford: Oxford University Press.

Sperling, Valerie. and Lisa McIntosh Sundstrom. 2021. "New and Enduring Forms of Feminist Activism in Contemporary Russia." NYU Jordan Center (blog), October 15, https://jordanrussiacenter.org/news/new-and-enduring-forms-of-feminist-activism-in-contemporary-russia/.

Stella, Francesca. 2015. *Lesbian Lives in Soviet and Post-Soviet Russia: Post/Socialism and Gendered Sexualities*. Basingstoke: Palgrave Macmillan.

Stoeckl, Kristina. 2020. "The Rise of the Russian Christian Right: The Case of the World Congress of Families." *Religion, State and Society*, 48(4), 223–38.

Stolyarova, Galina. 2008. "Matviyenko: Battle Ready." *Transitions Online*, May 27, www.ceeol.com/search/article-detail?id=81329.

Utkin, Roman. 2021. "Introduction." *Russian Review*, 80(1), 7–16.

Utrata, Jennifer. 2015. *Women without Men: Single Mothers and Family Change in the New Russia*. Ithaca: Cornell University Press.

Valodzin, Uladzimir. 2020. *Criminal Prosecution of Homosexuals in the Soviet Union (1946-1991): Numbers and Discourses*. EUI Working Paper. Florence: European University Institute.

Vasiakina, Oksana, Dmitrii Kozlov, and Sasha Talaver. 2020. *Feministskii samizdat. 40 let spustia*. Moscow: Common Place.

Weber, Cynthia. 1994. "Something's Missing: Male Hysteria and the US Invasion of Panama." *Gender Journal*, 19, www.academia.edu/26889809/Somethings_Missing_Male_Hysteria_and_the_U.S._Invasion_of_Panama.

Wilkinson, Cai. 2014. "Putting 'Traditional Values' into Practice: The Rise and Contestation of Anti-Homopropaganda Laws in Russia." *Journal of Human Rights*, 13(3), 363–79.

2020. "LGBT Rights in the Former Soviet Union: The Evolution of Hypervisibility." In Michael J. Bosia, Sandra M. McEvoy, and Momin Rahman (eds.), *The Oxford Handbook of Global LGBT and Sexual Diversity Politics*, pp. 233–49. New York: Oxford University Press.

Yuval-Davis, Nira. 1997. "Gender and Nation." In Linda McDowell and Joanne P. Sharp (eds.), *Space, Gender, Knowledge: Feminist Readings*, pp. 403–07. London: Routledge.

Zakharova, Svetlana. 2013. *Gendering Soviet Dissent: How and Why the Woman Question Was Excluded from the Agenda of Soviet Dissidents (1964–1982)*. Budapest: Central European University.

Zdravomyslova, Elena, and Anna Temkina. 2005. "Gendered Citizenship in Soviet and Post-Soviet Societies." In Vera Tolz and Stephanie Booth (eds.), *Nation and Gender in Contemporary Europe*, pp. 96–115. Manchester: Manchester University Press.

8 | The Foreign Policy of an Aspiring Great Power

ANDREI P. TSYGANKOV

Fig. 8.1 President Vladimir Putin heads a Security Council meeting at the Kremlin in Moscow on April 11, 2008. Credit: Dmitry Astakhov / Stringer / AFP / Getty Images.

[I]nternational relations today are too complex a mechanism to be managed from one center. This is vividly borne out by the outcome of American interference: There is essentially no longer a state in Libya; Iraq is balancing on the verge of disintegration; and so on. Problems in the modern world can be solved effectively only through serious and fair cooperation between leading states and their associations in the interests of common tasks. Such cooperation should consider the multivariate nature of the modern world, its cultural and civilizational diversity, and reflect the interests of key components of the international community.

Sergei Lavrov, "Razmyshleniia"

Abstract

Following the breakup of the Soviet Union, Russia has aspired to remain a major power in international relations. The status of "great power" has remained essential to Russia even after end of the period of Soviet grandeur and the post-Soviet transition. Until the mid-2000s, the country's leaders sought to revive its great power status in partnership with Western nations. Since the mid-2000s, Russia has moved in the direction of challenging Western global priorities by stressing values of national sovereignty and patriotism. More recently, Russia has sought to establish areas of mutual noninterference in relations with the West. In 2022, this approach resulted in Russia's invasion of Ukraine and the escalation of tensions and confrontation with the United States and NATO. Outside the West, Moscow has aspired to take advantage of global economic and geopolitical opportunities including in Asia, Africa, the Middle East, and Latin America. The chapter reviews the main developments in Russian foreign policy since 1991, giving an overview of the country's relations with Western and non-Western countries, while focusing on recent years. Studying Russian foreign policy in general, and historical and contemporary goals in particular, is important for both policy-relevant and theoretical reasons. This chapter addresses these goals as well as policy choices following the dissolution of the USSR and discusses both realist and liberal explanations of Russian foreign policy and its limitations. Finally, this analysis will help formulate a framework to assess Russia's ambition to become a major power in international relations in the future.

8.1 Introduction

Following the dissolution of the Soviet Union, Russia has aspired to remain a major power in international relations. Moscow has increasingly challenged the Western nations to accept Russia's special role in European, Eurasian, and Middle Eastern affairs by demonstrating strong military and diplomatic skills and by developing a partnership with China and other non-Western powers. Moscow assumes that, as a **great power,** Russia has a right to shape the security environment in more than one region in accordance with its interests. The first post-Soviet decade taught Russian leaders that the West is prepared to accept the Russian Federation as a junior partner, but not as a major power with a distinctive and legitimate system of values and interests in the world. When faced with the choice between closer ties and collaboration with the West and **great power status,** Russia has historically opted for the latter. The post-Soviet years have generally confirmed this rule. Except for a brief period in the early 1990s, Russia has not been prepared to sacrifice its great power status for special relations with Western nations.

Identity as a great power has remained essential to Russia throughout the three decades of the post-Soviet transition. Since the mid-2000s Russia has moved in the direction of challenging Western global priorities by stressing values of national sovereignty and patriotism. The Russian parliament passed laws and implemented policies designed to marginalize pro-Western opposition and limit the West's political and financial influence in the country. Over the past several years, Russia has gone further in adopting a defensive approach in relations with the West by seeking to establish clear "**red lines**" or areas of mutual noninterference and issues of limited cooperation. The US–Russia summit of June 2021 has been indicative of both sides' awareness of the danger of continued confrontation and escalation of relations. However, in 2022, such a confrontation occurred following Russia's demands of **security guarantees** from the West and the invasion of Ukraine. Outside the West, Moscow has aspired to take advantage of global economic and geopolitical opportunities including in Asia, Africa, the Middle East, and Latin America.

The chapter reviews the main developments in **Russian foreign policy** since 1991, focusing on recent years and selected regional directions. After addressing the significance of studying the country's foreign policy, I review its historical and contemporary goals as well as policy choices following the dissolution of the Soviet Union. Moscow is aware that even as a major power Russia remains vulnerable in several areas and must be selective in its goals and means abroad. Because of the West's global prominence, Russia's relations with the United States and European countries remain critically important. The chapter also shows that strengthening bilateral and multilateral ties outside the West is increasingly central to Russian foreign policy and discusses what this means for relations in Eurasia, the Middle East, and Asia. What we can expect for the future of Russian policy is that in the near term it will be greatly affected by US–China relations, the security situation in Eurasia and Europe, and the US approach to building ties with Moscow. The final section reflects on expectations of Russian foreign policy in the future and prospects for the country's development as a major power in international relations. I identify three possible scenarios – the status quo, destabilization, and increased cooperation between major powers.

8.2   The Significance of Studying Russian Foreign Policy

Studying Russian foreign policy is both policy-relevant and theoretically important. The first reason to devote attention to Russia's external relations concerns the country's significance: Given its determination and resilience as a major international power, Russia is essential to understanding current and potential developments in world politics. It has been an important contributor to the global transition from the US-centered unipolar world to a more diverse and multipolar organization of the international system. Over the past fifteen years, Russia has recovered its capabilities as a major power, built strong relations with China, capitalized on its diplomatic and military skills in Eurasia and the Middle East, and demonstrated to Western nations the importance of engaging Moscow in dialogue and mutually acceptable cooperation. In fact, Russia has demonstrated exceptional resilience and determination to remain an important player in international affairs, even as major crises – including the economic breakdown during the 1990s, the collapse of oil prices in 2008 and 2015, and COVID-19 in 2020 – have threatened to expose fragilities in its economy.

Western sanctions for the annexation of Crimea, support for separatism in the Donbas, interference in Western politics and cyberspace, and human rights violations inside Russia have not altered the country's foreign policy. While experiencing economic difficulties, Russia has remained actively engaged abroad. Against the commonly articulated expectations of Russia's reduced international ambitions, Moscow did not principally change its assertive approach in Eurasia (Ukraine) and the Middle East (Syria). In 2022, Russia went as far as to intervene militarily in Ukraine despite unprecedented economic sanctions and political pressures by the West. What is likely to matter and affect international relations is how the country's leadership engages with international affairs and to what extent it is prepared to cooperate with other members of the international system.

A second reason to devote close attention to Russian foreign policy is theoretical and concerns the analysis of domestic/foreign interrelations and the role of domestic politics in the formation of international policy, particularly in non-Western settings. Scholars of foreign policy lack a thorough understanding of policy formation in this context and are frequently guided by flawed theories and assumptions. Western analysts have tended to assume that a nondemocratic Russia will necessarily engage in belligerent and anti-Western international politics, while a democratic Russia will advance a cooperative policy toward the West. There is the tendency to assume that regime considerations are the drivers of foreign policy and that an "autocratic" Russia is mostly concerned with propping up dictators in the face of popular uprisings and democratic developments. Such analysis is not always incorrect, yet it misses important sources of Russian foreign policy, including its national values and geopolitical conditions.

In reality, a democratic Russia has not always been cooperative, while a nondemocratic Russia has occasionally displayed a willingness to strengthen relations with the United States and European countries (Gunitsky and Tsygankov 2018). The structure of Russia's values and politicoeconomic interests is quite different from those of Western nations. Yet this does not mean that Russia will necessarily act to undermine the West in international politics. It merits our attention if we are to understand

Russia's internal dynamics and policy directions. Knowledge of these processes will also contribute – by way of comparison with countries outside Russia – to our understanding of foreign policy in general. In addition to learning about foreign policy by studying its domestic politics, we can gain knowledge of domestic processes by analyzing changes in the country's international behavior. More or less active Russian foreign policy can be indicative of the leadership's confidence or lack thereof with respect to the country's economic and political foundations.

Finally, in the world of great power rivalry and a rapidly evolving international system, Russia presents an interesting puzzle. Moscow continues to speak and act as a great power despite the relative weakness of the country's economic and demographic capabilities. Since the 2010s, Russia has built an impressive military capacity, including in areas such as hypersonic and nuclear weapons, information and cyberwarfare, and air defense. Moscow has also projected its power beyond the Eurasian region by intervening in Syria and using its information and cyber capabilities to influence domestic politics in Western countries. These developments have surprised scholars and politicians, puzzling those who, like President Joseph Biden (2021), believe that Russian foreign policy exceeds the country's true capacity and therefore is not sustainable. For example, in July 2021, he stated that Russia's President **Vladimir Putin** "has a real problem" because "he's sitting on top of an economy that has nuclear weapons and oil wells and nothing else" (Biden 2021). Biden, like many other American politicians, has a long record of underestimating Russia's international capabilities, a propensity that is at the root of many problems in US–Russia relations.

8.3 Goals, Power, and the Military

Russia's foreign policy goals have evolved throughout history depending on the ambitions of the country's rulers and its relations with the outside world. Ever since the Turkish conquest of Byzantium in the fifteenth century, Russia has emerged as the stronghold of Eastern Christianity well aware of and insistent on its cultural distinctiveness. The country's religious tradition has differed from both that of Catholic Rome, on the one hand, and from those of non-Christian nations, on the other. The intense interaction with European countries has placed Russia within the larger European civilizational context, yet it also reinforced its distinct identity. Russia is a non-Catholic Christian nation, a large territorial polity with a strongly centralized state that borders Europe, Asia, and the Middle East. Its expansive territory and geographical location between West and East have also mattered greatly. With a vast territory, and as a land-based transcontinental empire, Russia has had to defend its sovereignty and security from powerful neighbors aspiring to exploit its wealth, territory, and geopolitical location.

These historical and geographical preconditions have formed a continuity in Russian foreign policy goals. Traditionally, these goals prioritized national security, sovereignty, and great power status. The achievement of these goals has depended on the country's ability to balance ambitions of other major powers including by preserving sufficient influence over its neighboring territories. The country's leaders have relied on diverse means of exerting such influence including economic sanctions and mobilization of soft power.

These considerations informed Russian foreign policy both before and after the Soviet dissolution. The Soviet Union's domestic politics and its international relations were deeply shaped by its ideological nature and global political ambitions. The Soviet Union presented a global alternative to Western capitalism, one that charted a new direction and was far more ambitious than traditional Russian foreign policy goals. The Soviet state and Western nations cooperated in defeating the Nazis in World War II but this alliance broke down soon after the war. During much of the Cold War, the two great powers sought to contain each other and their respective spheres of influence across Latin America, Africa, and Asia. The Soviet Union and the United States were engaged in an existential ideological conflict and could not agree on the ground rules and principles of the international system, despite the two systems' attempts to cooperate in the area of arms control during the 1960s and 1970s and a tacit agreement over some spheres of influence following World War II. After the collapse of the USSR in 1991, Russia abandoned Soviet ideological ambitions, while remaining committed to the preservation of great power status and aiming to restore its traditional influence in international affairs.

Each state has in its possession certain powers and resources to ensure the implementation of foreign policy goals. Russia's means to ensure the stated goals and great power status have been more limited since the disintegration of the Soviet Union. The country lost one-sixth of its territory, and the state was weakened to the point that some observers at one point called it a "failed state" (Willerton, Beznosov, and Carrier 2005). The economy also greatly suffered and, in a world of international competition and Western sanctions, it remains a point of vulnerability. Russia's economy has been declining in constant prices since 2015 (Russia Matters 2021), following Moscow's annexation of Crimea.

Over the past fifteen years, Russia has recovered and developed important tools to protect its interests. Such tools include energy, military power, nuclear and cyber capabilities, diplomacy, cultural/historical capital, and technological expertise. While Russia may not be comparable to the West in some areas, it is strong in other areas and capable of protecting its national sovereignty, securing its national borders, and maintaining its geopolitical influence in Europe and Eurasia (for assessments of Russia's power, see Kofman 2020; Saradzhyan and Abduallaev 2021; Stoner 2021).

The military has been especially important for Russia's ambitious foreign policy. Driven by the need to have a sufficient defense, Russia is no longer committed to the Soviet-like objectives of achieving parity with Western armies: It spends less than 3 percent of its GDP on the military. Since the mid-2000s, Russia has reformed its military to address the perceived gaps in the country's security and status relative to other major powers. The main sources of the reform included the army's less-than-smooth performance during the five-day conflict with Georgia in August 2008 (Renz 2018) and the need to respond to Western policies and technological developments. The latter included the United States' decision to abandon the Anti-Ballistic Missile Treaty, which was negotiated during the Cold War and which Russia considers the cornerstone of strategic stability. By withdrawing from the treaty in December 2001, the US leadership opted for the development of a global missile-defense system (MDS).

Responding to this US policy, Russia developed new hypersonic weapons capable of penetrating the MDS, including the hypersonic nuclear cruise missile Kinzhal and hypersonic intercontinental ballistic missile (ICBM) Avangard. While announcing these developments in his annual address to the Federal Assembly, Putin (2018) also presented the new heavy ICBM, Sarmat, designed to replace the older version, known as Voevoda or the SS-18 Satan. In addition to Russia's own nuclear build-up, Moscow cooperates with Beijing in opposing the US development of MDS (Macias 2018).

The other area of Western policy concerned the expansion of the North Atlantic Treaty Organization (NATO) toward Russian borders by gradually extending membership in the alliance to neighbors of Russia, thereby making it more vulnerable from a security standpoint. Following Moscow's role in annexing Crimea and supporting east Ukrainian separatism, the West imposed sanctions against the Russian economy and took steps to strengthen NATO and Western preparations against Russia's potential aggression. The alliance has conducted massive military exercises in Eastern Europe, the Baltic states, and the Black Sea. NATO also established a High Readiness Joint Task Force and moved several battalions to Poland and the Baltic states, while NATO members have actively armed and trained the Ukrainian military.

Moscow has responded by conducting its own exercises and preparing for potential aggression by NATO or provocations by Ukraine against Russia-supported areas in the Donbas. In 2021, Russia's confidence in its military prompted the Kremlin to challenge the West's policy of NATO expansion and military support for Ukraine. On December 17, 2021, the Kremlin made public its proposals to ensure guarantees for national security. The published documents included a demand to stop the expansion of the Western alliance, revoke promises of its future membership for Ukraine and Georgia, cease military cooperation with countries of the former Soviet region, and commit not to station nuclear weapons in Europe. Russia announced that it would respond by using force if the West ignores the Kremlin's proposals (*Moscow Times* 2021). On February 24, 2022, following two months of diplomatic negotiations with the West, Russia launched a military intervention in Ukraine. Putin justified his decision by the need to protect the security of Russia and the people of the Donbas from NATO and Ukraine's militarism and "Nazism" (Bloomberg 2022).

Because of the military reform, exercises, and combat participation, the Russian Army has emerged as one of the most competent in the world. The military has built new skills and competencies including a rapid reaction force, a sophisticated air defense system, hypersonic weapons, and others. In addition to conducting regular military exercises on land and sea in various parts of the world, Russia has tested some of its newly acquired skills and weapons in battle in Syria, Africa, and Ukraine. For example, the Crimea annexation took place with the involvement of specially trained forces who secured the peninsula's territory and arrested opposing Ukrainian officers without a single shot being fired. Russian airpower was applied in Syria, where Moscow refrained from deploying ground troops and launched thousands of airstrikes, hitting groups of anti-Damascus militants, command points, oil fields, and other targets. Russia also used the advanced S-400 air defense system and deployed Iskander ballistic missiles, all of which proved sufficient for accomplishing important victories on the ground. In Africa, Russia relied on semi-private organizations, such as the Wagner Group, to work with interested governments and enhance Russia's influence on the continent.

8.4   Stability and Change

Since 1991, the Russian Federation has gone through at least two important periods in relations with the outside world. This section reviews these periods and proposes an explanation of the changes by stressing the role of ideas and perception of national interests by the Russian leadership. This explanation is consistent with the constructivist theory that focuses on cultural identity and perceptions in international relations. The leaders' ideas/beliefs and perceptions ranged from more liberal and pro-Western to those favoring sovereignty and independence. In theoretical debates of international relations, there are also explanations that highlight the importance of power and the domestic political system/regime in the formation of foreign policy. Each of these explanations is insufficient to account for the change in Russian foreign policy.

Until the mid-2000s, the country sought to revive its status as a responsible major power in partnership with Western nations. Both **Boris Yeltsin** and Vladimir Putin aimed to develop strong relations with the West, albeit from different foundations. Yeltsin wanted Russia to join the community of Western nations by rebuilding domestic institutions and aligning the country's foreign policy with those of the United States and European nations. This vision runs into difficulties in its implementation. Western nations grew critical of Russia's domestic policies in Chechnya and elsewhere and did not accept Moscow's definition of the country's international interests. The contemporary political leadership in the Kremlin no longer aims to bring Russia's political system closer to Western standards. Putin's idea of a state is quite different from that of Yeltsin, although scholars have noted that Putin's political system is partly built on policies and political practices left over from Yeltsin's years (Shevtsova 2007; Wood 2020). Partly because of a deepening disagreement with the West in foreign policy, Russia has increasingly diverged from Western nations in organizing domestic political order.

Putin's beliefs and worldview have made convergence between Russian and Western political institutions ever more difficult. In foreign policy, his vision stressed the need to cooperate with the West based on the common threat of global terrorism, rather than on common values. Like Yeltsin, Putin aspired to be recognized by the West, but as a distinct geopolitical actor rather than a democratic partner. Even before Putin's rise to power, he proclaimed, "Russia will not become a second edition of, say, the United States or Britain, where liberal values have deep historic traditions. Our state and its institutions and structures have always played an exceptionally important role in the life of the country and its people. For Russians, a strong state is not an anomaly to be gotten rid of. Quite the contrary, it is a source of order and the main driving force of any change" (Putin 1999).

Since the mid-2000s, Russia has increasingly relied on its own power to achieve its goals. Its foreign policy has become more assertive and proceeded from an understanding that the West is a rival and competitor, rather than a partner. By the 1990s, Russia's second foreign minister, Yevgeny Primakov, had already adopted this view of Western nations, especially the United States, and proposed that Russia build a strategic axis with China and India to counterbalance the West. However, operating from internally weak foundations and under US global dominance, Russia was in no position to act on Primakov's recommendations. By the mid-2000s, the Russian economy had greatly improved – partly because of the sharply increased world prices for oil and the completion of economic reforms during the 1990s. The Kremlin also modernized the military. With the exception of the 2009–11 period – the years of a young and relatively pro-Western president **Dmitry Medvedev** – Russia has sought to achieve its international goals by challenging the positions of Western nations in Europe, Eurasia, and the Middle East. The Ukraine crisis of 2014 and Russia's annexation of Crimea was a defining moment in the conflict between Russia and the West, resulting in a new level of Russia's alienation from Europe and the United States.

In domestic affairs, Putin has worked to marginalize opposition to his rule by building a party-dominant political system with the power to pass laws in the State

Duma. By exploiting the system, the Russian government has sought to undermine the influence of the West inside the country and built what has become known as a "sovereign democracy." The deputy head of the Presidential Administration, Vladislav Surkov, introduced the term to provide ideological support for Putin's vision. Other chapters in this book expand on how the system has evolved by increasing the political power of the Kremlin at the expense of the West-connected nongovernmental organizations and civil society (see Chapters 2 and 18). Putin's power has become further consolidated following international crises and foreign policy interventions, such as those in Georgia in 2008, Ukraine in 2014, Syria in 2015, and Ukraine in 2022.

There are at least two competing explanations for the identified shift in Russian foreign policy. Realist theories tend to stress the country's preoccupation with having the security and capabilities of a great power, as well as the West's insensitive reaction to the Kremlin's concerns. John Mearsheimer and others have attributed Russia's assertive foreign policy to the expansion of Western economic, political, and military infrastructure in Europe and Eurasia. In Mearsheimer's (2014) words, "the United States and its European allies share most of the responsibility for the crisis. The taproot of the trouble is NATO enlargement, the central element of a larger strategy to move Ukraine out of Russia's orbit and integrate it into the West." Realists are correct to highlight Moscow's security concerns, yet they underestimate Russia's readiness to cooperate with the West based on shared economic interests and pan-European identity. Medvedev's term, for example, demonstrated the potential for Russia–West cooperation. The two sides made progress in political and economic relations while continuing to disagree on important security issues. Russia and the United States signed and ratified the New START (Strategic Arms Reduction Treaty), limiting the number of nuclear missiles to 1,500 and banning their delivery in outer space. Russia and Western nations cooperated on stabilizing Afghanistan and controlling the Iranian nuclear program. Russia has also joined the World Trade Organization. In addition, Medvedev proposed a new pan-European security treaty, although Western countries did not reciprocate, being satisfied with the NATO-centered security structure.

Liberal scholars trace Moscow's assertive foreign policy to Putin's "authoritarian" instincts and his political regime's "autocratic" nature (McFaul 2020). Liberals are correct to identify possible links between domestic political vulnerabilities and the tendency to use force in foreign policy as a way of diverting public attention away from pressing problems at home. However, such explanations are difficult to support with facts. One can claim – with at least the same plausibility – that Russia's political system does not have to rely on aggressive foreign policy for internal stability. Even if the liberal logic works, it may apply to both "autocratic" and democratic political systems. It also cannot work as a consistent method to ensure regime stability beyond the short-term perspective. Indeed, in the medium term, an aggressive foreign policy can seriously undermine regime stability.

Moreover, liberal explanations misunderstand the nature of Russia's political system. Even though it differs from a Western-style system, scholars of Russia's internal politics often identify various informal checks and balances that constrain Putin. These scholars define the system as a hybrid or semi-authoritarian regime (Robertson 2011; Flikke 2017), implying that the country's system is hardly a dictatorship in terms of power distribution. Nor is the system necessarily confrontational to the West in foreign policy. The autocracy-centered explanations, therefore, have difficulties explaining Medvedev's attempts at rapprochement with the West. After all, Putin remained the major power-broker acting in Medvedev's shadow.

Finally, liberals tend to dismiss Russia's security concerns as driven by its search for status and Western recognition. For example, they rarely seriously consider the process of NATO expansion as a key reason for Russia's annexation of Crimea and assertive foreign policy (McFaul 2014). However, the rise of Russia's security class in domestic and foreign politics – the so-called *siloviki* – has resulted not only from domestic but also from international sources. The *siloviki* constitute a powerful group within the political establishment, who are mobilized and empowered by the Kremlin each time Western nations deny the country recognition of its status and security interests (Tsygankov 2022).

Realist and liberal explanations are therefore incomplete and partially incorrect. They each point to a limited number of factors shaping Russian foreign policy, thereby refusing to recognize its complexity. Security, power, and the political system, as stressed by realists and liberals, each play a role in the formation of foreign policy, yet none of them can serve as the decisive influence. Depending on state perception of potential gains from cooperating with the West, Russian leaders can advance distinct definitions of national interests.

8.5   Relations with the West

Russia's contemporary relations with Western nations – defined largely as the United States and Western Europe – are best described as an **asymmetric rivalry** (Tsygankov 2019). "Rivalry" indicates the two sides' principal conflict over the nature of the international system and emerging new world order, as well as their determination to challenge each other's position by available means short of a military conflict. "Rivalry" implies an adversarial type of relation. It rises above the level of interstate competition while not reaching the level of (cold) war. The two sides are prepared to engage in a military confrontation in terms of their capacity, yet each side wants to avoid such an outcome and is prepared to cooperate on a limited number of issues that do not define the nature of the international system. The rivalry between Russia and the West is "asymmetric" in the sense that Russia's overall power does not match that of Western nations, yet it is sufficient to ensure the country's security and considerable global influence.

The list of important disagreements between Russia and the United States includes arms control, the US missile defense system in Europe, the expansion of NATO, the militarization of outer space, routes of energy transportation, cybersecurity, and others. These disagreements have been accumulating since the 1990s, and none has been fully resolved. Relations between Russia and the West reached a low point following Putin's return to the presidency in 2012 as well as, especially, following the Euromaidan Revolution in Ukraine in 2013–14 and Russia's invasion of Ukraine in 2022. Blaming the United States for the revolution and change of power in Kyiv, Russia annexed Crimea and provided support for separatists in eastern Ukraine (the Donbas). In 2022, the Kremlin demanded that the West exclude Ukraine from any considerations for future membership in NATO and pressured Kyiv to accept the Minsk Protocol by granting the Donbas regional autonomy. Western nations responded to Russia's military interventions by introducing personal and economic sanctions against Russia and by demanding Moscow withdraw its military from Ukraine.

Under the presidency of Donald Trump, Russia has had to deal with polarized decisionmaking in Washington. Trump and Putin developed good personal relations and proceeded from a similar set of beliefs about international politics as shaped by great powers and the art of diplomacy. However, the US establishment treated Trump as an outsider and an exceptionally egocentric and unpredictable politician. His own generals had low confidence in Trump's judgment and were fearful that his decisionmaking might cause international crises. In addition, his own political class largely perceived him as a potential traitor, involved in making secret deals with Putin. As a result, Trump has never been fully accepted in political circles as a legitimate president and could not act on his beliefs. Despite his eagerness to "do business" and "get along" with Russia (New York Times 2020), he only had one meeting with Putin, in Helsinki on July 16, 2018. The meeting took place during Special Counsel Robert Mueller's investigation into Trump's "collusion" with Russia on impeachment charges led by his Democratic opponents. Having established several working groups with Russia, including in the economic and cyber areas, Trump could never accomplish anything of value in bilateral relations with the Kremlin. The fact that allegations about treason and collusion have been proven untrue has not helped to improve US–Russia relations.

Relations with the United States have remained tense following the election of Joseph Biden as the country's president in 2020. The two sides extended START, negotiated during the years of Medvedev and Barack Obama's presidencies, for five years. In January 2021, shortly after his inauguration, Biden called Putin to initiate the renewal of the treaty – a move opposed by Trump, who was aiming for the development of US military superiority including in the area of nuclear weapons. However, beyond this example of strategic cooperation, the two sides have been divided by different interests and opposing political values and have had a long list of disagreements about international security and world order.

The United States–Russia summit conducted on June 16, 2021, had the potential to establish a new framework of relations, in which the countries remain rivals while at the same time pursuing limited cooperation on some issues of mutual importance. The latter could include arms control, cybersecurity, climate, and others. Following the meeting, the two sides have engaged in consultations over cybersecurity and strategic negotiations in Geneva. They have also pledged cooperation in preventing further global warming, including coordinating policies in the Arctic and limiting carbon releases.

The two sides have also inched toward more cooperation and lowered the stakes of their competition in energy markets. In July 2021, Biden signaled his acceptance of Nord Stream 2, a gas pipeline connecting Russia and Germany, extremely important for both countries and nearly complete at that point. Biden promised not to oppose Nord Stream 2 in exchange for German chancellor Angela Merkel's pledge to introduce swift sanctions against Russia should it ever exploit the pipeline for political purposes (Lewis and Shalal 2021). In the fall of 2021, responding to fears of Russia's potential invasion of Ukraine, German officials repeated the promise to introduce tough sanctions and not rely on the pipeline's exploitation. In March 2022, following Russia's invasion of Ukraine, Nord Stream 2 became nonoperational while Western nations imposed a freeze on Russia's foreign currency reserves and imposed severe economic sanctions. They also introduced personal sanctions on the country's **oligarchs** (wealthiest businesspeople) and on many politicians, including Vladimir Putin.

Russia and the United States, therefore, have remained rivals engaged in global political competition. Washington intends to preserve the United States' leadership in the international system, which Moscow does not accept. Jointly with China, Russia argues for a principled change in the global order based on multilateralism, a multipolar balance of power, and diversity in regions and political systems (for the divergence of Russian and US perspectives on the international system, see Tsygankov 2019; Ziegler 2021; Safranchuk and Lukyanov 2021). Following the US military withdrawal from Afghanistan and the emergence of the Taliban regime in the country, Washington has attempted to engage with Moscow on counterterrorism cooperation. Putin, however, has chosen to address the issue through the Shanghai Cooperation Organization (SCO), essentially rejecting American attempts to cooperate in this realm. It remains to be seen whether Russia and the United States can cooperate on preventing Afghanistan from slipping into becoming a renewed source of instability and terrorism in the region.

Similar yet distinct dynamics have characterized relations between Russia and Europe. The difference here is that Russia has had extensive historical ties to Europe and has been economically and politically interdependent with European nations. In its culture and identity, Russia is partly European, which has been reflected in Moscow's desire for mutually advantageous relations, albeit not at the expense of Russia's interests and international status. In 1994, Russia and the EU have signed an agreement on partnership and cooperation, yet over the past decades the differences between the sides have widened. Despite original expectations, they have not liberalized the visa regime and have not established a mutually acceptable framework of multilateral energy cooperation. Nor have they made progress in security relations. Russia has remained mistrustful of activities by the Organization of Security and Co-operation in Europe (OSCE) and NATO. Moscow has also been critical of the European Parliament's political views and preferred to build relations with European countries on a bilateral basis, rather than with the EU as an organization.

In their turn, European countries and the EU have criticized Russia's political system and human rights record, as well as its economic and energy policies. The list of the two sides' disagreements is long and growing. It includes issues such as Russia's annexation of Crimea, intervention in Ukrainian affairs, use of energy for achieving political objectives, interference in European elections, poisoning of the British citizen and former Russian military officer Sergei Skripal on March 4, 2018, supporting Belarus's leader Alexander Lukashenko following his fraudulent reelections as that country's president in August 2020, the poisoning and arrest of opposition leader **Alexei Navalny**, and so on. Since the 2014 Ukraine crisis, the EU has reacted to these developments by introducing various sanctions against Russia and expelling Russian diplomats. The EU has also ceased to conduct regular summit meetings with Moscow, although various European officials have traveled to Russia and have sought to maintain a bilateral dialogue with the Kremlin.

Russia has responded to European pressures by engaging in assertive policies toward those nations in Eastern and Central Europe that have been highly critical of Moscow, while cultivating bilateral relations with governments and political movements interested in strengthening ties with Russia. In particular, Moscow has severed relations with the Baltic states and Poland, but maintained strong contacts with Serbia, Austria, Italy, Hungary, and Slovenia. Russia has also supported various political movements such as France's Front National and the German political party Alternative für Deutschland. The reason for these relations had partly to do with shared goals of challenging the West-centered global order along with protecting Russia's interests and great power status in Europe.

During this period, Moscow preserved relatively strong political and economic relations with France and Germany, despite the latter's criticisms of Russia's human rights record and handling of Ukraine. For example, both countries have criticized

Russia's elections to the State Duma as insufficiently transparent and democratic. Moscow, in turn, has been highly critical of NATO's military activities intended to contain Russia's power in Europe, the Baltic Sea, and the Black Sea. Responding to the Western alliance's annual exercises with the involvement of Ukraine, Georgia, and several other former Soviet nations, Russia has conducted large-scale military drills of its own with the participation of allies including China and members of the Russia-initiated Collective Security Treaty Organization (CSTO).

Since 2020, Russia has worked to bilateralize its relations with European nations further. Following Biden's efforts to revive US transnational ties with Europe and increase political pressures on Russia to comply with Western norms and priorities, Moscow threatened to sever any communication with the EU. During a February 2021 visit to Moscow by the head of the EU's foreign policy Josep Borrell Fontelles, Russian foreign minister Sergei Lavrov refused to discuss any issues concerning Russia's human rights record. The Kremlin also signaled in 2021 that the country was rethinking its membership in the Council of Europe and that Russia intended to limit relations with the EU to those relating to energy supplies and political stability in Ukraine and the wider European continent. Moscow had revoked its membership in the Parliamentary Assembly of the Council of Europe over the threat of intensifying sanctions against the Russian economy. Russia returned to the organization in June 2019 following its invitation and assurances of fair treatment; the country was expelled in March 2022 over its invasion of Ukraine. In December 2021, following the Putin–Biden online summit, Russia initiated a discussion of mutual security guarantees with the United States, rather than European nations (Russian Federation, Ministry of Foreign Affairs 2021). The message from the Kremlin, again, was that it did not see a dialogue with Europeans as sufficient for satisfying Russia's interests.

Following Moscow's invasion of Ukraine in 2022, Russia's already fragile relations with the West suffered an unprecedented blow and are not likely to recover any time soon. Scholars and politicians have raised the specter of a new cold war with the emergence of pronounced economic, political, and social divisions, rather than the establishment of a secure and inclusive international order.

8.6 Relations with the Former Soviet Region

Consideration of Russia's interaction with the former Soviet region includes post-Soviet economic, political, and security relations. Russia seeks to exploit these relations in order to minimize threats to its security and maximize opportunities for development. In particular, the Kremlin has demonstrated that it is determined to limit the presence of other major powers' military infrastructure on the territory of states adjacent to Russia. Russia fought a war with Georgia and undermined

Ukrainian sovereignty in 2014 and 2022 by annexing Crimea, supporting the Donbas, and invading Ukraine in part to prevent the latter joining NATO and further developing its military ties with Western nations.

By 2021, the Russian leadership had determined that Kyiv, supported by the West, had gone too far and was undermining Russia's security interests. Russian officials made multiple statements arguing that Ukraine's aspiration to join NATO and Kyiv's growing military cooperation with the United States and the Western military alliance were not acceptable. Responding to Ukraine's military preparations, including in the Donbas area, as well as Ukraine–Western countries' joint military exercises in the Black Sea and other areas close to Russia, Moscow concentrated a large number of troops on the Ukrainian border. On February 21, 2022, following several days of heightened military tensions in the Donbas, Russia recognized its political independence and promised to provide security for the people of the region. Three days later, Russian troops attacked Ukraine from the south, east, and north.

In addition to military and political measures, Russia has sought to mobilize available economic and energy tools in relations with Ukraine. The completion of Nord Stream 2 directly to Germany was one of these. Because Moscow has heavily relied on Ukrainian transportation for gas supplies to Europe, the new pipeline – should it ever become operational – would provide Moscow with an additional advantage against Kyiv. Ukraine remains dependent on transportation of Russia's gas for its budget revenue. (By some calculations, Russia's diversion of gas supplies to the pipeline with Germany may cost Kyiv as much as $5–6 billion annually in a budget of around $39 billion – that is, about 12–15 percent of the overall budget [Izotov 2021]. Ukraine's overall budget in 2021 was $39.18 billion. This calculation assumes that Russia will cease transporting its gas through Ukraine – Russia denies this intention.) For these reasons, the Ukrainian government was firmly opposed to Nord Stream 2, arguing for its sanctioning by Western nations. The West imposed such sanctions following Russia's military intervention in Ukraine.

Russia has also sought to preserve security relations and a military presence in Central Asia, the Caucasus, Belarus, and Transnistria (in Moldova). In November 2020, Russia brokered peace in the war between Azerbaijan and Armenia over the territory of Nagorno-Karabakh. Following the war, Russia deployed additional troops to the region for peacekeeping purposes (Strokan', Krivosheev, and Khalatian 2020). In 2021, Moscow has made progress in strengthening the Russia–Belarus economic and political union. On September 9, 2021, responding to perceived security threats from the West, the two countries signed twenty-eight agreements, promising the integration of currency systems, the free movement of goods and people, a common taxation regime, and the future unification of parliamentary and judicial systems. In addition, Minsk agreed to establish a Belarus–Russian military training center and host Russian air defense systems near the border with Poland. Russia and Belarus shared a common perception of the threat presented by the West that grew stronger in the context of Russia's invasion of Ukraine in February–March 2022. In January 2022, Russia also strengthened its influence in Kazakhstan by sending in, upon the government's request, peacekeeping forces. According to Kazakhstan's government, there was a need to stabilize the country during chaotic and violent public protests (Jacobs 2022).

Russia has therefore continued to view itself as a major power, responsible for preserving stability in the former Soviet region. In 1992, Moscow initiated the establishment of the CSTO – a security pact with an obligation to protect its members (Russia, Armenia, Belarus, Kazakhstan, Kyrgyzstan, and Tajikistan) from foreign attacks. In 2021, following the United States' withdrawal from Afghanistan, Moscow made clear that it would not tolerate the presence of American troops or personnel in the region. Washington had previously asked several Central Asian governments to consider hosting US military personnel and migrants from Afghanistan.

With respect to geoeconomic developments, Russia has strived to build energy infrastructure for transporting resources to Europe, Asia, and the Middle East. As a country rich in minerals, Russia remains interested in and is greatly dependent on the export of natural gas, oil, and other resources. It transports energy over land (through Ukraine, Belarus, and Central Asia) and water (via the Black Sea, Baltic Sea, and Arctic Ocean). Russia has also built economic relations with neighbors within available multilateral frameworks such as the Eurasian Economic Union and the SCO.

8.7 Other Significant Relations

Russia maintains interests and relations outside the West and the former Soviet region. Moscow has also remained interested in expanding commercial ties and arms sales and has cultivated special relations with selected countries across the globe (for overviews of Russia's relations with non-Western nations, see Trenin 2017; Karaganov and Suslov 2018; Salzman 2019; Spechler and Spechler 2019; Lukin and Diesen 2020). In pursuance of its ambitions to remain a major global power, Russia has strong ties with Asia, Latin America, and Africa. Nevertheless, Russian foreign policy is gradually returning to its pre-Soviet roots by concentrating on Europe, Asia, and the Middle East as regions of primary significance for national security and development. Russia's new National Security Strategy, adopted in July 2021, has strengthened the Kremlin's ambition to deter the West and engage with non-Western nations such as China and India (Saradzhyan 2021). Three directions stand out as especially important to Russia outside the West: Eurasia, China, and the Middle East.

In Eurasia, Russia aims to establish foundations for a new international order, which the Kremlin imagines as *multi*polar, *multi*cultural, and *multi*lateral (for analyses of Russian perspectives on the contemporary international system, see Tsygankov 2019; Ziegler 2021; Safranchuk and Lukyanov 2021). Moscow now makes sense of Eurasia outside the boundaries of the Soviet Union and in the broad geographic and geopolitical sense – as the region that includes and interconnects Europe, Asia, and the Middle East and has the greatest promise for the twenty-first century's development. Russian analysts have written extensively on the new image of the region, which they visualize as a greater Eurasia, stretching from the Atlantic Ocean to the Pacific, and in which Russia, Asian, Middle Eastern, and European countries cooperate based on jointly established economic and political rules (Karaganov and Bordachev 2018; Kotlyakov and Shuper 2019). In particular, the Kremlin has proceeded from a vision of greater Eurasia acting to build special relations with Asian powers, especially China, and Middle Eastern countries, such as Turkey and Iran.

China has emerged as a critically important partner for Russia. Since the 1990s and Primakov's efforts to strengthen ties with Beijing, relations have acquired a strategic dimension. The two countries have settled territorial disputes, signed a declaration of friendship, bridged perceptions of security threats, and reached a qualitatively new level of economic/energy cooperation. Their annual mutual trade now approaches $150 billion. The two countries have built bilateral energy pipelines and have conducted business predominantly in local currencies, eliminating US dollars from their mutual transactions.

Regionally, Russia perceives China as a premier economic and security partner. Each of the two countries has initiated its own geoeconomic scheme in Eurasia. China's "Belt and Road" initiative is global and incorporates Russia and Eurasia in terms of transportation routes and sources of energy. The Russia-initiated Eurasian Economic Union (EEU) is a narrower geographic project, which is nevertheless essential as a transportation bridge connecting China to Europe. In addition to Russia, the EEU members are Armenia, Belarus, Kazakhstan, and Kyrgyzstan. The organization benefits from trade openness for its members, as well as from Chinese investments. In May 2015, the two countries signed an agreement on cooperation between the EEU and the "Belt and Road" initiative (BBC Russia 2015).

Russia–China security relations are not without tensions, yet the two sides have managed them as compatible and even complementary. China has not recognized either Russia's annexation of Crimea or the independence of South Ossetia and Abkhazia (following the Russia–Georgia conflict of August 2008). Nevertheless, Moscow and Beijing have developed a similar preference for a multipolar international system and a similar perception of global threats as related – to a significant degree – to the United States' ambition to preserve the West-centered world order. Since the late 1990s, Russia and China have been issuing joint statements on their vision of a multipolar world and conducting joint military exercises on land and at sea. They have also cooperated within the SCO to address regional security threats. With the US withdrawal from Afghanistan in August 2021, the two countries may cooperate further to stabilize the region. Previously, they had maintained relatively smooth relations in Central Asia, where China has been active in economic and energy affairs, while Russia has preserved military dominance (Kaczmarski 2016, 2; for a Russian perspective on relations with China, see Lukin 2018; Denisov and Lukin 2021). Importantly, China and India, alongside other major non-Western powers, have refused to sanction Russia for its invasion of Ukraine in 2022.

In the Middle East, Turkey has been both the most important, and the most difficult, partner for Russia. Extensive trade and tourist relations have brought the two countries together. In some years, their mutual trade was around $30 billion (Russell 2021, 2), which is several times greater than Russia's trade with any other country in the region. Russia has also built important pipelines through Turkey and the Turkish sector of Black Sea waters to deliver natural gas to South European markets. Turkey has expressed interest in various Eurasian and global projects, such as BRICS, organized by non-Western powers including Russia (Erşen and Köstem 2020, 235). In addition, the two countries have developed strong military ties. Moscow sold Ankara the long-range aid defense system S-400, alongside China and India (Erşen and Köstem 2020, 234). Turkey purchased the system despite US opposition and the threat of sanctions. Finally, as with Putin–Trump relations, the Russian leader's international outlook is closer to that of the Turkish president than to Western liberal beliefs.

However, Turkey's great power ambitions in the region have created tensions in relations not only with Western powers but also with Russia. In one scholarly assessment, Turkish foreign policy has made a transition from the logic of interdependence to the logic of "strategic autonomy" defined in terms of balancing the US-led hierarchical order in regional and global settings (Kutlay and Öniş 2021). In particular, Turkey has worked to increase its influence in Syria, the Black Sea, and the Caucasus. In all three areas, Russian and Turkish interests have been dramatically different. Ankara has refused to recognize the Moscow-propped Bashir Assad as the legitimate leader of Syria and has undermined the country's attempts at territorial consolidation and unity. In the Black Sea area, Turkey has developed political and military relations with Ukraine by refusing to recognize Crimea as a part of Russia and providing Kyiv with military assistance. Following the start of the Russia–Ukraine war in 2022, Ankara proposed itself as the mediator of the conflict but Moscow declined the offer. In the Caucasus, Turkey not only sided with Azerbaijan in the war against Russia's ally Armenia, but Ankara also provided Baku with logistical and military support.

Since the Arab Spring in 2011, Russia has increased cooperation with other Middle Eastern countries including Egypt, Syria, Israel, Iran, Saudi Arabia, and others (Galeeva 2021). Moscow has built military and energy ties with Egypt despite Egyptian criticism of Assad in Syria. In October 2017, Russia also signed an important agreement with Saudi Arabia that included a new political assessment of the region, a decision to jointly limit production of oil, and a pledge to develop economic and military ties (Barmin 2017). Despite some disagreements, Russia's and Iran's assessments of economic, political, and military relations in the region have been quite similar due to a correlation of interests in defending Assad from foreign pressures, overcoming Western sanctions, and limiting the United States' role in the Middle East. In September 2021, Russia supported Iran's full membership in the SCO.

8.8   Russian Foreign Policy in the Future

In the short term, several areas of international relations are likely to influence Russian foreign policy. Especially important among them are the United States' relations with China, the security situation in Eurasia and Europe, particularly with respect to Ukraine, and the US strategy of managing relations with the Kremlin. The United States' relations with China have been defining the international system since Trump's attempts to increase pressures on Beijing and contain China's growing power. Biden has continued with the policy of containment, viewing China as the most important challenger for the West-centered international order. Assuming that US–China competition continues, Russia will be increasingly challenged to demonstrate its independence and the ability to steer clear of American and Chinese political pressures. Demonstration of such independence is a test of Russia's great power capabilities.

The security situation in Eurasia and Europe, particularly with respect to Ukraine, is unlikely to improve in any significant way. Indeed, it has deteriorated further, given the military conflict in Ukraine and the continuous tensions between Russia and European countries. Issues such as Russian energy supplies to Europe and Moscow's violation of Ukrainian sovereignty and territorial integrity will continue to be divisive in Russia–Western relations. Western sanctions against Russia, as well as military support for Kyiv, will have a strong influence on the Kremlin's overall foreign policy.

Finally, the US strategy of managing relations with the Kremlin will have an important role in shaping Russia's future foreign relations. In particular, if the overall emphasis of the United States' policy is on China and global issues such as strategic stability, cybersecurity, and climate, then Washington may have to move beyond its current approach. The latter has largely focused on containing Russia through sanctions and military deterrence (Charap 2021). A more complex and comprehensive policy will have to be based on a different perception of global threats and areas of potential cooperation.

The status quo scenario assumes the current level of tension in US–China relations, Russia's frozen security relations in Europe and Eurasia, and a US–Russia rivalry that does not develop in a more dangerous direction. Under this scenario, the Kremlin may stabilize relations with Ukraine and NATO and be compelled to limit its global role and concentrate on addressing outstanding issues of economic and political development in greater Eurasia and inside the country. Improving social welfare institutions, providing additional incentives for small and medium-sized businesses, developing transportation infrastructure, and ensuring political stability and a smooth succession of power could be among Russia's internal priorities. Regionally, the Kremlin may expedite the search for a strategy of mutually beneficial economic and energy-based relations with China, Turkey, Iran, and other countries. The Kremlin may also be open to cooperation with the United States on a limited number of global issues.

The second scenario assumes that the current global transition obtains additional destabilizing dynamics. US–China relations may escalate into a full-blown cold war and even include possible military incidents. Russia's relations with Europe and the United States may deteriorate further over the war in Ukraine or other security-related issues. Russian foreign policy will then be likely to become even more security-centered and focused on developing an appropriate military response and capabilities, especially within the Eurasian space. With respect to the West, Russia's foreign policy will then limit cooperation on global issues to a minimum while returning to active assertiveness and demonstration of power based on Russia's contemporary geopolitical advantages rather than long-term economic and social potential. In a long-term perspective, such a policy may translate into the country's internal decline and its greater dependence on China.

There is also a possibility of increased cooperation in the international system between major powers over issues of global importance. These issues are already on the agenda of international relations and include climate change, cybersecurity, strategic stability, and others. Assuming sufficient political will among major powers such as the United States, China, India, Russia, France, and Germany, among others, they may prioritize the development of new behavioral principles and international institutions based on the need to address these pressing global issues. Given the level of contemporary international tensions, this scenario seems less likely. However, if progress in international cooperation takes place, Russia will be less concerned with national security and more encouraged to adopt a more globally minded foreign policy.

DISCUSSION QUESTIONS

1. Why was Boris Yeltsin not successful in implementing his vision of integrating Russia with the West? What role, if any, did the West play in Russia's transformation during the 1990s?

2. How has Russian foreign policy changed since the mid-2000s? Did it become more or less cooperative in relations with the West? Which academic theory is best at explaining the change?

3. Has Russian foreign policy changed since 2019? Has Russia continued its assertiveness or become more cooperative or defensive in relations with the West and with non-Western nations? Give evidence to support your answer.

REFERENCES

A number of themes in this chapter are also discussed in Andrei P. Tsygankov, *Russia's Foreign Policy*, 6th ed. (Lanham, MD: Rowman & Littlefield, 2022).

Barmin, Yury. 2017. "What's behind the Saudi King's Historic Visit to Russia." *Moscow Times*, October 4.

BBC Russia. 2015. "Rossiia i Kitai podpisali dogovor o 'Shelkovom puti.'" May 8, www.bbc.com/russian/rolling_news/2015/05/150508_rn_china_putin_jingping_silk_route.

Biden, Joseph. 2021. "Remarks by President Biden at the Office of the Director of National Intelligence." July 27, www.whitehouse.gov/briefing-room/speeches-remarks/2021/07/27/remarks-by-president-biden-at-the-office-of-the-director-of-national-intelligence/.

Bloomberg. 2022. "Transcript: Vladimir Putin's Televised Address on Ukraine." February 24, www.bloomberg.com/news/articles/2022-02-24/full-transcript-vladimir-putin-s-televised-address-to-russia-on-ukraine-feb-24.

Charap, Samuel. 2021. "Expanding the Scope for Statecraft in US Russia Policy." *War on the Rocks*, May 14, https://warontherocks.com/2021/05/expanding-the-scope-for-statecraft-in-u-s-russia-policy/.

Denisov, Igor, and Alexander Lukin. 2021. "Russia's China Policy: Growing Asymmetries and Hedging Options." *Russian Politics*, 6(4), 531–50.

Erşen, Emre, and Seçkin Köstem. 2020. "Turkey's Interest in Closer Relations with Russia: Global, Regional and Domestic Dynamics." *SİYASAL: Journal of Political Sciences*, 29(2), 232–42.

Flikke, Geir. 2017. "The Sword of Damocles: State Governability in Putin's Third Term." *Problems of Post-Communism*, 65(6), 434–46.

Galeeva, Diana. 2021. "How Have Russia's Policies in the Middle East Changed since the Arab Uprisings?" Middle East Institute, Washington, DC, April 21.

Gunitsky, Seva, and Andrei P. Tsygankov. 2018. "The Wilsonian Bias in the Study of Russian Foreign Policy." *Problems of Post-Communism*, 65(6), 385–93.

Izotov, Sergei. 2021. "Slili v trubu. Kak sdelka SShA i Germanii po 'Severnomu potoku-2' zastavit Ukrainu izmenit' otnoshenie k Rossii?" Lenta.ru, July 30, https://lenta.ru/articles/2021/07/30/v_trubu/.

Jacobs, Harrison. 2022. "Russia-Led Alliance Troops Have Arrived in Kazakhstan after Mass Protests." NPR, January 6, www.npr.org/2022/01/06/1070840030/police-say-dozens-have-been-killed-in-kazakhstan-unrest.

Kaczmarski, Marcin. 2016. "The Asymmetric Partnership? Russia's Turn to China." *International Politics*, 53, 415–34.

Karaganov, Sergei, and Timofei Bordachev (eds.). 2018. *Vpered k Velikomu okeanu – 6*. Moscow: Valdai Club.

Karaganov, Sergei, and Dmitri Suslov. 2018. "A New World Order: A View from Russia." In Peter W. Schulze (ed.), *Multipolarity: The Promise of Disharmony*, pp. 59–82. Frankfurt-on-Main: Campus Verlag.

Kofman, Michael. 2020. "Bad Idea: Dismissing Russia as a Declining Power in US Strategy." *Defense360*, December 18, https://defense360.csis.org/bad-idea-dismissing-russia-as-a-declining-power-in-u-s-strategy/.

Kotlyakov, V. M., and V. A. Shuper (eds.). 2019. *Russia in the Forming Greater Eurasia*. Moscow: "Kodeks" Publishing House.

Kutlay, Mustafa, and Ziya Öniş. 2021. "Turkish Foreign Policy in a Post-Western Order: Strategic Autonomy or New Forms of Dependence?" *International Affairs*, 97(4), 1085–1104.

Lavrov, Sergei. 2017. "Razmyshleniia na novom etape mezhdunarodnogo razvitiia." *Rossiia v global'noi politike*, 3, no. 6 (Nov./Dec.), https://globalaffairs.ru/articles/istoricheskaya-perspektiva-vneshnej-politiki-rossii-3/.

Lewis, Simon, and Andrea Shalal. 2021. "US, Germany Strike Nord Stream 2 Pipeline Deal to Push Back on Russian 'Aggression.'" Reuters, July 21, www.reuters.com/business/energy/us-germany-deal-nord-stream-2-pipeline-draws-ire-lawmakers-both-countries-2021-07-21/.

Lukin, Alexander. 2018. *China and Russia: The New Rapprochement*. Cambridge: Polity Press.

Lukin, Alexander, and Glenn Diesen (eds.). 2020. *Russia in a Changing World*. New York: Palgrave.

Macias, Amanda. 2018. "China and Russia Are 'Aggressively Pursuing' Hypersonic Weapons, and the US Can't Defend against Them, Top Nuclear Commander Says." CNBC, August 8, www.cnbc.com/2018/03/20/china-and-russia-aggressively-are-pursuing-hypersonic-weapons-general.html.

McFaul, Michael. 2014. "Moscow's Choice." *Foreign Affairs*, 93(6)(November–December), 169–75.

2020. "Putin, Putinism, and the Domestic Determinants of Russian Foreign Policy." *International Security*, 45(2), 95–139.

Mearsheimer, John. 2014. "Why the Ukraine Crisis Is the West's Fault." *Foreign Affairs*, September–October, www.foreignaffairs.com/articles/russia-fsu/2014-08-18/why-ukraine-crisis-west-s-fault.

Moscow Times. 2021. "Russia Demands 'Urgent' US Talks, Warning of 'Military Response' to NATO Activity." *Moscow Times*, December 20, www.themoscowtimes.com/2021/12/20/russia-demands-urgent-us-talks-warning-of-military-response-a75880.

New York Times. 2020. "Trump Praises Himself for Wanting to 'Get Along' with Russia." *New York Times*, September 3, www.nytimes.com/live/2020/09/03/us/trump-vs-biden.

Putin, Vladimir. 1999. "Rossiia na rubezhe tysiacheletii." *Nezavisimaia Gazeta*, December 30.

2018. "Presidential Address to the Federal Assembly." March 1, http://en.kremlin.ru/events/president/news/56957.

Renz, Bettina. *Russia's Military Revival*. Cambridge: Polity.

Robertson, Graeme. 2011. *The Politics of Protest in Hybrid Regimes: Managing Dissent in Post-Communist Russia*. Cambridge: Cambridge University Press.

Russell, Martin. 2021. "Russia–Turkey Relations: A Fine Line between Competition and Cooperation." European Parliamentary Research Service, February, www.europarl.europa.eu/thinktank/en/document/EPRS_BRI(2021)679090.

Russia Matters. 2021. "Claim in 2021: Russia's GDP Per Capita Is 30% Lower than in 2013." August 25.

Russian Federation, Ministry of Foreign Affairs. 2021. "Press Release on Russian Draft Documents on Legal Security Guarantees from the United States and NATO," December 17, www.mid.ru/en/foreign_policy/news/1790809/.

Safranchuk, Ivan, and Fedor Lukianov. 2021. "Sovremennyi mirovoi poriadok. Strukturnye realii i sopernichestvo velikikh derzhav." *Polis: Political Studies*, 2, 57–76.

Salzman, Rachel S. 2019. *Russia, BRICS, and the Disruption of Global Order*. Washington, DC: Georgetown University Press.

Saradzhyan, Simon. 2021. "Russia's New Security Strategy: Deter US, Ignore EU, Partner with China and India." *Russia Matters*, July 15, https://russialist.org/russias-new-security-strategy-deter-u-s-ignore-eu-partner-with-china-and-india/.

Saradzhyan, Simon, and Nabi Abduallaev. 2021. "Measuring National Power: Is Putin's Russia in Decline?" *Europe–Asia Studies*, 73(2), 291–317.

Shevtsova, Lilia. 2007. *Russia Lost in Transition: The Yeltsin and Putin Legacies*. Washington, DC: Carnegie Endowment for International Peace.

Spechler, Dina R., and Martin C. Spechler. 2019. *Putin and His Neighbors: Russia's Policies toward Eurasia*. Lanham, MD: Rowman & Littlefield.

Stoner, Kathryn E. 2021. *Russia Resurrected: Its Power and Purpose in a New Global Order*. Oxford: Oxford University Press.

Strokan', Sergei, Kirill Krivosheev, and Aik Khalatian. 2020. "Edunstvenno mirnoe reshenie. Karabakhskuiu voinu zavershila Rossiia." *Kommersant*, November 11, www.kommersant.ru/doc/4566102.

Trenin, Dmitry. 2017. *What Russia Is up to in the Middle East*. Cambridge: Polity Press.

Tsygankov, Andrei P. 2019. *Russia and America: The Asymmetric Rivalry*. Cambridge: Polity Press.

    2022. *Russia's Foreign Policy*, 6th ed. Lanham, MD: Rowman & Littlefield.

Willerton, J. P., M. Beznosov, and M. Carrier. 2005. "Addressing the Challenges of Russia's 'Failing State.'" *Demokratizatsiya: The Journal of Post-Soviet Democratization*, 13(2), 219–40.

Wood, Tony. 2020. *Russia without Putin: Money, Power and the Myths of the New Cold War*. London: Verso.

Ziegler, Charles E. 2021. "A Crisis of Diverging Perspectives: US–Russian Relations and the Security Dilemma." *Texas National Security Review*, 4(1)(Winter), 11–33.

PART II
Political Economy

9 Property Rights: Forging the Institutional Foundations for Russia's Market Economy

JORDAN GANS-MORSE

Fig. 9.1 "Raiders are attacking us! Help!" Credit: Vladimir Mashatin / PhotoXPress.

> Who cares about criminals? Inspectors can close you in a matter of seconds. This is itself a kind of mafia system.
>
> Small business-owner, Moscow (author interview, 2009)

Abstract

Institutions that protect property rights, enforce contracts, and resolve business disputes are essential for a market economy to function smoothly. These institutions may be formal or informal, ranging from courts to the reputation of prospective business partners. But in the chaotic transformation from Soviet-era economic planning to a market economy, firms in Russia came to utilize far more extreme strategies for securing property, including services provided by organized crime and corrupt public officials. This chapter traces the evolution of Russian firms' strategies for protecting property rights, enforcing contracts, and resolving business disputes from the early days following the Soviet Union's collapse through the contemporary Putin era. The focus is on "everyday" Russian firms, rather than on oligarchs, state-owned enterprises, or conglomerates in the natural resource sector. We will see that a central challenge of Russia's post-Soviet transformation has been to forge state institutions strong enough to prevent chaos and coercion by criminals yet also constrained enough to curtail predation by powerful state officials.

9.1   Introduction

For market economies to function efficiently, institutions that protect property rights, enforce contracts, and resolve business disputes are essential. These institutions reduce uncertainty, provide firms with vital information, mitigate conflicts, and reduce the overall costs of market transactions. In countries with long-established market economies, such institutions often developed gradually and in piecemeal fashion over decades or centuries, creating an impression that, where markets emerge, the necessary institutional underpinnings naturally follow. Russia's rapid transformation from a planned to a market economy in the 1990s, however, vividly demonstrated that the emergence of effective market-supporting institutions cannot be taken for granted. This transformation also illustrated the challenges firms face in their absence. Thrust into a chaotic environment in which institutions ranging from courts to better business bureaus were either nonexistent or ineffective, firms in post-Soviet Russia were forced to rely on extreme measures for securing property and enforcing contracts, including services provided by organized crime and corrupt state officials.

   This chapter traces the evolution of Russian firms' strategies for protecting property rights, enforcing contracts, and resolving business disputes from the early days of the Soviet Union's collapse through the contemporary era of **Vladimir Putin**, as well as the evolution of the key institutions that shaped these strategies. The primary focus of the chapter is on "everyday" Russian firms, rather than on **oligarchs**, powerful state-owned enterprises, or large conglomerates in strategic sectors such as oil and gas. In line with the general argument of this book, the story of property rights in post-Soviet Russia features elements of both stability and fragility. On the side of stability, business disputes throughout the entire post-Soviet era have been characterized by unusually high levels of private actor violence, state actor corruption, or both. On the side of fragility and change, the specific types of illicit coercion firms face have continuously evolved, as have firms' strategies for dealing with novel threats to property security.

   The chapter is divided into four main sections. Section 9.2 first introduces key theoretical concepts. Section 9.3 then offers an overview of property rights and business disputes during the period of the Soviet collapse and the chaotic emergence of Russia's market economy. Recently created formal legal institutions during this period remained largely ineffective, and firms often relied instead on the protection services of various private actors, including organized crime groups. Section 9.4 turns to property rights in the final years of **the Boris Yeltsin era** and during the first decade of Putin's rule. In the early 2000s, Russia made considerable progress at improving the effectiveness of formal legal institutions, and firms increasingly came to use courts and lawyers. However, the empowerment of state agencies without an accompanying increase in accountability also strengthened corrupt state actors. These corrupt officials provided illicit protection services to some firms while simultaneously posing a major threat to others. Section 9.5 then analyzes how the system that would come to be known as **"Putinism"** undermined much of the progress that had been made in the early Putin period, ultimately creating a highly unstable environment in which the costs of market transactions remain high and firms continue to face significant threats to the security of their property. Putin's decision to invade Ukraine in February 2022, and the economic collapse resulting from the subsequent sanctions and boycotts, greatly exacerbated these negative trends, raising significant questions about Russia's political and economic trajectory in years to come.

The concluding section takes a step back and examines two lessons to be drawn from consideration of property rights in post-Soviet Russia. The first is that there is nothing automatic and inevitable about the emergence of effective market-supporting institutions. Building institutions requires time, political will, and the support of the citizens or firms most likely to rely on these institutions. The second is that creating effective market-supporting institutions requires an incredibly delicate balancing act on the part of the state. Too weak a state leads to chaos and widespread coercion by private actors, as seen in Russia following the Soviet collapse. But too powerful a state leads to predation and corruption by unconstrained state officials, as seen in Russia as Putin increasingly consolidated power.

9.2 Property Rights in the Context of Weak State Institutions

The Nobel Prize–winning economist Douglass North (1990, 3) famously defined **institutions** as "the rules of the game in a society" or "the humanly devised constraints that shape human interaction." Of the many institutions that support the efficient functioning of market economies, few are as important as **property rights**, which frequently are defined as the rights to use an asset, derive income from it, and transfer it to another owner (Barzel 1997, 3). However, the concept of "rights" presupposes the existence of a functioning state apparatus, which publicly codifies the law, identifies citizens' privileges and obligations, and establishes the distinction between legitimate and illegitimate ownership – in other words, a state apparatus that establishes and enforces the "rules of the game" governing market activity. During the chaotic years following the collapse of the Soviet Union, the Russian state often lacked the capacity to fulfill these functions. In this context, the very notion of "rights" becomes problematic. Instead, as in other places where states have been weak, as well as in points in history prior to the emergence of modern states, it makes more sense to consider the ways that firms in the post-Soviet period sought to accumulate and protect *claims* to property, often via coercive means.

The weakness of formal institutions in the post-Soviet period creates other challenges for understanding property rights in this context. Formally, the Russian constitution of 1993 and a series of laws issued in the 1990s clearly set out the rules of the game for *allocating* property rights. The problem was that formal institutions capable of *enforcing* these rules were almost entirely lacking. The result was a striking divergence between formal rules of the game and the actual rules that firms, state officials, citizens, and criminals understood to govern everyday behavior. While informal rules of the game are sometimes considered to be "informal institutions" (Helmke and Levitsky 2004), the process of identifying and documenting these largely unwritten, sometimes illegal, and frequently changing rules in the Russian context is no easy task. This chapter offers insights into the evolution of institutions, both formal and informal, by focusing on the strategies firms used to secure their claims to property and resolve business disputes, tracing – in a manner advocated by the anthropologist Alena Ledeneva (2006, 22) – the ways that these strategies "infringe on, manipulate, or exploit formal rules and ... make use of informal norms and personal obligations for pursuing goals."

Firms do not, of course, choose strategies in a vacuum. The surrounding institutional environment, as well as the types of threats firms face, both shape and are shaped by firms' strategies. Proceeding chronologically, the sections that follow situate firms' use of a wide range of strategies, employing a mix of violence, corruption, and law, in the context of evolving legal and regulatory institutions and ever-changing threats to the security of property from both private and state actors.

9.3   Property Rights in the Aftermath of the Soviet Collapse

The Soviet Union was a socialist **command economy** (Kornai 1992; Åslund 1995, ch. 1). Other than personal possessions, all property, including firms, farms, land, and natural resources, belonged to the state. The state planning agency, Gosplan, allocated resources to enterprises and set output targets for enterprise directors. Prices existed for administrative purposes but bore little relation to the supply and demand of goods and services.

The institutional underpinnings of the Soviet system differed dramatically from those critical to the functioning of market economies. In the absence of privately owned firms, there was no need to protect property rights, nor was there a need for specialized regulatory institutions such as agencies that oversee securities markets or antitrust policy. While Soviet enterprises relied on contracts with trading partners, these contracts operated within the framework devised by the state planning apparatus, not as voluntary agreements among economic actors (Belova 2005). Enterprises could turn to Gosarbitrazh, a hybrid judicial–administrative system of arbitration courts, to help resolve interenterprise disputes, but in practice enterprise directors often preferred to rely on informal negotiations, sometimes involving powerful political patrons who would intervene on behalf of favored enterprises (Hendley 1997).

The Soviet economy began to stagnate by the 1970s, but ground along for nearly two more decades, thanks in part to large oil and gas reserves and high oil prices. When **Mikhail Gorbachev** became general secretary of the **Communist Party of the Soviet Union** in 1985, he prioritized the revival of economic growth. To boost efficiency, Gorbachev decentralized many allocation decisions to the enterprise level and legalized independent worker-owned cooperatives. These reforms, known as *perestroika*, or rebuilding, loosened the constraints of the command economy. To mobilize societal support for his economic reform efforts, Gorbachev then initiated *glasnost*, a policy of greater openness that allowed for significant increases in freedom of speech and citizens' rights to organize politically.

Gorbachev's reforms stopped short of the creation of full capitalism and democracy, but they liberalized the Soviet system enough to unleash opposition forces that would tear the Soviet Union apart. By the time of the union's official demise in December 1991, the economy was in free fall, and Boris Yeltsin, president of the newly independent Russia, took steps to transition to a full-fledged market economy. At the beginning of 1992, nearly all controls on retail prices were abolished, allowing individuals and firms to buy, sell, and trade with whomever they pleased and at whatever price the market would bear. Yeltsin's reformers next moved to transfer state-owned enterprises to private hands. In the brief four-year span between 1992 and the end of 1995, more than 100,000 small enterprises and nearly 18,000 medium and large enterprises were transferred to private owners (Blasi et al. 1997, 189), a redistribution of assets on a scale never before witnessed in human history. By the mid-1990s, the key **elements of a market economy** – freedom of trade, free prices on most goods and services, and widespread private ownership – were in place. But the institutional underpinnings that allow market economies to function smoothly were not.

9.3.1 Early Post-Soviet Legal Institutions: "Excellent on Paper . . . Irrelevant for Business"

The Soviet Union disintegrated in a remarkably short period of time. Yeltsin's economic team recognized that building new and complex legal institutions would take far longer, but they believed that they had to push forward rapidly with market reforms nevertheless. In the uncertain months following the Soviet collapse, they feared that a return to communism would remain possible until they smashed the backbone of the command economy – the state ownership of all productive assets. They additionally believed that they had only a short amount of time at their disposal, or what their contemporary, the Polish reformer Leszek Balcerowicz, frequently referred to as a short "window of opportunity" of "extraordinary politics" in which interest groups that might oppose reforms had yet to organize (Balcerowicz, Blaszchyk, and Dabrowski 1997). Justified or not, the rush to build markets *before* market-supporting institutions inevitably created an institutional vacuum. By 1995, for example, privatization had created thousands of joint-stock companies with millions of shareholders – yet the Russian parliament did not manage to pass essential commercial and capital market laws until 1996. Starkly illustrating the challenges of governing market economies in the absence of key institutions, foreign legal advisors who participated in drafting this legislation noted that, until these laws were placed on the books, the Russian legal lexicon did not even have terminology for concepts indispensable to the functioning of joint-stock companies, such as "fiduciary duty" and "self-dealing" (Black, Kraakman, and Tarassoav 1999, 1752).

While institution-building clearly lagged behind market reforms, Russia's reformers nevertheless managed to develop legal and regulatory institutions at a formidable pace. **Commercial courts** (*arbitrazhnye sudy*) were created in 1992 on the remnants of the Gosarbitrazh system discussed above. These courts were tasked with hearing cases among firms and between firms and state agencies. They comprised part of an emerging tripartite judicial system, the other branches of which consisted of a Constitutional Court and the courts of general jurisdiction (*sudy obshchei iurisdiktsii*), which were to hear cases related to noncommercial civil litigation and criminal matters. A new constitution, ratified in 1993, enshrined both the right to private property (Articles 8 and 35) and the principle of an independent judiciary (Article 120). Parts I and II of a new Civil Code came into force in 1995 and 1996, respectively, providing a legal basis for contracting between private entities, and laws governing bankruptcy, the securities market, and joint-stock companies were in place by 1996. An antimonopoly commission formed during the Gorbachev era prior to the Soviet collapse continued to function until 1998 when it was upgraded to the status of a ministry, and a federal securities commission was established in 1994 (Gans-Morse 2017, ch. 4). By the mid-1990s, just half a decade after the fall of the Soviet Union, the legal scholar Kathryn Hendley (1997, 236) surveyed Russia's legal institutions and concluded that, "[f]or the most part, the legal infrastructure needed for a market economy has been created – at least on paper. Relatively stable rules exist by which citizens can order their behavior, and institutions have been created that are charged with enforcing those rules. Taken as a whole, the accomplishment is impressive."

The existence of formal institutions does not guarantee, however, that these institutions govern everyday interactions or that laws on the books constitute the binding constraints that shape firms' strategies. In the first years after their formation, the commercial courts experienced a sharp decline in their annual caseloads, an approximately 40 percent drop from around 340,000 cases in 1992 to just over 200,000 in 1994, as firms turned away from the formal legal system and relied on extralegal means of resolving disputes (Gans-Morse 2017, 58–61). Accordingly, Hendley (1997, 246) continued her assessment of Russia's emerging legal infrastructure by warning that "Russia stands in grave danger of becoming a country with an excellent legal system on paper, but one that remains largely irrelevant for business."

Firms' lack of confidence in Russia's newly created legal institutions in part reflected a realistic assessment of their effectiveness. To their credit, a sliding scale for filing fees made the commercial courts relatively accessible even to less wealthy litigants (Hendley 1998, 96–100), and the courts exhibited impressive efficiency, meeting the statutorily imposed deadline for issuing rulings within two months for 95 percent of applicable cases (Hendley 2003, 372). But the courts suffered from an inability to enforce their rulings. Nonpayments and barter were so extensive in the 1990s that few firms had funds in their bank accounts for courts to garner, and overloaded bailiffs faced a case flow that according to some estimates would have required enforcement of a case every two hours in order to keep pace (Kahn 2002, 159). The courts also suffered from a lack of financial resources, remaining, in the words of the political scientist and legal scholar Peter Solomon (2008, 66), "shabby places," which hindered efforts to raise the symbolic status and authority of the judiciary. To top off these challenges, Soviet-era judges faced the near-impossible task of adjudicating disputes over market transactions despite having received their legal educations and lived nearly their entire lives in a society with a nonmarket economy, a consideration that raised questions about their competence (Black, Kraakman, and Tarassova 1999, 1752–53; Gans-Morse 2017, 76).

Firms had even less reason to have confidence in law enforcement agencies to effectively offer property rights protection. Law enforcement agencies, suffering no less than courts from a deficit of funding, found themselves literally outgunned, with smaller weapons, slower cars, and fewer resources than the criminals they pursued (Gerber and Mendelson 2008, 10; Favarel-Garrigues 2011, 183). Lack of competent cadres compounded law enforcement problems, as law enforcement officials abandoned collapsing state structures to enter the growing private security market. By one estimate, in 1993 less than half of personnel at the Ministry of Internal Affairs (MVD), the ministry that oversees Russia's police force, had more than three years of experience (Taylor 2011, 189).

The judiciary's and law enforcement agencies' lack of capacity was far from the only reason Russian firms avoided formal institutions in the early post-Soviet period. The formative experiences of Russia's emerging business class had taken place either within the Soviet industrial sector or in the semi-legalized markets of the *perestroika* era, both of which habituated a reliance on informal means of resolving disputes. Observing the balance of Russian firms' legal and extralegal strategies for enforcing contracts in the mid-1990s, the legal scholar Katharina Pistor (1996, 87) determined that "the early institutional changes aimed at providing a court system for handling commercial disputes have so far proved to be largely ineffective," but that "the main reasons for this appear to lie less in the inefficiency of the system than in the lack of demand for the services that it offers." But, then, on whose services were Russian firms relying?

9.3.2   Post-Soviet Russia's "Violent Entrepreneurs"

Even in societies with well-developed legal systems, firms and individuals usually turn to litigation or law enforcement only as a last resort, preferring instead to resolve conflicts based on personal relationships, informal norms, private arbitration, or other strategies often referred to under the rubrics of **relational contracting** or **private ordering** (Macaulay 1963; Ellickson 1991; McMillan and Woodruff 2000). But, in post-Soviet Russia, firms' avoidance of the formal legal system reflected a reliance on far more extreme methods of securing property and enforcement contracts, including threats of violence, contract killings, and services provided by criminal protection rackets. This extraordinary role of private coercion in the Russian business world in turn reflected the unusual challenges that emerged from the institutional void left by the Soviet collapse. Whereas in most countries organized crime is limited to illegal sectors such as prostitution, drugs, arms trafficking, fraud, and money-laundering, in the early post-Soviet period organized crime groups and other providers of private protection services in Russia – a set of actors whom the sociologist Vadim Volkov (2002) evocatively labeled **"violent entrepreneurs"** – became deeply intertwined with the daily business of otherwise legitimate firms. These violent entrepreneurs simultaneously posed a grave threat to property security while fulfilling the fundamental protective and adjudicative functions usually fulfilled by modern states.

The roots of private coercion in the Russian business world were directly tied to the creation of private property. Gorbachev's *perestroika* and *glasnost*, discussed above, produced new opportunities not only for aspiring private entrepreneurs but also for the criminal underworld, for the rapid emergence of entrepreneurial ventures and open-air markets created ideal conditions for extortion. The criminal protection rackets originally formed to extort street-market kiosks in the late 1980s soon evolved into far more complex operations. Criminal gangs, often referred to as *bandity*, offered entrepreneurs protection from other extorters in exchange for a percentage of their profits, a service known as providing a "roof" (in Russian, a **krysha**). As the privatization of state-owned enterprises in the early

1990s produced tens of thousands of shops and small businesses, these enterprises proved to be valuable targets for criminal groups – and simultaneously in desperate need of protection services. Protection rackets' portfolio of services expanded accordingly, coming to include contract enforcement, debt collection, and intelligence gathering on prospective business partners (Volkov 2002, chs. 3–4). In the absence of an effective court system, a system of "shadow justice" formed, in which the *krysha* of one firm would meet with the *krysha* of another to negotiate on behalf of their respective clients or, if need be, to resolve the dispute by force (Skoblikov 2001).

Estimates by Russian law enforcement suggested that in the early 1990s up to three-fourths of Russian businesses paid protection money (Webster 1997, 2–3). Such estimates are difficult to verify, but rigorous research conducted in the mid- to late 1990s confirmed the widespread prevalence of criminal rackets, particularly among smaller firms. A 1996 survey of small retail shops in Moscow, Ulianovsk, and Smolensk revealed that more than 40 percent of respondents recounted having contact with a criminal group in the previous six months (Frye and Zhuravskaya 2000), while a 1997 survey of enterprises from across twenty-one Russian regions similarly found that approximately 40 percent of respondents reported personally experiencing violent extortion or threats of physical coercion "sometimes" or "often" (Radaev 1999, 36–40).

During this period, private security agencies also proliferated, offering services, many of dubious legality, similar to those provided by criminal rackets. The collapse of Soviet security structures responsible for intelligence, counterintelligence, internal security, and secret police functions, and in particular the reorganization of the largest and most powerful of these agencies – the Committee for State Security (KGB) – created a supply of highly trained unemployed security specialists. Already by 1993 there existed approximately 5,000 officially registered private security agencies, and this number would double by the end of the decade (Volkov 2002, 138; Gans-Morse 2017, 48). Rather than outsourcing security, larger firms created internal security services, which the journalist David Hoffman (1997) colorfully described as "private armies of security agents, bodyguards and commercial spies." In some cases, labeling these services as "armies" was quite apt: The security department of Russia's natural gas monopoly Gazprom in the 1990s numbered 13,000 employees and was led by a former KGB colonel (Volkov 2002, 134–35).

To a certain extent, Russia's violent entrepreneurs provided an effective substitute for more formal market-supporting institutions that were either lacking or ineffective. Private contract-enforcement services often allowed firms to engage in transactions that otherwise might not have taken place due to concerns about bad faith on the part of suppliers or customers. Private provision of business intelligence services facilitated deals that otherwise might not have been feasible due to a lack of information about prospective partners' reputational histories. But a market

economy in which criminal *kryshas* and private security agencies were key providers of property security, contract enforcement, and dispute resolution came with
significant costs. Throughout 1993, sixty-one car and street bombs exploded in
Moscow as criminal groups battled for territorial control (Hoffman 2002, 277). In
1994 the MVD catalogued 562 contract killings, an official count that undoubtedly
represented only a fraction of the total (Statkus 1998, 66).

The level of violence was unsustainable, and by the mid-1990s criminal protection rackets were being forced from the marketplace. In a bloody process of
competition among criminal groups, stronger organizations pushed the weaker from
the battlefield, and the number of criminal groups peaked in 1995 (Modestov 1996;
Volkov 2002, ch. 3). Many of the criminal leaders who survived the early 1990s with
their wealth intact either fled Russia for early retirement in Southern Europe or
became more deeply invested in legitimate business ventures and came to recognize
the need for order and stability. As one *bandit* reportedly stated, "In this kind of
environment, who can do any business?" (cited in Handelman 1994, 93).

From the mid-1990s onward, a wide range of evidence points to a shift away from
reliance on private violence and coercion. A sociological analysis of business
conflicts in Russia's Central Federal District identified a noteworthy decline in the
annual number of businesspeople murdered in the course of conducting business,
from 213 in 1997 to 33 in 2005 (Matveeva 2007, 86). Journalists and Russian
security experts similarly reported a drop in contract killings during this period.
These sources additionally observed that many of the contract killings that persisted
into the 2000s were not directly related to business conflicts but instead targeted
journalists and human rights activists (Gans-Morse 2017, 49). Additionally, by the
second half of the 1990s, firms themselves were seeking to avoid criminal protection
rackets' services. The 1997 survey of firms from twenty-one regions cited above
found that, in response to threats and extortion, only 15 percent of respondents
would turn to criminal groups, while about the same number would turn to the
police. The largest category of respondents, 34 percent, said they would rely on
themselves to deal with the threat (Radaev 1999, 42–43). Similarly, in contrast to the
40 percent of respondents who reported recent contact with rackets in the previously
referenced 1996 survey conducted in Moscow, Ulianovsk, and Smolensk (Frye and
Zhuravskaya 2000), less than 25 percent of small shops in a 1998 survey conducted
in the same three cities reported such encounters (Frye 2002). By 2010, a survey of
firms from eight Russian cities found that less than 8 percent of the small businesses
in the sample (and less than 4 percent of the overall sample) reported contact with
criminal rackets in the previous three years. Less than 5 percent of respondents in
the survey said that they or their employees had "sometimes" or "often" been
subjected to threats or physical coercion (Gans-Morse 2017, 49–50).

The shift away from violence was also evident in the private security sector.
Although the number of registered private security agencies continued to grow,

reaching 30,000 by the late 2000s (Gans-Morse 2017, 48), most differed little from their Western counterparts as Russia entered its second post-Soviet decade. Experts estimated that provision of basic physical security of buildings, cargo, and business executives accounted for 70 percent of the sector's revenues, with the remainder consisting of information security, legal services, and the installation of cameras and alarms. As the security concerns of Russian businesspeople evolved, the notion of "economic security" (*ekonomicheskaia bezopasnost'*) came to be understood as responses to new and complex threats such as computer virus attacks by competitors or semi-legal raids utilizing complicated legal schemes to acquire assets. Firms specializing in economic security came to rely on lawyers, accountants, IT specialists, and former law enforcement officials rather than on violence and force to counter these emerging challenges (Gans-Morse 2017, 52).

In summary, by the end of the 1990s, the era of overt private violence and coercion as a widespread tool of mainstream Russian firms was largely fading, with legitimate businesses relying on *bandity* for protection, adjudication, and contract-enforcement services almost exclusively in remote and underdeveloped regions (Pravotorov 2006; Volkov 2002, 152). Organized crime remained a significant problem, but it was no longer a regular player in everyday business transactions in Russia. Instead, as Elena Panfilova, the director of the anticorruption organization Transparency International's Moscow office, explained in a 2009 interview, it remained active in those illegal sectors "where it belongs" (cited in Gans-Morse 2017, 45). Meanwhile, Russian firms increasingly eschewed violence and turned to legalistic means of protecting assets through the courts and other formal legal institutions, as detailed in the following section. Nevertheless, many firms in Russia continued to face unusual threats and to engage in illicit strategies for securing property. The form of both threats and strategies, however, was shifting. In place of threats of violence from private actors, firms increasingly faced extortion from corrupt state actors and, instead of employing the services of criminal protection rackets or private protection agencies, firms began to rely more extensively on services provided by corrupt public officials.

9.4 Property Rights in the Early Putin Era

By 2000, when Yeltsin transferred power to Putin, laws were on the books, a court system was in place, and a rudimentary regulatory apparatus was emerging. Upon his rise to power, first as prime minister in 1999 and then as president beginning in 2000, Putin set out to restore the Russian state's capacity. For Russia to return to its former status as a major geopolitical player, its economy would need to thrive. For its economy to thrive, a state capable of fulfilling fundamental protective and adjudicatory functions would be needed.

Beginning with an open letter to voters during the 2000 presidential campaign, Putin emphasized the importance of establishing a "**dictatorship of law**" (Putin 2000). Western analysts struggled to parse the meaning of this phrase, but the very ambiguity of Putin's terminology foreshadowed the contradictory trends in Russia's state legal capacity that have characterized the Putin era. On the one hand, Putin improved the legislative framework for and dramatically increased the financial resources available to courts, law enforcement agencies, and other legal and regulatory institutions, in many ways improving their effectiveness. On the other hand, high-profile political interventions in the judicial system and corruption within law enforcement and regulatory agencies undermined judicial independence and limited formal institutions' effective provision of contract enforcement and dispute resolution. Corrupt state officials, like the *bandity* who preceded them, came to pose significant threats to property security while also serving as important service providers for firms seeking to secure property, enforce contracts, or resolve disputes using extralegal means.

9.4.1   Legal Institutions under Putin's "Dictatorship of Law"

In the first three years of his presidency, Putin leveraged his popularity and influence to push through legislation that had succumbed to political gridlock and the fragmentation of political authority during the Yeltsin era. The Russian government brought the new Civil Code to completion and introduced new procedural codes for criminal law, civil law, and the administration of the commercial courts. Previously, Russia had operated under a Soviet-era Civil Procedural Code and Criminal Procedural Code, leaving key constitutional rights unenforceable nearly a decade after the adoption of the constitution. Among other innovations, these new Putin-era codes shifted the burden of proof in criminal matters to the state and transferred significant elements of authority over arrest and pretrial detention from the Procuracy (*prokuratura*) to the judiciary (Solomon 2008, 66–67).

Beyond these notable legislative achievements, Putin significantly increased the financial resources devoted to legal institutions. Funding for the judicial system increased more than fivefold during the first decade of Putin's rule, leading to higher salaries for judges, the repair of court buildings, and the computerization of court administrations (Gans-Morse 2017, 81). Also noteworthy was an effort by the Russian government to increase transparency by mandating the creation of court websites and public access to online databases of judicial decisions. The need to publicly justify decisions, reformers hoped, would improve the quality of court rulings and act as a partial safeguard against corruption or political interference (Solomon 2008, 67). By the end of the 2000s, commercial courts were posting the majority of their decisions online.

With respect to accessibility and efficiency, the commercial courts continued to perform well. Despite rapidly rising caseloads, judges in the commercial courts by and large still managed to close cases within statutorily defined timeframes. Problems with enforcement of court decisions persisted, but the booming economy mitigated some of the troubles prevalent in the 1990s, such as the challenge of trying to collect from penniless debtors. Various reforms to the Arbitrazh Procedural Code in 2002 also empowered the Bailiffs Service, such as a change that extended the validity of court orders to seize funds from debtors' bank accounts from six months to three years, making it more difficult for debtors to hide by avoiding the use of their bank accounts (Hendley 2003, 375). In terms of competence, judges and other state officials possessed a decade of experience regulating and living within a market-based society by the time the Putin era began, and increased funding for courts, higher salaries (now paid on time), and improved physical security created far stronger incentives to remain within the corps of judges, although recruitment of judges remained a problem (Hendley 2007, 108).

Not all of Putin's early institutional reforms conducted in the judicial sphere, however, were without controversy. Most notably, changes to the Law on the Status of Judges that imposed an age limit of sixty-five on federal judges and allocated to nonjudges one-third of the seats on Judicial Qualification Commission, the sole bodies that could remove tenured judges from the bench, threatened to undermine judicial independence. Related reforms made it easier to open criminal proceedings against judges and impose other forms of disciplinary action. While concerns about judicial autonomy and self-governance were not without merit, liberal pockets within the government, such as the Ministry of Economic Development and Trade, supported some of these changes, perceiving them to be important steps toward reducing corruption and improving the accountability of judges (Solomon 2008, 68). Nevertheless, despite the infrequent occurrence of judge dismissals, a handful of high-profile instances in the early 2000s created the impression that an independent judiciary was under attack (Hendley 2006, 356–57).

Whatever concerns persisted about the effectiveness of the commercial courts, they paled in comparison to concerns about the effectiveness of law enforcement agencies. As with the judiciary, funding for law enforcement increased considerably under Putin, rising nearly threefold in the first decade of the 2000s (Taylor 2011, 53–54; Gans-Morse 2017, 81). But, despite increased resources, turnover and recruitment problems among law enforcement officials remained grave. The head of the MVD in 2005 declared the personnel situation within law enforcement to be "catastrophic," noting that, among local-level MVD employees, more than half were under thirty years of age with minimal experience. Well into the 2000s, MVD officials faced personnel shortages of up to 50 percent for key positions, such as criminal investigators (Taylor 2011, 190). Citing such problems, Solomon (2005, 233) declared that "policing in Russia is less professional now than it was in the late Soviet period." Law enforcement officials' continued engagement in supplementary work outside their official duties, ranging from basic work as security guards to sophisticated protection rackets for private enterprises, compounded these personnel problems. Surveys throughout the 2000s found more than half of all law enforcement officials to be reliant on unofficial income streams, often of a magnitude exceeding their formal salaries (Dubova and Kosals 2013, 50–51).

Overall, law enforcement officials remained ineffective at fulfilling their official duties to provide protection to society as a whole, but their increased funding, status, and authority turned them into fearsome competitors to the violent entrepreneurs who had provided protection services to firms in the 1990s. Increased clout unmatched by improved professionalism or increased constraints on corruption also turned law enforcement and other state officials into a potent threat to property security.

9.4.2   Evolving Threats, Evolving Services: From Violence to Corruption

As Russian firms turned away from private coercion in the mid- to late 1990s, they began to utilize strategies that relied on corruption – that is, on services provided by state actors but offered selectively to private clients for the purpose of state officials' private profit. Foremost among these was the type of protection racket offered by law enforcement officials, which was known as a *mentovskaia krysha* – a reference to the term *menty*, a common but semi-derogatory term for police – as opposed to the criminal racket, known as a *banditskaia krysha*. Law enforcement protection rackets offered many of the same services previously provided by criminals, including debt collection, contract enforcement, and adjudication of disputes. By some estimates, approximately 30 percent of MVD personnel offered some form of *krysha* in the 1990s (Webster 1997, 30). The most sought-after services were those provided by the MVD's State Directorate for the Struggle with Organized Crime and its regional branches, as well as by units from the KGB's successor, the Federal Security Service (FSB), devoted to economic and organized crime (Sborov 2003; Pravotorov 2006).

Even before Putin's rise to power strengthened law enforcement's clout, private security agencies and law enforcement rackets had increasingly squeezed criminal rackets out of the market for protection services (Volkov 2002, 169–79; Taylor 2007, 45). As a Russian business journalist reported, "By the end of the 1990s, the majority of entrepreneurs capable of making money were 'voluntarily' providing support to the law enforcement authorities. It could be said that the country had been divided into zones of 'police patronage'" (Sborov 2003). By the early 2000s, leaked internal cables from the US Embassy in Moscow to the State Department in Washington, DC, provided evidence that this trend of firms utilizing law enforcement rackets in place of criminal rackets had only grown stronger: "Moscow business owners understand that it is best to get protection from the MVD and FSB (rather than organized crime groups) since they not only have more guns, resources and power than criminal groups, but they are also protected by the law. For this reason, protection from criminal gangs is no longer so high in demand" (Chivers 2010).

The corrupt provision of protection services by state officials threatened to subvert formal state institutions, undermining the defining role of modern states as providers of public goods that are accessible, at least in theory, to all tax-paying citizens and firms. Yet according to some accounts in the Russian business press, the abandonment of private coercion was something to be applauded. In the words of one Russian journalist, "the classic *krysha* is becoming irreversibly a thing of the past. In our day 'protection' of businesses appears to be more civilized" (Pravotorov 2006). Such analyses seemed to overlook the extent to which the services provided by corrupt government officials extended beyond mere protection. Firms were learning that there were safer, more efficient means than private coercion to undercut competitors or settle disputes. As one businessman explained, "In the past, if someone refused to pay they could damage the shop or just burn it. Now they've understood that it is cheaper and safer to get fire inspection to close it down for a week or two. And the effect is the same" (cited in Volkov 2002, 50–51). An even more fearsome tool was the "**contract investigation**" (*zakaznoi naezd*), whereby a competitor or counterparty in a dispute would bribe a prosecutor or investigator to open a criminal case. Taking advantage of judges' willingness to allow pretrial detention without bail even for nonviolent crimes, law enforcement officials could effectively imprison victims for extended periods of time until they agreed to settle disputes on terms favorable to the attacker (Gans-Morse 2017, 88–90).

Corrupt judicial officials also became entangled in attacks on property rights, particularly those involving **illegal business raiding** (*reiderstvo*). While the term is taken from the American usage, it involves far more than buying up a company's shares in a bid to change management. Prior to a 2002 reform to the Law on Bankruptcy, one common scheme was to acquire a company's debt and then utilize legal loopholes to initiate forced bankruptcy, despite the firm's sound financial health. Raiders would then bribe a judge to appoint a loyal bankruptcy trustee, who would facilitate the theft of the targeted firm's assets. Other schemes that continued to be used throughout the 2000s involved forgery of internal corporate documents or the creation of a second set of documents by paying corrupt government officials, which could then be used to acquire a majority of voting stock or to create a friendly board of directors (Volkov 2004; Firestone 2008).

As corrupt state officials came to recognize their essential role in orchestrating raids, they increasingly became the initiators of such attacks acting on their own volition, rather than at the behest of paying private-sector clients. Bureaucrats leveraged their regulatory powers by selling illegitimate licenses or extorting bribes from firms seeking to bypass red tape or inspectors' fines. Strikingly, despite deregulatory reforms undertaken during Putin's first term as president, more than half of all licenses in the mid-2000s continued to be issued for activities which by law did not require licensing (Shetinin et al. 2005, 7). Corrupt law enforcement officials, meanwhile, continued using the threat of criminal prosecution to force firms to pay bribes or to sell off assets at below-market prices. By the 2010s, more than 100,000 businesspeople were incarcerated for crimes such as fraud, misappropriation or embezzlement, and money-laundering (Kramer 2013). The fact that only 10 to 15 percent of cases related to fraud and embezzlement in this period resulted in sentencing, in stark contrast to murder and rape, which, once initiated, nearly always led to sentencing, suggests that a disturbing portion of these prisoners were victims of law enforcement raiders, not bona fide criminals (Volkov, Paneyakh, and Titaev 2010).

The abuse of the Criminal Code to pressure entrepreneurs became grave enough to attract attention at the highest levels. In 2010 President **Dmitry Medvedev** signed a law prohibiting the pretrial detention of businesspeople accused of nonviolent economic crimes. Without the leverage of pretrial detentions at their disposal, corrupt law enforcement raids declined, and the number of recorded economic crimes subsequently fell (Gans-Morse 2017, 90). But, as discussed below, the problem would soon resurface.

9.4.3   Firms' Rising Demand for Law

As reliance on private coercion decreased and state officials replaced criminal elements in the private security market, Russian firms also increasingly came to rely on formal legal institutions. The number of annual cases firms initiated in Russia's commercial courts quintupled between 1994 and 2010, rising from around 200,000 to more than 1 million. Evidence from numerous surveys of Russian firms demonstrates that beginning in the late 1990s, and particularly by the mid-2000s, Russian firms were utilizing the commercial courts extensively, with around one-third of smaller firms and two-thirds of larger firms reporting litigation experience (Gans-Morse 2017, 58–61). Particularly noteworthy was firms' growing use of legal remedies even in disputes with state authorities, something that firms in many countries seek to avoid out of fear of retribution by state officials or due to a lack of confidence in state-appointed judges' willingness to rule impartially in cases involving the state (Hendley 2002, 144–45). Between 2000 and 2008, cases against the tax authorities increased 280 percent, and by the end of the decade overall litigation against state agencies represented nearly 20 percent of all cases initiated by firms. Notably, win rates for plaintiffs in cases against tax authorities were quite favorable, growing from around 60 percent at the end of the 1990s to above 70 percent in the late 2000s (Gans-Morse 2017, 60–61).

In some circumstances, rising caseloads can result from a growing number of disputes rather than increased willingness to turn to legal institutions, but survey data suggest that such considerations cannot account for the trends observed in Russia throughout the early 2000s. Between 2000 and 2007, legal violations reported by firms in fact declined (Yakovlev 2008). Meanwhile, the 2010 survey of firms from eight Russian cities cited above found that 54 percent of respondents indicated that, compared to ten years earlier, they would be more willing or significantly more willing to turn to the courts in response to violations of their legal rights, compared to just 6 percent of respondents who indicated that their willingness had declined. Of the remaining respondents, 33 percent indicated that their willingness to use the courts remained unchanged, and 7 percent were undecided as to how to answer (Gans-Morse 2017, 59–60).

Most business disputes, of course, do not end up in court, meaning that litigation rates attest to only a portion of firms' actual increase in reliance on lawyers and law. But many other indicators offer broader evidence that law had come to play an increasingly important role in the Russian business world. From the late 1990s through the 2000s, the number of Russian lawyers increased, indicating a perceived demand for the profession (Hendley 2006, 364). Estimating the number of Russian lawyers is complicated because the legal profession in Russia is divided among *advokaty* and *iuristy*, a distinction that is a holdover from Soviet times, during which the former were the rough equivalent of defense attorneys and the latter the rough equivalent of in-house counsel. Only *advokaty* are required to take a bar exam and pay bar membership dues, and, accordingly, only the exact number of *advokaty* is known, even though they represent the minority of all lawyers. But among *advokaty* there was a dramatic increase between 1996 and 2010, from around 26,000 to more than 63,000, a 140 percent change (Gans-Morse 2017, 61).

Lawyers themselves, moreover, reported significant changes in their profession's role in business. As one of Russia's top tax lawyers recalled, by the late 2000s, there was booming demand for his services, whereas in the 1990s his "main problem was not winning, but convincing businesspeople that it is worth going to court." A young litigator confirmed that "Previously, everything was decided with a handshake. Previously, there was no point in signing a contract, because nevertheless no one was going to win anything in court, or enforce a court decision. Now it's not like this . . . A court case already means a lot, and it's easy to enforce a decision." Nor were these developments limited to major cities such as Moscow. When asked about the extent to which firms use the court system, a lawyer from the Siberian town of Barnaul observed that "people more or less have come to resolve disputes in a civilized way, by going to court." He noted that the courts had become so packed with litigants that "to move through the corridors of a courthouse is now impossible" (cited in Gans-Morse 2017, 62–63).

Firms' evaluations of their reliance on lawyers and courts relative to other means of securing property, enforcing contracts, and resolving disputes also provide striking evidence of the increasingly important role of formal legal institutions in post-Soviet Russia. Even by the late 1990s, surveys showed that firms considered the use of courts to be one of the more effective means for addressing contractual problems with suppliers or customers (Hendley, Murrell, and Ryterman 2000, 635–36). By 2010, when asked in surveys to rank their likeliness of using various strategies to collect a debt or resolve an interfirm conflict over control of a valuable asset, Russian firms for both types of disputes indicated that their two most probable courses of action would be to use lawyers to resolve the conflict out of court or to file a claim in the commercial courts. These legalistic strategies ranked higher even than direct negotiations with the other firm's management, which is often considered an early step in resolving disputes even in the most litigious of societies (Gans-Morse 2017, 64–65).

To be sure, some of Russian firms' use of legal institutions in the 2000s reflected bribery and judicial corruption, or the types of illegal raiding schemes described above, rather than legitimate reliance on legal institutions for their formally prescribed purposes. But both analyses by knowledgeable legal scholars (Hendley 2006, 251) and interviews with Russian lawyers themselves (Gans-Morse 2017, 68) indicate that cases involving raiding or corruption were a small minority of the overall caseload by the 2000s, particularly in the commercial courts. Corruption remained a more pressing problem in the courts of general jurisdiction. Indeed, raiders and corrupt law enforcement officials regularly exploited this fact by targeting victim firms with criminal charges, over which the more professionalized and competent commercial courts had no jurisdiction, rather than with civil or administrative infractions. Nevertheless, neither raiding nor judicial corruption was extensive enough to support the claim that Russian firms in the 2000s were engaging with formal legal institutions primarily out of corrupt motives. Rather, by the end of Russia's second decade after communism, firms consistently and frequently had come to rely on lawyers, law, and legal institutions, even as they continued to face novel threats from corrupt state officials or unsavory competitors willing to pay for the services these officials corruptly provided.

9.5   Property Rights in the Era of Putinism

To circumvent constitutional limits on consecutive terms, Putin from 2008 to 2012 installed his longtime aide, Dmitry Medvedev, as president, while he himself assumed the post of prime minister. Upon his return to the presidency in 2012, the Russian political system – and, accordingly, its governance of the economy – changed dramatically. From Putin's ascent to power in 1999 through the world financial crisis of 2008–09, Russia's economy had enjoyed an enviable annual average growth rate of nearly 7 percent. But it never fully regained steam after the crisis, and international sanctions imposed in response to Russia's illegal annexation of Crimea in 2014 exacerbated the economic slowdown. Unable to derive political support and legitimacy from economic growth, Putin's hold on power required a new social contract.

The system that emerged after 2012, often referred to as Putinism, is a highly personalistic form of authoritarianism in which Putin's legitimacy and popularity rest on a mix of populist appeals and socially conservative policies at home and an assertive foreign policy designed to bolster Russia's geopolitical stature abroad (Fish 2017). The new model requires significant repression and censorship both to prevent political unrest and to manage the narrative of Russia's foreign policy adventurism. Compared to the model of governance that characterized the earlier years of the Putin era – a political system that, while far from democratic, nevertheless exhibited elements of political competition, targeted its repression narrowly, and remained modestly responsive to the concerns of the business community – consolidated Putinism is far less conducive to the types of institutional reforms needed to improve the security of property rights.

9.5.1 Putinism's Incompatibility with Institutional Reform

The logic of Putin's power and popularity in the early 2000s had been favorable for property rights security. Political support required economic growth, growth required investment, investment required secure property rights, and secure property rights required institutional reforms. But property rights have played a much less central role in Putin's calculations since 2012: His popularity and legitimacy for the next half-decade would derive from feats such as bringing Crimea under the Russian flag and projecting Russian power in the Middle East to shape the outcome of Syria's civil war, and these endeavors had little to do with protecting everyday firms' property rights.

The one notable change to legal institutions since Putin's return to the presidency involved the 2014 abolishment of the Supreme Commercial Court (Vysshyi Arbitrazhnyi Sud), which previously had been the court of last appeal for the commercial courts. Russia's Supreme Court (Verkhovnyi Sud), the court of last appeal for the courts of general jurisdiction, subsumed the Supreme Commercial Court's duties, thereby curtailing the institutional autonomy from the rest of the judicial system that the commercial courts had enjoyed since their founding. Putin justified the reforms by emphasizing the importance of uniform interpretation and application of law across the commercial courts and courts of general jurisdiction, but critics perceived a power play to rein in the commercial courts' independence and predicted that the judicial restructuring would have a detrimental impact on lower courts' rulings in economic disputes (Pomeranz 2013; Treshchev 2013). Debate over the reforms' effects continues to this day, but critics' concerns seem to have been overstated (Kashanin et al. 2019; Pavlova 2019), and, as discussed below, firms' reliance on the commercial courts has continued to rise.

Despite the deprioritization of institutional reform after 2012, the economic slowdown created pressure for Russia's top leadership to take steps to minimize corrupt officials' siphoning of resources from the state budget. Additionally, the widespread protests that erupted at the end of 2011 and continued into the spring of

2012 – a response both to the fraudulent December 2011 parliamentary elections and to economic stagnation and rising corruption more broadly – unsettled Russia's ruling elite and forced them to recognize the political risks of unconstrained corruption and predation (Rochlitz, Kazun, and Yakovlev 2020). In his third term as president, Putin therefore initiated a series of high-profile campaigns aimed at demonstrating support for the business community, including the creation of the post of a presidentially commissioned Ombudsman for Entrepreneurs' Rights, amnesties for businesspeople convicted of economic crimes, a temporary suspension of regulatory inspections for small businesses, and the implementation of anti-corruption measures requiring state officials to publicly declare their and their families' assets and sources of income online.

These measures appear to have produced a modest reduction in overall levels of corruption, at least among lower-level officials (Rochlitz, Kazun, and Yakovlev 2020). But in many ways the measures were more performative than substantive. The 2013 amnesty for economic crimes was worded so narrowly that it resulted in the release of fewer than 2,000 imprisoned businesspeople (Buckley 2014). A second amnesty in 2018, designed purportedly to encourage Russian entrepreneurs who had fled abroad to return to Russia, fared little better: One of the first to return found himself arrested (Krylova, Deane, and Shelley 2021, 19). By the time Putin won reelection to a fourth term in 2018, it was clear that the business community had little hope of relying on the state to hold predatory officials to account.

9.5.2 Demand for Law vs. the Predatory State prior to Russia's Invasion of Ukraine

In the years prior to Russia's 2022 invasion of Ukraine, the threats posed by corrupt state actors to the property security of Russian firms remained severe. From 2014 to 2019, the number of economic crimes initiated by law enforcement officials rose by nearly 60 percent. From 2018 to 2019, the Investigative Committee of the Russian Federation, a rough equivalent to the FBI in the United States, reported a 135 percent increase in illegal business raiding. And the Ombudsman for Entrepreneurs' Rights continued to receive tens of thousands of reports annually of legal violations committed by state authorities against Russian firms (Krylova, Deane, and Shelley 2021, 8–10).

Some Russian firms undoubtedly continued to rely on protection services provided by corrupt state officials, but the trends toward use of formal legal institutions that emerged in the 2000s have also persisted, despite the significant challenges that firms have encountered over the past decade. With international sanctions and low oil prices weighing down the Russian economy, some firms, particularly in regions such as the Far East, responded by moving operations into the unofficial economy, both to cut costs and to avoid extortion by predatory state officials (Blyakher 2019). Firms that operate unofficially often hesitate to turn to courts or other formal legal institutions out of concern that their own semi-legal or illegal practices may be exposed in the process (Gans-Morse 2017, 99-110). Also of concern in recent years have been the periodic high-profile murders of prominent businesspeople, leading one newspaper to question whether these represent a return to the "criminal '90s." But businesspeople probed by journalists expressed the view that such events remain a rarity, not a harbinger of private coercion's reemergence as a normalized way of doing business (Kharitonova 2020).

Flareups of violence and some firms' retreat to the informal economy notwithstanding, firms' use of the commercial courts continued to climb. Having increased from around 340,000 in 2000 to more than 1 million in 2010, the number of annual cases initiated by firms reached nearly 1.5 million in 2016 before dipping marginally in 2017 and 2018 (Gans-Morse 2020, 55–56). Annual surveys of its members conducted by Russia's largest business association, the Russian Union of Industrialists and Entrepreneurs (RUIE), point to similar trends. In 2020 a remarkable 80 percent of respondents, including around 60 percent of small and medium enterprises and more than 90 percent of large firms, had been a litigant in the commercial courts. Even more notable was that an overwhelming majority of firms – around 80 percent – indicated turning to the courts as one of the most effective strategies for protecting their legal rights and resolving conflicts (survey respondents were instructed to choose up to three strategies). In contrast to the near-consensus on the effectiveness of courts, respondents displayed far less agreement about the utility of other strategies. The second and third most endorsed strategies – to act independently to protect oneself or to seek support from federal agencies – were each chosen as among the most effective by just 30 percent of respondents (RUIE 2021, 61–64).

As Putin entered his third decade of ruling Russia, the security of property rights was at the mercy of two countervailing trends. On the one hand, Russia's private sector had largely abandoned its violent past and quite extensively come to rely on law as the primary tool for resolving business disputes. On the other, predation by state officials continued largely unabated. Predicting which trend would prevail was difficult even before Russia's invasion of Ukraine in February 2022. With Russia's economy in tatters due to sanctions and boycotts, it remains to be seen whether Putinism will survive and, if it does, what form it will take, what types of novel threats to property rights will emerge, and how Russian firms will adapt during the challenging times that lie ahead.

9.6   Conclusion

The case of post-Soviet Russia vividly illustrates the importance of market-supporting institutions that protect property rights, enforce contracts, and help to resolve business conflicts. In the first years after the Soviet Union's collapse, formal legal institutions were ineffective or nonexistent. Firms consequently turned to a range of informal and extralegal means to secure claims to property. The most extreme of these involved the services of criminal protection rackets. By the 2000s, the effectiveness of Russia's formal legal institutions had improved. During his early years in power, Putin oversaw a number of reforms to Russia's legal infrastructure, and significant increases in funding boosted the capacity of the commercial courts. As firms turned away from reliance on the violence that had characterized the 1990s, they came to rely more extensively on law and formal legal institutions. At the same time, many firms continued to utilize illicit services to secure property and enforce contracts, but increasingly these were provided by law enforcement rather than criminal rackets. As the Putin era proceeded, threats to the property security of firms from illegal business raiding and predation by state officials grew. Such threats persisted throughout the period of consolidated Putinism that began after 2012 and, as Russia's political system has become less conducive to institutional reforms, its capacity to constrain state officials' extortion and raiding has diminished. Faced with high levels of public-sector corruption and predation, firms nevertheless have continued to utilize formal legal institutions.

Two significant insights can be drawn from this turbulent evolution of firms' strategies for securing property, enforcing contracts, and resolving business disputes in post-Soviet Russia. The first is that markets cannot function efficiently without effective market-supporting institutions. Without proper institutional underpinnings, transactions are likely to be guided not by Adam Smith's invisible hand but by the violent fist of organized crime groups, unscrupulous business-owners, and corrupt state officials. Nor can it be assumed that the necessary institutions will evolve as soon as the fundamental elements of a market economy – freedom of trade, free prices on most goods and services, and widespread private ownership – are put in place. Institution-building requires time, political support, and a constituency of private citizens and firms ready to lobby for and then utilize newly created institutions.

The second insight to be drawn from the case of post-Soviet Russia concerns the delicate balancing act between state weakness and strength. Russia in the 1990s suffered from a weak state, resulting in widespread use of private coercion even in otherwise legitimate sectors of the economy. By contrast, Russia under Putin suffers from a resurgent state that has resources and capacity at its disposal but not the capacity to constrain the arbitrary practices of corrupt state officials. Secure property rights require a goldilocks state that is strong enough to protect property rights yet simultaneously constrained enough to refrain from property expropriation. It is this challenge of threading the needle between too little and too much state strength that led Douglass North, the economist and Nobel laureate whose seminal work first drew attention to the importance of market-supporting institutions, to declare paradoxically that, "The existence of the state is essential for economic growth; the state, however, is the source of man-made economic decline" (North 1990, 20).

Unlike the 1990s, the Russian state today has the capacity to provide institutions that will facilitate economic growth. But, given Putin's choice of irredentism over prosperity and development, the Russian state is more likely to contribute to economic decline.

DISCUSSION QUESTIONS

1. Why is it problematic to analyze property *rights* – as distinct from property *claims* – in contexts where the state is weak?
2. What can the study of property rights in post-Soviet Russia teach us more broadly about how market economies function and the challenges of making markets work well?
3. In what ways might law enforcement protection rackets be less damaging to society than criminal protection rackets? In what ways might they be more damaging?

REFERENCES

Åslund, Anders. 1995. *How Russia Became a Market Economy.* Washington, DC: Brookings Institution Press.

Balcerowicz, Leszek, Barbara Blaszczyk, and Marek Dabrowski. 1997. "The Polish Way to the Market Economy." In Wing Thye Woo, Stephen Parker, and Jeffrey D. Sachs (eds.), *Economies in Transition: Comparing Asia and Eastern Europe*, pp. 131–60. Cambridge, MA: MIT Press.

Barzel, Yoram. 1997. *Economic Analysis of Property Rights.* New York: Cambridge University Press.

Belova, Eugenia. 2005. "Legal Contract Enforcement in the Soviet Economy." *Comparative Economic Studies*, 47(2), 387–401.

Black, Bernard, Reinier Kraakman, and Anna Tarassova. 1999. "Russian Privitization and Corporate Governance: What Went Wrong." *Stanford Law Review*, 52, 1731–1808.

Blasi, Joseph R., Maya Kroumova, Douglas Kruse, and Daria Panina. 1997. *Kremlin Capitalism: The Privatization of the Russian Economy.* Ithaca: Cornell University Press.

Blyakher, Leonid. 2019. "Regions in Search of a Violent Entrepreneur." *Demokratizatsiya: The Journal of Post-Soviet Democratization*, 27(1), 51–74.

Buckley, Neil. 2014. "Amnesty Will Do Little to Improve Russia Business Climate." *Financial Times*, January 16.

Chivers, C. J. 2010. "Below Surface, US Has Dim View of Putin and Russia." *New York Times*, December 1.

Dubova, Anastasia, and Leonid Kosals. 2013. "Russian Police Involvement in the Shadow Economy." *Russian Politics and Law*, 51(4), 48–58.

Ellickson, Robert C. 1991. *Order without Law.* Cambridge, MA: Harvard University Press.

Favarel-Garrigues, Gilles. 2011. *Policing Economic Crime in Russia: From Soviet Planned Economy to Privatization.* New York: Columbia University Press.

Firestone, Thomas. 2008. "Criminal Corporate Raiding in Russia." *International Lawyer*, 42(4), 1207–30.

Fish, M. Steven. 2017. "What Is Putinism?" *Journal of Democracy*, 28(4), 61–75.

Frye, Timothy. 2002. "Private Protection in Russia and Poland." *American Journal of Political Science*, 46(3), 572–84.

Frye, Timothy, and Ekaterina Zhuravskaya. 2000. "Rackets, Regulation, and the Rule of Law." *Journal of Law, Economics, and Organization*, 16(2), 478–502.

Gans-Morse, Jordan. 2017. *Property Rights in Post-Soviet Russia: Violence, Corruption, and Demand for Law.* New York: Cambridge University Press.

  2020. "Taxes, Banking, and Legal Development in Russia: Lessons about Institutional Complementarities and the Rule of Law." *Demokratizatsiya: The Journal of Post-Soviet Democratization*, 28(1), 47–75.

Gerber, Theodore P., and Sarah E. Mendelson. 2008. "Public Experiences of Police Violence and Corruption in Contemporary Russia: A Case of Predatory Policing?" *Law and Society Review*, 42(1), 1–44.

Handelman, Stephen. 1994. "The Russian Mafiya." *Foreign Affairs*, 73(2), 83–96.

Helmke, Gretchen, and Steven Levitsky. 2004. "Informal Institutions and Comparative Politics: A Research Agenda." *Perspectives on Politics*, 2(4), 725–40.

Hendley, Kathryn. 1997. "Legal Development in Post-Soviet Russia." *Post-Soviet Affairs*, 13(3), 228–51.

  1998. "Remaking an Institution: The Transition in Russia from State Arbitrazh to Arbitrazh Courts." *American Journal of Comparative Law*, 46, 93–127.

  2002. "Suing the State in Russia." *Post-Soviet Affairs*, 18(2), 122–47.

  2003. "Reforming the Procedural Rules for Business Litigation in Russia: To What End?" *Demokratizatsiya: The Journal of Post-Soviet Democratization*, 11(3), 363–80.

  2006. "Assessing the Rule of Law in Russia." *Cardozo Journal International and Comparative Law*, 14(2), 347–91.

  2007. "Putin and the Law." In Dale Herspring (ed.), *Putin's Russia: Past Imperfect, Future Uncertain*, 3rd ed., pp. 99–124. Lanham, MD: Routledge.

Hendley, Kathryn, Peter Murrell, and Randi Ryterman. 2000. "Law, Relationships and Private Enforcement: Transactional Strategies of Russian Enterprises." *Europe–Asia Studies*, 52(4), 627–56.

Hoffman, David. 1997. "Banditry Threatens the New Russia." *Washington Post*, May 12.

  2002. *The Oligarchs: Wealth and Power in the New Russia.* New York: Public Affairs.

Kahn, Peter L. 2002. "The Russian Bailiffs Service and the Enforcement of Civil Judgments." *Post-Soviet Affairs*, 18(2), 148–81.

Kashanin, A. V., A. B. Kozyreva, N. A. Kurnosova, D. V. Malov, and V. D. Churakov. 2019. "Ekonomicheskoe pravosudie v Rossiiskoi federatsii 2014–2018. Analiticheskii obzor." Tsentr razvitiia sovremennogo prava, црсп.рф/wp-content/uploads/2020/05/Экономическое-правосудие-в-2014-2018.pdf.

Kharitonova, Ekaterina. 2020. "Opros predprinimatelei. Oshchushchaete li vy vozvrashchenie kriminalnykh 90-kh?" Realnoe vremia.ru, September 5.

Kornai, Janos. 1992. *The Socialist System: The Political Economy of Communism*. Princeton: Princeton University Press.

Kramer, Andrew. 2013. "Russia's Stimulus Plan: Open the Gulag Gates." *New York Times*, August 8.

Krylova, Yulia, Judy Deane, and Louise Shelley. 2021. "Reiderstvo 2.0: The Illegal Raiding Pandemic in Russia." Working paper, Terrorism, Transnational Crime and Corruption Center at George Mason University. June, https://traccc.gmu.edu/wp-content/uploads/2022/03/Reiderstvo-2.0-The-illegal-raiding-pandemic-in-Russia-1.pdf.

Ledeneva, Alena. 2006. *How Russia Really Works: Informal Practices in Politics and Business*. Ithaca: Cornell University Press.

Macaulay, Stewart. 1963. "Non-Contractual Relations in Business: A Preliminary Study." *American Sociological Review*, 28, 55–69.

Matveeva, N. S. 2007. "Kriminologicheskii analiz sostoianiia zashchishchennosti predprinimatelei ot tiazhkogo nasiliia v Tsentral'nom Federal'nom okruge." In A. I. Dolgova (ed.), *Kriminalnaia ekonimika i organizovannaia prestupnost'*, pp. 86–90. Moscow: Russian Criminological Association and Nizhgovorod Academy of the MVD.

McMillan, John, and Christopher Woodruff. 2000. "Private Order under Dysfunctional Public Order." *Michigan Law Review*, 98(8), 2421–58.

Modestov, Nikolay. 1996. *Moskva banditskaia*. Moscow: Tsentrpoligraf.

North, Douglass. 1990. *Institutions, Institutional Change and Economic Performance*. New York: Cambridge University Press.

Pavlova, Zinaida. 2019. "Kak likvidatsiia VAS RF otrazilas' na sudebnoi praktike." *Advokatskaia Gazeta*, April 5.

Pistor, Katharina. 1996. "Supply and Demand for Contract Enforcement in Russia: Courts, Arbitration, and Private Enforcement." *Review of Central and East European Law*, 22(1), 55–87.

Pomeranz, William. 2013. "Russia's Fading Judiciary." *National Interest*, October 28.

Pravotorov, Mikhail. 2006. "Proshchai, 'krysha'!" *Profil*, October 4.

Putin, Vladimir. 2000. "Open Letter to Russian Voters." *Izvestiia*, February 25.

Radaev, Vadim. 1999. "The Role of Violence in Russian Business Relations." *Problems of Economic Transition*, 41(12), 34–61.

Rochlitz, Michael, Anton Kazun, and Andrei Yakovlev. 2020. "Property Rights in Russia after 2009: From Business Capture to Centralized Corruption?" *Post-Soviet Affairs*, 36(5–6), 434–50.

RUIE (Russian Union of Industrialists and Entrepreneurs). 2021. "Doklad RSPP o sostoianii delovogo klimata v 2020 godu." Report, RUIE (Moscow), https://media.rspp.ru/document/1/0/a/0a140bd76442296880d5190932d0bf73.pdf.

Sborov, Afanasiy. 2003. "Oborotni v pogonakh." *Vlast'*, July 21.

Shetinin, Oleg, Oleg Zamulin, Ekaterina Zhuravskaya, and Evgeny Yakovlev. 2005. "Monitoring the Administrative Barriers to Small Business Development in Russia (5th Round)." CEFIR Policy Paper Series No. 22, Center for Economic and Financial Research, Moscow.

Skoblikov, Petr. 2001. *Imushchestvennye spory i kriminal v sovremennoi Rossii*. Moscow: Publishing House DELO.

Solomon, Peter H. 2005. "The Reform of Policing in the Russian Federation." *Australian and New Zealand Journal of Criminology*, 38(2), 230–40.

  2008. "Assessing the Courts in Russia: Parameters of Progress under Putin." *Demokratizatsiya: The Journal of Post-Soviet Democratization*, 16(1), 63–74.

Statkus, V. F. 1998. "Raskrytie prestuplenii – vazhneishee sredtsvo borby s prestupnost'iu." *Gosudarstvo i pravo*, 4, 68–73.

Taylor, Brian. 2007. "Russia's Power Ministries: Coercion and Commerce." Working paper, Institute for National Security and Counterterrorism (INSCT), Syracuse University, Syracuse, NY (October).

  2011. *State Building in Putin's Russia: Policing and Coercion after Communism.* New York: Cambridge University Press.

Treshchev, Sergei. 2013. "Ob"edinenie sudov." Lawfirm.ru, December 17.

Volkov, Vadim. 2002. *Violent Entrepreneurs: The Use of Force in the Making of Russian Capitalism.* Ithaca: Cornell University Press.

  2004. "Hostile Enterprise Takeovers: Russia's Economy in 1998–2002." *Review of Central and East European Law*, 29(4), 527–48.

Volkov, Vadim, Ella Paneyakh, and Kirill Titaev. 2010. "Proizvolnaia aktivnost' pravookhranitel'nykh organov v sfere borby s ekonomicheskoi prestupnost'iu." Analytical Paper, Institute for the Rule of Law, https://enforce.spb.ru/images/analit_zapiski/Policy_memo_crimestat_v2_26.pdf.

Webster, William H. 1997. *Russian Organized Crime: Global Organized Crime Project.* Washington, DC: Center for Strategic and International Studies.

Yakovlev, Andrei. 2008. "Pravo i pravoprimenenie v Rossii glazami biznesa. Chto izmenilos' za sem' let." In Yurii Tikhomirov (ed.), *Pravoprimenenie: teoriia i praktika*, pp. 214–39. Moscow: Formula Prava.

10 Economic Policies and Russia's Global Economic Integration

LAURA SOLANKO

Fig. 10.1 Financial district, Moscow. Credit: Westend61 / Westend61 / Getty Images.

> However, I want to note ... the norm in the international community, in the world today, is also harsh competition – for markets, for investment, for political and economic influence. And in this fight Russia needs to be strong and competitive.
>
> Vladimir Putin, "Annual Address, 2002"

Abstract

Over the past two decades, the quest for economic stability and security has become a leading principle of contemporary Russian macroeconomic policies. To understand the genesis of these fundamental building blocks of Russia's macroeconomic policies, the chapter provides a chronology of key policy choices and macroeconomic developments from the financial crisis of August 1998 to the aftermath of the global financial crisis ten years later. The painful fallout of recurring economic crises, most notably in the 1990s and after the global financial crisis of 2008, has shaped Russia's recent policy choices in fiscal, monetary, and trade policies. During President Vladimir Putin's first two terms in office in 2000–08, the Russian government reformed public finances, restructured sovereign debt, and wisely created a Stabilization Fund for a rainy day. These fiscal buffers cushioned the economy against some direct effects of the 2008 and 2014 crisis. Since 2012, it has become clear that conservative fiscal and monetary policies alone are not enough to support economic growth or increase household welfare. The sanctions and trade restrictions that are the result of geopolitical tensions with the West added further weight and urgency to Russia's search for economic security at the expense of other economic priorities, such as social policy or improving the investment climate.

10.1   Introduction

Russia's economy is dependent on global markets. Trade in goods and services and access to global financial markets are crucially important for the country's welfare. This is not unusual for upper-middle-income countries, but Russia is more vulnerable to swings in the global markets than the average economy. Crude oil, oil products, and natural gas constitute well over half of the value of Russian exports and provide a quarter of public-sector revenues. Any abrupt changes in these revenue streams have immediate effects in domestic financial markets and in the external value of the Russian ruble. Managing these vulnerabilities is a key challenge for the Russian government. The tumultuous years of economic transition in the 1990s and the recurring financial crises have further heightened demands for a stable and predictable macroeconomic environment. Under President **Vladimir Putin**, the quest for stability and economic security has become a leading principle of Russian economic policies.

Managing external vulnerabilities and providing stability and security for domestic actors constitute the traditional field of any government's fiscal, monetary, and trade policies. In this chapter, I will examine how tools and outcomes of these major macroeconomic policy areas have evolved in Russia over the past decades. A particular focus of the discussion is how external shocks and internal structural weaknesses continue to create economic fragility, and how robust economic growth and conservative economic policies have helped bring stability to the Russian economy. The 1990s and early 2000s were a period of unprecedented globalization in trade and finance, as multilateral agreements eased restrictions on foreign trade and capital flows almost everywhere, making trade less costly for everyone. Russia, a newly independent country after 1991, was thus integrated into the global economy precisely at a time when markets for goods and capital were becoming both fiercely competitive and quite volatile.

As a matter of definition, **fiscal policy** refers to the use of government spending and taxation powers to influence the domestic economy. One could argue that existence of fiscal policy is a defining feature of an independent state. Secondly, **monetary policy** means actions taken by a central bank to maintain the stability of prices and the financial sector in order to support stable economic growth. To this end, central banks use various tools to influence the price and availability of money in the economy. Traditionally, this primarily means steering a policy interest rate charged on central bank operations. For some central banks, managing or controlling the foreign exchange rate is the key task, while others focus solely on domestic prices. Thirdly, **trade policy** refers to government regulations and (bilateral or multilateral) agreements on foreign trade and crossborder investments. Trade in goods and services is shaped by import and export tariffs as well as by nontariff barriers, for example, local content requirements that require firms to use domestic goods or services.

Russia's fiscal and monetary policies have changed dramatically since the collapse of Soviet Union. The oftentimes chaotic liberalization, privatization, and decentralization of the early 1990s ended in a major fiscal failure. Russia defaulted on its sovereign debt in August 1998, which forced the government to cut spending and to balance the budget. In the years that followed, tax reforms and increasing oil prices helped in balancing the budget and then in paying back the remaining Soviet-era public debt by summer 2006. In the 2000s, Russia became a country with almost no sovereign debt controlling one of the world's largest foreign exchange reserves. Following international best practice, the Russian monetary policy framework was completely overhauled in the 2010s, and the central bank switched to targeting inflation in the following decade. In just two decades Russia had become a textbook example of countercyclical, conservative fiscal policies and prudent monetary policy.

Over the past decade, Russian fiscal policies have continued to be shaped by three distinct features: avoidance of sovereign borrowing, dependence on global oil prices, and an expenditure structure tilted toward pensions and the military. Russia's sizable fiscal buffers and moderate inflation have greatly improved macroeconomic stability and eased vulnerability to external shocks. Given the chaotic starting point, this is a remarkable achievement.

Nevertheless, sound macroeconomic policies are not sufficient to diversify the economy. Russia today is as dependent on revenues from the hydrocarbon sectors as it was two decades ago, with about a quarter of Russia's GDP created in the oil and gas sectors. Russia's **global economic integration** has mainly occurred via energy and raw material exports and capital flows. Russian producers have always imported foreign technologies, but they were never very tightly linked to global production networks, and the current trade policies make importing foreign technology and knowhow increasingly costly. Russia has, however, pursued financial openness, and unrestricted crossborder capital flows have remained an important factor in the policy mix, despite economic nationalist rhetoric. This implies that any abrupt changes in global financial and energy markets will continue to cause havoc in the Russian economy.

Diversifying the economy away from hydrocarbons has been a goal of the Putin government since the early 2000s, but the reform process would require potentially risky reforms along with new policies aimed to increase competitiveness in the nonenergy sectors. Since 2014 Russia's import-substitution policies have increasingly shielded domestic manufacturers from international competition, but at the same time these policies have increased the costs of diversification. Over the past decades, Russia's government has favored rigid rules and stability over flexibility and innovation in economic policies. This has slowed the diversification away from hydrocarbons. Meanwhile, Russia's main export markets, especially in Europe, are tightening carbon neutrality targets. This may seriously challenge the wisdom of Russia's current economic policy choices.

The state plays an important role in Russia's economy. In most economies where democratic institutions are weak and the rule of law is selective, the overall role of the public sector tends to be much larger than the share of government expenditure would suggest. In Russia too, state-owned or state-controlled corporations typically control much of energy, finance, and transportation sectors. Further, where formal institutions are weak, de facto implementation of laws and regulations tends to allow various state actors wide powers to shape economic outcomes, as Chapters 2 and 5 address.

Within two weeks after Russia's attack on Ukraine in February 2022, the Russian economy faced an unprecedented crisis. Western sanctions that target the Russian Central Bank and major commercial banks have brought about the near-collapse of Russia's financial system. Another set of Western sanctions, coupled with the ruble's devaluation, will severely limit Russia's options to import foreign technologies for years to come. Sanctions and potential Russian countersanctions may also restrict Russia's income from exports of raw materials. The final economic shock will come via increased risk and uncertainty, likely to lead to a significant drop in both domestic and foreign investments. As of mid-March 2022, it is impossible to evaluate the total cost of the war and sanctions on the Russian economy. But it is clear that Russia will have to rely on wide range of capital controls, more state regulation, and all that is left of the fiscal buffers to evade an economic crisis akin to that of the early 1990s.

10.2 How Stability and Sovereignty Became the Cornerstones of Russian Macroeconomic Policies

I begin this section by examining how the Russian crisis of 1998 ended the first decade of post-Soviet transition in Russia and why tight fiscal policy became a cornerstone of macroeconomic policies for the years to come. I then examine how new fragilities emerged and how sizable fiscal and monetary buffers were not enough to fight off the effects of a global crisis.

10.2.1 Setting the Stage

The first decade of the economic transformation from the Soviet planned economy to what turned out to be a poorly functioning market economy was devastating for all countries of the former Soviet Union and formerly socialist Central Europe. The early years of price liberalization and privatization and the collapse of old networks were especially destructive in Russia, where real GDP shrank by about 40 percent between 1988 and 1995. The standard prescription of necessary reforms for post-Soviet economies in the late 1980s and early 1990s was a long list of liberalization, privatization, stabilization, and structural reforms, a canon known as the **Washington Consensus**. In Russia, liberalization and privatization generally were pushed ahead relatively swiftly by **Boris Yeltsin**'s team of liberal reformers, a policy that was later labeled "shock therapy," distinct from a more gradual, step-by-step strategy to the post-socialist economic transformation. Russia's liberal reforms, however, were hampered by the Yeltsin government's failure to pursue fiscal and financial stability early on. Price liberalization was not coupled with simultaneous reforms in public expenditure, which meant that the government continued to pay enterprise subsidies, state-sector wages, costs for social services, and so on, while failing to collect taxes and fees to finance the outlays. Unable to balance expenditures and revenues, Russia generated sizable federal budget deficits for much of the 1990s.

By the mid-1990s, Russian securities markets started to emerge, and an increasing share of the budget deficit could be financed by government bonds. The new means of deficit financing allowed the government to reduce its dependence on central bank financing, thereby giving the central bank some room to conduct monetary policy. But issuing government bonds also allowed the government to avoid the inherently unpleasant decisions to cut public spending.

Foreign trade was gradually liberalized by removing most quotas for imports and exports, and many export tariffs were lowered substantially in 1992–95. In general terms, the quality and variety of Russian products were far below what was available in global markets. Russians thus imported foreign goods for consumption, and companies invested in technological updates as a first step to increase economic wellbeing. Nevertheless, imports remained subject to various tariffs, and in these early years of the post-Soviet transformation the Russian government was already showing a preference for protecting import-competing domestic industries.

Import of foreign capital was, however, welcomed, and the government bond market was opened to foreign investors in early 1996. Very high yields and the fixed ruble-to-United States dollar (USD) exchange rate made the short-term government bonds known as GKOs (*gosudarstvennye kratkosrochnye obligatsii*), highly attractive for anyone with a fair dose of risk appetite and access to global money markets. Many Russian banks took foreign loans and invested in the booming GKO market. Initially the outstanding stock of these bonds was very small, but it started to grow quickly. New bonds were auctioned weekly, with the most common maturity being only three months. This meant that every week increasing volumes of new bonds had to be issued simply to pay back the maturing bills.

As the Asian financial crisis hit global financial markets in 1998, Russia's mounting short-term debt became a signal of looming disaster. Foreign investors began to withdraw their bets from emerging markets, which meant that liquidity in Russian markets quickly dried up. To make matters worse, falling oil prices led to growing deficits in both the current account and the federal budget. A classical financial crisis was in the making. In August 1998 the authorities had no choice other than to devalue the ruble, declare a default on ruble-denominated debt, and force a moratorium on all foreign debt payments. The fragile macroeconomic stabilization that had been achieved in 1997 was wiped out almost overnight. Overall, Russian GDP decreased by 5 percent in 1998, and inflation peaked at over 100 percent.

The **Russian crisis of 1998** came to symbolize the perils of rapid financial liberalization and loose fiscal policies. Internationally, events in August 1998 strengthened discussions on the future of the global financial system and especially on the relative merits of financial globalization in emerging economies. In domestic politics, Russian decisionmakers had to take fiscal consolidation seriously. In the midst of a financial crisis the only way to do that was to drastically cut expenditure, in particular the complex and opaque web of enterprise subsidies. General government expenditure (federal, regional, and local budgets combined) was cut by a whopping 10 percentage points from 36 percent of GDP in 1997 to 26 percent of a much smaller GDP in 1999. The fiscal deficits that seemed impossible to limit in the early years of transition had all but disappeared by the end of 1999.

After immediate macroeconomic stability was achieved, the new economic policy team nominated by President Putin finally embarked on major tax reforms in late 2000. A team led by Finance Minister Aleksei Kudrin put forward a new Tax Code that introduced significant changes. Several tax rates were cut significantly, tax bases were unified, and many tax breaks and some regulatory loopholes were abolished. Most importantly, a strict oil-taxation regime was put in place. Oil

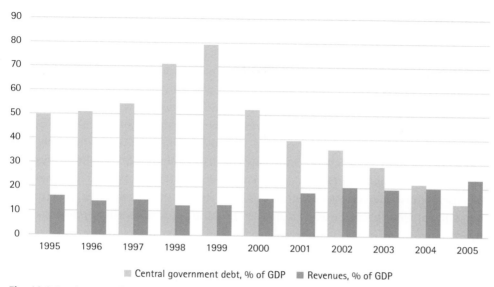

Fig. 10.2 Russian central government revenue and debt, 1995–2005.
Source: Created by author from BOFIT Russia Statistics.

companies had typically been able to minimize their tax payments by using barter payments, transfer pricing, and on- and offshore tax havens. As Russian corporate accounting on profit and loss statements was notoriously unreliable, the new oil taxation was based on physical quantities produced and exported. The mineral extraction tax became an ad valorem tax calculated based on the price of Urals crude, not on domestic prices. All these reforms aimed to decrease tax avoidance and thereby increase government revenue. On most accounts, they succeeded (see Figure 10.2).

Overall, the experience of an extremely violent financial crisis created an economic policy consensus on the necessity of maintaining a balanced budget. This **policy consensus** included a shared mistrust of foreign borrowing by the government. Never again should sovereign Russia be left at the mercy of international financial markets. Very cautious and conservative fiscal policy soon became the only game in town. Importantly, apart from the ninety-day moratorium, no major capital controls were put in place. Russia remained highly dollarized and private-sector foreign funding was not seen as a threat to stability. Therefore, the new policy consensus did not entail economic isolationism. Policymakers wanted to see Russia joining the global economy, but on more cautious terms.

10.2.2 The Great Economic Boom and the Bust

In the 1990s, oil prices rarely exceeded US$ 20 per barrel, and during the 1998 crisis crude prices temporarily dropped below $10 (all prices are in US dollars). **Oil prices** started to recover in 2000, and the price for Urals crude, the major Russian export variety, followed suit. It traded at around $23 per barrel in 2001–02, but the price more than doubled to $50 in 2005. During Putin's first term in office, a new Tax Code and oil tax regime had been put in place, which meant that Russia was exceptionally well placed to benefit from the unprecedented boom in global trade. Federal budget revenues that equaled 15 percent of GDP in 2000 had grown to 24 percent of GDP by 2005, and the federal budget was running a surplus of 7 percent of GDP. The next big economic policy discussion was about how best to use the surpluses. Many commentators made compelling cases for using the windfall monies to support an impoverished population or to fund much-needed infrastructure investments. The fiscal conservatives, however, argued that significant increases in government expenditure would mostly lead to higher inflation with little effect on long-term growth. Instead, it would be preferable to use some of the funds to pay back Soviet-era public debt and store the rest in a sovereign reserve fund.

The fiscally conservative strategy won the debate in the end. Thanks to this policy choice and rapid increase in global oil prices, Russia repaid all remaining Soviet-era public debt in August 2006. By the end of 2006, the newly created Stabilization Fund had ballooned to $90 billion. If in 1998 Russia had been a textbook example of irresponsible fiscal management, by 2006 it had started to look like a model student.

Better legal frameworks, macroeconomic stability, and the overall economic boom also fostered growth in modern banking in Russia. However, the domestic banking system at the time was small in relation to the investment needs of large corporations such as Gazprom or Rosneft. In contrast to most former socialist countries in Central Europe, the role of foreign banks has never been significant in the Russian banking sector. No major bank was ever privatized, and foreign entry remained restricted.

Large fixed investments had to be financed out of retained earnings or by borrowing from abroad. Whereas sovereign foreign borrowing was nonexistent, **private-sector foreign debt** started to accumulate. The Russian Federation had received an investment grade rating from all three major rating agencies by the end of 2005. This helped the large Russian companies raise funding and meaningfully decreased lending costs. The piecemeal liberalization of capital accounts continued, and most remaining restrictions on financial flows were lifted in 2007.

The **exchange rate**, meanwhile, remained tightly managed until 2014. The central bank had a dual mandate of promoting stable exchange rates and maintaining moderate inflation, but the former policy goal was much more important. As inflation in Russia remained above the levels in the United States, the ruble continued to appreciate in real terms, making imports increasingly attractive.

Successful macroeconomic stabilization, the maturing of the structural transformation of the 1990s, and a favorable external environment supported economic growth in Russia. On average, between 2000 and 2007 Russian GDP grew by

7 percent annually. This unprecedented pace of economic growth rapidly created wealth. The number of billionaires more than doubled, and real incomes increased for almost everyone. This was not unnoticed by international investors. Global foreign direct investment inflows increased in four consecutive years and reached record levels in 2007.

Overall, the policy choices of President Putin's first two terms in office made the Russian government almost debt-free, with one of the world's largest foreign exchange reserves and a sizable sovereign wealth fund. Many aspects of Russia's legal and regulatory framework were improved. But Russia's economy remained plagued by the weak rule of law, corruption, and a cumbersome bureaucracy. The unprecedented economic boom made neglecting these issues all too easy.

A decade after the dramatic economic crisis of 1998, Russia's economy was once again threatened by **global financial instability**, this time originating in the collapse of the US subprime mortgage markets. In late 2008 global investors rushed to move their liquid assets to safe havens from emerging markets, causing havoc in Russian markets. And, as the period of global economic boom ended abruptly, global raw material prices duly collapsed. A global crisis once again hit the Russian economy.

This time, however, Russian state finances were in much better shape than in 1998, and the government did not hesitate to use the spending powers at its disposal. Despite powerful **fiscal and monetary policy support**, the Russian GDP shrank by a whopping 8 percent in 2009, more than in any other large economy of the G20 group. The global financial crisis had a devastating effect on the Russian economy, even though its macroeconomic fundamentals were in excellent shape. This underlines how interconnected Russian economy is with the rest of the world and how vulnerable it is to abrupt changes in global commodities and financial markets.

To limit this vulnerability, diversification of the economy away from hydrocarbons would be needed. But planning measures to promote innovation and fair competition require a different set of administrative capabilities than balancing the state budget. Moreover, implementing such reforms requires strong political backing. Both of these have been in short supply, especially after the 2009 crisis. Avoiding risks took precedence over bold reforms, and macroeconomic policies once again focused on balancing the budget. Sizable fiscal buffers and central bank reserve assets were regarded as necessary to fight off the effects of future external shocks.

What is more, oil prices recovered quickly, which meant that Russia could delay structural reforms and fall back on hydrocarbon revenues. Once global growth resumed in 2010, Russia's economy grew rapidly, surpassing the precrisis level of GDP in 2011. For a short while, it seemed that the economic growth based on increasing oil prices and benefits of earlier reforms would continue to provide stability and relative prosperity for Russian citizens. Yet, it soon became clear that

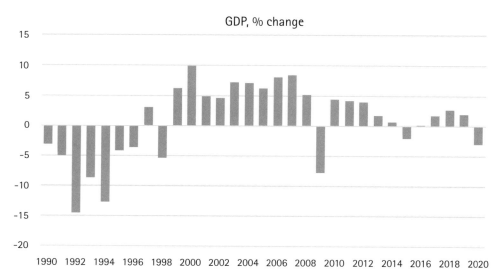

Fig. 10.3 Russian GDP growth, 1990–2020.
Source: Created by author from BOFIT Russia Statistics.

stability alone would not return Russia to a path of fast economic growth. In 2012–20, since President Putin has reassumed the presidency for a third and fourth term, Russian GDP has grown by a meager 1 percent annually, what essentially amounts to nearly a decade of stagnation (see Figure 10.3).

10.3   Stability, Security, and External Shocks

Fiscal, monetary, and trade policies in contemporary Russia were deeply influenced by the government's quest for economic stability, which in turn is a response to the external and internal fragilities that have shaped policy choices and policy outcomes in these areas.

Managing Russia's public finances is highly demanding due to country's volatile oil tax revenues, and tackling this volatility was the primary task of the government's fiscal policy team. Since the global financial crisis, monetary policy has been largely mandated to a technocratic team of central bank economists tasked with bringing down inflation and thereby increasing macroeconomic stability. With support from the president, the central bank implemented a bold monetary policy change in 2014 and switched to full inflation targeting. Two further changes in foreign economic policy have critically shaped Russia's integration into the global economy: Russia's "Pivot to Asia" and its import-substitution policies. As a result of these policies, Russia's economy has become more self-sustaining in a few narrow fields, but it has not become less dependent on raw material exports.

10.3.1 Conservative Fiscal Policies Continued

Russian fiscal policies continue to be shaped by three distinct features: avoidance of sovereign borrowing, dependence on global oil prices, and public expenditure heavily tilted toward pensions and the military. The background for the first feature, very conservative budgeting and maintaining a balanced budget, we are already familiar with. This quest for stability has also resulted in Russian fiscal policies being a textbook example of countercyclical fiscal policy. Increases in government expenditure have been mainly linked to countervailing negative effects of external shocks or explained by traditional political business cycles. In more tranquil times, however, public expenditure has grown more slowly than the economy overall. Political economy setups in most Western nations have made such expenditure cuts nearly impossible.

10.3.1.1 Revenues Tilted toward Oil and Gas

The second feature is self-evident, but too often neglected. As an **oil-exporting country**, Russia's revenue structure is tilted toward taxes and fees on oil production and exports. As a rule of thumb, half of federal revenues come from the oil and gas sector via a mineral extraction tax and export duties. Since the federal budget covers about half of the total government budget, this means that about a quarter of the total Russian government revenues originate directly from the oil and gas sector. Personal income tax and corporate profit tax together only bring in about a fifth of general government revenue.

The proceeds of the single largest revenue source are linked to inherently volatile oil export prices. Russia, therefore, faces the typical problem of resource-dependent economies: how best to manage volatility of government revenue. Discussions on various ways to smooth government consumption over time have been at the very core of Russian economic policy discussions since the mid-1990s. From early on, international advisors, such as the International Monetary Fund (IMF), proposed adhering to a predetermined **oil price rule** for fiscal policy. An oil price rule would limit the use of oil revenues if export prices exceeded a baseline price. The challenge is how to determine a baseline price level for a commodity as volatile as crude oil. Should the baseline be based on prices in the past and, if so, would that mean prices in the past five years or in the past decade or over an even longer period of time? Should that price reflect price level in dollars or in domestic currency? There are no obvious correct answers to these questions, and it is therefore not entirely surprising that finding a solution was not easy. Financial hawks like the Ministry of Finance typically tended to favor a very low baseline price, whereas the Ministry of Economy and some sectoral ministries naturally argued for a higher baseline price and higher public spending.

After various attempts, the current oil price rule was adopted in 2017. The rule states that "surplus" oil and gas revenues that accrue to the federal budget when oil prices are above a predetermined level are to be saved in the **National Welfare Fund**. As the fund's assets have increased, so have discussions on how to use them. The fund is still largely seen as a stabilization fund, a buffer against global shocks. But surely some of the assets could be used to support domestic investments in infrastructure or in manufacturing? In the early 2000s the Ministry of Finance succeeded in arguing that large-scale use of excess budget revenue to prop up domestic investments would bring few tangible benefits. Now, in the 2020s, as prospects for economic growth are much more moderate, the temptation to use some of the funds for various goals is again on the rise.

10.3.1.2   Public Expenditure Tilted toward Pensioners and the Security Apparatus

The single largest expenditure item in the Russian consolidated budget is social security. That is true for many economies globally, but in Russia cash payments to pensioners alone equal almost a quarter of total expenditure. Russia's low birth rates and increasing life expectancy threaten to increase this share further. However, reforming the pension system and increasing the pension age have proven to be especially unpopular reforms. Russia's approximately 43 million pensioners constitute about 40 percent of all eligible voters.

The second-largest public expenditure item is the combination of national defense, internal security, and public order. Assessing the true extent of Russian military expenditure is a tedious task, as some expenditure items categorized as internal security, education, housing services, and national economy are in fact directly linked to the armed forces. Moreover, an increasing share of these non-military budget items has been classified as secret in the Russian budget laws, making it impossible to assess their real uses. The Stockholm Peace Research Institute (SIPRI) estimated 2020 Russian military expenditure at slightly above 4 percent of GDP, among the highest in the world.

In most countries, debate on the composition of public spending is often at the heart of economic policy debates. In Russia such discussions are all but nonexistent, as cutting pensions and criticizing military expenditure are politically highly sensitive. Although the government did undertake two very unpopular important social policy reforms, first in 2005, when in-kind benefits were monetized, and most recently raising the pension age in 2020, as Chapter 13 will detail. Russia's public expenditure is geared toward ensuring stability and security at the expense of investments in human capital such as education and healthcare. For a country aspiring to modernize and diversify its economy, that is worrying.

10.3.2   Monetary Policy and Financial Market Stability

Following the stepwise devaluation of the ruble in early 2009, the Central Bank of Russia (CBR) continued to actively intervene in the foreign exchange markets.

These interventions far outweighed all other instruments the central bank could use to control domestic interest rates and money supply. It became clear that Russia in the early 2010s was a prime example of what academics and practitioners call the **impossible trinity** (the **trilemma**). The trilemma states that a country can simultaneously choose only two of the three policy goals of global financial integration, independent monetary policy, and a fixed exchange rate. Supported by sizable foreign reserves, Russia was trying to choose all three. The result was persistently high inflation, leading to real appreciation of the ruble and declining price competitiveness of domestic producers. Therefore, one of these goals had to be dropped.

First, international financial markets had become essential to Russian business elites both as a source of funding and as a means of storing wealth. Investments in foreign assets offer wider options for risk management and potentially better property rights than domestic investments. Russian elites and policymakers shared a clear commitment to maintain financial integration and free movement of capital. Imposing capital controls was never seriously discussed. Secondly, giving up sovereign monetary policy was clearly out of question. Moreover, it would have been difficult to imagine a country as large and heterogeneous as Russia to align its interest rates to those of any foreign country. Therefore, if something had to be adjusted, the only option was to abandon the **managed exchange rate**. Since the early 2000s, most central banks globally had opted for a combination of floating exchange rate and a full inflation targeting to avoid the trilemma. In Russia a gradual shift in focus from exchange rate targeting to inflation targeting was mentioned in relevant policy documents as early as 2004. The trouble was that successful inflation targeting requires relatively well-functioning financial markets and sophisticated market-based monetary policy tools. The inherited structure of the banking sector made attaining these difficult.

As a legacy of the 1990s, the Russian banking sector remained fragmented and prone to bank runs. Many of the small and obscure financial firms behaved more like casinos than banks, often preferring speculation in foreign exchange markets to lending activities. Others were merely accounting units for large corporations, focused on servicing one client: the bank's owner. In the early 2010s, there were still more than 1,000 banks operating in the market, most of them tiny and owned by a handful of increasingly wealthy individuals. Weeding out at least the most obscure institutions was a process that was long overdue. Lack of trust among financial market actors also meant that the interbank markets worked poorly, and this had a bearing on the effectiveness of central bank monetary policy actions. As only a few banks had access to central bank auctions, interest rate changes barely affected bank lending rates.

All of this started to change in the 2010s. A significant change occurred in 2013 as the Central Bank of Russia became a financial markets mega-regulator with an explicit financial stability mandate. The CBR assumed responsibility for the regulation of insurance and pension markets, professional security market participants, investment funds, actuarial activities, rating agencies, and microfinance organizations, as well as for the development of financial market infrastructure. The new financial markets mega-regulator enjoyed a clear political mandate to clean up the financial sector. The number of banks decreased on average by 100 annually in 2013–15, with no discernible negative effect on financial stability. At the same time the CBR started to use more market-based interest rates to signal its monetary policy stance. The CBR announced that it would have measures in place to allow a free-floating ruble by the end of 2014.

Maintaining the managed exchange rate did come to an end during 2014. Following the annexation of Crimea in March 2014, the CBR intervened extensively in the currency markets, selling more than $26 billion worth of its currency reserves in a single month to prop up the ruble. As oil prices started to fall in summer 2014, instead of further interventions the CBR relaxed its mechanism for steering the exchange rate and began cautiously to increase the main monetary policy rate. As oil prices continued to fall and Western sanctions on Russia were imposed, the value of the ruble duly collapsed. Finally, in mid-December 2014, the ruble was allowed to float freely, and the key policy rate was more than doubled to 17 percent. To the surprise of many, in midst of a crisis Russia had resolutely switched to a new monetary policy regime of **inflation targeting**. The central bank no longer has a target for nominal exchange rate, and instead the 4 percent inflation target was taken seriously. The trilemma was solved.

The banking sector cleanup continued. Of the 834 banks at the end of 2014, fewer than half existed by the end of 2020. Additionally, several faltering banks in the top fifty were taken over by the CBR in the latter half of 2017, and many more were assigned to the Deposit Insurance Authority for rehabilitation. Despite the decreasing number of credit institutions, bank lending grew constantly. Of the remaining banks, an increasing share was modern universal banks, serving both households and corporate clients.

As expected, the **floating exchange rate** has helped make the economy less vulnerable to external shocks. When oil prices rise (or fall), the ruble tends to appreciate (or depreciate), making export revenues less volatile in ruble terms. This in turn translates into less volatile oil tax revenues in the federal budget. The CBR has focused on controlling inflation and maintaining financial stability. Inflation in 2016–20 was, on average, quite close to the 4 percent target level, a remarkable achievement given Russia's past inflation history (see Figure 10.4).

The move to a floating rate was neither easy nor without its skeptics. A fixed foreign exchange rate had been one of the few relatively stable and predictable economic indicators during the previous decades. A significant share of bank deposits was in foreign currency, and Russians were accustomed to pricing

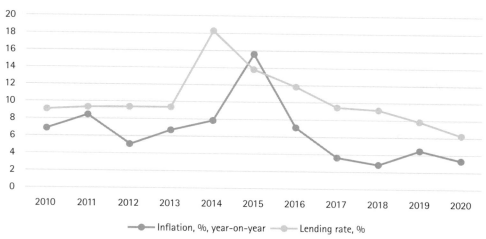

Fig. 10.4 Inflation and average lending rate in Russia, percentage, 2010–2020.
Source: Created by author from BOFIT Russia Statistics and Central Bank of Russia. Data points are annual averages. Lending rate is the average rate on ruble-denominated short-term (less than 12 months) corporate loans.

high-ticket items and upmarket rental agreements in US dollars. Another line of argument was based on the observation that the high and volatile inflation rate had kept real interest rates low or even negative for most of the previous decades. Therefore, Russian corporations had become accustomed to negative loan interest rates, and a change in monetary policy would cause widespread havoc.

Yet, despite these concerns, the Russian economy quickly adapted to the new policy regime. Low and predictable inflation supported financial stability and growth of the banking sector. When inflation slowed down, nominal interest rates also declined. Russian monetary policy now closely resembles that of other large central banks such as the European Central Bank and the United States Federal Reserve. The challenges are similar, and the policy toolkits include broadly similar instruments. Details naturally differ. But the broad lesson of this policy shift is that the Russian economy is not so unique after all. Russian economic actors react to increasing (or decreasing) prices in much the same way as actors anywhere else. Institutions differ but, where they are similar, so are the outcomes.

10.3.3 Trade Policies and Foreign Economic Relations

As discussed in section 10.3.2, free movement of capital has remained a largely uncontested policy choice in Russia. Free movement of goods and services, however, has garnered less political support, even if the economic boom in the early 2000s was largely built on imported machinery and foreign technologies. Promoting imports as a means of increasing competition, productivity, and links to global value chains has never attracted much support in Russia.

Russia was a latecomer to the World Trade Organization (WTO), joining only in 2012. Russia had signaled its intent to join much earlier, as WTO accession was part of Russia's policy in the 1990s to join all the major international organizations and multilateral agreements that govern the global economy. The delay was in part due to Russia's desire to protect domestic manufacturing and service sectors from foreign competition, and in part shaped by the fact that Russia exports few manufactured goods that would benefit from lower trade barriers. Russia's key export items are raw materials that are mostly exempted from import tariffs everywhere.

Over the past decade, two key policy objectives – a pivot to the East and import-substitution – have shaped Russian trade policies and foreign economic relations more than WTO membership. These two objectives became more urgent when relations with many Western countries deteriorated, but neither was a direct consequence of the geopolitical troubles. Both were launched soon after the immediate effects of the global financial crisis began to wane.

10.3.3.1   Pivot to the East

In the 1990s and early 2000s, Russia's conception of economic globalization was defined by increasing trade links and crossborder finance with the economies in the western hemisphere, with the European Union countries in particular. This was natural for several reasons, not least because Russia's existing export infrastructure connects Russia to Eastern and Western Europe, and many firms in these economies were eager to enter the Russian market. By the early 2010s, however, the driving force of global economic growth had changed dramatically. Asian economies had become the world's largest and fastest-growing markets, which meant that Russia's main export items (crude oil, natural gas, and hard coal) were increasingly in demand by Asian customers. Even though global economic growth halted in 2009, China continued to grow quickly and surpassed the United States as the world's largest primary energy consumer.

President Putin first outlined Russia's "Pivot to the East," that is, a shift in policy emphasis to Asia, in 2009. At the time the Pivot simply acknowledged the new realities of the global economy. **Diversification of export markets** is a reasonable policy objective, and a focus on Asia is essential for securing future export markets for Russian hydrocarbons. Opening new oil and gas export routes to the East required developing new production areas in eastern Siberia and building two vast pipeline systems across thousands of kilometers. An oil pipeline from Siberia to the Pacific coast with a connection to China was commissioned in 2009–12 and a natural gas pipeline to China in late 2019. Thanks to these new pipelines, China has become one of Russia's main trading partners over the past ten years, leading to a significant diversification of Russia's oil and gas export markets. Consequently, the share of the EU countries in Russian crude oil exports has declined, but was still about one-half in 2020.

Over time, the pivot to the East and closer cooperation with China came also to align more closely with Russia's broader foreign policy goals of breaking US hegemony and creating a multipolar world order. Indeed, China and Russia have increased their cooperation on many fronts, including cooperation in the defense sphere with, for example, high-profile joint military exercises. Chinese technology has become essential in many Russian oil and gas fields. Both countries also share doubts about the dollar's preeminent status in global trade finance. Cooperation has resulted in increased use of the ruble and the yuan in bilateral trade, and Russia's Central Bank now holds some of its foreign exchange reserves in yuan. Further, a small number of large Russian corporations have secured loans from Chinese development banks.

Despite high-profile statements, however, changes on the ground have been less favorable to Russia. Growth in exports to China has only increased Russia's dependence on hydrocarbons, as the share of manufactured goods in Russian exports to China is even smaller than their share in Russia's exports globally. In many branches, the competitiveness of Chinese manufactured products is much better than that of the Russian alternatives. Even in the defense industry, Chinese expertise is beginning to outstrip Russia's arms export offerings. Moreover, Chinese corporations have not been interested in making large direct investments in the Russian economy. Less than 10 percent of Russia's trade with China is invoiced in rubles, and Russia's sovereign payment system has not become a viable alternative to its Chinese analog or to the Belgium-based international SWIFT system.

While intensifying economic relations with other major Asian countries is critical in cementing the success of Russia's Pivot to Asia, Russia's relations with other Asian economic giants, particularly Japan, India, and South Korea, are lukewarm at best. If this does not change, the Pivot to Asia may become "Bow to China" instead (see Figure 10.5).

10.3.3.2 Import-Substitution Is Everywhere

High dependence on imports has always been met with suspicion in Russia, and the 2005 National Priority Programs enshrined the notion of increasing self-sufficiency in agriculture. By the early 2010s the need to protect and support domestic production began to gain increasing attention in policy discussions. As dependence on foreign debt was deemed dangerous for public finances, dependence on imported goods was increasingly seen as a potential threat to economic sovereignty and security. High-profile **import-substitution** (*importozameshchenie*) programs soon became the primary tool to increase Russia's economic sovereignty.

Increasing import-substitution, that is, favoring domestic goods at the expense of imported ones, stems partly from the need to diversify the economy away from oil and gas. Blocking imports should direct demand toward domestic goods and thereby help in reviving sectors outside oil and gas. Russian import-substitution policies

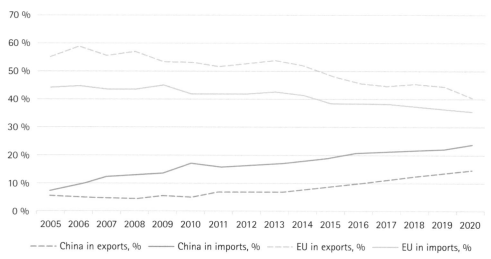

Fig. 10.5 Share of China and the EU in Russia's foreign trade, percentage of total, 2010–2020. *Source*: Created by author from BOFIT and Russian Customs.

initially focused on agriculture and four branches of manufacturing: metals, machinery and equipment, automobiles, and aviation. Domestic production in these sectors was to be supported via localization requirements, government subsidies, and preferences in public procurement.

However, in 2014 the EU, the United States, and their allies introduced **economic and political sanctions** against Russia in response to Russia's actions in Ukraine. Initially, the restrictive measures were relatively mild, mostly consisting of travel restrictions and the freezing of assets of individuals directly linked to the illegal annexation of Crimea. Business contacts with entities located in Crimea were also sanctioned. Since July 2014, the EU and the United States have enforced a broad set of sectoral economic sanctions against Russia. These include embargos on arms exports and exports of dual-use goods for military use. Exports of goods and services related to deep sea, Arctic, and shale oil exploration and production were also banned. The most significant set of sanctions restricts the use of dollar- and euro-based funding by the largest Russian banks and some energy companies. These measures effectively curtailed access to the EU and US financial markets.

The sanctions regime remained relatively stable until spring 2018, when the US government acted to punish Russia for interference in the 2016 elections and for global malign practices by sanctioning wealthy Russian individuals. Around the same time the EU imposed additional sanctions on Russian individuals and entities in response to Russia's use of the military-grade nerve agent in the poisoning of double agent Sergei Skripal in the UK. Ever since then, the US and EU sanctions have gradually tightened, and new individuals and entities have been added to the sanctions lists. Due to the extraterritorial nature of the US sanctions, in practice all financial institutions globally have to comply with the US measures. This has meant increased scrutiny and higher costs for nonsanctioned Russian customers too.

Russia's immediate response to economic sanctions was to broaden its import-substitution policies. Since 2015, policies favoring domestic goods and services have steadily intensified and the number of affected sectors has increased. Import-substitution is now promoted in areas such as IT, electronics, Arctic oil and gas exploration, and pharmaceuticals. Since 2015, the narrative around import-substitution policies has changed, and economic security has taken precedence over supporting economic growth and diversification. Dependence on foreign goods and services is increasingly seen as a concern for national security, and promoting import-substitution is meant to strengthen domestic alternatives to Western systems. Russia is certainly not alone in increasing trade barriers and supporting import-competing industries. This line of thinking goes well together with the recent global rise in economic nationalism and protectionism. According to the Global Trade Alert Database, Russia's policies have been especially restrictive in electronics, transportation, and communication equipment.

In the short term, restricting imports may bring some benefits, but it is a costly way to support domestic producers. Russia's ban on food imports is a prime example. In line with Russia's Food Security Doctrine of 2010 and in response to Western economic sanctions, the import of many fruits and milk and meat products was severely restricted in 2014. Import restrictions and the sharp devaluation of the ruble decreased imports of foodstuffs in 2014–15. Consequently, food prices increased, and the selection of goods offered shrank, decreasing Russian consumer welfare. Import bans and subsidies undoubtedly increased the profitability of Russian agribusinesses, but it remains unclear if the corporate benefits outweigh the loss of Russian consumers. The best available estimates conclude that these import bans create a small but enduring deadweight loss on the Russian economy (Volchkova and Kuznetsova 2019). If equivalent domestic production simply does not exist, import-substitution policies are likely to create even more distortions. Building a homegrown industry is a risky strategy that is unlikely to increase welfare for all, unless the protected sectors exhibit significant positive externalities on the rest of the economy. At least until now, these policies have contributed to the decade-long stagnation in real incomes of Russian households.

The irony is that the real threat to Russia's economic sovereignty and security is its dependence on oil and gas exports. Building fiscal buffers, maintaining sensible monetary policies, diversifying export routes, and restricting imports will bring stability and sovereignty only if policymakers succeed in pushing for a real diversification of economic activity. Turning inward and restricting competition are hardly a good recipe for building internationally competitive, skill-intensive industries capable of outliving the hydrocarbons sectors. Only time will tell if going it alone on projects without Western partners will result in research and development that pays back in the form of innovation or exportable products. In the short run, import-substitution pushes up production costs and slows down investment projects.

10.4 Conclusion

The Russian economy and economic policymaking have changed dramatically from the chaotic years of the early 1990s. The policy consensus that emerged in the late 1990s has greatly improved fiscal and financial stability in the country and helped the government build sizable fiscal buffers. In this sense, Russia has become a textbook example of prudent fiscal policies. The overarching goal of promoting stability and sovereign decisionmaking is reflected also in the current composition of public expenditure, which is tilted toward pensions and security over investments in human capital.

Russia's global economic integration deepened remarkably in the 2000s. Russian corporations benefited from increased funding opportunities provided by the global financial markets. Foreign jurisdictions became popular destinations for storing financial wealth. Increasing global demand for hydrocarbons and metal products provided lucrative opportunities for Russian exporters.

After the fiscal reforms of the early 2000s, the most significant change in the macroeconomic policy framework was the change in monetary policy regime in late 2014. The move to inflation targeting did help in bringing down stubbornly high inflation, thereby making the domestic economic environment more stable and predictable. Further, a floating ruble exchange rate has partly insulated Russian budget revenues from volatility in global oil prices.

Better macroeconomic policies have brought stability, but sensible fiscal, monetary, and trade policies are not enough to insulate the Russian economy from external volatility. Global oil prices collapsed in 1998, 2008, 2014, and 2020, and all of these caused severe recessions for the Russian economy. Russia will remain vulnerable to global shocks as long as its economy is dependent on exports of raw materials.

Nor have better macroeconomic policies alone been sufficient to support high economic growth. Since the global financial crisis, growth in Russia has lagged behind most emerging economies. In 2010–20 Russian GDP grew on average by 1 percent annually, compared to 2.4 percent globally. Economic growth has been especially disappointing compared to what could be hoped for. Most government development plans and forecasts envision at least 3 percent annual growth, but program papers have typically shied away from discussing how this would be achieved.

Instead of finding ways to support entrepreneurship and promote private-sector innovations, the Russian authorities increasingly rely on import-substitution policies. Early on, promoting domestic production at the expense of imports was seen as a way to revitalize the domestic economy. But, lately, restrictions on the use of imported goods and services are increasingly seen as an efficient means to insulate the Russian economy from external threats. By and large, Russia's macroeconomic policies are being subordinated to security concerns.

Given this state of affairs, what will the future of Russia's global economic integration look like? Over the past twenty years, the main channels of economic integration have been financial markets and energy exports. Following Western sanctions, access to global financial markets has been severely curtailed for many large Russian banks and corporations. Consequently, Russian state banks have become an increasingly important source of investment financing for Russian investors. This may lead to investment decisions being tilted toward supporting security policy preferences instead of increasing productivity. On the other hand, the long-term prospects of Russia's energy exports may be seriously hampered by carbon neutrality targets in the EU and China. The increasing competitiveness of renewable energy sources and proposed carbon taxes may seriously undermine the very foundation of Russia's fiscal policies. Up to now, Russian energy policies have not taken global energy transition seriously. Unless this changes, the future looks bleak at best.

DISCUSSION QUESTIONS

1. Why is maintaining a balanced budget and avoiding deficits considered so crucial by Russian economic policymakers? What might be the economic costs and benefits of such a policy line?
2. The Russian economy is dependent on oil and gas exports. How does this limit Russia's macroeconomic policies and prospects for economic growth in the future?
3. What do you think are the most important factors shaping Russian economic policies in the next five to ten years? How will they shape Russia's role in the global economy?

FURTHER READING

Alexeev, Michael, and Shlomo Weber (eds.). 2013. *The Oxford Handbook of the Russian Economy.* Oxford: Oxford University Press.

Åslund, Anders, Sergei Guriev, and Andrew Kuchins (eds.). 2010. *Russia after the Global Economic Crisis.* Washington, DC: Peterson Institute for International Economics. (An excellent collection of articles written immediately after the 2009 crisis.)

DiBella, Gabriel, Oksana Dynnikova, and Slavi Slavov. 2019. "The Russian State's Size and Its Footprint: Have They Increased?" International Monetary Fund Working Papers No. 19/53, March.

Frye, Timothy. 2021. *Weak Strongman: The Limits of Power in Putin's Russia*. Princeton: Princeton University Press.

Fungáčová, Zuzana, Iftekhar Hasan, Laura Solanko, and Paul Wachtel. 2019. "Banking in the Transition Countries of Central, Southern, and Eastern Europe and the Former Soviet Union." In Alain Berger, Philippe Molyneux, and John O. S. Wilson (eds.), *The Oxford Handbook of Banking*, 3rd ed., pp. 1132–51. Oxford: Oxford University Press.

Gustafson, Thane. 2021. *Klimat: Russia in the Age of Climate Change*. Cambridge, MA: Harvard University Press.

Kudrin, Alexey, and Evsey Gurvich. 2015. "A New Growth Model for the Russian Economy." *Russian Journal of Economics*, 1, 30–54.

Melchior, Arne. 2019. "Russia in World Trade: Between Globalism and Regionalism." *Russian Journal of Economics*, 5(4), 354–84.

Miller, Chris. 2018 *Putinomics: Power and Money in Resurgent Russia*. Chapel Hill: University of North Carolina Press.

Sutela, Pekka. 2012. *The Political Economy of Putin's Russia*. London: Routledge. (For an analysis of the 1990s and 2000s, up to the global financial crisis.)

REFERENCES

Unless otherwise noted, all macroeconomic data referred to in the text is retrieved from the BOFIT Russia Statistics, www.bofit.fi/en/monitoring/statistics/russia-statistics/.

Putin, Vladimir. 2002. "Annual Address to the Federal Assembly of the Russian Federation, April 18, 2002," http://en.kremlin.ru/events/president/transcripts/21567.

Volchkova, Natalia, and Polina Kuznetsova. 2019. "Skol'ko stoiat kontrsanktsii. Analiz blagosostoianiia." *Journal of New Economic Association*, 3(43), 173–83.

11 Russia's Oil and Gas Industry: Soviet Inheritance and Post-Soviet Evolution

MIKHAIL STROKAN AND RUDRA SIL

Fig. 11.1 Oil pumps in the Russian Far North. Credit: Alexyz3d / iStock / Getty Images Plus.

> There is something about petroleum that is controversial and intriguing. And there is something about Russia that is mystifying and absorbing. When the two converge in the study of Russian petroleum, the result is bound to be tantalizing and engrossing.
>
> Marshall Goldman, *Petrostate*

Abstract

This chapter traces the evolution of the Russian oil and gas sector. We argue that, at least since 2000, Russia's vast natural resources have been a source more of stability than of fragility for the economy. This is in part due to the distinctive history and role of fossil fuels in the context of a Soviet economy that was designed to be self-sufficient and thus diversified. While this did not prevent economic stagnation in the late Soviet period (1970s–80s) or a steep decline in production during the early years of post-Soviet transition (1992–99), it created the foundations for a petrostate that gradually came to be more resilient and adaptable in the face of fluctuations in energy prices, financial crises, and increasingly contentious relations with the West. Following 2000, while the state played an increasingly assertive role in the oil and gas industry, the government also adopted various measures to limit dependence on resource rents, to reduce vulnerability to sudden shifts in global energy prices, and to increase economic stability in the face of new geopolitical challenges. These included a Stabilization Fund, new budgetary practices to control spending and support other industries, diversification of supply flows and export composition, and intensified investment in new infrastructural projects. While there are now growing concerns over carbon emissions and the technological demands of further exploration, hydrocarbons have been mostly a positive force in the Russian economy. Whether that holds true following the war in Ukraine and the imposition of massive Western sanctions in 2022 remains to be seen.

11.1   Introduction

This chapter examines Russia's evolving efforts to manage its vast hydrocarbon resources and the revenues they generate. Although shale fracking has recently enabled the United States to take over the top spot in **oil and gas production**, Russia remains the leading exporter of natural gas and is second only to Saudi Arabia in oil exports. Russia also accounts for 12 percent of total oil output while remaining home to the world's largest **gas reserves**. While total natural resource rents now represent a smaller share of the economy than in the early 2000s, they still account for 10–15 percent of Russia's GDP. And, since 2000, **fuel exports** have accounted for 50 to 70 percent of total export earnings (World Bank 2021).

These figures suggest that Russia is a "**petrostate**" – a state that regularly generates a significant portion of its revenue by capturing rents from the export of fossil fuels. Petrostates are thought by some to be vulnerable to a "**resource curse**": The rents generated from the extraction of natural resources are thought to forestall economic and political reforms while allowing other sectors of the economy to lag behind. Some also view this "curse" as a source of vulnerability for ambitious petrostates that depend too heavily on resource rents and find their economies contracting in the face of sudden drops in energy demand. However, the "resource curse" thesis has been also critiqued by scholars (such as Smith and Waldner 2021) who argue that the impact of natural resources varies substantially depending on regional conditions and domestic institutions.

This chapter essentially affirms the latter view, emphasizing the unusual historical trajectory of Russia's oil and gas industry from Soviet times and painting a more complete picture of its role in the economy of post-Soviet Russia. That is not to say that Russia's petrostate is unaffected by sudden declines in global energy demand or that the rest of the economy is immune to the impact of falling oil prices. Indeed, during the late Soviet period (the 1980s) and the first decade of the post-Soviet era (the 1990s), it appeared that natural resources did little to aid, and may well have impeded, efforts to revitalize the wider economy. Yet, in contrast to petrostates that have little domestic production outside the energy sector, Russia's petrostate in the twenty-first century has continued to invest in other sectors while devising new strategies to mitigate the impact of fluctuating energy prices and adapt to new external challenges and opportunities. Thus, although Russia's economy must now contend with unprecedented challenges in the face of Western sanctions imposed following the **2022 Ukraine war**, the oil and gas industry has generally been more of a contributor to the country's relative stability than a source of its fragility.

Our chapter begins with the distinctive history of oil and gas extraction from the late nineteenth century through the period of Soviet **industrialization**. As section 11.2 outlines, the Soviet oil and gas sector was part of a development strategy aimed at creating a relatively autarkic and internally diversified planned economy (Gustafson 2017; Luong and Weinthal 2010; Vatansever 2021). Starting in the 1970s, the Soviet Union began to export oil and gas beyond the Soviet bloc, relying increasingly on resource rents to offset economic stagnation and budgetary shortfalls. Following the breakup of the USSR, as section 11.3 describes, the oil and gas sector was characterized by greater fragility, as production continued to drop during the 1990s. This decline was in part due to low oil prices and plummeting domestic demand in a shrinking Russian economy, and in part the result of choices of a new cohort of oil **oligarchs** who took control of state assets at firesale prices and initially focused more on turning a profit rather than quickly restoring production.

In the early 2000s, the Russian oil and gas industry would rebound dramatically. Section 11.4 examines the strategies adopted by **Vladimir Putin** and his associates to rein in the oil oligarchs and reassert state control over much of the oil and gas sector. During Putin's first two terms (2000–08), oil and gas prices soared and the Russian economy grew at an impressive pace, earning it a place among the "BRIC" economies (alongside Brazil, India, and China). Over time, however, new challenges and opportunities would appear, requiring more adjustments and new policies, as described in section 11.5. These included the use of a **Stabilization Fund** to mitigate the negative effects of global financial crises and fluctuations in energy prices. There were also other measures to offset the pressures generated by economic sanctions applied by the West, to increase investments in new infrastructure and exploration projects, and to leverage the growing demand for energy in China and across the developing world (in spite of global concerns over carbon emissions).

While Russia is very much a petrostate and is thus impacted by fluctuating energy prices, our conclusion emphasizes that Russia is no ordinary petrostate. Both in terms of the extent of its resource dependence and in terms of its approach to managing oil and gas rents, the Russian petrostate appears to have more in common with Norway than with the petrostates of the Gulf. Specifically, Russia has taken a wide range of steps to buffer the economy from the impact of falling global energy prices, while following budgetary rules to limit and govern the spending of resource rents. This implies that the performance of the Russian economy should not be viewed solely as a function of energy prices and that falling energy prices should not be viewed as inevitably or irreversibly weakening the Russian petrostate.

11.2 The Soviet Inheritance: The Expanding Yet Atypical Role of Fossil Fuels

Although not considered an energy superpower until the past two decades, Russia has long been one of the world's largest producers of petroleum, dating back to the late nineteenth century. From 1898 to 1901, Russia surpassed the United States for the top spot in oil production worldwide. By the start of World War I, Russia already accounted for 30 percent of global oil production. At the time, oil was mainly extracted in the North Caucasus (in present-day Chechnya) and in the west Caspian (in present-day Azerbaijan). Following the devastation of World War II, the Soviet Union expanded its production into Siberia, eventually becoming the world's top oil producer from the mid-1970s through the 1980s (Goldman 2008).

11.2.1 From the Late Nineteenth Century through World War II

The early development of the Russian oil industry preceded the Bolshevik Revolution and featured a prominent role for foreign entrepreneurs and companies. In 1876, the Nobel brothers, Robert and Ludvig, founded the Branobel Petroleum Production Company in Baku (their younger brother Alfred Nobel also benefited from the resulting fortune, which would later fund the Nobel Prizes). With the construction of the Baku–Batumi railway in 1883, the Rothschild family also made a major investment in Russian oil-refining and -exporting facilities, drawing upon the services of Russian engineer Vladimir Shukhov, who had designed one of the world's first oil pipelines. Thanks to these efforts, oil from the west Caspian could be transported to Russian Black Sea ports and then shipped anywhere in the world. After the Bolshevik Revolution of 1917, private companies were nationalized, causing production to sharply decline; yet some foreign companies, such as John Rockefeller's Standard Oil Company (now known as ExxonMobil), continued to work with the Bolsheviks in the 1920s to restore oil production (Antipova and Kulakova 2020; Yergin 2008).

Starting with **Vladimir Lenin**, the Soviet state made hydrocarbon exploration one of its top priorities. The nascent Soviet state placed all available knowledge, expertise, and resources under a unified system of central planning that immediately produced dividends. Between the 1930s and the 1950s, in spite of the traumatic consequences of Joseph Stalin's purges and the devastation brought by World War II, the Soviet economy experienced rapid industrialization at a breakneck pace, spurring further efforts to expand the production of fossil fuels. The Volgo-Urals basin emerged as a new site for major exploration and came to account for 45 percent of Soviet oil production by the 1950s (Antipova and Kulakova 2020).

Importantly, unlike most oil and gas producers at the time, Soviet hydrocarbon production between the 1930s and the 1950s was initially designed not to earn export revenues but to support a massive, centralized program of rapid industrialization and autarkic development. That is, oil and gas production in the Stalin era was tied to the creation of infrastructure for domestic distribution and supported the establishment of a wide array of other domestic industries (steel, chemicals, machine-building, and so on). This aspect of Russia's hydrocarbon sector development would have important ramifications for the extent and impact of resource dependence in post-Soviet Russia's economy.

11.2.2 Soviet Oil and Gas in the Post–World War II Era

In the post–World War II period, oil extraction expanded eastward, and gigantic oil fields were set up east of the Urals in western Siberia. These new Siberian oil fields quickly rose in prominence due to their sheer size and helped the USSR generate massive surpluses, pushing down the price of oil being exported by the Gulf states and triggering the creation of OPEC (Organization of the Petroleum Exporting Countries) in 1960. At this point, Soviet central planners still prioritized the domestic needs of Soviet industries and households while supplying Moscow's allies in the Soviet bloc with low-cost fuel. Oil was transported to the latter through the ambitious Druzhba (Friendship) pipeline, which was finished in 1964 and later grew into the longest oil pipeline system in the world. Of course, this arrangement had costs: Not only was the price of oil and gas subsidized, but payment was frequently made in the form of shipments of other goods from Eastern Europe to the Soviet Union, rather than hard currency that may have facilitated the acquisition of more technologically advanced goods (Shaffer 2009). Nevertheless, these trade and barter arrangements made sense as part of a program designed to meet the needs of a Soviet bloc that wanted to remain self-sufficient while seeking to close the gap with the West in technology and manufacturing capabilities (Goldman 2008).

The 1970s saw a major shift in the Soviet oil and gas industry in that the export of fossil fuel to countries beyond the Soviet bloc became an increasingly important

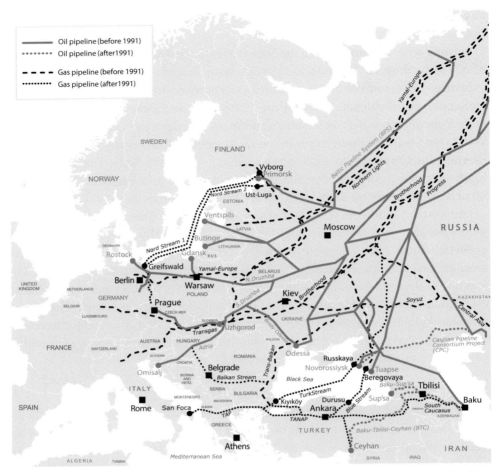

Map 11.1 Oil and natural gas pipeline systems of European Russia (as of 2021). Credit: Mikhail Strokan.

part of the economy. By the end of the 1960s, the USSR was generating enough surplus in hydrocarbons that Soviet foreign minister Andrei Gromyko floated a "gas-for-pipes" deal with West Germany: The latter would annually purchase 3 billion cubic meters of Soviet gas in exchange for exporting large-diameter pipes to the USSR. This paved the way for the construction of new gas pipelines in the 1970–80s (see Map 11.1), including the 1700-mile Soyuz (Union) pipeline as well as the Bratstvo (Brotherhood) and Progress pipelines. During this period, the demand for Russian oil continued to increase in Europe, which led to the construction of the Druzhba-2 oil pipeline, which more than doubled export capacity.

Thus, since the 1970s, the Soviet Union could be reasonably classified as a petrostate. Even if not oriented toward efficiency and profit maximization, the oil and gas sector was proving to be a major asset for one of the two global superpowers during the Cold War. Oil and gas rents in the USSR started to increase in the early 1970s and reached a Soviet-era peak in the early 1980s, with earnings rising approximately eightfold between 1970 and 1980 (Gaddy and Ickes 2013).

Ironically, this was also the time when the Soviet economy began to enter a period of stagnation, as the costs of energy production began to rise. The Soviet energy sector, while initially quite competent in developing its own methods and tools for extraction, had not been able to take advantage of the most advanced techniques being developed elsewhere (Goldman 2008). This was in part because of a Soviet preference for self-reliance and in part because the United States was seeking to effectively embargo exports of advanced equipment and technology. Oil production, in particular, began to stagnate, as obsolescent technologies made it difficult to continue to cheaply extract oil beyond the more easily accessible deposits in Siberia. In fact, the US Central Intelligence Agency in 1977 even predicted that, despite its vast reserves, the USSR could turn into a net importer of oil (Goldman 2008; Shaffer 2009).

While this scenario never materialized, the Soviet oil and gas industry went through a sharp downturn during the 1980s. Revenues from oil and gas exports, counted upon in the 1970s to compensate for stagnation in other sectors, declined sharply as world oil prices dropped from more than $100 a barrel in 1981 to under $30 a barrel in 1986 (all prices are in US dollars). In any case, more than 70 percent of the extracted oil and gas was still being consumed domestically by uncompetitive industries or being exported to East European allies at below world prices (Ermolaev 2017). Moreover, during the 1980s, with little being invested in the agricultural sector, the Soviet Union went from being self-sufficient in food to a net importer. Thus, whatever hard currency the Soviet oil and gas sector was still generating was being used not in the development of new technology or upgrading of infrastructure but simply to pay for food imports. It is these challenges that led to the initiation by **Mikhail Gorbachev** of *glasnost* and *perestroika* as part of a last-ditch effort to revitalize the Soviet economy, a project that included the transformation of the Soviet Ministry of Gas Industry into Gazprom (which would evolve into the largest Russian joint-stock company, albeit with half its shares owned by the Russian government).

These developments during the last decade of the USSR could be interpreted as evidence of a distinctive Soviet-style "resource curse" – marked by overreliance on hard currency, stagnating production, and shifting patterns of domestic consumption affected by fluctuations in oil prices and export revenues (Goldman 1983). At the same time, although the economy sputtered, overall national income in Soviet Russia continued to grow throughout the 1980s, even if at a lower rate than in the 1960s–70s. The decline in oil prices in the 1980s did not lead to nearly as steep a decline in industrial output in nonextractive sectors as would prove to be the case during the 1990s (when industrial output was cut nearly in half). And, despite the economic stagnation plaguing the USSR during its last two decades, the GDP of the Russian Soviet Federative Socialist Republic (RSFSR) in 1990 remained higher than at any point during the first decade of post-Soviet transition.

Thus, the story of the Soviet petrostate, while it does affirm certain aspects of the resource curse thesis during the 1970s–80s, also reveals some distinctive features tied to a broader history of Soviet economic development. In particular, the push for oil and gas production was always intertwined with an ambitious program to promote an autarkic, diversified industrial economy within the Soviet bloc. This is one key reason why, in the post-2000 period, the oil and gas sector would become more a source of stability than a point of vulnerability for the Russian economy as a whole. Before getting to this point, however, it is worth understanding the roots of the precarious conditions in which the Russian energy sector found itself during the 1990s.

11.3 The Russian Energy Sector in the 1990s: Privatization without Production

The first decade of post-Soviet transition was not simply a matter of liberalizing the economy, but of setting up the foundations of a market economy while dismantling a centrally planned one. The process was initially steered by proponents of "**shock therapy**" such as Yegor Gaidar, President **Boris Yeltsin**'s most trusted economic advisor in the early 1990s. While Gaidar's team, backed by US economic advisors and International Monetary Fund officials, predicted some "growing pains" during the transition, they expected these to be largely temporary. There were others who favored a more gradual approach and warned of price distortions and social costs that would arise from moving too quickly on liberalization and privatization in an uncertain environment. But these cautions were set aside by proponents of shock therapy, who preferred to move as quickly as possible to extricate the state from the economy and preempt any backsliding toward communism. A market economy did emerge during the 1990s – but not without a significant cost imposed upon ordinary Russians (Stiglitz 2002). With the sudden removal of price controls, ordinary citizens found themselves facing triple-digit hyperinflation through 1995. Production plummeted, and many factories lay idle and fell into decay, while unemployment rose dramatically. Russia's GDP fell by more than 30 percent between 1990 and 1998, a contraction comparable to, or even greater than, that of the US economy during the Great Depression (1929–33).

11.3.1 Privatization and the Divergent Fates of Oil and Gas

This was the turbulent environment within which Yeltsin's government set out to privatize Soviet state assets, including the vast facilities of the oil and gas industry. Although privatization was an integral component of postcommunist reforms, the manner and environment in which it was carried out greatly affected oil and gas production. The "mass privatization" program initiated in 1994 was designed to distribute millions of vouchers among the country's citizens so they could acquire shares and become stakeholders in newly privatized firms. Yet, given the extreme anxiety triggered by rising unemployment, shrinking or unpaid wages, and the sharply increased costs of basic necessities, millions of Russian citizens gladly exchanged their vouchers for small stacks of cash handed out by representatives of a savvy and well-networked group of entrepreneurs. The latter – Russia's first oligarchs – thereby acquired, at rock-bottom prices, controlling shares in massive state assets, including the fields, refineries, and other facilities of the former Soviet oil and gas industry.

While oil and gas are both hydrocarbons and frequently discussed in tandem, it is worth noting that the gas industry is quite different from oil, and that privatization of these two sectors also proceeded along different paths. Before the advent of liquefied natural gas (LNG), gas moved through huge trunk pipes built in the 1970s–80s which were under state control and would continue to require state coordination. Unlike the Soviet system of oil wells and refineries, which could be broken up and privatized, natural gas in the 1990s still had to operate essentially as what Gaidar termed a "natural monopoly" (Gustafson 2017, 71). Even if one could imagine private owners taking control of natural gas and transporting it to a border, they would not have found a way to sell the gas at the border since there was still no spot market for gas in Europe (Gustafson 2017, 58). What is more, gas was vital for Russia's domestic consumption, more so than oil, as it is used to heat ordinary apartment buildings and homes in the winter and to generate electricity to power most other industries across Russia. This is precisely why the Yeltsin government decided to preserve state control in the gas sector. Facilities associated with the production and distribution of natural gas, rather than being privatized, ended up being transformed into a state-managed association of enterprises that functioned as a single joint-stock company. This company became Gazprom, the largest publicly listed natural gas company in the world, with the state holding controlling shares (initially 100 percent, now just over 50 percent). At present, Gazprom is the largest company in Russia in terms of revenue.

The oil sector neither had nor did it require such a degree of central coordination. While some in the former Soviet oil and gas ministry wanted to set up a single corporate structure for the oil industry, it was difficult for them to find a plausible rationale or sufficient support for pursuing this path. Instead, in November 1992, President Yeltsin signed Presidential Decree No. 1403, setting up three large holding companies – Lukoil, Yukos, and Surgutneftegas – that would incorporate all smaller enterprises and subsidiaries involved in the full cycle of production, from extraction and refining to transportation, storage, marketing, and the processing of byproducts. These and other vertically integrated oil companies (VIOCs) effectively facilitated a high degree of organizational integration and centralized coordination of different phases and aspects of the production and marketing. When these VIOCs were privatized in 1996, the new owners found themselves in control of the best possible asset they could get their hands on: a fully integrated multidivisional oil company acquired at firesale prices.

Oil industry directors who resisted being absorbed into one of these holding companies came together under a "temporary" state company that took control of all remaining assets (Gustafson 2017, 72–76). This company, Rosneft, would prove to be anything but temporary. In fact, Rosneft today occupies the headquarters of the former USSR Ministry of Oil and is now Russia's third-largest company and the second-largest state-controlled company (after Gazprom) in terms of revenue. How it grew to be so large is discussed in section 11.4. During the 1990s, however, the future of the oil industry was thought to lie not in the hands of Rosneft but in the hands of those who took charge of the newly privatized VIOCs.

The 1990s also saw the growth of foreign ownership in the oil sector. The Russian government established a process for negotiating "production-sharing agreements." The first of these was signed in 1994 and involved "Sakhalin Energy," with shares initially distributed among Royal Dutch Shell, Mitsui, and Mitsubishi. Other global energy giants such as Exxon, Total, BP, and ConocoPhillips set up joint ventures. But at the center of all of these collaborative arrangements were the oligarchs, who had managed to take control of a majority of the interest in all of Russia's newly privatized energy companies. By 2002, 80 percent of the oil production in Russia came from the private companies, half of which were the ones owned by oligarchs (Gustafson 2017, 101).

11.3.2 The Decline in Demand and Production

The first decade of postcommunist economic reform did not see the positive results that private ownership and a market economy were supposed to bring. In fact, oil and gas production continued to fall, as a result of a sharp decline in domestic energy use and low global energy prices. As industrial production was collapsing, annual energy use fell 33 percent from about 6,000 kg in oil equivalent per capita in 1990–91 to around 4,000 kg in the 1996–99 period (World Bank 2021). Global demand also sagged during these years and then declined steeply during the 1997–98 Asian financial crisis, which impacted the entire global economy and contributed to Russia's own crisis in 1998. The average monthly price of Brent crude (which would hit $100 per barrel in early 2008) hovered between just $15 and $20 per barrel during most of the 1990s, before crashing to a low of $10 per barrel in November 1998 (US EIA 2021). The drop in external demand was also connected to the economic transition of Central and East European economies that sought to integrate rapidly into a European and global economy where alternative suppliers of energy could be sought. All of this was compounded by problems that had already surfaced in the Soviet period: the inefficient use of existing oil wells and the lack of investment in new fields and technologies. Consequently, the capacity for extraction continued to decline as the "easy" fields exploited during Soviet industrialization started to get depleted (Gustafson 2017).

With the convergence of all these unfavorable conditions, Russia's oil output at the end of the 1990s had fallen to just over half of the level seen at the Soviet-era peak of 1987 (Vatansever 2021, 62). The share of oil rents as a percentage of GDP, which was just 4 percent annually between 1992 and 1997, fell to under 2 percent (of a much lower GDP) in 1998. Yet, the "new Russians" who had taken over the privatized oil and gas companies did not themselves suffer; in fact, they proceeded to amass huge fortunes and, in some cases, gain political influence, as noted in Chapter 12. Despite sagging demand and declining production, the bargain-basement prices at which the oil and gas assets had been acquired meant that reselling even at low prices produced enormous profits. The new owners had less interest in investing their newfound wealth in the development of new oil fields or the improvement of production efficiency, instead diverting most of their export earnings to offshore tax havens (Goldman 2008). This undercut any possibility of reversing the steady decline in production capacity or leveraging resource rents to reverse the steep decline in the national economy.

11.4 Hydrocarbons in the Putin Era: The Return of the State

A new era was ushered in with the appointment of Vladimir Putin as the new president of the Russian Federation on New Year's Day 2000. A new group of advisors and staffers gained positions of prominence and influence in the Kremlin. Among them were a number of high-ranking *siloviki* (political elites from the military or security organs) drawn from Putin's past contacts in the KGB/FSB (the KGB was the Soviet-era Committee for State Security, which became the FSB, the Federal Security Service in 1991). They staffed key cabinet positions alongside some extremely capable economists and longtime associates from his period in the St. Petersburg mayor's office. The start of the Putin era coincided with a dramatic turnaround in the Russian economy. Over the next eight years, Russia recorded annual GDP growth rates between 5 and 10 percent (World Bank 2021) and came to be touted as one of the rising BRIC economies. While this growth was driven by a number of factors, it was certainly aided by the dramatic rise in oil and gas rents – and by a concerted effort to reassert state control over the energy sector.

11.4.1 The Reining in of the Oil Magnates

At the time that Putin came to power, some oil oligarchs – such as Mikhail Khodorkovsky – were already making their own plans to negotiate deals with foreign companies and build new private pipelines. Such moves, had they been coordinated with the government, may well have yielded some dividends for the oil sector and the economy as a whole. However, Khodorkovsky's fiercely independent stance and his growing political ambitions made this more of a zero-sum game for the Kremlin. Thus, it is no surprise that the reassertion of state control in the energy sector was most dramatically symbolized by the government's move to imprison Khodorkovsky on tax evasion and embezzlement charges while breaking up the Yukos oil company into several chunks, the largest of which would be absorbed by the state-controlled Rosneft (which essentially tripled in size as a result).

The Yukos affair is often viewed in the West as an act of political repression against a would-be opponent of the Kremlin or a blunt attempt at expropriation by the state. Such views may have a kernel of truth to them. But, in reality, the actions taken against Khodorkovsky and Yukos were part of a broader program of reasserting state control in the strategically critical energy sector which, during the 1990s, appeared to have slipped irretrievably beyond state control. The broader program was already evident at a meeting in the oil city of Surgut in western Siberia in March 2000, when Putin excoriated oil executives for exporting capital out of Russia and declared bluntly: "In the end, the mineral resources belong to the state" (Gustafson 2017, 253). In 2003, Putin also ruled that the state-controlled Transneft would be the sole owner of all oil-export pipelines in the country (Gustafson 2017, 269–70). The stakes of foreign companies were also curtailed as Putin dismissed the 1990s production-sharing agreements as a "colonial practice." The Russian state gradually increased its control of the energy pie by purchasing shares of companies. The stakes owned by foreign companies (which were never able to capture a significant portion of the Russian hydrocarbon industry to begin with) ended up shrinking to just 3.2 percent of oil production and 3.6 percent of gas production in Russia, which is comparable to the output of smaller oil companies such as Russneft and Bashneft (Zaslavskii 2011).

These moves were not merely a naked attempt to capture the growing revenues accompanying rising oil prices. In fact, the first moves to reassert state control in the oil sector occurred during Putin's first term, when Brent crude oil prices rose only modestly, remaining mostly within the $25–35 per barrel range. It was only later that oil prices would surge past the $100 per barrel mark, reaching a peak of more than $140 per barrel in mid-2008. In effect, Putin and his advisors were already committed to a statist program without much regard for the price of oil. As oil export revenues climbed from $36 billion in 2000 to $173 billion in 2007, no doubt private owners in the oil sector benefited. But the state also had in place instruments and policies to tax the superprofits and greatly increase government revenue. Whereas the percentage of GDP accounted for by oil rents had fallen to under 2 percent at the time of the 1998 financial crisis, between 2003 and 2008 oil rents came to represent 10–13 percent of a much larger GDP (World Bank 2021).

11.4.2   The Gas Sector after 2000: Gazprom

The distinctive requirements of production and distribution in the gas sector, as noted in section 11.3, meant that Gazprom was never officially privatized. However, by the late 1990s, it had gradually moved away from the Kremlin's control. Even though the state retained a controlling interest in the company, Gazprom seemed to be undertaking activities that reflected the goals and priorities of its general director at the time, Rem Viakhirev. Viakhirev increasingly placed many of his relatives and closest friends into key positions, while expanding into other sectors such as metals and petrochemicals, presumably violating the borders of autonomy authorized by the Kremlin. Thus, when Viakhirev's contract expired in 2001, it was not renewed. Instead, Putin replaced him with Aleksei Miller, a 39-year-old former staffer from when Putin had headed the Committee on External Relations in the St. Petersburg mayoralty.

Miller conducted a systemic purge of the senior ranks of Gazprom, and reestablished state control over the company, while at the same time consolidating its leading position in the gas industry (Gustafson 2017, 267). Some liberal reformers in Russia criticized Putin for not using this moment to completely restructure the gas industry by breaking up Gazprom and allowing greater competition. It is difficult to know how such a move would have fared amid the geopolitical and economic challenges that would appear over the next two decades. What is evident is that Miller's unquestioned and continuous control over Gazprom since 2001 coincided with large-scale investments in giant infrastructure projects designed to vastly expand the production and export of natural gas. These projects included new pipelines to Europe (Blue Stream, Turk Stream, and Nord Stream 1 and 2), the Power of Siberia pipeline (to export gas to China as part of a thirty-year deal signed in 2014), and the initiation of LNG projects to enable shipping of natural gas. There were also new efforts to increase exploration in the Arctic region. In effect, whatever benefits may have been gained through breaking up Gazprom were traded away for a long-term strategy that ensured state control of the world's largest natural gas reserves while reinforcing Russia's position as the world's top exporter of gas.

11.4.3   Toward a "Public–Private Partnership" – Russian-Style

This "return of the state" in the energy sector should not be mistaken for a return to a planned economy. Certainly, many of the *siloviki* with an interest in the energy sector, most notably Igor Sechin (currently president of oil giant Rosneft), were more than happy to support a more active state that was regaining control over the energy sector and developing a coherent program for managing resource rents. Yet, many liberal reformers could also get behind the changes of the 2000s because the state left space for profit-generating activities for private actors in the sector. Even as state-controlled Rosneft expanded, several oil companies continued to operate independently and in a semi-competitive environment (Vatansever 2021).

Table 11.1 Seven largest Russian oil and gas companies

| | | Predominantly oil | |
| | | Predominantly natural gas | |
Company name	Ownership structure as of March 2022	Headquarters	Annual revenue in billions USD (2018)
Gazprom	50.23% state-owned	St. Petersburg	131.2
Lukoil	Private	Moscow	119.3
Rosneft	50% state-owned	Moscow	113.2
Surgutneftegas	Private	Surgut, Khanty-Mansi Autonomous Okrug	24.8
Transneft	78.55% state-owned	Moscow	14.9
Tatneft	36% state-owned plus veto power over key strategic decisions	Almet'evsk, Republic of Tatarstan	12.7
Novatek	Private	Tarko-Sale, Yamal-Nenets Autonomous Okrug	9

In the gas industry, despite the dominance of Gazprom, new private companies emerged and thrived, including Novatek, which has become a leader in the production of LNG (see Table 11.1).

Moreover, the state's role was not merely that of dictating policies from above or of seeking to capture rents. The government actively supported extensive research and analysis, including at economic thinktanks set up with abundant funding from the Presidential Administration. These included the Center for Strategic Projects, led by German Gref and staffed by a team of liberals, many of whom had served in the St. Petersburg mayor's office in the 1990s (Gustafson 2017, 254). Also part of the brain-trust was the highly regarded economist Aleksei Kudrin, Putin's longtime associate who initiated a major tax reform designed to simplify the calculation and collection of taxes, one based on production and another on exports. Kudrin also led the effort to research sovereign funds of other energy exporters prior to rolling out Russia's own Stabilization Fund (discussed in section 11.5). Thus, a broad consensus was forged on the value of what might be called a Russian-style "public–private partnership" in the hydrocarbon sector. The partnership maintained space for private entrepreneurial activities while giving the state the instruments to leverage resource rents and develop new policies in pursuit of national developmental goals.

The state's dominant role in the energy sector – in particular its control over the two "national champions," Rosneft and Gazprom – have likely helped some close to the Kremlin become very wealthy. Yet, what is often overlooked is that the bulk of the revenue enabled the state to achieve a variety of important national goals during Putin's second term. Apart from the aforementioned investments in the gas industry, Russia managed to pay off debts to foreign creditors (including the debts of the USSR, which were taken on in their entirety by the Russian Federation in 1992). The government was able to invest in other exporting industries, which dramatically boosted output and spearheaded Russia's economic rebound in the early 2000s. New resources were made available for public infrastructure projects (including roads and bridges) as well as kindergartens, hospitals, and research institutes. The state was also able to launch initiatives to boost the incomes of ordinary Russians and prop up those Soviet-era *monogoroda* (single-industry or single-enterprise cities) that were struggling to adapt to a globalized market economy. Finally, it is worth noting that the Russian economy benefited from a perennial trade surplus, one that would exceed $100 billion in nine of the ten years between 2006 and 2015 (World Bank 2021).

11.4.4   Energy Prices and the Russian Economy

It is important to recognize here that Russia's post-2000 economic growth was not simply a function of rising energy prices, as is frequently assumed. It was also the result of expanding production and leveraging resource rents to spur production in other sectors. In 2000, when Russia's GDP grew by a whopping 10 percent, Brent crude oil prices remained under $30 a barrel. While this was well above the 1998 average of $12 a barrel, it was not much higher than the $24 a barrel it was in January 1996 when Russia's economy was in a shambles. Yet, oil rents still climbed from below 2 percent of GDP during the 1998 crisis to more than 14 percent of a larger GDP in 2000, suggesting that the increase in oil rents was not just about oil prices, but also about oil and gas production rising again.

It is also noteworthy that, as Russia's GDP in PPP (purchasing power parity) nearly tripled between 2000 and 2008, oil rents remained at 11–13 percent of GDP even though oil prices had been rising much more rapidly (reaching and surpassing $100 per barrel). This suggests that much of the economic growth was coming from the restoration and expansion of productive capacity in sectors outside oil and gas. Moreover, while it is true that fuel exports represented 60–70 percent of total export value during the 2006–15 period, Russia's overall annual exports during that same period averaged more than $400 billion a year – four times the value of total exports in 2000. This also means that the average value of yearly nonfuel exports in 2006–15 was at least triple the value recorded in 2000. At the very least, the growth in Russia's nonfuel exports since 2000 has kept pace with the rise in nonfuel exports worldwide (World Bank 2021).

While these figures demonstrate the limits of the view that Russia is "cursed" by excessive resource dependence, proponents of that view might still point to the impact of the steep drop in oil prices in the second half of 2008, which was followed by Russia's GDP contracting by nearly 8 percent in 2009. However, it is important to view these trends in the context of a devastating financial crisis that led to the world economy as a whole contracting for the first time in more than half a century. This global crisis was spurred not by falling energy prices but by the United States' subprime mortgage collapse, which also sent many other economies into recession. In 2009, while Russia's economy contracted sharply, reduced demand for energy around the world clearly played a significant role. At the same time, the European Union saw its economy shrink by 4 percent, Germany's economy contracted by nearly 6 percent, and the Baltic countries saw their economies shrink by more than 14 percent. Thus, while falling energy prices did contribute to Russia's economic contraction in 2009 and created new challenges for the Kremlin, it is important to note that this occurred in a year when the entire global economy and several of the world's largest economies were shrinking as well.

These observations are not intended to suggest that Russia's energy sector or the economy writ large is in excellent shape. Indeed, there are still major challenges ahead and significant efficiency gains to be realized. Yet, the above discussion does imply that broader economic trends in Russia, while no doubt affected by fluctuations in energy prices, are at least partly a result of the performance of other sectors and of global economic conditions that also affect other countries. The following section examines more closely the strategies and policies adopted by the Kremlin so as to better manage Russia's natural resources (and the revenues they generate).

11.5   The Management of Natural Resources: Adapting to Challenges

In comparing petrostates, there is a tendency to focus on the level of resource dependence and to discount the choices and actions undertaken by key decision-makers. A closer look at the strategies, policies, and institutional shifts in Russia since 2000 reveals a concerted effort to achieve two broad objectives with respect to hydrocarbons. The first is to limit the outflow of superprofits generated by the production and exporting of oil and gas. The second is to mitigate the extent of resource dependency and, in particular, the negative effects of fluctuations in hard currency inflows tied to fossil fuel exports.

In pursuing these goals, Putin has relied heavily on the aforementioned Aleksei Kudrin, who had been in the St. Petersburg administration with Putin in the early 1990s before being named deputy finance minister under Yeltsin and then becoming minister of finance from 2000 to 2011. In 2000, neither Putin nor Kudrin could imagine oil prices reaching $100 per barrel in 2008. Indeed, looking back at the crisis of 1998, when oil prices averaged $12 per barrel, Kudrin (2020, 50) recalled: "I prayed to God for the price to be higher than $20." What Kudrin did recognize was that the status quo following privatization was unsustainable, given the stagnation of production and investment in the energy sector. At the same time, he was all too aware of the dangers of becoming overly dependent on resource rents. On the one hand, a sudden drop in prices could destabilize the Russian economy. On the other hand, sustained high oil prices could also produce a Russian version of the "Dutch disease" (where an increase in resource rents increases the currency's value and reduces exports in other sectors because of their higher prices abroad): A sharp rise in the ruble's value would increase the price of Russia's nonfuel exports (and thus lower the demand for these goods). While Putin was largely responsible for reorganizing the structure of ownership (as discussed in section 11.4), it was Kudrin who set out to design fiscal practices and budgetary rules to maintain stability in the face of fluctuations in revenue streams from oil and gas exports.

11.5.1 The Stabilization ("Rainy Day") Fund

In 2001, Kudrin initiated a large-scale investigation – carried out within the Ministry of Finance and various new thinktanks – to examine the organization of sovereign funds in developed countries (Kudrin 2020). Kudrin zeroed in on Norway, a top-fifteen oil producer that had maintained a high standard of living while buffering itself from sudden drops in energy prices through a sovereign wealth fund, created in 1990 to manage revenues generated from oil exports. Under Kudrin, a similarly structured Stabilization Fund went into operation in 2003. The fund was designed to stash away a portion of the growing revenues generated by oil and gas exports, capped at 10 percent of annual GDP.

In its first two years (2003–04), the fund was used to pay down external debt, including that taken over from the USSR. Subsequently, it served as a "rainy day" fund that could be utilized to stabilize budgetary flows in the event of sudden drops in energy prices and export earnings. Perhaps most importantly, by taking some of the resource rents out of circulation, the fund helped to keep the ruble from becoming overvalued and preempted a bout of Russian-style "Dutch disease" that might have otherwise hampered the growth of other export sectors. Also worth noting is that, starting in 2003, Russia's Ministry of Finance began to introduce a series of rules to guard against overspending from the revenues generated by oil and gas exports. These included separate lines in the budget for oil and gas revenues and for revenues from other sources, along with a new rule setting a cap (at 3.7 percent in 2021–22) for expenditures drawing on the former stream (Russian Federation, Ministry of Finance 2021). This ensured that the government would not develop spending habits predicated on high inflows from fossil fuel exports.

Of course, the Stabilization Fund could not prevent a decline in GDP of nearly 8 percent in 2009, following an unprecedented slide in oil prices from a high of $144 a barrel in June 2008 to just $34 only six months later. While Kudrin and his team had been planning for price volatility, they were unprepared for a global financial crisis that would severely curtail energy demand and contribute to an extraordinarily steep decline in oil rents. Moreover, Kudrin's team had not yet learned to manage the sovereign wealth fund efficiently, permitting the government to use it to shore up the salaries of public-sector employees (for example, teachers and soldiers) and selectively boost investment in certain large industries. This meant that not as much was done to guard against the impact of the unexpectedly massive oil price hike between 2005 and mid-2008, a period during which the ruble's value rose by more than 20 percent (from 29 rubles to the dollar to 23). This may not have seemed like a big problem so long as oil prices continued to climb – or at least remained stable. But, when oil prices plummeted in the second half of 2008 against the backdrop of a global financial meltdown, the ruble fell precipitously, losing 57 percent of its value. In response, the government used up a large portion of the sovereign fund merely to support the ruble rather than to stabilize the macroeconomic environment and support other sectors of the economy.

At the same time, the crisis of 2008–09 provided the impetus for further policy shifts designed to create a buffer that could withstand bigger fluctuations in energy prices than could have been envisioned during Putin's first term. In 2008, the Stabilization Fund was split into two separate funds: the National Wealth Fund (used to balance the pension budget and support voluntary pension savings) and the National Reserve Fund (used to manage inflationary pressures and balance the budget in the event of a decline in energy export revenues). While this served the purpose of making sure that a substantial portion of the fund remained available for managing inflation and the budget, in February 2018, the two funds were remerged. It is likely that, in anticipation of an overhaul of the pension system (including raising the pensionable age) to come that summer, the government decided that it would have more flexibility working with a unified National Wealth Fund. As of 2021, that fund held assets valued at more than $180 billion; the fate of these assets remains unclear as successive rounds of sanctions linked to the Ukraine war begin to have an effect.

11.5.2   A More Resilient Petrostate

Other important measures would be introduced following Putin's return as president in 2012 (following the 2008–12 term when **Dmitry Medvedev** held the presidency with Putin in the role of prime minister). Starting in 2013, a new budget rule was introduced by the government, in which estimates for oil and gas revenues would be based not on then-current oil prices but rather on an average of oil prices over the previous five years. This was designed to guard against any excessive optimism on expected revenues. Subsequently, the government adopted an even tougher standard, using a fixed oil price. This was set initially at $50 per barrel before being reduced to the present level of $40 per barrel. It is true that the price of oil has dipped below $40 per barrel on several occasions (for example, between December 2015 and March 2016, and again in early 2020, during the first months of

COVID-19 lockdowns across much of the world). But, during most of the past decade, oil prices have held well above $40 per barrel, with average monthly prices in 2021 ranging between $55 and $85 per barrel (US EIA 2021). Thus, the budget rule and the other measures have helped to keep budget deficits at or below 4 percent of GDP since 2010, while facilitating a budget surplus in four of these years (Trading Economics 2021; Reuters 2021).

Moreover, independently run energy companies have recently started to become a more significant part of the oil and gas sector. The state-backed "national champions," Rosneft and Gazprom, remain the largest companies in the sector. But private companies serve as additional vehicles for maintaining output and generating investment in new technologies and infrastructure. They also effectively apply pressure on the larger companies to improve their efficiency and productivity. The most revealing example is the aforementioned Novatek, a natural gas company in which the majority of shares are not controlled by the government (in contrast to Gazprom and Rosneft). Laws that previously gave Gazprom a monopoly on the transportation of gas have been revised to permit Novatek and other companies to get involved in the export of LNG. Novatek is leading the massive Arctic LNG-2 project on the Yamal peninsula, a project that also serves Russia's wider ambitions of securing its foothold in the increasingly competitive Arctic Circle. And, in the context of Russia's pivot to China, it is worth noting that Novatek has been permitted to sign agreements independently with the China National Petroleum Company (CNPC) and the China National Offshore Oil Company (CNOOC), enabling the latter to become a shareholder in the Novatek-led Arctic LNG-2 project (Sassi 2021).

All of these changes appear to have helped the energy sector to better absorb the negative effects of fluctuations in energy prices and of global economic and political uncertainties. This is evident in the aftermath of a more sustained decline in oil prices in 2014–15, during which oil prices dropped over the course of eighteen months from $115 per barrel to $28 per barrel. While there was no global financial crisis, Western sanctions linked to the crisis in Ukraine and the takeover of Crimea intensified the impact of falling energy export revenues. The sanctions decreased foreign investment, intensified capital outflow, and shut down some new joint investment projects. And, yet, the overall impact on the energy sector and the economy writ large was much more limited and contained.

This time around, the government did not have to rely on the Stabilization Fund to prop up the ruble, but instead maintained the free flow of currency while focusing its efforts on maintaining fiscal discipline and boosting domestic output in other sectors. The latter effort proved more effective than expected. For example, with renewed investment in agriculture, Russia became the world's leading exporter of wheat and a "food superpower," with wheat rising to become Russia's third-largest export (Wegren 2021; Wengle 2022). While the Russian economy did contract in 2015, it was by a mere 2 percent (as opposed to nearly 8 percent in 2009).

And, while export revenues declined by 31 percent in 2015, this was a smaller drop than had occurred in 2009 and compares favorably to what happened to OPEC producers such as Saudi Arabia and Kuwait, whose fossil fuel export revenues in 2015 fell by more than 40 percent (World Bank 2021).

The combination of Western sanctions and the crisis in Ukraine (through which most Russian-sourced gas traveled to Europe) also spurred new efforts at diversification of both pipelines and markets. On the European front, while the most ambitious project, Nord Stream 2, would be canceled following the war in Ukraine, new pipelines were constructed to Turkey to expand distribution across Europe (including to Austria, Hungary, Romania, and Serbia, among others). Energy cooperation with China was also scaled up, marked by a massive $400 billion gas deal that included construction of the Power of Siberia pipeline to take gas to China. In addition, through productive cooperation arrangements with other post-Soviet energy producers – notably Kazakhstan, Azerbaijan, and Turkmenistan – Russian pipelines provided transport for hydrocarbons sourced from other places. And, with its expanding capabilities in production and transportation of LNG, Russian gas is now in a position to reach other parts of the developing world, where energy demand is projected to keep rising for at least the next two decades.

Looking ahead, it is evident that the story of oil and gas is about to enter a new chapter in view of the massive Western sanctions triggered by the 2022 Ukraine war (which are far more severe than earlier rounds of sanctions introduced right after the 2014 crisis in Ukraine). Preparations are under way for a possible ban on imports of Russian hydrocarbons. Although some countries (such as Hungary) have signaled opposition to a total ban on Russian gas given the costs and risks, it is possible that these countries can be exempted from a ban, even as most of the EU moves to cut off imports from the country that accounts for 40 percent of its natural gas. On the flipside, if Russia were to significantly curtail gas exports (as it has done with Bulgaria and Poland for their refusal to pay for Russian gas in rubles), it would be cutting off a huge source of government revenue.

Absorbing the costs of these moves and adjusting to new realities will take time: It may take years before Europe finds adequate substitutes for Russian gas, just as it will take Russia time to scale up hydrocarbon exports to other regions to make up for the loss of the European market. It is certain, however, that this process will involve major disruptions for Europe and Russia while fundamentally transforming global energy markets for the foreseeable future.

11.6   Conclusion: No Ordinary Petrostate

Following Russia's 2009 economic contraction, Paul Krugman questioned Russia's inclusion among the BRIC countries and asserted that Russia's "petro-economy" was structurally more similar to Saudi Arabia's than to China's or India's (Bloomberg News 2011). Krugman is right insofar as Russia *is* a petrostate and *is* structurally quite different from emerging economies such as China and India. There is, however, a vast difference in the level of resource dependence between Saudi Arabia and Russia. Between 2000 and 2019, while the percentage of Russia's GDP accounted for by oil rents ranged from 5 to 15 percent, the same figure for Saudi Arabia ranged from 19 to 54 percent (World Bank 2021). To take into account population, during this same period, per capita oil and gas rents (PPP) in Russia ranged from $600 to $3,300, while the corresponding figure for Saudi Arabia was $7,800 to $24,000.

This chapter suggests that, when comparing petrostates, Russia should be viewed as closer to Norway than to Saudi Arabia. For one thing, Russia shares with Norway a historical pattern whereby industrialization efforts during the twentieth century had borne fruit well before oil and gas exports became an important source of hard currency. This puts them in a situation that is far different from most OPEC members, which began to rely upon oil and gas exports to finance the purchase of manufactured goods before attempting to invest in domestic nonenergy industries. Thus, even if all petrostates benefit from fossil fuel rents, a much larger percent of the GDP of Russia and Norway is accounted for by other sectors. Oil and gas rents, calculated on a per capita basis, also place Russia much closer to Norway than to Saudi Arabia; in 2015, for example, oil and gas rents in Russia amounted to $2,110 per capita (in PPP, using current US dollars) – even lower than the $3,269 for Norway and just one-sixth of the $12,560 for Saudi Arabia (World Bank 2021). Similarly, in terms of exports, Russia's fuel exports in 2015 accounted for 63 percent, much closer to Norway's 58 percent than to Saudi Arabia's 78 percent (World Bank 2021). More importantly, the past two decades reflect a conscious effort to develop policies in Russia that are partly modeled on those previously introduced in Norway, as a means to guard against volatility in global demand and energy prices.

What this implies is that, at least until the outbreak of the 2022 war in Ukraine, the Russian petrostate was more robust and resilient than commonly assumed. Russia inherited an economy that, despite its inefficiencies and eventual stagnation, was diversified and featured significant infrastructure. While this did not prevent economic stagnation in the late Soviet period or a steep decline in production during the 1990s, for most of the post-2000 period, Russia's vast hydrocarbon deposits have been more a source of stability than of fragility for the Russian economy. While there remain problems with respect to inefficiency, corruption, technological limitations, and the concentration of wealth among oligarchs, the positive impact of high oil and gas rents on the rest of the economy has been more durable and substantial than has the negative impact of dependence on hydrocarbons. During periods of high energy prices, production and investment in other sectors have increased substantially, and the economy as a whole has grown. And, in times of economic crises or falling prices, the contraction of the economy has not been severe or sustained enough to reverse the gains accrued during the years of economic growth. At least for the two decades between 2000 and 2021, the governance of natural resources in Russia, far from being static, involved the active identification and management of new challenges while adapting to changing conditions through a mix of policies and strategies. The question now is whether the Russian petrostate can adapt even further and find new ways to survive – and to support the rest of the Russian economy – as it contends with the full impact of Western sanctions linked to the Ukraine war.

DISCUSSION QUESTIONS

1. Why does it matter that oil and gas extraction in the USSR was established as part of a development strategy aimed at self-sufficiency and rapid industrialization?
2. Was the decline in oil and gas production during the 1990s inevitable? Why or why not?
3. How did the state increase its control over the oil and gas industry after 2000? On balance, did this help or hurt the performance of the energy sector?
4. Some say that a country relying too much on hydrocarbon exports is "cursed" because other sectors of the economy suffer or remain undeveloped. How true is this of Russia?
5. What makes Russia's petrostate different from the petrostates of the Gulf countries that are members of OPEC?

REFERENCES

Antipova, K. A., and O. A. Kulakova. 2020. *Istoriia neftegazovoi otrasli*. Samara: Samara State Technical University.

Bloomberg News. 2011. "Russian 'Petro-Economy' Doesn't Belong among BRICs, Krugman Says." September 9, www.bloomberg.com/news/2011-09-09/russian-petro-economy-doesn-t-belong-among-brics-krugman-says.html.

Ermolaev, Sergei. 2017. "The Formation and Evolution of the Soviet Union's Oil and Gas Dependence," Working Paper, Carnegie Moscow Center (March 29).

Gaddy, Clifford G., and Barry W. Ickes. 2013. "Russia's Dependence on Resources." In Michael Alexeev and Shlomo Weber (eds.), *The Oxford Handbook of the Russian Economy*, pp. 309–40. New York: Oxford University Press.

Goldman, Marshall. 1983. *USSR in Crisis*. New York: W. W. Norton.
  2008. *Petrostate: Putin, Power and the New Russia*. Oxford: Oxford University Press.

Gustafson, Thane. 2017. *Wheel of Fortune: The Battle for Oil and Power in Russia*. Cambridge, MA: Belknap Press of Harvard University Press.

Kudrin, Aleksei. 2020. *Ekonomicheskoe razvitie Rossii. Tom 1*. Moscow: Delo.

Luong, Pauline Jones, and Erika Weinthal. 2010. *Oil Is Not a Curse: Ownership Structure and Institutions in the Soviet Successor States*. Cambridge: Cambridge University Press.

Reuters. 2021. "Russia Heading for Budget Surplus, even with Putin Spending Goals – Analysts." July 13, www.reuters.com/article/us-russia-budget/russia-heading-for-2021-budget-surplus-even-with-putin-spending-goal-analysts-idUSKBN2EJ1JU.

Russian Federation, Ministry of Finance. 2021. "Federal Budget of the Russian Federation," https://minfin.gov.ru/en/statistics/fedbud/.

Sassi, Francesco. 2021. "Energy Partnership Bolsters China–Russia Relations." East Asia Forum, April 8, www.eastasiaforum.org/2021/04/08/energy-partnership-bolsters-china-russia-relations/.

Shaffer, Brenda. 2009. *Energy Politics.* Philadelphia: University of Pennsylvania Press

Smith, Benjamin, and David Waldner. 2021. *Rethinking the Resource Curse.* New York: Cambridge University Press.

Stiglitz, Joseph. 2002. "Russian People Paid the Price for Shock Therapy." *The Times* (UK), June 22.

Trading Economics. 2021. "Russia: Government Budget," https://tradingeconomics.com/russia/government-budget.

US EIA (US Energy Information Administration). 2021. "Petroleum and Other Liquids," www.eia.gov/dnav/pet/hist/LeafHandler.ashx?n=PET&ts=RBRTE&f=M.

Vatansever, Adnan. 2021. *Oil in Putin's Russia: The Contests over Rents and Economic Policy.* Toronto: University of Toronto Press.

Wegren, Stephen. 2021. *Russia's Food Revolution.* New York: Routledge.

Wengle, Susanne. 2022. *Black Earth, White Bread: A Technopolitical History of Russian Agriculture.* Madison: University of Wisconsin Press.

World Bank. 2021. World Bank Open Data, www.data.worldbank.org/indicator.

Yergin, Daniel. 2008. *The Prize: The Epic Quest for Oil, Money and Power.* New York: Free Press.

Zaslavskii, Aleksandr. 2011. "Inostrannye kompanii i Rossiiskaia neft." *Pro et Contra,* (September–October), 40–50.

12 Russia's Oligarchs

STANISLAV MARKUS

Fig. 12.1 *Lady Anastasia* moored on the island of Majorca, seized and under investigation by Spanish authorities to ascertain whether it belongs to a Russian oligarch targeted by sanctions, March 15, 2022. Credit: Jaime Reina / AFP / Getty Images.

There are no billionaires in Russia, only people working as billionaires.

Russian joke

Abstract

Russia's superwealthy and politically influential elites – or oligarchs – were created during the privatization of the 1990s. After Putin came to power in 2000, he subordinated the oligarchs to the state: The oligarchs could keep their fortunes as long as they supported the Kremlin's priorities. Under Putin, state procurement became the new engine of oligarchic enrichment. Three types of oligarchs can be distinguished today: Putin's friends, the silovarchs, and the outsiders. As a whole, the oligarchs seek more predictability from the Kremlin and more security for their assets – but they do not necessarily desire democracy or the rule of law proper. The oligarchs cannot force the Kremlin to guarantee their property rights due to the internal divisions among themselves, as well as the Kremlin's complete control of coercion. While several oligarchs have also attempted to push for democratization, they have mostly failed. Internationally, the oligarchs present the West with several challenges, including the projection of Russia's political influence abroad and Russian money-laundering in the West. Finally, a comparative and historical perspective suggests that oligarchs have good reasons to fear democracy, but this fear can be overcome. Yet, in the Russian context, the gap between the oligarchs and the population at large will remain dramatic.

12.1   Introduction

"*Oligarkh*" is a politically loaded word in Russia. This chapter will help you understand who the mysterious Russian **oligarchs** are; how their relationship with the Kremlin has evolved; what the prospects of oligarchs shaking up the authoritarian stability in Russia are in the future; and what the international ramifications of Russia's oligarchs are.

The original Greek word *oligarkhia* means "government by the few," as opposed to *demokratia* or "government by the many." In social science (Winters 2011) and popular discourse, the term "oligarchs" has acquired an additional connotation: the superwealthy elites. Indeed, Russian oligarchs are, above all, tycoons whose extreme wealth sets them far apart from the rest of the population and endows them with disproportionate political influence.

Make no mistake: Russia has no shortage of oligarchs. While Russia is a middle-income country (with a GDP per capita similar to countries like Turkey and Greece), the country is among global leaders in terms of the number of billionaires. Russia's wealth inequality, in other words, is dramatic. The top 1 percent of Russian wealth-holders own 58 percent of total household wealth, the highest share in the world, followed by Brazil (50 percent), India (41 percent), and the United States (35 percent) (Shorrocks, Davies, and Lluberas 2021). Let us examine next who the "1 percent" are in Russia, where their wealth comes from, and what role they play in Russian politics.

As this chapter explains, while Russia's oligarchs played an outsized political role during **Boris Yeltsin**'s administration in the 1990s, they were "cut down to size" after **Vladimir Putin** came to power in 2000. The deal offered to the oligarchs was simple: Stay out of politics, and keep your property. The oligarchs who called Putin's bluff and tried to challenge the Kremlin met with swift expropriations and jail terms. Today's Russia mostly features politically tamed oligarchs who, at least publicly, toe the Kremlin's line. At a deeper level, however, the oligarchs crave more security for their assets and better relations with the West – yet this implicit demand has not been translated into effective pressure on the Kremlin. Overall, the oligarchs are a source of stability for the system that Putin built – at least as long as they remain highly unpopular with the public, and the Kremlin retains effective control of coercion.

12.2   Enter the Oligarch

12.2.1   Origins of the Oligarchs

In 1991, the Soviet Union collapsed, and Russia emerged as an independent country convulsed by political and economic crises. The USSR had been an autocracy, featuring the unelected Communist Politburo as the ultimate unaccountable policymaker. However, despite this dramatic asymmetry in political power (with most of the population having none), the Soviet Union was a relatively equal society when it came to income and wealth distribution. To be sure, the elites of the **Communist Party of the Soviet Union** lived much better lives than the rest (especially because they could escape the shortage economy through privileged access to various goods and services). Yet the gap in living standards was not extreme by modern standards. At the same time, the Soviet state owned all productive assets such as factories and shops.

Against this background, Russia's two-stage privatization process – including voucher privatization and for-cash sales – drove the initial accumulation of extreme wealth in the 1990s. Decisions about privatization in Russia were made in the context of creeping anarchy at the enterprise level. Gaps and contradictions in the existing legislation facilitated the "spontaneous" and semi-legal conversion of state property into private assets. By 1992, the theft of factory assets by managers was widespread; labor discipline and output collapsed; and the supply of goods dried up. While looted factory assets flooded the black market, shortages of food and consumer goods in the shops sparked popular outrage. In this setting, reformers (led by the prime minister Yegor Gaidar) argued that formally privatizing productive assets would return discipline to the shop floor in the short run while creating efficient incentives for owners and managers in the long run.

The supporters of voucher privatization also hoped that the requisites of fairness and justice could be satisfied through a free distribution of assets to the public, albeit at the expense of budget revenues and capital investment in the firm, as the proponents of privatization via sales pointed out. In addition to the economic and fairness-based criteria, privatization held a political promise. It would make, many argued, the communist defeat irreversible through the creation of a wide stratum of property-owners with a stake in a market economy.

The **voucher privatization** was designed as a free transfer of industrial wealth to Russian citizens: Every adult could pick up (free) vouchers at their local bank, and use these vouchers to bid on enterprise equity at auctions. In reality, however, the 1992–94 voucher privatization of medium-sized and large enterprises involved significant concessions to "red directors," the managers of old Soviet-era state-owned enterprises. The red directors lobbied successfully for a compromise with Gaidar's government, allowing them to purchase shares in their firms, up to a controlling stake, at a discount before any equity was offered to the general public. While the vouchers were successfully distributed to 150 million Russian citizens, an active class of small stockholders – which the reformers had hoped for – did not emerge. Still, Russia's voucher privatization was completed within two years, an astounding record considering that almost 14,000 medium-sized and large firms were transferred into private ownership.

This period coincided with the explosive growth of independent private entrepreneurship (previously illegal in the USSR). Given the weak rule of law during these early years of the post-Soviet transformation, corrupt or criminal business ventures often had a competitive advantage in achieving profitability (since they could buy off state officials or force competitors out of business; see also Chapter 9). Indeed, this budding rich class became known as *novye russkie* ("new Russians"), described by a Russian social scientist as "physically strong, poorly educated, assertive, devoid of moral prohibitions, materially wealthy types" (Simonian 2010).

Yet it is the second stage of privatization that gave birth to the oligarchs proper. It began in 1995, and involved for-cash sales to outsiders (that is, not the managers of state-owned enterprises scheduled for privatization), promising revenues for the state treasury as well as the imposition of discipline on enterprise management by the new owners. This phase was marred by corruption, resulting in the exclusion of competitive bidders and a pitiful treasury intake. While the voucher stage saw the state unburden itself of thousands of small shops and large loss-making state-owned enterprises, it was during this second stage of privatization that many highly profitable jewels of the Soviet economy – often in the natural resources sector – were privatized. And if the red directors triumphed in stage one, stage two gave rise to the post-Soviet oligarchs who were not always tied to the communist *nomenklatura*, and tended to be younger and more daring.

The second privatization stage culminated in the infamous "loans-for-shares" scheme (Treisman 2010). The government faced a budget shortfall, including Yeltsin's own cash-starved presidential reelection campaign of 1996. In this context, ownership stakes in twelve large state-owned enterprises were transferred from the government to select tycoons in exchange for loans these oligarchs extended to shore up the federal budget. Ostensibly, these equity stakes served as loan collateral, to be returned by the tycoons after the government repaid its debt. In reality, the government defaulted, allowing the creditors (oligarchs-to-be) to auction off the stakes in giant firms (such as Yukos, LUKoil, and Noril'sk Nikel), typically to themselves. Most Russians viewed "loans for shares" as an affront and injustice: Yeltsin's administration seemingly enriched a small group of oligarchs by effectively selling off the "commanding heights" of the Soviet economy at a hefty discount (Goldman 2003). This perception and ensuing anger continued even when the oligarchs managed their companies more efficiently than nonoligarchic owners (Guriev and Rachinsky 2005).

12.2.2   The Evolution of the Oligarchs' Relationship with the Kremlin

The relationship between the oligarchs and the Kremlin can be described rather simply: While in the 1990s the oligarchs had the upper hand, since the 2000s the Kremlin has been calling the shots. What is Russia's policy direction? Who should have power? Who may possess wealth? Against whom should the state's considerable coercive resources be deployed? Questions like these are almost exclusively settled in the Kremlin today, while in the 1990s the oligarchs had a big say.

The dramatic fate of Boris Berezovsky, one of the most flamboyant Russian oligarchs, epitomizes this evolution. In 1996, Berezovsky famously boasted to the *Financial Times* that he and six other tycoons controlled half of Russia's economy. Indeed, a new Russian word was coined to capture "the rule of seven bankers" (*semibankirshchina*) including Berezovsky himself (controlling ORT and Sibneft, among other companies), Mikhail Khodorkovsky (Yukos), Mikhail Fridman (Alfa Group), Petr Aven (Alfa Group), Vladimir Gusinsky (NTV), Vladimir Potanin (UNEXIM Bank), and Aleksandr Smolensky (Bank Stolichny). This group had built corporate empires that assured not only financial heft but also political influence. Multiple oligarchs assumed formal positions in the government, and anecdotes abounded describing coffers of cash being carried into the Kremlin in exchange for political favors (Hoffman 2011).

Yet the circumstances changed radically after Putin came to power in 2000. Berezovsky lost control of his vast portfolio of companies, including Russia's flagship airline Aeroflot, the oil company Sibneft, and the country's largest television broadcaster ORT. He fled to the UK where he was granted political asylum in 2003. Berezovsky apparently committed suicide in 2013, after a decade of his relentless public relations campaign against Putin (which included full-page advertisements in the *New York Times* and *Wall Street Journal*).

Why and how did this reversal of fortunes for the oligarchs occur in Russia? When Putin assumed the presidency in 2000, he elaborated the notion of "equidistance": Each oligarch would be equally removed from levers of power. Essentially, the proposed "deal" was that the oligarchs would stay out of politics, and the Kremlin would stay out of the oligarchs' businesses.

Yet the attempted accommodation between oligarchs and Putin failed (Tompson 2005). Neither the oligarchs nor Putin could resist the temptation to break the informal deal. Some oligarchs continued to interfere in politics (Markus 2008), for example, by financing political parties opposed to the Kremlin or by seeking out influential foreign allies. Meanwhile, Putin's agenda of restoring a strong Russian state was extended to crushing the oligarchs as independent bases of power (Volkov 2008). Oligarchs who controlled independent media networks – such as Vladimir Gusinsky, who ran the irreverent NTV channel – in particular, were targeted, and their media assets taken over by the Kremlin. As a result, some high-profile oligarchs went into exile. In 2003, Mikhail Khodorkovsky, Russia's richest man and the controlling shareholder of the Yukos oil giant, was jailed in a highly politicized trial that served as a watershed moment in the Kremlin–oligarch relationship.

Furthermore, popular disappointment with the privatization of the 1990s facilitated its partial rollback in the 2000s (Markus 2017b). Putin's Kremlin applied political pressure on enterprises in the strategic industries (media and natural resources in particular) to sell controlling stakes to the state, while legislating preferential treatment granted to the so-called state corporations. The Law on State Corporations granted these conglomerates preferential tax arrangements, wideranging regulatory exemptions, and operational independence from local state bodies. The Kremlin has also pushed the oligarchs to invest more in "corporate social responsibility" by cultivating economic projects beneficial to the broader communities in regions where they operate factories or extract natural resources. For example, Roman Abramovich (the owner of the English soccer club Chelsea, before he was forced to give it up after the February 2022 invasion of Ukraine) was made governor of Chukotka, a remote Siberian region, and invested considerable sums of his personal money in regional development.

Overall, while the oligarchs wielded substantial influence both in the economy and in politics toward the end of the 1990s, Putin's tenure terminated the era of "business as usual," that is, the rules of wealth accumulation and political influence established by the tycoons in the 1990s. However, as the rest of this chapter explains, new groups of superwealthy actors have emerged on Russia's political scene to take the place of Yeltsin-era oligarchs.

12.2.3   Oligarch Types in Today's Russia

To start, we must recognize the diversity of Russian business elites today. This matters because not all oligarchs are equally privileged. In terms of their proximity to power, three groups stand out (Markus 2017a).

First, Putin's friends are personally connected to the president. Such connections are often idiosyncratic. They may stem from the infamous Ozero dacha cooperative (a gated summerhouse community), from Putin's hobbies (such as judo), from his career, and so forth. This is the most exclusive network. Many of Putin's close friends have experienced a meteoric rise to extreme wealth that can be explained only through their connections to the Russian president. In many ways, this network around Putin resembles Yeltsin's inner circle, which was known in the 1990s as "the Family." Yet there is a critical difference, too: Putin's friends are almost entirely dependent on their patron's favor to continue their oligarchic existence. Among Putin's closest oligarch friends from St. Petersburg (where Putin grew up) are Yury Kovalchuk (often referred to as Putin's "personal banker"), Gennady Timchenko (whose key asset is the energy trading firm Gunvor), and the brothers Arkady and Boris Rotenberg (who own assets in construction, electricity, and pipelines).

Secondly, some of today's business elites in Russia have leveraged their networks in the FSB (Russia's security services, formerly the KGB, where Putin made his career prior to becoming president), the police, or the military to amass extreme personal wealth. The Russian word for cadres from the military and law enforcement is *siloviki*. Hence, the *siloviki*-oligarchs are referred to as the **silovarchs** (Treisman 2008). While the circles of Putin's friends and the silovarchs partly overlap, the silovarchs comprise a larger group, most of whose members are not Putin's personal friends. The silovarchs have also been painted as the resentful KGB (now FSB) officers of the 1990s who, once eager to take over control (and wealth) from the Yeltsin-era oligarchs, got their chance under Putin (Belton 2020). To conceal their personal wealth – which would raise questions about corruption, given their government jobs – silovarchs often let family members hold their assets. The sons of Yury Chaika, Russia's powerful procurator general (until 2019), for example, "amassed a huge business empire, thanks ... to their father's position and their ability to keep regional prosecutors onside" (Walker 2015). The man reputed to be the (informal) leader of the *siloviki* as well as the (formal) chair of Rosneft, the state's oil giant, is Igor Sechin – widely seen as the second most powerful person in Russia.

Thirdly, an even larger number of the super-rich in Russia are outsiders not personally connected to Putin, the military, or the FSB. Indeed, some current outsiders are the 1990s-era oligarchs: While Putin selectively crushed politically inconvenient or obstreperous oligarchs after coming to power, he did not seek to systematically "eliminate oligarchs as a class" as he had promised during his initial election campaign. For example, oligarchs such as Vladimir Potanin, Oleg Deripaska, and Alisher Usmanov, who accumulated their wealth in the 1990s, regularly feature in the lists of richest Russians today. Others are simply businesspeople who managed to build successful companies without the "political capital" of the silovarchs or Putin's friends.

While none of these three groups is monolithic, these categories are useful to highlight the distinct power resources at the oligarchs' disposal. Putin's friends possess the highly prized "access to the body" (*dostup k telu*), implying the privilege to be heard by – and possibly sway – the most powerful individual in Russia via informal conversations. It is quite evident that being Putin's friend increases an oligarch's wealth significantly.

Meanwhile, the silovarchs have direct access to coercion, either through their current appointments in the power agencies (the police, FSB, military, and so on) or their close personal contacts there. More than other groups, the silovarchs possess the power of (c)omission: They can implement Putin's orders – or fail to do so. Since 2003, Putin's friends and the silovarchs have steadily risen to control crony sectors of the economy and to hold important positions in the executive branch. These groups are disproportionately represented on corporate boards of the "state corporations," and they often own large stakes in firms from sectors where profitability depends on government favor (such as oil, utilities, telecommunications, defense, and construction).

Compared to Putin's friends and the silovarchs, the influence of outsiders is much more mediated. Some outsiders have held seats in the **Duma**. (While politically impotent in today's Russia, the parliament provides deputies with immunity from legal prosecution, which is attractive for some business elites.) Others have lobbied via the Russian Union of Industrialists and Entrepreneurs (RUIE), a business association representing large capital, formed in 1990 and at times influential in policy debates (Markus 2007).

The relative proximity to power of Putin-era oligarchs has determined their access to state contracts as key avenue for self-enrichment (Markus 2017b). Public procurement in Putin's Russia has played a role similar to privatization in the 1990s as the engine of enormous fortunes for politically connected individuals. Many sectors, including infrastructure, defense, and healthcare, have seen regular overcharging of the state treasury by private suppliers, sometimes at prices equal to double or triple the market rate and with kickbacks to the state officials involved.

As these dynamics imply, while the forms of Russia's post-Soviet corruption have changed, its extent has not. State power is continuously converted into private wealth and vice versa, weakening public accountability of the government and undermining the rule of law (Dawisha 2015).

12.3 Oligarchs as Agents of Change?

One of the main uncertainties on Russia's contemporary political stage relates to the pressure for change that the oligarchs might exert. This potential change refers, above all, to the balance of power between the oligarchs and the Kremlin (which, as described above, strongly favors Putin) – but also to Russia's democracy and rule of law writ large. This generates several important questions. Is there any demand for change on the part of the oligarchs in Putin's Russia? If so, what type of change do they seek? And, finally, to the extent such demand exists, do the oligarchs possess sufficient leverage to shift Russia's trajectory?

12.3.1   Demand for Change from the Oligarchs

For multiple reasons, oligarchs' demand for systemic change has not involved the rule of law. Let us analyze the issue in terms of "exit, voice, and loyalty," the classical conceptual responses to adversity (Hirschman 1970). In our context, adversity stands for the political disempowerment or even persecution of the oligarchs under Putin's rule. In this situation, "exit" implies the cessation of economic activity in Russia, for example, via capital flight; "voice" implies active disagreement with the Kremlin's policymaking and attempts to change it; and "loyalty" implies continuing economic activity in Russia without voicing any disagreements politically.

Consider exit. Unlike trapped constituencies such as blue-collar labor, Russia's business elites have ample possibilities to retire not only their capital but also themselves abroad, which may decrease their demand for institutional change at home (Sharafutdinova and Dawisha 2016). Russian oligarchs are indeed some of the most avid buyers of high-end real estate in prime locations across the world, and data on investor visas also show that Russian business elites are increasingly purchasing foreign residence permits (Gulina 2016). The top issuers of investor visas for Russian big capital are, in descending order, the United Kingdom, Portugal, the United States, and Austria. In these countries, investor visas leading to permanent residence or citizenship involve a minimum $1 million–3 million investment and sometimes proof of job creation.

The motivation to pursue a strategy that signals loyalty relates to the oligarchs' reasoning that it pays to support a system that has allowed them to prosper. For the oligarchs, it may be precisely the *lack* of rule of law that facilitates the expansion of riches, for example, through a variety of corrupt schemes commonly referred to as "raiding" (Markus 2015, 54–64; see also Chapter 9). To be sure, the environment of constant danger is not for the faint of heart. According to Mikhail Gutseriev, who left Russia in 2007 after being pressured to sell his company Russneft, "only in London did I realize that . . . back in Russia I had spent 20 percent [of my time] on business, and 80 percent on confrontation" (Reznik 2010). And yet, when given a chance in 2010, Gutseriev returned to Russia, suggesting that the risks of "confrontation" may be well worth the rewards. In a survey of the executives at 396 Russian manufacturing enterprises, 24 percent of the respondents agreed with this statement: "the poor protection of property rights presents not only a threat but also an opportunity for business growth" (Markus 2015, 111–12).

Finally, even when business elites voice their disagreement with the system, they may press the state for de facto accountability at the firm level via stakeholder alliances with labor, community, or foreign investors (Markus 2008, 2012). Such alliances allow business-owners to protect their specific firms while avoiding the need for country-level rule of law.

Taken together, the above factors imply that business elites are partly complicit in the persistence of **Putinism**, their complicity being not only self-fulfilling (Hale 2015) but also self-serving. Indeed, most of the unfortunate Russian billionaires who lost their billionaire status in 2006–15 were not victims of the state, but rather of market conditions or unscrupulous rivals (Treisman 2016).

12.3.2   What Do Oligarchs Want?

Yet to conclude that the oligarchs are content with the status quo is premature. To identify what the oligarchs want, let us move beyond the "rule of law" as the benchmark.

Russia's super-rich may not want institutionalized accountability writ large (competitive and honest elections, plus legislative and judiciary independence). But there is likely to be demand for de facto elite accountability. From the oligarchs' perspective, the latter could theoretically be achieved in several ways, including (1) a relatively impartial elite arbiter, like Leonid Brezhnev in Soviet times or Ukraine's Leonid Kuchma before the Orange Revolution; (2) an empowered oligarch-controlled parliament, like the Ukrainian Rada after the Orange Revolution; (3) Singapore-style authoritarian legality guaranteeing property rights without competitive politics; or (4) powerful associations of large businesses that can check the state, as in Mexico in the late nineteenth century.

The demand for such de facto elite accountability, in whatever form, is rising, particularly since the imposition of sanctions on Russia by the West in the 2010s and 2020s. The conditional nature of oligarchic ownership – subject to Kremlin's approval – in Russia has long been acknowledged, at least since the 2003 expropriation of Khodorkovsky's Yukos company. Yet the conditionality imposed on the oligarchs by Putin early in his first tenure ("stay out of politics, and keep your property") is becoming unreliable given Putin's unilateral departures from the informal agreement.

The contrast between the 2003 case of Mikhail Khodorkovsky and the 2014 case of Vladimir Yevtushenkov, both oligarch targets of Putin's Kremlin, is telling. One could easily argue that Khodorkovsky flouted Putin's "rules" by financing opposition parties and threatening to interfere with Russia's foreign policy (via plans for Yukos's pipelines and asset sales to US firms). Yevtushenkov, by contrast, epitomizes oligarchic loyalty to Putin. Yevtushenkov abandoned his patron Yury Luzhkov, the former mayor of Moscow to whom Yevtushenkov owes his fortune, when Luzhkov's relations with the Kremlin grew tense in 2010. But no matter: Yevtushenkov's oil company Bashneft was expropriated, decimating the oligarch's wealth, despite the fact that Yevtushenkov's progressive buy-up of Bashneft shares in 2005–09 had been meticulously coordinated with the Kremlin. Igor Sechin,

Putin's favorite silovarch, in charge of Rosneft, reportedly masterminded the 2014 attack on Bashneft. The fact that Putin let a loyal oligarch (Yevtushenkov) be devoured by Sechin raises the question of what exactly loyalty to Putin is worth.

Another apolitical oligarch, Sergei Pugachev, has faced the Kremlin's wrath recently. In exile since 2012, Pugachev faces criminal charges in Russia and claims that the Kremlin had expropriated around $15 billion of his business assets. Formerly referred to as the "Kremlin's banker," Pugachev was notably in Putin's inner circle at the beginning of the 2000s.

The irregular application of unwritten rules has made Russia's business elites nervous. This is evident to a careful observer in the fact that the group of Putin's friends itself is rather fluid. By 2010, Putin distanced himself from friends of the late 1990s and his first presidency (including Pugachev), reaching out instead to friends from his younger years, that is, from the early to mid-1990s (for example, from the Ozero dacha cooperative) and even from childhood (as in the case of Arkady Rotenberg). Is there a guarantee that Putin will not "unfriend" some of them, too? Western jurisdictions (especially London) have seen a rising tide of commercial litigation by the Russian business elites (Nougayrède 2013): This trend suggests that, for the oligarchs, Putin is not living up to the role of an arbiter or the enforcer of authoritarian legality either.

Overall, there is demand for greater predictability in business–power relations on the part of the oligarchs – but no vision on how to achieve it. Given Putin's erratic decisions, the oligarchs have no reason to trust him with the role of a stabilizer or enforcer, even if he plays that role by default.

Yet, a more institutionalized form of authoritarian legality may also be unpalatable to many oligarchs, given how diligently the FSB has been collecting *kompromat* (evidence of legal wrongdoing that can be used for blackmail) on business elites, including the silovarchs themselves (Ledeneva 2013, 38). Since many oligarchs have broken the law in their careers, the "rule of law" would make them vulnerable (for example, subject to prosecution), given their past misdeeds.

Meanwhile, popular resentment of the super-rich in Russia makes honest and competitive elections a risky proposition. Russian business elites have watched the instability in Ukraine closely in the wake of democratization, including both the reprivatization attempt after the 2004 Orange Revolution (Markus 2016) and some anticorruption initiatives after the 2014 ouster of Viktor Yanukovych.

Finally, the oligarchs' experience with the RUIE and its mixed record in improving state–business relations (Markus 2007, 2015) has cooled business elites' enthusiasm for association-building. The RUIE's requests on behalf of Khodorkovsky and Yevtushenkov were ignored by the Kremlin. At the end of the day, the question facing the Russian oligarchs is urgent but unanswered: Which way from here?

In addition to greater predictability, another vector of implicit oligarchic demand for change aims at a more West-friendly foreign policy. This demand is driven by tangible personal losses from Western sanctions experienced since 2014 by Putin's friends and some of the silovarchs. Multiple waves of sanctions have been applied to Russia by the administrations of Barack Obama, Donald Trump, and Joseph Biden. These sanctions constitute the US response to the Russia-sponsored invasion of Ukraine in 2014; to Russia's repeated cyberattacks against the United States, including for the purposes of electoral interference; to Russia's state-sponsored chemical attacks against Sergei Skripal (a defector from the FSB) in the UK in 2018 and against **Alexei Navalny** (a key opposition leader) in 2020; and – most dramatically – to Russia's renewed full-scale invasion of Ukraine in 2022.

Beyond the crucial issue of sanction-related losses by the oligarchs close to the Kremlin, all types of oligarchs desire to keep the West as a viable exit option. The latter implies that the Russian super-rich want to prevent the reputational damage abroad from spiraling entirely out of control. Yet, Putin's Kremlin has remained utterly unmoved by the sanctions, both in its antagonistic foreign policy vis-à-vis the United States and in its increasingly authoritarian domestic policymaking. Hence, it is reasonable to assume that the oligarchs are growing (even) more anxious.

12.3.3   Lack of Oligarchic Leverage

Most Russian oligarchs would benefit from a shift in Russia's trajectory toward greater de facto elite accountability and less hostility vis-à-vis the West. But is this implicit demand matched by the oligarchs' capacity to achieve it?

The answer is no. The key reason is a **collective action problem**, that is, the oligarchs' inability to act together to achieve a common purpose. While in smaller economies the actions of a single larger-than-life oligarch (for example, Bidzina Ivanishvili in Georgia) may change the status quo, the sheer number of Russia's super-rich, all equipped with their own power resources, implies that sustainable leverage requires cooperation. Cooperation, however, is not the Russian oligarchs' strong suit.

For Putin's friends and the silovarchs, the problem resides in the competitive nature of the Russian kleptocracy. Russia's "piranha capitalism" (Markus 2015) is defined by individual state employees at all levels of the executive hierarchy competing with each other to extract rents from the economy. Even if Putin wanted to be a trusted arbiter among the oligarchs, the implementation of his decisions would be a challenge in a system whose executive branch is pulled apart by competing kleptocrats, not least the silovarchs, who have effectively undermined a number of Putin's priorities, including international defense contracts, Gazprom's strategy in Europe, electoral manipulation, and so on.

To be sure, oligarchic clans offer a form of collective action, but they have always been fragmented, overlapping, and changeable. Even Putin's closest friends are not above mutual sabotage, including that of their patron: consider analysis by The Economist (2012) showing that a state-linked Russian oil trader, Gunvor, was regularly driving down the price for Urals crude, a Russian export oil mixture, for the private profit of Gennady Timchenko, a supposed Putin loyalist. When nominal loyalty yields to predatory temptations, group cohesiveness suffers. Russia's independent TV channel Dozhd has reported that Putin's former St. Petersburg friend, Sergei Pugachev, embezzled oligarchic donations to Putin's election campaigns, including a $50 million donation from Lukoil alone (Zygar' 2016, 21, 37).

The outsider tycoons, too, are anything but cohesive. This was most vividly demonstrated by the five-year struggle for Noril'sk Nickel between Vladimir Potanin (famous for engineering the loans-for-shares scheme in the 1990s) and Oleg Deripaska (affiliated with **Dmitry Medvedev**, Aleksandr Voloshin, and the vestiges of Yeltsin's "Family"). Potanin initially outsmarted Deripaska who, in turn, vowed to fight Potanin "to the death," as both oligarchs engaged their massive administrative resources at home while also suing each other abroad in a series of battles between 2008 and 2012.

Public knowledge of oligarchic rivalries almost certainly constitutes only the tip of the iceberg. The depth and acrimony of these struggles are likely far more severe, thereby making collective leverage by the super-rich in Russia an unlikely proposition. But collective lobbying is not the only path to leverage for the super-rich. Let us reconsider exit.

As noted above, from the oligarchs' perspective, their possibility of leaving Russia may reduce their demand for change. However, from Putin's perspective, capital flight or even its implicit threat may put pressure on the system, by depriving the Russian economy of investment, jobs, and tax revenue. In other words, exit may reduce the oligarchs' explicit demand for better arrangements from the state while simultaneously increasing their implicit leverage to get such arrangements. Exit as a form of leverage does not depend on collective action, since every oligarch can exercise it *individually*.

In Russia, it is more difficult for individual silovarchs and friends of Putin – as compared to outsider oligarchs – to rely on exit as an implicit threat, due to the intimate connections to the state apparatus of Putin's friends and the silovarchs, as well as the progressive tightening of (Putin-inspired) legislation restricting state employees' foreign asset ownership.

In any case, for a long time Putin has been starkly insensitive to the implicit exit threat of Russia's individual capital owners. As one oligarch noted in his comment on the Bashneft attack, "the Kremlin certainly would understand that it was going to hurt the stock market; that it's going to add to the whole economic situation; that it was going to frighten the business community … They went ahead anyway … because they wanted to deliver a message: 'Behave yourself'" (Myers and Becker 2014).

Instead of counteracting capital flight by improving the investment climate, the Kremlin has tried to force capital back to Russia, most prominently through a "de-offshorization" campaign launched in 2013. This campaign has targeted oligarchs' options to conceal their wealth via foreign-registered accounts (often to evade Russian taxes). Until recently, individual oligarchs could decide separately on whether to (a) keep their physical profit-generating assets in Russia; (b) register their assets and cash flows in Russia or offshore; (c) personally reside in Russia or abroad; and (d) let their family members reside in Russia or relocate them abroad. The winning formula for many oligarchs has been to keep their physical productive assets in Russia but register them offshore while also securing foreign residence permits for themselves and/or their extended family.

The de-offshorization campaign may indicate a shift in the Kremlin's attitude regarding these possibilities of exit. At the unlikely extreme, Putin may push the oligarchs to decide: Either keep your business in Russia and register it here – or liquidate your assets in Russia and leave the country altogether. So far, many top companies such as RusAl, Metalloinvest, MTS, RusHydro, and KamAZ have pledged to stop registering businesses offshore and to repatriate their physical productive assets held abroad.

If the oligarchs' reaction to Western sanctions and economic decline is any indication, then the oligarchs' influence on Russia's trajectory will remain limited. The RUIE has pointedly kept silent on Russia's economically ruinous foreign policy since the conflict in Ukraine unfolded. Despite their substantial wealth losses from sanctions, Putin's friends paraded their readiness to sacrifice even more for their leader in various interviews. Of course, the propaganda aspect of such statements aside, the oligarchs care deeply about their billions.

Yet their strategy of defending their wealth has been indirect: Instead of pushing Putin to change course, the oligarchs have sought compensation from the state. In September 2014, the Duma adopted a law according to which Russian citizens who lost assets abroad due to sanctions would be compensated from the Russian treasury. The law sparked a popular outcry, as Russian taxpayers balked at the prospect of bailing out the oligarchs. Putin's reaction to these attempts at personal compensation by the oligarchs was negative (both the Russian government and the Supreme Court rejected the Duma law). Meanwhile, some strategically important companies, particularly Rosneft, have received ample help from the state.

After Russia launched a broad war against Ukraine in 2022, at times purposely targeting civilians, the international community imposed unprecedented sanctions targeting trade (especially in energy products), investments (seizing the assets of Russian oligarchs in the West), and global connectivity (via the SWIFT banking network for financial transactions). This time, even the oligarchs' extensive philanthropic activity in the West (for example, donations to universities and museums) came under close scrutiny, and, in many cases, donations were subsequently rejected by the recipient. Vladimir Potanin, for example, had to exit the governing board of New York's iconic Solomon R. Guggenheim Museum. This philanthropic activity had been conducted at least partly to give the oligarchs "political insurance" (Markus 2008), a safe haven in the West if the situation in Russia became untenable. The global backlash against the Russian oligarchs (spanning countries as diverse as the United States, Japan, and Portugal, among many others) after the 2022 invasion demonstrated that this "insurance" strategy had failed.

How did the oligarchs react? Mikhail Fridman, Oleg Deripaska, and Vagit Alekperov were among the first oligarchs to speak out, ever so cautiously, against the war – although, notably, not against Putin or Russia's system of rule. Putin, for his part, fully embraced the policy of "import-substitution," which implies that Russia is aiming at economic self-sufficiency achieved through domestic production of all necessary goods (Markus 2022a). Notably, this not only reduces the impact of sanctions but also has the potential to further enrich the Russian oligarchs through state contracts for goods that had been previously imported (Gabuev 2022).

The bottom line is: Absent greater cooperation by the oligarchs, or higher responsiveness of the Russian leadership to the threat of capital exit, Russia's business elites have little leverage to shape the country's trajectory and the degree of personalism in Putin's rule. One potential exception to this is the silovarchs because it is the guns – not the money – that speak loudest in wartime Russian elite politics (Markus 2022b). However, it is too early to tell.

12.3.4   Renegades and Trojans

Eppur si muove! While the oligarchs' leverage in Russia is systemically limited, cases of vocal – if so far inconsequential – opposition to the Kremlin by business elites do exist in Russia's recent history. Two types of instance come to mind.

First, the **renegade oligarchs** such as Khodorkovsky, Yevgeny Chichvarkin, or the late Berezovsky had experienced persecution by the Russian state, left the country, and then invested in opposition to Putin's regime from abroad. Prior to his 2013 death, Boris Berezovsky had conducted a broad informational campaign against Putin, including the financing of a film that implicated the FSB in the 1999 apartment bombings in Russia. Berezovsky also wrote open letters to Putin ("Volodia, . . . as a typical dictator, you are not ready to surrender power through elections"), to Patriarch Kirill ("Your Holiness, . . . help Putin come to his senses . . . take power from his hands and peacefully, wisely, Christian-like, give that power to the people"), to George W. Bush, and so on.

Mikhail Khodorkovsky was pardoned by Putin in 2013 after a politically motivated ten-year imprisonment. The oligarch has since reanimated his foundation Open Russia, which provided logistical backing to hundreds of independent and opposition candidates in the 2016 Duma elections. Khodorkovsky has forcefully criticized Russia's military actions in Ukraine as well as the imprisonment of Navalny in 2021, while predicting significant change in Russia around the presidential elections of 2024. He has also hired a substantial staff of professional journalists to fuel his growing online presence. Yevgeny Chichvarkin, the extravagant erstwhile owner of Yevroset' (Russia's largest mobile phone retailer), fled to London in 2008 after losing his business in a series of raiding attacks by the police. Though the fabricated criminal cases against Chichvarkin in Russia were closed in 2011 (the oligarch personally appealed to Medvedev on the matter), he chose to stay in London and engage in opposition activity.

In 2016, Chichvarkin joined forces with Khodorkovsky. The two oligarchs conducted an online press conference in April 2016 from London, streaming live to the Moscow offices of Open Russia. Chichvarkin suggested at the conference that "color revolutions" – the mass pro-democracy uprisings in post-Soviet countries – should not be feared. According to Khodorkovsky, Chichvarkin's experience in mass communications would benefit the "political–educational" mission of Open Russia. Despite their diverging political visions – Khodorkovsky calls himself a statist while Chichvarkin identifies as a libertarian – both agreed at the conference that the current Russian power is "hurtling toward a dead end" (said Chichvarkin). When that dead end is reached, the renegades plan to oversee a two-year "temporary administration" in Russia in order to ensure subsequent honest elections.

The renegade oligarchs face significant challenges in their quest to democratize Russia. They lack the support of the Russian population at large. They are also disconnected from influential elites at home. If a political opening occurred in Russia, the renegades could potentially return and help steer the country – but they are unlikely to be the cause of that opening. So far, the renegades' strategy is to (a) invest heavily in communications capacity; (b) nurture and showcase a cadre of young politicians in Russia's parliamentary elections; and (c) wait for the Kremlin to make a mistake. Putin has not been prone to mistakes, however: not when it comes to power preservation.

Secondly, oligarchs such as Alexander Lebedev and Mikhail Prokhorov have engaged in the formal political process while living in Russia. We can refer to such oligarchs as the "Trojans," after the legendary Greek tactic to defeat the opponent from the inside (by smuggling warriors disguised in a statue of a "Trojan horse" through enemy gates). As do the renegades, the Trojans advocate democratization and rule of law. However, the Trojans have stopped short of criticizing Putin directly, focusing on systemic shortcomings instead. More so than the renegades, the Trojans emphasize gradual, evolutionary change.

Alexander Lebedev is a banker, media owner (he co-owns *Novaya Gazeta* with **Mikhail Gorbachev**, plus several British papers), and former KGB officer. Lebedev ran for mayor in Moscow in 2003, but lost to Luzhkov. He also sought to run for mayor of Sochi in 2009, but he was disqualified as a candidate. Lebedev successfully ran for the Duma, where he was a deputy in 2003–07, switching his party affiliation from Rodina to **United Russia** to independent during his term. Lebedev has devoted resources to exposing high-level corruption in the Russian bureaucracy, cooperating with Navalny at one point, but he has distanced himself from the prominent opposition activist since 2012.

Mikhail Prokhorov has owned major assets in mining, finance, and media (as well as the Brooklyn Nets). He ran as an independent candidate in the 2012 presidential elections. In 2011, Prokhorov had become the leader of the Right Cause party. After losing the presidential elections to Putin, the oligarch launched a new party, Civic Platform. Prokhorov's political involvement is the most high-profile to date by a Russian oligarch. His respectable share of the vote in the 2012 presidential elections, 8 percent, despite the domination of the media by Kremlin-friendly outlets, suggests that the Trojans are better connected to Russian citizens and elites than the renegades. Furthermore, it demonstrates that divisions among the Kremlin insiders can help the Trojans. Prokhorov's political rise would have been impossible without the intensifying competition between the teams of Prime Minister Putin and President Medvedev at the time.

However, Prokhorov's experience also demonstrates two limitations of the Trojans. First, the Trojans are no match for the Kremlin's political technologists when it comes to strategy in the Byzantine world of authoritarian populism. Secondly, the Trojans have shown a limited commitment to political life. (In the midst of his presidential campaign, for example, Prokhorov left for a one-month vacation in Turkey.) Unlike the renegades, the Trojans seem to play politics rather than to live politics. Opposition activity as a hobby – even when pursued by talented, charismatic, and wealthy individuals – will not upset Russia's political equilibrium.

12.4   The International Dimension

If Russian oligarchs were a purely domestic phenomenon, our analysis could stop here. It is the international dimension of Russia's oligarchs that presents urgent policy challenges for the West.

First, Russia's provision of employment, loans, and donations to potential political decisionmakers abroad has allowed the country to place bets on political players who may offer strategic value in the future. The Russian bank First Czech–Russian Bank loaned 9 million euros in 2014 to the populist anti-EU party of Marine Le Pen in France. Russia's biggest private oil company Lukoil paid a $1.4 million state fine for Martin Nejedly, a key advisor to the Czech president in 2016, allowing Nejedly to keep his influential position. Germany's former chancellor Gerhard Schröder has been employed by Gazprom in its Nord Stream pipeline projects for more than ten years. In 2010, Renaissance Capital, a Russian investment bank, paid $500,000 to former US president Bill Clinton for a speech whose timing coincided with the review by the Committee on Foreign Investment in the United States of a sensitive purchase by Rosatom, the Russian nuclear agency, of a Wyoming uranium mine. It is noteworthy that such monetary benefits are not directly provided by the Russian government but rather by Russian companies or banks. It is likely that at least some oligarchs initiate geopolitically significant transactions voluntarily to create rapport with the Kremlin. In the 2000s, the strategies of Russian oligarchs to protect their companies from the Kremlin centered on cultivating foreign investors (Markus 2008). Today, they seem to involve "geopolitical volunteering" on behalf of the Kremlin (Markus 2017b).

Secondly, consider the effects of massive flows of Russian capital to Western jurisdictions, both onshore and offshore. According to government figures, since Putin came to power in 2000, Russia has experienced a total net outflow of more than $550 billion; some independent experts put the total at more than $1 trillion. Some of this money was legally earned. Of concern here is dirty money which is, in effect, laundered in the West. Funds obtained through bribery, stolen from the Russian treasury, or plundered from the Russian bank deposits find safe haven in the West through luxury investments and, most importantly, through secret bank deposits.

The ramifications of this arrangement are profound. To begin with, the availability of Western havens for dirty cash adversely changes the incentives of the Russian elites. Why invest in any future-oriented policy (state-building, economic growth, rule of law, societal peace) if one can plunder and hide the proceeds successfully? By dramatically lowering the risk of domestic exposure and punishment for corruption or theft, foreign offshore havens reward such behavior.

Furthermore, the deluge of corrupt proceeds from Russia, China, and many other developing countries has created an entire money-laundering industry in the West, involving bankers, lawyers, accountants, and other professionals, who instruct their Russian clients on the specifics of shell companies, artificial bankruptcies, reputation-enhancing investments, and financial secrecy (Judah 2016). This manifold Western money-laundering industry is a vested interest in the status quo on behalf of Russian corrupt officials and oligarchs, particularly in countries such as Switzerland, the UK, Austria, the United States, Luxembourg, and others. The expectation that closer socioeconomic engagement would transform economic elites in the developing countries was rather naïve – the transformation goes very much both ways.

Thirdly, weak enforcement of anti-money-laundering laws in the West further undermines its soft power in Russia by exposing the promise of clean government, a key attraction of Western democracy that inspired two Maidan Revolutions in Ukraine, as hypocritical. The Russian state media have been at pains to criticize Western governance model: The fact that the West indirectly encourages Russian corruption by accepting and safeguarding its dirty cash supports that narrative.

The United States has already begun to address some of these issues. If initially the United States erred on the side of attracting foreign capital by not fully implementing the anti-money-laundering standards of the Organisation for Economic Co-operation and Development (OECD), its Department of Justice has recently aggressively pursued suspect foreign cash. The government's Kleptocracy Asset Recovery Initiative, launched in 2010, combines the expertise of the Department of Justice, the FBI, and other enforcement agencies to confiscate corrupt proceeds of foreign officials (and, if possible, return them to the countries harmed). Furthermore, the Bank Secrecy Act requires financial intermediaries to know their customers and report any suspected unlawful activity.

Perhaps the greatest challenge, with respect to Russia and more generally, concerns the anonymity of global offshore finance. On this front, the US administration would find some cooperation from Moscow. Economically, the Russian treasury has been losing vast sums to offshores. Politically, the Kremlin is keen to strengthen its control over bureaucrats and oligarchs, two groups for whom offshore nest eggs provide an alternative to Putin's Russia. A joint US–Russian effort, however limited, at ending the anonymity of corrupt cash flows into Western jurisdictions would serve the interests of both countries.

Finally, not all international ramifications of Russia's big capital are negative. Some individual oligarchs and their companies, for example, have leveraged foreign courts to impose more accountability on the Kremlin at home. A notable, albeit partial, success case here is Yukos. The shareholders of Khodorkovsky's expropriated company have scored multiple legal and monetary victories against the Kremlin in European and American courts (Markus 2015).

12.5   Conclusion

Regardless of their proximity to power, most Russian oligarchs have been quiescent in the face of attacks by the Kremlin, Western sanctions, and economic decline. Those who have pushed for change remain marginalized. Will this situation last? Two overarching lessons can be gleaned from other countries to forecast the political behavior of Russia's business elites (Markus 2017a).

12.5.1   Comparative Lessons for Russian Oligarchs

First, oligarchs have good reason to fear democracy, but this fear can be overcome.

For the oligarchs, democratization involves multiple threats that have materialized to some extent across the world after the introduction of greater political competition. These threats include trust-busting and demonopolization reforms (South Korea); pressure for higher taxes and redistribution (Argentina, Brazil, Mexico); collapse of order and spiraling violence (Indonesia); and revision of privatization results (Ukraine).

However, democratization is by no means anathema to the super-rich. They are more likely to accept it or push for it when some of the following conditions hold: economic prosperity (South Korea); declining dependence of business profits on government connections (Western Europe, Mexico, Brazil); high dependence of political elites on big business for political finance (Ukraine); or a sharp increase in the autocrat's attacks on business elites (Kyrgyzstan, Ukraine, Belarus, Kazakhstan). Of course, just because the oligarchs voice their support for democratization does not mean that political change will follow. This brings us to the next lesson.

Secondly, to effect change, the oligarchs need the people. Mikhail Prokhorov may empathize with the late Chung Ju-yung, the founder of Hyundai, who established a new political party and ran for president in 1991–92 in a bid to challenge the ruling Democratic Justice Party and the incumbent. Yung ran on a platform stressing competence and professionalism, just like Prokhorov. The *chaebol* leader suffered a humiliating defeat, despite the fact that Korea's business elites had closed ranks behind the need for change. Though fed up with economic incompetence of the regime, the *chaebol*s remained alienated from the population at large. Collective action by the oligarchs is not enough.

The importance of popular support should be self-evident for the renegades and the Trojans, that is, for all oligarchs who openly advocate liberalization. But, even for the Russian business elites who care more about their material interests than any political vision, popular support is crucial if the Ukrainian experience is any guide. Quantitative analysis of the Ukrainian super-rich suggests that business wealth is more resilient against various shocks (including authoritarian expropriation) for oligarchs who pursue "flexible" strategies aimed at legitimacy (via media and political parties) than for oligarchs who rely on direct power or asset mobility (Markus and Charnysh 2017). (The darker side of the Ukrainian lesson is that adaptability and deniability, which these flexible strategies assure, can make the oligarchs immune to democratic pressures.)

While the gulf has always been enormous between Russia's business elites and the general population, the Kremlin's economic (since 2009) and foreign (since 2011) policies have driven a further wedge between the tiny fraction of Russia's "1 percent" and the rest. The Kremlin's military–economic populism has combined an aggressive stance abroad with patriotic propaganda and the financial support of vulnerable population layers at home. In budget terms, this policy paradigm is too expensive amidst economic recession. Yet while the oligarchs pick up the bill – in the form of new taxes on oil revenue, Western sanctions, and lost trade – citizens at large applaud Putin.

The oligarchs understand Putin's game. The fugitive oligarch Sergei Pugachev cannot be alone in thinking that "today, personal friendship and loyalty don't mean anything … why does Putin need friends when 85 percent of Russians support him?" (Meyer and Reznik 2015). The billionaire Yury Kovalchuk, Putin's friend who replaced Pugachev in his informal capacity as the president's personal banker, captured the prevalent mood best in his reaction to Western sanctions: "Put yourself in my place. If I start annoying him, like Kudrin does, telling him what he does not like, arguing back – how will that end for me? I will reduce my access to 'the body,' punishing myself even more than the Europeans did. What for? For whom?" (Zygar' 2016, 370).

12.5.2   Parting Thoughts

In Ayn Rand's libertarian manifesto *Atlas Shrugged*, which has inspired generations of teenagers as well as Evgeny Chichvarkin, large capitalists pull out of a state-dominated economy, forcing its collapse, and then take over leadership. Although some of the Russian oligarchs have resorted to exit, it has not been sufficient for the Kremlin to change course. Meanwhile, divisions among the oligarchs as well as between the oligarchs and the population have prevented the former having an effective "voice."

Internationally, Russian big capital presents acute challenges for the West to the extent it is earned illegally and retired abroad, or to the extent it is used to achieve Kremlin's foreign policy goals. At the same time, international experience suggests that, while the interests of the Russian oligarchs might be jeopardized by democratization, the oligarchs would also find greater leverage vis-à-vis the Kremlin if they could align themselves more effectively with the people.

DISCUSSION QUESTIONS

1. What is the meaning of the Russian joke used as the epigraph for this chapter?
2. Was the rise of the Russian oligarchs in the 1990s inevitable? Which factors facilitated their emergence? What might the Yeltsin administration have done differently to prevent a group of bankers from becoming "oligarchs"?
3. Why have oligarchs been unable to change Russia's trajectory under Putin? Is this likely to change in the future?

REFERENCES

Belton, Catherine. 2020. *Putin's People: How the KGB Took Back Russia and Then Took on the West*. New York: Farrar, Straus and Giroux.

Dawisha, Karen. 2015. *Putin's Kleptocracy: Who Owns Russia?* New York: Simon and Schuster.

Economist, The. 2012. "Gunvor: Riddles, Mysteries and Enigmas." May 5.

Gabuev, Alexander. 2022. "Why Vladimir Putin and His Entourage Want War." *The Economist*, February 19.

Goldman, Marshall. 2003. *The Piratization of Russia: Russian Reform Goes Awry*. London: Routledge.

Gulina, Olga. 2016. "Rossiiskie den'gi na Zapade." *Intersection*, April 27.

Guriev, Sergei, and Andrei Rachinsky. 2005. "The Role of Oligarchs in Russian Capitalism." *Journal of Economic Perspectives*, 19, 131–50.

Hale, Henry. 2015. *Patronal Politics: Eurasian Regime Dynamics in Comparative Perspective*. Cambridge: Cambridge University Press.

Hirschman, Albert O. 1970. *Exit, Voice, and Loyalty: Responses to Decline in Firms, Organizations, and States*. Cambridge, MA: Harvard University Press.

Hoffman, David. 2011. *The Oligarchs: Wealth and Power in the New Russia*. London: Hachette UK.

Judah, Ben. 2016. *The Kleptocracy Curse: Rethinking Containment*. Washington, DC: Hudson Institute.

Ledeneva, Alena. 2013. *Can Russia Modernise? Sistema, Power Networks and Informal Governance*. Cambridge: Cambridge University Press.

Markus, Stanislav. 2007. "Capitalists of All Russia, Unite! Business Mobilization under Debilitated Dirigisme." *Polity*, 39, 277–304.

　　2008. "Corporate Governance as Political Insurance: Firm-Level Institutional Creation in Emerging Markets and Beyond." *Socio-Economic Review*, 6, 69–98.

　　2012. "Secure Property as a Bottom-up Process: Firms, Stakeholders, and Predators in Weak States." *World Politics*, 64, 242–77.

　　2015. *Property, Predation, and Protection: Piranha Capitalism in Russia and Ukraine*. Cambridge: Cambridge University Press.

　　2016. "Sovereign Commitment and Property Rights: The Case of Ukraine's Orange Revolution." *Studies in Comparative International Development*, 51, 411–33.

　　2017a. "The Atlas That Has Not Shrugged: Why Russia's Oligarchs Are an Unlikely Force for Change." *Daedalus*, 146, 101–12.

　　2017b. "Oligarchs and Corruption in Putin's Russia: Of Sand Castles and Geopolitical Volunteering." *Georgetown Journal of International Affairs*, 18, 26–32.

　　2022a. "Long-Term Business Implications of Russia's War in Ukraine." *Asian Business and Management*.

　　2022b. "Meet Russia's Oligarchs, a Group of Men Who Won't Be Toppling Putin Anytime Soon." *The Conversation*, online, March 4.

Markus, Stanislav, and Volha Charnysh. 2017. "The Flexible Few: Oligarchs and Wealth Defense in Developing Democracies." *Comparative Political Studies*, 50, 1632–65.

Meyer, Henry, and Irina Reznik. 2015. "The Chilly Fallout between Putin and His Oligarch Pals." Bloomberg.com, January 22

Myers, Steven, and Jo Becker. 2014. "Even Loyalty No Guarantee against Putin." *New York Times*, December 26

Nougayrède, Delphine. 2013. "Outsourcing Law in Post-Soviet Russia." *Journal of Eurasian Law*, 3, 383–450.

Reznik, I. 2010. "Ia nikogda ne torgoval Rossiei." *Vedomosti*, May 19.

Sharafutdinova, Gulnaz, and Karen Dawisha. 2016. "The Escape from Institution-Building in a Globalized World: Lessons from Russia." *Perspectives on Politics*, 15(2), 361–78.

Shorrocks, Anthony, James Davies, and Rodrigo Lluberas. 2021. *Global Wealth Report 2021*. Zurich: Credit Suisse Research Institute.

Simonian, Renald. 2010. "O nekotorykh sotsiokul'turnykh itogakh rossiiskikh ekonomiches-kikh reform 90-kh godov." *Mir Peremen*, 98–114.

Tompson, William. 2005. *Putin and the "Oligarchs": A Two-Sided Commitment Problem?* Oxford: Oxford University Press.

Treisman, Daniel. 2008. "Putin's Silovarchs." *Orbis*, 51, 141–53.

  2010. "'Loans for Shares' Revisited." *Post-Soviet Affairs*, 26, 207–27.

  2016. "Russia's Billionaires." *American Economic Review*, 106, 236–41.

Volkov, Vadim. 2008. "Standard Oil and Yukos in the Context of Early Capitalism in the United States and Russia." *Demokratizatsiya: The Journal of Post-Soviet Democratization*, 16, 240–64.

Walker, Shaun. 2015. "The Luxury Hotel, the Family of the Top Moscow Prosecutor and Russia's Most Notorious Gang." *Guardian*, December 12.

Winters, Jeffrey. 2011. *Oligarchy.* Cambridge: Cambridge University Press.

Zygar', Mikhail. 2016. *Vsia kremliovskaia rat'*. Moscow: Intellektual'naia Literatura.

13 | Inequality and Social Policy in Russia

ILYA MATVEEV AND SARAH WILSON SOKHEY

Fig. 13.1 Need, charity, and oblivion in central Moscow, 2019. Credit: Yuri Kadobnov / AFP / Getty Images.

The main problems of Russia come from the seizure of power by a narrow group of people and monstrous inequality that has arisen as a result. Inequality of wealth and inequality of possibilities ... Especially the extreme wealth in Russia is illegal and unjust. The overwhelming majority [of those responsible] are not successful entrepreneurs building businesses, but the participants in mass privatization and the bureaucrats.

Alexei Navalny, "Pora vybirat'"

As for the abyss [between rich and poor], unfortunately, it exists – that's the first thing. Secondly, unfortunately, it is also that, as a rule, it's a global tendency to a large degree, at least in the larger economies this is happening ... We should, of course, take this into account. We should, at a minimum, reduce the number of people living in extreme poverty, that's true.

Vladimir Putin (cited in RIA Novosti, "Putin prizval")

Abstract

Inequality in Russia skyrocketed in the 1990s. The wealthiest businesspeople became oligarchs while average Russians struggled to cover the cost of their basic needs. In this chapter, we examine the rise of inequality in postcommunist Russia, and the role that social services – like healthcare, education, and pensions – played in socioeconomic wellbeing. This chapter details the evolution of inequality and public opinion about economic issues. We show that, with increasing inequality, the provision of social services and other public goods suffered due to the government's lack of capacity and finances. In the 2000s, Putin ushered in a period of rising oil prices and better economic performance. Inequality has decreased to some degree in recent decades, and the provision of social services has dramatically improved since the early 2000s. After the 2009 financial crisis, a renewed period of stagnation began, and a number of protracted problems in the provision of public goods persist. We discuss some social policy promises that have been unfulfilled in the lead-up to Putin's fourth election in 2018, and the consistently low level of spending on social services. These unfilled promises matter because they affect everyday realities for many Russian citizens and raise the question whether economic inequality and poor public services may influence regime stability in Russia in the long run. Survey research suggests, though, that poor economic conditions and lacking social services have so far frustrated, but only rarely enraged the Russian public and are unlikely to undermine support for the regime on their own. Whether socioeconomic factors contribute to stability or fragility in Russia today depends on how these issues are utilized by the political opposition.

13.1   Introduction: The Nature of Inequality in Russia

Inequality matters for citizens' individual wellbeing and for general economic growth and stability. This is why inequality has received so much international attention in the present era where the gap between the poor and the wealthy is steadily growing. Thomas Piketty (2014), for instance, highlights the rapidly increasing rates of inequality around the world. Others note the significant social harm done by high and persistent levels of inequality, including the erosion of trust, limited social mobility, and increased mental illness (Wilkinson and Pickett 2011). Indeed, at certain junctures, inequality has resulted in large protest movements, such as the Occupy Wall Street movement that erupted after the 2009 financial crisis (Levitan 2021).

Since the early 1990s, inequality has plagued Russia and risen dramatically. The wild and unregulated nature of setting up a market-based economy in Russia in the

1990s led to the dark quip by some that "capitalism is everything Marx said it would be." By the mid-1990s, it is estimated that around twelve wealthy businesspeople controlled something on the order of 85 percent of the Russian economy (Hoffman 2011). In less than ten years, the country had gone from being dominated by the state with most citizens living in relatively equitable economic conditions (albeit relatively poor conditions by Western standards) to a country with one of the highest rates of inequality in the world, on a par with inequality in Brazil and the United States.

In this chapter, we discuss the nature of inequality in Russia. We chronicle the history of inequality in Russia in the Soviet era, the 1990s, and the 2000s under **Vladimir Putin,** and then turn to a discussion of social policies that directly and indirectly address inequality. Government policies play an important role in why inequality persists or increases. Tax policy, for instance, is critical in understanding rising rates of inequality. Indeed, one of Piketty's main proposals for addressing inequality is to introduce a global tax on the rich. Finally, we conclude with a consideration of how inequality and social policy may affect regime survival in Russia. Inequality and social policy responses offer invaluable insight into the domestic politics of Russia today. Growing public dissatisfaction with inequality may not be the direct cause of the regime's demise, but it will provide a crucial context for the future battles between the regime and the opposition – battles in a war whose outcome is still uncertain. Inequality and social policy are at the heart of the tension between stability and fragility for the current Russian regime.

13.1.1   A Brief History of Inequality from the Soviet to the Early Post-Soviet Period

Inequality in the Soviet Union was very low by international standards. Inequality is often measured with the **Gini coefficient** (a standard measure of monetary income inequality). Interestingly, Soviet income inequality was low, but was still slightly higher than in the Scandinavian social democracies in the late 1980s. The Gini coefficient for the USSR as a whole in 1988 was 0.29, while for the Russian Soviet Federative Socialist Republic (RSFSR) it was 0.264 – comparable to that of Denmark (0.262), but slightly higher than in Finland (0.222), Norway (0.246), and Sweden (0.231). Importantly, though, monetary income was a poor measure of inequality in the Soviet context due to the peculiar nature of Soviet economic and social organization. Within the centralized, administratively controlled system of distribution of goods, different parts of the country were supplied with food, consumer goods, and durables of different standards. Even if Soviet citizens had similar wages, they experienced vastly different standards of living, depending on where a citizen lived. Residents of Moscow, St. Petersburg, and smaller cities with strategic defense factories had access to a wider variety of goods than the rest of the country.

In addition, high-level government officials, **Communist Party** elite, and a number of specific occupational groups had access to a large number of nonmonetary privileges (Filtzer 2014). While all citizens of the Soviet Union were entitled to free, universal education, healthcare, and other public services, for instance, employees of certain large organizations such as the Ministry of Railways and the Ministry of Internal Affairs had access to separate, more advanced healthcare systems and other facilities, giving Soviet society a distinctly corporatist flavor. The Communist Party leadership, popularly known as the *nomenklatura*, was especially privileged: High-ranking members of the Communist Party were provided with better-quality food and clothing, comfortable housing, and myriad other goods that were unavailable to the rest of the country, turning the *nomenklatura* into a separate caste, even though the official salary of the general secretary of the Communist Party was only 4–5 times higher than that of a skilled manual worker. As Mikhail Voslensky, a student (and former member) of the *nomenklatura* noted, "at this level everyone lives in luxury at state expense without opening his purse" (Voslensky 1984, 225). In the post-Soviet period, monetary inequality overshadowed nonmonetary privileges, yet some of the latter survived to this day: High-level public officials still enjoy access to a separate healthcare system as well as government-provided housing that they often privatize and sell, or pass on to their children.

13.1.2   The Explosion of Income and Wealth Inequality in the 1990s

The marketization of the Russian economy in the 1990s was accompanied by a dramatic rise in income and wealth inequality. According to the official data published by Rosstat, Russia's statistical agency, the top quintile's share of the aggregate monetary income in 1990 was 32.7 percent. By 1995 (the first post-Soviet year for which statistics are available), this figure jumped to 46.3 percent, while the Gini coefficient for that year was 0.387. In a few short years, Russia went from being one of the most equal countries in the world to one of the most unequal, on a par with the United States – a dramatic and painful transformation. Part of the rise in inequality reflects a historically unique decompression of wages. In the Soviet Union, wage levels were determined in a centralized manner, and differences were kept to a minimum. With the advent of the market economy, returns on education increased as the newly created market economy rewarded certain types of workers, especially those trained and highly educated in booming sectors. The decompression of wages, while statistically significant, in fact accounted for only a fraction of the overall rise in Russia's wage inequality at that time (Lukiyanova 2011, 133). Differences between industries and sectors turned out to be far more important than differences in levels of education. Workers in some sectors, such as finance and resource exports, fared relatively well during the transition, while wages in other sectors – agriculture, manufacturing, public services – did much worse. Within-sector differentiation grew as well: Some enterprises proved to be more competitive than others, hence their ability to pay higher wages. Finally, regional differences made the biggest contribution to the overall rise in wage inequality: Just like some industries, some regions fared better during the turbulent period of the 1990s, while others were particularly hurt by the transition to the market economy. As a result, by 1995, the average wage in the poorest region (the Caucasian republic of Dagestan) was 10 times less than the average wage in the richest region (oil-producing Yamal-Nenets Autonomous Area) (Lukiyanova 2011, 138).

Capitalist development in Russia has thus been highly uneven, creating a deep divide between a few successful regional economies and the rest of the country. More broadly, beyond the increased differences between salaried employees, we could think of the dramatic rise in inequality in the early 1990s as reflecting the emergence of the new super-rich. While the contribution of the highest earners to overall income inequality is hard to quantify because of their underrepresentation in the social surveys, the gap between the so-called **oligarchs** (a new group of the ultrawealthy) and the rest of the country was clearly enormous. According to one estimate, by 2001 the six largest conglomerates, owned by a few powerful insiders, controlled almost 20 percent of finance and industry in Russia (Kotz and Weir 2007, 220). The endless ambition and opulent lifestyle of the new business elite left a lasting impression on the social psyche, becoming the symbol of post-Soviet inequality. Timothy Frye (2006) argues that shady privatization deals that allowed the oligarchs to amass their wealth turned into an "original sin" of Russian capitalism, undermining the legitimacy of property rights in the eyes of the public.

Grotesque riches on one end of income and wealth distribution coexisted with extreme poverty and destitution on the other. By 2000, 29 percent of Russians lived below the official poverty line, which at the time was only $43 per month (the average monthly wage was $80). With such low incomes, many people were food-insecure. In 2000, 28 percent of Levada survey respondents indicated that they sometimes could not afford to buy food. Another 46 percent stated that they had enough money to buy food, yet had difficulty purchasing clothes or any other consumer durables (Levada Center 2021). Near-universal hardship and the collapse of government institutions left deep scars in Russian society for decades to come.

13.2   Inequality in Putin's Russia

While the explosive rise of inequality in the 1990s is a rather uncontroversial point among scholars, the dynamics of inequality in the subsequent period are subject to debate. Indeed, according to Rosstat, the Gini coefficient for income inequality in 2019 (0.411) was slightly higher than in 2000 (0.395). However, the Russian Longitudinal Monitoring Survey (RLMS), an independent survey run by the

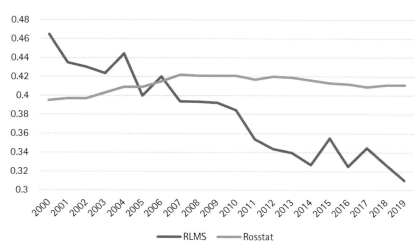

Fig. 13.2 Inequality in Russia, 2000–2019.
Source: RLMS, Rosstat.

Higher School of Economics, paints a different picture. The RLMS shows a substantial decline in inequality over the same period. The Gini coefficient for income inequality in 2000 was 0.46, while in 2019 it was 0.31 (see Figure 13.2).

Works that rely on the RLMS have offered several explanations for the decline in inequality in the 2000s and 2010s. Yuriy Gorodnichenko, Klara Sabirianova Peter, and Dmitriy Stolyarov (2010) posit that income inequality in the 1990s was exaggerated in the survey data due to widespread wage arrears. While some workers reported zero income in the previous month, others, who had finally been paid several months' worth of wages, reported an unusually high income; hence there was an artificial increase in the Gini coefficient. Since the early 2000s, wage arrears have become less common, leading to a gradual decrease in observed inequality. Paula Calvo, Luis Felipe López-Calva, and Josefina Posadas (2015), also using the RLMS, found that the decrease in inequality was not just a statistical artifact, but was caused by real, substantive changes. Specifically, wages grew faster at the bottom of the distribution, narrowing the gap between the poor and the middle class. This was made possible by sustained economic growth, increases in the minimum wage, better remuneration in the public sector, and interregional convergence in wages. Indeed, the gap between the average wage in the poorest and the richest regions narrowed quite substantially. By 2007 Dagestan remained the poorest region and Yamal-Nenets Autonomous Area was still the richest, but the gap in the average wage between them narrowed to 6.5 times (as compared to 10 times in 1995).

Other research questions the optimistic conclusions of the abovementioned studies. Thomas Remington argues that social surveys like the RLMS end up underrepresenting top income-earners. The generous compensation packages for the top management, particularly in finance and natural resource industries, are not well captured by income surveys (Remington 2018). Instead, Remington uses the official Rosstat data on inequality, which are based on survey responses, yet undergo statistical transformations to partially account for the underrepresentation of the highest earners; hence the difference with the RLMS (see Figure 13.2). He also relies on indirect indicators, such as payroll contributions to the Pension Fund. Remington concludes that income inequality in Russia has a tendency to increase during periods of economic growth.

Indeed, the concentration of wealth among Russia's wealthiest is hard to reconcile with the notion that inequality has been declining in the past twenty years. According to research by Credit Suisse, a Swiss bank with many Russian clients, the number of millionaires (in dollars) in Russia increased from 14,000 in 2000 to 246,000 in 2019 (Shorrocks, Davies, and Lluberas 2019, 147). The number of billionaires rose from 17 in 2003, when the first Russian Forbes list was published, to 96 in 2017 (Matveev 2019, 401). Filip Novokmet, Thomas Piketty, and Gabriel Zucman (2018) reveal the dramatic expansion of wealth and income at the top of the distribution. By combining surveys with national accounts and tax data, they came up with a Gini coefficient of 0.54 for 2015. They argue that Russia is in fact one of the most unequal countries in the world.

Overall, the data on inequality in Putin's Russia are rather contradictory and incomplete. Nevertheless, existing research allows us to make certain informed assumptions. It is likely that the strong economic performance of the 2000s remedied at least some of the gravest issues that had emerged in the previous decade. Wages in the worst-hit industries and regions improved, narrowing the gap between the bottom and the middle of the income distribution. However, the distance between the economic elite and the rest of the country most likely has increased even further over the past twenty years. Economic growth was particularly beneficial to the executives who received large bonuses as part of the global trend toward the rise of the "supermanagers" (Piketty 2014, 302). Booming commodity prices and easy access to global finance fueled the expansion of the billionaire class. Corruption has also been an important factor in the rise of inequality during Putin's rule, although a very hard one to quantify. Top government officials amassed enormous wealth that does not appear in surveys or tax records. A combination of these factors has made inequality a sensitive political issue for most Russians.

13.3 Public Attitudes and Official Rhetoric toward Inequality

The lack of a functioning state in the 1990s fueled extreme inequality and inspired popular movies that focused on inequality and related social issues. For example, the movie *Brat* (Brother, 1997) depicts a Russia in the 1990s plagued by poverty, crime, and drugs. The main character, a veteran of the First Chechen War, cannot find employment except with criminals. Other films like *Tycoon: A New Russian* – a 2002 movie called *Oligarkh* in Russian – showed a fictionalized and critical life story of an oligarch based on the real-life **Boris Berezovsky**, who became one of the richest men in Russia in the 1990s before fleeing the country in the early 2000s. Although these fictional movies exaggerate in some ways, they reflect the very real extreme inequality that emerged in postcommunist Russia.

Russian popular culture betrays a fascination with extreme wealth, but also a strong sense of injustice at inequality. Despite the growth of inequality, Russians possess strong egalitarian and redistributive attitudes. In 2019, 92 percent of survey respondents agreed that income differences in Russia were too high (as compared to 81 percent in high-income countries and 77 percent in middle-income countries) (Figure 13.3). Similarly, an overwhelming majority of Russians believes that the government should be responsible for reducing inequality (Figure 13.4); 83 percent claim that the government should provide a decent standard of living for the unemployed, while 85 percent express their support for progressive taxation (although, incidentally, at the time of the survey Russia was one of the few countries in the world with a flat income tax). Russians support universalistic welfare policies; 60 percent consider it unjust that people with higher incomes can buy better health-care than people with lower incomes (for education, the figure is 64 percent).

These egalitarian and redistributive attitudes are pervasive in Russian society. In all key respects, the middle classes are no different from the rest of the country

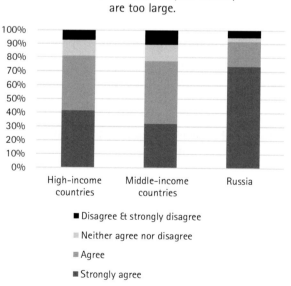

Fig. 13.3 Public opinion in Russia about income inequality, 2019.
Source: ISSP Research Group 2021.

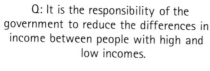

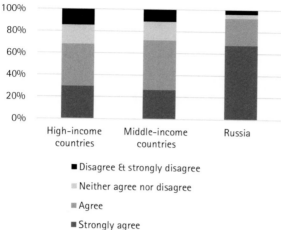

Fig. 13.4 Public opinion in Russia about government responsibility for inequality, 2019.
Source: ISSP Research Group 2021.

(Mareeva 2021). Nor are these attitudes solely the product of the Soviet period. In fact, the preference for **redistribution** (referring broadly to transferring money from wealthier individuals to those with less) has been continually growing since the early 1990s. In 1993, 65 percent of survey respondents agreed that the government should take action to reduce inequality. This figure increased to 82 percent in 1999, 86 percent in 2009, and, finally, 92 percent in 2019. Another longitudinal survey conducted by the Levada Center shows similar results. While in 1992 only 29 percent of survey respondents still clung to the planned economy, this figure has been growing throughout the 1990s and finally stabilized at around 50–55 percent (Figure 13.5).

The interpretation of these results is rather straightforward. In the immediate wake of the market reforms of the early 1990s, Russians were tired of the Soviet system and were hopeful that capitalism would bring an improvement in standards of living. However, the ensuing hyperinflation and rampant inequality quickly changed their mind. A joke circulating in Moscow at the time went as follows: "What has one year of capitalism in Russia done that seventy years of communism were unable to accomplish?" The answer: "It's made communism look good" (Kotz and Weir 2007, 192). Subsequent economic recovery in the 2000s failed to improve the reputation of the market economy.

Growing aversion to capitalism went hand in hand with growing preference for redistribution. The economic stagnation of the 2010s further increased the

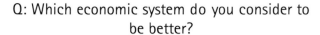

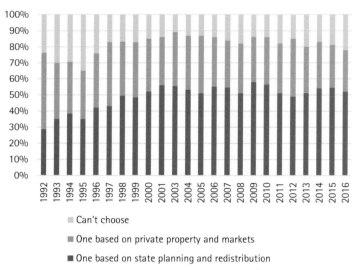

Fig. 13.5 Preference for economic system in Russia, 1992–2016.
Source: ISSP Research Group 2021.

importance of inequality in public opinion. According to the survey conducted by the Russian Academy of Sciences in 2013, 71 percent of Russians felt that income inequality was a painful problem for society as a whole, while 47 percent maintained that it was a painful problem for them personally. By 2018, these figures increased to 84 percent and 69 percent, respectively (Mareeva 2015, 2018). Similarly, the share of respondents who strongly agreed that income differences in Russia were too high increased from 62 percent in 2009 to 74 percent in 2019 (ISSP Research Group 2021). The concern for inequality among the Russian public has likely never been higher.

During his annual press conference in 2018, Vladimir Putin acknowledged the problem of inequality in Russia. However, in his view, this was a common problem for all large economies. He indicated that the government should take inequality into account, yet he did not offer any specific solutions for this problem, focusing on poverty instead. This seems to be part of a pattern. Whenever asked about inequality in the Russian context, Putin talks about poverty, refusing to recognize inequality as a separate problem worthy of government action.

Strategy 2010, an official public policy roadmap adopted by the government in 2000, did mention inequality, although it was overwhelmingly focused on competition and growth. The only solution for inequality brought up in the document was the reorientation of the welfare system to target those most in need. By contrast, Strategy 2020, a roadmap developed in the late 2000s to replace Strategy 2010, offered an extensive discussion of inequality. The new strategy mentioned the high psychological toll of inequality and its divisive effects (Mau and Kuzminov 2013, 372). The authors of the new document continued to advocate means-testing as a solution for inequality; however, they also suggested several changes to the tax system, such as the introduction of real estate taxes for individuals, tax breaks for families with children, and increased progressivity of payroll taxes as well as the new "solidarity tax" on high salaries (Mau and Kuzminov 2013, 385–86). Nevertheless, unlike Strategy 2010, Strategy 2020 has never become law. The actual policy choices of the Russian government have reflected very limited recognition of inequality as a social problem.

13.4   Social Policy and Inequality in Russia

If inequality was increasing starkly in Russia at certain points in the 1990s and 2000s, what was the Russian government doing about it? And why was the Russian government not better able to address this pressing challenge? One of the main tools the government has to address inequality is **social policies** such as education, healthcare, pensions, and well-designed labor policies that ideally promote labor productivity and flexibility while providing a social safety net. We address attempts to provide social policy in two periods: first, the 1990s, when many social policy reform attempts were limited and ended up failing; and secondly in the 2000s when socioeconomic conditions and social policy provision improved for a decade before beginning to stagnate.

13.4.1   The 1990s: Failed Provision and Failed Reform

As the first Russian president, **Boris Yeltsin** inherited the obligations of the Soviet **welfare state**, that is, a whole set of policies related to social wellbeing and largely synonymous with the term "social policies." The Soviet welfare state provided many universal benefits including education, healthcare, childcare, and pensions (Cook 1993). Many of these benefits had previously been provided in-kind and directly through the recipient's employer. A common model was that a factory or company would provide meals at a cafeteria, housing for employees, daycare for their children, and sometimes even electricity, heating, and transportation for the whole town in the case of large state-owned firms. Some benefits, such as pensions and maternity leave, were handled by the Soviet state at the national level. Many of these in-kind and monetary benefits – including pensions – were expensive to maintain, but were not overly generous (Cook 2007).

In moving away from the Soviet welfare state, Yeltsin and his team of advisors, especially the most influential advisors like Anatoly Chubais (minister of privatization in 1991) and Yegor Gaidar (prime minister in 1992), were motivated by a pro-market neoliberal reform ideology that was prevalent among the post-communist countries (Appel and Orenstein 2018). The neoliberal economic agenda favored rapid privatization of state-owned property, removal of state control over the economy including ending price controls, and reducing state spending. Postcommunist countries pursued this agenda to varying degrees. In Russia, the liberalization part of reform happened quickly, with an abrupt end to the state's control over wages and prices, but privatization was delayed (Gustafson 1999). Many social benefits, such as pensions, were not eliminated, but the state lacked the money and capacity to provide these benefits in the 1990s.

Most domestic and foreign advisors agreed that Russia's economic transformation should be brought about through the restructuring of Russia's large, previously state-owned enterprises. Instead of serving as quasi-welfare providers, they should focus on becoming profitable private enterprises that paid taxes which would, in turn, finance a functioning state that could provide adequate social services. The problem was that Russia lacked a strong functioning state in the 1990s, and federal authorities lacked the power to collect taxes from burgeoning oligarchic empires. Yeltsin faced an uncooperative **Duma**, with many representatives strongly opposing his economic reforms, and he was largely unable to exercise much authority vis-à-vis the incumbent and newly emerging economic actors. The managers of former state-owned enterprises were opposed to the breakup of their large firms and the loss of power over the significant resources they controlled; they therefore blocked the reforms proposed by Chubais and Gaidar.

Yeltsin had limited success in enacting his package of market-oriented reforms. He often attempted to pass major economic reforms using executive decrees, which were then countered by contradictory legislation coming from the Duma. Indeed, the 1993 failed coup attempt to oust Yeltsin was spurred by a constitutional crisis fueled by the unpopularity of Yeltsin's economic reform agenda. The collection of federal taxes, which would have helped finance better social policy provision, was especially abysmal in the 1990s (Ponomareva and Zhuravskaya 2004).

As a result, in the 1990s social policy spending suffered, and regional inequality increased as the government shifted the responsibility for funded social policies to the regional governments. In the 1990s, there was a sharp dip in government income as tax revenue declined, both because of a fall in profits and because the state was too weak to effectively collect taxes.

The lack of revenue combined with a weak state meant that many state-provided benefits to which Russian citizens were entitled (such as pensions) were simply not paid or provided in the 1990s. While inequality boomed in the 1990s, social policy spending languished. Spending on healthcare, education, and pensions would not have been a cureall for the severe economic inequality in Russia in the 1990s, but it certainly could have helped to cushion the impact of the economic crisis and reduce some of the extreme poverty.

13.4.2   The 2000s: Improvement then Stagnation

The economic situation improved dramatically in the 2000s in large part due to rising oil prices. Putin also enjoyed a more cooperative Duma with the rising new party of power, **United Russia,** which supported his agenda and which controlled a legislative majority. The provision of social services in Russia improved dramatically in the 2000s. Pensions that were owed were now being paid out, and services to which citizens were entitled were more readily available. The Russian government was much better at providing social services, but the public goods that most helped the average Russian were still not a priority for the government.

Nonetheless, spending as a percentage of Russia's total GDP remained low compared to levels in other European countries. The average European country spends about 7 percent of GDP on healthcare every year, and about 5 percent on education. By contrast, since 2000 the Russian government has spent about 5 percent of GDP on healthcare and about 3 percent per year on education (World Bank 2021). Spending alone does not tell us much about how a country's welfare system works, but the fact that the Russian government has not increased its spending over a twenty-year period – during parts of which the economy was doing quite well – indicates that social services were not a priority.

A number of important changes were made to social policy services in the early 2000s. This was part of a larger package of economic reforms backed by Putin. One of Putin's first orders of business in office was tax reform. He also introduced a unified social tax. Employers would be obligated to pay a set percentage of wages as a unified social tax which would be pooled to finance many social services. This went along with Putin's introduction of the flat tax and his plan to reduce the overall tax burden, in part to increase compliance. Putin and United Russia also introduced a number of changes intended to modernize the Russian welfare state, including pension reforms and attempts to reform healthcare insurance and the quality of medical care.

13.4.3   Pension Reforms

Pensions are a good example of the nature of social policymaking in Russia, and how the government failed to pursue stable and well-thought-out social policies that might mitigate inequality. Importantly, pensions are the most directly redistributive policy, meaning they have the potential to most directly alleviate inequality in the short term (Popova, Matytsin, and Sinnot 2018). Pensions are the biggest single area of expenditure for many developed countries, including Russia. Moreover, support from pensioners at the polls is tremendously important to Russian leaders (Javeline 2003). Indeed, one of Putin's early popular successes was in getting pensions paid, in part by putting pressure on the regional governments to disburse payments for benefits that had often gone unpaid in the Yeltsin era. Pensions matter so much, in fact, that the Russian government has increased pension benefits before every presidential election in the postcommunist era (Wilson

Sokhey 2018). In short, the Russian government likely cares about making pensioners happy more than any other social group.

Putin achieved an enormously popular measure that Yeltsin never did. He managed to get state-provided pensions paid in the early 2000s, after many retirees had survived a decade of benefits that were paid out inconsistently at best. Putin then backed a potentially transformative pension reform designed to transfer some of the risk and burden of paying for pensions from the state to citizens. The Soviet pension system was not overly generous, but was expensive for the state to maintain. Russia's aging and shrinking population, combined with a very low retirement age (fifty-five for women and sixty for men), made it difficult for the government to continue paying state-provided pensions. These state-provided pensions are equivalent to what is called social security in the United States and the basic state pension in the United Kingdom. In Russia, there simply were not enough younger working people paying taxes for the state to easily cover the current and growing state-provided pension payments.

During his two decades in office, Putin backed several types of reforms related to the pension system and pensioners. His first attempt to reform the system was the introduction of a pension reform in 2002, by which mandatory retirement savings would be allocated to individual accounts which would, in principle, be privately managed and invested – a reform often referred to as **pension privatization** (Wilson Sokhey 2017). A portion of current contributions was being diverted to individual accounts instead of being used to pay current pension benefits. In the short term, pension privatization increased the government's spending obligations even though in the long term it was supposed to cut costs. Furthermore, Russia lacked a well-developed group of private pension funds, which the system necessitated. After the financial crisis of 2008–09, pension privatization was abandoned. Russians largely ignored both the introduction and the reversal of what was a potentially transformative pension reform. In short, there were significant limits to the ability of even Putin to accomplish market-oriented reforms.

A second type of reform included the **monetization** of in-kind benefits (*l'goty*), which began in January 2005 for pensioners and other groups, including public-sector employees, veterans, and disabled people (Wengle and Rasell 2008). Monetization meant that, instead of being entitled to and receiving in-kind goods and services such as transportation, utilities, and stays in health clinics paid for by the state, individuals would get cash payments to compensate them for their use of essential services. This was not, strictly speaking, a pension reform – it did not alter the state pension system – but it was highly relevant to a very large segment of pensioners, and indeed it was pensioners who largely protested these measures when they went into effect.

The main challenge of the monetization of *l'goty*, or in-kind benefits, was that the payments pensioners would receive in many cases would not be sufficient to cover the costs of the benefits. There were mass protests in January 2005 when the reform was rolled out. These were the largest protests since the coalmining strikes of 1989 under the Soviet system. Nonetheless, survey evidence from the time showed that most of the public was not strongly opposed to monetizing benefits, and the reform stood (Remington 2011). The government did not abandon the monetization of benefits because of the protests, but Putin did backtrack on some of the measures (Wengle and Rasell 2008).

Finally, in arguably the least popular move Putin has backed in office, in the summer of 2018 the Russian government raised the age at which individuals can retire and receive state-funded benefits, after he had recently been reelected in the spring of 2018. Raising the **retirement age** was extremely unpopular. Indeed, for eighteen years Putin had promised that he was opposed to this reform. Observers had long pointed out that Russia's retirement age of fifty-five for women and sixty for men was well below the European average, and was fiscally unsustainable. In other words, the Russian government needed people to work longer before it started paying them pensions.

Despite its being an extremely unpopular reform, Putin backed the legislation that passed in late 2018 mandating raising the retirement age from fifty-five to sixty-three for women and sixty to sixty-five for men. While the fiscal challenge of paying the state pensions was indeed enormous and the subsidy to the Pension Fund became the biggest outlay in the federal budget, some experts pointed out that the government had not exhausted all available options before "pushing the red button" of raising the retirement age. Part of the problem in financing the pension system was a lack of contributions to the Pension Fund by those who were employed in the "shadow economy," that is, those who lacked an official labor contract and did not pay taxes or paid less than they were supposed to. According to different estimates, between 20 and 30 percent of Russian workers are employed informally and semi-formally (Gimpelson and Kapeliushnikov 2015). Limiting the size of the "shadow economy" and expanding formal employment could have been enough to reduce the Pension Fund deficit, thus preventing the need to raise the retirement age. However, such a reform would have been very complex and quite possibly beyond the capacity of the Russian state in its present form. Instead, the Kremlin went for a simpler, but deeply unpopular option. In this example, we see that the lack of state capacity forced the government to adopt unpopular measures, ultimately undermining support for the regime at least in the short term.

13.4.4   Other Broken Social Policy Promises

Pensions are just one area of social policy. The Russian government has fallen through on a number of other promises in the arena of social policy. Putin and other leaders have long agreed to improve the quality of healthcare and education in the country and have consistently failed to do so. There is very high inequality across the regions of Russia. Some regional governments can provide adequate and even high-quality education and healthcare systems, while many others cannot. Conditions in healthcare and education have been stagnating in Russia in recent times. The government regularly makes promises to provide better hospitals and schools, but its actual record in doing so is mixed at best.

The 2009 global financial crisis hit Russia hard, as it did many countries. Russia, however, had its Stabilization Fund that had been set up and financed by revenue from state-owned natural resources. The Stabilization Fund was created in late 2003 to put aside funds "for a rainy day" or, in more macroeconomic terms, to keep the budget balanced if oil prices fell or some other fiscal crisis occurred (Tabata 2007). When that very rainy day came during the 2009 global financial crisis, the Russian government spent down the Stabilization Fund and was able to successfully offset some of the worst effects of the financial crisis. The result, though, was that the Stabilization Fund was largely depleted by the end of 2010 (Ketenci 2010).

Since the financial crisis, economic conditions have improved in Russia, but living standards are still stagnating. The depletion of the Stabilization Fund has also meant growing pressure on the government to cut spending. Another economic crisis hit in 2014–16, resulting in the Russian government strategically cutting spending on social services and benefits. In particular, we can see that the Russian government dramatically cut spending in certain areas (such as education) and in certain regions (Matveev 2020). Spending on pensions – always considered a politically sensitive area – was largely protected.

In 2017, **Alexei Navalny** and his Anti-Corruption Foundation unveiled a documentary detailing the extreme wealth of **Dmitry Medvedev**, a former president (2008–12) and prime minister (2000–08 and 2012–20). The documentary – *On Vam Ni Dimon* (He's Not Dima to You) – can be viewed in its entirety on YouTube with English subtitles and on the website https://dimon.navalny.com. Navalny and his associates reveal Medvedev's astonishing wealth, including vineyards and lavish homes with their own luxury houses just for ducks. Rubber duckies became a running gag to mock Medvedev and his corrupt network of cronies. Russian protesters in 2017 held signs with pictures of rubber ducks and slogans such as "Pathetic Cowardly Thief" and "Corruption Steals the Future."

By the time Putin was elected for the fourth time in 2018, we saw an increasing gap between what the Russian state promises its citizens and what it actually delivers. Most recently, the COVID-19 pandemic that reached Russia in the early spring of 2020 only further strained Russia's healthcare system and systems of social support. Interestingly, the government's response to the pandemic, while lackluster, did not provoke mass disapproval from the Russian public. This may be because some Russians generally approve of the quality of the Russian healthcare system, while those who do not have such low expectations that the pandemic did not trigger a backlash against the government (Wilson Sokhey 2021). If the pandemic continues to undermine general economic outcomes, this is likely to have a bigger direct effect on individuals' political behavior.

Many efforts to improve socioeconomic conditions have fallen short. Ilya Matveev and Anastasia Novkunskaya (2020) reveal this growing gap in what the state promises and what it does. In 2012, Putin backed legislation to raise public employees' salaries, but implementation was so bungled and so reliant on regional financing that in many cases it made local conditions worse. Regional governments often had to take on huge debts to finance the reforms, and in some cases hospitals and schools had to fire workers. The modest salary gains have since been entirely negated by rising inflation. In areas such as maternity care services, the effects of this poorly implemented reform can be seen in stark relief. In many cases like this, what is needed is simply more money from the federal government.

In 2017, the Russian newspaper *Vedomosti*, a source often more critical of the Kremlin than others, ran an article in the run-up to the 2018 presidential election in which it detailed the failures of the government to follow through on a number of its promises. Table 13.1 summarizes the promises and the track record published by the newspaper.

As Table 13.1 shows, the government failed to deliver in key areas like building more schools, improving the quality of life (instead the numbers living under poverty increased during this period), housing stock renovation, and mortgage affordability, providing more affordable utilities, and fighting corruption. The only promise that had been fulfilled was the promise not to raise the retirement age. As noted above, Putin reneged on even this decades-long promise and backed a proposal to increase the pension age after his fourth election in 2018.

13.5 What Inequality and Social Policy Mean for Russian Politics and Regime Stability

Inequality and the provision of public goods like education and healthcare play an important role in Russian regime stability that is often overlooked. A prime example of this is the significant constitutional amendments that Putin proposed in January 2020, which included an array of social policy promises discussed in the following sections.

13.5.1 Social Policy Promises and the 2020 Constitutional Amendments

In January 2020, Putin proposed constitutional amendments. A referendum was held from June 25 to July 1, having been postponed from May 2020 due to the

Table 13.1 Status of Putin's 2012 campaign promises after five years

2012 Promises	Accomplished by 2017?
Increase pensions	**Mixed:** Pensions increased just 5.4 percent, which has not kept pace with inflation and the cost of living.
Not raise the retirement age	**Yes:** Against the advice of some of his own advisors, Putin has refused to back any increase in Russia's relatively low retirement ages.
Improve social wellbeing	**No:** The number of people living beneath the poverty line has increased by several million people.
Increase wages, especially in areas such as education	**Mixed:** Average wages have slightly increased, but increases in prices and the devaluation of the ruble have hurt the purchasing power of many Russians. Salaries in the education sector are still lower than average salaries.
Build 1,000 more schools; increase available spots for preschoolers and kindergartners	**No:** The number of schools has declined by about 7,000. In November 2016, there were more than 391,000 children under the age of 3 waiting for a spot in preschool and 65,000 waiting for a spot in kindergarten.
Limit utilities expenses to promote affordable housing	**No:** The costs for utilities have increased across the board. The costs for heating and electricity rose by nearly 50 percent, and the cost of hot water by 57 percent. These increases outpaced the rise of consumer prices, which was only 43 percent.
Decrease mortgage rates	**No:** Mortgage lending rates have actually increased slightly from 12.32 percent in 2011 to 12.67 percent in 2016.
Fight corruption	**No:** According to several world organizations including Transparency International, Russia's corruption ranking has worsened since the previous election.

Source: Adapted from Wilson Sokhey 2017 and Illarionov 2017.

COVID-19 pandemic. The amendments passed, with 68 percent turnout and with support from just under 78 percent of those who voted (Teague 2020). Critically, the amendments allowed Putin to run for two more terms as president beginning in 2024, but also included a wide array of promises on healthcare, education, pensions, and more. The inclusion of these significant social policy promises reveals how important socioeconomic conditions and public goods are to the Russian domestic audience.

The constitutional amendments were notable for promises about improving healthcare, education, labor rights, and pensions (Wilson Sokhey 2020). Conspicuously missing were promises about housing renovations, a recent and controversial area of reform for the Russian government (Smyth 2020; Morris, Semenov, and Smyth 2021). Although they were not included in the constitutional amendments, housing issues are yet another area in which the Russian government must balance public demands for improvement with the government's actual capacity to make things better.

Regarding healthcare and education, a revised Article 71 of the constitution includes new language about scientific–technical endeavors and creating a single legal system to improve healthcare, upbringing (meaning childrearing) and education, and continuing education. Article 72 further commits to the provision of sufficient and quality healthcare and to protecting public health in order to raise the quality of life. Labor rights are addressed in new sections of Article 75, which promises that workers' rights will be respected and that there will be a minimum wage that is not less than a living wage.

Article 75 also includes new promises regarding the indexation of pensions, which implies a promise to regularly increase them. Article 75 also indicates that the government will create a pension system based on equity, justice, and intergenerational solidarity (Smyth and Wilson Sokhey 2021). This language was likely to address any potential objections from younger Russians about bearing the brunt of the cost for providing for older Russian retirees' benefits. Notably, even the constitutional amendments reveal a conception of social citizenship in which some citizens are more valued than others (Smyth and Wilson Sokhey 2021). For instance, there are still a number of special categories of pensioners who are exempt from the increase in retirement age and who may also receive additional pension payments.

It is critical to remember that these promises were bundled together with a crucial amendment: resetting the term limits for the presidency, thereby enabling Putin to run for two more terms beginning in 2024. The social policy promises were bundled together with these changes to the term-limits clock to make the whole package more attractive to voters. It was not possible to support some amendments and reject others, as it was a yes or no vote for all the amendments simultaneously.

The social policy promises in the constitutional amendment are vague and not credible, particularly in that there is no mechanism to hold the government accountable for breaking these constitutional promises. Furthermore, these promises bolster a system in which there are expectations for social benefits that cannot be met. These statements are best understood as declarations of intent and commitment to the Russian public. Similar statements have been made in previous drafts of the Russian constitution and in political speeches and public policy documents. The inclusion of social policy promises in the constitution is a strong signal that the Russian regime and Putin think that the public cares about these issues.

13.5.2 Socioeconomic Dissatisfaction Alone Is Unlikely to Topple the Russian Regime

Survey evidence indicates that Russians are most concerned with general economic conditions. In a nationally representative survey of Russians conducted in August

2021, the most pressing issue was rising prices (63 percent of respondents), followed by poverty (36 percent) and unemployment (33 percent). Only 9 percent of respondents thought the most important issue was the provision of public welfare benefits like unemployment benefits, pensions, and other benefits. Past Levada Center survey data show that from 1996 to 1998 about 65 percent of Russians thought the most socially pressing issue was the payment of welfare benefits. By 2001, that number had dropped to only 10 percent and has not risen above 11 percent since then. In short, we see a stark contrast in public opinion on welfare state provision between the 1990s and the 2000s. Many Russians thought welfare was the most pressing issue in the 1990s, but do not think the same in the 2000s.

Although Russians are well aware of stagnation in the provision of public goods in Russia, dissatisfaction with healthcare and education alone is unlikely to result in significant political turnover or regime change. Rather, general economic conditions – which are very much affected by social policies – are likely to be the most directly influential on Putin's popularity and regime support.

Ultimately, even the most pressing concerns, like poverty, inequality, and material deprivation, do not necessarily pose a threat to the regime by themselves. Economic issues, however, are increasingly politicized by the opposition. The anti-Putin movement was much more liberal ten years ago. In 2021, due mostly to Navalny's influence, it is more populist, and inequality plays a big role. Navalny constantly criticizes the oligarchs, even from prison via newspaper opinion pieces and with his supporters' help in maintaining his website at https://navalny.com. His brave and vocal criticism of the Kremlin won him the European human rights, the Sakharov Prize.

Navalny is best known for his work exposing corruption and mobilizing the public to vote strategically against United Russia in elections. Less well known is that Navalny was one of several opposition leaders who helped organize protests against raising the retirement age. Other groups, such as independent trade unions and the **Communist Party of the Russian Federation**, also organized protests because raising the retirement age was almost universally unpopular. However, while trade unions wanted as broad a coalition as possible, Navalny mostly refused to cooperate with other groups in organizing protests, preferring to have his own protests rather than participate in joint events. Nonetheless, Navalny's stance against inequality and issues like raising the retirement age are notable, if not always influential.

Ten years of stagnant incomes and economic turbulence take a toll on any regime's legitimacy. This is why the Russian regime gets more and more repressive with each year (Freedom House 2021). This is also why authoritarian strategies are best understood as a combination of repression and rewards. Repression becomes more necessary when there is greater popular dissatisfaction. At some point, there could be a tipping point at which the regime cannot maintain enough repression or make enough people content enough for the regime to stay in power. It can, however, take a long time to reach that tipping point. The question is whether the current Russian regime can survive in these stagnating conditions, with the people getting angrier (see also Chapter 14) and the oligarchs getting more and more scared of personal sanctions (see Chapter 12). Countries like Iran show that extreme and rigid authoritarianism can survive for many decades, but Iran's authorities have a strong religious legitimacy that Russia lacks.

In countries other than Russia, we might discuss the influence of labor and unions in organizing people and lobbying the government for different policies. Labor demands have a unique role in Russian politics. Labor has not generally been considered to be very politically influential in Russia, although there are a handful of notable exceptions when workers have mobilized to pressure the government to keep large factories afloat (Crowley 2021). In general, organized labor in Russia has been very weak since 1990. There is one large labor organization, a holdover from the Soviet era, which is still backed by the state today. Independent labor organizations are heavily restricted, having to do things like announce when strikes will end before the strike begins (Crowley 2021). Nonetheless, the Russian government's restrictions on independent labor organizations suggest a serious concern that labor demands could be more destabilizing if there were greater freedom of organization and expression. Furthermore, current dissatisfaction focuses on the lack of state-provided goods. The weakness of organized labor means that specific labor demands are not likely to be influential.

The future of the current Russian regime is difficult, even impossible, to predict. The most honest answer to the question of whether the Russian regime can keep this delicate balance of repression and rewards is: maybe. We can say that socio-economic demands will persist and the average Russian citizen has a lot to complain about. Opposition leaders and movements could capitalize on this dissatisfaction, but their success in challenging the current regime and leadership will depend on their ability to organize citizens and subvert restrictions on their freedom of expression. Inequality and low-quality public goods – like stagnating conditions in healthcare and education – cannot alone take down the current Russian government.

13.6 Conclusion

Postcommunist Russia saw a historically unprecedented surge in economic inequality in the 1990s that accompanied the marketization of the country's economy. We contrasted this trend with the relative equality in terms of incomes in the Soviet era, though we also showed that access to many goods and services was de facto unequally distributed. Inequality has declined but has persisted in the 2000s under

Putin. Though social policy reforms brought important changes in how the neediest could access benefits, overall, state-provided social support has done little to offset the inequality in postcommunist Russia. Nevertheless, high levels of economic inequality and stagnating social conditions alone are unlikely to bring down the current authoritarian regime in Russia. This may be surprising to observers in Western countries, but it is important to remember that many countries around the world have suffered persistent economic crises without experiencing significant challenges.

Economic inequality and social policy responses are a vital part of understanding Russian domestic politics today. Economic inequality presents an opportunity for opposition groups in Russia to exploit when they try to challenge Putin and United Russia. This is why we see the opposition figure, Alexei Navalny, taking a very populist approach in his political agenda. Citizens care about their living standards, their opportunities, their education, and their jobs. The question is, as always in politics, how these demands will be translated into political organization and political and policy changes. This chapter has shown how inequality and social policy can contribute to both the stability and fragility of the current Russian regime and leadership.

DISCUSSION QUESTIONS

1. What are some of the causes of inequality in Russia? Why was inequality not a concern in the Soviet communist era, but is a very big concern in the postcommunist era of the 1990s and 2000s? How and why is corruption related to the high economic inequality in Russia?
2. How and why do social policies exacerbate or alleviate economic inequality? Which social policies most directly influence economic inequality, and why? Do you think that social policies can fix inequality?
3. Do you think inequality and dissatisfaction with social policies are likely to undermine support for Putin and the current regime? Why or why not?

REFERENCES

Data on inequality come from the World Development Indicators published by the World Bank and the Russian State Statistical Agency. Public opinion data and data on income inequality are taken from surveys conducted by the Levada Center, the Russian Longitudinal Monitoring Survey (RLMS), and the International Social Survey Programme. The independent Levada Center survey organization has regularly polled Russians since the early 1990s on a whole range of issues, including standard questions about approval of leaders and socioeconomic conditions, providing reliable indicators about public opinion.

Appel, Hilary, and Mitchell Orenstein. 2018. *From Triumph to Crisis: Neoliberal Economic Reform in Postcommunist Countries.* Cambridge: Cambridge University Press.

Calvo, Paula, Luis Felipe López-Calva, and Josefina Posadas. 2015. "A Decade of Declining Earnings Inequality in the Russian Federation." World Bank Policy Research Working Paper, no. 7392.

Cook, Linda. 1993. *The Soviet "Social Contract" and Why It Failed: Welfare Policy and Workers' Politics from Brezhnev to Yeltsin.* Cambridge, MA: Harvard University Press.

2007. *Postcommunist Welfare States: Reform Politics in Russia and Eastern Europe.* Ithaca and London: Cornell University Press.

Crowley, Stephen. 2021. *Putin's Labor Dilemma: Russian Politics between Stability and Stagnation.* Ithaca: Cornell University Press.

Filtzer, Don. 2014. "Privilege and Inequality in Communist Society." In Stephen A. Smith (ed.), *The Oxford Handbook of the History of Communism*, pp. 504–21. Oxford: Oxford University Press.

Freedom House. 2021. "Freedom in the World 2021: Russia," Freedom House: Washington, DC, https://freedomhouse.org/country/russia/freedom-world/2021.

Frye, Timothy. 2006. "Original Sin, Good Works, and Property Rights in Russia." *World Politics*, 58(4), 479–504.

Gimpelson, Vladimir, and Rostislav Kapeliushnikov. 2015. "Between Light and Shadow: Informality in the Russian Labour Market." In Susanne Oxenstierna (ed.), *The Challenges for Russia's Politicized Economic System*, pp. 33–58. London: Routledge.

Gorodnichenko, Yuriy, Klara Sabirianova Peter, and Dmitriy Stolyarov. 2010. "Inequality and Volatility Moderation in Russia: Evidence from Micro-Level Panel Data on Consumption and Income." *Review of Economic Dynamics*, 13(1), 209–37.

Gustafson, Thane. 1999. *Capitalism Russian-Style.* Cambridge: Cambridge University Press.

Hoffman, David. 2011. *The Oligarchs: Wealth and Power in the New Russia.* New York: Public Affairs.

Illarionov, Andrei. 2017. "10 nevypolnennykh obeshchanii Putina i Medvedeva." *Vedomosti*, May 5.

ISSP Research Group. 2021. International Social Survey Programme: Social Inequality V – ISSP 2019. GESIS Data Archive, Cologne, Germany, ZA7600 Data file Version 1.0.

Javeline, Debra. 2003. *Protest and the Politics of Blame: The Russian Response to Unpaid Wages.* Ann Arbor: University of Michigan Press.

Ketenci, Natalya. 2010. "Major Determinants of Current Account in Russia." *Transition Studies Review*, 17, 790–806.

Kotz, David, and Fred Weir. 2007. *Russia's Path from Gorbachev to Putin: The Demise of the Soviet System and the New Russia.* London: Routledge.

Laruelle, Marlene, Mikhail Alexseev, Cynthia Buckley, Ralph S. Clem, J. Paul Goode, Ivan Gomza, Henry E. Hale, Erik Herron, Andrey Makarychev, Madeline McCann, Mariya Omelicheva, Gulnaz Sharafutdinova, Regina Smyth, Sarah Wilson Sokhey, Mikhail Troitskiy, Joshua A. Tucker, Judyth Twigg, and Elizabeth Wishnick. 2020. "Pandemic Politics in Eurasia: Roadmap for a New Research Subfield," *Problems of Post-Communism*, 68(1), 1–16.

Levada Center. 2021. "Chelovek sovetskii. Kak menialis' vospriiatie rossiianami samikh sebia i ikh otnoshenie k SSSR." January 14, www.levada.ru/2021/01/14/chelovek-sovetskij-kak-menyalis-vospriyatie-rossiyanami-samih-sebya-i-ih-otnoshenie-k-sssr/.

Levitan, Michael. 2021. "Occupy Wall Street Did More Than You Think." *Atlantic*, September 14.

Lukiyanova, Anna. 2011. "Effects of Minimum Wage on the Russian Wage Distribution." Higher School of Economics Research Paper No. WP BRP 09/EC/2011.

Mareeva, Svetlana. 2015. "Spravedlivost' i neravenstvo v obshchestvennom soznanii rossiian." *Journal of Institutional Studies*, 7(2), 109–19.

  2018. "Sotsial'nye neravenstvo i sotsial'naia struktura sovremennoi Rossii v vospriiatii naseleniia." *Vestnik Instituta Sotsiologii*, 9(3), 101–20.

  2021. "Middle-Class Perceptions of Inequality Compared to Other Russians: Consensus or Disagreement?" *Sotsiologicheskie Issledovaniia*, no. 2, 177–88.

Matveev, Ilya. 2019. "Big Business in Putin's Russia: Structural and Instrumental Power." *Demokratizatsiya: The Journal of Post-Soviet Democratization*, 27(4), 401–22.

  2020. "State, Capital, and the Transformation of the Neoliberal Policy Paradigm in Putin's Russia." In Berch Berberoglu (ed.), *The Global Rise of Authoritarianism in the 21st Century: Crisis of Neoliberal Globalization and the Nationalist Response*, pp. 33–50. New York: Routledge.

  2021. "Benefits or Services? Politics of Welfare Retrenchment in Russia, 2014–2017," *East European Politics*, 27(3), 534–51.

Matveev, Ilya, and Anastasia Novkunskaya. 2020. "Welfare Restructuring in Russia since 2012: National Trends and Evidence from the Regions." *Europe–Asia Studies*, 74(1), 50–71.

Mau, Vladimir, and Yaroslav Kuzminov (eds.). 2013. *Strategiia-2020. Novaia model' rosta – novaia sotsial'naia politika*. Moscow: Delo.

Morris, Jeremy, Andrey Semenov, and Regina Smyth. 2021. *Urban Activism in Contemporary Russia*. Bloomington: Indiana University Press.

Navalny, Alexei. 2016. "Pora vybirat': Aleksei Naval'nyi – kandidat v presidenty Rossii." YouTube, December 13, www.youtube.com/watch?v=wkN8sSrUbdY.

Novokmet, Filip, Thomas Piketty, and Gabriel Zucman. 2018. "From Soviets to Oligarchs: Inequality and Property in Russia 1905–2016." *Journal of Economic Inequality*, 16(2), 189–223.

Piketty, Thomas. 2014. *Capital in the Twenty-First Century*. Cambridge, MA: Belknap Press.

Ponomareva, Maria, and Ekaterina Zhuravskaya. 2004. "Federal Tax Arrears in Russia: Liquidity Problems, Federal Redistribution or Regional Resistance?" *Economics of Transition*, 12(3), 373–98.

Popova, Daria, Mikhail Matytsin, and Emily Sinnot. 2018. "Distributional Impact of Taxes and Social Transfers in Russia over the Downturn." *Journal of European Social Policy*, 28(5), 535–48.

Remington, Thomas. 2011. *The Politics of Inequality*. Cambridge: Cambridge University Press.

  2018. "Russian Economic Inequality in Comparative Perspective." *Comparative Politics*, 50(3), 395–416.

RIA Novosti. 2018. "Putin prizval umen'shit' chislo rossian, zhivushchikh za chertoi bednosti." December 20, https://ria.ru/20181220/1548338677.html.

Shorrocks, A. F., J. B. Davies, and R. Lluberas. 2019. *Global Wealth Databook 2019*. Zurich: Credit Suisse Research Institute.

Smyth, Regina. 2020. "Explaining Urban Protest in Illiberal Regimes: An Emphasis on Russia." *APSA Newsletter*, Issue 1, Spring.

Smyth, Regina, and Sarah Wilson Sokhey. 2021. "Constitutional Reform and the Value of Social Citizenship." *Russian Politics*, 6, 91–111.

Solnick, Steven. 1998. *Stealing the State: Control and Collapse in Soviet Institutions.* Cambridge, MA: Harvard University Press.

Tabata, Shinichiro. 2007. "The Russian Stabilization Fund and Its Successor: Implications for Inflation." *Eurasian Geography and Economics*, 48(6), 699–712.

Teague, Elizabeth. 2020. "Russia's Constitutional Reforms of 2020." *Russian Politics*, 5, 301–28.

Voslensky, Mikhail. 1984. *Nomenklatura: The Soviet Ruling Class.* Garden City, NY: Doubleday.

Wengle, Susanne, and Michael Rasell. 2008. "The Monetisation of L'goty: Changing Patterns of Welfare Politics and Provision in Russia." *Europe–Asia Studies*, 60(5)(Jul.), 739–56.

Wilkinson, Richard, and Kate Pickett. 2011. *The Spirit Level: Why Greater Equality Makes Societies Stronger.* New York: Bloomsbury Publishing.

Wilson Sokhey, Sarah. 2017. *The Political Economy of Pension Policy Reversal in Post-Communist Countries.* Cambridge: Cambridge University Press.

2018. "Buying Support? Putin's Popularity and the Russian Welfare State." Report, Foreign Policy Research Institute, Philadelphia.

2020. "What Does Putin Promise Russians? Russia's Authoritarian Social Policy." *Orbis*, Summer, 390–402.

2021. "Russia's Response to Covid-19: Leveraging Pre-Pandemic Data to Theorize about Public Approval." *Problems of Post-Communism*, online, July 20.

World Bank. 2021. *World Development Indicators.* Washington, DC: World Bank, http://data.worldbank.org/data-catalog/world-development-indicators.

Zubarovich, N. V., and S. G. Safronov. 2013. "Neravenstvo sotsial'no-ekonomicheskogo razvitiia regionov i gorodov Rossii 2000-kh godov. Rost ili snizhenie?" *Obshchestvenie Nauki i Sovremennost'*, No. 6, 15–26.

14 Russian Labor: Between Stability and Stagnation

STEPHEN CROWLEY

Fig. 14.1 Worker at the AvtoVAZ factory in Tolyatti, Russia, 2009. Credit: Bloomberg / Bloomberg / Getty Images.

I turned off the television and saw the light.

> Aleksei Borisov (cited in Vulikh, "Ia otlip ot televizora i prozrel'")

Abstract

Does Russia's working class form a pillar of popular support for the Putin regime? Or are workers and their communities struggling with stagnating standards of living, so that their social and economic concerns might become demands for political change? There is ample evidence to support both views. This chapter will attempt to reconcile those contradictory views regarding labor in Russian politics and society. In doing so, it will point to a substantial dilemma for Russia's leadership. Seeking to rejuvenate Russia's slow-growth economy will almost certainly entail hardship for Russia's workers, which could lead to social protest and political instability. Yet failing to rejuvenate the economy will likely result in prolonged stagnation, which could also lead to protest and instability.

14.1   Introduction

Russia inherited a large industrial infrastructure – **working-class** cities and factory towns – from the Soviet period. While many residents of these communities are grateful that the **Vladimir Putin** era brought about substantial improvements from the cataclysmic 1990s, continued stability can come to be seen as **stagnation**. Yet reviving economic growth might entail bankruptcies and closures of unprofitable workplaces, which could generate greater dissatisfaction and even protest from a core part of Putin's social base. Russia's largest **labor union**, the **Federation of Independent Trade Unions of Russia** (FNPR), is a hold-over from the communist era when unions were government-controlled, and remains largely subservient to the Kremlin. This means that Russia's workers have few legally effective channels to express economic and social grievances, with the result that protests can erupt spontaneously and have the potential to escalate. Hence, Russian leaders face a stark dilemma: Efforts to promote social stability, especially in Russia's many working-class communities, might lead to slower economic growth, which could in turn lead to social, and perhaps political, instability. Yet efforts to boost economic growth would entail restructuring Soviet-era factories, leading to worker layoffs, which could likewise create protest and instability in the factory towns.

To make sense of all this, the historical background that forms the setting for the current situation matters critically, since the large majority of Russia's industrial centers and towns were created under the specific conditions of the Soviet era. Then we can turn to three sets of challenges for labor in Russia: economic, social, and political. Given the central theme of this book, most attention will be placed on the political challenge. For Russia's political regime, the challenge is to maintain stability, while the challenge for workers is to make sure their concerns are heard and addressed.

14.2   The Soviet Labor Legacy

While the Russian Revolution of 1917 and the Bolshevik seizure of power were ostensibly a workers' revolution, Russia was still a largely rural society, and as much as 80 percent of the population were peasants before Stalin's rapid industrialization drive began in 1929. The industrialization that then took place was virtually unprecedented in speed and scale. More than 1,000 new cities were built in the early decades of the Soviet Union, the majority in the 1930s, many of which were "born and raised as Soviet-style company towns, in the shadow of one industrial establishment or with several establishments dividing responsibility or competing for control." These enterprises provided "housing and whatever meager services" there were (Taubman 1973, 54). With cities built around the workplaces, the factories themselves became known as "city-forming enterprises" (*gradoobrazuiushchie predpriiatiia*).

14.2.1   The Soviet Coal and Steel Economy

To be sure, many Soviet citizens lived in larger cities such as Moscow and Leningrad (later renamed St. Petersburg) that were not tied to industrial plants. But a sizable part of the Soviet population – much more sizable than in Western countries of the same era – continued to live in factory towns and industrial-based cities up until the end of the Soviet Union in 1991. This rapid industrialization created what some referred to as the Soviet "coal and steel economy," centered on large enterprises specializing in heavy industry, such as steel-making and machine-building. The enterprises were indeed large: While the biggest steel factory in the United States, the Gary Works outside Chicago, employed more than 30,000 workers at its height, the biggest Soviet steel plant in Magnitogorsk employed more than 70,000.

The Soviet economic system was able to industrialize rapidly and sent the first satellite and cosmonaut into space. But it was also characterized by **shortages** for all kinds of goods, which were not rationed by price as they are in a **market economy** (most people will not buy a good, for instance, if it is too expensive). This meant that factories often were short on critical inputs to assemble products that the central planners asked for. The shortages included labor. Labor shortages were created because it was fairly cheap for a given factory to hire additional workers. Soviet managers were first and foremost charged with fulfilling the plan, that is meeting the level of output given to them by higher-ups; whether their operations were profitable or costly was far less relevant. Factories sought to retain workers – especially the most skilled – by supplying them with **in-kind goods and benefits** that were in short supply elsewhere, including housing and basic consumer goods. For instance, a worker might get a factory-supplied apartment, daycare for children, a stay at the plant's vacation resort, and a daily meal at the plant's cafeteria. Trade unions in the Soviet system did not operate like unions do in a capitalist society; rather than bargaining with management on behalf of workers, Soviet unions were more like an arm of management and were largely responsible for distributing the scarce goods and benefits that the workplace offered in order to retain workers and keep them from seeking work elsewhere. Meanwhile, Soviet workers did not have to fear being fired, since given the labor shortage they could seek work elsewhere.

Workers tended to stay in one job if they benefited from or depended on the housing and other essential items that were provided through their workplace and were in short supply elsewhere.

14.2.2   The Wage Arrears Crisis of the 1990s

Much was to change with the collapse of the Soviet planned economy in 1991. In January 1992, almost immediately upon becoming president of independent Russia, **Boris Yeltsin** liberalized prices, allowing them to be set by supply and demand. Prices – which had essentially been frozen under the old system – suddenly skyrocketed. The labor shortage quickly disappeared and was replaced by a labor surplus and the fear of unemployment. Formerly state-owned enterprises were rapidly privatized by new owners now seeking profit. Outmoded Soviet technologies were suddenly faced with global competition, and factories teetered on bankruptcy, with the potential for massive levels of unemployment. Besides the loss of jobs, the broader impact on the industrial cities and towns would have been devastating. Given how dependent workers and their families had become on their factories and industrial communities, which provided much more than employment, there was a palpable fear of a "social explosion."

However, despite Russia suffering an economic decline in the 1990s that was even worse than that experienced by the United States during the Great Depression, the result was not massive unemployment (which in the US case had exceeded 25 percent). Instead of a loss of jobs, wages dropped dramatically. Many workers became impoverished, but they were technically still employed. Most of the old Soviet factories somehow survived and often held on to a large workforce, sometimes relying on barter and other arrangements rather than profit to remain afloat (Woodruff 1999). Wages became so low that it eventually led to a crisis of "**wage arrears**" – that is, wages went unpaid altogether. At its height in late 1998, the crisis of wage arrears meant that approximately two-thirds of Russian workers reported overdue wages, with those affected reporting close to five months' pay in arrears on average (Earle and Peter 2000). Workers sometimes got "paid" with unsold goods their factories produced – in one case coffins – and many survived by growing food on small plots of land.

Graeme Robertson (2011, 153) convincingly argues that wage arrears "had become the dominant economic problem in Russia in the second half of the 1990s." One might argue it had become a major social and political problem as well. Besides predictions of massive layoffs, there were also widespread expectations of mass protest – the feared "social explosion." But, for the most part, given extensive impoverishment and a disorienting array of social changes, workers and their families appeared to be struggling to get by rather than engaging in protest. However, protests did grow, leading to a wave of strikes. As Samuel Greene and Graeme Robertson (2010) point out, more than 95 percent of strikes at the time were about unpaid wages that were legally owed by employers. In 1999 unpaid coal-miners blockaded the Trans-Siberian Railway, Russia's main transportation artery, in what became known as the "rail wars."

That was the same year that Vladimir Putin came to power, first as prime minister and then, in 2000, as president. The timing was propitious for him – a boom in oil prices boosted the Russian economy from its nadir. The wage arrears crisis soon ended, with wages rising considerably, and living standards improved overall. For a time, Putin certainly seemed to fulfill his promise of providing stability after the tumultuous 1990s. However, the oil-fueled economic growth obscured a number of significant challenges from view. More worrisome for Russia's leadership, that growth did not last indefinitely, which created challenges for maintaining stability.

Chris Miller argues that there is a hierarchy of goals at work in Russia's political economy: "first, political control; second, social stability; third, efficiency and profit" (2018, 97). Yet there are obvious contradictions in such a goal ranking. Political control cannot rely indefinitely on repression and propaganda, especially if the third goal – an efficient economy that provides some public benefit – is not being met. Yet, as we shall see in what follows, prioritizing that third goal of economic efficiency, which would almost certainly entail hardship for Russia's industrial communities, risks undermining the second goal and ultimately the first.

14.3   Economic Challenges

Russia inherited an industrial economy that was built to meet the demands of planners, not to compete on world markets. Making products of the highest quality at the lowest possible price was a new challenge, one made especially difficult when the existing technological base often lagged behind that found in the leading capitalist economies. The challenge was deepened by what some called "**overman-ning**": that is, employing more workers than would be needed in a comparative enterprise purely focused on profit-making. Further still, many of the factory towns that arose around "city-forming enterprises" depended on the plants to provide essential services for the community. Thus, restructuring these factories to make them truly competitive would mean mass layoffs in many cases, and abandoning the services that the plants provided to the local municipalities.

An example of just how challenging that restructuring could be comes from a seemingly successful case: that of AvtoVAZ, Russia's largest automobile plant. The factory dominates the city of Tolyatti, Russia's largest *monogorod* (pl. *mono-goroda*), sometimes referred to as "Russia's Detroit." The plant and the city around it were built in the 1960s, with the car factory producing the ubiquitous Russian Lada, based on Italian Fiat technology. Well into the post-Soviet period, the plant employed more than 100,000 workers in a city of 700,000, with many other residents employed by firms connected to AvtoVAZ. Yet even when offered at a very low price, once Russians could choose from other options on the car market, few preferred the Lada, which had been upgraded only marginally from the 1970s. The plant was privatized in 1992, but once it had quickly accumulated huge debts and generated fears of worker unrest, it was effectively renationalized three years later, and received massive government subsidies. By the 2000s, in order to protect jobs at AvtoVAZ and other Russian car plants, the government hiked tariffs on auto imports. That, however, led foreign automakers to open plants in Russia, making the Lada even less competitive (many of those foreign firms subsequently left in the 2010s, when the Russian economy and demand for cars worsened).

With the global recession of 2008, the government took further steps to protect jobs at AvtoVAZ, by raising tariffs on used car imports (since many Russians preferred even used imports to a new Lada). But that led to another problem for the government: protests from importers and consumers of used cars, especially in the Far East, where there was a large market for used Japanese cars. The protests in cities such as Vladivostok grew and quickly became politicized, with some put down by riot police flown in from Moscow.

Still, by 2009, AvtoVAZ was on the verge of bankruptcy, despite having slashed hours and pay, which pushed the lowest-paid workers below the poverty line. Roughly 27,000 workers were let go. Yet many had already reached pension age, with others simply moved to subsidiary operations under the AvtoVAZ orbit. When that failed to bring the firm to profitability, the Russian government turned to the French automaker Renault, which had been a minority shareholder in AvtoVAZ.

Renault then became the majority owner, meaning that AvtoVAZ was transformed from a large Russian employer in a company town that also sought to make a profit (or at least break even) into a moneymaking firm within a multinational corporation that happened to be based in Russia. Not surprisingly, the foreign ownership slashed the workforce even further, reducing it to 44,000 workers in 2014 (down from the 1990s level of 100,000). Even though most of those workers were given jobs elsewhere, protests grew. Much of the anger was centered on Renault's pick for CEO, who was referred to by workers as "that American" (he was actually Swedish) during a time of heightened nationalist tensions in Russia. The Russian government made sure he was soon fired.

With subsidized employment provided for many of the laid-off AvtoVAZ workers, the greatest conflicts arose with workers in the many local firms supplying auto parts to the plant. The Renault leadership decided that those parts lacked in quality, preferring parts imported from its own supply chain. The result was that several of those Russian firms went bankrupt. The workers let go by those firms demanded the promised back pay, which in some cases had gone unpaid for more than two years. When one worker complained to the regional governor in a public forum about unpaid wages, the governor – a Putin appointee – created a scandal with his absurd and rambling response that tried to blame the problem on the American ambassador and the US Central Intelligence Agency (the governor was soon replaced).

In short, massive downsizing was carried out in Russia's largest *monogorod* firm, but not without costly subsidies and open conflict that had the potential to become much worse. To this day, tensions remain high in Tolyatti.

14.3.1   Low Wages

Beyond some notable exceptions such as AvtoVAZ, substantial restructuring of the post-Soviet industrial infrastructure was largely avoided, arguably because doing so might well have resulted in a "social explosion." Before the Soviet collapse, Russian society had not experienced unemployment since the 1920s, and there was no existing "safety net" to cushion the fall for those suddenly left without work. When forced to cut costs in the attempt to become competitive, enterprises throughout Russia chose not to cut the number of workers on the payroll, but rather to cut their wages. In a country like the United States, employment levels rise and fall depending on economic conditions; in Russia, it is wages that do so (see Figure 14.2).

The result is that wages in Russia are still extremely flexible. While wages started to climb with economic growth in the 2000s, workplace managers retained considerable control over how much individual workers got paid. This was in part due to the inability of trade unions – most of which were holdovers from the Soviet era – to influence wage and salary levels (about which more below). But it was also because the official wage paid to workers was very low. This was partly so that employers could avoid paying their share of wage taxes. But it was also due to the extremely low level of Russia's minimum wage. Despite promises going back to the year 2000, Russia's legally defined minimum wage has only recently been raised to meet the officially determined "minimum subsistence wage," below which an individual is said to be in danger of not consuming enough calories to maintain his or her body weight. Hence employers often paid workers a very low nominal wage, with supplemental pay being given as a bonus, often as cash "in the envelope" and thus free from taxation. This gave managers a tremendous amount of leverage over workers, since they could simply add or subtract the level of the bonus from each worker almost at will.

While wages generally rose during Putin's first years in office, they only did so relative to the extremely low levels of the previous decade. It was only in 2007 (the year before the global recession) that average wages in Russia officially exceeded those of 1991 (the year of the Soviet collapse). And with that global recession Russia's flexible wages contracted once again.

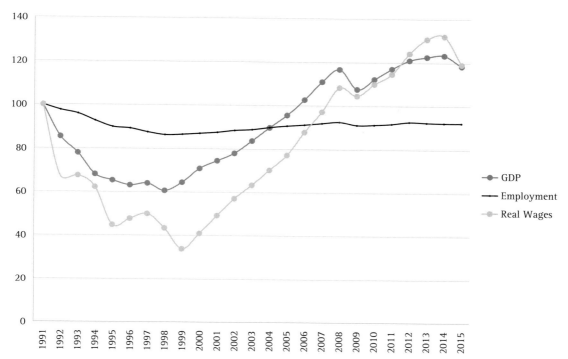

Fig. 14.2 Changes in GDP, employment, and real wages in Russia, 1991–2015.
Source: Created by author, based on data by Gimpelson, Kapeliushnikov, and Roshchin 2017 and Rosstat 2018.

14.3.2   Low Productivity and the "Middle-Income Trap"

Low wages, however brutal for workers, can in theory become a country's comparative advantage on the world market, provided that the economy is centered on the export of labor-intensive products. However, this is simply not the case in Russia, where – outside certain firms in the metals sector and military industry – Russian manufacturing exports are noncompetitive. Low wages, in turn, fail to create incentives for workers to invest in education and for employers to invest in technology. Why spend money on expensive machinery when you can add more workers cheaply, and pay them even less when times are tough?

The problem for Russia's economy is that paying workers cheaply and failing to invest in education and technology reduces productivity. As the economist Paul Krugman (1990, 11) has noted, "productivity isn't everything, but in the long run it is almost everything. A country's ability to improve its standard of living over time depends almost entirely on its ability to raise its output per worker." Yet Russian labor productivity is very low by comparative standards. According to the Organisation for Economic Co-operation and Development (OECD), for every hour worked, a Russian worker contributes the equivalent of $23 to GDP, while the comparative figure for both the US and Germany is $68. Indeed, Russian labor productivity is lower than that of Chile and Turkey. Of thirty-six OECD comparator countries, Russia outranks only Mexico and South Africa.

Besides low wages, the labor productivity of Russian workers is hindered by the many large factories inherited from the Soviet era, particularly those in auto manufacturing (beyond AvtoVAZ), machine-building, and older steel plants. Essentially, rather than shrinking the workforce and paying remaining workers a higher salary, a typical Russian firm has chosen to retain a comparatively large workforce, while paying workers low salaries. As of 2014, 80 percent of Russian workers employed in manufacturing were working in large enterprises, defined as companies employing 250 or more workers. This is by far the highest proportion of the thirty-six comparator countries surveyed by the OECD. In almost all of those countries the majority of manufacturing workers were employed in small and medium-sized firms, which tend to be much more productive.

While large Russian industrial plants remained afloat during the 1990s, during difficult times, they also avoided major transformation during the oil boom, when Russia's economic fortunes improved. Note that this strategy has been encouraged by the Putin government that fears unemployment and resulting labor unrest. This kept workers employed, but given low productivity levels the overall result was that Russia became stuck in what economists call a "**middle-income trap**": that is, the inability of a country to generate enough economic growth to advance to the level of the wealthier countries of the world, such as those in North America or Western Europe (Doner and Schneider 2016). Thus, stability began to look like stagnation, with a significant impact on living standards. Beyond economics, all of this had social – and ultimately political – implications.

14.4   Social Challenges

Beyond the economic concerns, the Russians who live in the many industrial communities throughout the country often struggle to get by on low wages and precarious employment. Their life experiences are often quite different from the Russians who live in more prosperous major cities. Such social divisions are widened by Russia's vast geography, with working-class regions often located far from metropolitan centers, many in harsh climates.

14.4.1   "First Russia" versus "Second Russia"

Russia's major cities, especially Moscow and St. Petersburg, have largely thrived in the post-Soviet era, with Moscow in particular the center not only of government but of the bulk of the country's corporate and financial enterprise. Russian geographer Nataliia Zubarevich (2011) has referred to such cities as "**first Russia**." Some have argued that the best way for the Russian economy to become more productive and escape the middle-income trap is to invest in a handful of other Russian cities, lifting them to the level of Moscow and St. Petersburg. That would seem to make sense, since a number of people have argued that "superstar cities" are the engines of growth in a global economy, as they become centers of technological change, receive a disproportionate share of capital investment, and house the world's leading-edge companies. Some have described the professionals drawn to such cities as the "creative class" (Florida 2004; Mellander et al. 2014). Kremlin advisor Aleksei Kudrin (2017) has drawn on such arguments to propose that Russia should invest in "cities, instead of oil," as a way to end the country's dependence on the export of oil, gas, and other commodities.

The challenge, however, is that doing so would ignore what Zubarevich calls "second Russia," that is, its many factory towns and industrial communities in Russia's heartland. These include more than 300 cities and towns that are officially designated as *monogoroda*: towns that are in a sense "company towns," almost entirely dependent on a single factory or one industry. These towns were built around "city-forming enterprises," meaning that the factories provided many of the municipality's vital services. In such places, if the factory goes bankrupt and closes, the very survival of the community is threatened. The official list of such towns may be revised downward, with the government proposing changes to the definition of "*monogorod*," restricting their number to roughly 150. Yet, beyond the officially designated *monogoroda*, there are many other cities and towns outside Moscow and St. Petersburg that are reliant on manufacturing and related industries for their continued wellbeing, and many of those industries struggle to remain competitive and profitable.

The challenges that such communities face can be seen in the example of Pikalevo, a *monogorod* in Leningrad Oblast. In 2009, amidst the global economic crisis, the town's three interconnected factories (producing alumina, cement, and potash) had shut down, with one-fifth of the city's population laid off, and many workers owed back wages. Without revenue, the town was in debt for its gas bill, and the town's heating plant was shut down, depriving the city's residents of hot water. In response, residents stormed the mayor's office and then blockaded a major highway, creating a 400-kilometer traffic jam, bringing the conflict, as we shall see, to the attention of Putin himself.

14.4.2   Rustbelt Immobility

Across Russia's many regions, there are several that are particularly dependent on industrial manufacturing, such as Sverdlovsk and Chelyabinsk, and others, like Kemerovo and Komi, that are dependent on coalmining. These regions contain a large number of cities and towns reliant on one or more industrial concerns. Though Russia lags behind the advanced capitalist economies of the world, it also seeks to become a "postindustrial society," but in doing so must confront the reality of declining industrial regions commonly referred to as "rustbelts."

Some observers argue that a major reason the Russian economy experiences low growth or even stagnation is that it pursues a policy of "keeping the lights on," that is, using subsidies and other means to keep factories open even when it makes little economic sense to do so (Gaddy and Ickes 2013). The World Bank (2011, 82) has urged the Russian government to take a different approach: "to become a dynamic economy, Russia will have to be more flexible – to constantly move human resources and productive capital from low-value to high-value opportunities. This usually entails shifts of labor and capital from declining regions to expanding regions." In other words, Russia should encourage workers and their families to move from rustbelt regions to more vibrant cities.

The economic logic behind such recommendations is hard to deny. In the long run it may be true, as commentator Leonid Bershidsky (2019) argues, that "the Grim Reaper is coming for the once-bustling little towns where people had moved from the villages. In a country with too much space and too few people, much of [Russia's] territory is doomed to be a huge flyover zone." Yet the evidence suggests that many Russians do not rely on economic logic in choosing where to live. Even given economic hardship, and even when offered monetary incentives to relocate, many Russians prefer to remain in their communities (even those beyond the Arctic Circle) where they have long-established friendships and other ties (Bolotova, Karaseva, and Vasilyeva 2017). As Jeremy Morris (2016) has described it, many in Russia's *monogoroda* find ways to make their struggling communities "habitable," that is, livable enough so that one can get by. When pushed to relocate, either by economic hardship or government incentives, even if they do not openly protest – about which more below – they can engage in what Greene (2018) has termed "aggressive immobility."

Hence, unless the process of relocating families from declining areas to more vibrant cities happens very gradually – a pace that would likely undercut the goal of economic growth – attempts to uproot people from places they call home will almost certainly be resisted. Beyond economic and social concerns, this has significant political implications. As another observer has noted, "voters in the Russian rustbelt form the bedrock of political support for the regime, which fears the anger that would follow from aggressive enterprise closure" (Hedlund 2014).

14.5   Political Challenges

As we have seen, economic hardship has the potential to generate social conflict. Especially in a relatively closed political regime like Russia's, such conflict could very well lead to political instability. To understand better why that might be so, we need to look at the role of Russia's trade unions, as well as the country's experience with labor protest.

14.5.1 Russia's Trade Unions

As introduced at the outset, labor unions under the Soviet system were largely controlled by management and ultimately by the **Communist Party of the Soviet Union**, and acted less as advocates for workers' interests than as arms of management, distributing goods and benefits in order to retain employees at a given workplace. In the postcommunist period, Russia's main labor federation, the FNPR, became what some have termed a "legacy union": that is, a union largely shaped by its past as an integral part of an authoritarian regime (Caraway, Cook, and Crowley 2015). While no longer controlled by the Communist Party, the FNPR is now closely allied with **United Russia**, the Kremlin-backed party that dominates the Russian **Duma**. As a federation, the FNPR contains more than 120 member organizations – with thirty-eight unions organized by profession or "trade," and eighty-two associations based in Russia's various regions – almost all of which it inherited from the Soviet past. As was true then, most FNPR unions act less as advocates for workers than as managers of them.

Union membership has dropped from the once-compulsory membership of the Soviet period to a total of about 20 million members. One-quarter of those employed in Russia are union members, and about half of all those working in large and medium enterprises belong to unions, almost all of which are in turn affiliated with the FNPR (Gimpelson, Kapeliushnikov, and Roshchin 2017, 22). At one point, the head of the FNPR, Mikhail Shmakov (2001), could claim that the FNPR remains "the biggest non-governmental association in the Russian Federation." Yet the membership ties, that is the commitment of union members to the organization itself, remain quite weak. In a finding that is troubling not just for unions but for Russia's civil society generally, public opinion surveys have repeatedly found that labor unions are among the less-trusted social institutions in the country. Close to thirty years after the collapse of the Soviet Union, an independent poll by the Levada Center (2021) found that when respondents were asked which institutions deserve trust, labor unions were ranked third from the bottom out of nineteen political and social institutions, above only "large Russian businesses" and "political parties."

Nominally at least, the Russian government and the FNPR sought to create a West European–style system of "social partnership" for industrial relations, with tripartite commissions on various levels including representatives from unions, employers, and the state. Rather than an avenue for bargaining and compromise, however, with the FNPR's acquiescence such institutions have largely aimed at defusing conflict. Even in the wake of the 2008–09 economic crisis, when union members were experiencing the greatest hardship they had faced in years, the labor federation prided itself on ensuring social stability above all. The FNPR commissioned an "independent study" of its activities during the crisis that reached "an important conclusion: In times of crisis the value of trade unions to ensure social stability has increased significantly" (Tribuna 2010; see also Ashwin 2004).

There are newer, alternative unions in Russia, and they tend to be fairly militant and inclined to protest, and in fact have often formed as a result of a labor conflict. One such union, the MPRA (Interregional Labor Union of Automobile Workers) was quite active during the oil boom period of the 2000s at AvtoVAZ and other auto plants. But alternative unions are small in number and, not surprisingly given Russia's political climate, are sharply constricted by law and often harshly repressed. Those that have received solidarity support from unions abroad are typically labeled "foreign agents."

14.5.2   Labor Protest

In defending their interests, workers are constrained not only by ineffectual or repressed unions, but also by legal restrictions that make lawful strikes extremely difficult to carry out. Engaging in unauthorized work stoppages can be grounds for dismissal. Since only legal strikes are officially recognized, this can create misleading statistics. For instance, during the depth of Russia's economic crisis in 2009, the statistical agency Rosstat claimed that only one strike took place during the entire year. Yet Russian observers record much larger numbers of labor protests. Those protests can take a variety of forms: Beyond work stoppages (whether legally recognized or not) they can include petitions, marches and demonstrations, work slowdowns, and, in extreme cases, hunger strikes, public self-mutilation, and threats of suicide. While the latter cases are few in number (though much greater during the wage arrears crisis in the late 1990s), they illuminate the lack of effective institutional mechanisms for resolving economic and social problems in Russia's workplaces.

Indeed, while the Putin regime has seemingly reduced the threat of labor protest by either restricting unions or making them compliant, and significantly reducing the scope for lawful strikes, the labor protests that do break out are often uncontrolled events. Most such protests are spontaneous and "wildcat," that is, they take place without any union participation at all (FNPR unions often become involved later, to try to "dampen" the conflict). As such, they are often acts of desperation, when workers can find no other way out, as the extreme acts of protest vividly illustrate.

This points to another rather unique feature of Russian labor protest. At least in advanced capitalist countries, strikes tend to happen when economic conditions are good, and when the labor market is "tight," that is, when there is greater demand for workers, who then have leverage because they have greater opportunity to find work elsewhere. In Russia the reverse is true: Labor protest typically happens when economic conditions are poor and wages decline or even go unpaid (Crowley and Olimpieva 2018). Once again, we see a connection between the state of the economy and social, and ultimately political, stability.

14.5.3 Pikalevo and the Crisis of 2008–2009

As I noted, the Russian economy benefited greatly from the oil boom, with considerable growth from 1999 to 2008. But then the global crisis hit Russia, once again raising fears of social unrest. Suddenly there were concerns about the forgotten *monogoroda*, and how they might be impacted by the economic turbulence. In November 2008, the economist Evgenii Gontmakher (2008) caused a sensation when he published an article in the newspaper *Vedomosti* about the potential for social unrest in *monogoroda*, provocatively titled "Novocherkassk, 2009!" As Russians well remember, Novocherkassk was the name of a town in southern Russia where, in 1962, twenty-five workers protesting food price increases were shot and killed by Soviet authorities, with another seven later executed and many more injured and imprisoned. Well into the postcommunist era, Novocherkassk remains synonymous with spontaneous labor uprising and state repression in Russia (a feature film portraying the events, titled *Dear Comrades*, was released in Russia in 2020). In fact, just months before Gontmakher's article appeared, in February 2008, President Putin had visited Novocherkassk and laid flowers at a memorial to the workers killed.

The article sketched out a hypothetical scenario where a labor protest in a single *monogorod* quickly spread, leading to unrest and violence all the way to Moscow. Soon thereafter Russia's Federal Mass Media Inspection Service warned *Vedomosti*'s editor-in-chief that the article "could be considered an attempt to incite extremist activities" (Oreshkin 2008) and thus in potential violation of Russia's antiterrorism law.

Just five months later, the residents of the *monogorod* of Pikalevo rose in protest. Putin, then prime minister, soon arrived in the town by helicopter to personally intervene in the crisis, in large part by dressing down **oligarch** factory-owner Oleg Deripaska. Putin forced Deripaska to accompany him on a tour of the town's cement factory, asking as the cameras rolled, "Why has your factory been so neglected?" before adding, "They've turned it into a rubbish dump. Why was everyone running around like cockroaches before my arrival? Why was no one capable of taking decisions?" (Elder 2009). In an act of ritual humiliation shown on all the national television channels, Putin compelled Deripaska to sign a document promising that the town's factories would resume operation, in a scene that became known as the "bending of an oligarch." With a scathing look, Putin asked, "Oleg Vladimirovich, did you sign this? I don't see your signature." Once the disgraced Deripaska had signed the document, Putin gruffly demanded his pen back. Much of this was staged: As one source put it, a "solution had already been negotiated the day before

Putin's dramatic visit to the town, one which was in fact generous to Deripaska" (Fortescue 2011, 280). Yet, for television viewers, the scene was a dramatic example of Putin acting as the nation's alpha male, defending Russia's working families against thieving oligarchs.

14.5.4   Igor Kholmanskikh and the "First Russia" Protests of 2011–2012

While Russia's economy bounced back following the downturn of 2008–09, Putin appeared to rely on working-class support when faced with a different challenge: Mass protests erupted in 2011 and 2012 over charges of election fraud, with protesters demanding a "Russia without Putin!" The protests were said to be driven by the "creative class" – educated professionals in Russia's largest urban centers, especially Moscow and St. Petersburg, that is, in "first Russia." When the protests were underway, in December 2011, Igor Kholmanskikh, a factory foreman at the Ural Tank Factory (UralVagonZavod) in Nizhnii Tagil, addressed Putin directly during one of the president's annual "direct line" call-in shows. Standing on the factory floor surrounded by his fellow workers and referring to the protests, Kholmanskikh told Putin that "if the militia ... can't handle it, then me and the guys [*muzhiki*] are ready to come out and defend stability" (Barry 2012).

Russia's state-controlled media played up this event considerably. Putin also appointed Kholmanskikh, despite his lack of relevant credentials, as the presidential representative for the Ural Federal Region, who was thereby singled out as the embodiment of Putin's working-class support (ITAR-TASS 2012). Following this, some commentators argued that Putin survived the liberal intelligentsia's discontent and protests by dividing and pitting "rural and Rust Belt Russia against urban and modernizing Russia" (Krastev and Holmes 2012, 44).

14.5.5   From Stability to Stagnation

Yet there are reasons to question the basis and durability of working-class support for Putin. For example, Kholmanskikh preceded the publicized portion of his 2011 remarks to Putin with these words: "Mr. Putin, you visited our plant in hard times and helped us ... Today, thousands of people at our plant have work, get paid for their work and have a good outlook for the future. This stability is important to us. We don't want to return to the past" (cited in Guillory 2017). Since that time, however, Russia's economy has stagnated, and real disposable incomes were 10 percent lower in 2021 than they were in 2013. Even worse for Kholmanskikh and his fellow workers, by 2015 – just four years after his remarks – their Urals Tank Factory was on the verge of bankruptcy (*Novaya Gazeta* 2016). Discontent in Nizhnii Tagil, the industrial town where the factory is based, has only grown since (Grove 2019).

Given this economic stagnation, might workers and others in the country's hinterlands join with the educated professionals in Russia's major cities in demanding "Russia with Putin"? From the perspective of Russia's leadership, such a protest alliance could result in a "**color revolution**," such as those that have removed political leaders in Georgia, Ukraine, and other post-Soviet states. While that would appear quite unlikely, not least given Putin's apparent popularity, the Kremlin quite clearly fears such an outcome. After all, the Russian-backed president of Ukraine, Viktor Yanukovych, fled the country following the uprising there in 2014.

In an effort to prevent that from happening in Russia, the leadership seeks to keep society divided, in part by maintaining a bulwark between protests centered around social and economic grievances – which are met with a degree of tolerance – and protests with explicitly political demands, which are harshly repressed. Yet, in practice, protests with social and economic grievances can become quickly politicized, especially in places like Russia, where the government controls (directly or indirectly) much of the country's economic activity. Still, a wide gulf separates Russia's urban centers from the country's extensive hinterland, and the different social classes and the life chances those regions represent. The Kremlin seeks to exploit that division, as the Kholmankikh episode illustrates.

14.5.6 Russia's Truckers and the Road to Radicalization

An illustrative example of both those phenomena – the rapid politicization of economic grievances, and the divisions between social classes – came in 2015. The Russian government announced a new road tax on load-bearing tractor-trailers, in order, it was argued, to help pay for the wear and tear heavy loads placed on Russia's highways. Russia's truck drivers, many of whom had been barely scraping by, united in protest almost instantly. Within days, truckers in forty-three of Russia's eighty-five regions and more than seventy cities took to the streets in various forms of protest. In some cases they drove in "snail" convoys at less than ten miles per hour, while in others they blockaded highways altogether. While the protesting truckers were met with harassment from the police, with those drivers in front of the convoys arrested, a number of truckers set up an encampment in Khimki on the outskirts of Moscow to continue their protest.

Reflecting their initial respect for Putin, the truckers first pleaded (in an echo of the old Russian saying "if only the tsar knew") "President, help us!" Some foreign observers therefore dismissed the trucker's protest as a "failed politicization" (Østbø 2017).

Some Russian intellectuals were harsher. The journalist and commentator Arkady Babchenko (2018) complained that Russian liberals "do not comprehend their own people." He then added bitterly, "when will you finally understand, my dear caring idealistic liberal friends," that there will be no revolution, because "the people" care only about small localized problems like trucker taxes and garbage dumps, and otherwise support Putin wholeheartedly. Instead of revolution, Babchenko argued crudely, "here there will be only uprisings ... of naked asses." While Babchenko's comments might appear extreme, other prominent liberal commentators repeatedly refer to average Russians as passive and unthinking "cattle," as if working-class Russians themselves were responsible for keeping Putin in power (as discussed in Morris 2021).

Yet, when faced with repression and silence of their plight on state-controlled media, the truckers quickly became radicalized, forming their own independent union. As Aleksei Borisov, a leader of the new union put it, "no one from the government would talk with us. The majority of the information from the mass media was either nonexistent or unreliable ... Much became clear. I turned off the television and saw the light" (Vulikh 2017). For a time, at least, they explicitly disavowed politics, claiming they distrusted the political system and political parties of every stripe. Within months, however, the truckers bridged the gap from economic grievance to political protest, calling for a general strike while demanding the government resign, and advancing their own leader, Andrei Bazhutin, to run as a presidential candidate against Putin. Bazhutin, who claimed he had been arrested a dozen times, had been fined 60,000 rubles, threatened with the loss of his apartment, and at various times deprived of his driver's license (and thus his means of income), was arrested again and gave up his presidential bid.

The Kremlin is clearly afraid that the bulwark separating social and economic demands from calls for political change might collapse. This is what made the opposition leader **Alexei Navalny** so threatening: By exposing and denouncing egregious levels of corruption by Russia's top leadership, including Putin himself, his protest movement promised to unite not only latte drinkers in "first Russia" demanding greater political freedoms, but also those preferring stronger drink in rustbelt towns concerned with economic issues such as declining wages. As one trucker put it while addressing a Navalny-inspired protest, Russia's potholed roads (the purported reason for the truck tax) were being ruined by yachts, not trucks.

14.5.7   Class Coalitions in Belarus

The prospect that such disparate groups would unite in protest might appear farfetched, yet precisely that happened in 2020 in neighboring Belarus. There, protesters demanding President Alexander Lukashenko step down after a clearly stolen election were soon joined by workers in factories and workplaces across the country. Employees in as many as eighty enterprises joined the protests. The thirty largest state-owned enterprises impacted by the protests produced more than one-quarter of the country's GDP (Artiukh and Gorbach 2020).

In a tangible message that they were seeking to break through the class stereo-types of industrial workers, workers from one plant marched with a large banner that read: "We are not sheep, not cattle, not 'little people.' We are the workers of the

Minsk Tractor Factory, and we are not 20 people, we are 16,000." There and elsewhere, workers marching in uniform out of factory gates were cheered by fellow protesters. Lukashenko himself appeared to hold a Soviet-era view of workers and their position vis-à-vis the state. The besieged president went to a factory to appeal to the workers – long seen as his core supporters – complaining that their protests were to him like a "stab in the back." They responded with boos and catcalls, and continued their protests. Overall, mass protests continued for several weeks.

Beyond their numbers – 16,000 in a single factory – protests by workers pose some particular challenges for leaders like Belarus's Lukashenko and Russia's Putin. Both leaders have portrayed workers as their core supporters; should workers express overt dissatisfaction rather than support, the leader's political legitimacy can quickly come into question. Protesting workers can shut down factories and other workplaces, creating economic costs in a way that is more difficult for students and other social groups to do. Further still, when such leaders call for repression against demonstrators, as they quite often do in Belarus and Russia, protesting workers can create a dilemma for the security services, the police, and the militia. It is one thing to be told to use your truncheon against some college-educated types infected by Western ideals; it is another to be ordered to smack the heads of factory-workers. Workers and low-level police and militia are likely to come from the same social milieu; that is, these groups lack the "social distancing" that make acts of aggression and violence against others easier to carry out. In Belarus, rank-and-file security officials began defying orders, and openly taking off and destroying their uniforms on social media. Arguably, without the firm backing that the Belarus government received from Russia, others might have joined them, and Lukashenko would most likely have been chased from office.

14.6   Conclusion: Russia's Labor Dilemma

To be sure, there is little evidence that such a coalition between Russia's working class, often found in industrial communities in the country's widespread regions, and educated liberals in the major cities is forming in Russia. The social as well as geographical distance between these groups remains vast. For that to change, liberal opposition leaders would need to avoid patronizing language, and to speak in a way that resonates across class and social divides. Navalny's language was a major exception, in that his denunciation of top-level corruption spoke to both economic anger and political frustrations (and this was arguably a major reason he was apparently poisoned and then imprisoned). Still, large segments of the population, including workers and others, remain concerned that a change in leadership, that is, the success of the opposition's call for "Russia without Putin," might bring about a rerun of the 1990s, which many vividly remember as a time of social chaos and economic dislocation. President Putin, his loyalists, and state-sponsored media have consistently stoked such fears, describing change as a likely descent into chaos, contrasting it with its own promise of stability (Sharafutdinova 2019).

However, while there are only limited signs of a potential crossclass coalition that could lead a Russian "color revolution," a continued reliance on the promise of stability has begun to create its own problems. This is especially true since living standards have been stagnating for some time now. The economic challenge is clear: How does Russia increase its labor productivity and escape from the "middle-income trap"? Some have suggested paths for doing so, such as closing down unprofitable workplaces and shifting workers and their families to more thriving metropolises. Yet doing so would almost certainly create a social challenge, as Russians in many rustbelt and rural communities have shown their unwillingness to accept such changes. Ultimately it could well become a political challenge, leading to open protest from the regime's purported core supporters.

Russia's leadership has made clear that it seeks by all means to prevent such protest. Hence, one might predict a policy of muddling through, that is, avoiding major disruptions to the country's social fabric, which major economic restructuring would almost certainly entail. Yet maintaining the status quo will likely create its own set of challenges, and might become its own source of social and even political unrest.

With the collapse of the Soviet Union, Russia inherited a legacy of an industrial economy that was not built in order to compete on world markets. This included a large number of cities and towns where the lives of workers and their families were dependent on one or more industrial concern. Contrary to predictions, during the economic crisis of the 1990s, Russia did not experience mass unemployment; instead, wages dropped and even went unpaid. As Putin came to power, the economy improved, wages rose, and his promise to restore stability to Russian lives appeared to be fulfilled. That changed with the global economic recession of 2008, when fears arose about protests in Russia's many single-industry towns, the *monogoroda*. When protest broke out in one such town, Pikalevo, Putin arrived to portray himself as the town's savior. He appeared to rely on support from workers in Russia's industrial hinterlands during another crisis in 2011–12 – political protests largely led by the "creative class" in Moscow and St. Petersburg. But, as economic growth continued to slow, and living standards stagnated, it became less clear that Putin could reliably count on workers being among his core supporters. The protests by Russia's truckers illustrate the difficulties of preventing social and economic protests from leading to demands for political change. Moreover, while a wide social and often geographical gulf separates Russia's liberal opposition and its "creative class" living in "first Russia" from those living in the industrial communities of "second Russia," the example of Belarus shows that in the right circumstances such divides can be quickly bridged.

All of this suggests a major reason why the Russian government has refrained from carrying out deep restructuring of its post-Soviet industrial landscape. But that has not allowed it to escape a looming dilemma: By preventing mass layoffs, the government can maintain social stability, but only at the cost of economic growth. But the lack of economic growth can itself become a potential threat to social, and ultimately political, stability.

DISCUSSION QUESTIONS

1. Why might the Putin regime be afraid of labor protest? Given all the power in the hands of the Russian government, are you persuaded that they are afraid?
2. Why might it be hard for working-class Russians and more educated and professional citizens to share common goals?
3. If you were an advisor to the Russian president, how might you suggest the country revitalize its economy without setting off social and political instability?

REFERENCES

Artiukh, Volodymyr, and Denys Gorbach. 2020. "Workers' Struggles in Ukraine and Belarus: Comparing Working-Class Self-Activity across the Post-Soviet Uprisings." *Rosa Luxemburg Stiftung*, November 4, www.rosalux.de/en/news/id/43290/workers-struggles-in-ukraine-and-belarus?cHash=25197f3015ef2d33cfd619cd5f50e8ce.

Ashwin, Sarah. 2004. "Social Partnership or a 'Complete Sellout'? Russian Trade Unions' Responses to Conflict." *British Journal of Industrial Relations*, 42(1), 23–46.

Babchenko, Arkadii. 2018. "Zdes' budet tol'ko bunt." Kasparov.ru, March 25, www.kasparov.ru/material.php?id=5AB76BF41B808.

Barry, Ellen. 2012. "Putin Reaches down to the Assembly Line for First Appointment." *New York Times*, May 18, www.nytimes.com/2012/05/19/world/europe/vladimir-putin-appoints-tank-factory-worker-who-offered-to-chase-antigovernment-protesters-off-moscow-streets.html.

Bershidsky, Leonid. 2019. "Putin Turns Swathes of Russia into Flyover Country." Bloomberg, March 7, www.bloomberg.com/opinion/articles/2019-03-07/putin-s-development-plan-picks-favorites-among-russian-regions.

Bolotova, Alla, Anastassia Karaseva, and Valeria Vasilyeva. 2017. "Mobility and Sense of Place among Youth in the Russian Arctic." *Sibirica*, 16(3), 77–124.

Caraway, Teri L., Maria Lorena Cook, and Stephen Crowley (eds.). 2015. *Working through the Past: Labor and Authoritarian Legacies in Comparative Perspective*. Ithaca: Cornell University Press.

Crowley, Stephen, and Irina Olimpieva. 2018. "Labor Protests and Their Consequences in Putin's Russia." *Problems of Post-Communism*, 65(5), 344–58.

Doner, Richard F., and Ben Ross Schneider. 2016. "The Middle-Income Trap: More Politics than Economics." *World Politics*, 68(4), 608–44.

Earle, John S., and Klara Sabirianova Peter. 2000. "Equilibrium Wage Arrears: A Theoretical and Empirical Analysis of Institutional Lock-In." SSRN ELibrary, September, http://papers.ssrn.com/sol3/papers.cfm?abstract_id=251999.

Elder, Miriam. 2009. "Vladimir Putin Takes Oleg Deripaska to Task." *Daily Telegraph*, June 4, www.telegraph.co.uk/news/worldnews/europe/russia/5446293/Vladimir-Putin-takes-Oleg-Deripaska-to-task.html.

Florida, Richard L. 2004. *The Rise of the Creative Class: And How It's Transforming Work, Leisure, Community and Everyday Life.* New York: Basic Books.

Fortescue, Stephen. 2011. "The Russian Economy and Business–Government Relations." In Graeme J. Gill (ed.), *Routledge Handbook of Russian Politics and Society*, pp. 274–87. New York: Routledge.

Gaddy, Clifford, and Barry William Ickes. 2013. *Bear Traps on Russia's Road to Modernization.* Abingdon, UK: Routledge.

Gimpelson, Vladimir, Rostislav Kapeliushnikov, and S. Iu. Roshchin (eds.). 2017. *Rossiiskii rynok truda. Tendentsii, instituty, strukturnye izmeneniia.* Moscow: Tsentra Trudovykh Issledovanii NIU VShE. https://publications.hse.ru/books/204342588.

Gontmakher, Evgenii. 2008. "Stenarii'. Novocherkassk-2009." *Vedomosti*, no. 210, November 6.

Greene, Samuel A. 2018. "Running to Stand Still: Aggressive Immobility and the Limits of Power in Russia." *Post-Soviet Affairs*, 34(5), 333–47.

Greene, Samuel A., and Graeme B. Robertson. 2010. "Politics, Justice and the New Russian Strike." *Communist and Post-Communist Studies*, 43(1), 73–95.

Grove, Thomas. 2019. "Russians in Heartland Sour on Vladimir Putin over Money Woes." *Wall Street Journal*, March 22, www.wsj.com/articles/russians-in-heartland-sour-on-vladimir-putin-over-money-woes-11553252400.

Guillory, Sean. 2017. "Whatever Happened to 'Russia without Putin'?" *New Eastern Europe*, no. 1, www.neweasterneurope.eu/articles-and-commentary/2235-whatever-happened-to-russia-without-putin.

Hedlund, Stefan. 2014. "Russia's Monotowns: Evidence of an Increasingly Obsolete Economy." *World Review* (blog). February 4.

ITAR-TASS. 2012. "President Appoints Railway Car Building Plant's Workshop Manager Presidental Envoy in Urals." ITAR-TASS, May 21, http://en.itar-tass.com/russianpress/675842.

Krastev, Ivan, and Stephen Holmes. 2012. "An Autopsy of Managed Democracy." *Journal of Democracy*, 23(3), 33–45.

Krugman, Paul R. 1990. *The Age of Diminished Expectations: US Economic Policy in the 1990s.* Cambridge, MA: MIT Press.

Kudrin, Aleksei. 2017. "Goroda vmesto nefti." *Vedomosti*, July 20, www.vedomosti.ru/opinion/articles/2017/07/20/724744-goroda-nefti.

Levada Center. 2021. "Doverie obshchestvennym institutam," October 6, www.levada.ru/2021/10/06/doverie-obshhestvennym-institutam/.

Mellander, Charlotta, Richard L. Florida, Bjørn Terje Asheim, Meric S. Gertler, and Regional Studies Association (Seaford, UK) (eds.). 2014. *The Creative Class Goes Global: Regions and Cities 69.* London: Routledge.

Miller, Chris. 2018. *Putinomics: Power and Money in Resurgent Russia.* Chapel Hill: University of North Carolina Press.

Morris, Jeremy. 2016. *Everyday Post-Socialism: Working-Class Communities in the Russian Margins*. Cham: Springer.

——— 2021. "Laying Homo Sovieticus to Rest, Part I: Who Are You Calling Bydlo?" *Postsocialism* (blog), August 6, https://postsocialism.org/2021/08/06/laying-homo-sovieticus-to-rest-part-1-who-are-you-calling-bydlo/.

Novaya Gazeta. 2016. "Al'fa-bank podal v Arbitrazhnyi sud Sverdlovskoi oblasti zaiavlenie o priznanii bankrotom 'Uralvagonzavod.'" *Novaya Gazeta*, June 10, www.novayagazeta.ru/news/2016/06/10/122397-alfa-bank-poprosil-priznat-uralvagonzavod-bankrotom.

Oreshkin, Dmitry. 2008. "The Second-Largest Potemkin Village in History." *Moscow Times*, December 17.

Østbø, Jardar. 2017. "Between Opportunist Revolutionaries and Mediating Spoilers: Failed Politicization of the Russian Truck Drivers' Protest, 2015–2016." *Demokratizatsiya: The Journal of Post-Soviet Democratization*, 25(3), 279–303.

Robertson, Graeme B. 2011. *The Politics of Protest in Hybrid Regimes: Managing Dissent in Post-Communist Russia*. New York: Cambridge University Press.

Rosstat. 2018. "Finansy Rossii – 2018 g. Statisticheskii sbornik." Federal'naia Sluzhba Gosudarstvennoi Statistiki, https://gks.ru/bgd/regl/b18-51/Main.htm.

Sharafutdinova, Gulnaz. 2019. "Russia's Struggle over the Meaning of the 1990s and the Keys to Kremlin Power." *PonarsEuarasia - Policy Memos*, May, www.ponarseurasia.org/memo/russias-struggle-over-meaning-1990s-and-keys-kremlin-power.

Shmakov, Mikhail. 2001. "Press Conference with Independent Trade Unions Federation Chairman Mikhail Shmakov." Federal News Service, December 3.

Taubman, William. 1973. *Governing Soviet Cities: Bureaucratic Politics and Urban Development in the USSR*. New York: Praeger.

Tribuna. 2010. "FNPR proshla nezavisimuiu e'kspertizu," No. 13, April 8.

Vulikh, Yekaterina. 2017. "'Ia otlip ot televizora i prozrel.' Pochemu riazanskie perevozchiki sobiraiutsia na vserossiiskuiu stachku." 7x7, March 22, https://7x7-journal.ru/articles/2017/03/22/ya-otlip-ot-televizora-i-prozrel-pochemu-ryazanskie-perevozchiki-sobirayutsya-na-vserossijskuyu-stachku.

Woodruff, David. 1999. *Money Unmade: Barter and the Fate of Russian Capitalism*. Ithaca: Cornell University Press.

World Bank. 2011. *Russia: Reshaping Economic Geography*. Washington, DC: World Bank.

Zubarevich, Nataliia. 2011. "Chetyre Rossii." Vedomosti.ru, December 30, www.vedomosti.ru/opinion/news/1467059/chetyre_rossii.

15 Everyday Economic Life on Russia's Margins

ANN–MARI SÄTRE AND LEO GRANBERG

Fig. 15.1 Café owner, Kamchatka. Credit: UNDP, Creative Commons.

It is very fortunate that locally there have probably remained many honest entrepreneurs, who want to work within the limits of the law and who earn money through their own work, and not by means of corrupt deals.

Small entrepreneur in Karelia (interview, 2014)

Abstract

This chapter introduces the reader to the economic conditions and challenges of citizens who live in Russia outside metropolitan areas, regional capitals, or rich oil- and gas-producing regions. In the Soviet era, life in villages and small towns was organized around large and often powerful state-run factories and collective farms, which were responsible for providing many public services. The privatization of these enterprises left towns and villages uncertain not only about jobs, but also about who would take over the provision of basic services and duties. As the 1990s wrought havoc on local economies, Russian citizens in these smaller towns and villages sought ways to survive. They tried to rely on subsistence farming and occasional local incomes, and to find new ways to make a living as entrepreneurs or farmers. They worked without salaries to keep their jobs or took advantage of opportunities for labor migration to more prosperous places in Russia.

This chapter details how people succeeded and failed in their attempts to survive and prosper in post-Soviet Russia and to find new ways to work together and with public authorities. Some political reforms addressed the dire situation in these villages and towns. Local administrations were reformed, opening possibilities for collaboration with citizens; many, however, perceived local administrations as more of a hindrance than a help for their initiatives. Some civil society organizations emerged in towns, while in the villages civic activism was mainly manifest in informal networks and social groups. The chaotic years of the 1990s were followed by a decade of stabilization and slowly emerging improvements even in Russian villages and remote towns, which we call the "**margins.**"

Since the years of robust growth ended in the 2010s, people in the villages and small towns have again faced economic and political difficulties. It has become more challenging to establish enterprises, political rights are limited, and foreign relations are tightly controlled.

15.1 Introduction: Economic Life in Russian Villages and Small Towns

This chapter takes us to Russia's small towns and villages and details the social and economic challenges and responses to these from citizens, entrepreneurs, civic organizations, and local authorities. In prerevolutionary Russia, most subjects of the Russian Empire lived in small towns and villages. Even after the October Revolution, the Soviet Union was predominantly rural, and Soviet-era farms and forestry enterprises formed the basis of most rural communities. Small towns were built for newly established processing industries. They were geographically and culturally distant from Russia's political and economic centers, St. Petersburg and Moscow, and often also from regional capitals. In the final decades of the Soviet Union and the 1990s, the share of Russia's population living in villages dwindled. According to Russian official statistics, 25.6 percent of Russia's population was rural in 2018. Officially, the size of the rural population has not changed much since the end of the Soviet Union.

In the Soviet era, **life in villages and small towns** was organized around state enterprises, **collective farms**, and forests and was integrated into the planned economy. Farms and enterprises were responsible for providing many public goods, such as social services, electricity, and garbage disposal. During the chaotic years of the 1990s, salaries were often delayed or sometimes not paid at all, **poverty** spread, and death rates increased. Public infrastructure crumbled, and private residences became derelict. The 1990s were followed by a decade of stabilization, crucial reforms, and improved state funding for local public services and administration. Poverty rates decreased, and economic growth during the first two terms of **Vladimir Putin**'s presidency brought improvements even to the Russian margins. As growth slowed in the 2010s, however, new and old challenges in villages reappeared.

The remainder of the chapter proceeds as follows: Section 15.2 describes how Soviet-era economic planning shaped rural areas and small towns as well as the main features of the transformation of the Soviet system to a market-based economy. Section 15.3 recounts the economic reorganization at the local level in the post-Soviet period: What happened when collective farms were closed or privatized and when private farms and enterprises were allowed. The section describes the main economic activities in the rural areas, how agriculture is differentiated according to local circumstances, the role of forestry in the north, and the rise of new small entrepreneurial businesses but also large-scale capital investments in rural areas. The section introduces poverty, which was experienced by almost everyone in the 1990s and remains a central legacy of that decade. The role of migration in rural areas is highlighted in section 15.4, while section 15.5 considers the ways in which socioeconomic challenges have been addressed by the state and by societal actors.

Russia is a large and diverse country. This chapter draws mostly on interviews and fieldwork conducted in northwestern and central Russia over the past two decades (Granberg and Sätre 2017). Overall, the chapter points to a central dilemma of Russian society and politics, namely that it is a country with huge natural resources that has not been especially successful in giving regular citizens access to these resources and providing for their wellbeing. The chapter shows what a lack of access to resources and institutional malfunctioning look like at the local level.

15.2   From the Soviet Past to the Tumultuous 1990s

Soviet-era villages and towns were integrated into the planned economy, which in turn was shaped by the political considerations of the Soviet leadership. Soviet-era planning decided which industries to prioritize, coming up with plan targets and calculating resource allocations based on these priorities. In the planned economy, high priority was given to energy, heavy industry, and the military industry. Relatively low priority was given to consumer goods industries and hospitals, for example. One of the characteristic problems of the planned economy was that output targets were not matched with requisite input deliveries, which caused problems at production sites, and therefore in towns and villages.

15.2.1 Soviet Economic Planning in Villages and Small Towns

Soviet-era agriculture was organized in **state farms** (*sovkhozy*) or in cooperative farms (**kolkhozy**), the original production cooperatives, which were established in the 1930s. In the North, there were many *leskhozy*, the state-owned enterprises responsible for organization of forest use, management, and protection. They were simultaneously the sole operations in charge of logging and conservation, a dual role that shaped how forests were managed and exploited. *Sovkhozy, kolkhozy,* and *leskhozy* were also responsible for the social life of local communities, and provided a large range of public services such as maintaining roads and bridges, energy production, waste management, and even running childcare facilities and cultural centers. Farms and enterprises received budgetary funds for each of these activities, though often not enough funds made it all the way to the village level. One of the features of Soviet-era rural life is that many villages were remote and scattered across the country's large territory. During the later decades of the Soviet era, the state tried to consolidate rural settlements by establishing "agrotowns" around farm centers and moving working families to them. Russia's settlement structure never-theless was defined by small villages spread across farflung areas.

Everyday life in most Russian villages was determined in many ways by the workings of collective and state farms, the *sovkhozy* and *kolkhozy*. In the hierarchy of Soviet planning, the priority of agriculture changed over time: As the state became increasingly concerned with the inefficiency of farms, resource allocations increased. Throughout the Soviet period, though, collective and state farms struggled to meet plan targets, which contributed to shortages.

In part because of shortages, many Soviet citizens developed entrepreneurial skills and coping mechanisms. An important feature of Soviet agriculture was that it included significant **subsistence production**, which could be seen as a societal response to shortages. Agricultural workers had the right to cultivate a small area of land and to keep some animals for household consumption. Subsistence production was extremely important during times of crisis, such as during World War II and again during the economic crises of the 1980s and 1990s, when rural citizens adapted to a collapsing village economy by growing their own food. At times, between a third and a half of the basic staples of the Russian diet was grown in these private plots, though for some commodities, such as potatoes, the share was even larger.

15.2.2   When the State Withdrew and Poverty Spread

The collapse of the Soviet system and the end of the planned economy ushered in a vicious downward spiral of economic and social conditions in villages. As state farms lost their incomes, they could not pay salaries and maintain local infrastructure (Sätre 2019). Low or unpaid salaries, in turn, went along with poor housing conditions, little or no access to healthcare, alcoholism, high death rates, orphaned children, and lost opportunities in education and in the socialization of new generations. Social problems accumulated, and poverty could affect any citizen, regardless of education or profession.

Families and relatives tried to help each other. Families in the countryside and small towns grew vegetables and often kept animals: some hens, one or two cows, goats, or other animals. People in the cities often had second houses (dachas) that had garden plots, in which they grew food to sustain them over the winter. The older generation gave their small pensions to help meet the family's common needs and might pay, for example, their grandchildren's educational costs. In the first post-Soviet decade, economic hardship was widespread and many citizens accepted poverty as normal. In more recent years, as more rural citizens have been able to found an enterprise or make a living in other ways, and thereby escape poverty, attitudes to poverty have changed. It has become more common for citizens of villages to think of poverty as a consequence of poor people's attitude to work.

15.3   Economic Reorganization and Entrepreneurship in the Villages

Even in the most chaotic years of the 1990s, the most enterprising rural actors tried to utilize local resources to survive, and some managed to thrive. Entrepreneurs engaged in agricultural production using the tools and farms from privatized collective farms. In many northern Russian forests, trees were cut and timber was sold illegally, which provided starting capital for commercial enterprises. Others legally rented forest land from the state. Success varied in these ventures.

After the end of socialism, small entrepreneurs often started businesses in local trade or in industries and services that had not been on the priority list earlier. In this sector, they would neither challenge the interests of big money nor awaken expectations to contribute financially to the needs of local and regional administrations.

Some of the new entrepreneurs succeeded in developing business activities out of nothing. Starting from small-scale trade in oranges, clothes, or vodka, for example, they collected the capital they needed to move from the informal economy to register their companies officially. The sharpest increase in the number of self-employed occurred between 1996 and 1998; it doubled during the same period when unemployment reached its peak. Generally each rural municipality has at least some new companies, working for example in fish farming, **tourism**, or logging. In many smaller towns a business club was founded, which brings together local entrepreneurs for support, an advisory center, and interconnected networks. It is also noticeable that quite a few women started businesses soon after the Soviet system was dissolved.

Starting in the early 2000s, a set of remarkable changes in state policy took place. With increasing incomes from oil and gas, the state was able to finance economic development programs and provide subsidies for economic and social aims. Some of these programs had remarkable effects in the countryside. The Putin government returned to more generous state support for agriculture and became more involved in forestry, after a policy of almost total laissez-faire during the 1990s.

15.3.1 Agriculture and Fish Farming

The 1990s were a decade marked by economic collapse for Russian farms. Russian gross agricultural production fell by almost half between 1990 and 1998. When the state farms were privatized, workers and pensioners received land shares, which they could either sell or keep and which entitled them to a piece of farmland that had formerly belonged to the collective. Others survived through subsistence gardening and keeping animals, a tradition from socialist times, when state farms could not guarantee food for the whole Soviet population. Yeltsin-era policymakers had expected that this would lead to the flourishing of family farming, which would produce for domestic and global markets. However, new small farms had neither the training nor an extension service to help make the transition to market conditions. What is more, farmers did not have access to credit, and market infrastructure was missing.

Ivan's story, for example, is an illustrative example of a farmer in Arkhangel'sk Oblast who faced challenges and was ultimately not successful.

> Ivan was a tractor driver of a former *sovkhoz* in a river valley in Arkhangel'sk Oblast. When the *sovkhoz* in the village closed in 2000, he established a small-scale farm with his wife to produce milk. Milk was often not available in stores at that time. During privatization, *sovkhoz* workers had the opportunity to gain ownership of farmland and machines. Ivan acquired five hectares of land (around twelve acres), a tractor, and ten cows and started milk production. He succeeded in starting production but marketing turned out to be a problem. Most of the villagers had one or two cows, and families without cows bought milk from their neighbors. Ivan had to sell milk outside the village. There was a dairy nearby, but that enterprise was unable to accept Ivan's milk as he could not provide proof of its quality. Ivan's attempts to run a dairy farm failed. He only succeeded in selling his cattle for food to the Roma village. He was grateful to

them. In future years, he made handicrafts from birch bark, produced honey, and has written a history of the village (interview, 2013).

The state farms' adaptation to market conditions was a difficult process. In northern regions about every second farm was closed, and only a few farms were developed to produce for the market. Although legal changes permitted the emergence of market-oriented farming, in reality Russia's institutional conditions presented many obstacles to small family farms. The state focused on large-scale farming, and therefore few family farms emerged in rural communities. Those farms often combined rural tourism or food-processing with farming. Many villagers did continue to keep some animals and grow food for household use, but few earned a living from this kind of farming. While some registered family farms developed, most households preferred to continue farming as informal units in order to avoid bureaucratic problems, the necessity of reporting to authorities, and fees. Sometimes these unregistered enterprises produced food quite effectively and professionally. In addition to villagers, dacha owners also produced food in rural areas that were within commuting distance from cities.

A cautious rural recovery started around the turn of the millennium, although livestock production continued to suffer for some time. Grigory Ioffe, Tatyana Nefedova, and Ilya Zaslavsky (2006) document the uneven recovery of agricultural production in the late 1990s and early 2000s. They compare developments in the northern and southern parts of Russia, using Kostroma Oblast as an example in the north and the Stavropol' Krai for the south, which is Russia's most fertile area and is known as the black-soil area or **black-earth region** (*chernozem*). Agricultural collapse was much more severe and recovery much slower in the Russian north. The end of state subsidies to agriculture contributed to the difficulties that farmers in non-black-earth regions faced.

The recovery of agricultural production was to a large extent made possible by money that was invested in Russian farmland and farms after the devaluation of the ruble in 1998 and a set of land reforms enacted in 2002 (Wengle 2018). In the early 1990s, Russia had enacted a moratorium on sales of farmland, excluding small plots owned by farm workers. This moratorium was lifted in 2002, triggering a large-scale transfer of farmland from collective farm workers to large corporate farms. Interest in farming was much greater in the south than in the north. Both Russian and foreign businesses started to invest in fertile areas in the south, buying or leasing land in order to establish large farm enterprises, though the volume of foreign investment declined over the years. A remarkable trend for all regions was that the recovery of agricultural production was concentrated around the cities.

In Russia's southern regions, many smaller farms and local rural households were farming their lands with good results (Mamonova 2016). High productivity was partly achieved through their mutualistic relations with some large farms, getting help with plowing, borrowing or buying cheap farm inputs, and sometimes grazing their animals on the farm's fields. Also, varying forms of relations were implemented to buy or lease land and to sign contracts between plot-owners and the leasing company.

After the devaluation of the ruble, meat imports became more expensive, which created demand for the organization of large-scale production. Countersanctions after the occupation of Crimea interrupted the import of Western agricultural products to Russia. This created protection for Russia's domestic food industry against foreign competition and helped agriculture to develop. As for the Russian government's policy, it favored large enterprises, and as a consequence large-scale poultry, pig, and dairy farms and, later, cattle ranches were established in some of Russia's regions, often near cities. This kind of production was led by what are called agroholdings, which specialized in vertically integrated production of meat, producing forage, raising animals, processing meat, and establishing brand names for these products (Wengle 2021). Some of these agroholdings employ rural workers, but they also largely focus on technology-intensive production, which meant that the overall share of employment in agriculture declined.

Despite the rise of agroholdings, then, citizens in small towns and villages continued to look for ways to make a living. In the Karelian economy, fish farms have played an important role. Sergei, a fish farmer from Murmansk, is an example of a new entrepreneur; he had bought an existing fish farm in a middle-sized lake and rented the fish factory building for processing fish products.

> Sergei had been a fisherman in a vessel in Murmansk for more than twelve years. Fishing in international waters was a highly profitable business in the 1990s, because catches were sold on the foreign market and purchased with foreign currency. He collected enough capital to buy the rights to the fish farm and made a deal with the district administration to employ local people and rebuild roads to the farm. In 2001 he started production next to the medium-sized lake. He contributed to the social wellbeing of the area, selling the catch to old people's homes in the region. We visited the farm twice, and the second time, in 2015, it was obvious that business was going well, even thriving. Now his son has taken the leadership of the farm and Sergei himself has moved to St. Petersburg, where he has established a hotel chain. Sergei and his son are producing, among other things, high-priced salmon roe for the hotel chain (interviews, 2003, 2015).

15.3.2 Forestry

Forestry was a most promising industry for starting an enterprise in the 1990s in Russia's forested northern regions, and it has remained an important sector throughout the post-Soviet period. The forest sector was already of high economic value both to forest settlements and to wider populations in (and before) Soviet times. When forestry and sawmills were complemented with paper and pulp mills, material prosperity spread into the whole community.

An early adopter was Igor, who established a timber company in Karelian Russia, with his brother.

> Igor's father was a *leskhoz* director in the 1990s, which helped the enterprise solve the crucial problems of that time caused by hyperinflation, the lack of a credit system, unclear legislation, and so on. The company started with a team of eight men, and within ten years the number of employees had grown to 200. At that time, they had a group of four separate enterprises that cut and processed timber. One of them was a joint venture with a Finnish entrepreneur. When Igor's brother retired, this branch closed. The original company still worked in logging, operated a sawmill, and built cottages. The third company was a pig farm, which provided food for workers, among others. The fourth company was intending to open a holiday village with a restaurant. At the time of our interview, the village was half built by a lake. It consisted of thirty wood buildings, and extensive plans existed for how to develop the village. In the end, it was not opened by Igor. Business conditions changed, unforeseen events happened, and a new owner emerged to take over the business. Igor's example shows the uncertainties and the limits of small entrepreneurship in Russia. However, Igor did continue in the original logging business for many years (interviews, 2002, 2006).

Since the dissolution of the USSR the number of people formally employed in the forest sector has fallen dramatically – from 2 million down to 800,000 in 2006. Soviet companies had offered a range of social services and infrastructure, from which the local population could also often benefit. As in agriculture, private actors invested in the forest sector. With privatization, the responsibilities for local social welfare functions were formally moved from enterprises to the local municipality.

Since the collapse of the Soviet planned economy, much of the activity in Russia's forestry sector happens illegally. The World Wildlife Fund of Russia estimated in 2012 that 10–35 percent of harvested timber came from illegal sources in Russia, and in some regions illegal logging was as high as 50 percent (Ulybina 2014, 143). At the same time, in some regions, vigorous entrepreneurial activity emerged in forestry. A *leskhoz* director in Karelia estimated that in the early 2000s there were about 600 private companies in Karelian Republic active in this sector, with around 30 companies using state-owned land through long-term leases (interview, 2002).

In 2006 a set of reforms was carried out in forest administration in an attempt to combat illegal activity. In the "Forest Code of the Russian Federation" *leskhozy* were discontinued; furthermore, the federal government was defined as the only owner of forests in Russia. The fundamental regulation of the forestry sector was defined through federal-level legislation, whereas a series of local issues, such as forest use for household needs, was delegated to the regions. Some of these changes affected local forestry entrepreneurs, and consequently local residents in forest-rich regions in Russia: Auctions were introduced as the main mechanism for forest resource distribution. The earlier method had been based on contracts between forest companies and local authorities. These were made after negotiations, in which local forest companies had more of a chance to get the contract than under the new system, depending on their personal relationship to authorities. Local companies could promise to provide jobs for local people and to take care of communal tasks, such as repairing bridges and maintaining the road network.

Ten years later a municipal director based in the forests in the middle of Arkhangel'sk Oblast described the consequences of this change. Previously he would have received a request from the district to organize forest work in the nearby forests and delegated this task to local companies. These entrepreneurs, mutually, took responsibility for some local projects. However, in the new system the rights to log the forest were decided by auction. This arrangement has meant that the local entrepreneurs have lost their harvesting rights, as richer and bigger companies from the Russian metropoles, with no respect for local needs, have arrived in their place (interview, 2013).

The timber industry did well in forest-rich regions due to investments by both foreign and Russian capital. Some of the companies in this sector had been reorganized into joint-stock companies in the early 1990s, which sold timber to international markets. Some of the most prosperous rural towns and villages are located around industrial timber plants.

Juha Kotilainen and colleagues studied four forestry and timber companies in northwestern Russia that existed in the Soviet planned economy; three were located in villages, where they offered almost the only available work for local people, and the fourth was located in a small town (Kotilainen et al. 2009). One went bankrupt twice before its activity became viable, and it continued under the ownership of a Russian company, free of debt and with formal responsibilities to maintain the infrastructure in the settlement. Three companies have acquired a long-term forest lease for forty-nine years, which has stabilized their prospects. The fourth and smallest one was not able to lease forestry land for periods longer than five years and has experienced severe difficulties in stabilizing its activity. Two of these enterprises do not pay significant amounts of tax into the district budget, while the taxes paid by the other two account for 46 and 70 percent of the budgets of their respective districts.

The three larger companies have retained a Soviet-era social norm that in the north the enterprises must, for example, provide the population with firewood either free or at very low prices. One enterprise has a long-term social program that is meant to benefit village citizens, and another is preparing a similar one. The program's aim is to support professional education of new workers; the enterprise promises to recruit workers from the local population, which also means refraining from hiring teams of loggers from other regions of Russia or migrant labor. While these four settlements were quite successful, there were many other settlements in which villagers lost opportunities to work in forestry, which had dramatic consequences for economic life in Russia's remote northern settlements.

15.3.3   Tourism

Small-scale tourism entrepreneurs played an important role in villages and small towns, where they built up small hotels and restaurants, provided work for local people, and supplied services for them. Travelers and tourists had traditionally found accommodation in villagers' homes, often free of charge. *Sovkhozy* sometimes had hotels. After the 1990s a few local entrepreneurs started to rent rooms in their houses, others built guesthouses or hotels, and those with more capital built holiday resorts. In the district of Priazha, Karelia, we found one moderate hostel in 2005. In 2021 the internet service bookings.com lists twenty-one accommodations closer than 25 km to the village center of Priazha. Tourism has rapidly grown into a significant branch of local economy in Russian Karelia, and not only there.

One strategy to obtain financial capital for the tourism business has been to engage in trade through the running of shops. Marina and Alexei are a couple, both teachers, who started a ski and tourism center and a sports school in Arkhangel'sk Oblast, offering free classes for children.

> Marina and Alexei's salaries as teachers were paid by the state. They owned a private shop in the village together with some relatives. Although they earned very little from this shop after the payment of salaries, taxes, and repayment of loans, some money was left to put into the development of a tourism business. As they rented out a shop, they earned rent and used the proceeds to build a house of their own to live in as well as other houses to rent to tourists. Their tourism business has been built up step by step. In 2016, nine houses were made available for rent to tourists, the first of which had been built in 2003. From the money they earned, they have also been able to build two saunas (which are very popular in the northern forest regions), a restaurant, and a building for administration and selling souvenirs. Gradually, the "ski and tourism center" was developed partly by state money and partly and increasingly with money from the private sector. In 2014, the owners found that their business was big enough to earn a decent income for their family (interviews 2002–16).

15.3.4   Women as Entrepreneurs

Setting up a private business was a new thing: It was not allowed in Soviet Union. During privatization, this was a new opportunity, and many women used it to set up businesses in traditionally female sectors that had low status and were underdeveloped during the Soviet era. In the early 1990s, female entrepreneurship was primarily oriented toward retail trade and services. Women in smaller towns and villages have set up trading firms, but they also set up firms to process berries and mushrooms, agricultural products, and even timber. Among female-owned businesses, enterprises with a small number of employees were dominant. Women also started small-scale businesses that provided childcare, healthcare, and education, or set up in small-scale tailoring, dressmaking, knitting, and handicrafts. Sometimes women entrepreneurs hire employees to ease their own double burden, of taking care of families and running a business at the same time.

There are many new possibilities for potential entrepreneurs, while there are also at times many unpredictable obstacles to overcome. The gendered labor market inherited from Soviet times is reflected in women's entrepreneurship: Businesses often develop slowly and gradually, and its thriving hinges on the networks of personal relationships of the owner. The lack of market infrastructure and the arbitrary enforcement of rules by authorities force female entrepreneurs to rely on personal networks and multiple sources of income. The prevalence of large, vertically integrated firms in Russia have further made it difficult to set up new firms. Authorities also prefer to deal with a few large firms rather than a larger number of small ones. Because the markets are controlled by entrepreneurs who are already solvent, newcomers are likely to be forced into existing hierarchical structures. Many small business-owners perceive that politicians and community officers are "in the hands of the **oligarchs**." This means that the larger firms do not have to worry about the rules that concern the smaller ones (see also Chapter 9). Despite these general trends, we also heard from local entrepreneurs of examples of local mayors helping small female business-owners with various facilities, letting locales for rent, or even lending money to them.

It has probably become more difficult to start small businesses in the 2010s than it was just after the privatization reforms in the 1990s. One reason is the increased focus among Russia's state officials on economic and political control. It was also initially possible to acquire equipment needed to get started as the entrepreneurs could take over equipment or buy it cheaply from old state firms. A third reason is that, over time, registration requirements and stricter rules for obtaining licenses came to be enforced. Many entrepreneurs do not want business partners or collaborators from outside the family. The perceived instability of the situation has meant that people were hired on an informal basis, especially in businesses run without licenses.

Despite many problems, women still try to start their own businesses. Since the mid-2000s, female participation in entrepreneurship has developed significantly, involving partially new spheres, such as the provision of social services to the population, catering, cosmetic and hairdressing services, medicine, art, and tourism. This is reflected in official policies to promote female entrepreneurship as part of national programs on entrepreneurship. In addition, the "National Strategy of Action for Women for 2017–2022" includes measures both to increase female entrepreneurial activity and to promote social entrepreneurship as an important branch of female entrepreneurship.

As seen from the following examples, there are women who have managed to build up businesses; however, other women continue to solve everyday problems by means of various traditional strategies for survival. At the time of writing, it is not known how hard the COVID-19 pandemic and the economic crisis caused by sanctions after the 2022 war have hit women running small businesses. It is safe to say that these events have likely made it even more challenging for any entrepreneur running a small business.

Zhanna is a textile entrepreneur, who has developed her textile enterprise little by little in the central village of a community in Arkhangel'sk region since the early 1990s.

> The shutdown of a state firm meant an opportunity for Zhanna, as a former employee, to take over a small number of sewing machines. She developed her textile enterprise slowly and did not invest in new, more technically advanced machines until there was enough capital within her own enterprise. Her husband invested money that he earned from logging timber in Zhanna's textile firm. She was sewing to order only, due to the limited buying capacity in the local sphere. Orders included ladies' clothes, suits, work uniforms for companies, and tablecloths for restaurants. She said the expansion of the business was limited by a lack of skilled staff in the local community. Her solution was to educate her staff herself. She ran sewing-related activities and workshops in the village. In 2008, she opened a new shop in a town some 250 miles away. But she decided to keep going in her own village, where the rents were low and where she had her roots, while also maintaining the sewing-to-order business in the larger town. In 2012 Zhanna had expanded her activity to curtains and interior design (interview, 2012).

Margarita is an early-years schoolteacher in Nizhny Novgorod Oblast; she started with a kiosk selling oranges during her maternity leave.

> Margarita is a successful entrepreneur; she now owns a new hotel in a small town. She had been a teacher who made her first small capital by selling oranges at a small roadside stand during her maternity leave. She survived the period of hyperinflation in the early 1990s by buying twenty tons of pasta, which she and her husband then sold with prices rising in line with inflation. After several years doing business as a kiosk operator, in small-scale agriculture, and in a café, she built her first hotel with two stories, good-quality

accommodation, the best restaurant in a small town, and even a new and popular banquet hall (interview, 2013).

15.4 Rural Migration

In Soviet times, between 1966 and 1980, the rural population decreased by 1–1.5 percent per year despite the restrictions on leaving state farms. Migration flows changed rapidly after the collapse of the USSR. In the first post-Soviet years, the population declines in the Russian countryside slowed for some years, in large part because of an influx of migrants from the former Soviet republics. In response to economic disparities and anti-Russian sentiments, Russians living in those countries together with foreign workers moved to Russian villages from the newly independent states. After 2000, the transformation to a market-oriented economy again set in motion significant **migratory flows**. Rural population outflows resumed, as citizens moved from rural areas to cities, and from small towns to large cities.

In the rural areas outside the black-earth region, populations became more concentrated in larger settlements and around larger cities. Villages in the remaining and outlying territories have very low populations; they are mostly occupied by summer visitors, with many of them abandoned and given back to nature. Remaining members of the local village populations take temporary or seasonal jobs in cities and in profitable industries, above all in the energy sector (see Chapter 11). In the southern regions, a massive inflow of urban and rural investment in agriculture has combined with a no-less-massive outflow of local rural residents taking temporary jobs in cities due to the decline in labor-intensive animal husbandry and modernization of crop production.

Even in Soviet times, daily commuting from the rural villages to nearby towns and cities was a normal phenomenon, and it helped to keep villages populated. Temporary migration remains very common in villages and small towns. People from settlements beyond the urban agglomerations find employment opportunities in the city regions through the Internet or acquaintances. Their family stays in the official place of residence, while the workers themselves travel often hundreds or thousands of kilometers to work and back. The rhythm of these movements is often one or two weeks at work and one or two weeks at home. It is estimated that the proportion of people who participate in this practice varies from 5 percent to 30 percent of the working-age population in villages and towns, depending on the distance from a large city, local demographic characteristics, and the range and state of local businesses (Makhrova, Nefedova, and Pallot 2016).

Russia has also experienced movements in the opposite direction, from the towns and cities to the countryside, most typically "**dacha migration**," moving to second houses and huts in rural areas in the holidays. Some estimates calculate that 15–20 million families own dachas in Russia, which amounts to about half of all urban residents. New dacha villages have been built around Moscow. In rural places, old houses are converted into second homes by relatives in the younger generations, and some of them are renovated. Here and there, a rich Russian builds a mansion with high fences, often perceived by locals as disturbing to the harmony of an old village. As a whole, strong seasonal suburbanization takes place when dachas come into use. People may move to dachas for longer periods or they may stay there on the weekends and for short summer holidays. A sociological survey from 2012 shows that food production is the primary function of a dacha for residents in smaller towns. For those from larger cities, recreation is more central than food production.

Migrants from former Soviet states play an important role in many of Russia's villages and small towns. They often bring skills and knowledge to Russian villages that the local residents did not have. Caucasian restaurants are common in many small towns, and the owners were often the first pioneers in their new municipalities to start an eating place, a hotel, family farm, or other activity.

Three cases of immigrants from the Caucasus illustrate this trend:

> A middle-aged man had arrived in southern Karelia in the 1990s and established a family farm with small cattle. He combined farming with tractor work, clearing snow in the winter from the village roads and offering help to the local population plow their garden plots in the springtime. It was not easy to get good contacts with local villagers but he stayed in the village and later he also started small-scale rural tourism.

> In another Karelian village, an entrepreneur from Baku worked for the municipality as a tourist guide and together with his wife established a hostel on his own property. By 2004, they rented rooms from their two-story house and a separate cottage with a *bania* (sauna) standing by a small stream.

> A man from Azerbaijan moved to a village near Luga in Leningrad Oblast. He was a shoemaker by profession. He had stayed in bigger towns on the way but found it more comfortable and safer to live in the village. He was an enthusiastic soccer fan, and by 2009 he had established himself as a trainer for a junior girls' team, with his own daughter participating.

15.5 Solving Social and Economic Problems

Both local administration and local civic actors have attempted to help solve social problems. In many villages volunteers have cooperated with local administration to address poverty. In 2002, in a small rural settlement by Lake Ladoga, for example, we observed that a local women's club was able to use a building belonging to the local administration, trying to do what they could to help children. They offered a place for the children to play and supplied a meal for children from poor families, and an escape from violence at home. Local authorities consented to this use of public infrastructure, allowing citizens to organize help for local social problems.

Local administration was reformed in 2006, when it received necessary, though meager, resources to help work in smaller communes. Civil society developed from various informal arrangements in rural areas to more formal organizations. We will see below how social and economic problems were addressed at the local level: how local administration is attempting to contribute to solving them, how civil society is acting in this sphere, and how and to what extent government programs facilitate such activity.

15.5.1 Administration without Resources

In rural areas, Russian subnational administrations, the oblasts or republics, have two lower levels of administrative structures: the district level and the local municipal level. In the Soviet era, the capacity of local administration was dependent on its relations with enterprises and higher-level administration. The district level had limited responsibilities and small budgets. Local and small-town administrations typically did not even have their own budget. Funding depended on negotiations with the district level on a case-by-case basis. The situation in the local settlements became critical during privatization, because many local administrative tasks were no longer fulfilled by any level of government. Complaints were made to higher levels, but seldom with any success.

The deputy director of a municipal administration in Karelia, Anna, illustrates the duties of the staff of a municipal administration. The director was Viktor, who had a wide range of responsibilities and was initially dealing with social and economic issues and issues of culture and development of the village. He was involved with constituencies and also worked with various higher agencies, in direct contact with the (district) administration. Anna explained that, in addition to Viktor and herself, the deputy director, two further employees handled public administration: There was Svetlana, who was the land expert, and Nina, who worked in the military registration office. The duties of the local director and deputy director overlapped. The land expert's duty was to solve issues concerning rentals and private ownership of land, sanitation conditions, rubbish dumps, and cemeteries, and to maintain a civil registry of certificates for family members, housing conditions and registration certificates. In the military registration office, Nina also managed the passport and visa services.

At the time of interview in 2004, the local administration was working with several difficult problems, because the privatized former state farm was essentially in a state of bankruptcy. The funding for local needs was insufficient, and the main worries for the administration were housing and unemployment. For example, they could not arrange housing for new teachers, which is a commitment in the legislation for new graduates who settle in rural areas. Therefore, this region could not get specialized teachers for the school.

15.5.2   New Local Administration

Regional and local administration often faced the practically impossible challenge of providing even the most basic local services during the 1990s. Healthier public budgets in the 2000s enabled local administrations to increase public-sector salaries and, most importantly, distribute pensions for rural residents. This improved standards of living in rural areas and led to an equalization of basic incomes across regions. The reform of local administration in 2006 altered the situation further. City districts were separated from municipal districts, and a two-level municipal system was established. For local administration – urban or rural settlements – this meant an important practical improvement: The new lowest level of local administration received its own budget to respond to local social and economic problems. Some of the higher positions of the new administrative level were filled by women.

Like before the reform, local authorities remained responsible for basic services in small towns and villages. It is up to the local authorities to find their own ways to deal with problems of shortfalls in resources and any specific acute improvements needed, whatever they may be. Although there is little access to profits from the energy resources and rents in many places, these places may have a relatively high level of freedom in terms of interference from the central level: "You just have to be active and try, and try again, not to let bureaucracy let you down" (interview, local head in a small town, Arkhangel'sk Oblast, 2012).

The quality of leadership in local administration varies, naturally, but many people on the local level try vigorously to solve different common problems caused by local circumstances and central orders. They work in different positions in society and often use any opportunities beyond their official duties and responsibilities. People in local administration may also be innovative, energetic, skillful, and respected by the residents in the community in question.

All around the country, the local administrations exist and act in a very similar context. Vertical administration implies that each place seems to be isolated from its neighbors and other places in a similar situation. The ability of administrations to support or to complicate the establishment of companies is highlighted when comparing two communities in Arkhangel'sk Oblast: One has several new types of firms (tourism, the berry industry, clothing); the other could not facilitate new companies while trying to protect – in vain – its old work units in the timber industry.

Relations between local authorities and enterprises that operate locally are crucial for whether and how social problems are addressed. Because of a chronic lack of funding for local needs, community leaders have to use different methods to find funds to address citizens' needs. This leads to a mutual dependence between authorities and companies. Local enterprises often accept what they call corporate social responsibility as a duty.

15.5.3 Putin-Era Responses to Rural Poverty

During the growth period in the Russian economy from 2000 to 2013, the state improved its policies relating to poverty and social problems, increasing state funding to a number of social programs and bringing new features to the local policy. First, new programs in healthcare, housing, education, and agriculture in 2005 offered much-needed funding for rural Russia. Many of these provided federal funding, but in addition were supported and enforced by regional governors. Secondly, to receive such funding, an application had to be submitted by a local organization, which required – thirdly – that local actors had to formulate and launch projects. These new features in political programs are in line with what is called new governance. One particular social program, for foster families, moved most children from children's homes to private families, offering a better future for children and an opportunity for rural residents to receive funding as foster parents.

According to Russian statistics, poverty began to increase again in 2013 (Sätre 2019). This theme returned to the political agenda in a presidential statement and a new federal law. President Vladimir Putin conceded in a 2018 speech to the Federal Assembly that large-scale poverty was an important problem and that the reduction of poverty by at least half would be the key goal for the next ten years (Putin 2018). In this connection, the importance of the social and civic activity of the Russian people was noted and, accordingly, socially oriented NGOs were welcomed to contribute to solve social problems. After the 2013 legislation obligated the state bodies of all levels to assist volunteer activity. In practice, various regions and municipalities implemented this legislation in very different ways.

The social sector needed political reform, and the government decided that social NGOs and social enterprises were potential contributors to work in the social sector. The privatization of social sector was started, and NGOs and enterprises were invited to take part in this process. New legislation from 2010 and 2015 promised socially oriented organizations an opportunity to receive state support in order to supply certain goods and services. Civil society was mobilized by this process in rural settlements as well as in urban ones. Project-based development methods by the government offered resources to NGOs. However, in the same period NGOs were also meeting with increasing suspicion and attempted control by political leaders, who did not like to be challenged by civic activism. Was this new form of governance still embracing the civil society sector?

Elena is an example of how an active administration can contribute to development. She is the deputy mayor in a district in Arkhangel'sk Oblast.

Elena explained how the district participated in a variety of federal-level programs and presidential priority projects. These were to construct infrastructure, develop sports and tourism, and build houses for elderly and for employees working in the budget sector. Elena outlined plans for the ski resort area: There was a need for more accommodation for upcoming skiing competitions. They participated in the regional program for building houses. With this activity Elena feels that she has actually been able to make a difference through her own actions (interview, 2014).

15.5.4   Local Civic Activity

The direst years of need also helped to give rise to an awakening of local civil society, often initially geared to helping poor children and families in need. Some Soviet-era social organizations were revived and reformed to adapt to new social challenges. Women's Councils were established in the 1960s as part of the state structure. In the 1990s, in many villages local women worked to address the consequences of poverty in the ruins of the Soviet state.

There is much evidence of civic activity in the 2000s. Some foreign initiatives are well documented. The Swedish Development Agency (SIDA) started a development program on the local level as early as 1998. Its goal was to facilitate non-agrarian development, especially but not solely for small entrepreneurs. The joint EU/Russian project "Ladoga Initiative" was an EU-funded crossborder project between Finland and Russia from 2011 to 2013. It worked relatively well, showing (in addition to its main aim) how local administration, active villages, and small enterprises could work together to reach a concrete goal. Only a few registered civic organizations existed in the target communities around Lake Ladoga. However, informal cooperation worked well: Grassroots-level entities participated intensively, building children's playgrounds, repairing sport sites, and establishing recreational facilities, and so forth. This process was not without problems, but none of the local projects was left undone. Networking took place between people and was based more on personal ties than on formal relations. Furthermore, the World Bank has funded a somewhat similar but larger project around Russia since 2005, called the "Local Initiatives Support Programme."

Russia launched also its own local development model called TOS (self-managed local association) to support short-term local projects. It is a special juridical form, which is suitable for short-term projects with a single goal, for instance, building a playground or a footbridge, or constructing a drainage system in cooperation with neighbors. Some Russian regions applied this form actively and experienced a boom in grassroots-level activities. A TOS is based on the common desire to carry out a concrete project jointly. TOS activity was remarkable in Arkhangel'sk Oblast, as an example, proving that people in Russia were able to design local projects to reach their common goals. It worked well when the question was of short-term projects in the local area with no need for a budget or for longer-term supervision of outcomes.

However, the reforms and investments of the Russian Federation are crucial for any larger local development in the country. The legislation allowing private companies, reform of local administration, National Priority Programs, and social policy programs are examples of measures that have provided opportunities for local improvements in Russia.

As for the local administration reform, it acknowledged the importance of small administrative units organizing services and activities on the very lowest local level. And the National Priority Programs were at least somewhat successful in providing improved social services. During our investigation we found many examples in which the programs succeeded in breathing new life into schools and recreational facilities (houses of culture) and in limiting local dependence on imported food. Pensions and salaries for teachers, doctors, cultural workers, and social workers were again paid regularly and were even increased. Villages bene-fited from these programs not only as a site for agricultural production but also as places for many types of enterprises. Local communities could and sometimes did apply for funding for improvements in their infrastructure. Federal funding has been flowing down into the construction of new family houses and other new buildings.

When coming to the 2010s we meet, simultaneously, the government's increasing attempt to control civic associations as well as the explicit wish on the part of the same government to mobilize citizens and to support local initiatives. The dividing line in the rulers' thinking lies somewhere between politicized activities and con-structive social and cultural initiatives.

Our research on local NGO activity in central Russia has clarified what is happening to local NGOs in the changed political climate. These NGOs worked to rehabilitate former drug users, to reduce domestic violence, to prevent homeless-ness, and so on. They were both formal and informal organizations, such as charity funds, registered associations, informal clubs, and local groups for mutual help and support. They had varying relations to the wider public as well as to Russian authorities. Any success in their activity was connected to citizens' trust in them.

The overall picture is that much depended on the reputation of the person in charge. There was no sign of internal democracy or collective decisionmaking in these NGOs: Strategic decisions were mostly taken by the leader. The Russian legislation on "foreign agents" (requiring NGOs that receive any money from abroad to register and to include the fact that they are a "foreign agent" on any publicity) means that NGOs are increasingly controlled by the state, and many independent

NGOs have been harassed by state agencies. Other NGOs have managed to adapt to new conditions and survive. Quite a few have reorganized their activities, some collaborating more closely with the local administration or the church. Some want to stay unregistered in order to avoid bureaucratic requirements; instead they cooperate with a registered NGO or an enterprise. And some NGO members establish a commercial enterprise to solve funding problems instead of the NGO itself. The study gives also evidence of charity as the main method of helping people rather than mobilizing them.

15.6   Conclusion

The new freedom to establish local businesses and the reform of local administration together opened a window of opportunities for local people to act for improvements. The types of economic activity and the level of development vary between as well as within communities. The competence, experiences, attitudes, and views of the local entrepreneurs who took charge were a decisive factor in shaping economic life in Russian villages. This is not to say that the right person could make a difference anywhere. Local circumstances are extremely important as well. Although community life is organized in various ways and the awareness of development trends and possibilities is rather diverse too, what is striking is the widespread conception of villagers and citizens of small towns that the communities appear to be working largely as isolated places.

Russian leaders and scientists are proud of the country's immense natural resources. Russia's human resources are remarkable as well, taking into account the size of the population, its ethnic diversity, and its high general level of education (offered since the Soviet era). What matters more than the overall total of the resources that Russia has at its disposal is how they are used. Energy exports filled state coffers and offered opportunities for economic investment and welfare policy reform, as well as for the government's other priorities, not least the rebuilding of Russia's military power. Mining and the metal industry complement energy production. Russia's extensive forested areas in the central and northern parts and the fertile agricultural lands in the south compete with any other country's similar resources. The latter areas have not been prioritized in Russian economic policy, however, in the same way as energy production.

Access to these resources by village residents is crucial for the wellbeing of local populations and their farms and enterprises. Whether and how local access materialized depended on preconditions such as laws and local governance, and local actors' educational, cultural, and social capital. To succeed with a business idea, an entrepreneur needs to have good relations with the local community and with partners or stakeholders outside it. A farmer or an entrepreneur without connections to the market is powerless.

The reform of local administration in 2006 gave some hope for a positive turn in local development. The vertical hierarchies in the Russian state favor, however, big companies in business and big agroholdings in agriculture. During the 2010s, it has become more difficult to establish and develop small businesses, although it is still possible. With Russia's war in Ukraine, and consequent sanctions on Russia, the economic life of citizens has once again been thrown into question. Villagers and citizens of smaller towns will likely have to fall back on gardening and other survival strategies practiced in decades past.

DISCUSSION QUESTIONS

1. Russia has rich natural resources. Can residents in villages and small towns make use of these resources in ways that benefit them and society as a whole? What could be done better?
2. In what ways have local social groups responded to poverty and other problems in Russian villages and small towns?
3. What kind of entrepreneurs does Russia have? In what ways are Russian entrepreneurs similar to and in what ways are they different from entrepreneurs in other countries – Western market economies and developing countries?

REFERENCES

Granberg, Leo, and Ann-Mari Sätre. 2017. *The Other Russia: Local Experience and Societal Change.* Oxford and New York: Routledge.

Ioffe, Grigory, Tatyana Nefedova, and Ilya Zaslavsky. 2006. *The End of Peasantry? The Disintegration of Rural Russia.* Pittsburgh: University of Pittsburgh Press.

Kotilainen, Juha, A. A. Kulyasova, I. P. Kulyasov, and Svetlana S. Pchelkina. 2009. "Re-Territorializing the Russian North through Hybrid Forest Management." In Soili Nystén-Haarala (ed.), *The Changing Governance of Renewable Natural Resources in Northwest Russia*, pp. 131–47. Farnham, UK: Ashgate.

Makhrova, Alla G., Tatiana G. Nefedova, and Judith Pallot. 2016. "The Specifics and Spatial Structure of Circular Migration in Russia." *Eurasian Geography and Economics*, 57(6), 802–18.

Mamonova, Natalia. 2016. "Rethinking Rural Politics in Post-Socialist Settings: Rural Communities, Land Grabbing and Agrarian Change in Russia and Ukraine." Ph.D. thesis, Erasmus University Rotterdam.

Nefedova, T. G. 2012. "Major Trends for Changes in the Socioeconomic Space of Rural Russia." *Regional Research of Russia*, 2, 41–54.

Putin, Vladimir. 2018. "Presidential Address to General Assembly," March 18, http://en .kremlin.ru/events/presidential/news/56957.

Sätre, Ann-Mari. 2019. *The Politics of Poverty in Contemporary Russia.* London and New York: Routledge.

Ulybina, Olga. 2014. "Russian Forests: The Path of Reform." *Forest Policy and Economics*, 38, 143–50.

Wengle, Susanne A. 2018. "Local Effects of the New Land Rush: How Global Capital Inflows Transformed Rural Russia." *Governance*, 31(2), 259–77.

  2021. *Black Earth, White Bread: A Technopolitical History of Russian Agriculture.* Madison: University of Wisconsin Press.

PART III
Politics and Society

16 Russia's Conservative Forces and the State: A Dynamic Balancing Act

MARLENE LARUELLE

Fig. 16.1 Residents walking near the Suzdal Kremlin and the Cathedral of the Nativity of the Theotokos. Credit: Max Ryazanov / Moment / Getty Images.

> Without the values embedded in Christianity and other world religions, without the standards of morality that have taken shape over millennia, people will inevitably lose their human dignity. We consider it natural and right to defend these values.
>
> Vladimir Putin, "Meeting of the Valdai International Discussion Club"

Abstract

Since the collapse of the Soviet Union, Russian society has been molded by different ideological forces. Those representing conservative values – understood as a combination of references to the national culture's exceptionalism, Orthodoxy, and a vague "traditional values" narrative – have historically comprised a plurality, and even sometimes a majority. The Presidential Administration under Vladimir Putin has been capturing that dynamic to its own advantage, trying to secure the political loyalty of these conservative-minded segments of the population and mobilize them in support of the regime. Within this conservative segment, the Russian Orthodox Church has been gaining in influence to the point that it is now Russia's key ideological entrepreneur, pushing for a "moralization" of society and politics and developing lobbying strategies to penetrate secular state institutions: the military, the school system, and the judiciary. Russia's 2022 invasion of Ukraine has dramatically shifted the conservative equilibrium toward justifying mass violence against Ukraine and repression at home.

16.1　Introduction

The Russian regime brands itself both domestically and on the international scene as a conservative power. While scholars disagree on whether this "conservative turn" has genuine ideological content (for example, Robinson 2019) or is merely an empty shell used by the regime to secure its legitimacy (for example, Pomerantsev 2014), it has certainly become a central narrative of the Russian state and informs some of its policies.

But what is the content of this **conservatism** that is promoted at such a high level? Conservatism wants to slow the pace of changes and challenges the need for permanent "progress." It believes that humanity shares ontological features that cannot easily be challenged or denied by individual will, and that identity (national, sexual, and gender) is not purely a social construct that can be changed if an individual feels dissatisfied with it.

As deployed by the Russian regime today, conservatism is understood as the need to reaffirm the supremacy of the state as the only guarantor of the survival of the nation, the need to avoid rapid political changes that could jeopardize the country's reassertion of itself on the international scene and the regime's stability at home, and the need for some values shared by citizens such as respect for national traditions (as reconstructed they may be) and social hierarchies. This conservative credo, by itself quite vague, has been operationalized in public policies through the promotion of so-called **traditional values** such as pro-family measures, defense of heterosexual marriage, patriotism, anti-Westernism, and so on. It has been articulated to a narrative on Russia's cultural specificity that has taken different identity languages about Russia's boundaries and relationship to neighboring territories

(Eurasianism, the **Russian World**, Russia as a specific civilization, Russia and Ukraine as one nation, and so on.)

The Russian government positions itself as promoting a moderate or healthy (*umerennyi* or *zdorovyi* in Russian) conservatism but rejects radical formulations that would empower more conservative actors too much. And, indeed, the Russian playground for conservatism is broad and occupied by myriad actors. Among them, the **Russian Orthodox Church** (ROC) dominates as a *primus inter pares*: It has become the main advocate of conservative values and the premier institution able to lobby for them in a relatively efficient way (see also Chapter 21). Around it, one may find many smaller actors with more specialized agendas and themes of predilection (pro-family, pro-monarchy, ethnonationalists). The ideological continuum between a Russian regime presenting itself as "moderate conservative" and groups pushing for more radical, reactionary, or fundamentalist narratives constituted the core ideological balancing act in Russia before the 2022 war – but also a potential liability to the regime's stability.

Indeed, ideational creativity and ideological stability have been a strength of **Vladimir Putin**'s regime for many years. For two decades, the regime has provided an "all you can eat" buffet of ideational products speaking to different audiences and filling ideological niches to create the broadest possible social consensus around the regime. This consensus relies on three pillars: the memory of the 1990s as a new Time of Troubles (Smuta, a reference to the early seventeenth century, when Russia faced a deep political crisis with the demise of the Rurik dynasty and several foreign interventions), a recurrence of which needs to be avoided at any cost; a celebration of Russia's history as uninterrupted over a millennium, whatever the political ruptures might be; and the idea that Russia is a unique civilization, distinct from the West and opposed to it, while still being part of a broader European culture.

While this consensual reading of national identity and national values was a strength for a long time, it gradually became a liability. The regime's gradual cooptation of conservative forces to fight the liberals, the church's rising influence, and a public opinion that became more and more polarized in terms of values together rendered the ideological consensus around the regime more fragile. The invasion of Ukraine has accelerated the ideological radicalization process and polarized public opinion.

16.2 The 1990s: Conservative Forces in Opposition

In the first decade after the end of the Soviet Union, conservative forces mostly defined themselves in opposition to the liberal and pro-Western government of

Boris Yeltsin. Yet, at that time, there already existed many gateways between conservative forces and some sections of the state, be they law enforcement agencies and the military, or conservative political parties and their leaders.

16.2.1　Conservative Forces in the Soviet Union

Many observers think of the Soviet Union as ideologically homogeneous. This view is incorrect. At least since Nikita Khrushchev's de-Stalinization in the mid-1950s, a number of conservative groups existing within the Soviet state apparatus and the **Communist Party of the Soviet Union** (CPSU) had tried to resist the softening of the totalitarian Stalinist regime. In the 1970s and the early 1980s, the administration of Leonid Brezhnev relaxed its ideological control over the society enough to allow several ideological groupings to compete with one another (Brudny 2000).

Inside state structures and official institutions such as the Writers' Union (the centralized institution providing official status to recognized writers), conservative forces were divided into two main groups: the **Stalinists**, who called for a return to a Stalinist regime as the only way to maintain control over Soviet society and avoid centrifugal tendencies; and the **Slavophiles** (those who believe in a specific Russian path and a joint destiny for eastern Slavic people), who were critical of the whole Soviet period and nostalgic for prerevolutionary Russia. The latter focused their critique on the Soviet destruction of the peasant world, the environmental impact of Soviet industrialization, and the risk that the Russian nation would be subsumed by the regime's internationalist ideology. Outside state institutions, in the Soviet underground, small groups of far-right forces – holding to fascism, Nazism, or interwar émigré ideologies – had long existed, although they were systematically repressed by the regime. Among these, one group stands out: the Golovin Circle, a group present in Moscow's bohemian cultural underground that was fascinated by European far-right ideologies and managed to avoid being dismantled by the authorities. **Aleksandr Dugin**, a key figure of post-Soviet far right, emerged from this group.

Conservative values and practices were also inherent in the communist narrative itself. The Bolshevik project was essentially a mission to modernize society by combining industrialization, secularization, and urbanization. Throughout the life of the Soviet Union, the communist party-state rhetorically emphasized its adherence to the idea of "progress" and its focus on the future and youth. Yet, allegiance to left-wing ideas – such as Marxism-Leninism, atheism, and socialism in politics and economics – was combined with right-wing sociocultural conservatism in the period after World War II. A notable element of state-sanctioned Soviet values was a kind of prudishness, manifest in the preaching of "high morals," the condemnation of adultery (wives complained about unfaithful husbands to Communist Party officials), criticism of premarital sex, and the criminalization of male homosexuality. State censorship monitored art, film, and literature for moral and political impropriety, even imposing a virtual ban mentioning or depicting sex in any of these media.

16.2.2   The Reemergence of the Russian Orthodox Church

Perestroika (reconstruction) and *glasnost* (openness) were launched by **Mikhail Gorbachev** in 1985–87 and amplified ideological debates already existing within the Soviet intelligentsia. Conservative forces united against Gorbachev's reforms first. Once Gorbachev was sidelined by Boris Yeltsin and his liberal supporters, who pushed for the complete dismantling of the Soviet Union and liberalization of Russian politics and economic reforms, some sided with the general secretary in the – failed – hope of slowing down the collapse of the established order.

It was the *perestroika* years that saw the reemergence on the Russian public scene of a central conservative institution: the Russian Orthodox Church, or **Moscow Patriarchate**. After decades of official Soviet atheism, which resulted in the repression of religion, the ROC was rehabilitated. In spring 1988, the Kremlin offered its full support for celebrations of the millennium of the Christianization of Russia, commemorating the baptism of Prince Vladimir of Kyiv in 988. Originally intended to be purely a church affair, state backing transformed the celebration into a national event, marking a turning point in *perestroika* and a major shift in Soviet religious policy. The Law on Religious Freedom passed in 1990 and the subsequent policy of transferring some religious edifices back to religious communities definitively transformed the domestic religious landscape.

The ROC's ideological position evolved dramatically over these early post-Soviet years. Between the last years of *perestroika* (1989–91) and the constitutional crisis that opposed the presidency and the **Duma** in fall 1993, the ROC rapidly shifted from a narrative stressing freedom of religion and expression as core democratic values to a discourse on the moral collapse of the state and society. Increasingly, the ROC advocated that religion become the main pillar of the political, cultural, and demographic revival of Russian society. This shift set the stage for the ROC's alliance with increasingly prominent conservative movements in Russian society and politics.

16.2.3   Political Conservatism, from the Margins to the Mainstream

Conservative forces and the ROC have seen their position on the Russian domestic scene evolving gradually from an existence at the margins of political discourse during the first Yeltsin years toward the mainstream at the end of the 1990s, foreshadowing trends during Putin's presidency.

Already in the early 1990s, the ROC had quickly found political partners that opposed the liberal Yeltsin government. They blamed Yeltsin and his team of reformers for the precipitous collapse of the state, the decline of Russia's status on the international scene, and the crime and violence that were ravaging the country's economy. The new **Communist Party of the Russian Federation (CPRF)**, led by

Gennady Zyuganov and built on the ruins of the by-then-forbidden Communist Party of the Soviet Union, crafted a new political language combining communist and Orthodox values. The party called for the revival of Russia's great power status and reconnection with its unique spiritual legacy (March 2002). The alliance between communist forces and the ROC was forged by two key figures, Aleksandr Prokhanov and Aleksandr Podberezkin. Together they crafted a new ideological strand that merged references to Orthodox spirituality, nostalgia for the Soviet regime, and a vague sense of Russia's greatness that transcended historical discontinuities. The ROC also courted the misleadingly named Liberal Democratic Party of the Russian Federation (LDPR) – led by Vladimir Zhirinovsky, a far-right politician known for his eccentricities and provocations – to celebrate Russia's unique spirituality in the face of a decadent West.

At that time, the main conservative language to reaffirm Russia's messianic role in the world, its great power status, and its unique civilization was Eurasianism. A doctrine born among Russian émigrés during the interwar period in Europe and Manchuria, Eurasianism called for Russia's de-Europeanization and de-Westernization by affirming its specific status of being a separate continent between Europe and Asia. It dreamed of a post-Bolshevik Russia in which revolutionary energy would be channeled to recreate a powerful empire led by a Eurasianist elite, whose values would be close to Italian fascism. In the 1990s, neo-Eurasianism emerged as a central trend among the so-called red–brown coalition (those nostalgic for Soviet greatness – the reds – and those inspired by fascism – the browns), embodied by Aleksandr Dugin, a central figure in the Russification of European fascist doctrines. Dugin's neo-Eurasianism has advocated an imperial structure as the most natural form of political regime for Russia, promoted the alliance of several civilizational blocs under Russia's leadership against the Anglo-Saxon world, and backed a totalitarian regime at home (Laruelle 2008). Born in nationalist countercultural circles in the 1990s, the notion of Eurasia has gradually become mainstream and then was captured by the Kremlin and largely emptied of its most radical features.

A plethora of small political and civil society movements representing conservative forces existed around the church, the Communist Party and the LDPR. Many of them were inspired by the Nobel Prize laureate Alexander Solzhenitsyn (1918–2008), one of the intellectual fathers of Russian nationalism who called for Russia to move away from modernity and go back to its national roots. Such movements included the Congress of Russian Communities (KRO), led by future Russian ambassador to NATO and deputy prime minister for the military–industrial complex Dmitry Rogozin, which advocated for the 25 million ethnic Russians living in the "near abroad" (the former Soviet space) and for an ethnocentric demographic revival. There were also several pro-Orthodox movements, among them the Transfiguration Brotherhood, the St. Andrew Foundation, and the Russian

Zemstvo Movement, which engaged the country's then-powerful governors and other high-ranking regional officials to turn their ideas into political reforms and social experiments at both the local and the federal levels (Grek 2022).

Notably, these and other grassroots far-right movements had emerged outside representative politics, which shows the vibrancy of Russia's "uncivil civil society." Chief among these far-right militia groups was Russian National Unity (RNU), a paramilitary movement led by Aleksandr Barkashov; it sent volunteers to post-Soviet conflicts, including to Transnistria, South Ossetia, Abkhazia, and Chechnya (Laruelle 2018). Its brigades received paramilitary training through the RNU's connections to the Ministry of Defense. **Cossacks** were also on the rise, especially in southern Russian cities such as Stavropol' and Krasnodar.

Historically, Cossacks were peasant-soldiers who lived in self-governing entities and were tasked with protecting the borders of the Russian Empire and securing newly conquered territories in Siberia, the Caucasus, and Central Asia. Largely liquidated during the Soviet regime, they reemerged during *perestroika* and obtained recognition of their special status in 1996–97. In 2005, a federal Law on State Service of the Russian Cossacks enabled them to work for all the power ministries: as border-guards for the **FSB** (Federal Security Service), as well as for the Ministry of Internal Affairs, the Ministry of Emergency Situations, and the Ministry of Defense. Today, around 100,000 Cossacks work for law enforcement agencies, either as volunteers or as paid civil servants. Some of them also act as vigilantes, with street action mostly directed against labor migrants, liberals, and pro-LGBTQ+ movements.

Leading up to the parliamentary and presidential elections in 1995–96, Yeltsin's hold on the presidency was increasingly contested by centrist conservatives around the future prime minister and minister of foreign affairs Yevgeny Primakov (1929–2015), Moscow mayor Yury Luzhkov (1936–2019), and General Aleksandr Lebed (1950–2002). These were powerful political actors, who held that Russia needed to avoid the dangers of liberalism and communism, depicted as two extreme ideological positions; instead, they advocated a middle way for Russia, one that put the interests of the state above all else. These centrist figures strengthened patriotic discourse and marginalized liberals and their pro-Western discourse with the ideas that Russia needed a strong state domestically and a great power internationally.

In the legislative elections of 1999, the idea of a specific Russian path of development became consensual even within parties considered liberal: All critically analyzed the country's situation and recognized the need for more authoritarian policies that could meet the Chechen security challenge. The new presidential party, Unity, deftly played on these sentiments, coopting the electoral niche established by Primakov and Luzhkov's rival Fatherland (Otechestvo) party to make Vladimir Putin the embodiment of national consensus and security (Laruelle 2009). Putin's first manifesto, published on December 31, 1999, announced many of the future features of the regime, opposing liberalism as it existed during the Yeltsin era, and advocating a strong state domestically, a revival of patriotism and spiritual values, and Russia's reassertion on the international scene.

16.3 Conservative Forces and the Putin Regime: Inspiration, Cooptation, Repression

Under Putin's long leadership, the relationship between state structures and conservative forces has evolved dramatically. State authorities have gradually coopted conservative groups and narratives, in pursuit of a resonant and consensual ideological construction that speaks to the majority of citizens and marginalizes those associated with pro-Western liberalism. While narratives related to mores, religion, and sexuality are often left to government-funded NGOs, the securitization of identity and memory is directly produced by the Presidential Administration and Putin's inner circles.

Cooptation has worked through offering conservative actors visibility in state-run media, official positions, and state funding, but also by increasingly marginalizing all those who refused this cooptation. During the 2012 "conservative turn" that followed the massive anti-Putin **Bolotnaia protests of 2011–12**, as well during the 2014 annexation of Crimea, the Kremlin allowed some far-right figures, with radical nationalist and reactionary positions (for instance, Aleksandr Prokhanov and Aleksandr Dugin), to access widely state-controlled media channels.

The alliances between conservative forces and the Russian state are multilayered, depending on the moment (whether the Kremlin feels threatened or not by the liberals) and the place (each city and region has its own distinct policy), as well as the different ruling groups. For instance, municipal authorities in some conservative cities of Russia's south, such as Stavropol' and Krasnodar, have allowed more vigilante activism by the Cossacks while some northern cities, for example, Murmansk and Arkhangel'sk, often with more progressive mayors, have restrained them.

All these ambiguities show, above all, how skilled the Kremlin is at coopting movements and ideas that might compete with its own legitimacy. This is especially the case for all those referring to Russian nationalism, which the authorities consider to be a potential mobilizing factor that may support the regime or oppose it, and therefore as something to be brought "under control." This "control" does not mean merely repression and coercion, but also giving some of these movements a space for expression, allowing them to satisfy the needs of some segments of the population, and defusing the possibility of creating a coalition of the unsatisfied.

16.3.1 The Kremlin's Ecosystems and the Conservatism Agenda

This ability to integrate new ideological agendas was made possible by the fact that the Russian regime is a conglomerate of different vested-interest groups, each with their own agenda. Each forms a specific "ecosystem" (a community of different things living together and interacting with each other) made up of institutions, funders, patrons, identifiable symbolic references, ideological entrepreneurs, and media platforms. These different ecosystems exist in permanent motion, making constant readjustments to maintain their equilibrium and trying to penetrate the Russian government and get their agenda adopted at the highest level (Laruelle 2021a).

One can identify four broad ecosystems that compose the "Kremlin": the Presidential Administration itself, the Orthodox realm, the military–industrial complex, and the security services. These four ecosystems interact closely with each other and may have links with groups outside the Kremlin: The military–industrial ecosystem, for instance, still has close links with the Communist Party of the Russian Federation, part of the so-called coopted opposition.

While the Presidential Administration is mostly a bureaucratic structure supervising the different ecosystems and managing their competing interests, as well as a public relations bureau for the president, each of the three other ecosystems contributes to the promotion of some aspects of the conservatism agenda. The Orthodox realm comprises the ROC and myriad small Orthodox civil society groups and lobbyists, more or less close to the church and more or less radical in their values, all united around the promotion of traditional family and sexuality. The military–industrial complex is focused on the advancement of a militarized patriotism and the upbringing of the society and especially of the younger generations. The security services have taken the responsibility of the securitization of history: The main figures from the different security agencies all chair some state-funded institutions in charge of protecting the "historical truth," especially in relation to the memory of World War II in competition with Central and East European countries.

All these ecosystems have contributed to the codification of a new identity language for Russia over the past decade, which culminated with the (second) invasion of Ukraine on February 24, 2022. This language is centered on the notion of Russia's "civilizational security," which includes its classic strategic security, but also a form of "spiritual immunity" against everything identified as the West or liberalism. One of these securitization strategies has been to consolidate a buffer zone between Russia and the North Atlantic Treaty Organization (NATO) and ensure that Ukraine will not join the latter. But this strategic goal has been intertwined with a more primordialist narrative about Ukraine's illegitimacy as a nation and a sovereign state and about its supposed destiny to be part of Russia's orbit – this entanglement was vividly reflected in Putin's speech of February 21, 2022, justifying the war.

Russia's official conservatism was also enshrined when, in the midst of the COVID-19 pandemic in July 2020, Russians were invited to approve a long series of amendments to the constitution, many of which officialized a new form of state ideology, organized around three key pillars: religion, patriotism, and nationalism. This trinity is a remarkably close echo of "Orthodoxy, Autocracy, Nationality," the official doctrine of the Russian Empire under Tsar Nicholas I (1825–55). Yet, unlike under Nicholas I, the contemporary ideological trinity is anything but a rigid doctrine: Its formulation remains evasive and deliberately ambiguous.

The 2020 constitutional amendments mention God ("safeguarding the memory of forefathers who passed on their ideals and faith in God"), allow only opposite-sex marriages, and insist on "family values." Yet, while God is now mentioned in the constitution, Orthodoxy is not recognized as a state religion. Nor does the amendment deny the secularity of the state; it refers to the "memory of fore-fathers," not to today's state institutions, such that the religiosity of society does not contradict the secularity of the state. Of the conservative values that are to be engraved into the new constitution, only opposite-sex marriage appears to be formulated in a manner so straightforward as to forbid the alternative at the highest legal level. The regime has thus tried to avoid legally binding pronounce-ments on divisive topics such as religion and nationalism, saving these for issues where consensus is already secured: patriotism, World War II narratives, and the outlawing of homosexuality.

Let us now focus on the ecosystem that is the most centered around conservatism per se, and not around patriotism or memory wars: the Orthodox realm. It comprises several segments: the church itself, the conservative activists emphasizing the traditional family and **monarchism**, and Russian Islamic institutions advocating their own form of conservatism.

16.3.2 The Church's Ideological Leadership: Successes and Limits

First among equals of these conservative worlds is the ROC, which has become a central actor on the Russian political scene, both institutionally and ideologically. While it drives a large part of the conservative agenda, it is also a complex conglomerate of multiple factions with different outreach to the political spectrum and different ideological views of what the relationship between church and state should be.

Over the past three decades, conservative factions have progressively taken over the Patriarchate, obtaining concessions from the former patriarch, Aleksei II (1990–2008). The latter did not belong to the fundamentalist wing, but he was concerned that some segments might secede and request to join the more conserva-tive and nationalist Russian Orthodox Church Outside Russia (ROCOR), the part of the church that refused to recognize the Soviet regime and was represented mostly among Russian émigré communities. This risk disappeared with the canonical reunification of the ROC and ROCOR in 2007, even if fundamentalist voices can still create dissension within the ecclesiastic institution (Papkova 2011).

Since 2008, the new patriarch, Kirill Gundiaev – formerly Aleksei II's second-in-command in charge of the church's Department of Foreign Relations – has been changing the Patriarchate's ideological line. Kirill has supported a more clearly nationalist narrative, stressing Russia's status as an Orthodox country and claiming a form of Russian ethnonationalism that somewhat conflicts with the state's more multiethnic narrative. Although Patriarch Kirill largely aligns himself with state historical policy – especially when it comes to commemorating the big dates of Russian history, including Soviet history – he has delegated some of the church's ideological initiatives to other influential figures who hold more reactionary views and do not hesitate to position themselves in opposition to the state's agenda. These include Metropolitan Tikhon, a prominent figure who leads a reactionary lobby inside the church.

Leaving aside a handful of small liberal parishes that exist locally but lack influence on the church's politics and policies, the Patriarchate is today divided into three broad groups: a mainstream that embraces Soviet culture and supports the church's rapprochement with the state (it includes mostly neophytes and those who have been ordained as priests over the past two decades) and two more radical strands. Of these more radical strands, the former is sometimes labeled "Orthodox Stalinism," as it combines Orthodox fundamentalism with a cult of strong power (whether that of Ivan the Terrible or Stalin), exalts a Holy Russia with a communist coloration, and criticizes the Moscow Patriarchate and the Kremlin for being too ideologically weak. The latter cultivates continuity with the underground church of the 1930s–50s: Some of its churchmen served time in the GULAG, and it is close to the ROCOR.

The church–state relationship is ambivalent: It is a mutually beneficial alliance that rests on a fragile search by the state to legitimate its hold on power, and the church's attempts to elevate its status as the main source of morality in Russian society. Both actors hope to keep society under control ideologically, yet they sometimes compete in terms of legitimacy (more secular for the state, religious in essence for the church) and long-term goals (regime survival for the state, existence over centuries for the church).

The ROC has invested heavily in its legal and symbolic status to be sure that its newly acquired position cannot be undermined again. Although the Patriarchate maintains that it does not prefer any particular type of political regime, its *Fundamentals of the Social Conception of the Russian Orthodox Church*, issued in 2000, pleads for a political regime grounded in Orthodoxy. The *Fundamentals* stipulates that the Patriarchate recognizes the separation of church and state, yet displays open sympathy for monarchy and theocracy, which the church considers superior forms of polity since they guarantee the symphony of spiritual and temporal powers.

To secure its status, the church has been working hard to become an indispensable and central symbolic resource for the state. In pursuit of this aim, the ROC has supported the Russian state under Putin in its main endeavors: reaffirming the continuity and preeminence of the state (*preemstvennost'*), notwithstanding historical ruptures and spatial discontinuities, and strengthening patriotic attitudes among Russian citizens, with a special focus on the patriotic upbringing of young people. Yet the church maintains its own memory policy independent from the state, with a much more critical view of the Soviet regime and especially of religious repressions. But, besides divergences in interpretation of the Stalinist past, the church and the state cooperate in silencing alternative voices and remembrance, and especially in taking away from the liberals the commemoration of Stalinism, as with the closure of the oldest and most respected civil society association Memorial in December 2021.

The church has also backed the state in its reassertion of a place on the international scene by developing an Orthodox paradiplomacy – with some nuances when the church sees its own interests as somehow contradicting those of the state, as in the relationship to Georgia and Ukraine. In relations to both countries, the Moscow Patriarchate tried to keep channels of communication open even at times of conflict: The Russian Orthodox Church and the Georgian Patriarchate have conducted significant paradiplomacy after the two countries stopped their diplomatic relations after the August 2008 war. After Crimea's annexation by Russia in 2014, the Russian Orthodox Church tried to keep a nuanced narrative that simultaneously affirmed that Ukraine is spiritually part of the "Russian World" and therefore should stay under the Moscow Patriarchate's umbrella, while at the same time preserving the sensibility of its numerous parishes based in Ukraine. That equilibrium game failed in 2018 with the recognition of the Ukrainian Church's ecclesiastical independence (autocephaly) by the Constantinople Patriarchate, and in 2022 with the Moscow Patriarchate's embrace of the Russian state's narrative about the invasion of Ukraine.

In exchange for its support for state policies, the ROC has gained the status of first among equals in terms of religious legislation and informal recognition; has secured its finances with the return of many ecclesiastical properties and some lucrative businesses; and has penetrated the army (the ROC and the Ministry of Defense signed their first partnership as early as 1994 [Adamsky 2019]), the penitentiary world, and more recently the school system, as well as the judicial system around family issues, albeit none of them at the level it would hope for.

Indeed, in recent years, the ROC seems to have plateaued in terms of its efforts to penetrate state institutions and public spaces without provoking discord. The introduction of school classes on "Basics of Orthodox Culture" as part of the portfolio of options offered under the broad umbrella of the course "Fundamentals of Religious Cultures and Secular Ethics," for instance, has not lived up to the church's expectations. In 2017–18, slightly over one-third of Russian families (37 percent) selected the class on Orthodoxy, while 42 percent opted for secular ethics, and 17 percent for world religious cultures (Iakimova 2020). The growing visibility of the church on the urban landscape, as it reclaims property and builds new religious edifices, has likewise sparked tenacious resistance, as in the case of St. Isaac's Cathedral in St. Petersburg, where more than 200,000 city residents petitioned against the cathedral's transformation from a museum into an active church; or in the cases of Torfianka park in Moscow and Malinovka park in St. Petersburg, where people protested against the erection of a new church on their urban green spaces.

Not only does the ROC face resistance from society, but it also tends to be undercut by fundamentalist groups within Russian Orthodox circles. In 2017, for instance, radical Orthodox activists were able to make their voices heard in defense of the last tsar, Nicholas II, as a holy figure. Controversy arose in response to the widely publicized film **Matilda**, which depicts the (well-documented) love story between the young Nicholas II, still only a tsarevich at that time, and ballerina Mathilde Kschessinska. Because the sexual life of the future tsar (and not with his future wife) featured prominently, several church figures argued that the film was blasphemous and called on believers to pray that it be banned, even though the Patriarchate itself did not make any official statements. Several radical Orthodox groups, including the Orthodox paramilitary group Sorok Sorokov, organized prayer sit-ins in the streets near theaters that were showing the film. A henceforth unknown group calling itself Christian State–Holy Russia threatened to commit violent acts if the film was released. It threw petrol bombs at the building that housed the film director's studio and torched cars near Moscow, where flyers displayed the slogan "Burn for *Matilda*."

Fundamentalists made themselves heard again in 2020 when Father Sergei, a charismatic monk in charge of the Sredneural'sk women's monastery in the Ural region, refused to stop mass services during the first months of the COVID-19 pandemic. Defying all public orders – including those of the ROC hierarchy, which he accused of having betrayed the faith – he organized resistance with the help of some Cossacks and mercenaries until he was forcibly arrested and excommunicated. During his dissidence, he contributed to spreading COVID-denialist and antivaccine narratives among a religious segment of the Russian population.

16.3.3 The "Traditional Values" Segment

After the church and closely linked to it, the most influential segment of the conservative field that has succeeded in penetrating state institutions are the groups promoting "traditional values." Very close to the ROC and benefiting from its legitimacy and lobbying, these groups aligned their goals and messages with state-backed patriotism and the "traditional values" agenda (Stoeckl 2016). A large network of conservative civil society organizations is, for instance, working to address some of Russian society's most pressing social ills (support for orphans, the sick and disabled, single mothers, older generations, and so on). Classified as "socially oriented NGOs," these pro-family organizations have benefited from generous grants from different levels of the state administration.

This pro-family segment has developed international connections, including with the World Congress of Families (WCF). Founded in the United States in 1997, the WCF presents itself as a multifaith, multinational coalition that endorses the militant defense of the "natural family" and supports governments with antigay agendas. In Russia, the WCF has worked closely with the Patriarchate to create circles of influence in Moscow around antiabortion campaigners. The pro-family segment focuses on influencing Russian legislation and has authored several of the conservative laws passed in Russia over the past decade, such as the blasphemy law that emerged in the aftermath of the Pussy Riot scandal and punishes "causing offense to religious feelings" (Borenstein 2020), the law forbidding swearing, the "gay propaganda" law, restrictions on abortion, and the law decriminalizing domestic violence. It has also influenced debates on juvenile justice.

Within the Russian government, the pro-family segment can rely on influential supporters among the ranks of senior officials, such as Yelena Mizulina, head of the Duma's Committee on Family, Women, and Children Affairs. Mizulina established an interdepartmental working group to draft antiabortion legislation, and in 2012 she made public a "State Concept of Family Policy until 2025," which was not enacted by the Duma but which proposed a tax on divorce, strengthening the role of the church in family-related legislation, and propaganda in favor of multi-child families, as well as condemning the birth of children out of wedlock. Mizulina is backed by Maksim Obukhov, father of the Russian pro-life movement and founder and chair of the church's antiabortion medical center, Zhizn'. She also worked closely with Father Dmitry Smirnov (1951–2020), who led the Patriarchate's Committee for Family Affairs and the Defense of Motherhood and Childhood. Smirnov was known for his close ties to the military–industrial complex; his blessing of nuclear weapons; and his provocative statements, such as calling common-law wives "unpaid prostitutes" and claiming that abortion in Russia is worse than the Holocaust.

Closely linked with the pro-family narrative one can find groups with a monarchist agenda. A small minority of them have been calling for the return of the Romanovs or wishing to see a new dynasty take the throne of Russia, while a bigger group advocates a form of "Putinian monarchism," that is, a presidential regime that would make Putin president for life (Laruelle 2020). They support a strong state and leader, reduced political rights, conservative or reactionary values, the establishment of Orthodoxy as the state religion, and an aggressive foreign policy. These monarchist figures all work closely with some segments of the ROC and all have entry points inside Putin's inner circles.

Among the most famous figures in this monarchist segment is the world-renowned film director Nikita Mikhalkov, who has produced a number of patriotic films expressing his nostalgia for imperial Russia. He published a *Manifesto of Enlightened Conservatism* that, without calling openly for a return to monarchy, laments the fall of the Romanovs, speaks of monarchism's place in modern Russian conservatism, and lists "imperial norms, principles, and mechanisms of state structure" as key elements of "enlightened conservatism." The Russian political scene has also seen the emergence of a new muse of monarchism, Nataliia Poklonskaia, who positioned herself more clearly in favor of its Romanov variant than its Putinian form. A former procurator general of the Republic of Crimea and then an MP in the Russian Duma, Poklonskaia became an iconic political star in today's Russia. She has demonstrated her devotion to the memory of Nicholas II, even declaring that one of his statues cried – a sign of sanctity in Christianity. In what was probably her most symbolic gesture, she marched in the Immortal Regiment parade of May 9, 2017, with a portrait of Nicholas II – an allusion to tsarism as Russia's core genealogy and Nicholas II as the father of the Russians.

Another proactive monarchist line has been promoted by Vladimir Yakunin, head of the Russian railways from 2003 until he was fired in 2015. Close to Putin since the early 1990s, he has remained one of the Kremlin's means of communicating with the Patriarchate. Yakunin runs the St. André I Foundation (or Andrei Protocletos), one of the largest – and richest – Russian Orthodox foundations, which finances restorations of churches and monasteries, the return of Orthodox relics to Russian soil, cultural exchange programs with the Orthodox churches of the Patriarchate of Jerusalem, celebrations of the reconciliation between the Patriarchate and ROCOR, campaigns to promote traditional family values, and a slew of patriotic programs designed to keep the nationalist flame burning in the hearts of the younger generation.

Since 2014, the new apostle and financial backer of monarchism has been the **oligarch** Konstantin Malofeev, who leads Marshall Capital Partners, an investment fund specializing in the telecommunications market. He founded the Philanthropic Fund of St. Basil the Great, which boasts some thirty programs advocating a broad range of family values (antiabortion groups, assistance to former convicts and single mothers, and so on), providing Orthodox religious education, and offering assistance to Orthodox churches and monasteries. In 2006, Malofeev opened the St. Vasily the Great *gymnasium*, a private boarding institution in the Moscow suburbs that claims to be forming the new Russian elite and instilling monarchist values in them. The gymnasium fosters a tsarist atmosphere, holding traditional balls and hanging portraits of the imperial family and the main aristocratic families on the walls. It reproduces the tsarist education program, with daily prayers in Slavonic and classes in Orthodoxy, Latin, calligraphy, and traditional etiquette. Malofeev launched the first monarchist television channel, Tsargrad – the old

Russian name for Constantinople – inspired, as he himself said, by Fox News, and then took a new step by inaugurating the Two-Headed Eagle, an organization that aims to achieve "the transformation of Russia into a full monarchy." He has been very close to the pro-family segment, funding it and supporting its entry into the political arena, as well as offering a new niche for the infamous Aleksandr Dugin, who broadcasts on Tsargrad.

16.3.4   The Islamic Segment

Of Russia's 146 million inhabitants (if we include the 2 million in annexed Crimea), about 15 million are nominally Muslims, in the sense that they belong to an ethnic group whose cultural background mostly refers to **Islam**. Of course, not all are believers, and even fewer practice Islam. Some self-identify mostly by reference to their ethnicity, without placing any significance on religion; many combine ethnic and religious identities; and a minority considers religious belonging to be the main criterion of their identity. To these 15 million nominally Muslim citizens should be added between 2 and 3 million labor migrants officially documented who come from formerly Soviet and culturally Muslim countries (Uzbekistan, Tajikistan, Kyrgyzstan, and Azerbaijan).

Not only is Islam an integral part of Russia's history and culture, but it has now spread beyond its historical regions (the North Caucasus and the Volga–Urals) to become a pan-Russian phenomenon. These transformations mean that Russia's Islam has gradually lost some of its ethnic and local features and has been normalized as a part of everyday Russianness. This is visible in the massive migration flows of Muslims from the North Caucasus across Russian territory and especially in all Russian metropoles; in the growing use of Russian as the language of Islamic debate; in the birth of a "Muslim public opinion" that transcends ethnic specificities; and in the role played by Muslim republics and constituencies in the Putin regime's electoral legitimacy and ideological construction (Laruelle 2021b).

Russia's main muftiates (the Central Spiritual Administration of Muslims, based in Ufa, Bashkortostan, and the Spiritual Administration of Muslims of the Russian Federation, based in Moscow), as well as leaders of Muslim republics, have played a central role in accompanying, and sometimes even preceding, the regime's progressive officialization of conservative values. The ideology constructed by Ramzan Kadyrov as head of Chechnya, for instance, has been able to blend a militant patriotism that celebrates support for President Putin and classic references to Russia as an Orthodox and ethnically Slavic country, on the one hand, with an ultraconservative Islam inspired by Islamic puritanism and strong anti-Westernism, on the other (Laruelle 2017).

Even leaving aside the extreme case of Kadyrovism, the two muftiates have been playing an active role in promoting conservative values. Islamic leaders have been following the ROC narrative on mores and values, supporting the church's proposal to abolish abortion, decriminalize domestic violence, and ban everything homosexual. The leader of the Spiritual Administration of Muslims of Tatarstan, Kamil Samigullin, for instance, expressed that the Russian constitution should strengthen "traditional moral values," the central one being that a family can be constituted only "by the union of a man and a woman" (Sibgatullina 2022). The ROC and the muftiates speak the same language in terms of Russia's promotion of conservatism against the supposed decadent West. The deputy mufti Damir Mukhetdinov has, for instance, portrayed Russia's Muslim community as grounded in "antiglobalism, defence of traditional values, traditional multiculturalism, and moderate conservatism" (Mukhetdinov 2016, 6–7).

More than a simple pragmatic cooperation between the two religions, a kind of blending of Russian Islam with the heavy symbolic politics of the ROC is observable. The chief mufti of the Ufa-based Central Spiritual Administration of Muslims, Talgat Tadzhuddin, has created for himself the title of "Mufti of All Russia," an obvious echo of his Orthodox counterpart's designation as "Patriarch of Moscow and All Russia." Similarly, he has publicly engaged in a "Muslim" version of some Orthodox rituals, such as sprinkling objects with holy water, and has used the expression "Holy Russia" on several occasions. Moreover, because Islam is interpreted using an Orthodox Christian vocabulary and increasingly in Russian, there is a growing convergence even at the semantic level (Sibgatullina 2020).

Each time the ROC feels that its values agenda is being attacked by the secular or liberal segments of society, it can count on the support of the muftiates in these new cultural wars. During the *Matilda* crisis, the Muslim authorities took the blasphemy charge against the film very seriously and were more repressive than many Russian regions: The autonomous republic of Tatarstan banned the film from public theaters (but not private ones), while local authorities in Chechnya and Dagestan, with the support of Moscow's main mufti, Albir Krganov, asked that the film be banned in their republics and called for a replacement film that would show the last tsar in a better light.

Yet, on some issues, the positioning of Islamic institutions is more complex. For instance, muftiates had to speak against the state on the issue of women being allowed to wear the hijab. Indeed, the muftiates are at risk of being bypassed by more radical, Salafi groups and figures and are increasingly denounced as weak institutions with no role beyond bureaucratic administration of Islam-related matters and little theological legitimacy. This has pushed them to partner as much as possible with both state institutions and the ROC to maintain the fragile balance between the most radical parts of their constituencies and the secular structures. As explained by Gulnaz Sigbatullina, "Muslim religious elites have to find a difficult balance between an endorsement of normative family models and gender roles, on the one hand, and maintaining a moderate interpretation of Islamic norms, on the other. In order to stay on the safe side, a few Muslim leaders follow the tactic of simply approving the ROC rhetoric" (Sigbatullina 2022).

16.3.5   The Ethnonationalist Segment

A final segment of the conservative spectrum, centered on ethnonationalism, exists somewhat more removed from influential political circles. Ethnonationalist circles bring together groups that are more concerned with issues of national identity, ethnicity/race, and immigration than with moral values *and* that opposed the regime during the 2011–12 period of civil protests against Putin's third mandate. These movement were largely dismantled by 2016–17 and have not yet reemerged (Laruelle 2018).

In the early 2000s, the Putin regime adopted a laissez-faire policy toward **far-right street groups**, letting them organize violence against North Caucasians and labor migrants from Central Asia. For years, skinheads – about 50,000 people in the mid-2000s, making Russia the country in the world with the most skinheads – enjoyed a great deal of impunity: The militia and the special forces of the Ministry of Internal Affairs (OMON) only half-heartedly intervened in their attacks and sometimes even tacitly supported them. However, these skinhead groups were gradually dismantled, as was the Movement against Illegal Immigration, one of the most active far-right groups, which sought to act as a power-broker between street activists and nationalist politicians. The Russian Image movement, which existed between 2008 and 2010, represented the last attempt at institutionalized "managed nationalism" – that is, the organization of a far-right group with direct connections inside the Presidential Administration (Horvath 2021). But, from 2010 to 2013, several pogroms against migrants pushed law enforcement agencies, which feared losing control of street violence, to become more repressive.

Since the 2011–12 mass anti-Putin protests, which saw nationalists unite with liberals in denouncing the Putin regime, the authorities have come to recognize the mobilizing potential of ethnonationalism and have become more proactive in limiting it. The Russian legislative framework has since adapted to better silence far-right violence by targeting not only organizations, but also individuals and online activities. Nationalists can be charged under the Criminal Code's "political" articles (prosecution for inciting hatred, that is, for xenophobic speeches at rallies and statements on social networks) or ordinary criminal charges (hooliganism or robbery).

During the 2014 Ukraine crisis that followed the annexation of Crimea, Russian nationalists found themselves divided. Some recognized Putin as having contributed to reunifying the Russian nation and therefore softened their opposition to him, as in the case of Eduard Limonov (1943–2020), the leader of the banned National Bolshevik Party. Others criticized the Kremlin for not "finishing" the job by annexing the region of the Donbas and possibly the rest of eastern Ukraine. They therefore organized the deployment of volunteer fighters to the cities of Donetsk and Luhansk, putting themselves in the ambiguous position of serving unspoken state interests while continuing to complain about the Kremlin's lack of genuine nationalist policies. The fight for Novorossiia – the name given to the territories of eastern Ukraine that were supposed to "rejoin" Russia – became a new battlefield for radical nationalists looking for war theatres. A third, minority group decided to support Ukraine against Russia, seeing in Ukrainian far-right and paramilitary movements such as the Azov Battalion the embodiment of their ideological convictions.

The period 2014–15 was a turning point in the stance taken by Russian authorities vis-à-vis these groups; the former have pursued a decidedly repressive policy against the latter. The main nationalist groups have been dismantled, their websites taken down, and their leaders jailed or forced into exile. The Russian Marches organized on November 4 for the Day of National Unity, long seen as the foremost nationalist demonstration, have also declined in popularity: Whereas between 2011 and 2013 they had around 6,000 participants, by 2019 there were just 1,500 people, divided into two competing marches. The trajectory of the ethnonationalist segment illustrates how refusing state cooptation leads to repression. Meanwhile, conservative movements whose ideological foci were more compatible with the state's objectives have been able not merely to survive, but even to grow in the public space.

16.4   Conservative Values and Russian Society

The success of conservative forces in today's Russia depends, in part, on reaching conservative constituencies with state-endorsed values that are congruent with their own. It remains difficult to identify who these conservative bastions are, as they may live in very different socioeconomic and cultural realities.

16.4.1   Identifying Conservative Constituencies

Russian society is more heavily fragmented in terms of ways of life, access to consumerism, and values than outside observers tend to assume. There are three very different conservative constituencies in society that are potentially of importance for conservative movements that seek to gain broader influence and resonance for their views (Byzov 2018; Laruelle 2022).

First are the **ethnic republics**, especially the traditionally Muslim ones, that have embraced conservative values. Russia's **Muslim population** shares more conservative views, especially on gender issues, than non-Muslim Russians. Moreover, North Caucasian republics, as well as Tatarstan and Bashkortostan, constitute the backbone of the regime's legitimacy, delivering a high share of votes for the presidential party, **United Russia**, and the president. In the last four presidential elections,

Vladimir Putin (**Dmitry Medvedev** in 2008) received on average 88.5 percent of the vote in Muslim republics compared to 67 percent nationwide, while in the parliamentary elections United Russia received an average of 79.5 percent there compared to 55.86 percent nationwide.

Second is the so-called traditionalist periphery, which includes rural villages and small, industrial, and depressed towns that have struggled to survive under the conditions of a market economy without state support. Depending on the region and the time, villages and small towns have tended to vote for the Communist Party and/or for the presidential party, though even when they vote for the communist opposition, they still constitute the "silent majority" on which the regime relies to promote conservative values and a more authoritarian system. They tend to be more conservative in terms of abortion, divorce, sex before marriage, and homosexuality than the residents of big cities.

Thirdly, a segment of the middle class has likewise been calling for social and political stability. This more "bourgeois conservatism" is in large part the result of the dependence on the state of Russia's middle class. The number of state-sector professionals whose jobs depend on the state's economic success (Rosenfeld 2020) grew during the Putin years, and they have demonstrated staunch support for the Putin-era resurgence of patriotism and a great-power narrative. This does not mean they are ready to put these narratives of moral conservatism into practice, as abortion, divorce, and sex before marriage remain very widespread.

16.4.2   Russian Public Opinion on Conservative Values

As conservative political movements have become strong in Russian politics, this raises the question whether these forces indeed speak for Russian society at large, and to what extent their values are shared by the general population. The evidence here is mixed, and varies when it comes to conservative discourses versus conservative practices.

Evidence from a survey conducted in spring 2021 found that only 55 percent of respondents reported belonging to a religion (LegitRuss 2021). Of these, 81 percent identified Orthodoxy as their religion, meaning that approximately 40 percent of Russian population identify as Orthodox believers. What is more, church attendance is very low, estimated at between 2 percent and 6 percent of the population depending on how the question is framed. This level of engagement in religious practice is low and quite similar to those in the most secular countries of Western Europe. This confirms that Russia shares with Europe the trend of "identitarian Christianism," referring to Christian roots as part of national culture and identity to oppose Islam, migrants, or – in the Russian case – the "decadent West," but significantly spurning religious practice.

Except for a small minority of genuine believers, Russians are also not swayed in the ROC's opinion on family matters such as abortion or church marriage. Although considered among the most trusted institutions (usually after Vladimir Putin and just before or just after the army and the security services), the church is still struggling to conquer hearts and minds: Religion ranks very low as a factor in Russians' national identity and a cause for pride. In a 2018 survey, the church was ranked eleventh of fourteen causes that Russians cared about, at only 9 percent, far below "our past and history" (53 percent) and "our land" (35 percent). Even among practicing believers, it stood at just 19 percent.

The conservative forces' ability to make Russian society more conservative faces mixed success. Over time, Russians have become less tolerant of abortion, but public opinion remains quite polarized on the issue. In 2021, Russians were divided almost equally between supporting and opposing abortion, at 46 and 47 percent respectively (LegitRuss 2021). Importantly, most survey data do not paint a picture of a particularly conservative society: Two-thirds favor equality of women and men in the job market (although only half support gender equality in politics), childcare duties are almost unanimously seen as something that should be shared by parents, sex before marriage is accepted by a little more than half of the population, and the ideal family size is held to be between two and three children. Similar trends are visible on the issue of divorce, with a slow rise in the proportion of respondents condemning divorce.

Yet, on many such issues, the gap between attitudes and behaviors is important. While conservatism may prevail discursively, actual behavior tends to be far more liberal, especially when it comes to practices inherited from the Soviet era. For instance, even though an increasing number of Russians describe divorce as reprehensible in public opinion polls, divorce remains common: Russia's ratio of marriages to divorces is in line with the European average. Vladimir Putin even divorced his wife while in office, a risk no American president would take. People across the country largely accept common-law relationships and single motherhood, approve of abortions when a family is poor, and do not believe the man must be the family's only breadwinner. On abortion, Russia's current legislation is more restrictive than its Soviet counterpart, but the restrictions are in line with those of many progressive European countries.

The only topic on which Russia appears unambiguously conservative is homosexuality. For a long time, Russia was only moderately conservative in terms of public attitudes toward homosexuality: In 2005, 51 percent of its population agreed fully or partly with the idea that homosexuals had the same rights as other citizens. But since the deterioration of relations with the West in 2011–14, homophobia has been weaponized by the Russian state as a tool in the competition with the West, encapsulated by the sloganeering of Gayropa, a disparaging portmanteau, "gay Europe" (Riabova and Riabov 2019; Tyushka 2021; Wilkinson 2014; Morris and Garibyan 2021). The peak of homophobic attitudes was reached in 2013, in parallel with state-backed narratives, to the point that we can quite confidently state that this is the most successful case of state influence on moral values. Yet it seems that popular homophobia is on the decline. In 2019, Levada registered the highest level of support for LGBTQ+ rights in the past fourteen years, with 47 percent of respondents agreeing with the statement that "Gays and lesbians should enjoy the same rights as other citizens," compared to 43 percent who disagreed.

16.5   Conclusion

During the first two decades of the new millennium, the Russian regime has succeeded in building an ideological consensus that still speaks to the majority – even if this majority is shrinking – based on a subtle equilibrium of "moderate conservatism," embodied by a series of heavily loaded narratives and restrictive public policies, yet without embracing the agenda of the most reactionary groups. This ideological balance combines broadly shared views on the need for law and order, a strong and efficient state, and the reassertion of great power status, with less consensual views on imposing moral order and regimenting behaviors of Russian citizens. This equilibrium has been an element of stability and strength for the regime, confirming its ability to adapt its ideological plasticity to new contexts and to coopt conservative forces when it needed support against liberal ideas.

Yet this equilibrium is dynamic, evolving, and a potential vector of fragility for the Putin regime. The Russian Orthodox Church has its own agenda of promoting cultural wars against secular ideology and institutions, a memory policy in relation to the Soviet past that diverges from the state one, and a much more conservative agenda in terms of mores than the one the Russian society aspires to. Russia's strongly conservative civil society also offers fertile soil for more radical groups who are ready to confront the state more openly or act as vigilantes, who are sometimes prone to violence, and may rely on a well-developed militia culture. Russia's Islam is shaken by many intracommunity tensions around the definition of "Muslimness," and the muftiates have faced a weakening of their theological and moral legitimacy. Some Russian Muslims call for a more fundamentalist reading of Islamic conservatism that would, here too, contradict the state position.

The invasion of Ukraine has shifted the already difficult equilibrium of the regime. A presentation of Russia's war as a fight between conservatism and depraved liberalism has been boldly formulated by Patriarch Kirill during his

March 6, 2022, sermon offering a metaphysical justification for the war: Loyalty to Western civilization or to Russian civilization would be tested through accepting or rejecting gay parades. But Putin's justification of the war did not mention the issue of conservative values, insisting instead on blaming NATO expansion and the preposterous historical "illegitimacy" of the independent Ukrainian state.

It remains to be seen how the new Russia will be able to maintain its conservative equilibrium post-February 24 or whether it will gradually be supplanted and penetrated by ultraconservative and more reactionary forces energized by the war. Russian society is itself increasingly polarized, with small pockets of vocal resistance to – or at least resilience against – the conservative mainstream and against the war. While conservative values have long helped to stabilize the consensus between the Russian state and society, the war has radicalized state narratives and repressive public policies and renewed legitimacy for the most reactionary groups to become the new normal.

DISCUSSION QUESTIONS

1. Do you see conservatism as a strength or a weakness for the Putin regime?
2. Do you see the war as the product of Russia's official conservatism?
3. How are conservatism and nationalism articulated in the case of Russia?

CORE READINGS

Blackburn, Matthew. 2020. "Mainstream Russian Nationalism and the 'State-Civilization' Identity: Perspectives from Below." *Nationalities Papers*, 49(1), 89–107.
Laruelle, Marlene. 2020. "Making Sense of Russia's Illiberalism." *Journal of Democracy*, 31(3), 115–29.

REFERENCES

Adamsky, Dima. 2019. *Russian Nuclear Orthodoxy: Religion, Politics, and Strategy.* Stanford: Stanford University Press.
Borenstein, Eliot. 2020. *Pussy Riot: Speaking Punk to Power.* London: Bloomsbury Academic Publishing.
Brudny, Yitzhak M. 2000. *Reinventing Russia: Russian Nationalism and the Soviet State, 1953–1991.* Cambridge, MA: Harvard University Press.
Byzov, Leontiy Georgievich. 2018. "Conservative Trends in Contemporary Russian Society." *Russian Social Science Review*, 59(1), 39–58.
Grek, Ivan. 2022. "Russian Conservative Civil Society: The Case of the Zemstvo Movement." *East European Politics*, forthcoming.
Horvath, Robert. 2021. *Putin's Fascists: Russkii Obraz and the Politics of Managed Nationalism in Russia.* London: Routledge.

Iakimova, Olga. 2020. "A Decade of Religious Education in Russian Schools: Adrift between Plans and Experiences." *PONARS Policy Memo*, 676, www.ponarseurasia.org/wp-content/uploads/2020/11/Pepm676_Iakimova_Nov2020.pdf.

Laruelle, Marlene. 2008. *Russian Eurasianism: An Ideology of Empire*. Washington, DC: Woodrow Wilson Press/Johns Hopkins University Press.

2009. *In the Name of the Nation: Nationalism and Politics in Contemporary Russia*. New York: Palgrave Macmillan.

2017. "Kadyrovism: Hardline Islam as a Tool of the Kremlin?" Russie.Nei.Visions, No. 99, March.

2018. *Russian Nationalism: Imaginaries, Doctrines and Political Battlefields*. London: Routledge.

2020. "Ideological Complementarity or Competition? The Kremlin, the Church, and the Monarchist Idea in Today's Russia." *Slavic Review*, 79(2), 345–64.

2021a. *Is Russia Fascist? Unraveling Propaganda East and West*. Ithaca: Cornell University Press.

2021b. "Russia's Islam: Balancing Securitization and Integration," Russie.Nei.Visions, No. 125, November.

2022. "A Grassroots Conservatism? Taking a Fine-Grained View of Conservative Attitudes among Russians." *East European Politics*.

LegitRuss. 2021. "LEGITRUSS: Values-Based Legitimation in Authoritarian States: Top-Down versus Bottom-Up Strategies – The Case of Russia." Report funded by the Research Council of Norway. Project number 300997.

March, Luke. 2002. *The Communist Party in Post-Soviet Russia*. Manchester: Manchester University Press.

Morris, Jeremy, and Masha Garibyan. 2021. "Russian Cultural Conservatism Critiqued: Translating the Tropes of 'Gayropa' and 'Juvenile Justice' in Everyday Life." *Europe-Asia Studies*, 73(8), 1487–1507.

Mukhetdinov, Damir, 2016. *Rossiiskoe musul'manstvo. Traditsii ummy v usloviiakh evraziiskoi tsivilizatsii*. Moscow: Medina.

Papkova, Irina. 2011. *The Orthodox Church and Russian Politics*. New York: Oxford University Press.

Pomerantsev, Peter. 2014. *Nothing Is True and Everything Is Possible: The Surreal Heart of the New Russia*. New York: PublicAffairs.

Putin, Vladimir. 2013. "Meeting of the Valdai International Discussion Club." President of Russia, September 19, http://en.kremlin.ru/events/president/news/19243.

Riabova, Tatiana, and Oleg Riabov. 2019. "The 'Rape of Europe': 2016 New Year's Eve Sexual Assaults in Cologne in Hegemonic Discourse of Russian Media." *Communist and Post-Communist Studies*, 52(2), 145–54.

Robinson, Paul. 2019. *Russian Conservatism*. DeKalb: Northern Illinois University Press.

Rosenfeld, Bryn. 2020. *The Autocratic Middle Class: How State Dependency Reduces the Demand for Democracy*. Princeton: Princeton University Press.

Sibgatullina, Gulnaz. 2020. *Languages of Islam and Christianity in Post-Soviet Russia*. Leiden: Brill.

2022. "Russia's Muslim Leaders on Women's and LGBT+ Rights." *Culture Wars in Europe and Eurasia*, no. 2, February, George Washington University, Illiberalism Studies Program, Washington, DC.

Stoeckl, Kristina. 2016. "The Russian Orthodox Church as Moral Norm Entrepreneur." *Religion, State and Society*, 44(2), 123–51.

Tyushka, Andriy. 2021. "Weaponizing Narrative: Russia Contesting Europe's Liberal Identity, Power and Hegemony." *Journal of Contemporary European Studies*, 30(1), 115–35.

Wilkinson, Cai. 2014. "Putting 'Traditional Values' into Practice: The Rise and Contestation of Anti-Homopropaganda Laws in Russia." *Journal of Human Rights*, 13(3), 363–79.

17 The Russian Media

SCOTT GEHLBACH, TETYANA LOKOT, AND ANTON SHIRIKOV

Fig. 17.1 Russians watch a televised broadcast by President Vladimir Putin, September 2005. Credit: Denis Sinyakov / AFP via Getty Images.

This chapter went to press on the eve of Russia's invasion of Ukraine in February 2022. With the war came unprecedented censorship and the closure of most of what remained of Russia's independent media – an atrocity that abetted a catastrophe.

We dedicate this chapter to those brave citizens, professionals, and amateurs alike, who at great risk continue to provide truthful information to the Russian public.

Abstract

From Gorbachev through Yeltsin to Putin, Russia's media landscape has undergone profound change since the late 1980s. The centralized Soviet system of **propaganda** collapsed, to be replaced by freewheeling broadcast media that were not fully independent of the oligarchs who owned or controlled them. Vladimir Putin brought these media under his control after assuming the presidency in 2000, but for some time he was content to let information circulate in other arenas. That changed with his return to the presidency in 2012. Since then, and especially since widespread protests in 2011 and 2012, state control of the media has been consolidated and extended in various directions, most especially online. Under Putin, new media have emerged, but they too have been subjected to various sanctions and restrictions. The Russian state has for now perfected its control of the media, with uncertain consequences for the stability of Putin's rule.

17.1 Introduction: Russia's Changing Media Landscape

The story of media in postcommunist Russia is a tale of escape from state control, followed by the gradual reemergence of that control under **Vladimir Putin** even as media technology evolved. During Russia's liberalization in the late 1980s and early 1990s, privately owned news organizations emerged, though often these served to promote their owners' political and business interests rather than the interests of a free society. This flawed independence helped to pave the way for the reestablishment of media control in the 2000s, when Vladimir Putin came to power and the government began to seize control of the media – first the broadcast media from which most Russians learned the news, and then a much broader array of media outlets, including in the new digital economy.

After two decades of Putin's rule, the mainstream Russian media – almost all television stations and many prominent newspapers and online media – have been placed firmly under the Kremlin's control, with only a few independent news outlets remaining. Nonetheless, the government's command of the media today is a far cry from Soviet times, when news organizations were all part of an enormous, centralized propaganda machine. Putin's regime has neither the need nor the capacity to censor every word that is uttered or written – not least because of growing **internet penetration** and the proliferation of social media. The Kremlin can make it difficult to access **independent media**, but it cannot silence critical voices completely, and even state-owned media must compete for viewers and advertising revenue. To a degree difficult to imagine under communist rule, curious and active citizens – including especially young Russians, who grew up with the Internet – are still able to acquire multiple perspectives on any unfolding political story.

17.2   The Soviet Era and Gorbachev's Reforms

For seven decades, the Soviet government and the ruling **Communist Party of the Soviet Union** prioritized reshaping society and creating a "new Soviet man" who would be, among other things, loyal to the party and infused with Marxist-Leninist ideology (Hoffmann 2011). In pursuit of this aim, all news and information made available to citizens was carefully filtered. The party and government ministries controlled all media in the country, from central television to local newspapers. A Soviet joke ran: "In Russia, we have two channels on TV. Channel One is propaganda. Channel Two is a KGB officer who tells you to turn back to Channel One" (Popson 1985). By the 1980s, the number of Soviet television channels had increased to six, but the political views they promoted were coordinated by the Propaganda Department of the Communist Party. This centralized control made it impossible for critical or ideologically inconsistent news stories to reach a wide audience. Information from abroad was typically blocked: Foreign radio stations, such as Radio Liberty, were often jammed (Nelson 1997), and only selected Western books and movies were allowed (Roth-Ey 2012).

In the late 1980s, many Russians tasted media freedom for the first time, as Soviet leader **Mikhail Gorbachev**'s reforms began to chip away at central party control. Gorbachev declared a policy of *glasnost* (openness), which held that Soviet citizens could criticize the government's shortcomings and debate its policies. This led to a relaxation of **censorship** and the beginning of real political discussion in the national media, as well as the emergence of tabloid-style journalism (McNair 1991). Popular media outlets such as *Moskovskie Novosti*, *Ogonek*, and *Literaturnaia Gazeta* published critical pieces on Stalin's repressions, the state of the Soviet economy, and other contentious issues.

The overwhelming majority of Russian media organizations were at this stage still owned and controlled by the state, and certain politically sensitive topics were still censored. Nonetheless, by 1990, Western media were allowed to circulate more freely, and vibrant commercial newspapers such as *Kommersant* and *Nezavisimaia Gazeta* and radio stations such as Ekho Moskvy were established. The Soviet state also began to relax control over television, once the pillar of the communist propaganda machine.

These changes played a key role in the anti-Gorbachev putsch of 1991, which foundered in part on the failure of the plotters – a group of communist hardliners – to establish monopoly control of the airwaves. Even as the State Committee on the State of Emergency ordered state media to broadcast pro-putsch messages – an order that was only partially fulfilled, as central state television gave voice to the opposition – protest rallies and other events on the ground were covered by Ekho Moskvy and Voice of America. The failure of the putsch deprived the Communist Party of its remaining legitimacy and accelerated the disintegration of the Soviet state, culminating in the collapse of the Soviet Union at the end of 1991. With the demise of the Soviet state, the former central television channels became separate television stations, some of which were subsequently privatized and commercialized.

17.3   Yeltsin and the Oligarchs: The Media Wars of the 1990s

Boris Yeltsin, the first president of independent Russia, found himself faced with a vibrant, if immature, media market. In this new environment, media – especially television – were often used as weapons in the struggle for power and money. Many commercial television stations, newspapers, and magazines were owned or controlled by "**oligarchs**" – politically powerful businesspeople who did not hesitate to order their employees to vilify business competitors or political enemies (Burrett 2011, 78). In 1996, for example, the television media circled their wagons around Yeltsin to prevent a return to power by the Communists. In 1997, in contrast, media under the control of two of the oligarchs – Boris Berezovsky and Vladimir Gusinsky – attacked the government in retaliation for awarding shares in telecommunications giant Svyazinvest to a rival. In 1999, the presidential fortunes of former prime minister Yevgeny Primakov, a formidable and experienced politician who was initially one of the favorites in the race, were thwarted through a series of malicious television reports. Such instrumental and cynical use of journalism helped to drive Russians' skepticism about the media, which continues to this day (Roudakova 2017).

Throughout the 1990s, Russian journalists enjoyed substantial freedom to criticize government officials, something they could have only imagined in Soviet times. Vladimir Gusinsky's television station NTV, for example, was critical of the First Chechen War, waged during Yeltsin's presidency, with coverage of military and civilian casualties and interviews with Chechen separatists, and NTV's reports on corruption by high-level government officials extended beyond the Svyazinvest episode. In a similar fashion, the newspaper *Nezavisimaia Gazeta*, then controlled by Berezovsky, reported in 1999 on embezzlement and fraud in the Russian Central Bank and other federal agencies, using information from internal government documents.

As a result of such critical reporting, Yeltsin's relationship with news organizations became increasingly tense. The collapse of the Russian state, however, left Yeltsin with less control over media than his Soviet predecessors had possessed, and Yeltsin himself may have been personally disinclined to reimpose that control. Whatever the combination of opportunity and motive, the president and his administration did occasionally attempt to pressure news organizations (Hoffman 1999), but Yeltsin refrained from more dramatic moves such as shutting down or censoring media outlets.

17.4   Putin and the Reemergence of Media Control

The Russian government's perception of such criticism shifted substantially during the first presidential term of Vladimir Putin, Yeltsin's designated successor. Putin emerged as a political actor during the 1990s, and he witnessed at first hand the powerful role that the media could play in political battles. For the new president, independent media were not an irritation but an existential threat.

Broadcast television had for decades been the most influential medium in Russia, given the robust infrastructure built during the Soviet period and the underdevelopment of cable networks and independent print media. This influence played a key role in the 1999 parliamentary elections, over which Putin presided as prime minister. For essentially random reasons related to geography and the placement of television transmitters, the independent television network NTV was available in some parts of the country but not others. The pro-Kremlin Unity party's vote share was about nine percentage points lower in areas where citizens were able to receive NTV's signal than in those where they were not (Enikolopov, Petrova, and Zhuravskaya 2011), a likely consequence of NTV's greater criticism of the government and the coverage it provided to opposition politicians.

Criticism of the government on the airwaves continued into the early months of Putin's presidency. Just before Putin's election as president in 2000, NTV's satirical show *Puppets* portrayed him as an evil gnome from a fairytale. Another major television station, ORT – formally owned by the state but in practice controlled by Berezovsky – had initially supported Putin's bid for power, but after a falling-out between Putin and Berezovsky in the spring of 2000, the station took a more independent stance. In the first major crisis of Putin's presidency, the sinking of the nuclear submarine *Kursk* in August 2000, ORT (as well as NTV) was openly critical, blaming the president for the deaths of the 118 crew members on board.

In actions that both preceded and followed these events, the new Presidential Administration made several decisive moves to restrict independent journalism. In May 2000, less than a week after Putin's inauguration, Vladimir Gusinsky's offices were searched, and a month later the oligarch himself was arrested and charged with fraud. Subsequently released and allowed to flee to Spain, Gusinsky lost control of his media assets, including NTV, which were acquired by the state-owned energy giant Gazprom. In the same year, the government initiated criminal proceedings against Berezovsky, forcing him to leave Russia and sell his stake in ORT to Roman Abramovich, an oligarch with established loyalty to Putin; ORT was renamed Channel One soon after its takeover by the government. Another of Berezovsky's television stations, TV-6, which had been highly critical of Putin's government, was shut down in 2001 on the formal grounds that the company's assets had fallen below its authorized capital.

In a not uncommon view, one observer called the takeover of NTV the beginning of the "prolonged strangulation" of Russian media; another believed it to be "the date of the funeral of the hopes for a new Russia" (both cited in Ennis 2011). Throughout the broadcast media, many leading journalists and media managers either left or were forced out, to be replaced by more loyal personnel. The loss of independence meant dramatic changes to news coverage. Tina Burrett describes the censorship practices newly instituted at Channel One: "The editor-in-chief person-ally watches all reports about President Putin and he alone decides what to cut ... The editor-in-chief receives directions on what to show and what not to show from [the] director general ... [who] receives his orders directly from the Kremlin Press Office" (Burrett 2011, 76). The Kremlin also provided TV managers with so-called stop lists of politicians or public figures who were not to be invited as guests or covered in the news. At least on television, the freewheeling – if often commercially biased – reporting of the 1990s was over.

17.5   The Limits of Media Control

Russia's backsliding into media authoritarianism did not, however, mean a return to Soviet-era censorship, when both television and the press were heavily constrained by the directives of the Communist Party, and their reporting reflected the official Soviet ideology. On the contrary, throughout the early Putin era, Russian media maintained some degree of pluralism (Oates 2007). Whereas television stations were put under the direct or indirect control of the government, many other media organizations remained relatively independent. As Putin himself stated in an inter-view with the US network NBC News in July 2006, with more than 3,500 radio and television companies and in excess of 40,000 print outlets, the Kremlin "could not control them all even if we wanted to" (Putin 2006).

In his premise, Putin was almost certainly correct. Putin was clearly willing to do what it took to hold on to power, but he was not interested in fundamentally changing society. During his first two terms in office, it seemed sufficient to seize the "**commanding heights**" of the media industry (Gehlbach 2010). First and foremost, this meant controlling the national television networks that provided most Russians with news about their country and the rest of the world.

Below the commanding heights, the Kremlin's control of the Russian media was therefore incomplete. What is more, some segments of the media market witnessed a substantial increase in professionalism during the first decade of Putin's rule. Several influential business newspapers and magazines emerged and became known for their journalistic integrity and the quality of their investigative reporting. That list included the business dailies *Kommersant* (owned until 2006 by the exiled oligarch Boris Berezovsky) and *Vedomosti* (initially a joint venture of the

Financial Times and the *Wall Street Journal*), as well as *Forbes Russia* and *BusinessWeek Russia*. The rise of independent business journalism was propelled by fast economic growth during Putin's first two presidential terms. A surge in entrepreneurial activity and in living standards created a robust advertising market that, in turn, supported professional journalism – between 2000 and 2008, print and radio advertising in Russia grew sixfold (ACAR 2019) – though this greater independence may have paradoxically created an incentive for the state to eventually seize control (Gehlbach and Sonin 2014).

Several other independent news outlets grew in popularity and influence. *Novaya Gazeta*, a newspaper founded in 1993 with the help of former Soviet leader Mikhail Gorbachev, soon turned into a prominent investigative outlet that reported on the war in Chechnya, government corruption, police brutality, and money-laundering, among other topics. The high-quality news magazine *New Times* played a similar role. Ekho Moskvy, a radio station formerly owned by Vladimir Gusinsky alongside NTV, became a household name among liberal-minded and pro-Western Russians, even though its majority shareholder was the state-owned Gazprom. (The station turned a profit, which may have helped to guarantee its independence, and the Kremlin may have valued the window on the urban intelligentsia that Ekho Moskvy provided.)

Finally, the emergence and development of new independent media were aided by the proliferation of the Internet (known colloquially in Russia as the **RuNet**). In 2000, when Putin became president, only 2 percent of the Russian population had internet access. By 2010, this had increased to 43 percent (ITU 2021). This new audience was younger, wealthier, and eager for news. The first to reap the benefits of this interest in online news were several media outlets established in the late 1990s and early 2000s, including Lenta.ru, Rbc.ru, and Gazeta.ru. Initially little more than news aggregators, by the early 2010s these outlets, alongside new entrants such as cable news station Dozhd, which attracted viewers with its extensive coverage of antigovernment protests in 2011, were putting substantial emphasis on original news reporting and investigative work.

17.6   Pressure on Independent Media

Although many Russian media remained private in the Putin era, they were often not free of Kremlin influence. In important cases, the Kremlin encouraged loyal oligarchs to take ownership. Such indirect control allowed the government to deny its involvement in editorial decisions, even as the new owners acted as de facto agents of the state.

In 2006, for example, Alisher Usmanov, a billionaire born in Uzbekistan who is best known in the West as a major shareholder of Arsenal Football Club in the UK, purchased the company that published *Kommersant*, replacing its top management. At first Usmanov appeared not to interfere with journalists' work, but over time the newspaper's coverage became less edgy and more favorable to the government. Journalists who covered politics with a critical eye were eventually fired; those who remained learned to be more careful when writing about the Kremlin or the opposition.

A similar story concerns Yury Kovalchuk, a close friend of Vladimir Putin. In 2008, Kovalchuk created the National Media Group (NMG), which quickly became one of Russia's largest media companies (Lipman 2014, 183). By late 2021, NMG had acquired control of four major national television stations, dozens of cable channels, and several prominent newspapers. Such a media conglomerate could not have emerged without the support of the Kremlin, and NMG responded in kind. Previously independent news outlets adopted a more propagandistic orientation, closely mirroring the political coverage of state-run television stations such as Channel One.

Independent media were also subjected to economic and legal pressure. Such tactics were on display in the case of Natalia Morar, an investigative journalist for the *New Times*. After reporting in late 2007 on a Kremlin slush fund used to finance political parties, Morar (a Moldovan citizen but permanent Russian resident at the time of the incident) was barred from entering the country, and the magazine's advertisers disappeared overnight (Lipman 2009).

In addition, many independent journalists faced the very real threat of physical violence. Between 1992 and 2021, eighty-two journalists were killed in Russia. The Committee to Protect Journalists suspects government or military officials in at least a third of these deaths (see https://cpj.org/data), including the 2006 high-profile killing of *Novaya Gazeta* investigative journalist Anna Politkovskaya, who had reported on human rights violations during the Second Chechen War and on murders and torture in postwar Chechnya. Although the involvement of state officials could not be proven definitively in most cases, the failure to bring the actual organizers of these crimes to justice created an atmosphere of impunity, such that the threat of death or physical harm remained a constant fear for many investigative journalists.

Russian media managers, especially at the national broadcast networks, learned to walk a fine line, generally echoing the Kremlin's position on issues of the day, while also crafting messages to avoid alienating viewers. It was an old lesson, relearned. Soviet TV professionals understood that unadulterated propaganda is generally ineffective: Viewers realize that they are being fed the party line, and they fall back on whatever they are predisposed to believe (Mickiewicz 2008). Media under state control therefore provide enough real information to keep viewers guessing about the line between fact and fiction. This can be especially effective when high-quality information is scarce. Such was the case during the 2008 Russo-

Georgian War, when Russian viewers were treated to a mix of images of genuine suffering by South Ossetians, whom the Russian government supported in their conflict with the Georgian government, and apparently inflated casualty counts. In contrast, when outside information is readily available, as when external oil price shocks cause the value of the ruble to decline, Russian television media are compelled to report bad news – but try to change the narrative by blaming external actors (Rozenas and Stukal 2019).

To a degree unimaginable during the Soviet period, **cable and satellite television,** and increasingly the Internet, compete for the public's time. Russian citizens are therefore more likely than were Soviet citizens to change the channel or simply turn off the television if they are dissatisfied with what is being broadcast. This was demonstrated in dramatic fashion after the takeover of NTV in early 2001. With the change in editorial policy and departure of many of the network's veteran journalists, NTV's market share dropped from 17.9 percent in 2000 to 12.6 percent in 2001 (Gehlbach and Sonin 2014). The lesson, which the Kremlin learned the hard way, is that control of the commanding heights may not be sufficient to ensure a captive audience for propaganda. As a result, the state turned to control of other media, as discussed below. In addition, state media employees worked to make news reports more engaging, producing a hybrid format of propaganda that has been called "agitainment" (Tolz and Teper 2017). To that end, journalists enjoyed at least a measure of creative, though not political, freedom (Schimpfössl and Yablokov 2014) – a situation again reminiscent of the Soviet period, when film directors worked to produce "quality" films that nonetheless conveyed a propaganda message (Belodubrovskaya 2017).

17.7   The (Re)Consolidation of Media Control

The decade since 2012 has seen a tightening of state control over traditional and online media, alongside the growing exclusion of opposition actors from mainstream news. State-sponsored propaganda has largely replaced real news in the federal broadcast media, with news bulletins and talk shows such as Dmitry Kiselev's *Vesti Nedeli* promoting an agenda that extols the virtues of a strong and sovereign Russian state that stands in opposition to so-called Ukrainian fascists and an "immoral" West that promotes homosexuality. Everything – from the Sochi Olympics (hosted by Russia in 2014, the Olympics were trailed by numerous allegations of corruption and widespread evidence of doping that were not reported in state media) to the annexation of Crimea and the ensuing war with Ukraine – is placed into a strategic narrative that emphasizes a powerful yet benevolent "Russian World." Highly staged and ritualistic televised events, such as Putin's annual call-in show *Priamaia Linia* (see Wengle and Evans 2018; Chapman 2021), help convey an image of competence that forestalls the need for overt repression (Guriev and Treisman 2019, 2020).

Meanwhile, however, independent investigative media and opposition actors have come to rely on digital platforms and networked media to spread alternative narratives about infighting, corruption, and human rights violations among Russian officials. December 2011 was a pivotal moment in this transformation. Widespread allegations of fraud in that month's parliamentary elections pushed the Russian population into the streets and the online public sphere, sparking the largest mass protests since the early 1990s. Russian opposition forces and intellectual elites were able to mobilize large rallies in Moscow and smaller protests across the country, with participants decrying electoral abuses and calling for an end to Putin's rule.

Shut out by the mainstream media, the organizers of this "winter of discontent" turned to comparatively unobstructed Internet-based media and to social media to boost engagement, coordinate protest rallies, and provide evidence of protest numbers, which the state media tended to downplay. A "war of frames" emerged between state-controlled media and independent sources around the potential impact of the protests (Oates and Lokot 2013). While state-run news channels admitted only that citizens were dissatisfied with the political process, most independent private media and Internet-based sources were far more critical of the regime.

The Kremlin grew increasingly worried about the Internet's destabilizing potential following these events. It went to considerable lengths to wrest control of the digital space away from diverse private actors and to centralize internet governance, media censorship, and content regulation. Roskomnadzor – the Russian government's regulatory body overseeing the Internet, media, and telecommunications – took on a more prominent role in enforcing rules and restrictions. A host of new laws limiting foreign ownership of media and policing online speech, as well as recent legislation aimed at securing greater control over national internet infrastructure, exemplifies this push for consolidation of state control.

17.8   New Restrictions on Media Freedom and Online Expression

Spooked by the unrest, Russian authorities quickly approved a series of repressive regulations aimed at further restricting media freedom and stifling free expression online. Criminal defamation was reintroduced in a law adopted in 2012, providing for large fines or weeks of forced labor as punishment. Another restrictive law that came into force in 2012 granted unprecedented blocking powers to Russian telecommunications regulator Roskomnadzor and other state bodies (Rothrock 2012). Still another 2012 federal law mandated the creation of a "blacklist" registry of websites that disseminated allegedly illegal or otherwise harmful material. Websites could be added to the blacklist extrajudicially, and critics worried the new measures would be used to directly censor online content (Rothrock 2012).

Alongside restrictions aimed at impeding the role of the Internet as an alternative source of news and a space for debate, the Kremlin further expanded its efforts to control independent media outlets. In typical fashion, this was achieved primarily through the transfer of media ownership, as well as through indirect political pressure. An example of the latter came in January 2014, when Dozhd, one of the few independent television channels in Russia to openly cover the 2011 protests, faced state pressure over a controversial audience poll about the siege of Leningrad during World War II that asked viewers whether Soviet authorities should have surrendered Leningrad to the Germans to save hundreds of thousands of lives. After multiple complaints and an investigation, the channel was removed from Russian cable networks and forced to abandon its broadcasting studio, temporarily moving to a private apartment to continue broadcasting online.

Such developments were not limited to broadcast media. In March 2014, Russia's top news website, Lenta.ru, lost its editor-in-chief, Galina Timchenko, who was fired by owner Aleksandr Mamut after repeated warnings from Russian censors; Timchenko was replaced by a pro-Kremlin editor with experience at a pro-Kremlin internet publication. This personnel change at the top led to mass resignations among Lenta.ru's staff, who went on to found Meduza, a new independent media outlet based in Latvia, with Timchenko at the helm. Meduza began work in October 2014 and quickly gained popularity for its Russia-focused reporting and investigations. Alongside Dozhd, Meduza regularly covers issues that receive little to no coverage in state-run media, including corruption, attacks on free speech, domestic violence, and Russia's involvement in international conflicts.

Several new media laws have created challenges for these and other independent media outlets. These laws impose high penalties on newsrooms and journalists for violating "anti-extremist" regulations (discussed further below) and set limits on the share of foreign ownership in media companies (Wijermars and Lehtisaari 2020). The business daily *Vedomosti*, jointly owned by three Western publishing houses, was sold to Russian media entrepreneur Demyan Kudryavtsev in 2015, ahead of a new law prohibiting foreign entities from owning more than 20 percent of Russian media companies; the chief editor was replaced two years later. In 2020, the newspaper changed hands once again. The new editor-in-chief, Andrei Shmarov, was accused of censoring articles critical of Putin's constitutional reforms and investigations into state oil giant Rosneft; several editors resigned in protest.

A similar fate befell the online business news outlet RBC, owned by oligarch Mikhail Prokhorov, which faced pressure in May 2016 after reporting on corruption among Putin-friendly elites as part of the Panama Papers investigation. Its editorial team was ousted, and the new editors caused a scandal in July 2016 by introducing "new rules" for acceptable reporting and "double white lines" that RBC's journalists could not cross; details of the editorial meeting were soon leaked to the media. Such self-censorship complemented the legal restrictions, further limiting independent reporting.

17.9 The Rise of New Russian Media

To fill the void left by the crackdown on Russia's increasingly fragile media sphere, new independent outlets emerged. Some, like Meduza, operated in exile, while others resorted to crowdfunding to keep their operations afloat. This period also saw the significant diversification of the independent media sector and the emergence of advocacy-oriented outlets. MediaZona, founded by members of the feminist protest and art collective Pussy Riot, began shining a light on Russia's labyrinthine prison system in 2013. Takie Dela started reporting on human rights, social issues, and charity work in 2015. The second half of the 2010s was also characterized by the proliferation of outlets focused on regional and local reporting, such as Holod, Batenka.ru, 7x7, and Bumaga.

A number of new investigative media projects specializing in anticorruption investigations and open-source intelligence also emerged during this period, including The Insider, Proekt, Otkrytye Media, and Vazhnye Istorii (IStories). Their sleuthing, in turn, has faced tough competition from nonjournalist civic organizations doing similar anticorruption work, such as **Alexei Navalny**'s Anti-Corruption Foundation. Navalny's slickly produced video blockbusters targeting the illicit wealth of top Kremlin officials and oligarchs have racked up millions of views on YouTube and made Navalny and his allies the prime targets of Kremlin ire.

These innovative independent newsrooms had to compete for attention with emerging popular Kremlin-friendly media tabloids such as LifeNews, as well as the Byzantine network of anonymous channels publishing political commentary, conspiracy theories, and insider leaks on Telegram, Russia's most popular messaging platform (Lokot 2018; Klishin 2020).

To keep up with the changing media landscape and to capitalize on the growing role of information-sharing online, the Russian state also hastened to reform its own media assets. In 2013, a presidential decree liquidated two of Russia's oldest state-media institutions, the state-owned news agency RIA Novosti (established in 1941) and the Kremlin's international radio station, Voice of Russia (founded in 1929). In their place emerged the new international media holding Rossiia Segodnia, or Russia Today. This new entity, headed by fervently pro-Kremlin TV anchor Dmitry Kiselev, was branded by critics as an even more powerful state "propaganda machine" (in the words of liberal website editor Roman Fedoseev, as quoted by Stephen Ennis [2013]). It also incorporated RT, the state-funded foreign-language TV station led by

Margarita Simonyan, which was formerly known as Russia Today (hence the name of the new company).

The proliferation of state efforts to usurp media audiences in both traditional and online media spaces is evidence of the Kremlin's growing realization that it is no longer enough to retain control of national broadcast media alone. The diversification of Russians' media consumption habits and the relatively low bar for creation of successful digital media operations have led Russian regulators and officials to seek pervasive control of both national media and the Internet.

17.10   The Perfection of Control

Kremlin control over the media expanded still further in the late 2010s and early 2020s, as control over digital media and communications became part of a national governance and security agenda. Driving this change was further dramatic growth in internet penetration – up from 43 percent in 2010 to 85 percent in 2020 (ITU 2021). As this chapter was written, some 42 and 39 percent of Russians, respectively, received their news from social media and internet news sites (Levada Center 2021).

Key legislative changes have contributed to the further normalization of state censorship in digital spaces, targeting media outlets, NGOs, and private citizens. These include an infamous "bloggers' law" that required popular bloggers with more than 3,000 daily views to register with the state and disclose their personal information; a law creating a state-run list of "organizers of information distribution" and requiring social networks, portals, and similar sites to register and share certain data with the state; and measures limiting the anonymous use of public wi-fi networks and banning sales of prepaid SIM cards to customers without a state ID.

Some of the most far-reaching censorship- and surveillance-oriented measures have been adopted in the past several years. These include a data localization law that came into force in 2016, requiring internet companies to store Russian users' data on servers located within Russia. Although some companies (for example, eBay, Booking.com, and Samsung) have complied with the demands, others have yet to do so and have been fined or threatened with being blocked. The professional social network LinkedIn has been blocked in Russia since 2016 for failing to comply with the legal requirements (Lunden 2016).

Another comprehensive legal tool is an "anti-extremism" package of amendments, which was adopted in the summer of 2016 and took effect in 2018. This includes measures such as increased sentences for the use online of "extremist" language (a designation that state authorities can apply with great discretion), a push for internet companies to share encryption keys with the state and to decrypt user communications, and requirements to store user communications for six months and metadata for up to three years (Luganskaia 2017). In 2018, Russian censors used these legal grounds to block the Telegram messaging service after it refused to share encryption keys with law enforcement. The attempt proved mostly unsuccessful due to Telegram's sophisticated circumvention efforts and the state's clumsy blocking approach; the ban was lifted in 2020.

Social media content is regularly deleted or blocked on grounds of intolerance or disrespect toward government officials, and users have been fined and even jailed for posting, sharing, or liking content deemed to contain extremist language, calls to mass disorder, or unverified information about public figures. Data from Russia's Supreme Court show that convictions under the extremism charge more than tripled between 2012 and 2017; a large number of these have involved online activity (Gainutdinov and Chikov 2018).

The Kremlin's persistent efforts to gain greater control over online communications and critical expression on the Russian Internet came to a head in 2019 with the implementation of a comprehensive "sovereign Internet" strategy. A set of new regulations and technical upgrades aimed at more autonomy and state control over internet infrastructure, the "sovereign Internet" was presented as a means of protecting Russian cyberspace from external threats (Epifanova 2020). So far, however, it has mostly been used to consolidate control over information flows within Russia's borders, imposing new centrally controlled and less transparent website-blocking mechanisms and targeting opposition websites and social media platforms.

The first half of 2021 saw yet another wave of targeted economic and legal attacks on independent media: Multiple outlets and individual journalists were designated "foreign agents" by the state. The label applies to those deemed to be "involved in political activity" in the interests of "foreign entities" or "receiving assistance from abroad." Meduza, The Insider, and Dozhd have all made the list, along with the US-funded Radio Free Europe/Radio Liberty. The foreign agent legislation requires designated organizations and individuals to register with the state, regularly report on their activities, and indicate their foreign agent status with an obligatory label on any content they distribute, including social media posts (Kartsev 2020). Those labeled have already seen a swift decline in advertising revenues, and a number of independent journalists have left Russia, fearing further persecution. These developments indicate that independent media in Russia are facing an increasingly uncertain and fragile future, even as state-run outlets continue to enjoy government funding.

These ongoing efforts to install tight controls on information flows and news coverage demonstrate the Russian state's push for further control of the media.

This now extends across traditional media operations and less formal digital information channels, where state-sponsored propaganda and the censorship of critical voices combine to skew political debate and coverage of elections and social unrest. Some scholars have described this evolving regime as "**networked authoritarianism**" (Maréchal 2017; Greene 2012), as the state aspires to control political and social life more tightly, while investing in digital technologies and communications infrastructure. As a result of these efforts, Russians have less access to reliable information and unbiased media coverage. Alternative viewpoints are still available, but increasingly they are restricted to those with a substantial interest in current affairs and a high degree of media sophistication, including those young Russians who are able to navigate obstacles online in search of unbiased information.

17.11   Conclusion

Putin's first two terms in office, from 2000 to 2008, saw the imposition of state control over the most important national broadcast media. Since his return to the presidency in 2012, this control has been expanded in various directions, including most especially online. Although independent voices are still available, to an extent inconceivable during the Soviet period, the space for free expression has steadily shrunk over time. What in 2008 seemed a fragile system of censorship and propaganda today is more all-encompassing, as direct control of the "commanding heights" and indirect control through proxy owners is buttressed by legislation that extends the state into new arenas and imposes sanctions for critical expression.

Time will tell whether this new system contributes to the stability of the Putin regime. The dilemma of authoritarian rule is that censorship deprives not only the general public, but also the autocrat himself of information (Wintrobe 1998). The momentary "perfection" of information control may paradoxically leave the regime blind to destabilizing changes in Russian society. Yet creating space for criticism poses its own risks, as Putin surely remembers from Gorbachev's policy of *glasnost*. Either path is a gamble. For now, it seems that Putin has chosen the former.

DISCUSSION QUESTIONS

1. Were Russian media free and independent in the Yeltsin era? Why or why not?
2. Compare the relationship between the Russian government and the media under Boris Yeltsin and under Vladimir Putin. What was similar and what was different in these two eras?
3. What is the role of independent media in authoritarian regimes such as Putin's Russia? Can these media influence the politics of such countries?

REFERENCES

ACAR (Association of Communication Agencies of Russia). 2019. "Ob"em reklamnogo rynka Rossii v 2000–2018," www.akarussia.ru/node/7849.

Belodubrovskaya, Maria. 2017. *Not According to Plan: Filmmaking under Stalin.* Ithaca: Cornell University Press.

Burrett, Tina. 2011. *Television and Presidential Power in Putin's Russia.* London: Routledge.

Chapman, Hannah. 2021. "Participatory Technologies and Regime Support in Putin's Russia." *Comparative Political Studies*, 54(8), 1459–89.

Enikolopov, Ruben, Maria Petrova, and Ekaterina Zhuravskaya. 2011. "Media and Political Persuasion: Evidence from Russia." *American Economic Review*, 101(7), 3253–85.

Ennis, Stephen. 2011. "Ten Years On from the 'Storming' of Russia's NTV." BBC Blogs, April 21, www.bbc.co.uk/blogs/collegeofjournalism/entries/39d401d5-f936-319a-ac7a-8e3104979810.

2013. "Putin's RIA Novosti Revamp Prompts Propaganda Fears." BBC News, December 9, www.bbc.com/news/world-europe-25309139.

Epifanova, Alena. 2020. "Digital Sovereignty on Paper: Russia's Ambitious Laws Conflict with Its Tech Dependence." *Russia File,* Kennan Institute, Wilson Center, October 23, www.wilsoncenter.org/blog-post/digital-sovereignty-paper-russias-ambitious-laws-conflict-its-tech-dependence.

Gainutdinov, Damir, and Pavel Chikov. 2018. "Internet Freedom 2017: Creeping Criminalisation." Agora International, http://en.agora.legal/articles/Report-of-Agora-International-"Internet-Freedom-2017-Creeping-Criminalisation"/8.

Gehlbach, Scott. 2010. "Reflections on Putin and the Media." *Post-Soviet Affairs*, 26(1), 77–87.

Gehlbach, Scott, and Konstantin Sonin. 2014. "Government Control of the Media." *Journal of Public Economics*, 118, 163–71.

Greene, Samuel A. 2012. "How Much Can Russia Really Change? The Durability of Networked Authoritarianism." Policy Memo, PONARS Eurasia, www.ponarseurasia.org/memo/how-much-can-russia-really-change-durability-networked-authoritarianism.

Guriev, Sergei, and Daniel Treisman. 2019. "Informational Autocrats." *Journal of Economic Perspectives*, 33(4), 100–27.

2020. "A Theory of Informational Autocracy." *Journal of Public Economics*, 186, 104–58.

Hoffman, David. 1999. "War Reports Limited on Russian TV." *Washington Post*, October 10.

Hoffmann, David L. 2011. *Cultivating the Masses: Modern State Practices and Soviet Socialism, 1914–1939.* Ithaca: Cornell University Press.

ITU (International Telecommunications Union). 2021. "Percentage of Individuals Using the Internet: Russia Country ICT Data 2021," www.itu.int/en/ITU-D/Statistics/Documents/statistics/2021/PercentIndividualsUsingInternet_Nov2021.xlsx.

Kartsev, Dmitry. 2020. "What You Need to Know about Russia's Updated 'Foreign Agent' Laws." Meduza, December 28, https://meduza.io/en/feature/2020/12/28/what-you-need-to-know-about-russia-s-updated-foreign-agent-laws.

Klishin, Ilya. 2020. "Anonymous Telegram Channels Are Shaping Russia's Daily Life." *Moscow Times*, September 29, www.themoscowtimes.com/2020/09/28/anonymous-telegram-channels-are-shaping-russias-reality-a71588.

Levada Center. 2021. "Sotsialnye seti v Rossii." February 23, www.levada.ru/2021/02/23/sotsialnye-seti-v-rossii/.

Lipman, Maria. 2009. "Media Manipulation and Political Control in Russia." Chatham House Programme Paper 09/01, Chatham House, London, https://carnegiemoscow.org/2009/02/03/media-manipulation-and-political-control-in-russia-pub-37199.

——— 2014. "Russia's Nongovernmental Media under Assault." *Demokratizatsiya: The Journal of Post-Soviet Democratization*, 22(2), 179–90.

Lokot, Tetyana. 2018. "Telegram: What's In an App?" Point and Counterpoint. PONARS Eurasia, www.ponarseurasia.org/point-counter/telegram-whats-app.

Luganskaia, Dariia. 2017. "OpenEconomy: Kak Rossiiskie vlasti budut kontrolirovat' Internet. Tri osnovnykh sposoba." OpenRussia, April 23. https://openrussia.org/notes/708721/.

Lunden, Ingrid. 2016. "LinkedIn Is Now Officially Blocked in Russia." TechCrunch, November 17, https://techcrunch.com/2016/11/17/linkedin-is-now-officially-blocked-in-russia/.

Maréchal, Nathalie. 2017. "Networked Authoritarianism and the Geopolitics of Information: Understanding Russian Internet Policy." *Media and Communication*, 5(1), 29–41.

McNair, Brian. 1991. *Glasnost, Perestroika and the Soviet Media*. London: Routledge.

Mickiewicz, Ellen. 2008. *Television, Power, and the Public in Russia*. Cambridge: Cambridge University Press.

Nelson, Michael. 1997. *War of the Black Heavens: The Battles of Western Broadcasting in the Cold War*. Syracuse: Syracuse University Press.

Oates, Sarah. 2007. "The Neo-Soviet Model of the Media." *Europe–Asia Studies*, 59(8), 1279–97.

Oates, Sarah, and Tetyana Lokot. 2013. "Twilight of the Gods? How the Internet Challenged Russian Television News Frames in the Winter Protests of 2011–2012." *SSRN Electronic Journal*, June 28, https://papers.ssrn.com/sol3/papers.cfm?abstract_id=2286727.

Popson, Tom. 1985. "From Russia, With Jokes: Soviet Comedian Yakov Smirnoff Starts." *Chicago Tribune*, January 11.

Putin, Vladimir. 2006. "Interview with NBC Television Channel (USA)." July 12, http://en.kremlin.ru/events/president/transcripts/23699.

Roth-Ey, Kristin. 2012. *Moscow Prime Time: How the Soviet Union Built the Media Empire That Lost the Cultural Cold War*. Ithaca: Cornell University Press.

Rothrock, Kevin. 2012. "Russia: A Great Firewall to Censor the RuNet?" Global Voices, July 10, https://globalvoices.org/2012/07/10/russia-a-great-firewall-to-censor-the-runet/.

Roudakova, Natalia. 2017. *Losing Pravda: Ethics and the Press in Post-Truth Russia*. Cambridge: Cambridge University Press.

Rozenas, Arturas, and Denis Stukal. 2019. "How Autocrats Manipulate Economic News: Evidence from Russia's State-Controlled Television." *Journal of Politics*, 81(3), 982–96.

Schimpfössl, Elisabeth, and Ilya Yablokov. 2014. "Coercion or Conformism? Censorship and Self-Censorship among Russian Media Personalities and Reporters in the 2010s." *Demokratizatsiya: The Journal of Post-Soviet Democratization*, 22(2), 295–311.

Tolz, Vera, and Yuri Teper. 2018. "Broadcasting Agitainment: A New Media Strategy of Putin's Third Presidency." *Post-Soviet Affairs*, 34(4), 213–27.

Wengle, Susanne, and Christine Evans. 2018. "Symbolic State-Building in Contemporary Russia." *Post-Soviet Affairs*, 34(6), 384–411.

Wijermars, Mariëlle, and Katja Lehtisaari. 2020. "Introduction: Freedom of Expression in Russia's New Mediasphere." In Mariëlle Wijermars and Katja Lehtisaari (eds.), *Freedom of Expression in Russia's New Mediasphere*, pp. 1–14. London: Routledge.

Wintrobe, Ronald. 1998. *The Political Economy of Dictatorship*. New York: Cambridge University Press.

18 Civil Society in Russia: Compliance with and Resistance to the State

NATALIA FORRAT

Fig. 18.1 Regional administration building, Kemerovo, Russia, March 2014. Credit: Author's photo.

The bearer of sovereignty and the only source of power in the Russian Federation shall be its multinational people.

Constitution of the Russian Federation, Article 3.1

Abstract

Russian citizens view the state simultaneously as their leader and their oppressor. They want their state to be a strong, benevolent, and fair leader, but just as often they feel mistreated by it. In post-Soviet Russia, Vladimir Putin's government has used the desire of Russians to have a strong and fair state as a leader in order to coopt civil society. It created incentives for civil society organizations to pursue their causes through cooperation with state officials rather than through demanding accountability and confronting the state. Russian civil society organizations face a choice whether to accept such offers and collaborate with the state or not, weighing the benefits and repercussions of both paths. This chapter discusses Russia's civil society in the context of this choice, separating the "collaborating" and the "resisting" parts of it, considers their role in Russian politics, and demonstrates the forces inside civil society that contribute to the stability and fragility of the Putin regime.

18.1 Introduction

How do Russians view their state? Do they trust it? Are they proud of it? Do they avoid contact with it? These questions receive different answers depending on the context in which they are asked. On the one hand, public opinion polls show that **Vladimir Putin**'s approval ratings have always been moderate to high. The army, the president, and the national security services are the most trusted political institutions in the country (Gudkov 2020). For many Russians, these institutions are associated with defending the country from external threats, which is eminently important for how Russians view their own history. Sticking with the state in dangerous times and following its leadership are signs of patriotism. Such sentiments motivate people not just during times of war, such as World War II (called the Great Patriotic War in Russia); the same patriotic motives also drive participation in ambitious state-led initiatives, such as the **All-Russia People's Front** (ARPF, a state-organized alliance between the **United Russia** party and a plethora of Russian NGOs) and the youth patriotic organization Yunarmia, which is funded by the Russian government (Hemment 2015).

On the other hand, public opinion polls also show that only about 30–35 percent of respondents trust institutions such as the police, regional and local authorities, the procurator's office, and the courts (Gudkov 2020). What is more, only about 10 percent of Russians believe that the state has the same interests as the Russian people, and close to 90 percent say that the state elites ignore the people's interests and only serve their own (Khamraev 2018). These sentiments reveal a distrust of the state that has been common in Russian society since at least late Soviet times. Then, people often said one thing publicly and thought another thing privately. In the late Soviet period, state projects were often quietly sabotaged at the local level, and reports sent to the central ministries were falsified, which was symptomatic of the disconnect between the state and society. In post-Soviet Russia, civil society structures questioning and resisting state authority emerged alongside those loyal to the state (Greene 2014).

Another question related to whether Russians trust their state is whether Russians trust each other. This kind of social trust determines whether society can act collectively: If people do not trust each other, they fail to organize concerted political action. Here, too, the answers are contradictory. On the one hand, Russia, as the successor of the Soviet Union, is commonly thought of as a collectivist society. This kind of collectivism is often associated with a lack of respect for human rights and private property and with the general priority of collective interests over individual ones. On the other hand, many researchers describe Russia as an atomized society and Russian people as having low levels of interpersonal trust. Their trust circles usually encompass only family and close friends, and they view public activists as suspicious and driven by hidden material interests (Volkov 2020).

In this chapter, I will talk about the link between Russian people's views of the state and their views of collective action. All the opposing views described above reflect real and important trends in Russian society, and I will discuss how all of them can be true simultaneously. The most important aspect of state–society relations in Russia examined in this chapter is that Russian people view the state as both their leader and their oppressor, which makes them both loyal and disobedient to the state. In a sense, the Russian state is a paternalistic one taking on the role of a provider for citizens but also often acting as an abusive parent. Russian citizens are attached to the state as the institution that has historically provided collective protection and public goods. At the same time, they are also often disgruntled and resentful of the state since this protection historically has gone along with a history of abuse and control of citizens. As a result of these contradictory attitudes, Russians eagerly join state-led collective actions to defend the country from external enemies, but also often find themselves faced with oppression by the state. The former pushes them toward loyalty, the latter toward resistance, and each civil society actor must find a way to resolve this contradiction.

Understanding these dynamics will allow us to answer several questions about Russian politics, civil society, and the prospects for democratization in the future. First, it will allow us to understand whether, in contemporary Russia, civil society is independent or largely controlled by the state. Secondly, it will highlight Russians' attachment to the state as one of the sources of the authoritarian regime's stability in both the Soviet and the post-Soviet period. And, thirdly, it will allow us to see how abuse of its citizens by the Russian state makes the regime fragile and how social resistance to this abuse may lead to political change in Russia.

18.2   What Is Civil Society?

The term "civil society" usually refers to a wide variety of organizations including NGOs, labor unions, community groups, charities, professional associations, and so on. It is also sometimes referred to as "the third sector," the first two being commerce and the government. There is no strict definition that would drive the usage of this term, but most definitions place civil society at the intersection of the **nonprofit** and **nongovernmental** realms. These organizations are usually advancing some **collective cause** or defending a collective interest, rather than making a profit. At the same time, they are usually **organized by citizens** rather than by the government, and they exist at all societal levels, from local to international (Kenny 2016).

When talking about civil society, we must also remember that this term is closely connected to the ideas of Western modernity and has a normative component in it. It originates in European thought of the eighteenth and nineteenth centuries, when Enlightenment-era thinkers conceptualized civil society as the self-organization of autonomous and rational individuals operating under free market conditions. This kind of civil society was seen as a precondition of democracy (Kenny 2016). In contemporary Western thought, civil society is often associated with social capital – horizontal trust networks between individuals that facilitate collective action – which is also often considered to be a prerequisite of democratic development (Putnam, Leonardi, and Nanetti 1994). Even though later research has demonstrated that civil society and social capital may also serve antidemocratic ends (Berman 1997; Putnam 2001; Riley 2010), the idea of civil society as a precondition of democracy continues to dominate the discourse of academics and practitioners looking for solutions to social issues in developing countries (Kenny 2016).

Applying the term "civil society" to countries other than Western liberal democracies is often problematic because the nonprofit and the nongovernmental boundaries may look very different in societies with other political histories and economic systems (Chebankova 2015). Civil society in the Soviet Union and Russia, for example, has had a strong tradition of nonprofit work. During Soviet times, there were numerous citizens' associations – intellectual and sports clubs, professional societies, neighborhood councils, women's organizations, and so on. They contributed to community-building, fulfilled the role of social workers, and served as a platform for people to organize around common interests. According to different estimates, between 5 and 15 percent of the Soviet adult population participated in community self-help organizations (Friedgut 1979, 244). In contemporary Russia, there are many "socially oriented nongovernmental organizations" running charity projects and helping alleviate social problems, which highlights the nonprofit character of their work (Bindman 2015).

At the same time, the nongovernmental boundary of civil society in the Soviet Union and Russia has been severely compromised. Soviet-era civic organizations could exist only within the boundaries allowed by the Soviet party-state, which retained the right to prohibit any organization criticizing it and threatening its political monopoly. Dependence on the party-state did not necessarily mean that people were forced to participate in these organizations. With a few exceptions, such as the Young Pioneers – the Soviet-era youth organization often compared to the

Scouts – people could stay uninvolved without many adverse consequences. Participation required some individual initiative and enthusiasm for the cause. But that enthusiasm could by and large only fill the molds pre-approved by the party-state officials (Friedgut 1979). In contemporary Russia, the state also increasingly controls the activities of civil society organizations, creating favorable conditions for the loyal or apolitical ones and persecuting those that challenge state authority (Gilbert 2016). Later in the chapter, I will discuss these recent trends in more detail.

18.3   Two Tales of Civil Society Organizations in Russia

To better understand how Russians view their state and collective action, let us look at two contemporary civil society organizations from different Russian regions. Both are examples of the phenomenon that had its roots in Soviet-era civic activism: nonprofit organizations driven by enthusiastic citizens who care about a common cause, but not those who might be willing to disagree with the state or act against it. The first example is a residential council in Kemerovo, a local community organization of people living in the same neighborhood; the second example is the Alena Petrova Foundation, a fund helping children with cancer and their families. As you read about these examples, pay attention to how people view the role of the state in collective action and to whether these organizations fit the nonprofit and nongovernmental categories.

18.3.1   A Residential Council in Kemerovo City

Svetlana was an enthusiastic woman in her late twenties whom I met in 2014 in Kemerovo city, the capital of Kemerovo Oblast situated in the south of western Siberia (all information about this case comes from author interview with Svetlana [name changed for confidentiality], Kemerovo, March 2014). A few months earlier, she, her husband, and their young son had moved to a new suburban neighborhood a short drive from the city center. The neighborhood comprised low-rise apartment buildings, townhouses, and private homes along with a school, a hospital, several parks, and children's playgrounds. The city government subsidized mortgages for public-sector employees, such as teachers and doctors, to buy property in this neighborhood, and the population of the neighborhood increased to several thousand people in a few years.

The neighborhood had a residential council, and Svetlana was one of the council members. The council developed community rules, resolved issues with the construction company that built the neighborhood, and organized community events. For example, they developed a set of rules about pet-walking and trash collection.

They gathered complaints about the places where rainwater accumulated and forced the construction company to install more storm drains.

Svetlana was particularly excited about the community events that the council organized. She told me how they were able to pull together the resources and skills of their community for the events that made social life in the neighborhood more fun. For example, they worked with the local school to have the school band and the dance team perform at community events. They looked for sponsors who could provide the prizes for children's competitions. The residents of the neighborhood also contributed their own skills and resources: For example, someone knew how to do face painting, and they organized a face-painting station at a community festival. Someone else was able to arrange a free rental of lifesized puppets, which were very popular with the children. The population of the neighborhood consisted primarily of families with small children, and Svetlana said that many residents were eager to contribute to this community work.

So far, this residential council looks like a usual self-governing institution that is easy to imagine not just in Russia but in many other countries too. One unusual thing about this council, though, was that its creation was not initiated by the residents of the neighborhood. It was the administration of the Kemerovo city that contacted them and suggested they put together such a council. It was supposed to work together with the city administration to resolve various local issues and do community work. The meaning of "working together" in that offer was very literal: One of the city officials became a member of the council. Besides this official, members of the council included the head of the utility company that provided services in the neighborhood, and the principal of the neighborhood school. The council, therefore, was less of a group of activists who represented the neighborhood residents in communications with the city administration, the utility company, and the school, and more of a way to include the community activists into the city government organizational structure.

Even more interesting is that Svetlana's council was far from the only one in Kemerovo city. Starting from the late 1990s, the city administration created more than 7,700 residential councils across the city, which had a population of about 500,000, or 1 council per 67 residents on average. To manage this large number of councils, it also created forty-nine community centers spread out across the city and staffed with inspectors whose salaries came from the city budget. An organizational hierarchy like this would be difficult to create without a significant degree of cooperation and enthusiasm from below, from people like Svetlana. Where this enthusiasm comes from will be one of the main questions I discuss in this chapter.

18.3.2   The Alena Petrova Foundation, a Pediatric Cancer Charity

A second case of civic activism that helps us understand contemporary Russian state–society relations comes from another Siberian city, Tomsk, and our second character is Elena, Elena Alekseevna if we use the name and patronymic, as is customary in Russia (all information about this case comes from author interview with Elena Alekseevna, Tomsk, June 2014). Elena Alekseevna used to work as a dentist in a Tomsk suburb until her life was turned upside down when her middle child, a girl named Alena, was diagnosed with blood cancer at the age of thirteen. For almost two years, Alena fought for her life; sadly, she succumbed to the disease in 2006.

After Alena's death, Elena Alekseevna devoted her life to helping children diagnosed with cancer and their families. From her own experience, she knew that cancer treatment required significant financial resources and that the existing healthcare system did not always provide the best treatment options and did not cover many extra costs. Families had to contribute their private money for their children to have the best care and the highest chances of survival, and not all families could afford it. To help such families, Elena Alekseevna created a charity fund named after her daughter: the Alena Petrova Children's Fund. A local businessperson paid for her training at the Center for Development of Nonprofit Organizations in St. Petersburg, where she learned best practices of nonprofit-organization management, including state-of-the-art fundraising strategies. She focused on working with the media to attract public attention to her cause and on financial transparency of her organization, and in a few years the fund grew into the most well-known charity organization in the region and an exemplary one nationwide. Publicity and transparency helped to maintain a stable stream of private donations both from large business donors and from small private ones, as well as some revenue from the governmental money designated for nonprofit grants.

The resources Elena Alekseevna managed to attract allowed the fund to develop a comprehensive support system for children with cancer in Tomsk Oblast. The fund provides direct financial help to the families that cannot cover the treatment costs. It also provides the cancer department in the main regional hospital with some home appliances and supplies, which make the hospital stay more comfortable for the little patients, such as fridges, microwaves, TVs, and toys for the playroom. Besides this direct help, the fund also offers the services of professional psychological support to children and their families, rehabilitation services in the special center built for this purpose, and educational and entertainment activities, including cultural tours and summer camps for cancer survivors and their parents. The fund helps parents to navigate the bureaucratic process, through which they must go for their children to receive treatment or get certain benefits from the state. Finally, the fund organizes conferences, workshops, and other public events on the topic of children's cancer; these connect different stakeholders involved in the issues related to children's cancer in the region.

Elena Alekseevna's efforts have been appreciated by authorities both at the regional and the national levels. She and her fund received multiple honors from the regional government and several presidential grants. It was invited to join the All-Russia People's Front (ARPF) – an organization uniting a broad range of civic activists, which Vladimir Putin created in 2011 to "control the implementation of presidential decrees and fight corruption" (ONF 2021a). In my conversation with her, Elena Alekseevna praised the ARPF for providing the opportunity for the activists to meet personally with Putin, raise their issues, and often resolve them in minutes. One of the many examples she raised was about treating children with rare diseases. During one of the ARPF sessions chaired by Putin, a head physician of a regional hospital requested that the treatment of children with rare diseases be funded from the federal budget rather than from the regional ones, since it was very expensive. He said that there are only 117 such children in the whole country, and their treatment required 3.5 billion rubles (about $100 million). Putin immediately asked the minister of health, who was also present at the meeting, why they could not find the money for these 117 children. She responded that they, in fact, do have this money, and Putin asked her to prepare the necessary documents as soon as possible, so that the children could receive the treatment within three months.

Despite the many achievements of Alena Petrova Children's Fund, Elena Alekseevna's activities sometimes attract public criticism. One such criticism says that she never participates in the public protests that some other activists organize to attract attention to the issues in the healthcare system. Elena Alekseevna responds to her critics that her priority is providing real help rather than protesting. She agrees that the state must do more to help cure children with cancer: She has said that for a country that organized the extremely expensive Olympic Games in Sochi, not being able to find 10 million rubles (about $300,000) to treat a child's cancer is shameful. But, in her view, it was the job of people like her and organizations like the ARPF to close the gap between the state and the people. She believed that the bureaucrats were detached from real life and people's problems, as they saw the world through governmental statistics. ARPF meetings were an opportunity to communicate a different vision of the real problems on the ground to them. She deeply respected Putin, both for creating the ARPF and simply because one "must respect the leader of one's country." During the electoral campaign for the 2018 presidential election, she became one of a few hundred of Putin's "trusted representatives" – public figures, such as celebrities, artists, doctors, and nonprofit leaders – who publicly supported his reelection.

18.4 The State as the Leader and the Oppressor

These civil society organizations in Kemerovo and Tomsk both have two important qualities. They are civic-minded, that is, they work to advance a public cause and help other people. At the same time, their logic of interaction with the state is not one of protest and demand but the one of collaboration and teamwork (Bindman 2015; Cheskin and March 2015). These features illustrate the social norm informing societal activism in Russia – the norm that holds up the state as a leader.

Russians consider it normal and right when the state and public officials take on leadership of civic activism. Importantly, this notion of the state's role is distinct from, and runs counter to, the notion of the state and public officials acting as servants catering to people's individual needs, as public service is often envisaged in Western countries. In Russia, participation in state-led collective action is considered patriotic, as the state is seen as the legitimate leader. Russian patriotism encompasses attachment not only to the country's land and the community of people who live there but also to the state as the institution critical for the country's existence. Historically, the Russian state had to grow and consolidate under perpetual external threats as Russia's geographical location made it vulnerable to foreign invasion on multiple fronts. Over time, the central state and the tsar as its symbol managed to elevate their authority over other institutions, such as the church and the aristocracy.

The Soviet-era communist regime, therefore, did not create the norm of state leadership but rather capitalized on it. Even though Marxism-Leninism posits that communism was to be a stateless social formation, the Bolshevik Party managed to reconcile these elements of Marxist doctrine with the political tradition of the strong state in Russia. Although the Russian Empire and the Soviet Union were a world apart in some respects, the role of the state as the sole legitimate leader of collective action was characteristic of both.

Russia, as a society with a strong, dominant state, is sometimes called paternalistic, highlighting the similarity between the authority of the state leader and the authority of the father in a traditional family. This characteristic is accurate, with two very important caveats. First, Russian state paternalism does not mean that Russians have no individual initiative and rely solely on entitlements, such as free healthcare, free education, a stable income, and so on. As we saw in the examples above, the norm of state leadership coexists with individual initiative as long as individuals see themselves as members of the same team as the state, that is, working toward the same shared goals. Most Russians, therefore, do not expect the state to do everything for them, but they absolutely expect the state to provide strategic leadership for their collective effort. Secondly, compliance with authority and with the leader who represents one's identity group is not unique to Russians. Everywhere in the world, citizens organize in groups and follow the leaders who speak to their group identity most powerfully (Haslam, Reicher, and Platow 2011). The difference lies in what those groups are, for example, states, religious groups, ethnic groups, or political parties, and in how many of them are simultaneously acting in the political space. Russia is different from many countries because its political space is dominated by one institution, the state, rather than a plethora of parties, ethnic groups, and religions. At the individual level, however, Russians' motivation for collective action, for belonging to a group, and for following their group leader is very similar to the motivation of people in other countries (Forrat 2021).

State leadership also has its dark side. When most citizens believe in the virtue of state authority, this opens the possibility for abuse of public office by agents of the state. Many Russians intuitively want their state to be a wise father who cares for his children, protects them from dangers, and provides them with support and advice when they are in trouble. But the Soviet and Russian state has often behaved as an abusive parent. It has promised to provide citizens with some protection and resources for physical survival but at the same time has little respect for individual rights (*Moscow Times* 2020). For at least two centuries, the Russian state has had special police forces to repress any actions that questioned the authority of the state. In the twentieth century, during Joseph Stalin's time, state repression took on a mass character. In contemporary Russia, the law enforcement system often works to defend the political and economic interests of the state apparatus and the state elites while depriving ordinary citizens of resources, opportunities, and dignity.

How does the idea of the state as a leader coexist with the idea of the state as an oppressor in the minds of Russians? The answer to this question is very important for understanding the relationship of Russians with their state, which is shaped by both loyalty and distrust. Russians' attachment to the state does not mean that they always approve of what the state does. Quite the opposite: The most common attitudes among Russians to the state are distrust and feelings of betrayal. As I mentioned at the beginning of the chapter, the vast majority of Russians say that the interests of the state and those of the people are completely different. The important thing, though, is not that Russians distrust their state; it is what they envision as the best solution to this problem. In other countries, where state authority is not nearly as powerful, people's distrust of the state makes them demand that the state minimize its interference with people's lives. In Russia, the distrust of the state triggers a different reaction: People do not want the state to leave them alone because they feel very insecure without it; instead, they want the state to become a better leader, to stop caring only about its own interests and pay attention to people's needs, that is, to stop abusing its own citizens and start loving them (Gudkov 2016; Forrat 2021).

Russian state leaders have learned to use the people's desire to see the state transform from a bad leader to a good one to stabilize their regimes and consolidate support. Vladimir Putin has portrayed himself as a good leader by initiating and supporting politically benign civic initiatives. At the same time, there are signs that the norm of state leadership has been slowly eroding over the past decades, and now there is a small but visible section of Russians who are willing to challenge the state political monopoly. In the rest of this chapter, I will explore this tension between stability and fragility, speaking in more detail about the development of civil society in post-Soviet Russia.

18.5   The Civil Society Landscape

In the early 2020s, Russian civil society organizations are highly professional, using some of the best practices in the NGO toolkit from all over the world. At the same time, this sphere is strongly regulated by the Russian state. What exactly does Russian civil society look like these days? And how did it develop after the collapse of the Soviet Union and the communist party-state to get to where it is now?

18.5.1   How Many Civil Society Organizations Are There and What Do They Do?

The question of how many civil society organizations there are in Russia is not easy to answer. The vague definition of what exactly a civil society organization is and the existence of de facto organizations that are not registered as legal entities as well as those that are no longer active complicate the task of counting such organizations. For the purposes of our current discussion, let us focus on the nonprofits that work to solve some social issue or advance a social cause, and exclude organizations such as business associations or universities. Looking at both the official statistics and the information collected by civil society organizations themselves, we can say that there are currently between 12,000 and 17,000 active legally registered civil society organizations in Russia (Iaznevich et al. 2021; EMISS 2021).

This set of organizations is very diverse. It includes charities that collect money for expensive medical treatments and organizations that help homeless people, people with addictions, victims of natural disasters, migrants, the elderly, and orphans. A number of organizations work on environmental causes, such as animal rights and protecting the national landmark of Lake Baikal. Some associations are focused on maintaining the cultural traditions of the multiple ethnic communities that live in Russia. There are also amateur sports associations and organizations similar to the Scouts for children and youth, with a patriotic education curriculum. A separate group of organizations is dedicated to preserving historical memory of the Great Patriotic War and political repressions in the Soviet Union. Finally, there are human rights defenders who help the victims of violence, from domestic violence to prison torture, and initiatives that work to increase transparency of Russian elections.

All these diverse bodies have different relationships with the state. Some of them are effectively state-controlled organizations, which either survived the collapse of the Soviet Union or were newly established by the government in post-Soviet

Russia. A small number are completely independent from the state, such as some anticorruption and electoral transparency initiatives. A big chunk of civil society organizations, though, are in between these two poles: They are not completely controlled by the state and have a significant degree of autonomy, but they often work in collaboration with the state. To understand why collaboration with the state is difficult to avoid and what kind of dilemmas Russian civil society organizations currently face, let us briefly look at the historical development of civil society in post-Soviet Russia.

18.5.2 How Did Russian Civil Society Develop after the Collapse of the Soviet Union?

In the 1990s, Russian civil society, together with the rest of the country, was transforming. Many Soviet civil society organizations stopped functioning because the government could not support them any longer. At the same time, the collapse of the communist regime opened the country's political space to a wide variety of new initiatives, which were now supported by the foreign donors. Among the foreign donors there were both governments and private organizations. The largest absolute contributors of government funds were the United States and the European Union, and the largest private foundations were the **MacArthur and Ford Foundations** as well as **George Soros's Open Society Institute.** Western states generally devoted under 10 percent of their foreign assistance budgets for civil society support, with the bulk of money going to economic reforms or nuclear security (Sundstrom 2006, 36). But even these limited funds combined with private foundation resources allowed the creation and support of many civil society organizations across Russia as well as bringing the institutional experiences of Western NGOs to Russian soil.

Toward the mid-2000s, two things changed: First, Russia became richer and, secondly, Vladimir Putin's regime began its consolidation. Since 2006, Russian civil society organizations have begun receiving so-called **presidential grants** for projects that address social issues, such as poverty, as well as educational, cultural, youth, and human rights projects (Jakobson and Sanovich 2010, 294). In the 2000s, some rich businesspeople in Russia established private charity foundations that supported education, science, the arts, and social projects: **Vladimir Potanin's Foundation** started its first program in 2000, **Dmitry Zimin's Dynasty Foundation** was established in 2001, and **Mikhail Prokhorov's Foundation** began its work in 2004. At the same time, in the mid-2000s, the Russian government started using increasingly hostile rhetoric toward Western donors to Russian civil society organizations. They were accused of trying to weaken Russia by destabilizing Russian domestic politics, and, by the end of the decade, Western foundations significantly reduced their presence in Russia.

In the 2010s, the funding and political trends of the previous decade continued. The total budget for the presidential grants increased from 473 million rubles in 2006 to 4 billion rubles in 2016 (TASS 2017), and the regional governments also began developing grant programs for local NGOs (author interview with regional state official, Rostov-on-Don, Russia, April 2014). Some civil society organizations began using crowdfunding facilitated by the spread of noncash payments and quick money transfers (Javeline and Lindemann-Komarova 2020).

The increasing availability of domestic sources of funding was coupled with the increasing strengthening of state leadership of civil society organizations. In 2011, Vladimir Putin created the All-Russia People's Front (mentioned above) – an organizational platform uniting political parties, including United Russia, and a large number of civil society organizations. The ARPF board included university leaders, doctors, businesspeople, NGO leaders, famous athletes, state officials, and parliamentary deputies (ONF 2021c). The activities of the ARPF covered most areas of nonprofit work: from historical memory projects to labor, feminist, local, environment, poverty relief, and human rights issues (ONF 2021b).

For the civil society organizations that still dared to work against the state, repressive tools were developed. In 2012, after a large wave of protests against electoral falsifications, the Russian parliament adopted the **"foreign agent" law**, which remains the main tool of political repression of civil society a decade later. According to this law, civil society organizations that engage in "political activities" and receive any funding from abroad, even if it is very small, must submit detailed reports to the Russian Ministry of Justice and label all their public materials with a disclaimer that they were produced by a "foreign agent." Noncompliance is punished with very high fines and imprisonment of up to two years. The requirement to label all public materials as produced by "foreign agents" severely limits the ability of these organizations to reach out to the wider Russian public. In the Russian language, the expression "foreign agent" has a strong association with being a spy. Most Russians, especially those who do not follow politics closely and receive a lot of information from state-controlled outlets, would be cautious about engaging with these organizations or trusting the information from them.

Thus, by the early 2020s, the Russian state had developed both carrots and sticks for civil society. It supported these organizations financially while having enough legal tools to limit their activities or even shut them down. Many civil society organizations are now facing an important choice: Should they collaborate with the state, which would provide them with the necessary financial and networking resources to benefit their cause, or should they try to maintain their independence from it?

18.6   Russian Civil Society and Politics

In the changed political environment, many civil society organizations in Russia have developed closer ties with the Russian state. They apply for grants from the federal and regional governments and participate in state-directed initiatives (Polishchuk, Rubin, and Shagalov 2021). Many of them sincerely welcome the opportunities such collaboration provides as they feel they can do a lot more for their cause if they work in connection with state structures. Elena Alekseevna, the head of Alena Petrova Children's Fund, whom we met earlier in the chapter, is an example of an NGO leader who views her participation in All-Russia People's Front as a great opportunity to do more to help children with cancer.

There is nothing wrong in collaboration of civil society organizations with the state as such. More than that, state–society partnerships are often considered best practice in many areas of nonprofit work. They allow the state to make state programs more efficient and receive timely feedback, and help the efforts of the state and civil society complement each other in solving the problem. Such partnerships can also become the hubs in which civil society organizations with different expertise can be matched for joint innovative projects. All these effects are present in Russia, and this is why some Russian NGO leaders value collaboration with the state.

However, in societies with a strong state authority and lack of robust institutions of state accountability, such as independent parliaments and judiciary, cooperation between civil society and the state also has another effect. It promotes the image of the state as a good leader caring for its people. Such an image stabilizes the authoritarian regime, strengthens the state political monopoly even further, and makes it more difficult for the public to turn a critical eye on the state (McCarthy, Stolerman, and Tikhomirov 2020). That critical eye is very important if the issue at stake goes against the interests of the state apparatus. State officials are usually happy to make improvements to the governance process, for example, to remove bureaucratic obstacles for curing children with cancer. But resolving problems such as large-scale corruption involving the interests of top state officials or torture practices in Russian prisons requires significant pressure from a society with a healthy distrust of state authority. Social projects supported by the state resonate with the already existing desire of the people that their state behaves as a good caring leader. They neutralize the distrust of the state and make it difficult to maintain societal pressure on other issues.

Collaboration between civil society organizations and the state also helps the authoritarian regime divide civil society in the eyes of the public. The organizations that cooperate with the state are publicly praised and portrayed as examples of positive and productive attitudes to social problems, with their leaders being true

Russian patriots working for the good of the people. At the same time, the organizations and activists who work against the interests of the state apparatus and question state authority are condemned and presented as driven by hostile foreign governments eager to weaken Russia and by the personal greed of the activists paid by those foreign parties. Public opinion research shows that many Russians indeed view the leaders of civil society organizations with suspicion. They often question their motives and suspect that they may be running their organizations to misappropriate the money for their own purposes (Volkov 2020). This public image makes it difficult for the organizations not endorsed by the state to obtain wide societal support.

The tension between the "**collaborating**" and the "**resisting**" civil society has been intensifying in Russia at least since the early 2010s. These two groups do not have clear boundaries, and not all organizations can be qualified as one or the other. However, this tension presents a very real choice that more and more Russian civil society organizations face (Yaffa 2020). Below are a few examples of individuals and organizations who resolved this tension differently for themselves.

18.6.1   The "Collaborating" Civil Society

Chulpan Khamatova is a famous Russian actress. Since the late 1990s, she has appeared in many well-known Russian movies and theater performances, for which she has received dozens of awards. She is also one of the founders of a charity fund Podari Zhizn' (Give the Gift of Life) that helps children with cancer. In 2012, right before the presidential election, she recorded a 30-second video, in which she praised Vladimir Putin for keeping his promises and providing real help to her fund and the doctors who worked with it (vote4putin 2012). Shortly after publication of this video, Khamatova accompanied Putin on a visit to a recently built children's cancer clinic, built by a leading cancer research center in Moscow, which was broadcast by the major Russian TV channels. These videos divided the people who praised Khamatova as an actress but were critical of Putin. Some of them said it was a moral failure to support Putin as the person behind the corruption that plagued the country. Others said that it probably was not Khamatova's free choice and that she was threatened with reduction in the state's funding for her charity. Yet others believed she did everything right because children's lives were a lot more important than her ephemeral reputation.

Khamatova herself provided almost no comments about these videos. In a rare interview with the BBC in April 2012, shortly after the election, she said, "One must set priorities, and I have done that. All the rumors that I was tortured and forced . . . are, of course, not true. This was my choice." "I want to give the children a chance. It is disgusting for me to know that the children can die simply because they don't have the money, don't have the medicine. For me, it is unacceptable. I would not be able to continue living with it" (BBC News Russian Service 2012). Years later, in

2019, she said in another interview that, had she known in 2012 that Putin would start the war in eastern Ukraine and people would die there, she would not have recorded the video (Shikhman 2019, sec. 12:45).

Our next example is Niuta Federmesser – the founder of Hospice Foundation "Vera" named after her mother, Vera Millionshchikova, a doctor and pioneer of palliative medicine in Russia. Palliative medicine aims at helping terminally ill patients to die with dignity and without pain. As a teenager, Federmesser volunteered in Russian and British hospices; in 2006, she founded the Hospice Foundation "Vera"; and in 2013 she became the head of the Palliative Center funded by the Moscow Department of Health. Over the years, she has worked with the federal and regional governments, professional associations, and civil society organizations to make palliative care available for terminally ill patients in Russia. Among the many issues she addressed was access to painkillers, which are heavily regulated as addictive drugs by the Russian legislation. Many doctors are afraid to prescribe them even to terminally ill patients in pain because of possible criminal charges.

In 2018, during the Moscow mayoral election campaign, Federmesser supported Sergei Sobianin, the current mayor of Moscow and a close ally of Vladimir Putin. In November that year, she joined the federal board of the All-Russia People's Front, which, she said, opened the doors of regional governments for her palliative care projects. In May 2019, she agreed to a suggestion from Sobianin's team to run for the Moscow parliament because she thought that charity organizations should be represented there (Allenova 2019). This decision to run would have been less controversial if she had not been running against **Lyubov Sobol** – a close ally of **Alexei Navalny**, the main Russian opposition figure. Sobol recently sued the company of one of Putin's friends for supplying poor-quality lunches to Moscow schools, which resulted in the poisoning and hospitalization of dozens of children. The Moscow government clearly did not want to see Sobol in the city parliament, and Federmesser was supposed to split the opposition vote (Ruvinskyi and Zheleznova 2019). Navalny wrote an open letter to Federmesser asking her not to run and not to be a tool in the regime's hands (Navalny 2019). After this letter and other public criticism, Federmesser changed her decision and decided not to run, saying she preferred to devote her time to helping people rather than to dirty politics (Levchenko and Pertsev 2019). The Moscow electoral commission had to deny Lyubov Sobol registration as a candidate based on "procedural violations" to prevent her being elected to the city parliament (Eremenko 2019).

In these and other examples of civil society supporting Putin's regime, the common theme is always "we want to help people with whatever means are available to us." Many such activists say they are ignorant about politics and only care about advancing the cause they deeply understand. They also emphasize that they criticize the state when necessary but criticism is not their goal; they are looking for practical solutions to problems, and, in contemporary Russia, this is impossible without collaboration with the state.

18.6.2   The "Resisting" Civil Society

Another section of civil society has increasingly pursued a path of challenging the state. Unlike the "collaborating" civil society, which focuses primarily on charitable and nonpolitical causes, the "resisting" part is much better defined, not least due to the 2012 foreign agent law mentioned earlier. The goal of this law was precisely to identify the civil society actors whom Putin's regime considers a threat. A few organizations ended up on the foreign agent registry almost randomly. Most, however, were included because state officials had a reason to believe they were too independent, or even openly opposed to the current regime, so this registry is a useful guide to the "resisting" civil society in Russia (OVD-Info 2021).

Between 2012 and 2021, a total of 312 organizations were included in the foreign agent registry. Forty-two organizations were able to appeal the decision, usually by refusing small sums of foreign funding, and were subsequently excluded from the register. Of the remaining 270 organizations, 49 were banned in Russia, although they may have continued working abroad, and 106 chose to close permanently. This leaves us with 115 organizations; since 2019, these have been joined by 67 individuals, who could now be added to the register if they (1) make public statements and (2) receive any kind of income from abroad.

Figure 18.2 shows the breakdown of these organizations and individuals by activity area. The largest category is independent mass media and journalists. It includes, among others, the only national independent TV channel **Dozhd**, news portals **Meduza** and **The Insider**, investigative media **IStories** and **Bellingcat**, and several media outlets funded by grants from the US Congress, such as **Radio Liberty**, **Voice of America**, and **Current Time**.

Most organizations in the category of electoral rights and political associations are affiliated with the civic movement **Golos**. Since 2002, it has been training independent electoral observers and implementing projects aimed at increasing election transparency. Human rights organizations include, among others, Memorial, an organization created to preserve the memory of political repression victims in the Soviet Union and continuing to fight political repression and human rights abuses (see https://memo.ru/en-us/); the media project **OVD-Info**, which emerged during the electoral protests in Russia in 2011–12, and several organizations specializing in women's rights and the rights of prisoners, migrants, and LGBTQ+ people. The category of education and research includes independent social science research organizations that study public opinion and gender issues, and develop outreach projects related to historical memory and human rights. The status of the organizations on the foreign agent list continues to change. For example, on December 29, 2021, the Russian Supreme Court ordered the shutdown of Memorial,

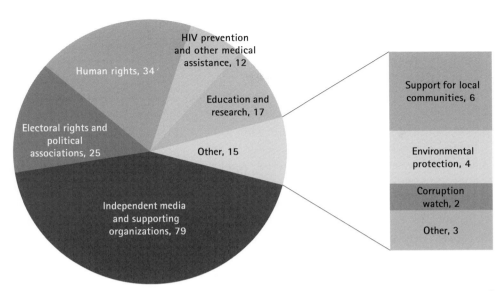

Fig. 18.2 Organizations and individuals included on the "foreign agent" registry by the Russian Ministry of Justice, by activity area.
Source: Author calculations based on https://ovdinfo.org/data/inoteka. Only organizations still active on December 31, 2021, are included.

formally based on minor violations of the foreign agent law, and the process of organizational closure was finalized in early 2022.

The "resisting" civil society tends to work on the issues that challenge the authority of the state and undermine the stability of the Putin regime. The state can address the criticism about the lack of palliative care by inviting the activists to work together with state officials and hospitals to improve the situation. However, if the criticism relates to ongoing electoral fraud or corruption accusations, it is much more difficult to use the same approach. Public conversations about the victims of Stalin's repressions and torture in Russian prisons raise questions about the limits of state power in people's minds. Environmental causes often tap into commercial interests of state and business elites. And the free media challenge the image of the state as a good leader. To be sure, Putin's functionaries attempt to coopt journalists or environmental activists too, but it is often more difficult to do than in the case of charity organizations with uncontroversial and politically benign causes such as children's cancer (Daucé 2014).

18.7 The Russian Invasion of Ukraine and Russian Civil Society

On February 24, 2022, shortly before this chapter was finalized, Russia invaded Ukraine and started a bloody war, which will have major consequences for the lives of millions of people as well as the histories of both countries and the world. The reaction of Russian society to this war highlights two important points discussed in this chapter: the split between collaborating and resisting civil society and the dark side of state leadership.

Even though by the start of this invasion the "resisting" civil society was significantly suppressed, during its first days, we witnessed dozens of collective letters and petitions opposing the war. They came from doctors, teachers, lawyers, scholars, journalists, psychologists, pilots, actors, writers, publishers, chefs, and many other professional groups (*Zhurnal "Kholod"* 2022). A petition on Change.org, which was started by Lev Ponomarev, a famous human rights activist, collected more than a million signatures during the first week, becoming the fastest signature collection for a petition in Russia and one of the fastest in the world (Ponomarev 2022). Antiwar protests and pickets took place in dozens of cities, but all these actions still amounted only to a small movement relative to the size of the country and the urgency of the moment. The authorities moved swiftly to suppress the antiwar movement with police crackdowns, new legislation imposing heavy criminal sentences on those involved in the movement, and the closure of all independent media outlets in the country.

At the same time, there were also celebrities and a few professional groups, such as the Russian Rectors' Union (the union of Russian university presidents), which issued statements in support of the war and the official narrative about it (Russian Rectors' Union 2022). While not all signatures on this statement should be seen as completely voluntary, anecdotal evidence and a few public opinion polls available so far suggest that a large part of the Russian public generally trusts the official propaganda narrative about the causes of this war. This narrative changes quickly, almost daily, but all its versions play on the motive of the external threat to the country, which is so often viewed uncritically by the Russian people. Earlier in the chapter, I talked about the oppression from the state that the Russian people endure because they view the state as their leader; this war demonstrates that the failure to control the state poses danger not only to Russians themselves, but also to people in other countries. It also raises the question of the historical and moral responsibility of the Russian nation for such failures and for the wars that the Russian state leads on their behalf – a question that will be reckoned with by generations of intellectuals after this war is over.

18.8   Conclusion

The dualistic attitude of Russians to their state, which they see as both their leader and their oppressor, produces tension between the "collaborating" and the "resisting" parts of civil society. This chapter has argued that Russians have historically favored collaborating with the state. In the ideal world, they prefer their state to be a benevolent leader, so that all public issues are resolved via teamwork rather than political confrontation. Putin's regime has used this preference to coopt civil society not only through repressions but also through the promise that the state will work together with the activists to improve people's lives.

Since the early 2010s, however, popular support for the "resisting" civil society in Russia has been growing, though it is difficult to single out one cause of such growth. Russia in the early 2020s, at least before the war with Ukraine, is a world apart from the Soviet Union: It has a marketized economy, with many citizens working in the private sector and owning their own homes. The Russian middle class travels abroad, and people of all backgrounds increasingly consume information from the Internet, which remains a lot less controlled than TV. All these factors, together with generational change, contribute to the growing resistance to the state and to the fragility of Putin's regime. This support is still relatively small and unstable, but even a small amount of resistance can start a cascade of mobilization, the likes of which have toppled authoritarian regimes in the past. The intensified repression of Russian civil society in recent years is a clear sign that Putin's regime considers the challenge serious.

It is very difficult to predict how the tension between the forces of regime stability and fragility in civil society will develop. Nurturing resistance to the state in a society whose identity is attached to the state is a slow process, which has its ups and downs. The war with Ukraine, which is far from over at the time of this writing, together with the economic crisis that is bound to follow will play a major role in this process. There is little doubt that Vladimir Putin's regime will continue repressing any challenges to the state authority, and it is possible that these repressions will slow down the resistance significantly. However, the political opposition and the "resisting" civil society are also changing, learning to work under harsh conditions, and finding new ways to reach out to the people and gain their support. Ultimately, the true democratization of Russia will depend on the growth of such resistance and its institutionalization in both civil society organizations and political structures.

DISCUSSION QUESTIONS

1. What are the differences and similarities between the civil society organizations you read about in the chapter and the ones you have encountered in your life? Where do these similarities and differences come from?
2. What would you do if you wanted to build a cancer hospital with cutting-edge equipment and cure many children from cancer, but the only sure way of getting the requisite resources was through publicly supporting a leader like Putin? Why?

3. Is strong state authority good or bad for democracy? What about the countries where state authority is extremely weak and the power largely belongs to local strongmen, such as Afghanistan?

REFERENCES

Allenova, Olga. 2019. "V sushchestvuiushchei v nashei strane sisteme bolezn' – eto prestuplenie." *Kommersant*, May 5, www.kommersant.ru/doc/3961780.

BBC News Russian Service. 2012. "Chulpan Khamatova. Menia ne pytali i ne prinuzhdali." April 9, www.bbc.com/russian/russia/2012/04/120405_chulpan_khamatova_interview.

Berman, Sheri. 1997. "Civil Society and the Collapse of the Weimar Republic." *World Politics*, 49(3), 401–29.

Bindman, Eleanor. 2015. "The State, Civil Society and Social Rights in Contemporary Russia." *East European Politics*, 31(3), 342–60.

Chebankova, Elena. 2015. "Competing Ideologies of Russia's Civil Society." *Europe–Asia Studies*, 67(2), 244–68.

Cheskin, Ammon, and Luke March. 2015. "State–Society Relations in Contemporary Russia: New Forms of Political and Social Contention." *East European Politics*, 31(3), 261–73.

Daucé, Françoise. 2014. "The Government and Human Rights Groups in Russia: Civilized Oppression?" *Journal of Civil Society*, 10(3), 239–54.

EMISS (Edinaia mezhvedomstvennaia informatsionno-statisticheskaia sistema). 2021. "Deiatel'nost' sotsial'no orientirovannykh nekommercheskikh organizatsii. Itogi vyborochnogo statisticheskogo nabliudeniia," https://fedstat.ru/indicator/60324.

Eremenko, Ekaterina. 2019. "Liubov Sobol' ne pustili na vybory v Mosgordumu." *Vedomosti*, July 16, www.vedomosti.ru/politics/articles/2019/07/16/806649-lyubov-sobol.

Forrat, Natalia. 2021. "The Social Roots of Authoritarian Power: State–Society Relations and the Political Machines in the Russian Regions." Typescript under review.

Friedgut, Theodore H. 1979. *Political Participation in the USSR*. Princeton: Princeton University Press.

Gilbert, Leah. 2016. "Crowding Out Civil Society: State Management of Social Organisations in Putin's Russia." *Europe–Asia Studies*, 68(9), 1553–78.

Greene, Samuel A. 2014. *Moscow in Movement: Power and Opposition in Putin's Russia*. Stanford: Stanford University Press.

Gudkov, Lev. 2016. "Mekhanizmy krizisnoi konsolidatsii." *Kontrapunkt*, no. 5 (September), 1–14.

  2020. "Doverie institutam." September 21, www.levada.ru/2020/09/21/doverie-institutam/.

Haslam, S. Alexander, Stephen Reicher, and Michael Platow. 2011. *The New Psychology of Leadership: Identity, Influence, and Power*. New York: Psychology Press.

Hemment, Julie. 2015. *Youth Politics in Putin's Russia: Producing Patriots and Entrepreneurs*. Bloomington: Indiana University Press.

Iaznevich, Elizaveta, Karina Pipia, Valeria Gubkina, Natalia Aluferova, Mikhail Vasenin, Anna Zheltoukhova, and Lev Kertman. 2021. "Fandraizing v Rossii. Kto i kak privlekaet sredstva? (2021)." Fond "Nuzhna pomoshch'," https://tochno.st/materials/fandrayzing-v-rossii-kto-i-kak-privlekaet-sredstva-2021.

Jakobson, Lev, and Sergey Sanovich. 2010. "The Changing Models of the Russian Third Sector: Import Substitution Phase." *Journal of Civil Society*, 6(3), 279–300.

Javeline, Debra, and Sarah Lindemann-Komarova. 2020. "Financing Russian Civil Society." *Europe–Asia Studies*, 72(4), 644–85.

Kenny, M. 2016. "Civil Society." *Encyclopedia Britannica*, May 25, www.britannica.com/topic/civil-society.

Khamraev, Victor. 2018. "Rossiiane trebuiut ot gosudarstva zaboty." *Kommersant*, August 23, www.kommersant.ru/doc/3720460.

Levchenko, Grigorii, and Andrei Pertsev. 2019. "Niuta Federmesser snialas' s vyborov v Mosgordumu. Ona ballotirovalas' v tom zhe okruge, chto i Liubov Sobol'." Meduza, June 15, https://meduza.io/feature/2019/06/15/nyuta-federmesser-snyalas-s-vyborov-v-mosgordumu-ona-ballotirovalas-v-tom-zhe-okruge-chto-i-lyubov-sobol.

McCarthy, Lauren A., Katherine Stolerman, and Anton V. Tikhomirov. 2020. "Managed Civil Society and Police Oversight in Russia: Regional Police–Public Councils." *Europe–Asia Studies*, 72(9), 1498–1522.

Moscow Times. 2020. "Russia's Share of European Human Rights Cases Hits 7-Year High." January 30, www.themoscowtimes.com/2020/01/30/russias-share-of-european-human-rights-cases-hits-7-year-high-a69099.

Navalny, Aleksei. 2019. "Pis'mo Anne Konstantinovne (Niute) Federmesser." May 7, https://navalny.com/p/6129/.

ONF (Obshcherossiiskii narodnyi front). 2021a. "Istoriia ONF," https://onf.ru/structure/istoriya-onf/.

2021b. "Proekty," https://onf.ru/projects/.

2021c. "Tsentral'nyi shtab," https://onf.ru/structure/rukovodstvo-0/.

OVD-Info. 2021. "Inoteka." October, https://ovdinfo.org/inoteka-en.

Polishchuk, Leonid, Alexander Rubin, and Igor Shagalov. 2021. "Managing Collective Action: Government-Sponsored Community Initiatives in Russia." *Europe–Asia Studies*, 73(6), 1176–1209.

Ponomarev, Lev. 2022. "Ostanovit' voinu s Ukrainoi!" Change.org, February 24, www.change.org/NetVoyne.

Putnam, Robert D. 2001. *Bowling Alone: The Collapse and Revival of American Community*. New York: Simon & Schuster.

Putnam, Robert D., Robert Leonardi, and Raffaella Y. Nanetti. 1994. *Making Democracy Work: Civic Traditions in Modern Italy*. Princeton: Princeton University Press.

Riley, Dylan J. 2010. *The Civic Foundations of Fascism in Europe: Italy, Spain, and Romania, 1870–1945*. Baltimore: Johns Hopkins University Press.

Russian Rectors' Union. 2022. "Obrashchenie Rossiiskogo soiuza rektorov." March 4, https://rsr-online.ru/news/2022-god/obrashchenie-rossiyskogo-soyuza-rektorov1/.

Ruvinskii, Vladimir, and Maria Zheleznova. 2019. "Za khospisy ili za detei." *Vedomosti*, May 14, www.vedomosti.ru/opinion/articles/2019/05/14/801262-za-hospisi-detei.

Shikhman, Irina. 2019. "Chulpan Khamatova. Kak spasti detei i ne okazat'sia dlia vsekh plokhoi. A pogovorit'?," www.youtube.com/watch?v=N1OAC8Mzf4w.

Sundstrom, Lisa McIntosh. 2006. *Funding Civil Society: Foreign Assistance and NGO Development in Russia*. Stanford: Stanford University Press.

TASS. 2017. "Prezidentskie granty dlia NKO. Dos'e." November 21, https://tass.ru/info/4483700.

Volkov, Denis. 2020. "Pochemu rossiiane boiatsia activisma i blagotvoritel'nosti." September 14, www.levada.ru/2020/09/14/pochemu-rossiyane-boyatsya-aktivizma-i-blagotvoritelnosti/.

vote4putin. 2012. "Khamatova golosuet za Putina," www.youtube.com/watch?v=I6x2y-pX0Tc.

Yaffa, Joshua. 2020. *Between Two Fires*. New York: Tim Duggan Books.

Zhurnal "Kholod." 2022. "'Net voine'. Spisok vsekh otkrytykh pisem protiv vtorzheniia v Ukrainu." February 27, https://holod.media/2022/02/27/otkrytye-pisma/.

19 | Protest in Russia: Discovering Power

SAMUEL A. GREENE

Fig. 19.1 People march to protest against Russia's invasion of Ukraine in central St. Petersburg, March 1, 2022. Credit: Olga Maltseva / AFP / Getty Images.

> Who's the power here? We're the power here! (In Russian, "Kto zdes' vlast'? My zdes' vlast'!")
>
> Protest slogan, December 5, 2011, Moscow

Abstract

Protest is politics at its most primal, its most emotional, its most exciting, and sometimes its most consequential. But, at its core, protest is a learning process, one in which people "at the top" and people "at the bottom" struggle to discover where the real power lies, and then to wield that power once they find it. Protest has been an integral part of the dramatic and often traumatic processes of social and economic transformation that Russia has witnessed over the past forty years, both as a driver of that transformation and as a result of it. Moreover, recent years have seen the Russian state reorganize itself and its relationship with society in order to suppress grassroots mobilization in general and protest in particular. This chapter reviews that history and the contemporary landscape of protest in Russia and asks what is being learned – and who is doing the learning – when Russian citizens take to the streets.

19.1   Introduction: Why Should We Care about Protest?

Protest is exciting. It provokes strong emotions, instilling hope in some, dread in others. Protest captures the imagination, allowing people we do not usually think of as powerful to imagine a real change in how society functions – and forcing people at the top of the political and economic food chains to do the same. It captures headlines, too, for the same reasons. Protest is politics at its most raw and its least predictable. Protest occurs when the usual ways of solving conflicts break down or are stifled. When that happens, **uncertainty** reigns: uncertainty about what is possible, about what the rules are, and about who is really calling the shots. Indeed, it is that very uncertainty that makes protest so interesting – particularly when it occurs in a country like Russia, where politics have seemed so certain, so predictable, and so dominated by a single individual for more than two decades.

19.1.1   Protest as a Learning Process

Most people do not spend most of their time protesting, of course. In fact, most people do not spend any of their time protesting, ever. But, from the outside, it might seem that Russian citizens protest less than most. Political scientists and sociologists spent much of the 1990s trying to understand why more Russians did not come out to protest the severe economic and social hardship caused by the end of the Soviet Union and the transition from a centrally planned, state-owned economy to private ownership and market-oriented capitalism. Many of the same researchers – and a new generation of analysts, too – then spent the 2000s struggling to explain why Russians did not turn out in greater numbers to resist threats to the country's democratic achievements and its slide back into political authoritarianism. But, even as scholars were asking these questions, many Russians were actually protesting. In varying ways, places, and numbers, Russian citizens came out to demand social, economic, and political change, to demand greater accountability, or simply to demand that their voices be heard. They did this when protest was relatively safe, and when it was almost certainly dangerous. They protested when everyone expected them to, and when no one did. And, time and again, even as institutions of democratic participation faltered, they forced significant political change – though not always in the direction they wanted.

That, then, is the other reason why we should care about protest, in Russia or anywhere else: Protest is a learning process, and observers of Russian politics can learn a lot from the lessons that protest teaches its participants. When protests erupt, it teaches governments and people in power – what political scientists call "**incumbents**" – that they have misjudged public sentiment. When incumbents decide how to respond to protests, perhaps by conceding to the protesters' demands or by repressing them, the people that political scientists call "**challengers**" learn how far the political establishment can be pushed. Those same challengers learn about themselves when they come out into the streets: how numerous they are, how much solidarity there is, how much risk they and their comrades are willing to take. Ordinary citizens sitting at home and watching the protests on television or via social media also learn about the issues that divide their society, about the level of confrontation and even violence that incumbents and challengers are willing to countenance, and about whether the conflict occurring in the streets concerns them – whether it is a fight they, too, need to join, on one side or the other.

In most other textbooks about politics in Russia and elsewhere, political scientists focus on the power that resides in formal institutions: in presidencies and parliaments, in laws and courts, in corporations and churches and all of the other structures present in citizens' social, economic, and political lives. All of those institutions are powerful because people expect them to be and behave accordingly. Protest, however, occurs when those expectations break down, when people begin to behave on the basis of how they think things *should be*, rather than how they *are* or *have been* up to that moment. And so the biggest lesson learned as a result of protest is where the power really lies: Who has the ability to establish a new set of expectations when the old ones have broken down? That is why political scientists and sociologists study protest, and that is the question at the heart of this chapter.

19.1.2 How This Chapter Works

To answer that question – how protest reflects, shapes, and reshapes the distribution of power in Russia – this chapter will review the history and patterns of protest in Russia with a focus on that learning process, asking along the way what lessons "challengers" and "incumbents" are learning, and what we as analysts can learn from those lessons. As we do that, we will review key moments and events, but this chapter is not an encyclopedia of Russian protest or even a comprehensive history. The landscape of Russian protest, like the landscape of Russian politics in general, is too complex to chronicle completely in a single chapter. While every attempt has been made to cover the phenomena that matter most to understanding this learning process, there are undoubtedly important things that have not made it in. What is more, the landscape of Russian protests and politics is evolving continuously, and realities on the ground will already be different by the time this book lands on your desk. This chapter provides a framework for understanding the rapidly evolving landscape of protest, and readers should see the bibliography as a guide for more in-depth research.

Focusing on what might broadly be seen as the period of **Vladimir Putin**, the bulk of this chapter is devoted to a sector-by-sector overview of Russia's contemporary landscape of protest. Local and environmental protests, protest on labor and other social and socioeconomic issues, ethnic and nationalist protest, protest involving gender and sexuality, and protest about politics itself take center stage. All of this will build toward some general conclusions – and questions for further thought – about what all of this protest tells us about the broader theme of this book: stability and fragility in Russian politics.

Prior to that, however, the chapter will begin with a bit of history, starting in the late Soviet period and running through the 1990s and the rise to power of Vladimir Putin. This is not only – and not even mainly – because it is important to know our history (although it is). Rather, if protest and power have to do with expectations, then we need to look at people's previous experiences and the stories of power and confrontation that inform their sense of how their political world works.

19.2   History: Protest in Russia before Putin

We usually think of the Soviet Union as a highly repressive state, in which protest was either anathema or virtually impossible – despite the fact that it was born out of protests that helped make tsarist rule impossible and eventually grew into the **Bolshevik Revolution**. This is, of course, mostly true. Protest was usually rare, on occasion brutally repressed, and always frowned upon until **Mikhail Gorbachev** began to loosen restrictions on political life in the mid- to late 1980s. But it is not entirely true, and protest was an important, if infrequent, part of Soviet political life well before Gorbachev gave permission for it to be.

19.2.1   Protest in the Soviet Union: Breaking the Ice

Expressly political protest in the Soviet Union was most notable for its absence: As expectations go, the idea that political or ideological challenges to the supremacy of the **Communist Party of the Soviet Union** – as **Vladimir Lenin** said, the "mind, honor, and conscience of the people" – would not be tolerated had been clear from the beginning, and, until the constitutional guarantee of the party's monopoly was removed in 1989, no one had ever sent a signal to the contrary. That did not stop people from trying from time to time, however. Perhaps most notably, a group of **dissidents** unfurled a banner on Red Square in 1968 condemning the Soviet Union's invasion of Czechoslovakia to remove a reform-minded government there. Within minutes, the protesters were arrested, and most were given lengthy jail sentences. After that, the Soviet political dissident movement – made up mostly of white-collar workers and intellectuals in Moscow, Leningrad, Kyiv, and other major cities – learned to mobilize anonymously and without posing a direct public challenge to the Kremlin, mostly through the publication and distribution of alternative news and opinion journals, referred to as *samizdat*.

Expectations for blue-collar workers were different, however. The Soviet Union, after all, was the workers' state: At least in theory, then, that should have lent some legitimacy to their voices, especially because they tended to call not for less socialism, but for more. The first Soviet-era social protests about which we know very much are the **strikes** that began in the late 1950s and early 1960s. Triggered by rising food prices and encouraged – to a very limited extent, and mostly unintentionally – by Nikita Khrushchev's political thaw after the terror of Joseph Stalin, a wave of strikes across the country culminated in a strike in the southern Russian city of **Novocherkassk** in 1962. There, thousands of workers occupied the local party headquarters, demanding intercession from above. Attempts to remove them turned violent, and at least five people were killed (Cook 1993; Baron 2001). While that protest and the resulting deaths were effectively covered up by the Soviet press, meaning that almost no one in the Soviet Union knew about them, important lessons were nonetheless learned by the authorities. Among these, apparently, was the importance of paying closer attention to the material conditions of workers, in order to head off such protest in the future – either by preventing anger from emerging, or by repressing potential protest organizers after anger had already arisen.

19.2.1.1   Protest after *Glasnost*

As a result, the peace was kept for nearly twenty years. Workers began to strike again only in the late Soviet period, after Gorbachev had announced the policies of *glasnost* and *perestroika* – "openness" and "restructuring" – effectively giving permission to workers to challenge the hierarchy. Almost all of these new strikes were at the grassroots, as workers complained about layoffs, poor pay and working conditions, and unfair pressure to meet production targets despite the lack of supplies and equipment (Cook 1993). By the summer of 1988, the official government newspaper *Pravda* reported that things had gone too far: "The strike fever is too high a price for us and *perestroika* . . . It is a terrible blow to the country's economy," the newspaper wrote (Cook 1993, 155).

The next summer, however, things got much worse. Miners in the Kuzbas region of western Siberia and the Donbas region of eastern Ukraine – two key Soviet industrial heartlands – struck in their hundreds of thousands. What had once been local wildcat strikes now formed a nationwide movement, rejecting official trade unions and Communist Party mediation and complaining that the burden of economic reform was falling disproportionately on common workers. Strikers demanded direct control over their enterprises, the ability to sell their coal at higher prices and retain more of the profits, less interference from the state, and more investment in their communities (Cook 1993).

As life worsened for all Soviet citizens – with inflation, shortages of food and consumer goods, falling incomes, and increasing corruption by everyone from political leaders to factory managers – workers in the country's heavy industries began to recognize how critical they were to the Soviet Union's continued survival: Electricity, heat, and the basic functioning of the economy all rested on their shoulders. They also began to recognize the power that this gave them, and that recognition spread: Soon, the coalminers were joined on the picket lines by oil workers, potassium miners, transportation workers, and others. The state responded as often as not by making concessions – and then by restricting workers' right to strike. By that point, of course, it was too late.

Gorbachev's policy of *glasnost* also opened the door for more explicitly political protest, including for challenges to how the Soviet Union was governed – and even to its structure as a state. Dissidents calling for improvements to the country's human rights record and an honest chronicling of the horrors of the past were not the only ones taking advantage of this new freedom, however. Ethnonationalist separatist groups in various parts of the Soviet Union – including the three Baltic republics of Estonia, Latvia, and Lithuania, Ukraine, and the South Caucasus republics of Georgia, Armenia, and Azerbaijan – rallied publicly for national self-determination, often claiming the right to secede from the USSR. For their part, ethnic Russian nationalist organizations, such as the virulently antisemitic group Pamyat', called for the establishment of a specifically Russian state, with roots in prerevolutionary (and often premodern) traditionalism. This cacophony came together in a truly massive uprising in August 1991, when hardline members of Gorbachev's government launched a coup, attempting to remove him from power. Crowds thronged central Moscow, denouncing the coup and calling on the military and police to join the people. When government forces refused to open fire, the coup was over – and so, effectively, was the Soviet Union.

19.2.2   Protest in the 1990s: Whose State Is It, Anyway?

Boris Yeltsin – elected president of the Russian Soviet Federative Socialist Republic (RSFSR) when it was still part of the USSR – helped lead the protests that ended the coup against Gorbachev in 1991. By the end of that year, he and the leaders of the Ukrainian and Belorussian Soviet Socialist Republics negotiated the peaceful dissolution of the Soviet Union, and Yeltsin became president of the newly independent Russian Federation. Yeltsin declared that Russia's future would be democratic and economically liberal, and his government began an ambitious program of economic reform, transferring property to private ownership, setting up financial markets, and opening up the country to the rest of the world.

For the vast majority of Russians, even if they supported Yeltsin and his aims, it was a time of tremendous hardship. Thus, within two years Yeltsin found himself facing down crowds of his own, not wholly unlike those that had helped end the hardline coup in 1991. In August 1993, supporters of nationalist, communist and generally antiliberal political forces – a broad spectrum of political and social groups opposed to Yeltsin, including many smarting over the loss of the Soviet Union in its various aspects – mobilized to block the approval of Russia's new constitution. In scenes reminiscent of the standoff between Yeltsin himself and the Soviet hardline coup plotters who had attempted to depose Gorbachev in 1991, Yeltsin's opponents barricaded themselves in the parliament building, took up arms, and declared themselves the rightful seat of power in Russia. This time, however, violence won out. The protesters were eventually forced out under an artillery bombardment. In **Duma** elections – under the new constitution – that December, some of the same forces took to the ballot box in support of the spectacularly misnamed Liberal Democratic Party of Russia (LDPR), a hard-right nationalist party led by Vladimir Zhirinovsky, who railed against Jewish conspiracies and American plots. The LDPR took the largest number of votes in that election, shocking the political establishment, but it was just the tip of a much larger nationalist iceberg. Other groups – such as Russian National Unity – were openly neo-Nazi, and the nationalist right remained a vocal and often violent presence in many Russian cities, particularly provincial cities, throughout the 1990s (Tolz 2003).

19.2.2.1 Protest and Patience in the 1990s

As in the 1980s, however, it was material concerns that motivated most of the country's protesters in the 1990s. Workers in the Kuzbas – who had risen up so powerfully against the Soviet Union in 1989 – took to the streets again in 1994, this time over unpaid wages, a growing problem in the cash-starved post-Soviet Russian economy. Taking advantage of both their numbers and their geographical position, some of these workers even blocked the Trans-Siberian Railway, cutting off the main artery connecting east to west and forcing Moscow to pay attention. They also appeared to throw their weight behind Zhirinovsky and his LDPR, who had plunged politics into disarray by winning the largest share of the votes in the previous year's parliamentary elections (Crowley 2021).

This provided a lesson about the power of cooperation both to workers and to politicians interested in challenging Yeltsin's Kremlin. Regional governors opposed to Yeltsin found common cause with industrial workers suffering from unpaid wages in cities from Siberia to the Far East, again blocking key railways and even occupying squares in central Moscow (Crowley 2021). This time, however, the government could not have granted concessions even if it had wanted to: In August 1998, even as miners banged their hardhats on Gorbatyi Bridge in the heart of the capital, the government defaulted on its debts, effectively declaring bank-ruptcy. For the second time in less than a decade, protesters were present at the fall.

While almost all Russian citizens experienced significant dislocation in the 1990s – as hyperinflation evaporated their savings and incomes, wages and pensions went unpaid, healthcare and social services went undelivered, enterprises closed, and jobs were lost – very few of them protested. There are multiple explan-ations for what some commentators have seen as "passivity," but most research has put paid to the idea that Russians were actually passive. Rather, their apparent "patience" – as Sarah Ashwin called it – was born of their reliance on a thick web of relationships of favors and mutual assistance which centered on the workplace, and which helped them to cope with the difficulties of post-Soviet life (Ashwin 1999). One result was that a great deal of Russian protest in the 1990s and even the early 2000s came to be managed – much like its democracy – from the top down, as competing political and economic interests latched onto grassroots grievances, at times stoking them up and directing the rage of the streets toward their opponents (Robertson 2010).

19.3 Russia's Landscape of Protest

It goes without saying, but Russia is a big country, and a diverse one, too: Some 140 million people live spread across 85 regions, some in cities whose wealth rivals the capitals of Europe, others in villages and towns whose quality of life has not changed much since the late nineteenth century. Protest occurs every day in a multiplicity of ways and over a multiplicity of issues. It would be a fool's errand to attempt to catalogue and understand it all in one go – and that is certainly not the ambition here. But considerable research over the past two decades has shed a lot of light on the broad trends and patterns, which are indeed enlightening.

19.3.1 Overview

One of the most consistent attempts to catalogue Russian protests – conducted by political scientist Graeme Robertson (2014) – traces trends in Russian mobilization from 1997 (early in Boris Yeltsin's second term) through 2011 (just before Vladimir Putin began his third term). Robertson finds four key trends. These are:

(1) A general decline in the volume of protest after a peak during the 1998 financial crisis (although things spiked a bit in 2008–09, in the aftermath of Russia's version of the global financial crisis of 2007–08).

(2) A change in the geographical distribution of protest, from being predominantly focused outside Moscow and St. Petersburg under Yeltsin, to being increasingly centered on Russia's political and cultural capitals under Putin.

(3) A striking (in a manner of speaking) shift in the content of protests. In 1997–2000, when Yeltsin was in power, 41 percent of the protests in Robertson's database were labor strikes, accompanied by a further 8 percent that were blockades of railways and highways. Traditional demonstrations – when people turn out in public squares to raise awareness and grab attention for their cause – made up only one-third of the events in the dataset. Compare that to the Putin period of 2007–11, when strikes and blockades fell to less than 6 percent of the database, and demonstrations rocketed to 84 percent. In other words, protest under Putin became less material and more political.

(4) A shift in protest repertoires, corresponding with a massive diversification of the issues at stake. In the Yeltsin-era protests, fully 72 percent involved unpaid wages, pensions, or other obligations. Under Putin, issues involving wages and obligations made up about 16 percent of protests, while 28 percent focused on the environment and development, 22 percent on government policy, 16 percent on civil rights, and the rest on a hodgepodge of other issues, ranging from history and foreign affairs to commercial disputes and elections.

A somewhat more recent database of Russian protest events, compiled by the political scientists Tomila Lankina and Katerina Tertytchnaya (2019), catalogued 5,824 protest events from 2007 through 2016, of which 41 percent were political in nature, 23 percent focused on social issues, 18 percent were about economic issues, 14 percent concerned legal issues, 9 percent focused on environmental problems, and 3 percent were cultural in nature. (Some protests involved more than one issue; hence the percentages do not add up to 100.) This paints a somewhat different picture from Robertson's research, but it confirms a general trend toward the increasing politicization of protest in Russia, as the regime itself has become more authoritarian.

19.3.2   Local and Environmental Protest

To the extent that the public had anything to do with the fall of the Soviet Union – an idea that is hotly debated but never entirely discounted – anger over environmental degradation is critical to that story. Public distress over the 1986 Chernobyl nuclear disaster, as well as the attempted coverup, fueled bottom-up demands for greater governmental transparency and accountability and accelerated Gorbachev's *glasnost* perhaps faster than the leader had himself anticipated. It also helped galvanize a broader environmental movement, channeling anger about the degree of destruction caused by industrialization and urbanization. These same background conditions carried on throughout the post-Soviet period, with more than half of Russian citizens – by the government's own estimates – living in areas that failed to meet basic standards for environmental health (Henry 2010). Nonetheless, as Laura Henry (2010) chronicles, an explosion in the number of environmental NGOs after the end of the Soviet Union – including the creation of Russian branches of the international movements Greenpeace and the World Wildlife Fund – did not coincide with large numbers of environmentally oriented protests. In the 1990s in particular, both the cash-strapped state and the cash-strapped ordinary citizen tended to see environmentalists as a nuisance, creating a socially and politically hostile environment (Yanitsky 1999). Notable recent exceptions include repeated protests against a pipeline encroaching on the protected watershed around Lake Baikal in the late 2000s, a 2013 approach by the Greenpeace ship *Arctic Sunrise* to an offshore drilling platform in the Russian Arctic, and protests against the environmental impact of construction for the 2014 Sochi Olympics.

Some of the most salient environmental protest was highly local in nature, straying into the realm of "NIMBYism," the acronym standing for "Not In My Back Yard" – a common element of protest around the world. Among the most prominent of these was a long-running movement in the Moscow suburb of Khimki, where citizens came together from 2009 through 2012 in an eventually vain attempt to block the construction of a new highway through a protected old-growth forest, first through letters and petitions to authorities, and eventually through street demonstrations and protest camps inside the forest itself (Evans 2012; Greene 2014b).

Beginning around 2016, environmental NIMBYism turned political. Protests began erupting in small towns around the country, which had found themselves inundated by rubbish shipped in from the country's largest cities, particularly Moscow and St. Petersburg. This led initially to protests in the Moscow suburb of Balashikha, just on the other side of the capital's beltway – a protest that even made national television and forced Putin to issue a public order that Moscow's rubbish be sent elsewhere (Flikke 2021). One of those "elsewheres" turned out to be Shies, a small town in Russia's Arctic North, which beginning in 2017 became the epicenter of nearly three years of public standoffs between protesters and authorities, leading both to the arrests and imprisonment of protest leaders, and to the dismissal of the regional governor (Flikke 2021). While nerves in Shies and elsewhere remain frayed, officials at the highest levels of power – including Putin himself – learned that even something as seemingly mundane as where a city's trash is deposited can have major political consequences, and thus needs to be carefully managed.

19.3.3 Social and Labor Protest

As we saw earlier, concerns about the material conditions of people's lives, from pay and pensions to housing and healthcare, which had dominated protest in the 1980s and 1990s, became less central to the protest agenda after Putin took power. In part, this was because Putin worked hard to keep both employers and labor unions under control, and his increasing monopolization of power meant that the use of protest as a means of political competition among members of the ruling elite was less relevant. Of course, the economy itself was also a factor: If the 1980s and 1990s were times of hardship, the period from 1999 to 2008 saw uninterrupted high levels of economic growth, creating more prosperity than ordinary Russians had ever known – even if that prosperity was unequally distributed in the economy, with **oligarchs** claiming the lion's share. Indeed, that inequality has played an important role in the social and labor protests that do still emerge under Putin.

19.3.3.1   Protest over Benefits and Livelihoods

In January 2005, demonstrations erupted in Moscow and other major cities, involving pensioners, students, and others – backed by trade unions, left-wing political parties, and a smattering of NGOs – angered by the passage and implementation of a law that turned many of their **social benefits into cash handouts**. At a time when the state was cash-rich – even creating a special fund to capture some of the extraordinary profits generated by oil and gas exports, preventing them from causing inflation and distorting the economy – many at the lower end of the income spectrum felt that this was a bait-and-switch operation, designed to let the government and its friendly oligarchs hold onto more of the money it was collecting. The protests went on for weeks, eventually forcing the government to back down on some parts of the law, while allowing authorities in particularly restless cities – including Moscow – to restore important parts of the old way of doing things (Cook 2007; Greene 2014b).

The 2005 benefits protests sent the message out to other groups that mobilization was both possible and potentially fruitful. Over the next couple of years, grassroots groups sprang up to resist everything from housing reform (changing the way apartment buildings were owned, managed, and financed), to car owners protesting rules that would make their automobiles obsolete, and citizens trying to protect Lake Baikal from industrial encroachment (Clement 2008). Sociologists studying these and other protest movements in Putin's second term also found that the "patience" that had helped keep disaffected Russian citizens off the streets in the 1990s was fading, as the networks and coping mechanisms that had helped people survive were no longer solving their problems: Increasingly, people were coming to the conclusion that only a communal effort could do that (Clement 2008; Greene 2014b).

19.3.3.2   Labor Mobilization

Almost dormant since Putin's rise to power, workers, too, began protesting again in 2006, in a wave of mobilization that would last until the global financial crisis hit Russia in 2008. This time, instead of fighting for protection in a failing economy, workers – at places ranging from Ford and Renault automobile assembly plants and beer breweries to retail chains and suburban Moscow railways – struck to get a bigger piece of Russia's unprecedented economic boom (Greene and Robertson

2010). However, unwilling to be coopted the way they had been in the 1990s – and wary of the Kremlin's increasing intolerance of anything that smacked of political opposition – Russia's new strikers avoided open politics altogether. The Kremlin, meanwhile, put pressure on factory-owners and managers to settle the strikes quietly, getting workers back to their jobs both without provoking anger and without giving other workers the sense that mobilization might work (Greene and Robertson 2010; see also Chapter 14).

When the 2007–08 financial crisis rolled into Russia, the Kremlin acted on lessons its earlier occupants had learned in 1989 and 1998. Rather than let economic dislocation erupt into protest – yielding perhaps a Russian version of the United States' Occupy Wall Street or Spain's Indignados – the Russian government put pressure on major employers to avoid layoffs at all costs. One result was that, while the Russian government, Russian corporations, and ordinary Russian citizens all took a financial hit, relatively few workers lost their jobs, and the streets remained quiet. To ice the cake, Putin made a public show of dressing down those oligarchs whose employees did protest over lost jobs and wages (Crowley 2021).

19.3.3.3 Social and Labor Mobilization after Crimea

Russia likewise managed to avoid significant social and labor unrest during its most recent economic downturn, which began in 2014 and saw six years of declining or stagnant real incomes – brought on by a combination of structural factors in the Russian economy and pressure from international sanctions imposed after Russia's annexation of Crimea and invasion of eastern Ukraine. To a great extent, whatever unease Russians may have had about the state of the economy was submerged by a powerful "rally around the flag" effect, as the annexation of Crimea and confrontation with the West supported a patriotic euphoria (Greene and Robertson 2020). But the Kremlin also learned to manage the pain and spread it as evenly as possible, without creating clear geographic or social pockets of hardship, and thus avoiding the sense of relative deprivation that can often lead to protest (Zubarevich 2018). As a result, cutbacks in spending on healthcare and education and even an **increase in the pension age** – while all unpopular and damaging to the approval ratings of the **United Russia** party and Putin himself – failed to produce much protest.

But when government policies did target identifiable groups in ways they felt were unfair, the protest was significant. For example, in 2015 when the government imposed a new tax on long-distance truck drivers, many of whom work as freelancers rather than on fixed employment contracts, the drivers organized a series of protests, driving slowly around the Moscow beltway and other thoroughfares to disrupt traffic (Østbø 2017). And in 2017, when Moscow city authorities launched a program to demolish thousands of 1950s-era apartment buildings – forcibly relocating potentially hundreds of thousands of residents – it provoked a campaign of active resistance that persisted through the time this chapter was written (Bainova,

Eroshkin, and Suliagina 2021). Two things are notable about these cases: First, in both movements, participants actively resisted attempts to politicize the protest, refusing to build alliances with opposition groups, even as official media and United Russia mouthpieces called them stooges of anti-Russian forces. Secondly, in both instances the authorities were forced to make significant concessions to the protesters.

19.3.4 Ethnic and Nationalist Protest

After the Soviet Union broke up into its nominally ethnic constituents – Russia, Ukraine, Georgia, Kazakhstan, and so on – many Russian citizens and Russia watchers worried that those centrifugal forces would carry over into post-Soviet Russia. After all, many of the constituent parts of the now-independent Russian Federation were "republics" or "autonomous oblasts" nominally affiliated with a titular ethnic group: Thus, there were the Turkic republics of Tatarstan and Bashkortostan, the Finno-Ugric republics of Karelia, Udmurtia, and Mordovia, the significantly Buddhist Asian republics of Buryatia, Tuva, and Altai, and the predominantly Muslim republics of the North Caucasus, including Chechnya, Ingushetia, and Dagestan – to name just a few. As discussed elsewhere in this book (see Chapters 3 and 21), many of these regions did challenge the supremacy of Moscow and the integrity of the new Russian state: Moscow fought two civil wars in Chechnya and continues to fight separatist movements in the North Caucasus, while Tatarstan fought (and lost) a long but peaceful political battle for increased sovereignty (Giuliano 2000; Lankina 2004).

19.3.4.1 Minority Ethnic Mobilization

While the Russian state held together – mostly peacefully, outside the North Caucasus – mobilization demanding greater autonomy continued in many of the ethnic republics throughout the 1990s and into the early 2000s. These were at their most powerful – and most resonant – when participants saw their ethnic identity as intrinsically connected to socioeconomic injustice (Giuliano 2011). They also played into struggles between regional leaders and Moscow, particularly during Yeltsin's presidency (Robertson 2010). As these struggles subsided, however, so did the mobilization that accompanied them, and the leaders of Russia's ethnic republics turned their attention to subduing potentially disruptive ethnonational protest at home.

Occasionally, however, minority ethnic protest has spilled out into the open – sometimes with support from regional leaders, and sometimes without. In 2017, for example, hundreds of thousands of Chechens and others from the North Caucasus demonstrated in Grozny, Moscow, and elsewhere against the Kremlin's failure to distance itself from government of Myanmar, which was violently suppressing its Muslim minority population. This was broadly understood to be a power play by

Chechen president Ramzan Kadyrov, although it also underscored the difficulties he himself faces in managing public opinion within his own constituencies (Shendrikova 2017). And in 2020 protesters in Bashkortostan mobilized to block a mining project on Kushtau Hill, a site sacred to local communities. A standoff between protesters and security forces of the local administration and the mining company turned violent, and the impasse lasted until authorities revoked the mining permit (Barbashin and Irisova 2020).

19.3.4.2   Slavic Nationalism

Slavic nationalist protest, on the other hand, has been much less subdued. Russian National Unity – an openly neo-Nazi group numbering at its peak as many as 100,000 members, led by Aleksandr Barkashov – emerged out of the violent constitutional confrontation of 1993 and dominated the radical nationalist scene until it was gradually suppressed in the late 1990s, as the Kremlin began to see it as a direct threat (Laruelle 2018). Other groups, less violent but no less radical – including the National Bolshevik Party headed by Eduard Limonov, and the Red Youth Vanguard led by Sergei Udal'tsov – combined nationalism with Soviet and great power nostalgia into a potent mix, which continued to spill out into small-scale protest and pickets into the 2000s, particularly on key dates such as October Socialist Revolution Day and Stalin's birthday.

In the late 1990s and early 2000s, Russian authorities used a series of anti-extremism and antihate speech laws to crack down on the hardest of the hard-nationalist groups, but the movement never quite went away. By 2005, a new wave of groups – including most prominently the Movement against Illegal Immigration (DPNI, by its Russian acronym, for Dvizhenie Protiv Nelegal'noi Immigratsii) – had organized into a loose nationalist coalition under the banner of the Russian March, an annual outpouring of chauvinist spirit in Moscow (Zuev 2013). An older movement – known loosely as Eurasianism, and symbolized by the right-wing philosopher Aleksandr Dugin – drew on a combination of old Slavophile philosophy and new, mostly geopolitical revanchism to add to the mix, becoming an important part of the response to the 2014 **Euromaidan Revolution** in Ukraine. Indeed, the Kremlin would eventually learn to draw on nationalist movements – and their ability to bring supporters out into the streets – as an important bulwark against more liberal opposition groups (Laruelle 2017).

Sporadic protest mobilization – often with violent consequences – arose as a result of the combination of economic precarity and migration, both of Russian citizens from the North Caucasus and of labor migrants from Central Asia and the South Caucasus. Among the most prominent was a series of events in the Karelian town of Kondopoga in 2006, where a bar-room brawl between ethnic Russian residents and internal migrants from Chechnya gave rise to mobilization on both sides, involving several thousand people overall. A protest by ethnic Russians descended into looting, and both sides were heavily suppressed by riot police brought in from other parts of Russia to quell the unrest (Shlapentokh 2010). Similar events occurred around the country, including in Moscow, where tens of thousands of nationalists descended on Manezhnaia Square, adjacent to the Kremlin, after a Russian football fan was killed in an altercation with a Russian citizen from the North Caucasus (Zakharov 2015). In 2013, days of riots and looting by Russian nationalists shook the working-class Moscow neighborhood of Biriulevo, also in response to altercations between Slavic and non-Slavic residents (Zakharov 2015). In all of these cases, protesters demanded something amounting to ethnic cleansing.

19.3.4.3 Managing Nationalism and Patriotism

In the aftermath of the 2004 Orange Revolution in Ukraine, as Russian authorities began to fear an uprising at home, the Kremlin invested in the creation of loyal youth groups, designed both to channel young Russians' ambitions in a more politically palatable (for the Kremlin) direction, and to help occupy key public spaces if and when oppositional mobilization were to arise. Chief among these was a group called **Nashi** – "Ours" or "Our Guys" – established in 2005. In addition to organizing training, summer camps, field trips, and networking opportunities for members, Nashi and similar groups (including Young Guard) themselves became part of the protest landscape – albeit in a capacity most researchers saw as "astroturf," rather than genuine grassroots activism (Hemment 2012). Some of this was directed squarely against the opposition, with large numbers of activists bussed in to shout down anti-Putin rallies. Almost from the beginning, however, the "activism" of Nashi and other state-linked groups took a distinctly nationalistic (though not ethnically chauvinist) turn. Thus, Nashi protested vocally against a decision by authorities in neighboring Estonia to relocate a monument to Soviet soldiers who died in World War II, sending members to Tallinn to protest, and hounding the Estonian and British ambassadors to Moscow (Lehti, Jutila, and Jokisipila 2008). And, in its framing of the opposition, Nashi almost instinctively – perhaps shaped by their very name – adopted an "us versus them'" rhetoric that pitched themselves as authentically Russian and patriotic, and their opponents as Western stooges (Atwal and Bacon 2012).

The result of these two strands – grassroots nationalist mobilization on the one hand, and top-down patriotic mobilization on the other – has been a fraught balancing act on the part of the Kremlin. On the one hand, the Kremlin has kept its distance from hard-right nationalist groups and their demands, clearly rejecting calls for ethnic cleansing. On the other, it has found itself increasingly reliant on nationalist sympathizers for patriotic mobilization, whether to counteract opposition rallies or for other purposes. Thus, nationalists formed an important part of both the "anti-Maidan" marches in Moscow and other major cities – designed to prevent the potential spread of revolutionary sentiment from Ukraine into Russia in 2014 – and the volunteer brigades that fought in the separatist war Russia has sponsored and supported in eastern Ukraine (Greene and Robertson 2019). But leaders of nationalist groups that claim genuine independence from the Kremlin have been repressed as severely as leaders of the liberal opposition, if not more.

19.3.5   Gender and Sexuality Protest

Even before the Kremlin made "traditional values" an explicit part of its political appeal – ostensibly defending Russia against homosexuality, feminism, and other supposedly destructive trends emanating from the West – the Russian political establishment had a distinctly patriarchal feel (see Chapter 7). Not only were women rare at the highest levels of Russian power, but men from Putin downward made their masculinity an important part of their political appeal – an approach that both resonated with and reinforced patriarchal tendencies in society more broadly (Sperling 2015). It should have been no surprise, then, that a feminist response would emerge. Pussy Riot – and the broader Voina political art movement of which it formed a part – was at the bleeding edge, but it was not alone (Johnson 2014).

LGBTQ+ mobilization has been severely suppressed in Russia for decades. LGBTQ+ communities began to come out into the open in the 1990s, after the Soviet-era law criminalizing homosexuality was repealed, but Western-style pride rallies were never a large-scale phenomenon in Russia. While smaller-scale pride events were held in Moscow, authorities stopped granting permission for pride rallies in 2006, and by 2017 activists had stopped trying (Buyantueva 2020). Instead, activists turned to single-person protests and flash mobs – which are harder for the authorities to prevent and police, but which can still carry some sanctions for participants. The largest of these on record was a 2012 flash mob in St. Petersburg, which gathered some 300 people (Buyantueva 2020). Conditions worsened as the government implemented a new law banning what it called "propaganda of non-traditional sexual relations" and effectively looked the other way when right-wing activists hounded and beat LGBTQ+ Russians.

Prior to Pussy Riot's performance in 2012, however, feminist protest in Russia was rare: Feminist groups were marginalized and unpopular, relegated to the fringes even of liberal civil society, despite the prominent role played by women in that civil society. What is more, Kremlin-organized youth groups – mobilized to help forestall the emergence of a Ukraine-style grassroots opposition – often used antifeminist appeals in their rhetoric (Sperling 2012). In part as a result, when feminist protest did erupt onto the scene, it was radicalized (Sperling 2014; Channell 2014). Indeed, Voina was responsible for Russia's previous high-profile feminist performance, in 2008, when a dozen or so members of the group copulated in a natural history museum, in a critique of then-president **Dmitry Medvedev**'s policies encouraging Russian women to have more babies (Channell 2014).

Indeed, much of the protest over issues of both gender and sexuality has taken a radical, performative turn. Most prominent, perhaps, was the artist Petr Pavlensky, who famously wrapped himself in barbed wire, sewed his lips shut, and nailed his scrotum to the cobblestones of Red Square. But while Pavlensky meant to speak on behalf of Russian citizens in general – sacrificing his body in apparent desperation – it is unclear how many of his compatriots saw themselves in him (Makarychev and Medvedev 2018).

19.3.6   Political Protest

The increasing personalization of politics – with many political scientists beginning to argue that Vladimir Putin himself was becoming the core institution of Russian politics, wielding power and influence above the office of the presidency or even the constitution – meant that Putin became the focal point for much political mobilization. By the time he returned to the presidency in 2012 from his four-year stint as prime minister, opposition-minded protesters saw Putin not simply as a symptom of the country's problems, but as their source, and they saw his removal as the key to a better future (Smyth 2014).

19.3.6.1   Attention Turns to Putin

To take a case in point, in 2009, protests erupted in Kaliningrad – an exclave around the formerly German city of Königsberg, sandwiched between Lithuania and Poland – demanding and eventually winning the removal of the local governor and reduced interference from Moscow. The movement grew out of a series of smaller-scale protests, targeted at much more specific grievances, including the tightening of customs restrictions in a region heavily dependent on crossborder trade, and the closure of a hospital. After Putin appointed Georgy Boos, a Moscow businessman-turned-politician, as Kaliningrad's governor, these smaller groups began to coalesce into a regionwide movement that saw Boos as the epitome of their problems and, increasingly, Putin as their source (Clement 2015). Similar protest bubbled up throughout Putin's second term in office and his stint as prime minister from 2008 to 2012, in places ranging from Vladivostok and Khabarovsk in the Far East, to Astrakhan in the south: In each case, local grievances spurred a movement that would eventually point the finger at Moscow.

Things came to a head in December 2011. Putin – who was wrapping up a four-year stint as prime minister, while Dmitry Medvedev had served as president – announced that he would be returning to the Kremlin the following year. Opposition-minded voters unhappy with this idea took out their frustrations on United Russia, the ruling party, in the December 2011 parliamentary elections. And, worried that their votes might not be properly counted, they also organized a large-scale election monitoring effort. When their fears were borne out and election results appeared to be falsified, they came out to protest. According to those who were there, organizers expecting to see a few hundred protesters at Chistye Prudy in central Moscow were surprised to find several thousand. Both angry and emboldened, the crowd marched on the nearby headquarters of the FSB security service at Lubyanka, chanting "*My zdes' vlast'!*" ("We're the power here!") There, of course, they were met by the police, where several of the loudest protest leaders – including **Alexei Navalny**, then an anticorruption blogger beginning to grow in prominence – were arrested, charged with violating public order, and sentenced to several days in prison (Greene 2014b).

19.3.6.2 The "Bolotnaia" Movement

With Navalny and others still in jail, a coalition of activists came together to create a coordinating council and begin what would turn into the largest organized challenge to Putin's rule since he came to power. Among the leaders were the journalist Sergei Parkhomenko, the civil rights activist Olga Romanova, the Khimki Forest protest leader Yevgeniia Chirikova, and representatives of older human and civil rights groups, voting rights groups, and more. The next week, they held a rally on Bolotnaia Square, within sight of the Kremlin, and kicked off a series of protests that would run until Putin was inaugurated for his third presidential term in May 2012.

Many of the same protest leaders – including Navalny, the radical left-wing activist Sergei Udal'tsov, and the Yeltsin-era reformer Boris Nemtsov – had been active in a long-running series of actions started in 2009 to hold protests on the thirty-first day of each month with thirty-one days, in honor of Article 31 of the Russian constitution, which guarantees the right to protest. While protesters gathered in cities across the country under the banner of "Strategy-31," only rarely did the protests feature more than a few dozen participants. The Bolotnaia protests of 2011–12 – which were also the first major protests in Russia to be enabled by online social media, much as the Arab Spring had been in the previous year or so in Tunisia, Egypt, and elsewhere – were different. They became a focal point for Russians upset about a range of issues, all of whom had come to see Putin as to blame for their grievances. This included, to be sure, those whose demands were purely political, who wanted to see genuine rotation in the Kremlin and a return to competitive politics, who had been complaining about human and civil rights abuses for years, and who were concerned about corruption at the highest levels. But it also included environmental protesters from Khimki and elsewhere demanding that government at all levels observe their own environmental protection laws, LGBTQ+ groups worried about increasing official and unofficial homophobia, and even nationalists concerned about immigration (Greene 2014a, 2014b). In this, they accomplished what earlier political protest movements could not.

Combining disparate protest movements into one movement was not without risks and difficulties. To take one prominent example, the Pussy Riot performance of 2012 – embedding a challenge to Vladimir Putin's legitimacy in a punk and feminist appeal and lending a radical aesthetic to the opposition's vision of Russia's future – gave the Kremlin an opportunity to push back, by appealing to the emotions of those whose vision of Russia's future was more conservative. The Kremlin thus responded not only by prosecuting the members of Pussy Riot and passing a law against offending the feelings of religious believers, but invited believers themselves to express their offense by protesting against the opposition, and by coming out to vote for Putin (Sharafutdinova 2018).

19.3.6.3 Protest and Coercion after Bolotnaia

Throughout most of the Bolotnaia protests, the Kremlin had been content to fight back through persuasion, rather than repression. Most of the protest events were given official permission, and the police kept a respectful distance. That changed on May 6, 2012, when protesters marched toward Bolotnaia Square – just across the river from the Kremlin – to voice their anger at Putin's impending third inauguration. Police blocked the route and tried to force the marchers back (or, it seemed to some, into the river itself). Hundreds were arrested in the resulting melee, sparking a series of trials that would send more than two dozen to jail for sentences as long as six years. That was the last time authorities approved a major opposition protest in central Moscow. From that point on, tactics shifted: Policing became harsher, preventative arrests became more frequent, and a series of laws was used to clamp down on media, social media, funding, and other resources crucial to opposition and protest movements more broadly. As Navalny emerged as the key figurehead of the movement (and especially after Nemtsov was assassinated in 2015), he and his allies became the target of numerous criminal investigations. Coercion gradually became the government's tactic of choice.

The opposition, however, kept at it. As a political force, they sought to contest every possible election: Navalny himself ran in the Moscow mayoral election of 2013, while he and his allies supported candidates running in local, regional, and national parliamentary elections at every opportunity. With their sights set on challenging Putin in the 2018 presidential election, Navalny's team began building a network of campaign offices around the country, while simultaneously ramping up online investigations published by the Anti-Corruption Foundation (known by its Russian acronym FBK, for Fond Bor'by s Korruptsiei) he created. In 2017, the foundation published an investigation into the wealth of Dmitry Medvedev – the ex-president then serving as prime minister – and used that to help motivate a series of nationwide protests. By this point, the movement itself had stopped expecting protest permission to be granted and in many cases had stopped asking. The resulting protests, which escalated again when Navalny was barred from running in the election, turned into a series of experiments, revealing the risks opposition supporters were willing to take, and the level of violence the police were prepared to use to get them off the streets.

This cycle continued to escalate through the summer of 2019, when protests erupted in Moscow over election officials' near-blanket refusal to register opposition candidates for city council elections. Peaceful protests were met with a level of police brutality that had not yet been seen in Russia (although less than the world witnessed in Belarus in 2020, or in many American cities during the Black Lives Matter protests). Protesters were beaten and arrested in their hundreds. And things escalated still further in January and February of 2021, when protesters turned out in Moscow and many other cities in response to the arrest and imprisonment of Navalny, who had returned to Russia after undergoing treatment in Germany for an apparent attempt to poison him. After more than 11,000 people were arrested in just three weekends of protest, and after Navalny's allied organizations were declared extremist and all collaboration with them was outlawed, those opposition leaders who remained free called a halt to protest. There were lessons, they said, to be learned.

Not all of the lessons, however, were negative. In 2019, thousands of ordinary Muscovites joined independent journalists in protesting against the arrest on trumped-up narcotics charges of the investigative journalist Ivan Golunov – a movement so sustained and so high-profile that authorities were eventually forced to back down, to drop the charges and release him, and even to investigate the police officers who had framed him (Henry 2022). In the midst of a general lesson about the power of physical coercion, both challengers and incumbents were also learning about the power of solidarity.

19.3.6.4 Antiwar Protest

On February 24, 2022, Russian troops launched a full-scale invasion of Ukraine, radically expanding a military intervention that had begun eight years earlier with Moscow's 2014 annexation of Crimea and involvement in a separatist war in the Donbas region of eastern Ukraine. The same day, thousands of ordinary Russian citizens began a wave of protests in more than sixty cities across the country, which continued throughout the early weeks of the war. Within the first three weeks, some 15,000 protesters had been arrested, easily outstripping the level of repression faced by those who came out in support of Navalny in early 2021 (OVD-Info 2022). Repressions, too, spread well beyond the streets, as the government moved to block access to independent Russian news sources – effectively shutting down longstanding independent media including Ekho Moskvy and Dozhd – foreign sources (such as the BBC Russian Service and Deutsche Welle), and most major international social media (including Facebook, YouTube, and Twitter). Under a new law passed shortly after the invasion began, protesters and anyone calling for protest or openly criticizing the war faced prison sentences of up to fifteen years.

These were not, however, the first antiwar protests in Russia. In March 2014 – when Russia's intervention in Crimea and the Donbas was beginning to materialize, but before the annexation – many of the leading figures and organizations involved in the Bolotnaia opposition movement rallied together for "Peace Marches," which drew 30,000 to 50,000 participants, primarily in Moscow and St. Petersburg (Tsvetkova and Bush 2014). Boris Nemtsov, the Yeltsin-era reformist politician-turned-opposition leader, emerged as one of the loudest and most consistent voices rallying antiwar protest, until his assassination in February 2015 (Nikolayenko 2019). An antiwar march he had planned to lead on March 1, 2015, turned into a 70,000-strong vigil in his memory, but the antiwar message remained, and many participants carried Ukrainian flags (BBC 2015).

In fact, Russia has an older tradition of antiwar protest. In 1989, at the height of Gorbachev's *glasnost*, activists came together to create "Committees of Soldiers' Mothers" – a nationwide advocacy campaign for the rights of conscripts that began to take shape in response to the horrors of the Afghan war and the harsh conditions of life in the Soviet army. These committees then became one of the most powerful voices challenging Yeltsin's catastrophic 1994–96 war in Chechnya, and they remained a powerful voice for military reform until the government stopped engaging with them not long after Putin first took office (Sundstrom 2006). While some Soldiers' Mothers activists did speak out against Russia's 2022 invasion of Ukraine, though, most of the protesters facing riot police and long prison terms across the country were the same people who had been protesting against Putin since 2011 – ideologically committed opponents of authoritarianism, many of whom heeded a rallying cry issued from his jail cell by Alexei Navalny (Reuters 2022). For them, this was not just about preventing Putin from committing atrocities in their name. It was an effort to stop Russia from sliding into outright totalitarianism.

19.4 Conclusion: Protest, Stability, and Fragility

Does the landscape of protest in today's Russia speak to the regime's stability, or to its fragility? Arguments could be made either way. The fact that the current arrangement of power in Russia has lasted as long as it has, through political booms and busts, and has seen off every challenger – that would seem to speak in favor of stability. On the other hand, the fact that protest keeps occurring, and that the state increasingly turns to coercion rather than persuasion to handle it – might that not suggest a kind of fragility?

This chapter suggests that we should approach that question somewhat differently, by dividing it into two. First, if protest occurs when expectations break down and institutions fail to dictate how political processes will go, then we need to pay attention to who has the upper hand in setting the new expectations, once the dust of political confrontation has settled. And, secondly, if protest is a learning process, then we need to ask which actors – the incumbents or the challengers – seem better able to grasp the lessons that protest teaches. If we can answer these questions, then we can get to grips with the broader issue of the stability or fragility of the Russian political system.

19.4.1   Expectations, Protest, and Revolution

If we think of a revolution as a fundamental shift in the nature of power – not just a change of who is in power, but a change of how power is acquired, maintained, and exercised – then the story outlined in this chapter contains at least one revolutionary moment, and perhaps two. When the hardline coup plotters tried to oust Gorbachev, the power of the street did not figure into their calculations: It was not part of their expectations. When the unexpected happened, the coup failed and the Soviet Union did, too. But, as revolutionary as the end of communism and the breakup of the state were, even more revolutionary was the establishment of a new set of expectations, one that would force politicians to take the street seriously. Yeltsin faced this again in 1993, this time from the other side and, while he won that fight with the street, he faced continuing struggles with popular mobilization throughout his presidency.

The second revolutionary moment, then, may have come somewhere in 2012, when, in deciding to switch from persuasion to coercion in its response to opposition mobilization, the Kremlin sought to shift expectations back in the other direction: to communicate to the street that it should no longer expect to play a role in how Russian power works. The extent to which the opposition had accepted those expectations has remained an open question even at the time this text was written, nearly a decade later. Those in power, though, very clearly continued to operate with this expectation in mind, and indeed that expectation seemed to harden over time, as the ferociousness of repression increased, and as more and more spheres of protest and popular mobilization found themselves under the gun. One reason, then, why more and more protest in Russia is becoming political is because the authorities are treating more and more protest as though it were political, regardless of what it was actually meant to be about.

And, yet, things may not be quite that straightforward. The Bolotnaia protest movement – even if it failed to change the "who" and "how" of Russian politics – had a major impact on the "what" and "why." It was, after all, the protests that prompted the government to turn to ideology and a degree of nationalism, fundamentally changing the ideological content of Russian politics. It was also the protests that pushed the authorities to become more repressive, to draw sharper divisions between "us" and "them," even at the risk of multiplying the number of disaffected citizens. These were not, of course, outcomes that the protesters sought, but they all suggest that the street continues to be highly relevant to Russian politics. Take, for example, the day that Navalny flew back from Berlin to

Moscow. After his supporters gathered at the capital's Vnukovo Airport to greet him – and to help prevent his arrest – the Kremlin gave orders for his flight to be redirected to Moscow's Sheremetyevo Airport instead, where no one was waiting. Those are not the actions of a system that has entirely discounted the power of ordinary citizens, or that does not fear the street.

19.4.2 Learning Lessons

Even when expectations are set, of course, they are not set in stone. The history of protest in Russia – and in the Soviet Union before – is testament to the rapidity and radicalness with which expectations can shift. And so politics and power are not simply a question of who gets the upper hand when expectations are reset, but also of who is better at learning and adapting to change.

The history and landscape reviewed in this chapter show learning on both sides. We see the late Soviet and then the early Russian state learn to take public interests on board. We see politicians in the 1990s learn to make use of protest, even to manipulate and manage it, but also to respect it, and perhaps to fear it. We see protesters learn how to use the interests of politicians and other leaders to further their own agendas, as well as how to avoid being captured and coopted by those whose interests they do not necessarily share. We see repertoires of action and reaction evolve in response to one another, as protesters take advantage of openings when they appear, and then learn to defend themselves when circumstances change.

Over time, however, the patterns of learning begin to diverge. Early on, we can see very clearly how challengers and incumbents learn together, how they push and pull one another, calculating opportunities and risks and deciding how to act. Even under Putin – particularly in his first two terms, but also later – we can see how protesters learn to get what they want, in part by avoiding outright politicization, while the regime learns to capitulate when need be and, when possible, to avoid provoking protest in the first place. In more recent years, though, it seems to be only the opposition that is doing the learning. For several years now, the authorities have responded in only one way: with repression and coercion. If they are learning anything, those lessons are not playing into the strategies and tactics they deploy. At the same time, protesters continue to evade and to innovate, and even – from time to time – to win victories.

We are left, then, with a decidedly mixed picture. On the one hand, we see a state that is clearly capable of pushing protest to the furthest margins of politics by using physical force to repress citizens taking to the streets, thereby undoing many of the democratic expectations that had emerged in the early post-Soviet period. On the other, we see the same state seemingly lose its ability to learn, and thus to adapt. What will it do if – when – expectations shift again? Perhaps, then, the answer is that stability and fragility coexist and that, in its quest for stability at almost any cost, the Russian political system is creating its own fragility.

DISCUSSION QUESTIONS

1. What drove the shifts in the content, geography, and type of protest in Russia from the Yeltsin era to the Putin era?
2. Why did the Russian government's approach to protest change after Putin came to power?
3. Why is some protest in Russia more radical in form than others?

REFERENCES

Ashwin, Sarah. 1999. *Russian Workers: The Anatomy of Patience*. Manchester: Manchester University Press.

Atwal, Maya, and Edwin Bacon. 2012. "The Youth Movement Nashi: Contentious Politics, Civil Society, and Party Politics." *East European Politics*, 28(3), 256–66.

Bainova, M. S., S. U. Eroshkin, and J. O. Suliagina. 2021. "Sotsial'nye problemy renovatsii zhil'ia v Moskve." *Sotsiologicheskie issledovaniia*, 7, 137–43.

Barbashin, Anton, and Olga Irisova. 2020. "Protesting in Russia in the 2010s: Rising Risks, Rising Costs." *SAIS Review of International Affairs*, 40(2), 111–19.

Baron, Samuel H. 2001. *Bloody Sunday in the Soviet Union: Novocherkassk, 1962*. Stanford: Stanford University Press.

BBC. 2015. "Boris Nemtsov Murder: Tens of Thousands March in Moscow," 1 March, www .bbc.com/news/world-europe-31677506.

Buyantueva, Radzhana. 2020. "What Motivates LGBT Activists to Protest? The Case of Russia." *Problems of Post-Communism*, forthcoming.

Channell, Emily. 2014. "Is Sextremism the New Feminism? Perspectives from Pussy Riot and Femen." *Nationalities Papers*, 42(4), 611–14.

Clement, Karine. 2008. "New Social Movements in Russia: A Challenge to the Dominant Model of Power Relationships?" *Journal of Communist Studies and Transition Politics*, 24(1), 68–89.

  2015. "From 'Local' to 'Political': The Kaliningrad Mass Protest Movement of 2009–2010 in Russia." In Kerstin Jacobsson (ed.), *Urban Grassroots Movements in Central and Eastern Europe*, pp. 163–93. London: Ashgate.

Cook, Linda J. 1993. *The Soviet Social Contract and Why It Failed: Welfare Policy and Workers' Politics from Brezhnev to Yeltsin*. Cambridge, MA: Harvard University Press.

  2007. *Postcommunist Welfare States: Reform Politics in Russia and Eastern Europe*. Ithaca: Cornell University Press.

Crowley, Stephen. 2021. *Putin's Labor Dilemma: Russian Politics between Stability and Stagnation*. Ithaca: Cornell University Press.

Evans, Albert B. Jr. 2012. "Protests and Civil Society in Russia: The Struggle for Khimki Forest." *Communist and Post-Communist Studies*, 45(3–4), 233–42.

Flikke, Geir. 2021. "Dysfunctional Orders: Russia's Rubbish Protests and Putin's Limited Access Order." *Post-Soviet Affairs*, 37(5), 470–88.

Giuliano, Elise. 2000. "Who Determines the Self in the Politics of Self-Determination? Identity and Preference Formation in Tatarstan's Nationalist Mobilization." *Comparative Politics*, 32(3), 295–316.

2011. *Constructing Grievance: Ethnic Nationalism in Russia's Republics.* Ithaca: Cornell University Press.

Greene, Samuel A. 2014a. "Beyond Bolotnaia: Bridging Old and New in Russia's Election Protest Movement." *Problems of Post-Communism*, 60(2), 40–52.

2014b. *Moscow in Movement. Power and Opposition in Putin's Russia.* Stanford: Stanford University Press.

Greene, Samuel A., and Graeme B. Robertson. 2010. "Politics, Justice and the New Russian Strike." *Communist and Post-Communist Studies*, 43(1), 73–95.

2019. *Putin v. the People: The Perilous Politics of a Divided Russia.* London: Yale University Press.

2020. "Affect and Autocracy. Emotions and Attitudes in Russia after Crimea." *Perspectives on Politics*, 20(1), 38–52.

Hemment, Julie. 2012. "Nashi, Youth Voluntarism, and Potemkin NGOs: Making Sense of Civil Society in Post-Soviet Russia." *Slavic Review*, 71(2), 234–60.

Henry, Laura A. 2010. *Red to Green: Environmental Activism in Post-Soviet Russia.* Ithaca: Cornell University Press.

2022. "People Power in Putin's Russia: Social versus Political Protests." In Nathan Stoltzfus and Christopher Osmar (eds.), *The Power of Populism and People: Resistance and Protest in the Modern World*, pp. 137–62. London: Bloomsbury.

Johnson, Janet Elise. 2014. "Pussy Riot as a Feminist Project: Russia's Gendered Informal Politics." *Nationalities Papers*, 42(4), 583–90.

Lankina, Tomila V. 2004. *Governing the Locals: Local Self-Government and Ethnic Mobilization in Russia.* Lanham, MD: Rowman & Littlefield.

Lankina, Tomila, and Katerina Tertytchnaya. 2019. "Protest in Electoral Autocracies: A New Dataset." *Post-Soviet Affairs*, 36(1), 20–36.

Laruelle, Marlene. 2017. "Is Nationalism a Force for Change in Russia?" *Daedalus*, 146(2), 89–100.

2018. *Russian Nationalism: Imaginaries, Doctrines, and Political Battlefields.* New York: Routledge.

Lehti, Marko, Matti Jutila, and Markku Jokisipila. 2008. "Never-Ending Second World War: Public Performances of National Dignity and the Drama of the Bronze Soldier." *Journal of Baltic Studies*, 39(4), 393–418.

Makarychev, Andrey, and Sergey Medvedev. 2018. "Biopolitical Art and the Struggle for Sovereignty in Putin's Russia." *Journal of Contemporary Central and Eastern Europe*, 26(2–3), 165–79.

Nikolayenko, Olena. 2019. "Framing and Counter-Framing a Peace March in Russia: The Use of Twitter during a Hybrid War." *Social Movement Studies*, 18(5), 602–21.

Østbø, Jardar. 2017. "Between Opportunist Revolutionaries and Mediating Spoilers: Failed Politicization of the Russian Truck Drivers' Protest, 2015–2016." *Demokratizatsiya: The Journal of Post-Soviet Democratization*, 25(3), 279–303.

OVD-Info. 2022. "Net voine. Kak rossiiskie vlasti boriutsia s antivoennymi protestami," https://reports.ovdinfo.org/no-to-war#2.

Reuters. 2022. "Jailed Navalny Calls for Anti-War Protests across Russia on Sunday," 11 March, www.reuters.com/world/europe/kremlin-critic-navalny-calls-anti-war-protests-across-russia-2022-03-11/.

Robertson, Graeme B. 2010. *The Politics of Protest in Hybrid Regimes: Managing Dissent in Post-Communist Russia.* Cambridge: Cambridge University Press.

2014. "Protesting Putinism: The Election Protests of 2011–2012 in Broader Perspective." *Problems of Post-Communism*, 60(2), 11–23.

Sharafutdinova, Gulnaz. 2018. "The Pussy Riot Affair and Putin's Demarche from Sovereign Democracy to Sovereign Morality." *Nationalities Papers*, 42(4), 615–21.

Shendrikova, Diana. 2017. "Why the Myanmar Crisis Makes Russia Choose between Muslim and Buddhist Minorities inside." ISPI Commentary, 7 September. Milan: Istituto per gli Studi di Politica Internazionale, www.ispionline.it/it/pubblicazione/why-myanmar-crisis-makes-russia-choose-between-muslim-and-buddhist-minorities-inside-17587.

Shlapentokh, Dmitry. 2010. "'Kondopoga': Ethnic/Social Tension in Putin's Russia." *European Review*, 18(2), 177–206.

Smyth, Regina. 2014. "The Putin Factor: Personalism, Protest, and Regime Stability in Russia." *Politics and Policy*, 42(4), 567–92.

Sperling, Valerie. 2012. "Nashi Devushki: Gender and Political Youth Activism in Putin's and Medvedev's Russia." *Post-Soviet Affairs*, 28(2), 232–61.

2014. "Russian Feminist Perspectives on Pussy Riot." *Nationalities Papers*, 42(4), 591–603.

2015. *Sex, Politics and Putin: Political Legitimacy in Russia*. Oxford: Oxford University Press.

Sundstrom, Lisa McIntosh. 2006. "Soldiers' Rights Groups in Russia: Civil Society through Russian and Western Eyes." In Alfred B. Evans Jr., Laura A. Henry, and Lisa McIntosh Sundstrom (eds.), *Russian Civil Society: A Critical Assessment*, pp. 178–96. Armonk, NY: M. E. Sharpe.

Tolz, Vera. 2003. "Right-Wing Extremism in Russia: The Dynamics of the 1990s." In Peter H. Merkl and Leonard Weinberg (eds.), *Right-Wing Extremism in the Twenty-First Century*, pp. 257–76. New York: Routledge.

Tsvetkova, Maria, and Jason Bush. 2014. "Ukraine Crisis Triggers Russia's Biggest Anti-Putin Protest in Two Years." Reuters, 15 March, www.reuters.com/article/ukraine-crisis-russia-rallies-idINL6N0MC0JC20140315.

Yanitsky, Oleg. 1999. "The Environmental Movement in a Hostile Context: The Case of Russia." *International Sociology*, 14(2), 157–72.

Zakharov, Nikolay. 2015. *Race and Racism in Russia*. London: Palgrave Macmillan.

Zubarevich, Natalya. 2018. "The Center–Regions Relationship: What Has Changed in Four Years of Crisis?" *Russian Politics and Law*, 56(3–6), 208–21.

Zuev, Denis. 2013. "The Russian March: Investigating the Symbolic Dimension of Political Performance in Modern Russia." *Europe–Asia Studies*, 65(1), 102–26.

20 | The Politics of the Environment in Russia: Extraction, Climate Change, and Indigenous Rights in the Russian Arctic

LAURA A. HENRY

Fig. 20.1 Yamal peninsula: Nentsy drive reindeer. Credit: Evgenii Mitroshin / iStock / Getty Images Plus.

> From time immemorial, mankind used nature to satisfy its
> needs, more and more ... First it was mushroom picking and
> animal hunting, later on it was mineral resources, metals,
> hydrocarbons. Can it be stopped? Of course not. It's impossible
> to stop. The question is how to use them sustainably, how to
> minimize the damage to nature or to bring it to zero.
>
> Vladimir Putin (cited in Myers and Roth,
> "Putin Defends Seizure")

Abstract

Environmental politics offers a useful entry point to evaluate the stability and
fragility of Russia's post-Soviet political and economic regime. The politics of the

environment in Russia intersects and interacts with a range of other issues – the state's capacity to enforce its laws; democracy and the ability of citizens to participate in politics; sources of economic growth and the regulation of the economy; inequality; and the diverse cultures of Russia's multinational society. Russia boasts tremendous ecological diversity and significant protected natural areas, but also faces a number of environmental challenges, not least of which are the effects of climate change. In the post-Soviet period, in an effort to recover from the instabilities of the 1990s, the Putin government developed an economic model based on natural resource exploitation and an increasingly authoritarian form of governance, justifying this system as a means of achieving prosperity and economic security for citizens. Today we see that Russia has strong environmental laws that are not always well enforced. Russians express a high level of concern about environmental issues, but the political climate is increasingly hostile to activism. Russia is also making a big bet on the Arctic region where natural resource extraction is expected to bolster Russia's future economic prospects and status as a great power, even as climate change and source of environmental degradation threaten Arctic inhabitants, wildlife, and ecosystems.

20.1   Introduction

On May 29, 2020, a massive oil spill – the largest fuel spill in Russia's history – occurred in Noril'sk, a city located above the Arctic Circle. Noril'sk is the home of Nornickel, one of the world's largest companies, engaged in the mining and smelting of palladium, nickel, and copper. Nornickel is owned by Vladimir Potanin, a prominent Russian **oligarch** who acquired the company in the controversial loans-for-shares privatization in the mid-1990s. At the Noril'sk–Taimyr Energy Company's Heat and Power Plant Number 3, a Nornickel subsidiary, 21,000 tons of diesel fuel leaked out of a storage tank, flowing into the surrounding soil and the Ambarnaya River (Meduza 2020). Efforts to clean up the fuel were complicated by the remote location, which allows only seasonal access for ground transport. Some observers speculated that climate change, which contributes to the thawing and subsiding of permafrost, may have played a role in destabilizing the storage tank. While this spill was unprecedented in scale, Noril'sk has been the site of severe pollution for decades, dating back to the Soviet era. Areas near the company's operations have been characterized as an **"industrial desert,"** a term describing "regions that arose because of the concentration of industry and its unabated pollution" during the Soviet period (Josephson 2007, 295). Air and water pollution and past fuel leaks have significantly degraded the traditional territories of Indigenous peoples in the region around Noril'sk – the Dolgans, Nenets, and Evenkis, among others (IWGIA 2020).

Responses from various political leaders and Russian government agencies were swift and harsh. The Federal Service for the Supervision of Natural Resources (Rosprirodnadzor) ordered Nornickel to pay a $2 billion fine, the largest sum ever paid by a Russian company as a legal penalty (RBK 2020a; RFE/RL 2021). The accident elicited especially strong words from Russia's president, **Vladimir Putin**. In his April 2021 Presidential Address to the Federal Assembly, Putin called for stricter environmental legislation:

> I would like to ask those responsible to accelerate the adoption of a law on the financial responsibility of enterprise owners for clearing up the accumulated pollution and for the reclamation of industrial sites. This is a very simple approach. Here it is: If you have benefited from polluting the environment, clean up after yourself. We must act harshly (Putin 2021).

Putin also assured the public that Nornickel's fine would be used to protect and improve environmental conditions in Noril'sk and the surrounding region (Reuters 2021). The company launched a public relations campaign following the spill with events such as a meeting with NGOs, environmentalists, and local community leaders (Nornickel 2021). In a video conference with President Putin, Potanin also promised that Nornickel would fund environmental remediation and programs to support Indigenous reindeer herding and the recovery of fishing areas.

The Nornickel fuel spill raises a number of questions about environmental politics in Russia, and more specifically in the Arctic. Environmental politics offers a useful entry point to consider the stability and fragility of Russia's post-Soviet political and economic regime, particularly how it has evolved under President Putin. The politics of the environment in Russia intersects and interacts with a range of other issues – the state's capacity to enforce its laws; democracy and the ability of citizens to participate in politics; sources of economic growth and the regulation of the economy; inequality; and the diverse cultures of Russia's multi-national society. The government acknowledges the public's concerns about environmental degradation and attempts to demonstrate its strict environmental policy, while often failing to implement laws and regulations. Moreover, features of Russia's political-economic model make it challenging to protect the environment in practice.

The following sections examine environmental politics from the Soviet period to the present, considering broad trends in environmental protection, activism, and public opinion, as well as offering a close look at environmental issues in the Russian Arctic, a region in which **natural resource extraction** is expected to bolster Russia's future economic prospects, yet climate change and source of environmental degradation threaten Arctic inhabitants, wildlife, and ecosystems.

20.2 Environmental Politics in Russia

Environmental issues are an area of great concern for many Russian citizens who value their health and their children's health, and who also favor the protection of natural spaces and wildlife. At times Russian citizens have come together to demand the enforcement of their constitutional right to a healthy environment. Yet Russia suffers from both chronic and severe environmental challenges, even as it hosts a significant percentage of the world's forests and protected natural territories. The subsections that follow consider how environmental politics in Russia is shaped by changes in political and economic governance, with particular attention to how this changing context of more democratic and more authoritarian governance has influenced environmental activism.

20.2.1 Changing Political and Economic Regimes, Changing Environmental Politics

The trajectory of environmental politics in Russia over the past four decades follows broader changes to the country's political regime, from a one-party authoritarian regime under the **Communist Party of the Soviet Union,** to a weak democracy in the 1990s, to a new, evolving style of hybrid authoritarian politics under President Vladimir Putin. Environmental activism was one type of civic engagement that grew rapidly during **Mikhail Gorbachev's** *perestroika* reforms of the late 1980s, which allowed for greater freedom of expression and association. Soviet citizens voiced concern about air and water pollution from industrial activity and nuclear contamination – a threat made obvious by the 1986 **Chernobyl** nuclear accident – among other issues (Yanitsky 1993).

In the last years of the USSR, the Institute of Geography in the Academy of Sciences published maps showing that 16 percent of Soviet territory was experiencing a "critical" or "catastrophic" environmental situation and 25 percent of the Soviet population lived in areas with "acute" environmental conditions due to pollution (Oldfield 2005, 26). In some of the Soviet republics, criticism of the Soviet regime by environmentalists became associated with nationalist independence movements (Dawson 1996), although this link was less developed in Russia. Following the disintegration of the Soviet system in the early 1990s, Russia's industrial activity dropped by almost half, leading to modest declines in air and water pollution, although Russia's economy remained highly energy- and pollution-intensive (per unit of GDP) compared to economies in Europe and North America.

In 1991, under the presidency of **Boris Yeltsin,** Russia wrote a new constitution and developed a raft of new environmental laws. The **Russian constitution** proclaims, "Everyone shall have the right to a favorable environment, reliable information about its state and restitution for damage inflicted to health and property from violations of environmental laws" (Chapter 2, Article 42). Other important laws were passed on ecological expertise (1995), protected natural areas (1995), wildlife (1995), waste (1998), and environmental protection (2002), as well as a new Water Code (1995) and Forest Code (1997) (Oldfield 2005, 70; Martus 2018, 22–23). In the 1990s, the Russian government also participated robustly in international efforts to address environmental issues. Russia has signed on to more than 100 international environmental agreements since 1991, and by 2020 was a formal participant in more than 190 multilateral environmental agreements (Mitchell 2021). These include the ratification of the Kyoto Protocol to the **UN Framework Convention on Climate Change** (UNFCCC), which brought the agreement to reduce greenhouse gas emissions into force globally.

Nevertheless, the institutional basis for environmental protection in Russia offers a mixed picture. After a period of bureaucratic instability, the **Ministry of Natural Resources and the Environment** was given the dual responsibility of overseeing the exploitation of Russia's resources and protecting the environment in 2008. Proponents of strong environmental protection have charged that the relevant departments and agencies are underfunded and understaffed, given the need to monitor such a huge territory and regulate powerful economic actors (Crotty and Rodgers 2012). As a result, Russia experiences an **"implementation gap"** between environmental laws on the books and how they are applied and enforced in practice (Nikitina and Kotov 2002).

The essential role of natural resources in Russia's economic development also shapes environmental politics. Natural resource industries engage in various forms of extraction – from oil and gas to mining, forestry, and fishing. Many of these industries play a large role in Russia's economy and some – notably in the energy sector – have relatively high rates of state ownership, indicating their strategic importance. Michael Bradshaw and Richard Connolly argue that "it is difficult to overstate the importance of natural resource exports to the functioning and per-formance of the Russian economy" (2016, 717), pointing toward the "extremely high" correlation between changes in annual export revenues and annual GDP growth. In 2013, at its peak, revenue from oil and gas exports was thought to account for more than 50 percent of Russia's federal budget (US EIA 2014), with more than 80 percent of the country's export revenue coming from natural resources (Bradshaw and Connolly 2016, 714). **Gazprom** and **Rosneft**, the state-owned gas and oil giants, are the largest taxpayers to the Russian government (Åslund and Fisher 2020; see Chapter 11). Given their importance to the economy, enterprises and their owners in these industries also wield significant political influence.

The natural resource focus of the economy is broadly accepted by elites and the public alike. Politicians who object to the conflation of political and economic power in Russia are generally marginal figures who do not wield legislative or budgetary power. For example, in 2009, the liberal party Yabloko charged that "'pollutioncrats' – those who are engaged in short-term welfare of the country at the expense of purposeful weakening of the mechanisms of protection of public ecological interests – are in power in Russia" (Yabloko 2009). However, the party received only 3.5 percent of the vote in the 2011 **Duma** elections, following this statement, and only 1.3 percent in the 2021 parliamentary vote. Overall, the coincidence of the weak enforcement of environmental law and powerful economic actors in the natural resource sector creates ongoing challenges for environmental protection in Russia, and these issues have not been high on the political agenda.

20.2.2   Emerging Environmental Activism in Post-Soviet Russia

While the first post-Soviet decade was more democratic than the previous Soviet system, it was also highly unstable and experienced a severe economic recession. Preoccupied by a host of pressing issues internationally and at home, President Yeltsin presided over a "negligent state" with regard to civil society as a whole (Henderson 2011, 12), and environmental activism in particular. Environmental NGOs (ENGOs) and movements were not repressed, but neither were they able to effectively partner with or pressure the government to implement and enforce environmental laws. In part, this lack of efficacy stemmed from ENGOs' lack of resources and the public's preoccupation with personal economic security during Russia's severe economic downturn in the 1990s. However, the lack of influence by environmental experts and activists can also be linked to the government's erratic policymaking process and low bureaucratic capacity as well as a lack of authority to implement laws across the country's vast territory. Sarah Henderson contrasts the state–society relationship under Yeltsin with the "vigilant state" approach of the Putin presidency, in which the government made a more concerted effort to engage civil society groups and also developed significantly more oversight of civil society (2011). In the early 2000s, more onerous requirements for legally registering and managing NGOs proved too burdensome for some grassroots citizen organizations (Gilbert 2016), some of which closed their doors even as other civic groups, particularly at the local level, persisted (Javeline and Lindemann-Komarova 2010).

Despite these shifting political conditions, the number of ENGOs in Russia grew throughout the 1990s and early 2000s. These were organizations of all types – from branch offices of international groups such as the World Wildlife Fund (WWF) and Greenpeace in Moscow, to small green political parties and environmental education clubs in provincial cities. Many of the larger environmental organizations sought support from foreign grant programs to launch their projects. Donors such as the US Agency for International Development (USAID), the National Endowment for Democracy (NED), the Eurasia Foundation, and other more environmentally focused foundations were eager to support community initiatives to pursue sustainable development projects or to experiment with recycling. The competition for resources to fund environmental activism privileged some groups over others, and those based in major cities, led by English-speaking activists, or with projects similar to those pursued in the West were more likely to receive funding (Henry 2010).

As the Russian economy revived in the 2000s, environmentalists expressed concern about continued pollution from industrial facilities and increasingly rapid natural resource extraction to fuel growth. The question of whether economic growth had to lead to ecological degradation became increasingly central to Russian debates in environmental politics. Environmentalists argued that Russia had a historic opportunity to break with the polluting practices of the past, while most elected officials prioritized reviving the international political and economic influence of the country, even at the expense of short-term environmental damage. During President Putin's first term in office, Aleksei Yablokov, former environmental advisor to President Yeltsin and president of Center for Russian Environmental Policy, a Moscow-based thinktank, criticized the government by asserting that the "ideology in Russia is that environmental protection is only for rich countries, and that when Russia is rich, it will be time to solve environmental problems" (Dresen 2005).

20.2.3 Environmentalism in Russia's Interests

By Vladimir Putin's third term as president (2012–18), space for environmental activism had begun to shift and contract. Formal and informal restrictions on civic activism resulted from multiple factors – some long-term trends in addition to new government laws enacted after protests following the 2011 parliamentary elections. These obstacles did not affect all forms of environmentalism equally. Over time, funding to Russia from foreign donors declined as other parts of the world exhibited greater need and priorities shifted. Major donors were also pushed out of Russia by the **2015 Law on Undesirable Organizations**. At the same time, Russian government rhetoric began to turn against NGOs that relied on foreign, rather than domestic, sources of financial support. This sentiment culminated in the **2012 "foreign agent" law**. Under this law, NGOs receiving funding from foreign sources and engaging in "political activity" were placed on a registry maintained by the Ministry of Justice, exposing the organization and its leaders to potential fines. A number of environmental organizations were affected by the law as the definition of political activity spanned efforts to change public opinion and complaints to regional government officials (Tysiachniouk, Tulaeva, and Henry 2018; Plantan 2020). These new laws and labels constrained the work of some of the oldest Russian environmental organizations and muted some critical voices, even as ENGOs have developed strategies to continue their work despite the unfavorable legal and political conditions. Thus far, these laws have not directly impacted **WWF-Russia** or **Greenpeace Russia** – ENGOs that are still operating in Russia as branches of their globally influential and high-profile international parent organizations – but many other ENGOs have been affected.

The use of the foreign agent law to curb some ENGOs does not mean that the Russian government is hostile to all forms of environmentalism. Under President Putin's third and fourth terms, the government began to encourage citizen activism that aligned with state goals, such as volunteerism, and to discourage or repress organizations and individuals who are openly critical of the regime and its policies or who make demands in conflict with the government's preferences. In fact, the regime promotes certain forms of "patriotic environmentalism." The Russian government increased domestic support for "socially oriented" NGOs and those groups deemed as having worthy projects, in part through the Presidential Grant Fund (Laruelle and Howells 2020). Putin himself is famous for his high-profile displays of concern for wildlife, albeit in a hypermasculine style, such as when he assisted scientists in tranquilizing and tagging a Siberian tiger and a polar bear, or when he flew an ultralight aircraft to introduce cranes born into captivity to migration. Putin also has repeated a perspective frequently heard among government officials that Russia, given its sheer size and ecological diversity, is an **environmental donor** to the rest of the world. For example, in 2016 on a Russia Today broadcast, he stated "Our country has colossal reserves of fresh water, forest resources, enormous biodiversity and [Russia] acts as an ecological donor of the world, providing it with almost 10% of biospheric sustainability" (RT 2016). Most recently, the Russian government and scientific communities have also more actively tried to understand and promote the role of Russia's vast forests to act as carbon sinks. The government also endeavors to acknowledge public environmental concern. The Russian government declared 2017 the Year of Ecology and in 2018 introduced the National Project "Ecology," which encompasses initiatives ranging from the reform of waste management to projects to protect fresh water and to establish new specially protected areas (Russian Federation, Government of 2018). This kind of rhetoric indicates that there is still space for state-sanctioned environmentalism, albeit of a particular type, in Russia today.

20.3 Public Concern about the Environment and the Potential for Protest

The Russian public remains concerned about environmental issues, and there is some evidence that concern is growing. In a 2020 Levada poll, Russian respondents ranked environmental pollution as the top threat to humanity in the twenty-first century, above terrorism and armed conflict, with climate change in fourth place (Levada Center 2020). Some environmental issues attract more attention than others. Polls reveal persistent concern about air and water pollution and waste disposal, objective problems that Russian citizens often experience at first hand. Supporting these poll results, in 2019, the Presidential Council for Civil Society and Human Rights noted the high level of "complaints and social protests caused by the violation of citizens' rights to health protection, sanitary and epidemiological well-being and a favorable environment when handling waste" in thirty regions and recommended that more be done to prevent waste through recycling and other measures (Presidential Council for Civil Society and Human Rights 2019). In addition, the year 2020 witnessed a record number of instances of high and extremely high air pollution in Russia (RBK 2020c), events that attracted widespread comment in online forums.

Public concern about **climate change** also appears to have grown over time, although polling on the issue is quite variable. In the early 2000s various government figures, including President Putin, voiced doubt about whether human activity was the primary cause of climate change. This form of climate skepticism shaped media coverage and public opinion in Russia, with many believing that concern about global warming was overblown (Tynkkynen and Tynkkynen 2018). However, in the 2020 Levada poll, 34 percent of respondents agreed that "global warming" is a serious threat (RBK 2020b). In a 2021 Public Opinion Foundation poll focused more narrowly on environmental issues, 67 percent of respondents agreed that global warming is underway; however, global warming is listed in ninth place among the most severe or dangerous environmental issues, attracting only 14 percent of respondents. Opinion is also mixed as to whether warming should be attributed to human activity or natural processes, with approximately a quarter of the population viewing climate change as a natural phenomenon in both polls (Public Opinion Foundation 2021). In a broader context, while international polls show Russians to be somewhat less concerned about climate change than the global average, they often rank higher than their counterparts in the United States in levels of concern (IPSOS 2020; Pew Research Center 2020).

Citizens surveyed generally assign the government the leading responsibility for environmental protection. Given the lack of real political party competition in Russia, however, public concern for the environment does little to shape the outcomes of elections, and green parties have failed to achieve a significant share of the vote. In the absence of access to responsive formal political institutions, at times Russian citizens have been willing to **protest** to try to prevent environmental damage (see Chapter 19). Recent notable public actions have occurred around the threatened loss of public green space to the construction of a new cathedral in Yekaterinburg, overflowing landfills in Moscow Oblast, and mining of Kushtau Hill, a sacred site in Bashkortostan. Direct experience with environmental degradation, which goes along with the proximity and visibility of the problem, may prompt public environmental mobilization on issues such as the cleanliness or safety of urban spaces, the visible quality of air or water, the availability of recreational spaces, and the ability to safely dispose of waste and not be plagued by the waste of others. At the same time, in a 2020 poll of Russian citizens, the majority of respondents stated that they did not believe that it was possible to address the country's problems through protests. Nonetheless, those polled who did offer examples of successful "meetings, pickets, or demonstrations" mentioned the protests for green space in Yekaterinburg and protests against landfills and new waste incinerators as examples of effective actions (Public Opinion Foundation 2020). However, given the ubiquity of environmental challenges in Russia, protests overall remain quite rare.

Many Russian citizens remain concerned about the environmental situation in the country. Overall, the Russian government has attempted to establish the regime's credibility as a steward of the environment through robust laws and programs focused on environmental protection, yet these laws are often poorly enforced. The government is willing to partner with and support pro-regime forms of environmentalism, but also has begun to repress environmentalists whose voices are perceived as more critical. Russian environmental politics is thus quite firmly controlled by the state, while citizens harbor persistent discontent and doubts about its willingness and ability to address the country's environmental challenges.

20.4   Tensions over the Environment and Extraction in the Arctic

In September 2013, two Greenpeace activists attempted to scale Gazprom's Prirazlomnoe oil platform, the site of Russia's first Arctic offshore oil-drilling project. Following the incident, thirty activists and crew members on the *Arctic Sunrise*, a Greenpeace ship, were arrested on charges of hooliganism. Justifying the effort at direct action, Greenpeace International pointed to the dangers of drilling for oil in the Arctic waters: "Icy waters, icebergs and the extreme weather make the drilling conditions much worse and much more risky" than at lower latitudes; Greenpeace also noted the "near-impossibility of cleaning up an Arctic oil spill" (Ayliffe 2013). In December 2013, after an international outcry, and in the run-up to the 2014 Sochi Winter Olympics, the activists were released from detention. However, the broader debate about the safety and sustainability of resource extraction in Russia's fragile Arctic ecosystem continues. The political, economic, and ideational significance of the Arctic region looms large in Russian politics. Given the rapid shifts in the Arctic ecosystem due to climate change, nowhere is the tension between stability and fragility more evident than in the Arctic.

20.4.1   Imagining the Arctic

The "North" has long played an outsized role in the Russian imagination as the source of distinctive traits and traditions in Russian culture. As a Russian literary scholar argued:

The most important thing, more important than the fact that the North cannot but touch the heart of each Russian person, is that it is the most Russian. It is not only spiritually Russian – it is Russian because it has played an outstanding role in Russian culture. It saved Russian bylinas, Russian ancient customs, and Russian wooden architecture from oblivion (Likhachev 1983, 7, as cited in Shabaev et al. 2016, 82).

Similarly, in the present day, "the Arctic" plays an essential role in the Russian government's vision of the country as a current and future "great power." The region has captured the imagination of many of Russia's political and economic actors as a site of a resource bonanza that will fuel future economic growth. Traveling in the Russian Arctic, one occasionally hears the saying: "Half of the Arctic is Russia's and half of Russia is the Arctic." While not technically true, this grandiose claim to Russia's status as the premier Arctic state is not far off the mark.

As a region, the Arctic has attracted grandiose thinking for generations. Historically, the Arctic was viewed as "terra nullius" – an empty land where intrepid explorers could seize territory in the name of their home country, a view that is echoed in current rhetoric about the "scramble for the Arctic" as countries lay claim to as-yet-undiscovered resources on the continental shelf under the Arctic Ocean (Sale and Potapov 2010; Emmerson 2010). The Arctic environment is also often perceived as pristine, untouched, and far from the human activities that lead to pollution in lower latitudes. Both of these conceptions are incorrect. The first premise ignores the presence of the Indigenous peoples of the Arctic, who have inhabited the region for millennia. Today Russian law recognizes 40 ethnic groups among the "**Indigenous small-numbered peoples of the North, Siberia, and the Far East,**" while Indigenous advocates have identified more than 180 distinct peoples (IWGIA 2021). The latter view misses the fact that the Arctic is a "sink" for persistent organic pollutants such as mercury, PCBs, and other contaminants produced by industry farther south and carried north through global air and water currents (Friedrich 2016). Microplastics also have been found in Arctic waters. These pollutants enter the food chain, adversely impacting Arctic inhabitants and wildlife. In addition, the Arctic region has felt some of the earliest and most severe effects of climate change. Diminishing sea ice and melting glaciers may reach a tipping point that will have global consequences for sea levels, ocean currents, and climatic patterns.

20.4.2 Industrializing the Arctic

The Russian Arctic was the site of earlier and greater industrialization than other Arctic territories due to the Soviet regime's vision for the region under the planned economy, the central organizing tool of Soviet governance. The government used the rhetoric of "conquering the North" to settle and develop the region (Hønneland

2020, 35). Most of Russia's Arctic cities were constructed around sites of resource extraction. In many cases, prisoners within the GULAG labor camp system living in harsh conditions in remote locales were forced to construct industrial facilities and transportation links from scratch. For example, Vorkuta was chosen as the site of a labor camp in order to develop coal reserves to supply the military, while Noril'sk grew out of the Norlag labor camp, which from the 1930s to 1950s housed thousands of prisoners who constructed the basis for the mining operation that continues today (Josephson 2014, 281–82). After World War II, these *monogoroda* – towns based on a single industry – were further developed using government subsidies to attract labor and improve infrastructure despite difficult climatic conditions. Pollution from these industrial sites was sometimes severe. Forest die-off extended downwind of cities such as Monchegorsk and Nikel' as chemical deposits from pollution acidified soil and water in the region (Bruno 2016, 171). The Soviet regime also brought "civilization" and "modernization" to the Indigenous inhabitants of the region by gathering traditional economic activities such as hunting and reindeer herding under the umbrella of new collective farms (Slezkine 1994, 193–209). However, when the Soviet Union collapsed, state subsidies to the Arctic region disappeared. Collective farms struggled to survive, and the most lucrative and profitable industries were fully or partially privatized, while inefficient enterprises closed. Many urban residents moved south, contributing to depopulation. The population of the Russian North (a somewhat broader categorization than "the Russian Arctic") declined by 20 percent between 1989 and 2013, with almost 2 million people departing for lower latitudes (Heleniak 2017, 70).

Today, the Arctic serves as a stage for Russia's national ambitions. In 2007, Artur Chilingarov, the polar explorer and Duma member, led an underwater expedition that planted a Russian flag made of titanium on the seabed of the Lomonosov ridge near the North Pole, symbolically claiming the territory for Russia (BBC 2007). While the action caused consternation and complaint from other Arctic states and carried no legal force, it reinforced the centrality of the Arctic for the Russian government. The Arctic is a linchpin of several goals – economic growth, security, international influence, and even the legitimacy of the regime. The Arctic is the site of current or planned projects for on- and offshore drilling of oil and gas, of ports and other infrastructure to service the Northern Sea Route from Asia to Europe, and of new military bases. In October 2020, the Russia government published a new "Strategy for Developing the Russian Arctic Zone and Ensuring National Security through 2035" (Russian Federation, Government of 2020b). Some of the goals listed include protecting Russia's sovereignty; developing the region as a strategic natural resource base to propel economic development; developing the **Northern Sea Route** for global transport; protecting the Arctic environment; and protecting the traditional way of life of Indigenous minorities. Marlene Laruelle argues that the

Russian government has a "nationalist reading of the Arctic" – in other words, "that of triumphant military industries and that of new technologies, that of hard power or soft power" (Laruelle 2015, 10). At the same time, achieving these goals may have significant environmental costs and negative impacts on Indigenous peoples and other Arctic residents.

20.4.3 Extracting Arctic Resources

Russia's political economic model – based in large part on resource extraction, often led by state-owned companies – is clearly visible in the Arctic. The region is also the epicenter of Russia's plan for sustained economic growth. By some estimates, Russia controls 80 percent of the mineral resources in the Arctic as a whole. The Russia Arctic is now responsible for 90 percent of the country's production of natural gas and 17 percent of its oil (Kluge and Paul 2020). Regions of the Far North such as **Yamal-Nenets** and **Khanty-Mansi** are the site of rapid expansion of the oil and gas industries, with Yamal-Nenets accounting for 80 percent of Russia's gas production in 2018 (Staalesen 2019). In 2020, these two subnational regions together contributed more than 17 percent of the federal budget's revenue (Tóth-Czifra 2021). In March 2019, Nikolai Korchunov, Russia's representative to the Arctic Council, announced an anticipated $86 billion investment in the Russian Arctic by 2025, and noted that the "Arctic regions in the country account for around 10 percent of GDP and almost 20 percent of Russian exports" (TASS 2019a). Expanding extraction in the Arctic relies on partnerships with multinational oil companies in some cases and technology transfer in others, so Russia's war in Ukraine and the resulting sanctions will likely affect these plans.

Russia also controls the Northern Sea Route (NSR), a shipping route traversing the Russian Arctic that is envisioned as the key future transport link between Asia and Europe. In 2020, sea ice along the Northern Sea Route reached a record low. As sea ice recedes and the NSR becomes navigable year-round, it may become the most efficient way for companies to ship goods globally by reducing the distance ships travel up to 40 percent, as compared the current routes through the Suez or Panama Canals. The Russian government's plan to develop the NSR by 2035 involves investment from major natural resource companies, including Gazprom Neft, Rosneft, Novatek, and Nornickel. These public–private initiatives around the NSR are designed to produce new ships, including nuclear-powered icebreakers, new ports, railways, and airports. The Russian gas company Novatek also is constructing liquefied natural gas (LNG) terminals on the Yamal and Gydan peninsulas, with fuel to be shipped to European and Asian consumers using the NSR. **Rosatom**, Russia's powerful State Atomic Energy Corporation, is responsible for Russia's fleet of nuclear-powered icebreakers and has been given increasing authority to coordinate the development of and manage the NSR (Sevastyanov and Kravchuk 2020).

20.4.4   Climate Change in the Arctic: A Challenge and an Opportunity

The Russian government's ability to achieve its goals in the Arctic is both made possible and imperiled by climate change. Certainly, the opportunity to develop the NSR would not exist without decreasing sea ice in Arctic waters. More broadly, Russian government officials conceive of climate change as both an opportunity and a threat. In December 2019, the Russian government presented the National Action Plan for Adaptation to Climate Change designed "to reduce the vulnerability of the population of Russia, the economy and natural sites to the impacts of climate change; and to seize the opportunities arising from such changes" (Russian Federation, Government of 2019). The plan outlines measures to mitigate the damaging effects of climate change and to "use the advantages" of warmer temperatures (Deutsche Welle 2020). The advantages listed in the official policy document included greater access to Arctic waterways, in addition to the expansion of agriculture and lower heating energy costs during winter. The government hopes to achieve these goals through projects such as the Arctic Hectare program, in which the government gives away land to Arctic residents to stimulate tourism, agriculture, and other economic activity (TASS 2021a). This dual strategy of trying to minimize the harmful effects of climate change, while seizing the territorial and natural resources revealed by melting sea ice will present a difficult balancing act over the next decades, with some scholars anticipating that by 2030 the direct, negative impacts of climate change will begin to outstrip any modest gains currently anticipated (Gustafson 2021).

Russia has been willing to engage in multilateral international cooperation on climate change and Arctic governance. Russia participates in the UNFCCC's international climate talks, in part to reinforce its role as a major world power and in part to seek opportunities to shape the agreement and identify advantages for investment and modernization goals at home. Russia is currently the fourth-largest emitter of greenhouse gases and has a highly carbon-intensive economy. Under the **Paris Climate Agreement**, the Russian government pledged that the country would reduce emissions by 30 percent below 1990 levels by 2030. In fact, due to the significant reduction in carbon dioxide emissions during Russia's severe post-Soviet economic recession, this target will actually allow the country to modestly increase emissions in the next ten years. In Russia's draft long-term strategy for diversifying economic development and reducing greenhouse gas emissions by 2050, the baseline scenario projects an 8.2 percent increase in emissions as the most likely outcome (Russian Federation, Government of 2020a); under the most intensive scenario Russia still only would be likely to reach carbon neutrality by the end of the twenty-first century. As a result, Russia's efforts to address climate change have been judged as "critically insufficient" (Climate Action Tracker 2021).

The **Arctic Council** is the major multilateral organization to shape governance in the region. Russia is serving as the chair of the Arctic Council from 2021 to 2023 and has pledged to act in four priority areas: the people of the Arctic, including Indigenous peoples; environmental protection, including climate change; socio-economic development; and strengthening the Arctic Council (Arctic Council 2021). In May 2021, Foreign Minister Sergei Lavrov described Russia's commitment "to promote the region's balanced and sustainable social, economic and environmental development," including "to promote the region's further adaptation to global climate change," even as he stated that "the key to a more complete unlocking of the Arctic's economic potential is the creation of a favourable environment for investment" (Russian Federation, Ministry of Foreign Affairs 2021). Although the Arctic Council has traditionally maintained cooperation during periods of international tension, such as Russia's 2014 annexation of Crimea, in March 2022 the seven non-Russian member states of the council announced that they are pausing their participation in the organization for an indefinite period (US Department of State 2022). Pavel Baev cautions that military power will continue to play an important role in shaping the Arctic region: "Although Moscow presents itself as an upholder of international law, it remains a firm believer in the ultimate importance of military force in interstate relations. Its commitment to strengthening international institutions governing the Arctic is therefore counter-balanced with the determination to rely on its own power in protecting its rich possessions" (Baev 2018, 411). Russia's previous attempts to balance international engagement and the maintenance of state sovereignty in the Arctic have been at least temporarily upended by its war in Ukraine.

20.4.5 Environmental Challenges in the Arctic

As the Arctic region emerges as a space where the Russian government pursues national and international goals, localized environmental and human impacts of ambitious development plans are often neglected. The region continues to experience significant environmental degradation linked to industrial activity. While the Nornickel fuel spill garnered headlines worldwide, experts estimate that there were 17,171 oil spills in Russia in 2019, most of which received little attention (Alykova and Uzhvak 2020). Many of these spills are due to aging pipelines inherited from the Soviet era. Companies are often able to avoid paying for cleaning up spills, either because they occur in remote areas and are not officially reported or because there are loopholes that allow companies to evade legal responsibility. Greenpeace Russia calls the lack of enforcement a "hidden subsidy" by the government to the oil and gas industry (Greenpeace Russia 2020). These spills pollute water and soil in the region, jeopardizing hunting, fishing, foraging, and other activities. In addition, extractive infrastructure such as pipelines can interfere with reindeer-herding routes and other Indigenous economic activities (Henry et al. 2016).

Other widespread environmental challenges in the Arctic are related to the effects of climate change, which are increasingly visible. Scientists estimate that temperatures in Russia are warming 2.5 times faster than the global average temperature increase, with the Arctic regions warming the most quickly (TASS 2019b). The year 2020 was the hottest ever recorded in history, and record-breaking heat continued in the Arctic the following year. In June 2021, temperatures in the Arctic town of Verkhoiansk in the Sakha Republic reached 100°F. One effect of hotter and drier conditions has been more frequent and larger forest fires across Siberia. During the summer of 2021, forest fires in Russia burned an area nearly twice the size of Austria (Gamillo 2021). Using satellite data, European scientists have confirmed that wildfires in Russia during 2021 released a record level of carbon (European Commission 2021). Unreported leaks of methane – a potent greenhouse gas – from natural gas infrastructure have also been identified by satellite data (Mufson et al. 2021). Warming temperatures have led to unprecedented thawing of the region's permafrost. In a 2019 paper, Dmitry Streletskiy and coauthors project significant damage to buildings, roads, and other infrastructure in Russia's northern regions due to the loss of permafrost, finding that the "total cost of fixed assets affected by permafrost in the nine administrative regions in 2016 was 248.6 bln USD or 7.5% of Russian GDP for that year" (Streletskiy et al. 2019). Some villages in the Arctic have also experienced an inundation of water as permafrost melts, turning once-frozen ground into impassable wetlands (Troianovski and Mooney 2019). The loss of Arctic sea ice has contributed to coastal erosion and has decreased habitat for wildlife, including polar bears which are forced to search for land-based sources of food, including in garbage dumps around Arctic towns (Interfax 2021).

20.4.6   Environmental and Indigenous Activism in the Arctic

As they work to address these severe problems, environmental and Indigenous activists in the Arctic face significant hurdles. The Arctic region is relatively lightly populated, transport links are minimal, and many local residents live in economically precarious conditions and in remote towns and villages that are only seasonally accessible. Environmental problems often develop in these remote areas and may be witnessed by only a few people.

However, in several prominent cases, Indigenous peoples and environmentalists have mobilized to draw attention to damage to the fragile Arctic ecosystem and violations of **Indigenous rights** (Sulyandziga and Sulyandziga 2020). On Sakhalin, an island located in Russia's Far East, environmentalists and Indigenous activists worked together in the Green Wave movement to pressure international financial institutions to investigate how oil pipelines and infrastructure constructed by Sakhalin Energy (a consortium led by Royal Dutch Shell) damaged the spawning grounds and migratory routes of salmon. These protests resulted in a revised process of consultation between oil companies and Indigenous communities (Tysiachniouk et al. 2018a). In the Komi Republic, longstanding grievances between local residents – including Komi and Nenets reindeer herders – and Lukoil over chronic oil spills culminated in a 2015 socioeconomic agreement to compensate the local Komi–Izhemtsi community for environmental degradation and to transfer resources to the community for education and other services (Tysiachniouk et al. 2018b). In Yamal, Indigenous residents sent a letter to the United Nations to protest the impact of the Yamal LNG project on reindeer pastures and fish stocks (Cultural Survival 2018). In these cases, despite vast differences in economic and political power between companies and local communities, activists attempted to leverage negative publicity to show how energy companies violate their own corporate social responsibility policies, and in so doing risked reputational damage for their shareholders, lenders, and corporate partners. These conflicts generally do not stop oil and gas projects from going forward, but they can mitigate some of the more visible forms of environmental damage or channel compensation to affected communities.

Another recent environmental campaign was the struggle against a planned landfill for waste from Moscow, to be located in Shies in Arkhangel'sk Oblast (a location in the Far North, if not technically in the Arctic). Acting under the slogan "The Russian North Is Not a Dump!" local residents staged intermittent protests between 2018 and 2020, even as a group of more radical activists camped near the construction site. Construction of the landfill was stopped by court order in 2021 (*Kommersant* 2021). In another 2020 campaign, the NGO Aborigen Forum and Indigenous activists from Russia called upon Elon Musk not to use nickel and other metals from Nornickel in the production of Tesla's batteries in the absence of an environmental impact assessment. The letter states, "The lands of indigenous people appropriated by the company for industrial production now resemble a lunar landscape, and traditional use of these lands is no longer possible" (Nilsen 2020). The campaign received widespread media coverage, even though it did not receive a formal response from Musk.

ENGOs and Indigenous associations that have been involved in this activism have faced repression, however. Several environmental and Indigenous organizations working in the Far North have been placed on the foreign agent list. For example, the Kola Eco Center of Murmansk, which worked to ensure citizens' right to a healthy environment, was declared a foreign agent in 2017 after receiving funding for joint projects with Norwegian environmental NGOs (Nilsen 2017). In 2013, the Russian Association of Indigenous Peoples of the North (RAIPON), the country's largest Indigenous association and also a permanent participant in the Arctic Council, underwent a leadership struggle over who would head the organization, with more critical voices replaced by a generally pro-regime leadership (Henry and Plantan 2021). The Moscow-based Centre for Support of Indigenous Peoples of the North (CSIPN) was listed as a foreign agent in 2015 and forced to close temporarily in 2019 (Digges 2019). Protesters at the site of the Shies landfill also faced sometimes violent repression by the police and private security services. In contrast,

Russian government officials have organized projects in the Arctic that exemplify the government's preferred forms of environmental activism, such as the Clean Arctic program, in which volunteers clean up scrap metal and informal landfills (TASS 2021b).

20.4.7   Could Russia Drill Its Way to a More Sustainable Future?

The persistence of, and in some cases increase in, environmental challenges, in the Arctic and across Russia, indicates that the regime is willing to overlook the environmental impact of its model of economic development to achieve economic growth, maintain state spending, and increase international influence for the immediate future. However, long-term challenges loom on the horizon. Some government officials in Russia and elsewhere have suggested that it might be possible to, in effect, drill a path to a greener future. They have argued that revenues from extraction could be invested in a green economy – renewable energy and nuclear power, as well as climate adaptation – and thus contribute to future **sustainability**. Russia's Arctic Council Chairmanship website states: "In the context of further development of the region it is important to take into account not only the vulnerability of the Arctic to climate change, but also its long-term contribution – due to its natural, energy and transport resources and solutions – in facilitating the transition to a low-emission economy and, accordingly, to the implementation of the goals of the Paris Agreement" (Arctic Council 2021). Russian government officials have also argued that the country's natural gas exports to Europe are the solution to some European countries' dependence on coal, which has higher carbon emissions. Critics argue that this **"Arctic paradox"** – in which climate change causes Arctic sea ice to recede, revealing yet more fossil fuel deposits that could further contribute to climate change – is leading resource-dependent countries to propose "shadow solutions" to the problems of climate change and sustainability (Palosaari 2019, 148).

Even if one sets aside environmental concerns, basing the future of the Russian economy on projections about oil and gas extracted from the Arctic has inherent challenges. Russia is "a price taker, not a price maker on global natural resource markets" (Bradshaw and Connolly 2016, 716) and is subject to price volatility. As such, "Russia relies to an exceptionally large degree on the extraction and sale of a range of goods over which it exerts very little in the way of price-forming influence" (Bradshaw and Connolly 2016, 718). Revenues can rise and fall quickly based on factors beyond the country's control (see Chapter 11). Moreover, Arctic oil drilling is both risky and expensive. Estimates of the necessary oil price to allow for the profitable development of offshore drilling in the Arctic vary dramatically, but the Russian Ministry of Energy estimates a range of $50–70 per barrel (Chanysheva and Illinova 2021), while other estimates tend to be much higher. Russia's war in Ukraine has contributed to a surge in global energy prices, but simultaneously isolated Russia's oil and gas companies due to sanctions as major multinational companies such as BP, Shell, and ExxonMobil have withdrawn from extractive projects in Russia (Toplensky 2022). In the end, price fluctuations and the risks of long-term investment in fossil fuel may do more to prevent Arctic natural resource extraction than environmental arguments.

20.5   Conclusion

Russia boasts tremendous ecological diversity and significant protected natural areas, but also faces a number of environmental challenges, not least of which are the effects of climate change. In the post-Soviet period, in an effort to recover from the instabilities of the 1990s, the regime developed an economic model based on natural resource exploitation and an increasingly authoritarian form of governance and justified this system as a means of achieving prosperity and security for citizens. This short-term stability contains inherent risks as long-term fragility may result from dissatisfied citizens, overreliance on a few economic sectors, a weak ability to enforce some laws, the accumulation of environmental problems, and the destabilizing effects of the war in Ukraine.

While the Russian government pursues economic goals despite environmental challenges, President Putin and other officials have frequently expressed environmental concern, whether for wildlife or for serious daily problems like waste. Even as they have repressed critical voices, the government has encouraged some forms of patriotic environmental action, opening up space for the next generation of environmentalists. As the government weighs public health challenges, linked directly or indirectly to the environment, and the costs (as well as the benefits) of climate change, intense debates about the tradeoff between economics and the environment are certain to continue.

DISCUSSION QUESTIONS

1. How has the Soviet legacy shaped environmental politics and politics in the Arctic today? Does the past political and economic system of Russia weigh heavily on its present and future, or it is a relatively minor factor?
2. Do you think that sustainable development – or a balance among environmental, economic, and social goals – is likely, or even possible, in the Russian Arctic?
3. When citizens are excluded from political decisionmaking, they sometimes turn to protest to express their grievances. What do you see as some of the challenges of engaging in protest on environmental issues in Russia today? Do you think that protest is likely to be an effective strategy in Russia today?

REFERENCES

Alykova, Yuliia, and Polina Uzhvak. 2020. "Neftianye avarii sluchaiotsia kazhdye polchasa. Issledovanie real'nykh masshtabov zagriaznenii prirody." IStories Media, October 15, https://istories.media/investigations/2020/10/15/neftyanie-avarii-sluchayutsya-kazhdie-polchasa-issledovanie-realnikh-masshtabov-zagryaznenii-prirodi/.

Arctic Council. 2021. "Russian Chairmanship 2021–2023," https://arctic-council.org/about/russian-chairmanship-2/.

Åslund, Anders, and Steven Fisher. 2020. "New Challenges and Dwindling Returns for Russia's National Champions, Gazprom and Rosneft." Atlantic Council, June 5, www.atlanticcouncil.org/in-depth-research-reports/report/new-challenges-and-dwindling-returns-for-russias-national-champions-gazprom-and-rosneft/.

Ayliffe, Ben. 2013. "10 Reasons to Take Action to Stop Gazprom's Prirazlomnaya Oil Platform." Greenpeace International, September 25, https://wayback.archive-it.org/9650/20200413155352/http://p3-raw.greenpeace.org/international/en/news/Blogs/makingwaves/10-reasons-to-take-action-to-stop-gazproms-pr/blog/46766/.

Baev, Pavel. 2018. "Russia's Ambivalent Status-Quo/Revisionist Policies in the Arctic." *Arctic Review*, 9, 408–24.

BBC. 2007. "Russia Plants Flag under N Pole." August 2, http://news.bbc.co.uk/2/hi/europe/6927395.stm.

Bradshaw, Michael, and Richard Connolly. 2016. "Russia's Natural Resources in the World Economy: History, Review and Reassessment." *Eurasian Geography and Economics*, 57(6), 700–26.

Bruno, Andy. 2016. *The Nature of Soviet Power*. Cambridge: Cambridge University Press.

Chanysheva, Amina, and Alina Ilinova. 2021. "The Future of Russian Arctic Oil and Gas Projects: Problems of Assessing the Prospects." *Journal of Marine Science and Engineering*, 9(5), www.mdpi.com/2077-1312/9/5/528.

Climate Action Tracker. 2021. "Russian Federation." September 15, https://climateactiontracker.org/countries/russian-federation/.

Crotty, Jo, and Peter Rodgers. 2012. "The Continuing Reorganization of Russia's Environmental Bureaucracy." *Problems of Post-Communism*, 59(4), 15–26.

Cultural Survival. 2018. "Observations on the State of Indigenous Human Rights in the Russian Federation." May, www.culturalsurvival.org/sites/default/files/UPR-Report-Russian-Federation-2017.pdf.

Dawson, Jane. 1996. *Eco-Nationalism: Anti-Nuclear Activism and National Identity in Russia, Lithuania, and Ukraine*. Durham, NC: Duke University Press.

Deutsche Welle. 2020. "Russia Unveils Plan to 'Use the Advantages' of Climate Change." January 6, www.dw.com/en/russia-unveils-plan-to-use-the-advantages-of-climate-change/a-51894830.

Digges, Charles. 2019. "Two Prominent Rights Groups Liquidated by Russia's 'Foreign Agent' Law." Bellona, November 7, https://bellona.org/news/russian-human-rights-issues/2019-11-two-prominent-rights-groups-liquidated-by-russias-foreign-agent-law.

Dresen, F. Joseph. 2005. "Economic Growth and Environmental Security in Russia." Wilson Center, March 16, www.wilsoncenter.org/publication/economic-growth-and-environmental-security-russia.

Emmerson, Charles. 2010. *The Future History of the Arctic*. New York: Public Affairs.

European Commission. 2021. "Copernicus: A Summer of Wildfires Saw Devastation and Record Emissions around the Northern Hemisphere." September 21, https://atmosphere.copernicus.eu/copernicus-summer-wildfires-saw-devastation-and-record-emissions-around-northern-hemisphere.

Friedrich, Doris. 2016. "The Problems Won't Go Away: Persistent Organic Pollutants (POPs) in the Arctic." Arctic Institute, July 1, www.thearcticinstitute.org/persistent-organic-pollutants-pops-in-the-arctic/.

Gamillo, Elizabeth. 2021. "More Than 40 Million Acres of Land Have Burned in Siberia." *Smithsonian Magazine*, August 16, www.smithsonianmag.com/smart-news/siberian-wildfires-are-larger-globes-total-blazes-year-combined-180978433/.

Gilbert, Leah. 2016. "Crowding Out Civil Society: State Management of Social Organisations in Putin's Russia." *Europe–Asia Studies*, 68(9), 1553–78.

Greenpeace Russia. 2020. "Tsena ekologicheskogo dempinga v neftianoi otrasli." July, https://greenpeace.ru/wp-content/uploads/2020/02/Eco_Dumping_MV_03.pdf.

Gustafson, Thane. 2021. *Klimat: Russia in the Age of Climate Change*. Cambridge, MA: Harvard University Press.

Heleniak, Timothy. 2017. "Boom and Bust: Population Change in Russia's Arctic Cities." In Robert W. Orttung (ed.), *Sustaining Russia's Arctic Cities: Resource Politics, Migration, and Climate Change*, pp. 67–87. New York: Berghahn Books.

Henderson, Sarah L. 2011. "Civil Society in Russia," *Problems of Post-Communism*, 58(3), 11–27.

Henry, Laura A. 2010. *Red to Green: Environmental Activism in Post-Soviet Russia*. Ithaca: Cornell University Press.

Henry, Laura A., Soili Nysten-Haarala, Svetlana Tulaeva, and Maria Tysiachniouk. 2016. "Corporate Social Responsibility and the Oil Industry in the Russian Arctic: Global Norms and Neo-Paternalism." *Europe–Asia Studies*, 68(8), 1340–68.

Henry, Laura A., and Elizabeth Plantan. 2021. "Activism in Exile: How Russian Environmentalists Maintain Voice after Exit." *Post-Soviet Affairs*, DOI: 10.1080/1060586X.2021.2002629.

Hønneland, Geir. 2020. *Russia and the Arctic: Environment, Identity and Foreign Policy*. London: I. B. Tauris.

Interfax. 2021. "Taianie l'dov zastavilo belykh medvedei goniat' gusei." February 26, www.interfax.ru/russia/753652.

IPSOS Global Advisor. 2020. "Kak mir vosprinimaet uzmenenie klimata i COVID-19?" April, www.ipsos.com/sites/default/files/ct/news/documents/2020-04/g_earth_day_2020_global_deck_v3_embargoed_until_22.04.20_confidential_rus.pdf.

IWGIA (International Work Group for Indigenous Affairs). 2020. "Russian Oil Spill Exposes History of Indigenous Peoples' Rights Violations." June 23, www.iwgia.org/en/news/3790-russian-oil-spill-exposes-history-of-indigenous-peoples%E2%80%99-right-violations.html.

   2021. "Indigenous Peoples in Russia," www.iwgia.org/en/russia.html.

Javeline, Debra, and Sarah Lindemann-Komarova. 2010. "A Balanced Assessment of Russian Civil Society." *Journal of International Affairs*, 63(2), 171–88.

Josephson, Paul. 2007 "Industrial Deserts: Industry, Science and the Destruction of Nature in the Soviet Union." *Slavonic and East European Review*, 85(2), 294–321.

2014. *The Conquest of the Russian Arctic.* Cambridge, MA: Harvard University Press.

Kluge, Janis, and Michael Paul. 2020. "Russia's Arctic Strategy through 2035." Stiftung Wissenschaft und Politik, November 26, www.swp-berlin.org/publikation/russias-arctic-strategy-through-2035.

Kommersant. 2021. "Ekoaktivisty ob"iavili protestnuiu kampaniiu protiv mysornogo poligona v Shiese okonchennoi." January 9, www.kommersant.ru/doc/4639443.

Laruelle, Marlene. 2015. *Russia's Arctic Strategies and the Future of the Far North.* New York: Routledge.

Laruelle, Marlene, and Laura Howells. 2020. "Ideological or Pragmatic? A Data-Driven Analysis of the Russian Presidential Grant Fund." *Russian Politics*, 5(1), 29–51.

Levada Center. 2020. "Environmental Problems." February 18, www.levada.ru/en/2020/02/18/environmental-problems/.

Likachev, D. S. 1983. "Vvedenie." In K. P. Gemp (ed.), *Skaz o Belomor'e*, pp. 4–9. Arkhangel'sk: Pomorskii Gosudarstvennyi Universitet.

Martus, Ellie. 2018. *Russian Environmental Politics: State, Industry and Policymaking.* New York: Routledge.

Meduza. 2020. "'Norilsk Nickel' Challenges $2 Billion Damage Assessment for Arctic Fuel Spill." July 8, https://meduza.io/en/news/2020/07/08/norilsk-nickel-challenges-2-billion-damage-assessment-for-arctic-fuel-spill.

Mitchell, Ronald B. 2021. International Environmental Agreements (IEA) Database Project, https://iea.uoregon.edu/country-members/Russian%20Federation?field_inclusion_auto_value=MEA.

Mufson, Steven, Isabelle Khurshudyan, Chris Mooney, Brady Dennis, John Muyskens, and Naema Ahmed. 2021. "Russia Allows Methane Leaks at Planet's Peril." *Washington Post*, October 19, www.washingtonpost.com/climate-environment/interactive/2021/russia-greenhouse-gas-emissions/.

Myers, Steven Lee, and Andrew Roth. 2013. "Putin Defends Seizure of Activists' Ship but Questions Piracy Charges." *New York Times*, September 25, www.nytimes.com/2013/09/26/world/europe/seizure-of-a-greenpeace-vessel-by-russia.html.

Nikitina, Elena, and Vladimir Kotov. 2002. "Reorganisation of Environmental Policy in Russia: The Decade of Success and Failures in Implementation and Perspective Quests." Social Science Research Network, https://ssrn.com/abstract=318685/.

Nilsen, Thomas. 2017. "Arctic-Based Russian NGO Labeled 'Foreign Agent' by Moscow – Eye on the Arctic." April 24, www.rcinet.ca/eye-on-the-arctic/2017/04/24/arctic-based-russian-ngo-labeled-foreign-agent-by-moscow/.

2020. "Russian Indigenous Groups Call on Elon Musk Not to Buy Battery Metals from Nornickel." *Independent Barents Observer*, August 7, https://thebarentsobserver.com/en/ecology/2020/08/russian-indigenous-peoples-call-elon-musk-not-buy-battery-metals-nornickel.

Nornickel. 2021. "Nornickel Took Part in Norilsk Public Chamber Hearings." July 29, www.nornickel.com:443/news-and-media/press-releases-and-news/nornickel-took-part-in-norilsk-public-chamber-hearings/.

Oldfield, Jonathan D. 2005. *Russian Nature: Exploring the Environmental Consequences of Societal Change.* Burlington, VT: Ashgate.

Palosaari, Teemu. 2019. "The Arctic Paradox (and How to Solve It): Oil, Gas and Climate Ethics in the Arctic." In Matthias Finger and Lassi Heininen (eds.), *The Global Arctic Handbook*, pp. 141–52. Cham: Springer.

Pew Research Center. 2020. "Science and Scientists Held in High Esteem across Global Publics." September, www.pewresearch.org/science/2020/09/29/concern-over-climate-and-the-environment-predominates-among-these-publics/.

Plantan, Elizabeth. 2020. "A Tale of Two Laws," In K. Koesel, V. Bunce, and J. Weiss (eds.), *Citizens and the State in Authoritarian Regimes: Comparing China and Russia*, pp. 167–91. Oxford: Oxford University Press.

Presidential Council for Civil Society and Human Rights. 2019. "Sovet po pravam cheloveka prinial rekomendatsii po itogam spetszasedaniia, posviashchennogo predotvrashcheniiu obrazovaniia otkhodov." June 17, http://president-sovet.ru/presscenter/news/sovet_po_pravam_cheloveka_prinyal_rekomendatsii_po_itogam_spetszasedaniya_posvyashchennogo_predotvra/.

Public Opinion Foundation. 2020. "Protesty. Otnoshenie i predstavleniia ob effektivnosti." September 2, https://fom.ru/Nastroeniya/14445.

2021. " Problemy ekologii. Global'noe poteplenie." March 26, https://fom.ru/Bezopasnost-i-pravo/14559.

Putin, Vladimir. 2021. "Presidential Address to the Federal Assembly." April 21, http://en.kremlin.ru/events/president/news/65418.

RBK. 2020a. "Rosprirodnadzor obosnoval otsenku ushcherba pri razlive topliva v Noril'ske." October 20, www.rbc.ru/business/02/10/2020/5f748a779a79478068822a48.

2020b. "Rossiiane nazvali zagriaznenie prirody ugrozoi strashnee terrorizma." January 23, www.rbc.ru/politics/23/01/2020/5e2893299a79472b28203508.

2020c. "V Rossii postavlen rekord po zagriazneniiu vozdukha za 16 let." 2020. November 7, www.rbc.ru/society/17/11/2020/5fb26d119a7947780c13f546.

Reuters. 2021. "Nornickel's $2 Billion Fine Will Be Used to Improve Arctic Environment – Putin." March 10, www.reuters.com/article/us-norilsknickel-arctic-idUSKBN2B215S.

RFE/RL (Radio Free Europe/Radio Liberty). 2021. "Russian Company Pays Largest Legal Award in History – Almost $2 Billion – for Devastating Arctic Fuel Spill." March 10, www.rferl.org/a/russia-arctic-fuel-spill-norilsk-nickel-massive-fine/31143392.html.

RT. 2016. "Putin zaiavil, shto Rossiia vystupaet ekologicheskim donorom mira." December 27, https://russian.rt.com/russia/news/345486-putin-rossiya-donor-mira.

Russian Federation, Government of. 2018. "Natsional'nyi Proekt 'Ekologiia,'" http://government.ru/rugovclassifier/848/events/.

2019. "National Action Plan for Adaptation to Climate Change to 2022 (Order No. 3183-R)," http://government.ru/news/38739/.

2020a. "Strategy for Russia's Long-Term Development with Low Carbon Emissions to 2050," https://economy.gov.ru/material/news/minekonomrazvitiya_rossii_podgotovilo_proekt_strategii_dolgosrochnogo_razvitiya_rossii_s_nizkim_urovnem_vybrosov_parnikovyh_gazov_do_2050_goda_.html.

2020b. "Ukaz Prezidenta Rossiiskoi Federatsii ot 26.10.2020 No. 645 'O Strategii razvitiia Arkticheskoi zony Rossiiskoi Federatsii i obespecheniia natsional'noi bezopastnosti na period do 2035 goda," http://publication.pravo.gov.ru/Document/View/0001202010260033.

Russian Federation, Ministry of Foreign Affairs. 2021. "Foreign Minister Sergey Lavrov's Statement at the 12th Arctic Council Ministerial Meeting, Reykjavik." May 20, www.mid.ru/en/press_service/minister_speeches/-/asset_publisher/7OvQR5KJWVmR/content/id/4738773.

Sale, Richard, and Eugene Potapov. 2010. *The Scramble for the Arctic: Ownership, Exploitation and Conflict in the Far North*. London: Frances Lincoln.

Sevastyanov, Sergey, and Aleksey Kravchuk. 2020. "Russia's Policy to Develop Trans-Arctic Shipping along the Northern Sea Route." *Polar Journal*, 10(2), 228–50.

Shabaev, Yuri P., Igor Zherebtsov, Kim Hye Jin, and Kim Hyun Taek. 2016. "Pomors, Pomor'e, and the Russian North: A Symbolic Space in Cultural and Political Context." *Sibirica*, 15(2), 73–102.

Slezkine, Yuri. 1994. *Arctic Mirrors*. Ithaca: Cornell University Press.

Staalesen, Atle. 2019. "Money Pours in for More Tundra Oil." *Independent Barents Observer*, December 11, https://thebarentsobserver.com/en/industry-and-energy/2019/12/money-pours-more-tundra-oil.

Streletskiy, Dmitry A., Luis J. Suter, Nikolay I. Shiklomanov, Boris N. Porfiriev, and Dmitry O. Eliseev. 2019. "Assessment of Climate Change Impacts on Buildings, Structures, and Infrastructure in the Russian Regions on Permafrost." *Environmental Research Letters*, 14(2), 025003.

Sulyandziga, Liubov, and Rodion Sulyandziga. 2020. "Indigenous Self-Determination and Disempowerment in the Russian North." In Timo Koivurova, Else Grete Broderstad, Dorothée Cambou, Dalee Dorough, and Florian Stammler (eds.), *Routledge Handbook of Indigenous Peoples in the Arctic*, pp. 304–19. New York: Routledge.

TASS. 2019a. "Investments in Russian Economy in Arctic to Exceed $86 Bln until 2025." March 28, https://tass.com/economy/1051080.

2019b. "Russian Climate Gets Warmer 2.5 Times Faster than World Average – Diplomat." March 30, https://tass.com/society/1051300.

2021a. "Arctic Hectares Are of Highest Demand in Murmansk Region, of Lower Demand in Nenets, Komi." October 22, https://tass.com/economy/1353063.

2021b. "Clean Arctic Volunteers Begin Work in Komi." September 30, https://tass.com/economy/1344325.

Toplensky, Rochelle. 2022. "Western Oil Companies Leave Russia to Their State-Run Rivals." *Wall Street Journal*, March 2, www.wsj.com/articles/western-oil-companies-leave-russia-to-their-state-run-rivals-11646229422.

Tóth-Czifra, András. 2021. "Moscow vs Regions: Who 'Feeds' Whom?" Institute of Modern Russia, February 4, https://imrussia.org/en/analysis/3230-moscow-vs-regions-who-%E2%80%9Cfeeds%E2%80%9D-whom.

Troianovski, Anton, and Chris Mooney. 2019. "In Fast-Thawing Siberia, Radical Climate Change Is Warping the Earth beneath the Feet of Millions." *Washington Post*, October 3, www.washingtonpost.com/graphics/2019/national/climate-environment/climate-change-siberia/.

Tynkkynen, Veli-Pekka, and Nina Tynkkynen. 2018. "Climate Denial Revisited: (Re)Contextualising Russian Public Discourse on Climate Change during Putin 2.0." *Europe–Asia Studies*, 70(7), 1103–20.

Tysiachniouk, Maria, Laura A. Henry, Machiel Lamers, and Jan P. M. van Tatenhove. 2018a. "Oil and Indigenous People in Sub-Arctic Russia: Rethinking Equity and

Governance in Benefit Sharing Agreements." *Energy Research and Social Science,* 37, 140–52.

2018b. "Oil Extraction and Benefit Sharing in an Illiberal Context: The Nenets and Komi-Izhemtsi Indigenous Peoples in the Russian Arctic." *Society and Natural Resources,* 31(5), 556–79.

Tysiachniouk, Maria, Svetlana Tulaeva, and Laura A. Henry. 2018. "Civil Society under the Law 'On Foreign Agents': NGO Strategies and Network Transformation." *Europe–Asia Studies,* 70(4), 615–37.

US Department of State. 2022. "Joint Statement on Arctic Council Cooperation Following Russia's Invasion of Ukraine." March 3, www.state.gov/joint-statement-on-arctic-council-cooperation-following-russias-invasion-of-ukraine/.

US EIA (Energy Information Agency). 2014. "Oil and Natural Gas Sales Accounted for 68% of Russia's Total Export Revenues in 2013." *Today in Energy,* July 23, www.eia.gov/todayinenergy/detail.php?id=17231.

Yabloko. 2009. "On Anti-Ecological Policies of the Russia's Authorities." December 24, https://eng.yabloko.ru/Press/2009/1224-congress-ecology.html.

Yanitsky, Oleg. 1993. *Russian Environmentalism: Leading Figures, Faction, Opinions.* Moscow: Mezhdunarodnoye Otnoshenie.

Ethnicity and Religion in Russia

ŞENER AKTÜRK

Fig. 21.1 President Vladimir Putin poses with Russia's Patriarch Kirill, Chief Mufti of Russia Talgat Tadzhuddin, Chief Rabbi of Russia Berel Lazar, and Russia's Mufti Council chief Rawil Gaynetdin in Moscow as they celebrate National Unity Day, marking the 403rd anniversary of the 1612 expulsion of Polish occupation forces from the Kremlin, November 4, 2015. Credit: Natalia Kolesnikova / AFP / Getty Images.

Take as much sovereignty as you can swallow.

> Boris Yeltsin (quoted in Beissinger, *Nationalist Mobilization*)

The great mission of the Russians is to unite and cement civilization . . .
[Russia is] a state-civilization that is able to organically solve the problem of integrating various ethnic groups and confessions.

> Vladimir Putin, "Rossiia. Natsional'nyi vopros"

Abstract

Russia is a multiethnic and multireligious polity, with a long history of managing ethnic and religious identities and group allegiances. This chapter first briefly introduces the Russian Empire's multireligious and multiethnic structure before proceeding to the critical transformations of ethnic and religious identities in the Soviet period. Soviet policies promoted and ideologically reformulated ethnolinguistic identities as the building blocks of a multiethnic federation. Soviet official policies toward religion were also a central element of a great transformation that elevated ethnicity and imbued it with socialist content as a primordial social identity, while persecuting and downgrading religious identities. The chapter then addresses the post-Soviet period and the changes in ethnic policies that took place from Yeltsin to Putin. In the Yeltsin years, the pendulum swung between two extremes of ethnic policies, represented by Yeltsin's call for ethnic republics to "take as much sovereignty as [they] can swallow" in 1990 and his decision to invade Chechnya in 1994. During this period, majority and minority religions experienced a significant revival. After the 2000s, official policies accelerated processes of assimilation, and the revival and salience of ethnic and religious identities are related to domestic power struggles and foreign policy. Putin has used the Russian Orthodox Church in support of his domestic and international political goals in a way no Russian leader has done since the tsars, and he also relied on ethnic Russian nationalism in legitimizing Russia's annexation of Crimea.

21.1   Introduction

States make policies that regulate the rights of ethnic and religious communities, which in turn have far-reaching consequences for political dynamics (Aktürk 2012). Of all the European great powers, Russia is certainly the one that includes and politically represents the most ethnically and religiously diverse population in its contiguous territory. The historical fact that the overarching state governing such a vast territory and its diverse peoples collapsed twice, in 1917–22 and 1991–92, and was reconstituted as a multiethnic and multireligious polity in the past century, is a testimony both to the fragility and the stability of Russia. The politics of ethnicity and of religion in Russia today bears the imprint of both Soviet and pre-Soviet imperial legacies, which shaped ethnic and religious identities in such distinctive and seemingly contradictory ways that Russia has been depicted both as a very tolerant and as an excessively repressive state in its governance of cultural diversity.

Religion was the most significant social and administrative identity category under the Russian Empire, which had a multiconfessional establishment (Werth 2014), including **Russian Orthodox Christianity** as the dominant religion, along with numerous other officially recognized non-Orthodox religions. In contrast, Soviet state policies severely repressed and criminalized religious identities, while codifying and institutionalizing ethnic diversity, thus making ethnicity the most important particularistic identity both officially and in everyday life (Slezkine 1994). In imperial Russia, where religion was the primary social identity, Orthodox Christianity was the dominant and official religion in a multireligious polity, whereas in the militantly atheist and socialist Soviet Union, where ethnically defined nations became the primary organizing principle, the socialist Russian ethnicity became the "first among equals" in official parlance. Since the dissolution of the Soviet Union, both ethnic and religious identities have witnessed a revival and various transformations that have shaped identity politics in Russia today. Most of these radical transformations can be traced to the relatively democratic and pluralist governments of **Boris Yeltsin** in the 1990s, but they were augmented, reinforced, and achieved their momentous results later during the increasingly authoritarian and assimilationist governments of **Vladimir Putin** in the twenty-first century. Putin came to power by relaunching the war in Chechnya in 1999, and revived his popularity with the occupation and annexation of Crimea in 2014, two critical turning points for Russian politics and society during his rule. Putin also engineered the dissolution of several institutions of multiethnic nationhood, while eroding the autonomy of ethnic republics and elevating the status of Russian ethnicity and Russian Orthodoxy in politics and society.

For five centuries, Russia's ethnic and religious composition saw significant changes, with the most radical transformations in state policies occurring in the Soviet period, which I review in the first two sections. Patterns of repression and reform varied both chronologically and geographically. In this chapter, we will see how these momentous transformations form the background for politics of ethnicity and religion in present-day Russia.

21.2 Imperial Russia

Russian historiography traces the origins of the Russian state to "the Baptism of the Rus," when Grand Prince Vladimir of Kyiv converted to Orthodox Christianity and "forcibly baptized his people" in 988. After the Ottomans' conquest of Constantinople in 1453, Muscovite Russia claimed to be the only independent Orthodox Christian state in the world (Smolkin 2018, 22–23).

21.2.1 Ethnic and Religious Diversity in Imperial Russia

The conquest of Kazan in 1552 brought very sizable Muslim (mostly Tatar) populations under Russian rule, and it is often taken as the turning point that transformed the relatively homogeneous Muscovy into the multiethnic and multireligious Russian Empire. The conquest of the Baltic region in 1710 brought significant Lutheran populations, and the first partition of Poland brought very large Catholic, Jewish, and Uniate populations under Russian rule (Werth 2014, 3).

Nonetheless, imperial Russian history after 1552 can also be divided into two periods with regards to the governance of ethnoreligious diversity. The first period was characterized by more assertive assimilation (including forced mass conversions), persecution, and repression of non-Christians, starting with the reign of Ivan the Terrible (1547–84), while the second period starting with the reign of Catherine the Great (1762–96) was characterized by remarkable toleration, followed by many episodes of reform and repression under different tsars. These reformist efforts peaked after the Constitutional Revolution of 1905, ending with the collapse of the tsarist regime in 1917. A distinctive feature of both periods is that religion, far more than ethnicity, was the salient identity and the building block of a diverse polity. However, ethnic and religious boundaries often overlapped, and thus in many cases ethnic and religious identities reinforced each other.

21.2.2 From Ivan the Terrible to Catherine the Great, 1533–1762

Ivan IV (the Terrible) was the first grand duke of Moscow (1533–47) to assume the title of tsar of all Russia in 1547. The nascent Russian state of Muscovy already included remarkable ethnic and religious diversity by the sixteenth century (J. Martin 2001). The conquest of the **Kazan Khanate** in 1552 was followed by the conquest of the Astrakhan' Khanate in 1556, both of which are important for how they changed the ethnoreligious composition of the population under Russian rule. Already prior to these conquests, the Kazan Khanate's estimated population of 400,000 was remarkably multireligious; it consisted mostly of Muslim Tatars but included various other non-Christian peoples (Khamidullin 2008, 402). By 1719, Muslim ethnic groups such as the **Volga Tatars**, **Bashkirs**, **Siberian Tatars**, and **Nogai** numbered around 595,000, and Buddhist ethnic groups such as the **Buryats** and the **Kalmyks** numbered around 247,800, along with non-Orthodox Christian ethnic groups such as the predominantly Protestant Estonians (309,200) and Finns (164,200), among others (Kappeler 2001, 396–98). This increase in religious diversity, however, was accompanied by greater repression of minority religions, due to the missionary impulse to forcibly convert these new subjects to Orthodox Christianity. For example, "[t]he period from the conquest of Kazan in 1552 to the coming to power of Catherine the Great in 1762 was marked by a policy of systematic repression of Muslims and the destruction of Muslim civilization within Russia's borders" (Hunter 2004, 6).

21.2.3   From Catherine the Great to Nicholas II, 1762–1917

In the three centuries that followed the conquest of Kazan, Russia acquired vast territories inhabited by non-Christian peoples speaking non-Russian and often non-Slavic languages, in particular with the annexations of **Crimea** in 1783 and the Kingdom of Poland in 1815. By the early nineteenth century, Catholics had become the largest non-Orthodox population, and Russia also included the largest number of Jews in the world. This diversity was even further augmented with the annexations of the South Caucasus and Central Asia in the nineteenth and early twentieth centuries, which made Muslims the largest non-Orthodox population once again (Werth 2014, 14, 25). According to the 1897 census, the Russian Empire's population included 87.1 million Orthodox Christians (69.3 percent), 13.9 million Muslims (11.1 percent), 11.5 million Catholics (9.2 percent), 5.2 million Jews (4.2 percent), 3.7 million Protestants (3 percent), and 2.2 million Old Believers (1.8 percent), among others (Werth 2014, 4). Since the sixteenth century, Muslims in particular but also Buddhists have been the first significant non-Orthodox Christian populations to come under, and remain under, Russian rule to the present day, whereas Catholics, Jews, and Protestants, who were also very numerous and politically significant historically, no longer exist in such great numbers in Russia today.

In Russia, the majority religious tradition, Orthodox Christianity, has been historically subordinate to the tsar. This subordination was institutionalized with Peter the Great's abolition of the **Patriarchate** and establishment of the **Holy Synod** "(a state administration under the authority of the tsar) to manage Church affairs in 1718" (Tolz 2001, 37), which limited the ability of religious authorities to turn against the tsar, while also strengthening the identification of Orthodoxy with the Russian state. In 1773, Catherine the Great established new institutions to govern the religious affairs of the two largest non-Orthodox populations, arguably drawing inspiration from the benefits of the Holy Synod model in terms of political control and religious regulation, and motivated by the annexation of Muslim-majority Crimea and Catholic-majority Poland. These reforms resulted in the creation of the Orenburg Muslim Spiritual Assembly for the Muslims of Volga–Ural region in 1788, the Tauride Muslim Spiritual Directorate for the Crimean Muslims in 1794, and the Roman Catholic Spiritual College in 1801 (Werth 2014, 49–51).

21.3   Ethnic and Religious Policies in the Soviet Union

The Soviet Union's policies supported and augmented but also radically transformed ethnic identities, while severely suppressing religious identities. Francine Hirsch has argued that "no issue was more central to the formation of the Soviet Union than the nationality question" (2005, 5).

21.3.1   Transformations of Ethnic Identities: "National in Form, Socialist in Content"

The Russian Revolution heralded a momentous transformation and in many ways was unprecedented in world history. It overturned the tsarist Russian Empire, a dynastic polity legitimated in great part by the Russian Orthodox Church. In its stead, the Bolshevik revolutionaries created the world's first socialist polity, which was a federation of fifteen ethnically defined republics, each with its own distinct language, and in which **"militant atheism"** became the official policy toward religion. Over the course of the decades that followed the October Revolution, it became clear that the Soviet Union could not eradicate religion. It did succeed in turning what was one of the most religious polities in Europe before 1917 into a very secular one, with a relatively low level of religious observance by the time the USSR dissolved in 1991. Soviet policies on ethnicity also had a longlasting influence that still shapes Russian politics and society.

21.3.2   The Origins of Soviet Ethnic Policies: World War, Civil War, and Leninist Ideology

How and why did the Bolsheviks establish a multiethnic federal state that institutionalized and promoted ethnic diversity at multiple levels? There are at least three plausible explanations for this puzzle: The experience of the Russian Civil War (1918–20), the lessons Bolsheviks drew from World War I, and their ideology and strategy for a socialist world revolution. First, the Civil War between the Bolsheviks ("Reds") and their opponents, who included the monarchist Whites, the Socialist Revolutionaries, the Kadets (constitutional democrats), the Green Army (armed peasant groups), anarchists, and the ethnoreligious nationalist movements, was a formative experience for the constitution of the Soviet Union as a multiethnic federation. In order to win the support or at least the acquiescence of the non-Russian ethnoreligious groups, Bolsheviks promised them wideranging cultural autonomy. For example, there were attempts to establish three large Muslim-majority republics in the Caucasus, the Volga–Ural region, and Central Asia, but these were stymied by the Bolsheviks with a mixture of cooptation and violent repression. Instead, five distinct Central Asian union republics, two autonomous republics in the Volga–Ural region, one union republic, and half a dozen autonomous republics with Muslim majorities were established in the Caucasus. Applying ethnic instead of religious categories significantly splintered Muslim populations into much smaller administrative territorial entities. What is more, several independent states had already been established – and had existed for a few years during the Civil War – by ethnonational groups that formerly lived under the Russian Empire, including the independent states of Armenia, Azerbaijan, Georgia, and Ukraine. These states were brought under Soviet rule by a mixture of military occupation and elite cooptation by 1921 and retained their status as ethnically defined territories within the Soviet Union.

Secondly, ethnocultural and administrative concessions were also motivated by the lessons that the Bolsheviks drew from the collapse of the multiethnic Habsburg and Ottoman Empires during World War I, and Soviet policies such as extensive measures of positive discrimination vis-à-vis non-Russian ethnic groups were all part of "a strategy designed to avoid the perception of empire" (T. Martin 2001, 19). **Vladimir Lenin** and Joseph Stalin were successful in achieving this goal insofar as they avoided the fate of the multiethnic Habsburg and Ottoman polities, since the Red Army soon took control of almost all the territories that had previously been ruled by imperial Russia during the Civil War, reconstituted as the Union of Soviet Socialist Republics, officially established in December 1922.

Thirdly, and relatedly, unlike Karl Marx, who saw imperialism as a progressive force, Lenin argued that there were "oppressor" and "oppressed nations" – similar to the bourgeoisie and the proletariat in every society – and he advocated allying with the oppressed nations against the oppressor nations as part of his strategy for a worldwide socialist revolution. Lenin argued that communists must fight imperialism both at home and abroad. Thus, Soviet ethnic policies were meant to support the cultures and languages of the oppressed ethnic groups against the chauvinism of ethnic Russians.

On the religious front, too, Bolsheviks' "early antireligious measures were aimed above all at the Orthodox Church" and "the party was willing to forge alliances with those religious groups that had been persecuted under the imperial autocracy" (Smolkin 2018, 28). For example, the Cathedral of Christ the Savior was destroyed in 1931. However, once the Bolsheviks consolidated their hold on power, the militant atheism of the regime also targeted major non-Orthodox religious groups, such as Muslims. While there were about 26,000 functioning mosques before the October Revolution, Stalin's antireligious campaign reduced this number to 1,312 by 1942 (Hunter 2004, 29–30). The Bolshevik regime initially allied with religious "reformists" – both among Orthodox Christians, such as the Renovationists and the founders of the Living Church (Hosking 1992; Smolkin 2018), and among Muslims, such as the Jadids (Khalid 1999) – in order to weaken the mainstream Orthodox Christian and Muslim leadership and institutions.

21.3.3   The Affirmative Action Empire: Indigenization, Census, and Passport Ethnicity

The Soviet regime's goal was to translate communist ideology into the language and culture of every non-Russian ethnic group in the USSR so that it would be more effective and convincing, rather than being perceived as another Russian imperial attempt at assimilating and eradicating non-Russian ethnicities. Lenin was probably influenced by the similar effort of the Russian Orthodox missionary and scholar Nikolai Ilminsky, who attempted to convert non-Orthodox subjects of the Russian Empire, including the Muslims in particular, by translating Orthodox Christian content (such as the Bible) into the Indigenous languages of the non-Orthodox people (Kreindler 1977). The popular slogan "national in form, socialist in content" is a pithy summary of the Soviet strategy and policies toward ethnocultural diversity, known as the "nationalities policy."

Positive discrimination, now often known in English as affirmative action, targeting non-Russian ethnic cadres in official appointments, was an important pillar of Soviet nationalities policy. This meant that the Soviet Union was in fact an "affirmative action empire" (T. Martin 2001). These policies were known as *korenizatsiia*, or **"indigenization"** and aimed to cultivate and promote a loyal communist elite in every ethnic group across the USSR. Indigenization would facilitate the dissemination of Soviet ideology and the governing of non-Russian groups through their ethnic kin. In 1932, the Soviet government issued a list of ninety-one "culturally backward" nationalities deemed to be most deserving of positive discrimination (T. Martin 2001, 166–67). Notably, affirmative action policies were not applied in the most powerful and high-level institutions such as the military high command, the secret police (NKVD, MVD, KGB), the Central Committee, or the Politburo, where non-Slavic and particularly Muslim nationalities were severely underrepresented (Hosking 1992, 430–31).

In order to ethnically discriminate, positively or negatively, the Soviet state first had to ethnically identify all of its citizens. This momentous task was achieved with the Soviet census of 1926, in which Soviet citizens were classified based on a list of 191 ethnonational categories (Hirsch 2005, 329–33). Some Soviet citizens did not identify with an ethnonational category, and instead identified with their religion, but the census-takers were instructed to insist on getting an ethnic category as the answer (Hirsch 2005, 118). The list of ethnonational categories for the 1939 census only had sixty-two categories, about one-third of the 1926 census (Hirsch 2005, 333–34), reflecting the official view that many ethnicities merged into larger ones in the process of building socialism. A critical step was taken with the institution of **"passport ethnicity."** Starting in 1934, Soviet citizens above the age of sixteen had their ethnicity inscribed in the fifth line of their obligatory internal passports (Akturk 2010). Once registered, an individual could not change his/her ethnicity, and it became hereditary. Only the children of parents with different ethnicities could choose between them while receiving their passports. Passport ethnicity remained an important tool of totalitarian control and population management in the Soviet Union.

21.3.4 Ethnic Russian Backlash, the Fatherland War, and the Punished Nations

The positive discrimination that benefited non-Russian ethnic groups led to resentment and backlash from ethnic Russians (T. Martin 2001). This was particularly the case in the teaching of history and language. Leading figures of prerevolutionary

Russian history such as Ivan the Terrible and Peter the Great, who were condemned after the Bolshevik Revolution, were rehabilitated in Soviet education and popular culture in the 1930s (Platt and Brandenberger 2006). Any historical figure who had contributed to the development of imperial Russia was reinterpreted in a positive light as someone who had inadvertently helped building the future homeland of the first socialist society.

The **Fatherland War**, as World War II is known in Soviet and Russian historiography, brought about two other notable changes in ethnic and religious policies. Epitomized by Stalin's famous toast to the (ethnic) Russian nation in celebrating the victory over Nazi Germany, the symbolic place of ethnic Russians as the first among Soviet nations was augmented. Moreover, the repression of the Russian Orthodox Church was eased once war began, with the patriarch praying for Soviet victory over Nazi Germany, which was a welcome development for Stalin and the communist leadership.

Another crucial development of the late 1930s and the 1940s was the official stigmatization and mass deportation of entire ethnic groups, turning the promise of positive discrimination into mass persecution. Ethnic groups living in the western borderlands with ethnic kin states across the border, such as the Finns and the Poles, were deported starting in 1935, but Koreans were the first ethnic group deported en masse in 1937 (T. Martin 2001, 328–35). These "national operations made up . . . about . . . a third of the total executions during the Great Terror," even though these ethnonational groups constituted a very small percentage of the Soviet population (T. Martin 2001, 338). Many other ethnic groups were accused of collaboration with Germany and deported en masse from their homelands during World War II, including Balkars, Chechens, Crimean Tatars, Ingush, Karachais, Kalmyks, Meshketian Turks, and Volga Germans. These were known as the "**punished nations.**"

Many of these allegations were patently absurd. Some of these ethnic groups, such as the Meshketians living around the Soviet–Turkish border, were so far removed from the military front lines that they did not have any contact, let alone widespread collaboration, with the Nazi German armies. Even those Crimean Tatars who had been awarded the title "Hero of the USSR" for their valor in fighting Nazi Germany were arrested and deported (Fisher 1978, 166–67). Up to 46 percent of the Crimean Tatar population died within the first couple of years after the deportation, and the Ukrainian parliament "recognized this forcible deportation as genocide of the Crimean Tatar People" in 2020 (OSCE 2020). Chechens, Ingush, Kalmyks, and Karachais "suffered a similar fate" in the "genocidal deportations of 1944," in which the "official death rate of 23.7 percent in the trains [corresponds to] a total of 144,704 people," while "indirect population loss among Chechens alone range from 170,000 to 200,000" of a total of 478,000 Chechens and Ingush at the time (Wood 2004, 13–14). These deportations became a major source of popular hostility vis-à-vis Moscow, as in the case of Chechens and Crimean Tatars to the present day (Tishkov 1997, 193–94). In 1952–53, the final years of Stalin's rule, the last ethnoreligious group that was unofficially targeted in a systematic campaign was the Jews, who were accused of anti-Soviet activities during the anticosmopolitanism campaign and the Doctors' Plot, in which doctors of Jewish origin were accused of plotting to assassinate Soviet leaders (Grüner 2008).

21.3.5   Khrushchev and Brezhnev: Building the Soviet Nation under Mature Socialism

When Nikita Khrushchev assumed the leadership of the Soviet Union after Stalin's death in 1953, he allowed most of the punished nations to return to their homelands on their own, except for the Crimean Tatars, Meshketian Turks, and Volga Germans (Fisher 1978; Mukhina 2007), but these rehabilitations were only partial (Human Rights Watch 1991). At the same time, Khrushchev also brought back the antireligious campaign with renewed vigor, launching a campaign that destroyed the majority of functioning mosques in the entire Soviet Union. Khrushchev virtually eliminated mosques, reducing their number to roughly 400 by 1963, less than 2 percent of the number that had operated in imperial Russia (Hunter 2004, 32).

Khrushchev promoted the idea of Soviet nation (*sovetskii narod*) as "a new historical community of people" transcending ethnolinguistic and other sociocultural differences (Aktürk 2012, 197–228). Throughout Soviet history, socialist nationalities were expected to go through three consecutive stages of flourishing (*rastsvet*) and rapprochement (*sblizhenie*), culminating in their merger (*sliianie*). The new emphasis on the Soviet nation was accompanied by the new education laws of 1958–59, which made education in their native language optional for the non-Russian titular ethnic groups, thus incentivizing linguistic Russification (Bilinsky 1962), and by Khrushchev's failed attempt to remove ethnicity from the internal passport (Aktürk 2012, 211–13). Following Khrushchev's ouster in 1964, the emphasis on the Soviet nation continued during Leonid Brezhnev's leadership (1964–82), also known as the era of "mature socialism," and yet another attempt to remove ethnicity from the passport failed (Zaslavksy and Luryi 1979, 149–50). Under Brezhnev, the same ethnic leadership remained in power in the union republics for roughly two decades or more (Suny 1993, 118–19) and, secure in their own privileges, cultivated their coethnic elites, thus furthering the indigenization of Soviet socialism among non-Russians.

21.4   Dissolution of the USSR and the Rise of Russian Federation

Only 43.4 percent of the Russian Empire's population was ethnic Russian in 1897. After eight decades of Soviet rule 50.6 percent of the Soviet Union's population was ethnic Russian, according to the last census in 1989 (Tishkov 1997, 27, 41). In 1991, following the disintegration of the Soviet Union into fifteen independent countries, ethnic Russians constituted approximately 78 percent of the population of the Russian Federation. While this is the most ethnically homogeneous population Russia had in many centuries, the Russian government still governs a country in which more than a fifth of the population is not ethnically Russian.

Patterns of ethnic and religious diversity within the Russian Federation today overlap considerably since all major groups that are religiously distinct from the Orthodox majority are also considered distinct ethnic groups, but the opposite is not necessarily the case: There are many Orthodox Christian ethnic minorities such as the Chuvash and the Udmurt peoples. Religious diversity in Russia today has two geographical concentrations, with the North Caucasus and the Volga–Ural regions having the overwhelming majority of non-Christian, primarily Muslim, ethnic groups. In contrast, there are three additional regions where ethnically non-Russian peoples concentrate: Altai region with various Turkic groups, central and eastern Siberia with Indigenous Siberian and Turkic groups, and northwestern Russia with numerous Finno-Ugric groups.

The ethnic policies and institutions of Russia at present bear the imprint of Stalin's legacy. The USSR dissolved exactly along the lines of the fifteen Soviet socialist union republics it constitutionally contained. Russia's borders with these post-Soviet states remain the same as they were within the Soviet Union, with the notable exception of Russia's annexation of Ukrainian Crimea in 2014. With the constitution of 1993, Russia was established as a federation consisting of eighty-nine subjects, including numerous oblasts, krais, and federal cities, but also twenty-one ethnic autonomous republics, ten ethnic autonomous okrugs, and one ethnic autonomous oblast (Herrera 2005, 24). Russia inherited this ethnic territorial structure from the Soviet Union. Following Soviet practice, each ethnic territorial unit is identified with the specific titular ethnic group that it is named after: For example, Tatars are the titular ethnicity in the Republic of **Tatarstan**. Moreover, Russia also inherited legal and institutional legacies of Soviet nationalities policies such as passport ethnicity and the Ministry of Nationalities.

With the removal of Soviet-era bans on public expressions of religiosity, Russia witnessed a moderate religious revival in the 1990s. The Cathedral of Christ the Savior, destroyed in 1931 as mentioned above, was rebuilt in its original place and reopened to the public in 1997 (Smolkin 2018, 243). Similarly, Kul Sharif Mosque in Kazan, Tatarstan, which was destroyed during the Russian conquest of Kazan in 1552, was also rebuilt. Despite such a symbolic revival in religious architecture, levels of religious observance in Russia remain relatively low compared to many other areas of the world.

21.4.1 Yeltsin's Rise to Power and the Renegotiation of the Federation: "Take as Much Sovereignty as You Can Swallow"

One pattern of Russian politics since 1990 has been Moscow's concessions to the regions, especially the ethnic republics, in times of close competition for leadership at the center. Boris Yeltsin, who was struggling for the leadership of Russia against **Mikhail Gorbachev,** the last general secretary of the **Communist Party of the Soviet Union,** famously told Tatars to "take as much sovereignty as you can swallow" in his speech in Kazan, the capital of Tatarstan, in 1990. The rise of Yeltsin against Gorbachev was paralleled by what scholars labeled "Russia's ethnic revival" (Treisman 1997) and the "parade of sovereignties" (Hale 2000). Nationalist mobilization was uneven across the former USSR with the Baltic states as the most and the Central Asian states as the least mobilized for independence (Beissinger 2002). For example, there was far more popular mobilization for independence in **Chechnya** and Tatarstan, two autonomous republics within Russia, than in Turkmenistan or Uzbekistan, two union republics in Central Asia, and yet the latter two became independent whereas the former two could not (Giuliano 2000; Wood 2004). Every entity that was designated as a "union republic" in the USSR was recognized as an independent state, but not a single "autonomous" republic was recognized as independent, including Chechnya, which fought two very costly wars for independence against Russia (Walker 2003).

The Russian Federation's 1993 constitution indicates that the country is both an ethnic and an asymmetric federation, two features that distinguish it from many other federal polities. Ethnic republics, autonomous okrugs, and the autonomous oblast are the ethnic subjects while the oblasts, krais, and the federal cities are the nonethnic subjects of the Russian Federation (Herrera 2005, 24). Under Yeltsin, the elected leaders of the ethnic republics acquired the privilege of being recognized as "presidents" instead of governors. Presidents of the ethnic republics negotiated bilateral treaties with the central government during Yeltsin's presidency, and ethnic republics with rich natural resources such as Tatarstan were able to get particularly favorable terms and more extensive autonomy (Sharafutdinova 2000). These bilateral treaties made Russia an asymmetric federation, with various regions acquiring different levels of autonomy. Furthermore, by even engaging in international diplomacy, "Tatarstan has been 'acting like a state' in order to be recognised by international actors" (Sharafutdinova 2003). Ethnic leaderships of these regions were in part the continuation of the Soviet-era Communist Party elites, the *nomenklatura,* which resulted from the policies of indigenization (Kryshtanovskaya and White 1996; Petrov and Nazrullaeva 2018, 112). Electoral cycles, but especially the closely contested presidential election of 1996, forced Yeltsin to make concessions to the regional elites.

21.4.2   The First Chechen War, 1994–1996

The most notable exception to the pattern of bilateral negotiations was Chechnya, where Yeltsin ordered a military operation to suppress a secessionist mobilization in December 1994. The origins of the First Chechen War had historical and structural but also contingent and proximate causes. The deportation of Chechens to Central Asia in 1944, with the huge loss of life mentioned above (Wood 2004, 13–14), had been deeply traumatic. Secondly, Chechens experienced economic and political disadvantages even within their ethnic republic. Thirdly, the leader of the Chechen independence movement, **Dzhokhar Dudayev**, was previously an air force general stationed in Estonia, the Soviet republic that had one of the most popular and sustained mobilizations for independence, which inspired him (Wood 2004). Following declarations of independence by many union republics, Chechnya declared independence on November 1, 1991.

After numerous failed attempts to topple or kill Dudayev, Yeltsin ordered a full-scale invasion of Chechnya in December 1994. The "principal reason was to bolster his own [Yeltsin's] declining popularity" with "a small victorious war" (Tishkov 1997, 218). The Russian military took the Chechen capital, Grozny, after massive bombing and heavy casualties in March 1995. Dudayev was assassinated in a rocket attack in April 1996, which coincided with Yeltsin's presidential election campaign, but Chechen rebels captured Grozny after Yeltsin's reelection in August. Chechen victory, combined with the unpopularity of the war with the Russian public and the media scrutiny of the conduct of the Russian military, forced Yeltsin government to sign the **Khasavyurt Accords** on August 31, 1996, recognizing Chechnya as "a subject of international law" but postponing the decision on independence to 2001. The casualties of the war were devastating, especially for a tiny republic whose population was barely 1 million: "Conservative estimates give 7,500 Russian military casualties, 4,000 Chechen combatants and no less than 35,000 civilians – a minimum total of 46,500; others have cited figures in the range 80,000 to 100,000" (Wood 2004, 22). For the next three years, Chechnya enjoyed de facto independence, and **Aslan Maskhadov** was elected president of Chechnya in the elections of January 1997, which were "described by the OSCE as 'exemplary and free'" (Wood 2004, 24–25). These developments made a deep impression on both domestic and international audiences, with some observers interpreting the Russian defeat as "the end of Russia as a great military and imperial power" (Lieven 1999, 1).

21.4.3   Passport Reform and the Search for a Civic Territorial Russian Nationhood

The attempt to remove ethnicity from the Russian internal passport was inextricably linked with the attempt to create a new, nonethnic, and civic territorial Russian nationhood by deemphasizing ethnic differences. The Yeltsin government brought a new elite into power, one that was opposed to many Soviet policies, and passport ethnicity was one of the best-known Soviet legacies. A number of prominent voices wanted to remove ethnicity from the internal passport in the Yeltsin governments. Advocates of building a civic territorial nation, liberals who opposed mandatory recording of ethnicity that enabled discrimination, those who perceived a security risk in the classification of the citizenry according to ethnicity after witnessing the dissolution of the USSR, the Jews who were discriminated against through passport ethnicity throughout Soviet history, and those in favor of a more assimilationist nation-state for which passport ethnicity was a major obstacle: All favored the removal of ethnicity from internal passports (Akturk 2010; Shevel 2011). In contrast, leaders of ethnic republics were against such a reform because they feared they might lose their privileges and autonomy based on their titular ethnic status but also because "[f]or many people, especially Russia's ethnic minorities, recording their nationality in a passport is virtually the only way they can preserve their ethnic identity" (Khannanova 2000).

Yeltsin removed ethnicity from the internal passport with an executive decree on March 13, 1997. Tatarstan's state council declared this to be "the biggest provocation in the history of Russia," while Tatar activists publicly burned the passport (Akturk 2010, 329). Representatives from Bashkortostan, Dagestan, Ingushetia, and Kabardino-Balkaria criticized and opposed the removal of ethnicity from the passport (Akturk 2010, 330). Valery Tishkov, the minister of nationalities under Yeltsin's first government in 1992, and the head of the Institute of Ethnology and Anthropology throughout the 1990s and the 2000s, publicly supported this reform and argued that the success of Russian state-building depended on the removal of ethnicity from the internal passport (Akturk 2010). He maintained that the state should foster allegiance to a civic and territorial definition of the nation, which he defined as the *Rossian* nation, denoting all inhabitants of Russia irrespective of ethnicity (Tishkov 1997). Yeltsin also vetoed the new birth certificates in June 1997, "for the simple reason that they included the compulsory registration of the parents' ethnicity" (Aktürk 2012, 252), thus demonstrating that the government's new policy of deemphasizing ethnic differences among its citizens was not limited to the passport reform.

21.5   The Russian Federation under Putin and Medvedev

There are many continuities between the governments of Boris Yeltsin, Vladimir Putin, and **Dmitry Medvedev** in terms of the new ethnic policies they adopted. They all continued assimilationist new policies in deemphasizing ethnolinguistic differences and energetically pushed for a single, overarching Russian identity. There are also some aspects that distinguish Putin's approach to ethnicity and religion from Yeltsin's. Due to high oil prices, Putin had far more resources at his disposal and could go much further in eroding institutional and legal dimensions of Russia's multiethnic regime than Yeltsin could. Putin's two most dramatic decisions with ethnoreligious connotations and both domestic and international consequences are his decisions to relaunch the war against Chechnya in 1999 and his decision to occupy and annex Crimea in 2014. In the one and a half decades between these two fateful decisions, Putin also reduced ethnic republics' political autonomy, representation, and weight in Russian politics, while also dissolving several institutions of multiethnic nationhood.

There are two other critical developments under Putin indicative of the changing state policies toward ethnolinguistic and religious identities. The first is the downgrading of non-Russian titular languages in education, and the second is the promotion of Orthodox Christianity publicly as the leading religion of Russia. The ban on non-Cyrillic alphabets under Putin is related to both ethnolinguistic and religious dimensions of the new Russian national identity in the making. Thus, the Putin governments moved in the direction of Russian monolingualism in education, while also elevating the public role of Orthodox Christianity.

21.5.1 The Politics of Ethnicity, Religion, and the Nation under Putin and Medvedev

Both Yeltsin in 1996 and Putin as early as 1999 emphasized the need for developing a "national idea" for Russia (Hunter 2004, 127). For Putin, the collapse of the Soviet Union was the greatest geopolitical disaster of the twentieth century, and the ethnic federal structure of the USSR was a central element in that outcome. Thus, Putin seems to perceive the Soviet legacy of ethnoterritorial autonomies and the segmentation of the population along ethnocultural lines as a liability. Four of the five most visited regions by both President Putin and President Medvedev are ethnic republics that are also Muslim (Tatarstan, **Bashkortostan**, Chechnya, and **Ingushetia**), which is indicative of the presidents' paramount concern with these regions of ethnoreligious distinctiveness (Petrov and Nazrullaeva 2018, 130).

21.5.2 From the Second Chechen War (1999–2000) to the Annexation of Crimea (2014)

Putin's rise to power was intricately linked with his launching of the Second Chechen War in 1999. Until his abrupt appointment as the acting prime minister by Yeltsin in early August 1999, Vladimir Putin was a politically unknown figure, albeit with a long career in the Soviet and Russian secret service (the KGB and the FSB, respectively). Yet Putin's popularity rose suddenly and meteorically after he relaunched the war against Chechnya following "a series of explosions in apartment buildings in Buinaksk, Volgodonsk and Moscow in late August and September – FSB collusion has repeatedly, and plausibly, been alleged – [that] prepared domestic opinion for the 'counter-terrorist operation'" (Wood 2004, 27; see also Belton 2020,

153–61) since Chechen terrorists were accused and convicted (in absentia) for these apartment bombings. In October 1999, about 100,000 Russian soldiers, four times as many as Yeltsin had deployed and corresponding roughly to one-tenth of Chechnya's entire population, invaded Chechnya and captured Grozny in February 2000, while Putin won his first and only somewhat competitive presidential election in March 2000 (Wood 2004, 28).

The war resulted in the "Chechenization" of Russia (Ware 2011), meaning that the administrative centralization, elimination of horizontal accountability (such as competitive elections), and excessive use of coercion that were first "successfully" applied in Chechnya were later extended to the rest of the North Caucasus and the Russian Federation at large. This strategy has had many disadvantages, however, and might be unsustainable in the long run. "Crimea and Chechnya are by far the most heavily subsidized regions in Russia" (Petrov and Slider 2019, 63), demonstrating the tremendous economic costs of conquest, in addition to the diplomatic isolation, sanctions, war crimes, and systematic human rights abuses that resulted from Russia's effort to occupy and keep both of these regions.

Russia's annexation of Crimea is arguably the most recent event that changed the nature of Russian nationalism, ushering in a period much more defined by Russian ethnic nationalism and revisionism than under Yeltsin or in the first fourteen years of Putin's rule. Crimea's annexation boosted Putin's popularity and endeared him to Russian nationalists, but this proved to be temporary as many Russian nationalists soon became critical of Putin for not sufficiently supporting the pro-Russian secessionists in the Donbas region of Ukraine (Kolstø 2016; Laruelle 2016). In justifying the annexation of Crimea, with its ethnic Russian majority, to the domestic public, the Russian state employed an official identity discourse that was revisionist and that depicted Russia almost as an ethnic nation-state, going against the civic territorial and statist conceptions of Russian nationhood that had been employed by Yeltsin and earlier by Putin himself (Putin 2012; Teper 2016). Ethnicization of Russian national identity as such is a challenge for Russian citizens of ethnic and religious minority backgrounds, who make up more than one-fifth of Russia's population. Russia under Putin invaded Ukraine in late February 2022 under the pretext of an alleged "genocide" against ethnic Russians in the Donbas. This invasion made clear that Russia's official nationalism had taken a decisively revisionist turn, because an attempt to change political borders through military occupation is an unmistakable symptom of revisionism. Furthermore, the pretext of protecting ethnic Russians in Ukraine is yet another symptom of the ethnicization of Russian nationalism.

21.5.3   Ethnic and Religious Minority Representation

The central government's control over the ethnic regions' political representatives increased significantly starting with Putin's first presidential term (2000–04). The most popular and assertive presidents of ethnic autonomous republics, such as **Mintimer Shaimiev** of Tatarstan (1991–2010) and **Murtaza Rakhimov** of Bashkortostan (1993–2010), were removed. Even earlier in his presidency, Putin had been able to remove another popular ethnic president, **Ruslan Aushev** (1993–2001) of Ingushetia (Sakwa 2007, 25–26). Following a similar pattern, which some scholars compare to a "pendulum swing," **Duma** elections were switched to pure proportional representation in 2007 to prevent regionally popular politicians such as the leaders of ethnic republics from getting elected (Petrov and Nazrullaeva 2018, 114–18). In 2016, the mixed electoral system was brought back.

Despite these changes in electoral systems, non-Russian ethnic groups maintain a roughly proportionate level of representation in the Duma. A study of all Muslim-origin members of the Duma, who also belong to non-Russian ethnic groups, demonstrates that their numbers are almost proportionate to the size of Russia's Muslim minority, and, as such, the Muslim minority in Russia is more proportionately represented than the Muslim minorities in most other East and West European countries (Aktürk and Katliarou 2021). This is, in great part, a continuing legacy of Soviet-era affirmative action policies.

Russia's ethnic and religious policies also have an international dimension. For example, Russia attempts to use Tatarstan's institutions and elites to convince Crimean Tatars to accept the annexation of the peninsula by Russia (Podobied 2019). Somewhat similarly, due to the heavily Islamic nature of the anti-Russian resistance in Chechnya, Russia takes special care to cultivate a positive image in Muslim countries in order to avoid being the primary target of Islamic and Islamist movements. This may explain in part why Russia sought and gained an observer status in the Organisation of Islamic Cooperation (OIC) in 2005. These examples demonstrate that Russia's treatment of its ethnic and religious minorities serves both domestic and international purposes.

21.5.4 Dissolution of the Ethnic Autonomous Okrugs and the Ministry of Nationalities

The ethnoterritorial structure of the Russian Federation was not only qualitatively but also quantitatively eroded. Six ethnic autonomous okrugs were dissolved within five years under Putin's governments: The Komi Permiak, Ust-Orda Buryat, Agin-Buryat, and Koryak Autonomous Okrugs were merged with Perm, Irkutsk, Chita, and Kamchatka Oblasts, respectively, while the Taimyrskii (Dolgano-Nenetskii) and Evenkiiskii Okrugs were merged with the Krasnoyarsk Krai (Aktürk 2012, 254) between 2004 and 2008. Some of these ethnic autonomous entities, especially Evenkiiskii, Koryak, and Taimyrskii Okrugs, were very sizable territories (Herrera 2005, 25, Map 1), approximately 2 million square kilometers in total, and with significant natural resources. Only four ethnic autonomous okrugs remain: Chukotka, Khanty-Mansi, Nenets, and Yamal-Nenets. Among these, **Khanty-Mansi**

Autonomous Okrug in particular has vast natural resources: Roughly half of Russia's oil is produced in this region (Newsru.com 2012). These mergers brought down the number of subjects of the Russian Federation from eighty-nine to eighty-three; with the addition of Crimea and the Crimean city of **Sevastopol** as two distinct federal subjects in 2014, this number increased to eighty-five.

Under Putin, yet another institution of multinationalism was demolished: the **Ministry of Nationalities**. A Soviet legacy, this ministry was a testimony to the utmost importance attributed to the multinational constitution of Russia. It continued throughout the Yeltsin administrations, with the first post-Soviet Russian minister of nationalities being Valery Tishkov in 1992. Although it appeared under eight different names under Yeltsin, it persisted as a distinct ministry, nonetheless, at a time when "the central government was increasingly Russified as representation of non-Russians dwindled in appointed offices" (Goode 2019, 151). However, under Putin this ministry was abolished and in its place a new Department of Interethnic Relations was first included under the Ministry of Regional Development in 2004 for about a decade (Aktürk 2012, 253–54); this department was placed under the Ministry of Culture in 2014; finally it too was abolished and replaced with the Federal Agency for Nationality Affairs in 2015 (Goode 2019, 151–52). This agency sponsors events that simultaneously emphasize the ethnic diversity and the "singular cultural code" of Russia (FADN 2021), which is in line with Putin's opinion on the "national question" that Russia is "a multiethnic civilization, held together by the [ethnic] Russian cultural core" and thus that it has a "singular cultural code" (Putin 2012).

21.5.5 A Shift toward Monolingualism in Education, the Ban on Non-Cyrillic Alphabets, the Promotion of Orthodox Christianity, and the Ukrainian Question

First, both the Russian constitution and the specific laws concerning non-Russian titular and native languages systematically privilege Russian as the first and only mandatory language, but also allow for the ethnic republics to institute and support a second language, while the preservation of non-Russian native languages is mostly left to the personal efforts of individual citizens (Zhemukov and Aktürk 2015, 48–65). As a result of such systematic official preference and support, the Russian language has become far more widely spoken at the expense of non-Russian native languages throughout the Russian Federation in the thirty years since the dissolution of the USSR. While the ten largest titular ethnic minorities in Russia all had at least two-thirds titular-language proficiency in 2002, just eight years later only five of the ten largest minorities (Chechen, Chuvash, Ingush, Tatar, and Yakut) had more than two-thirds titular-language proficiency among their members (Akturk 2017, 1110). Moreover, while only one of the ten largest titular ethnic minorities (the Ingush) had over 80 percent proficiency in Russian in 1989, all ten largest titular ethnic groups had between 89.4 and 99.6 percent Russian-language proficiency in 2010 (Akturk 2017, 1109). Linguistic Russification has occurred at a dizzying pace in just two decades, and the proportion of those who have lost their native-language proficiency in less than a decade, even among the largest titular ethnic groups, has been alarming. Moreover, two of Putin's most prominent rivals in the past decade have made ethnic Russian nationalist, antiminority, and anti-immigrant promises in their campaigns. Mikhail Prokhorov, who ran as an independent candidate against Putin in the presidential elections of 2012 and came in third with 8 percent of the national vote, "proposed to abolish the national republics," whereas **Alexei Navalny**, "who ran as the joint candidate of several opposition parties to be the mayor of Moscow, and came in second with 27 percent of the vote, promised to 'cut the number of migrants by 70 percent'" (Akturk 2017, 1102).

Secondly, Putin's public praise of Orthodox Christianity, his displays of personal piety that distinguish him from Yeltsin and the Soviet leaders, and the ever-strengthening and seemingly symbiotic relationship between the Moscow Patriarchate and the Russian state all suggest that Orthodoxy is being elevated to a public role and function higher than it has ever had since 1917 (see also Chapter 16). For example, a huge statue of Grand Prince Vladimir was erected in central Moscow in 2016, which could be interpreted as the restoration of Orthodox Christianity as Russia's leading religion and the revived source of legitimacy (Walker 2016, cited in Smolkin 2018, 246).

Orthodox Christianity also plays a major role in Russia's projection of soft power around the world, including in the Americas, Europe, and the Middle East (Aktürk 2019). In relation to the struggle over Ukraine, for example, Putin claimed that the "Russian world . . . retained those Christian values that were seen as lost elsewhere" (Feklyunina 2016). Religious identity is particularly important in projecting Russia's soft power as the only Orthodox great power in other Orthodox-majority countries such as Bulgaria, Greece, Montenegro, Romania, and Serbia, as evidenced in Putin's visit to the Mount Athos monastic complex in Greece in May 2016, in which Russian media claimed that he sat on the throne of Byzantine emperors (Aktürk 2019). The Moscow Patriarchate vehemently objected to the granting of autocephalous (autonomous) status to the Ukrainian Orthodox Church by the Ecumenical Patriarchate in Istanbul in January 2019, and the Russian Orthodox Church is establishing a Patriarchal Exarchate of Western Europe in France, as part of a global competition against the Istanbul Patriarchate, which is criticized in Russia for being pro-Western (Kelaidis 2019).

A measure was passed in the Russian parliament and swiftly signed into law by President Putin in 2002, "mandating that all ethnic republics use the Cyrillic alphabet for their titular national languages," thus effectively banning the use of Latin script, which Tatarstan was seeking to use for the Tatar language (Hunter 2004, 242). The choice of alphabet is symbolic not only for ethnolinguistic but often also for religious and civilizational identity. Many Turkic Muslim groups insisted, both in the early Soviet period and in present-day Russia, on a switch to the Latin alphabet, which has also been undertaken in post-Soviet Azerbaijan, Turkmenistan, Uzbekistan, and Kazakhstan as a form of "linguistic decolonization" (du Boulay and du Boulay 2021). These attempts to use the Latin alphabet for non-Russian titular languages have been stymied under Putin, because they represent attempts to accentuate the cultural difference of these non-Slavic titular ethnic groups from the ethnic Russian majority, while the Putin administrations have been increasingly emphasizing a "singular cultural code."

Finally, Russia's military intervention in Ukraine since 2014 denotes far more than an international conflict as it deeply relates to the debates over Russian national identity. The significance of the "Ukrainian question" for the current debates on Russian identity was emphasized at the highest level with the publication of Putin's article "On the Historical Unity of Russians and Ukrainians" in June 2021, where he explicitly argued that "Russians and Ukrainians [are] one people" with a common language and religion (Putin 2021). Russia's unprovoked invasion of the rest of Ukraine, starting in late February 2022, can be seen in this light.

21.6 Conclusion: From the Affirmative Action Empire to an Assimilationist Nation-State

The Russian Empire impressed foreign observers with its vast religious diversity. By the early twentieth century, Russia included the world's largest Orthodox Christian and Jewish populations, more Muslims than the Ottoman Empire, millions of Catholics and Protestants, and a nonnegligible number of Buddhists, all of which had at least one member in the imperial parliament, the Duma, at some point after 1905. Although very repressive toward religious groups, the Soviet Union was also unprecedented in modern history in the extent to which ethnic diversity was officially recognized and institutionalized at multiple levels. The large populations of Catholics, Jews, Lutherans, and Uniates who came under Russian rule during the eighteenth century are for the most part no longer part of the Russian polity, and Muslims remain the largest non-Orthodox religious minority by a large margin. Although Russia still has the most ethnically and religiously diverse population among the European great powers, in contrast to its tsarist and Soviet predecessors, Russia today does not appear nearly as exceptional in tolerating or institutionalizing ethnic or religious diversity. Russia's movement from being the "affirmative action empire" toward being an assimilationist nation-state since 1992 is observable in numerous changes in cadres, institutions, laws, and policies.

Despite major challenges, both ethnic and religious identities have been revived and politicized in Russia since the dissolution of the Soviet Union. This contrasts both with the Russian imperial period, when religious identities trumped ethnic identities in most cases, and with the Soviet period, when ethnic identities with socialist content were officially recognized and promoted but public expressions of religious identities were suppressed and criminalized. While Russian ethnicity was the first among equals in the socialist Soviet Union, and the Russian Orthodox Church was the dominant and official religion in imperial Russia, both Russian ethnicity and the Russian Orthodox Church have gained primacy over other ethnic and religious identities, both officially and unofficially, in Russian politics and society today.

DISCUSSION QUESTIONS

1. How did Soviet policies reshape and influence ethnic and religious identities in the long term, and in what ways do we still observe these effects in present-day Russia?

2. What are some of the direct and indirect consequences of Russia's movement toward authoritarianism under President Putin on ethnic and religious minorities?

3. Would Russia's democratization lead to the empowerment and more extensive expressions of ethnic and religious identities, or would democratization primarily empower the ethnic Russian and Orthodox Christian majority at the expense of the ethnoreligious minorities?

REFERENCES

Akturk, Sener [Şener Aktürk]. 2010. "Passport Identification and Nation-Building in Post-Soviet Russia." *Post-Soviet Affairs*, 26(4), 314–41.

2012. *Regimes of Ethnicity and Nationhood in Germany, Russia, and Turkey*. New York: Cambridge University Press.

2017. "Post-Imperial Democracies and New Projects of Nationhood in Eurasia: Transforming the Nation through Migration in Russia and Turkey." *Journal of Ethnic and Migration Studies*, 43(7), 1101–20.

2019. "Five Faces of Russia's Soft Power: Far Left, Far Right, Orthodox Christian, Russophone, and Ethnoreligious Networks." *PONARS Eurasia Policy Memo*, 623, www.ponarseurasia.org/wp-content/uploads/attachments/Pepm623_Akturk_Nov2019_1-8.pdf.

Akturk, Sener, and Yury Katliarou. 2021. "Institutionalization of Ethnocultural Diversity and the Representation of European Muslims." *Perspectives on Politics*, 19(2), 388–405.

Beissinger, Mark R. 2002. *Nationalist Mobilization and the Collapse of the Soviet State*. New York: Cambridge University Press.

Belton, Catherine. 2020. *Putin's People: How the KGB Took Back Russia and Then Took On the West*. New York: Farrar, Straus, and Giroux.

Bilinsky, Yaroslav. 1962. "The Soviet Education Laws of 1958–9 and Soviet Nationality Policy." *Soviet Studies*, 14(2), 132–57.

du Boulay, Sofya, and Huw du Boulay. 2021. "New Alphabets, Old Rules: Latinization, Legacy, and Liberation in Central Asia." *Problems of Post-Communism*, 68(2), 135–40.

FADN (Federal'nogo agenstva po delam natsional'nostei). 2021. "VII s"ezd obshchestven-nogo dvizheniia 'Assotsiatsiia finno-ugorskikh narodov Rossiiskoi Federatsii.'" December 15, http://fadn.gov.ru/press-centr/news/vii-sezd-obshhestvennogo-dvizheniya-%C2%ABassocziacziya-finno-ugorskix-narodov-rossijskoj-federaczii%C2%BB.

Feklyunina, Valentina. 2016. "Soft Power and Identity: Russia, Ukraine, and the 'Russian World(s).'" *European Journal of International Relations*, 22(4), 773–96.

Fisher, Alan W. 1978. *The Crimean Tatars*. Stanford: Stanford University Press.

Giuliano, Elise. 2000. "Who Determines the Self in the Politics of Self-Determination? Identity and Preference Formation in Tatarstan's Nationalist Mobilization." *Comparative Politics*, 32(3), 295–316.

Goode, J. Paul. 2019. "Russia's Ministry of Ambivalence: The Failure of Civic Nation-Building in Post-Soviet Russia." *Post-Soviet Affairs*, 35(2), 140–60.

Grüner, Frank. 2008. *Patrioten und Kosmopoliten. Juden im Sowjetstaat, 1941–1953*. Cologne: Böhlau.

Hale, Henry E. 2000. "The Parade of Sovereignties: Testing Theories of Secession in the Soviet Setting." *British Journal of Political Science*, 30(1), 31–56.

Herrera, Yoshiko. 2005. *Imagined Economies: The Sources of Russian Regionalism*. New York: Cambridge University Press.

Hirsch, Francine. 2005. *Empire of Nations: Ethnographic Knowledge and the Making of the Soviet Union*. Ithaca: Cornell University Press.

Hosking, Geoffrey. 1992. *The First Socialist Society: A History of the Soviet Union from within*, 2nd enlarged ed. Cambridge, MA: Harvard University Press.

Human Rights Watch. 1991. "'Punished Peoples' of the Soviet Union: The Continuing Legacy of Stalin's Deportation." Helsinki Watch Report, www.hrw.org/reports/pdfs/u/ussr/ussr.919/ussr919full.pdf.

Hunter, Shireen. 2004. *Islam in Russia: The Politics of Identity and Security*. Armonk, NY: M. E. Sharpe.

Kappeler, Andreas. 2001. *The Russian Empire: A Multiethnic History*. New York: Routledge.

Kelaidis, Katherine. 2019. "Moscow's Patriarch Eyes Paris, and an Orthodox Battle Brews," *Religion and Politics*, June 4, https://religionandpolitics.org/2019/06/04/moscows-patriarch-eyes-paris-and-an-orthodox-battle-brews/.

Khalid, Adeeb. 1999. *The Politics of Muslim Cultural Reform: Jadidism in Central Asia*. Berkeley: University of California Press.

Khamidullin, B. L. 2008. "Kazanskoe Khanstvo." In *Bol'shaia rossiiskaia entsiklopediia*, vol. XII. Moscow.

Khannanova, Gulchachak. 2000. "Bashkirs Miss Line Five." *Current Digest of the Post-Soviet Press*, 52(37), 3, October 11 (English-language version of original in *Kommersant*, September 9, p. 7).

Kolstø, Pål. 2016. "Crimea vs. Donbas: How Putin Won Russian Nationalist Support – and Lost It Again." *Slavic Review*, 75(3), 702–25.

Kreindler, Isabelle. 1977. "A Neglected Source of Lenin's Nationality Policy." *Slavic Review*, 36(1), 86–100.

Kryshtanovskaya, Olga, and Stephen White. 1996. "From Soviet *Nomenklatura* to Russian Elite." *Europe-Asia Studies*, 48(5), 711–33.

Laruelle, Marlene. 2016. "The Three Colors of Novorossiya, or the Russian Nationalist Mythmaking of the Ukrainian Crisis." *Post-Soviet Affairs*, 32(1), 55–74.

Lieven, Anatol. 1999. *Chechnya: Tombstone of Russian Power*. New Haven: Yale University Press.

Martin, Janet. 2001. "Multiethnicity in Muscovy: A Consideration of Christian and Muslim Tatars in the 1550s–1580s." *Journal of Early Modern History*, 5(1), 1–23.

Martin, Terry D. 2001. *The Affirmative Action Empire: Nations and Nationalism in the Soviet Union, 1923–1939*. Ithaca: Cornell University Press.

Mukhina, Irina. 2007. *The Germans of the Soviet Union*. New York: Routledge.

Newsru.com. 2012. "V Khanty-Mansiiskom avtonomnom okruge dobyta 10-milliardnaia tonna nefti." February 22, www.newsru.com/finance/22feb2012/ugra.html.

OSCE. 2020. "On Remembrance of the Victims of the Deportation of the Crimean Tatar People from Crimea by the Soviet Regime," delivered by Ambassador Yevhenii Tsymbaliuk, Permanent Representative of Ukraine to the International Organizations in Vienna, to the 1268th meeting of the Permanent Council, 21 May, www.osce.org/files/f/documents/0/2/453540.pdf.

Petrov, Nikolay, and Eugenia Nazrullaeva. 2018. "Regional Elites and Moscow." In Daniel Treisman (ed.), *The New Autocracy: Information, Politics, and Policy in Putin's Russia*, pp. 109–35. Washington, DC: Brookings Institution Press.

Petrov, Nikolai, and Darrell Slider. 2019. "Regional Politics." In Stephen Wegren (ed.), *Putin's Russia: Past Imperfect, Future Uncertain*, 7th ed. pp. 49–68. Lanham, MD: Rowman & Littlefield.

Platt, Kevin M. F., and David Brandenberger (eds.). 2006. *Epic Revisionism: Russian History and Literature as Stalinist Propaganda*. Madison: University of Wisconsin Press.

Podobied, Pavlo. 2019. "Moscow Is Trying to Weaken Crimean Tatar Resistance with the Help of Tatarstan." *Eurasia Daily Monitor* 16 (43), March 27, https://jamestown.org/program/moscow-is-trying-to-weaken-crimean-tatar-resistance-with-the-help-of-tatarstan/.

Putin, Vladimir. 2012. "Rossiia. Natsional'nyi vopros." *Nezavisimaia Gazeta*, January 23, www.ng.ru/politics/2012-01-23/1_national.html.

2021. "On the Historical Unity of Russians and Ukrainians." July 12, http://en.kremlin.ru/events/president/news/66181.

Sakwa, Richard. 2007. "Putin's Leadership." In Dale Herspring (ed.), *Putin's Russia: Past Imperfect, Future Uncertain*, 3rd ed., pp. 13–35. Lanham, MD: Rowman & Littlefield.

Sharafutdinova, Gulnaz. 2000. "Chechnya versus Tatarstan: Understanding Ethnopolitics in Post-Communist Russia." *Problems of Post-Communism*, 47(2), 13–22.

2003. "Paradiplomacy in the Russian Regions: Tatarstan's Search for Statehood." *Europe-Asia Studies*, 55(4), 613–29.

Shevel, Oxana. 2011. "Russian Nation-Building from Yel'tsin to Medvedev: Ethnic, Civic or Purposefully Ambiguous?" *Europe-Asia Studies*, 63 (2), 179–202.

Slezkine, Yuri. 1994. "The USSR as a Communal Apartment, or How a Socialist State Promoted Ethnic Particularism." *Slavic Review*, 53(2), 414–52.

Smolkin, Victoria. 2018. *A Sacred Space Is Never Empty: A History of Soviet Atheism*. Princeton: Princeton University Press.

Suny, Ronald Grigor. 1993. *The Revenge of the Past: Nationalism, Revolution, and the Collapse of the Soviet Union*. Stanford: Stanford University Press.

Teper, Yuri. 2016. "Official Russian Identity Discourse in Light of the Annexation of Crimea: National or Imperial?" *Post-Soviet Affairs*, 32(4), 378–96.

Tishkov, Valery. 1997. *Ethnicity, Nationalism and Conflict in and after the Soviet Union*. Thousand Oaks, CA: Sage.

Tolz, Vera. 2001. *Inventing the Nation: Russia*. London: Arnold.

Treisman, Daniel S. 1997. "Russia's 'Ethnic Revival': The Separatist Activism of Regional Leaders in a Postcommunist Order." *World Politics*, 49(2), 212–49.

Walker, Edward W. 2003. *Dissolution: Sovereignty and the Breakup of the Soviet Union*. Lanham, MD: Rowman & Littlefield.

Walker, Shaun. 2016. "From One Vladimir to Another: Putin Unveils Huge Statue in Moscow." *Guardian*, November 4, www.theguardian.com/world/2016/nov/04/vladimir-great-statue-unveiled-putin-moscow.

Ware, Robert. 2011. "Has the Russian Federation Been Chechenised?" *Europe–Asia Studies*, 63(3), 493–508.

Werth, Paul. 2014. *The Tsar's Foreign Faiths: Toleration and the Fate of Religious Freedom in Imperial Russia*. New York: Oxford University Press.

Wood, Tony. 2004. "The Case for Chechnya." *New Left Review*, 30, 5–36.

Zaslavksy, Victor, and Yuri Luryi. 1979. "The Passport System in the USSR and Changes in Soviet Society." *Soviet Union*, 6(2), 137–53.

Zhemukhov, Sufian, and Şener Aktürk. 2015. "The Movement toward a Monolingual Nation in Russia: The Language Policy in the Circassian Republics of the Northern Caucasus." *Journal of Caucasian Studies*, 1(1), 33–68.

Index

References such as "178–79" indicate (not necessarily continuous) discussion of a topic across a range of pages. Wherever possible in the case of topics with many references, these have either been divided into subtopics or only the most significant discussions of the topic are listed. Because the entire work is about "politics" and "Russia," the use of these terms (and certain others that occur throughout the book) as entry points has been restricted. Information will be found under the corresponding detailed topics.